Management Accoun
Third Edition

Colin Drury

The
University
Of
Sheffield.

CUSTOM
CENGAGE Learning·

Australia • Brazil • Japan • Korea • Mexico • Singapore • Spain • United Kingdom • United States

Management Accounting, 3rd Edition
University of Sheffield

Publishing Director: Linden Harris

Custom Editor: Isabel Florence

Production Editor – Custom Lead:
  Alison Cooke

Production Controller: Eyvett Davis

For product information and technology assistance,
contact **emea.info@cengage.com**.

For permission to use material from this text or product,
and for permission queries,
email **emea.permissions@cengage.com**.

British Library Cataloguing-in-Publication Data
A catalogue record for this book is available from the British Library.

ISBN: 978-1-4080-7582-1

Cengage Learning EMEA
Cheriton House, North Way, Andover, Hampshire, SP10 5BE,
United Kingdom

Cengage Learning products are represented in Canada
by Nelson Education Ltd.

For your lifelong learning solutions, visit
www.cengage.co.uk

Purchase your next print book, e-book or e-chapter at
www.cengagebrain.com

Printed in the United Kingdom by TJ International
1 2 3 4 5 6 7 8 9 10 – 14 13 12

Acknowledgements

The content of this text has been adapted from the following product(s):

Management Accounting for Business, 4th Edition
Drury, Colin (978-1-4080-1771-5)

Management and Cost Accounting, 8th Edition
Drury, Colin (978-1-4080-6431-3)

Full copyright details and acknowledgements will appear in the aforementioned publications.

Table of Contents

Chapters originally from Drury, Colin, *Management Accounting for Business,* 4th Edition

Chapters originally from Drury, Colin, *Management and Cost Accounting,* 8th Edition

CHAPTER 1
INTRODUCTION TO MANAGEMENT ACCOUNTING

LEARNING OBJECTIVES

After studying this chapter you should be able to:

- **distinguish between management accounting and financial accounting;**
- **identify and describe the elements involved in the decision-making, planning and control process;**
- **justify the view that a major objective of commercial organizations is broadly to seek to maximize future profits;**
- **explain the factors that have influenced the changes in the competitive environment;**
- **outline and describe the key success factors that directly affect customer satisfaction;**
- **identify and describe the functions of a cost and management accounting system;**
- **provide a brief historical description of management accounting.**

There are many definitions of accounting, but the one that captures the theme of this book is the definition formulated by the American Accounting Association. It describes accounting as

> the process of identifying, measuring and communicating economic information to permit informed judgements and decisions by users of the information.

In other words, accounting is concerned with providing both financial and non-financial information that will help decision-makers to make good decisions. An understanding of accounting therefore requires an understanding of the decision-making process and an awareness of the users of accounting information.

During the past two decades many organizations in both the manufacturing and service sectors have faced dramatic changes in their business environment. Deregulation combined with extensive competition from overseas companies in domestic markets has resulted in a situation where most companies are now competing in a highly competitive global market. At the same time there has been a significant reduction in product life cycles arising from technological innovations and the need to meet increasingly discriminating customer demands. To compete successfully in today's highly competitive global environment companies have made customer satisfaction an overriding priority. They have also adopted new management approaches and manufacturing companies have changed their manufacturing systems and invested in new technologies. These changes have had a significant influence on management accounting systems. Progression through the book will reveal how these changes have influenced management accounting systems, but first of all it is important that you have a good background knowledge of some of the important changes that have occurred in the business environment. This chapter aims to provide such knowledge.

The objective of this first chapter is to provide the background knowledge that will enable you to achieve a more meaningful insight into the issues and problems of management accounting that are discussed in the book. We begin by looking at the users of accounting information and identifying their requirements. This is followed by a description of the decision-making process and the changing business environment. Finally, the different functions of management accounting are described.

THE USERS OF ACCOUNTING INFORMATION

Accounting is a language that communicates economic information to people who have an interest in an organization – managers, shareholders and potential investors, employees, creditors and the government. Managers require information that will assist them in their decision-making and control activities; for example, information is needed on the estimated selling prices, costs, demand, competitive position and profitability of various products and services that are provided by the organization. Shareholders require information on the value of their investment and the income that is derived from their shareholding. Employees require information on the ability of the firm to meet wage demands and avoid redundancies. Creditors and the providers of loan capital require information on a firm's ability to meet its financial obligations. Government agencies like the Central Statistical Office collect accounting information and require information such as the details of sales activity, profits, investments, stocks, dividends paid, the proportion of profits absorbed by taxation and so on. In addition the Inland Revenue needs information on the amount of profits that are subject to taxation. All this information is important for determining policies to manage the economy.

Accounting information is not confined to business organizations. Accounting information about individuals is also important and is used by other individuals; for example, credit may only be extended to an individual after the prospective borrower has furnished a reasonable accounting of his private financial affairs. Non-profit-making organizations such as churches, charitable organizations, clubs and government units such as local authorities, also require accounting information for decision-making, and for reporting the results of their activities. For example, a tennis club will require information on the cost of undertaking its various activities so that a decision can be made as to the amount of the annual subscription that it will charge to its members. Similarly, local authorities need information on the costs of undertaking specific activities so that decisions can be made as to which activities will be undertaken and the resources that must be raised to finance them.

The foregoing discussion has indicated that there are many users of accounting information who require information for decision-making. The objective of accounting is to provide sufficient information to meet the needs of the various users at the lowest possible cost. Obviously, the benefit derived from using an information system for decision-making must be greater than the cost of operating the system.

An examination of the various users of accounting information indicates that they can be divided into two categories:

1 internal parties within the organization;
2 external parties such as shareholders, creditors and regulatory agencies, outside the organization.

It is possible to distinguish between two branches of accounting, which reflect the internal and external users of accounting information. **Management accounting** is concerned with the provision of information to people within the organization to help them make better decisions and improve the efficiency and effectiveness of existing operations, whereas **financial accounting** is concerned with the provision of information to external parties outside the organization. Thus, management accounting could be called internal reporting and financial accounting could be called external reporting. This book concentrates on management accounting.

DIFFERENCES BETWEEN MANAGEMENT ACCOUNTING AND FINANCIAL ACCOUNTING

The major differences between these two branches of accounting are:

- *Legal requirements.* There is a statutory requirement for public limited companies to produce annual financial accounts regardless of whether or not management regards this information as useful. Management accounting, by contrast, is entirely optional and information should be produced only if it is considered that the benefits from the use of the information by management exceed the cost of collecting it.

- *Focus on individual parts or segments of the business.* Financial accounting reports describe the whole of the business whereas management accounting focuses on small parts of the organization, for example the cost and profitability of products, services, customers and activities. In addition, management accounting information measures the economic performance of decentralized operating units, such as divisions and departments.

- *Generally accepted accounting principles.* Financial accounting statements must be prepared to conform with the legal requirements and the generally accepted accounting principles established by regulatory bodies such as the Financial Accounting Standards Board (FASB) in the USA the Accounting Standards Board (ASB) in the UK and the International Accounting Standards Board. These requirements are essential to ensure the uniformity and consistency that is needed for external financial statements. Outside users need assurance that external statements are prepared in accordance with generally accepted accounting principles so that inter-company and historical comparisons are possible. Thus financial accounting data should be objective and verifiable. In contrast, management accountants are not required to adhere to generally accepted accounting principles when providing managerial information for internal purposes. Instead, the focus is on serving management's needs and providing information that is useful to managers relating to their decision-making, planning and control functions.

- *Time dimension.* Financial accounting reports what has happened in the past in an organization, whereas management accounting is concerned with future information as well as past information. Decisions are concerned with future events and management therefore requires details of expected future costs and revenues.

- *Report frequency.* A detailed set of financial accounts is published annually and less detailed accounts are published semi-annually. Management requires information quickly if it is to act on it. Consequently management accounting reports on various activities may be prepared at daily, weekly or monthly intervals.

THE DECISION-MAKING PROCESS

The decision-making process encompasses planning and control activities. Because information produced by management accountants must be judged in the light of its ultimate effect on the outcome of decisions, a necessary precedent to an understanding of management accounting is an understanding of the *decision-making process*.

Figure 1.1 presents a diagram of a decision-making model (the decision-making, planning and control process). The first four stages represent the decision-making or the planning process. **Planning** involves making choices between alternatives and is primarily a decision-making activity. The final two stages represent the *control process*, which is the

FIGURE 1.1

The decision-making planning and control process

process of measuring and correcting actual performance to ensure that the alternatives that are chosen and the plans for implementing them are carried out. You should note that the decision-making model specified in Figure 1.1 is a theoretical model based on the assumption of rational economic behaviour. This assumption has been challenged on the grounds that such behaviour does not always reflect actual real world behaviour (Burchell *et al.*, 1980).

Identifying objectives

Before good decisions can be made there must be some guiding aim or direction that will enable the decision-makers to assess the desirability of favouring one course of action over another. Hence, the first stage in the decision-making process should be to specify the goals or **objectives of the organization**.

Considerable controversy exists as to what the objectives of firms are or should be. Economic theory normally assumes that firms seek to maximize profits for the owners of the firm or, more precisely, seek the maximization of shareholders' wealth. Some writers (e.g. Simon, 1959) believe that managers are content to find a plan that provides satisfactory profits rather than to maximize profits. Clearly it is too simplistic to say that the only objective of a business firm is to maximize profits. Some managers seek to establish a power base and build an empire; another goal is security; or the removal of uncertainty regarding the future may override the pure profit motive. Nevertheless, the view adopted in this book is that, broadly, firms seek to maximize future profits. While organizations may also pursue more specific objectives (such as producing high-quality products or being the market leader within a particular market segment), maximizing future net profits represents a broad core objective for most firms. The reasons for choosing this objective are as follows:

1 It is unlikely that any other objective is as widely applicable in measuring the ability of the organization to survive in the future.

2 It is unlikely that maximizing future profits can be realized in practice, but by establishing the principles necessary to achieve this objective, firms learn how to increase profits.

Search for alternative courses of action

The second stage in the decision-making model is a search for a range of possible courses of action (or **strategies**) that might enable objectives to be achieved. If the management of a company concentrates entirely on its present product range and markets, and market share and profits are allowed to decline, there is a danger that the company will be unable to survive in the future. To survive it is essential that management identifies potential opportunities and threats in its current environment and takes specific steps now so that the organization will not be taken by surprise by any developments that may occur in the future. In particular, the company should consider one or more of the following courses of action:

1 developing *new* products for sale in *existing* markets;

2 developing *new* products for *new* markets;

3 developing *new* markets for *existing* products.

The search for alternative courses of action involves the acquisition of information concerning future opportunities and environments; it is the most difficult and important stage of the decision-making process.

Select appropriate alternative courses of action

The process of choosing among alternative courses of action is decision-making. Decision-making requires that information about the alternatives is gathered. For example, information should be gathered relating to the potential growth rates of the alternative activities that have been identified, the ability of the company to establish adequate market share and the projected profits for each alternative activity. The alternatives should be evaluated to identify courses of action that best satisfy the objectives of an organization. One of the major functions of management accounting is the provision of information that facilitates decision-making. This aspect of management accounting will be examined in Chapters 3–6.

Implementation of decisions

Once the alternative courses of action have been selected, they should be implemented as part of the budgeting and long-term planning process. The **budget** is a financial plan for implementing the various decisions that management has made. Budgets for all the various decisions are expressed in terms of cash inflows and outflows, and sales revenues and expenses. These budgets are merged together into a single unifying statement of the organization's expectations for future periods. This statement is known as a **master budget**. The master budget consists of budgeted profit and cash flow statements. The budgeting process communicates to everyone in the organization the part that they are expected to play in implementing management's decisions. We shall examine the budgeting process in Chapter 9.

Comparing actual and planned outcomes and responding to divergencies from plan

The final stages in the process outlined in Figure 1.1 of comparing actual and planned outcomes and responses to divergences from plan represent the firm's control process. The managerial function of **control** consists of the measurement, reporting and subsequent correction of performance in an attempt to ensure that the firm's objectives and plans are achieved. In other words, the objective of the control process is to ensure that the work is done so as to fulfil the original intentions.

To monitor performance, the accountant produces **performance reports** and presents them to the appropriate managers who are responsible for implementing the various decisions. Performance reports consisting of a comparison of actual outcomes (actual costs and revenues) and planned outcomes (budgeted costs and revenues) should be issued at regular intervals. Performance reports provide **feedback** information by comparing planned and actual outcomes. Such reports should highlight those activities that do not conform to plans, so that managers can devote their scarce time to focusing mainly on these items. This process represents the application of **management by exception**. Effective control requires that corrective action is taken so that actual outcomes conform to planned outcomes. Alternatively, the plans may require modification if the comparisons indicate that the plans are no longer attainable.

The process of taking corrective action so that actual outcomes conform to planned outcomes, or the modification of the plans if the comparisons indicate that actual outcomes do not conform to planned outcomes, is indicated by the arrowed lines in Figure 1.1 linking stages 6 and 4 and 6 and 2. These arrowed lines represent **feedback loops**. They signify that the process is dynamic and stress the interdependencies between the various stages in the process. The feedback loop between stages 6 and 2 indicates that the plans should be regularly reviewed, and if they are no longer attainable then alternative courses of action must be considered for achieving the organization's objectives. The second loop stresses the corrective action taken so that actual outcomes conform to planned outcomes. Chapters 9–11 focus on the planning and control process.

CHANGING COMPETITIVE ENVIRONMENT

Prior to the 1980s many organizations in Western countries operated in a protected competitive environment. Barriers of communication and geographical distance, and sometimes protected markets, limited the ability of overseas companies to compete in domestic markets. There was little incentive for firms to maximize efficiency and improve management practices, or to minimize costs, as cost increases could often be passed on to customers. During the 1980s, however, organizations began to encounter severe competition from overseas competitors that offered high-quality products at low prices. By establishing global networks for acquiring raw materials and distributing goods overseas, competitors were able to gain access to domestic markets throughout the world. To be successful companies now have to compete not only against domestic competitors but also against the best companies in the world.

Excellence in manufacturing can provide a competitive weapon to compete in sophisticated worldwide markets. In order to compete effectively companies must be capable of manufacturing innovative products of high quality at a low cost, and also provide a first-class customer service. At the same time, they must have the flexibility to cope with short product life cycles, demands for greater product variety from more discriminating customers and increasing international competition. World-class manufacturing companies have responded to these competitive demands by replacing traditional production systems with new just-in-time production systems and investing in advanced manufacturing technologies (AMTs). The major features of these new systems and their implications for management accounting will be described throughout the book.

Virtually all types of service organization have also faced major changes in their competitive environment. Before the 1980s many service organizations, such as those operating in the airlines, utilities and financial service industries, were either government-owned monopolies or operated in a highly regulated, protected and non-competitive environment. These organizations were not subject to any great pressure to improve the quality and efficiency of their operations or to improve profitability by eliminating services or products that were making losses. Prices were set to cover operating costs and provide a predetermined return on capital. Hence cost increases could often be absorbed by increasing the prices of the services. Little attention was therefore given to developing cost systems that accurately measured the costs and profitability of individual services.

Privatization of government-controlled companies and deregulation in the 1980s completely changed the competitive environment in which service companies operated. Pricing and competitive restrictions were virtually eliminated. Deregulation, intensive competition and an expanding product range created the need for service organizations to focus on cost management and develop management accounting information systems that enabled them to understand their cost base and determine the sources of profitability for their products, customers and markets. Many service organizations have only recently turned their attention to management accounting. One of the major features of the business environment in recent decades has been the growth in the service industry and the growth of the management accounting function within service organizations.

CHANGING PRODUCT LIFE CYCLES

A **product's life cycle** is the period of time from initial expenditure on research and development to the time at which support to customers is withdrawn. Intensive global competition and technological innovation combined with increasingly discriminating and sophisticated customer demands have resulted in a dramatic decline in product life cycles. To be successful companies must now speed up the rate at which they introduce new products to the market. Being later to the market than competitors can have a dramatic effect on product profitability.

In many industries a large fraction of a product's life-cycle costs are determined by decisions made early in its life cycle. This has created a need for management accounting to place greater emphasis on providing information at the design stage because many of the costs are committed or locked in at this time. Therefore to compete successfully companies must be able to manage their costs effectively at the design stage, have the capability to adapt to new, different and changing customer requirements and reduce the time to market of new and modified products.

FOCUS ON CUSTOMER SATISFACTION AND NEW MANAGEMENT APPROACHES

In order to compete in today's competitive environment companies have had to become more customer-driven and make customer satisfaction an overriding priority. Customers are demanding ever-improving levels of service in cost, quality, reliability, delivery, and the choice of innovative new products. Figure 1.2 illustrates this focus on customer satisfaction as the overriding priority. In order to provide customer satisfaction organizations must concentrate on those key success factors that directly affect it. Figure 1.2 identifies cost efficiency, quality, time and innovation as the key success factors. In addition to concentrating on these factors organizations are adopting new management approaches in their quest to achieve customer satisfaction. These new approaches are illustrated in Figure 1.2. They are continuous improvement and total value-chain analysis, along with social responsibility and corporate ethics. Let us now examine each of the items shown in Figure 1.2 in more detail.

FIGURE 1.2

Focus on customer satisfaction

Cost efficiency

The first factor listed in Figure 1.2 highlights cost efficiency. Since customers will buy the product with the lowest price, all other things being equal, keeping costs low and being **cost efficient** provides an organization with a strong competitive advantage. Increased competition has also made decision errors due to poor cost information more probable and more costly. These developments have made many companies aware of the need to improve their cost systems so that they can produce more accurate cost information to monitor trends in costs over time, determine the cost of their products and services, pinpoint loss-making activities and analyse profits by products, sales outlets, customers and markets.

Total quality management

In addition to demanding low-cost product, customers are demanding high-quality products and services. Most companies are responding to this by focusing on **total quality management** (TQM). TQM is a term used to describe a situation where *all* business functions are involved in a process of continuous quality improvement that focuses on delivering products or services of consistently high quality in a timely fashion. The emphasis on TQM has created fresh demands on the management accounting function to expand its role by becoming involved in measuring and evaluating the quality of products and services and the activities that produce them.

Time as a competitive weapon

Organizations are also seeking to increase customer satisfaction by providing a speedier response to customer requests, ensuring 100 per cent on-time delivery and reducing the time taken to develop and bring new products to market. For these reasons management accounting systems now place more emphasis on **time-based measures**, which have become an important competitive variable. **Cycle time** is one measure that management accounting systems have begun to focus on. It is the length of time from start to completion of a product or service. It consists of the sum of processing time, move time, wait time and inspection time. Only processing time adds value to the product, and the remaining activities are **non-value-added activities** in the sense that they can be reduced or eliminated without altering the product's service potential to the customer. Organizations are therefore focusing on minimizing cycle time by reducing the time spent on such activities. The management accounting system has an important role to play in this process by identifying and reporting on the time devoted to value-added and non-value-added activities. Cycle time measures have also become important for service organizations. For example, the time taken to process mortgage loan applications by financial organizations can be considerable, involving substantial non-value-added waiting time. Thus, reducing the time to process the applications enhances customer satisfaction and creates the potential for increasing sales revenue.

Innovation

The final key success factor shown in Figure 1.2 relates to **innovation**. To be successful companies must develop a steady stream of innovative new products and services and have the capability to adapt to changing customer requirements. Management accounting information systems have begun to report performance measures relating to innovation. Examples include the total launch time for new products/services, an assessment of the key characteristics of new products relative to those of competitors, feedback on customer satisfaction with the new features and characteristics of newly introduced products and the number of new products launched.

Continuous improvement

Figure 1.2 highlights that organizations are attempting to achieve customer satisfaction by adopting a philosophy of **continuous improvement**. Traditionally, organizations have sought to study activities and establish standard operating procedures. Management accountants developed systems and measurements that compared actual results with predetermined standards. This process created a climate whereby the predetermined standards represented a target to be achieved and maintained rather than a policy of continuous improvement. In today's competitive environment, to compete successfully companies must adopt a philosophy of continuous improvement, an ongoing process that involves a continuous search to reduce costs, eliminate waste, and improve the quality and performance of activities that increase customer value or satisfaction. Management accounting supports continuous improvement by identifying ways to improve and then by reporting on the progress of the methods that have been implemented.

Benchmarking is a technique that is increasingly being adopted as a mechanism for achieving continuous improvement. It involves comparing key activities with best practices found within and outside the organization. External benchmarking attempts to identify an activity, such as customer order processing, that needs to be improved, and finding a non-rival organization that is considered to represent world-class best practice for the activity and studying how it performs the activity. The objective is to find out how the activity can be improved and ensure that the improvements are implemented. The overall aim should be to find and implement best practice.

Value-chain analysis

Increasing attention is now being given to **value-chain analysis** as a means of increasing customer satisfaction and managing costs more effectively. The value chain is illustrated in Figure 1.3. It is the linked set of value-creating activities starting with the acquisition of the raw material from suppliers through to the ultimate end-use product or service delivered to the customer. Coordinating the individual activities effectively creates the conditions to improve customer satisfaction, particularly in terms of cost efficiency, quality and delivery. It is also appropriate to view the value chain from the customer's perspective, with each link being seen as the customer of the previous link. For example, production and marketing can be viewed as being customers of the design function, marketing as a customer of the production function, and so on. If each link in the value chain is designed to meet the needs of its customers, then end-customer satisfaction should ensue. Furthermore, by viewing each link in the value chain as a supplier–customer relationship, the opinions of the customers can be used to provide feedback information on assessing the quality of service provided by the supplying link. Opportunities are thus identified for improving activities throughout the entire value chain. The aim is to manage the linkages in the value chain better than competitors and thus create a competitive advantage. Management accounting plays a major role in providing information to help managers administer linkages in the value chain.

FIGURE 1.3

The value chain

Social responsibility and corporate ethics

Figure 1.2 indicates that companies are also focusing on **social responsibility** and **corporate ethics** to enhance customer satisfaction. Customers are no longer satisfied if companies simply comply with the legal requirements of undertaking their activities. They expect company managers to be more proactive in terms of their social responsibility. Company stakeholders are now giving high priority to social responsibility, safety and environmental issues, as well as corporate ethics. In response to these pressures many companies are now introducing mechanisms for measuring, reporting and monitoring their environmental costs and activities. A code of ethics has also become an essential part of corporate culture. In addition, professional accounting organizations play an important role in promoting a high standard of ethical behaviour by their members. Both of the professional bodies representing management accountants in the UK (the Chartered Institute of Management Accountants) and the USA (the Institute of Management Accountants) have issued a code of ethical guidelines for their members and established mechanisms for monitoring and enforcing professional ethics. The guidelines are concerned with ensuring that accountants follow fundamental principles relating to integrity (not being a party to any falsification), objectivity (not being biased or prejudiced), confi-dentiality, professional competence and due care (maintaining the skills required to ensure a competent professional service).

Many companies advertise their ethical or socially responsible activities to help increase customer satisfaction. The environmentally friendly vehicle used by the supermarket Sainsbury's for home deliveries has zero emission.

IMAGE COURTESY OF J. SAINSBURY'S PLC

REAL WORLD VIEWS 1.1

A look at a key feature of easyJet's business

As one of the pioneers in the low-cost airline market, easyJet bases its business on a number of principles:

- Minimize distribution costs by using the internet to take bookings. About 90 per cent of all easyJet tickets are sold via the web. This makes the company one of Europe's largest internet retailers.
- Maximize efficient use of assets by decreasing turnaround time at airports.
- A 'simple-service model' means the end of free on-board catering.
- Ticketless travel, where passengers receive an e-mail confirming their booking, cuts the cost of issuing, distributing and processing tickets.
- Intensive use of IT in administration and management, aiming to run a paperless office.

Discussion point

How can the management accounting function provide information to support a low-cost strategy?

COURTESY OF EASYJET AIRLINE COMPANY LTD

SOURCE: EASYJET WEBSITE (WWW.EASYJET.COM)

THE IMPACT OF INFORMATION TECHNOLOGY

During the past decade the use of information technology (IT) to support business activities has increased dramatically with the development of electronic business communication technologies known as **e-business**, **e-commerce** or **internet commerce**. These developments are having a big impact on businesses. For example, consumers are becoming more discerning when purchasing products or services because they are able to derive more information from the internet on the relative merits of the different product offerings. E-commerce (such as bar coding) has provided the potential to develop new ways of doing things that have enabled considerable cost savings to be made from streamlining business processes and generating extra revenues from the adept use of on-line sales facilities (e.g. ticketless airline bookings and internet banking). The ability to use e-commerce more proficiently than competitors provides the potential for companies to establish a competitive advantage.

One advanced IT application that has had a considerable impact on business information systems is **enterprise resource planning systems** (ERPS). An ERPS comprises a set of integrated software applications modules that aims to control all information flows within a company. The modules cover most business functions (including accounting). Users can access real-time information on all aspects of the business: in other words, they can use their personal computers (PCs) that are connected to the organization's database to ascertain what is happening in the organization almost as it happens. Using real-time data enables managers to analyse the data from the information system quickly and thus continually improve the efficiency of processes.

The introduction of ERPS has the potential to have a significant impact on the work of management accountants. In particular, ERPS substantially reduces routine information gathering and the processing of information by management accountants. Instead of managers asking management accountants for information, they can access the system to derive the information they require directly by PC and do their own analyses. Because ERPS performs the routine tasks that were once part of the accountants' daily routines, accountants have had to expand their roles or risk possible redundancy. ERPS has provided the potential for accountants to use the time freed up from routine information gathering to adopt the role of advisers and internal consultants to the business. Management accountants have become more involved in interpreting the information generated from ERPS and in providing business support for managers.

INTERNATIONAL CONVERGENCE OF MANAGEMENT ACCOUNTING PRACTICES

This book has become an established international text. It is therefore assumed that the content is appropriate for use in different countries. This assumption is based on the premise that management accounting practices generally do not differ across countries. Granlund and Lukka (1998) provide support for this assumption. They argue that there is a strong current tendency towards global homogenization of management accounting practices within the industrialized parts of the world.

Granlund and Lukka distinguish between management accounting practices at the macro and micro levels. The macro level relates to concepts and techniques; in other words, it relates mainly to the content of this book. In contrast, the micro level is concerned with the behavioural patterns relating to how management accounting information is actually used. At the macro level Granlund and Lukka suggest that the convergence of management accounting practices in different countries has occurred because of intensified global competition, developments in information technology, the increasing tendency of transnational companies to standardize their practices, the global consultancy industry and the use of globally applied textbooks and teaching.

Firms throughout the world are adopting similar standardized software packages (e.g. ERPS) that have resulted in the standardization of data collection formats and reporting patterns of accounting information. Besides the impact of integrated IT systems, it is common for the headquarters/parent company of a transnational enterprise to force foreign divisions to adopt similar accounting practices to those of the headquarters/parent company. A large global consultancy industry has recently emerged that tends to promote the same standard solutions globally. Finally, the same textbooks are used globally, and university and professional accounting syllabuses tend to be similar in different countries.

At the micro level Granlund and Lukka acknowledge that differences in national and corporate culture can result in management accounting practices differing across countries. For example, national cultures have been categorized as the extent to which:

1 the inequality between people is considered to be normal and acceptable;
2 the culture is assertive and competitive as opposed to being modest and caring;
3 the culture feels comfortable with uncertainty and ambiguity; and
4 the culture focuses on long-term or short-term outcomes.

There is evidence to suggest that accounting information is used in different ways in different national cultures, such as being used in a rigorous/rigid manner for managerial performance evaluation in cultures exhibiting certain national traits and in a more flexible way in cultures exhibiting different national traits.

FUNCTIONS OF MANAGEMENT ACCOUNTING

A cost and management accounting system should generate information to meet the following requirements. It should:

1 allocate costs between cost of goods sold and inventories for internal and external profit reporting;
2 provide relevant information to help managers make better decisions;
3 provide information for planning, control, performance measurement and continuous improvement.

Financial accounting rules require that we match costs with revenues to calculate profit. Consequently any unsold finished goods stock or partly completed stock (work in progress) will *not* be included in the cost of goods sold, which is matched against sales revenue during a given period. In an organization that produces a wide range of different products it will be necessary, for stock (inventory) valuation purposes, to charge the costs to each individual product. The total value of the stocks of completed products and work in progress plus any unused raw materials forms the basis for determining the inventory valuation to be deducted from the current period's costs when calculating profit. Costs are

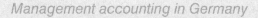

REAL WORLD VIEWS 1.2

Management accounting in Germany

In Germany management accounting is referred to as 'controlling' with management accountants referred to as 'controllers'. Although both words come from the English language, they are officially recognized in the German language.

So is a controller the same as a management accountant? In essence a controller performs a similar role to that of a management accountant. The principal functions of a controller are described as:

- planning a course of action to achieve business objectives;
- delivery of adequate, timely and understandable information;
- analysis and control using relevant performance measurements (feed-back control);
- keeping the business on course towards its objectives, taking corrective action in advance (feed-forward control).

These functions are quite similar to those mentioned in this chapter for management accounting. There are however some subtle differences. First, it is not normal for a controller to be a member of a professional body (such as a German equivalent of CIMA). Normally, controllers complete a *Betriebswirtschaftslehre*, which is similar to a business studies degree with a 'controlling' emphasis. It is also quite common to see the term 'controlling'combined with organization functions to create what is termed *Funktionalcontrolling* – for example Production-Controlling, Logistic-Controlling

or IT-Controlling. This does not mean there are multiple controllers in German businesses; rather controlling concepts are applied to each function. By controlling each business function the overall organizational objectives can be attained. Recent literature from Messner et al. (2008) suggests controlling is in fact a separate discipline and not a German synonym for management accounting. Whether or not controlling is a distinct discipline is a matter for debate. It does however seem that the tasks of a controller are similar to those of a management accountant.

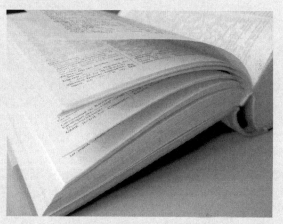

References:

Messner, M., Becker, A., Schaeffer, U. and Binder, C. (2008) Legitimacy and identity in Germanic management accounting research, *European Accounting Review*, 1, 1–31.

therefore traced to each individual job or product for financial accounting requirements in order to allocate the costs incurred during a period between cost of goods sold and inventories. This information is required for meeting *external* financial accounting requirements, but most organizations also produce *internal* profit reports at monthly intervals. Thus product costs are also required for periodic internal profit reporting. Many service organizations, however, do not carry any stocks, and product costs are therefore not required by these organizations for valuing inventories.

The second requirement of a cost and management accounting system is to provide relevant financial information to managers to help them make better decisions. Information is required relating to the profitability of various segments of the business such as products, services, customers and distribution channels in order to ensure that only profitable activities are undertaken. Information is also required for making resource allocation and product/service mix and discontinuation decisions. In some situations cost information extracted from the costing system also plays a crucial role in determining selling prices, particularly in markets where customized products and services are provided that do not have readily available market prices.

Management accounting systems should also provide information for planning, control, performance measurement and continuous improvement. Planning involves translating goals and objectives into the specific activities and resources that are required to achieve the goals and objectives. Companies develop both long-term and short-term plans and the management accounting function plays a critical role in this process. Short-term plans, in the form of the budgeting process, are prepared in more detail than the longer-term plans and are one of the mechanisms used by managers as a basis for control and performance evaluation. Control is the process of ensuring that the actual outcomes conform with the planned outcomes. The control process involves the setting of targets or standards (often derived from the budgeting process) against which actual results are measured. Performance is then measured and compared with the targets on a periodic basis. The management accountant's role is to provide managers with feedback information in the form of periodic reports, suitably analysed, to enable them to determine if operations for which they are responsible are proceeding according to plan and to identify those activities where corrective action is necessary. In particular, the management accounting function should provide economic feedback to managers to assist them in controlling costs and improving the efficiency and effectiveness of operations.

It is appropriate at this point to distinguish between cost accounting and management accounting. **Cost accounting** is concerned with cost accumulation for inventory valuation to meet the requirements of external reporting and internal profit measurement, whereas **management accounting** relates to the provision of appropriate information for decision-making, planning, control and performance evaluation. It is apparent from an examination of the literature that the distinction between cost accounting and management accounting is extremely vague with some writers referring to the decision-making aspects in terms of cost accounting and other writers using the term management accounting; the two terms are often used synonymously. In this book no attempt will be made to distinguish between these two terms.

You should now be aware from the above discussion that a management accounting system serves multiple purposes. The emphasis throughout the book is that costs must be assembled in different ways for different purposes. Most organisations record cost information in a single database with costs appropriately coded and classified so that relevant information can be extracted to meet each of the above requirements.

BRIEF HISTORICAL REVIEW OF MANAGEMENT ACCOUNTING

The origins of today's management accounting can be traced back to the Industrial Revolution of the nineteenth century. According to Johnson and Kaplan (1987), most of the management accounting practices that were in use in the mid-1980s had been developed by 1925, and for the next 60 years there was a slowdown, or even a halt, in management accounting innovation. They argue that this stagnation can be attributed mainly to the demand for product cost information for external financial accounting reports. The separation of the ownership and management of organizations created a need for the owners of a business to monitor the effective stewardship of their investment. This need led to the development of financial accounting, which generated a published report for investors and creditors summarizing the financial position of the company. Statutory obligations were established requiring companies to publish audited annual financial statements. In addition, there was a requirement for these published statements to conform to a set of rules known as generally accepted accounting principles (GAAP), which were developed by regulators.

The preparation of published external financial accounting statements required that costs be allocated between cost of goods sold and inventories. Cost accounting emerged to meet this requirement. Simple procedures were established to allocate costs to products that were objective and verifiable for financial accounting purposes. Such costs, however, were not sufficiently accurate for decision-making purposes and for distinguishing between profitable and unprofitable products and services. Johnson and Kaplan argue that the product costs derived for financial accounting purposes were also being used for management accounting purposes. They conclude that managers did not have to yield the design of management accounting systems to financial accountants and auditors. Separate systems could have been maintained for managerial and financial accounting purposes, but the high cost of information collection meant that the costs of maintaining two systems exceeded the additional benefits. Thus, companies relied primarily on the same information as that used for external financial reporting to manage their internal operations.

Johnson and Kaplan claim that, over the years, organizations had become fixated on the cost systems of the 1920s. Furthermore, when the information systems were automated in the 1960s, the system designers merely automated the manual systems that were developed in the 1920s. Johnson and Kaplan conclude that the lack of management accounting innovation over the decades and the failure to respond to its changing environment resulted in a situation in the mid-1980s where firms were using management accounting systems that were obsolete and no longer relevant to the changing competitive and manufacturing environment.

During the late 1980s, criticisms of current management accounting practices were widely publicized in the professional and academic accounting literature. In 1987 Johnson and Kaplan's book entitled *Relevance Lost: The Rise and Fall of Management Accounting*, was published. An enormous amount of publicity was generated by this book as a result of the authors' criticisms of management accounting. Many other commentators also concluded that management accounting was in a crisis and that fundamental changes in practice were required.

Since the mid-1980s management accounting practitioners and academics have sought to modify and implement new techniques that are relevant to today's environment and that will ensure that management accounting regains its relevance. By the mid-1990s Kaplan (1994) stated that:

> The past 10 years have seen a revolution in management accounting theory and
> practice. The seeds of the revolution can be seen in publications in the early to

mid 1980s that identified the failings and obsolescence of existing cost and performance measurement systems. Since that time we have seen remarkable innovations in management accounting; even more remarkable has been the speed with which the new concepts have become widely known, accepted and implemented in practice and integrated into a large number of educational programmes.

SUMMARY OF THE CONTENTS OF THE BOOK

This book is divided into five parts. Part 1 consists of two chapters and provides an introduction to management and cost accounting and a framework for studying the remaining chapters. Part 2 consists of four chapters and is titled 'Information for decision-making'. Here the focus is on measuring and identifying those costs that are relevant for different kinds of decisions. The title of Part 3 is 'Cost assignment'. It consists of two chapters that seek to provide an understanding of how costs are accumulated and assigned to cost objects, such as different products or services. In particular, this part describes the alternative approaches that can be used for measuring resources consumed by cost objects and the factors that should be considered in determining the sophistication of the cost accumulation system.

Part 4 consists of five chapters and is titled 'Information for planning, control and performance measurement'. This part concentrates on the process of translating goals and objectives of an organization into specific activities and the resources that are required, via the short-term (budgeting) and long-term planning processes, to achieve the goals and objectives. In addition, the management control systems that organizations use are described and the role that management accounting control systems play within the overall control process is examined. The emphasis here is on the accounting process as a means of providing information to help managers control the activities for which they are responsible. Performance measurement and evaluation within different segments of the organization are also examined.

Part 5 consists of two chapters and is entitled 'Strategic cost management and performance management'. The first chapter focuses on strategic cost management and the second on strategic performance management.

SUMMARY

The following items relate to the learning objectives listed at the beginning of the chapter.

● **Distinguish between management accounting and financial accounting.**
Management accounting differs from financial accounting in several distinct ways. Management accounting is concerned with the provision of information to internal users to help them make better decisions and improve the efficiency and effectiveness of operations. Financial accounting is concerned with the provision of information to external parties outside the organization. Unlike financial accounting there is no statutory requirement for management accounting to produce financial statements or follow externally imposed rules. Furthermore, management accounting provides information relating to different parts of the business whereas financial accounting

reports focus on the whole business. Management accounting also tends to be more future-oriented and reports are often published on a daily basis whereas financial accounting reports are published semi-annually.

- **Identify and describe the elements involved in the decision-making, planning and control process.** The following elements are involved in the decision-making, planning and control process: (a) identify the objectives that will guide the business; (b) search for a range of possible courses of action that might enable the objectives to be achieved; (c) select appropriate alternative courses of action that will enable the objectives to be achieved; (d) implement the decisions as part of the planning and budgeting process; (e) compare actual and planned outcomes; and (f) respond to divergencies from plan by taking corrective action so that actual outcomes conform to planned outcomes, or modify the plans if the comparisons indicate that the plans are no longer attainable.

- **Justify the view that a major objective of commercial organizations is broadly to seek to maximize future profits.** The reasons for identifying maximizing future profits as a major objective are: (a) it is unlikely that any other objective is as widely applicable in measuring the ability of the organization to survive in the future; and (b) although it is unlikely that maximizing future profits can be realized in practice it is still important to establish the principles necessary to achieve this objective.

- **Explain the factors that have influenced the changes in the competitive environment.** The factors influencing the change in the competitive environment are (a) globalization of world trade; (b) privatization of government-controlled companies and deregulation in various industries; (c) changing product life cycles; (d) changing customer tastes that demand ever-improving levels of service in cost, quality, reliability, delivery and the choice of new products; and (e) the emergence of e-business.

- **Outline and describe the key success factors that directly affect customer satisfaction.** The key success factors are cost efficiency, quality, time and innovation. Since customers will generally prefer to buy the product or service at the lowest price, all other things being equal, keeping costs low and being cost efficient provides an organization with a strong competitive advantage. Customers also demand high-quality products and services and this has resulted in companies making quality a key competitive variable. Organizations are also seeking to increase customer satisfaction by providing a speedier response to customer requests, ensuring 100 per cent on-time delivery and reducing the time taken to bring new products to the market. To be successful companies must be innovative and develop a steady stream of new products and services and have the capability to rapidly adapt to changing customer requirements.

- **Identify and describe the functions of a cost and management accounting system.** A cost and management accounting system should generate information to meet the following requirements: (a) allocate costs between cost of goods sold and inventories for internal and external profit reporting and inventory valuation; (b) provide relevant information to help managers make better decisions; and (c) provide information for planning, control, performance measurement and continuous improvement.

- **Provide a brief historical description of management accounting.** Most of the management accounting practices that were in use in the mid-1980s had been developed by 1925, and for the next 60 years there was virtually a halt in management accounting innovation. By the mid-1980s firms were using management accounting systems that were obsolete and no longer relevant to the changing competitive and manufacturing environment. During the late 1980s, criticisms of current management accounting practices were widely publicized in the professional and academic accounting literature. In response to the criticisms considerable progress has been made in modifying and implementing new techniques that are relevant to today's environment and that will ensure that management accounting regains its relevance.

KEY TERMS AND CONCEPTS

Each chapter includes a section like this. You should make sure that you understand each of the terms listed below before you proceed to the next chapter. Their meanings are explained on the page numbers indicated.

benchmarking (p. 10)

budget (p. 6)

continuous improvement (p. 10)

control (p. 6)

corporate ethics (p. 11)

cost accounting (p. 15)

cost efficient (p. 9)

cycle time (p. 9)

e-business (p. 12)

e-commerce (p. 12)

enterprise resource planning systems (p. 12)

feedback (p. 6)

feedback loop (p. 7)

financial accounting (pp. 3, 14)

innovation (p. 10)

internet commerce (p. 12)

management accounting (pp. 3, 16)

management by exception (p. 6)

master budget (p. 6)

non-value-added activities (p. 10)

objectives of the organization (p. 5)

performance reports (p. 6)

planning (p. 4)

product life cycle (p. 8)

social responsibility (p. 11)

strategies (p. 5)

time-based measures (p. 9)

total quality management (p. 9)

value-chain analysis (p. 11)

ASSESSMENT MATERIAL

The review questions are short questions that enable you to assess your understanding of the main topics included in the chapter. The page numbers in parentheses provide you with the page numbers to refer to if you cannot answer a specific question.

Subsequent chapters also contain review problems. These are more complex and require you to relate and apply to various business problems. Solutions to review problems are provided in a separate section at the end of the book. Additional review problems can be accessed by lecturers and students on the website (www.drury-online.com). Solutions to these problems are provided for lecturers in the *Instructors' Manual*. This is available on the lecturers' password-protected section of the website.

The website also includes over 30 case study problems. A list of these cases is provided on pages 389–392. The Electronic Boards case is a case study that is relevant to the introductory stages of a management accounting course.

REVIEW QUESTIONS

1.1 Identify and describe the different users of accounting information. *(pp. 2–3)*

1.2 Describe the differences between management accounting and financial accounting. *(pp. 3–4)*

1.3 Explain each of the elements of the decision-making, planning and control process. *(pp. 4–7)*

1.4 Describe what is meant by management by exception. *(p. 6)*

1.5 What is a product's life cycle? *(p. 8)*

1.6 Describe what is meant by continuous improvement and benchmarking. *(p. 10)*

1.7 Describe the different activities in the value chain. *(p. 11)*

1.8 Explain why firms are beginning to concentrate on social responsibility and corporate ethics. *(p. 11)*

1.9 Describe the different functions of management accounting. *(pp. 14–16)*

1.10 Describe enterprise resource planning systems and their impact on management accountants. *(pp. 12–13)*

1.11 Provide a brief historical description of management accounting. *(pp. 16–17)*

CHAPTER 2
AN INTRODUCTION TO
COST TERMS AND CONCEPTS

LEARNING OBJECTIVES

After studying this chapter you should be able to:

- **explain why it is necessary to understand the meaning of different cost terms;**
- **define and illustrate a cost object;**
- **explain the meaning of each of the key terms listed at the end of this chapter;**
- **explain why in the short term some costs and revenues are not relevant for decision-making;**
- **describe the three purposes for which cost information is required.**

In Chapter 1 it was pointed out that accounting information systems measure costs that are used for different purposes – i.e. profit measurement and inventory valuation, decision-making, performance measurement and control. Therefore different types of costs are used in different situations. Because the term 'cost' has multiple meanings, a preceding term must be added to clarify the assumptions that underlie a cost measurement. A large terminology has emerged to indicate which cost meaning is being conveyed. Examples include variable cost, fixed cost, opportunity cost and sunk cost. The aim of this chapter is to provide an understanding of the basic cost terms and concepts that are used in the management accounting literature.

COST OBJECTS

A **cost object** is any activity for which a separate measurement of costs is desired. In other words, if the users of accounting information want to know the cost of something, this something is called a cost object. Examples of cost objects include the cost of a product, the cost of rendering a service to a bank customer or hospital patient, the cost of operating a particular department or sales territory, or indeed anything for which one wants to measure the cost of resources used.

We shall see that the cost collection system typically accounts for costs in two broad stages:

1 It accumulates costs by classifying them into certain categories such as by type of expense (e.g. direct labour, direct materials and indirect costs) or by cost behaviour (such as fixed and variable costs).

2 It then assigns these costs to cost objects.

In this chapter we shall focus on the following cost terms and concepts:

- direct and indirect costs;
- period and product costs;
- cost behaviour in relation to volume of activity;
- relevant and irrelevant costs;
- avoidable and unavoidable costs;
- sunk costs;
- opportunity costs;
- incremental and marginal costs.

DIRECT AND INDIRECT COSTS

Costs that are assigned to cost objects can be divided into two broad categories – **direct** and **indirect costs**. Both categories can be further divided into direct and indirect material costs, and direct and indirect labour costs. Each of these categories is discussed in the following sections.

Direct materials

Direct material costs represent those material costs that can be specifically and exclusively identified with a particular cost object. Where the production of products or the provision of services represent the cost object, the cost of direct materials can be directly charged to the products or services because physical observation can be used to measure the quantity consumed by each individual product or service. In other words, direct materials become part of a physical product or are used in providing a service. For example, wood used in the manufacture of different types of furniture can be directly identified with each specific type of furniture such as chairs, tables and bookcases.

Direct labour

As with direct materials, **direct labour costs** represent those labour costs that can be specifically and exclusively identified with a particular cost object. Physical observation can be used to measure the quantity of labour used to produce a specific product or provide a service. The direct labour cost in producing a product includes the cost of converting the raw materials into a product, such as the workers on an assembly line at Nissan Cars or machine operatives engaged in the production process in the manufacture of televisions. The direct labour cost used to provide a service includes the labour costs in providing a service that can be specifically identified with an individual client in a firm of accountants or the labour costs that can be identified with a specific repair in a firm that repairs computers.

Indirect costs

Indirect costs cannot be identified specifically and exclusively with a given cost object. They consist of indirect labour, materials and expenses. Where products are the cost object the wages of all employees whose time cannot be identified with a specific product represent **indirect labour costs**. Examples include the labour cost of staff employed in the maintenance and repair of production equipment and staff employed in the stores department. The cost of materials used to repair machinery cannot be identified with a specific product and can therefore be classified as **indirect material costs**. Examples of indirect expenses, where products or the provision of a service are the cost objects, include lighting and heating expenses and property taxes. These costs cannot be specifically identified with a particular product or service.

The term **overheads** is widely used instead of indirect costs. In a manufacturing organization overhead costs are categorized as either manufacturing, administration and marketing (or selling) overheads. **Manufacturing overheads** include all the costs of manufacturing apart from direct labour and material costs. Administrative overheads consist of all costs associated with the general administration of the organization that cannot be assigned to either manufacturing, marketing or distribution overheads. Examples of administrative overheads include top-executive salaries, general accounting, secretarial, and research and development costs. Those costs that are necessary to market and distribute a product or service are categorized as marketing (selling) costs. These costs are also known as order-getting and order-filling costs. Examples of marketing costs include advertising, sales personnel salaries/commissions, warehousing and delivery transportation costs.

Figure 2.1 illustrates the various classifications of manufacturing and non-manufacturing costs. You will see from this figure that two further classifications of manufacturing costs are sometimes used. **Prime cost** consists of all direct manufacturing costs (i.e. it is the sum of direct material and direct labour costs). **Conversion cost** is the sum of direct labour and manufacturing overhead costs. It represents the cost of converting raw materials into finished products.

Distinguishing between direct and indirect costs

Sometimes, direct costs are treated as indirect because tracing costs directly to the cost object is not cost effective. For example, the nails used to manufacture a particular desk can be identified specifically with the desk, but, because the cost is likely to be insignificant, the expense of tracing such items does not justify the possible benefits from calculating more accurate product costs.

The distinction between direct and indirect costs also depends on the cost object. A cost can be treated as direct for one cost object but indirect in respect of another. If the cost object is the cost of using different distribution channels, then the rental of warehouses and the salaries of storekeepers will be regarded as direct for each distribution channel. Also consider a supervisor's salary in a maintenance department of a manufacturing company. If the cost object is the maintenance department, then the salary is a direct cost. However, if the cost object is the product, both the warehouse rental and the salaries of the storekeepers and the supervisor will be an indirect cost because these

FIGURE 2.1

Manufacturing and non-manufacturing costs

costs cannot be specifically identified with the product.

Assigning direct and indirect costs to cost objects

Direct costs can be traced easily and accurately to a cost object. For example, where products are the cost object, direct materials and labour used can be physically identified with the different products that an organization produces. Therefore it is a simple process to establish an information technology system that records the quantity and cost of direct labour and material resources used to produce specific products.

In contrast, indirect costs cannot be traced to cost objects. Instead, an estimate must be made of the resources consumed by cost objects using **cost allocations**. A cost allocation is the process of assigning costs when a direct measure does not exist for the quantity of resources consumed by a particular cost object. Cost allocations involve the use of surrogate rather than direct measures. For example, consider an activity such as receiving incoming materials. Assuming that the cost of receiving materials is strongly influenced by the number of receipts then costs can be allocated to products (i.e. the cost object) based on the number of material receipts each product requires. If 20 per cent of the total number of receipts for a period were required for a particular product then 20 per cent of the total costs of receiving incoming materials would be allocated to that product. Assuming that the product was discontinued, and not replaced, we would expect action to be taken to reduce the resources required for receiving materials by 20 per cent.

In the above illustration the surrogate allocation measure is assumed to be a significant determinant of the cost of receiving incoming materials. The process of assigning indirect costs (overheads) and the accuracy of such assignments will be discussed in Chapters 7 and 8 but at this stage you should note that only direct costs can be accurately assigned to cost objects. Therefore, the more direct costs that can be traced to a cost object, the more accurate is the cost assignment.

PERIOD AND PRODUCT COSTS

For profit measurement and inventory/stock valuation (i.e. the valuation of completed unsold products and partly completed products or services) purposes it is necessary to classify costs as either product costs or period costs. **Product costs** are those costs that are identified with goods purchased or produced for resale. In a manufacturing organization they are costs that the accountant attaches to the product and that are included in the inventory valuation for finished goods, or for partly completed goods (work in progress), until they are sold; they are then recorded as expenses and matched against sales for calculating profit. **Period costs** are those costs that are not included in the inventory valuation and as a result are treated as expenses in the period in which they are incurred. *Hence no attempt is made to attach period costs to products for inventory valuation purposes.*

In a manufacturing organization all manufacturing costs are regarded as product costs and non-manufacturing costs are regarded as period costs. Companies operating in the merchandising sector, such as retailing or wholesaling organizations, purchase goods for resale without changing their basic form. The cost of the goods purchased is regarded as a product cost and all other costs such as administration and selling and distribution

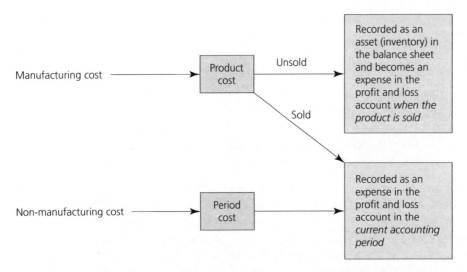

FIGURE 2.2

Treatment of period and product costs

expenses are considered to be period costs. The treatment of period and product costs for a manufacturing organization is illustrated in Figure 2.2. You will see that both product and period costs are eventually classified as expenses. The major difference is the point in time at which they are so classified.

Why are non-manufacturing costs treated as period costs and not included in the inventory valuation? There are two reasons. First, inventories are assets (unsold production) and assets represent resources that have been acquired that are expected to contribute to future revenue. Manufacturing costs incurred in making a product can be expected to generate future revenues to cover the cost of production. There is no guarantee, however, that non-manufacturing costs will generate future revenue, because they do not represent value added to any specific product. Therefore, they are not included in the inventory valuation. Second, many non-manufacturing costs (e.g. distribution costs) are not incurred when the product is being stored. Hence it is inappropriate to include such costs within the inventory valuation.

An illustration of the accounting treatment of period and product costs for income (profit) measurement purposes is presented in Example 2.1.

COST BEHAVIOUR

A knowledge of how costs and revenues will vary with different levels of activity (or volume) is essential for decision-making. Activity or volume may be measured in terms of units of production or sales, hours worked, miles travelled, patients seen, students enrolled or any other appropriate measure of the activity of an organization. Examples of decisions that require information on how costs and revenues vary with different levels of activity include the following:

1 How will costs and revenues change if activity is increased (or decreased) by 15 per cent?

2 What will be the impact on profits if we reduce selling price by 10 per cent based on the estimate that this will increase sales volume by 15 per cent?

3 How do the cost and revenues change for a university if the number of students is increased by 5 per cent?

EXAMPLE 2.1

The Flanders company produces 100 000 identical units of a product during period 1. The costs for the period are as follows:

	(£)	(£)
Manufacturing costs:		
Direct labour	400 000	
Direct materials	200 000	
Manufacturing overheads	200 000	800 000
Non-manufacturing costs		300 000

During period 1, the company sold 50 000 units for £750 000, and the remaining 50 000 units were unsold at the end of the period. There was no opening stock at the start of the period. The profit and loss account for period 1 will be as follows:

	(£)	(£)
Sales (50 000)		750 000
Manufacturing costs (*product costs*):		
Direct labour	400 000	
Direct materials	200 000	
Manufacturing overheads	200 000	
	800 000	
Less closing stock (50% or 50 000 units)	400 000	
Cost of goods sold (50% or 50 000 units)		400 000
Gross profit		350 000
Less non-manufacturing costs (*period costs*)		300 000
Net profit		50 000

Fifty per cent of the production was sold during the period and the remaining 50 per cent was produced for inventories. Half of the product costs are therefore identified as an expense for the period and the remainder are included in the closing inventory valuation. If we assume that the closing inventory is sold in the next accounting period, the remaining 50 per cent of the product costs will become expenses in the next accounting period. However, all the period costs became an expense in this accounting period, because this is the period to which they relate. Note that only product costs form the basis for the calculation of cost of goods sold, and that period costs do not form part of this calculation.

4 How do costs and revenues of a hotel change if a room and meals are provided for two guests for a three-day stay?

5 How many tickets must be sold for a concert in order to break even?

The terms 'variable', 'fixed', 'semi-variable' and 'semi-fixed' have traditionally been used in the management accounting literature to describe how a cost reacts to changes in activity. **Variable costs** vary in direct proportion to the volume of activity; that is, doubling the level of activity will double the total variable cost. Consequently, *total* variable costs are linear and *unit* variable cost is constant. Examples of variable costs in a manufacturing organization include direct materials, energy to operate the machines and sales commissions. Examples of variable costs in a merchandising company, such as a supermarket, include the purchase costs of all items that are sold. In a hospital variable costs include the costs of drugs and meals, which may be assumed to fluctuate with the number of patient days.

To illustrate how variable costs change with activity consider the example of a bicycle manufacturer such as the Raleigh Bicycle Company that purchases component parts. Assume that the cost of purchasing two wheels for a particular bicycle is £10 per bicycle. Figure 2.3(a) illustrates the concept of variable costs in graphic form. You can see that as the number of units of output of bicycles increases or decreases, the *total* variable cost of wheels increases and decreases proportionately. Look at Figure 2.3(b). This diagram shows that variable cost per *unit* of output is constant even though total variable cost increases/decreases proportionately with changes in activity.

Fixed costs remain constant over wide ranges of activity for a specified time period. Hence they differ from variable costs because total fixed costs are not affected by changes in activity. Examples of fixed costs include depreciation of equipment, property taxes, insurance costs, supervisory salaries and leasing charges for cars used by the sales force. Figure 2.4 illustrates how *total* fixed costs and fixed cost per unit of activity react with changes in activity.

You will see from this diagram that *total* fixed costs are constant for all units of activity whereas *unit* fixed costs decrease proportionally with the level of activity. For example, if the total of the fixed costs is £5000 for a month the fixed costs per *unit* of activity will be as follows:

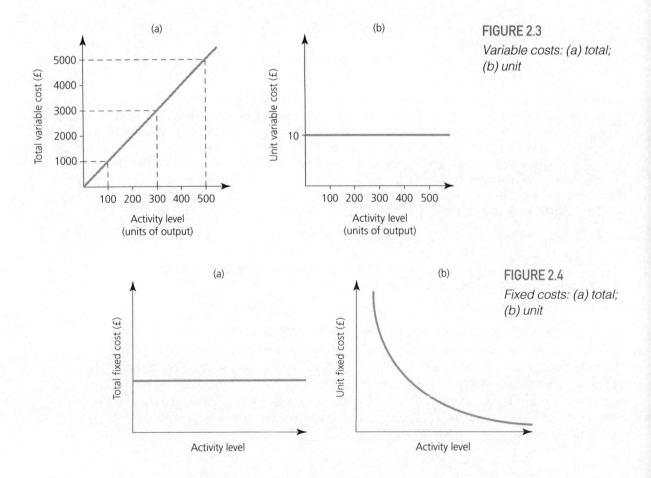

FIGURE 2.3
Variable costs: (a) total; (b) unit

FIGURE 2.4
Fixed costs: (a) total; (b) unit

Units produced	Fixed cost per unit (£)
1	5000
10	500
100	50
1000	5

Because unit fixed costs are not constant per unit they must be interpreted with caution. For decision-making, it is better to work with total fixed costs rather than unit costs.

The distinction between fixed and variable costs must be made relative to the time period under consideration. Over a sufficiently long time period of several years, virtually all costs are variable. During such a long period of time, contraction in demand will be accompanied by reductions in virtually all categories of costs. For example, senior managers can be released, machinery need not be replaced and even buildings and land can be sold. Similarly, large expansions in activity will eventually cause all categories of costs to increase. Within shorter time periods, costs will be fixed or variable in relation to changes in activity.

Spending on some fixed costs, such as direct labour and supervisory salaries, can be adjusted in the short term to reflect changes in activity. For example, if production activity declines significantly then direct workers and supervisors might continue to be employed in the hope that the decline in demand will be temporary; but if there is no upsurge in demand then staff might eventually be made redundant. If, on the other hand, production capacity expands to some critical level, additional workers might be employed, but the process of recruiting such workers may take several months. Thus within a short-term period, such as one year, labour costs can change in response to changes in demand in a manner similar to that depicted in Figure 2.5. Costs that behave in this manner are described as **semi-fixed** or **step fixed costs**. The distinguishing feature of step fixed costs is that within a given time period they are fixed within specified activity levels, but they eventually increase or decrease by a constant amount at various critical activity levels as illustrated in Figure 2.5.

Our discussion so far has assumed a one-year time period. Consider a shorter time period such as one month and the circumstances outlined in the previous paragraph where it takes several months to respond to changes in activity and alter spending levels. Over very short-term periods such as one month, spending on direct labour and supervisory salaries will be fixed in relation to changes in activity.

Note, however, that in the short term, even though fixed costs are normally assumed to remain unchanged in response to changes in the level of activity, they may change in

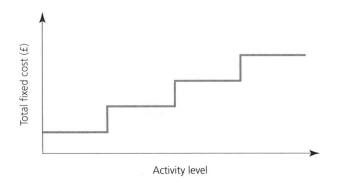

FIGURE 2.5
Step fixed costs

response to other factors. For example, if price levels increase then some fixed costs such as management salaries will increase.

Before concluding our discussion of cost behaviour in relation to volume of activity, we must consider **semi-variable costs** (also known as **mixed costs**). These include both a fixed and a variable component. If you refer to your telephone account for your land line you will probably find that it consists of a fixed component (the line rental) plus a variable component (the number of telephone calls made multiplied by the cost per call). Similarly the office photocopying costs may consist of a fixed rental charge for the photocopiers plus a variable cost (the cost of the paper multiplied by the number of photocopies). The cost of maintenance of equipment in a hospital may also be a semi-variable cost consisting of planned maintenance that is undertaken whatever the level of activity, and a variable element that is directly related to the level of usage of the equipment.

RELEVANT AND IRRELEVANT COSTS AND REVENUES

For decision-making, costs and revenues can be classified according to whether they are relevant to a particular decision. **Relevant costs and revenues** are those *future* costs and revenues that will be changed by a decision, whereas **irrelevant costs and revenues** are those that will not be affected by the decision. For example, if you are faced with a choice of making a journey using your own car or by public transport, the car tax and insurance costs are irrelevant, since they will remain the same whatever alternative is chosen. However, petrol costs for the car will differ depending on which alternative is chosen, and this cost will be relevant for decision-making.

Let us now consider a further illustration of the classification of relevant and irrelevant costs. Assume that in the past a company purchased raw materials for £100 but there appears to be no possibility of selling these materials or using them in future production apart from in connection with an enquiry from a former customer. This customer is prepared to purchase a product that will require the use of all these materials, but he is not prepared to pay more than £250 per unit. The additional costs of converting these materials into the required product are £200. Should the company accept the order for £250? It appears that the cost of the order is £300, consisting of £100 material cost and £200 conversion cost, but this is incorrect because the £100 material cost will remain the same whether the order is accepted or rejected. The material cost is therefore irrelevant for the decision, but if the order is accepted the conversion costs will change by £200, and this conversion cost is a relevant cost. If we compare the revenue of £250 with the relevant cost for the order of £200, it means that the order should be accepted, assuming of course that no higher-priced orders can be obtained elsewhere. The following calculation shows that this is the correct decision:

	Do not accept order (£)	Accept order (£)
Materials	100	100
Conversion costs	—	200
Revenue	—	(250)
Net costs	100	50

The net costs of the company are £50 less, or alternatively the company is £50 better off as a result of accepting the order. This agrees with the £50 advantage that was suggested by the relevant cost method.

In this illustration the sales revenue was relevant to the decision because future revenue changed depending on which alternative was selected; but sales revenue may also be irrelevant for decision-making. Consider a situation where a company can meet its sales demand by purchasing either machine A or machine B. The output of both machines is identical, but the operating costs and purchase costs of the machines are different. In this situation the sales revenue will remain unchanged irrespective of which machine is purchased (assuming of course that the quality of output is identical for both machines). Consequently, sales revenue is irrelevant for this decision; the relevant items are the operating costs and the cost of the machines. We have now established an important principle regarding the classification of cost and revenues for decision-making; namely, that in the short term not all costs and revenues are relevant for decision-making.

AVOIDABLE AND UNAVOIDABLE COSTS

Sometimes the terms **avoidable** and **unavoidable costs** are used instead of relevant and irrelevant cost. Avoidable costs are those costs that may be saved by not adopting a given alternative, whereas unavoidable costs cannot be saved. Therefore, only avoidable costs are relevant for decision-making purposes. Consider the example that we used to illustrate relevant and irrelevant costs. The material costs of £100 are unavoidable and irrelevant, but the conversion costs of £200 are avoidable and hence relevant. The decision rule is to accept those alternatives that generate revenues in excess of the avoidable costs.

SUNK COSTS

These costs are the costs of resources already acquired where the total will be unaffected by the choice between various alternatives. They are costs that have been created by a decision made in the past and that cannot be changed by any decision that will be made in the future. The expenditure of £100 on materials that were no longer required, referred to in the preceding section, is an example of a **sunk cost**. Similarly, the written down values of assets previously purchased are sunk costs. For example, if equipment was purchased four years ago for £100 000 with an expected life of five years and nil scrap value then the written down value will be £20 000 if straight line depreciation is used. This written down value will have to be written off, no matter what possible alternative future action might be chosen. If the equipment was scrapped, the £20 000 would be written off; if the equipment was used for productive purposes, the £20 000 would still have to be written off. This cost cannot be changed by any future decision and is therefore classified as a sunk cost.

Sunk costs are irrelevant for decision-making, but not all irrelevant costs are sunk costs. For example, a comparison of two alternative production methods may result in identical direct material expenditure for both alternatives, so the direct material cost is irrelevant because it will remain the same whichever alternative is chosen, but the material cost is not a sunk cost since it will be incurred in the future.

REAL WORLD VIEWS 2.1

Flying for free?

Many low-cost carriers like easyJet, Ryanair and Germanwings regularly offer flights to customers at a very low price or even free of charge. Ryanair, Europe's most profitable airline, wants to make air travel free, as in zero cost. By the end of the decade, 'more than half of our passengers will fly free', says Michael O'Leary, CEO of Ryanair.[1]

Surely there is a cost of providing a seat to a passenger, so how can one be given away for free? Is this a crazy pricing decision? The answer is no when one considers the nature of costs at low-cost carriers. Most costs are fixed in nature. First, the aircraft cost (of about $70 million for a Boeing 737) is fixed.[2] This cost is of course normally written off over the life of the aircraft as depreciation. Second, the salaries of the pilot, first officer and cabin crew are also fixed. And what about the fuel cost? This is also treated as a fixed cost as the carriers would say that the cost is incurred once the aircraft flies. Thus, if one additional passenger flies with a low-cost carrier, the variable cost associated with this passenger is zero and hence tickets could be given for free. It is also interesting to note how low-cost carriers often ground aircraft in off-peak periods, thus saving fuel and salary costs (they often use contract staff).

So how do lost-cost carriers make such large profits? Through the combination of a complex yield (revenue) management system, the sale of ancillary goods and services, and charges for additional services, profits abound for such operators. On the yield management side, not every seat will be free –

some will be quite expensive (if you want to travel at the last minute or a sporting event is taking place for example). Passengers are also being charged for food and drinks on board and even in some instances for checking in luggage. So if, for example, 50 per cent of the passengers on an aircraft have paid 'normal' fares that cover the fixed costs of the flight, revenue from additional passengers and services is 100 per cent profit.

Discussion points

1 Do you agree that the variable cost of a passenger can be zero?
2 How can a low-cost carrier improve or reduce its fixed costs?

References

1 *Business 2.0* magazine, 1 April 2006.
2 http://www.boeing.com/commercial/prices/

© T. LEHNE/LOTUSEATERS/ALAMY

OPPORTUNITY COSTS

An **opportunity cost** is a cost that measures the opportunity that is lost or sacrificed when the choice of one course of action requires that an alternative course of action is given up. Consider the situation where a student is contemplating taking a gap year overseas after completing his or her studies. Assume that the student has an offer of a job upon completion of his or her studies. The lost salary is an opportunity cost of choosing the gap year that must be taken into account when considering the financial implications of the decision. For a further illustration of an opportunity cost, look at Example 2.2.

It is important to note that opportunity costs cannot normally be recorded in the accounting system because they do not involve cash outlays. They also only apply to the use of scarce resources. Where resources are not scarce, no sacrifice exists from using these resources. In Example 2.2, if machine X was operating at 80 per cent of its potential capacity and the decision to accept the contract would not have resulted in reduced production of product A there would have been no loss of revenue, and the opportunity cost would be zero.

You should now be aware that opportunity costs are of vital importance for decision-making. If no alternative use of resources exists then the opportunity cost is zero, but if resources have an alternative use, and are scarce, then an opportunity cost does exist.

INCREMENTAL AND MARGINAL COSTS

Incremental (also called **differential**) **costs** and revenues are the difference between costs and revenues for the corresponding items under each alternative being considered. For example, a university department is evaluating the financial implications of a 20 per cent increase in the number of students. This would entail new full-time lecturers being appointed on a permanent contract at a cost of £150 000 per annum and an increase in the part-time lecturers budget of £15 000 (300 hours at £50 per hour) per annum. The difference in costs (i.e. the incremental cost) between the two alternatives of (1) no increase in the number of students and (2) 20 per cent increase in the number of students is £165 000.

Incremental costs may or may not include fixed costs. If fixed costs change as a result of a decision, the increase in costs represents an incremental cost. If fixed costs do not change as a result of a decision, the incremental costs will be zero. In the above example, let us assume that the part-time staff can be appointed on an hourly contract so that their employment can be matched exactly with the number of extra hours of teaching that are required from the increase in the number of students. In other words the employment of

EXAMPLE 2.2

A company has an opportunity to obtain a contract for the production of a special component. This component will require 100 hours of processing on machine X. Machine X is working at full capacity on the production of product A, and the only way in which the contract can be fulfilled is by reducing the output of product A. This will result in a lost profit contribution of £200. The contract will also result in *additional* variable costs of £1000. If the company takes on the contract, it will sacrifice a profit contribution of £200 from the lost output of product A. This represents an opportunity cost, and should be included as part of the cost when negotiating for the contract. The contract price should at least cover the additional costs of £1000 plus the £200 opportunity cost to ensure that the company will be better off in the short term by accepting the contract.

part-time staff can be classified as a variable cost. The full-time staff are a fixed cost. Therefore, the incremental cost in this example includes both fixed and variable costs.

If you have studied economics you will have noticed that incremental costs and revenues are similar in principle to the economist's concept of **marginal cost** and **marginal revenue**. The main difference is that marginal cost/revenue represents the additional cost/revenue of one extra unit of output whereas incremental cost/revenue represents the additional cost/revenue resulting from a group of additional units of output. We shall see that business decisions normally entail identifying the change in costs and revenues arising from comparing two alternative courses of action and where this involves a change in activity it is likely that this will involve multiple, rather than single units of activity.

THE COST AND MANAGEMENT ACCOUNTING INFORMATION SYSTEM

In the previous chapter we noted that a cost and management accounting information system should generate information to meet the following requirements:

1 to allocate costs between cost of goods sold and inventories for internal and external profit measurement and inventory valuation;

2 to provide relevant information to help managers make better decisions;

3 to provide information for planning, control and performance measurement.

With today's information technology a database can be maintained, with costs appropriately coded and classified, so that relevant cost information can be extracted to meet each of the above requirements. A suitable coding system enables costs to be accumulated by the required cost objects (such as products or services, departments, responsibility centres, distribution channels, etc.) and also to be classified by appropriate categories of expenses (e.g. direct materials, direct labour and overheads) and also by cost behaviour (i.e. fixed and variable costs). In practice, direct materials will be accumulated by each individual type of material, direct labour by different grades of labour and overhead costs by different categories of indirect expenses (e.g. rent, depreciation, supervision, etc.).

For *inventory valuation* in a manufacturing organization, the costs of all partly completed products (i.e. work in progress) and unsold finished products can be extracted from the database to ascertain the total cost assigned to inventories. The cost of goods sold that is deducted from sales revenues to compute the profit for the period can also be extracted by summing the manufacturing costs of all those products that have been sold during the period. We shall consider this process in more detail in Chapter 7.

Future costs, rather than past costs, are required for *decision-making*. Therefore costs extracted from the database should be adjusted for anticipated price changes. Where a company sells many products or services their profitability should be monitored at regular intervals so that potentially unprofitable products can be highlighted for a more detailed study of their future viability. This information is extracted from the database with costs reported by categories of expenses and divided into their fixed and variable elements. In Chapter 5 we shall focus in more detail on product/segmented profitability analysis.

For *cost control and performance measurement*, costs and revenues must be traced to the individuals who are responsible for incurring them. This system is known as **responsibility accounting**. Responsibility accounting involves the creation of responsibility centres. A **responsibility centre** may be defined as an organization unit or part of a business for whose performance a manager is held accountable. At this stage it may be easier to consider responsibility centres as being equivalent to separate departments within an organization. Responsibility accounting enables accountability for financial results and outcomes to be allocated to individuals (typically heads of departments) throughout the organization. Performance reports are produced at regular intervals for each responsibility centre. The reports are generated by extracting from the database costs analysed by responsibility centres and categories of expenses. Actual costs for each item of expense listed on the performance report should be compared with budgeted costs so that those costs that do not conform to plan can be pinpointed and investigated. We shall examine responsibility accounting in more detail in Chapter 10.

SUMMARY

The following items relate to the learning objectives listed at the beginning of the chapter.

- **Explain why it is necessary to understand the meaning of different cost terms**. The term 'cost' has multiple meanings and different types of costs are used in different situations. Therefore, a preceding term must be added to clarify the assumptions that underlie a measurement.

- **Define and illustrate a cost object**. A cost object is any activity for which a separate measurement of cost is required. In other words managers often want to know the cost of something and the 'thing' that they want to know the cost of is a cost object. Examples of cost objects include the cost of a new product, the cost of operating a sales outlet and the cost of operating a specific machine.

- **Explain the meaning of each of the key terms listed at the end of this chapter**. You should check your understanding of each of the terms listed in the 'Key terms and concepts' section below by referring to the page numbers that are shown in the parentheses following each key term.

- **Explain why in the short term some costs and revenues are not relevant for decision-making**. In the short term some costs and revenues may remain unchanged for all alternatives under consideration. For example, if you wish to determine the costs of driving to work in your own car or using public transport, the cost of the road fund taxation licence and insurance will remain the same for both alternatives, assuming that you intend to keep your car for leisure purposes. Therefore the costs of these items are not relevant for assisting you in your decision to travel to work by public transport or using your own car. Costs that remain unchanged for all alternatives under consideration are not relevant for decision-making.

- **Describe the three purposes for which cost information is required**. A cost and management accounting system should generate information to meet the following requirements:

    (a) to allocate costs between cost of goods sold and inventories for internal and external profit reporting and inventory valuation;

    (b) to provide relevant information to help managers make better decisions;

    (c) to provide information for planning, control and performance measurement.

A database should be maintained with costs appropriately coded or classified, so that relevant information can be extracted for meeting each of the above requirements.

KEY TERMS AND CONCEPTS

avoidable costs (p. 33)
conversion cost (p. 26)
cost allocations (p. 27)
cost object (p. 24)
differential costs (p. 35)
direct costs (p. 24)
direct labour costs (p. 25)
direct material costs (p. 24)
fixed costs (p. 30)
incremental costs (p. 35)
indirect costs (p. 24)
indirect labour costs (p. 25)
indirect material costs (p. 25)
irrelevant costs and revenues (p. 32)
marginal cost/revenue (p. 36)
manufacturing overheads (p. 26)

mixed costs (p. 32)
opportunity cost (p. 34)
overheads (p. 25)
period costs (p. 27)
prime cost (p. 26)
product costs (p. 27)
relevant costs and revenues (p. 32)
responsibility accounting (p. 37)
responsibility centre (p. 37)
semi-fixed costs (p. 31)
semi-variable costs (p. 32)
step fixed costs (p. 31)
sunk cost (p. 33)
unavoidable costs (p. 33)
variable costs (p. 29)

ASSESSMENT MATERIAL

The review questions are short questions that enable you to assess your understanding of the main topics included in the chapter. The page numbers in parentheses provide you with the page numbers to refer to if you cannot answer a specific question.

The review problems are more complex and require you to relate and apply the content to various business problems. Solutions to review problems are provided in a separate section at the end of the book. Additional review problems can be accessed by lecturers and students on the website (www.drury-online.com). Solutions to these problems are provided for lecturers in the *Instructors' Manual*. This is available on the lecturers' password-protected section of the website.

The website also includes over 30 case study problems. A list of these cases is provided on pages 389–392. The Electronic Boards case is a case study that is relevant to the introductory stages of a management accounting course.

REVIEW QUESTIONS

2.1 Define the meaning of the term 'cost object' and provide three examples of cost objects. *(p. 24)*

2.2 Distinguish between a direct and indirect cost. *(pp. 24)*

2.3 Describe how a given direct cost item can be both a direct and indirect cost. *(pp. 26–27)*

2.4 Provide examples of each of the following: (a) direct labour, (b) indirect labour, (c) direct materials, (d) indirect materials and (e) indirect expenses. *(pp. 25–26)*

2.5 Explain the meaning of the terms: (a) prime cost, (b) overheads and (c) cost allocations. *(pp. 26–27)*

2.6 Distinguish between product costs and period costs. *(pp. 27–28)*

2.7 Provide examples of decisions that require knowledge of how costs and revenues vary with different levels of activity. *(pp. 29–31)*

2.8 Explain the meaning of each of the following terms: (a) variable costs, (b) fixed costs, (c) semi-fixed costs and (d) semi-variable costs. Provide examples of costs for each of the four categories. *(pp. 29–32)*

2.9 Distinguish between relevant (avoidable) and irrelevant (unavoidable) costs and provide examples of each type of cost. *(pp. 32–33)*

2.10 Explain the meaning of the term 'sunk cost'. *(p. 33)*

2.11 Distinguish between incremental and marginal costs. *(p. 36)*

2.12 What is an opportunity cost? Give some examples. *(p. 35)*

2.13 Explain responsibility accounting. *(p. 37)*

REVIEW PROBLEMS

2.14 Classify each of the following as being usually fixed (F), variable (V), semi-fixed (SF) or semi-variable (SV):

   (a) direct labour;
   (b) depreciation of machinery;
   (c) factory rental;
   (d) supplies and other indirect materials;
   (e) advertising;
   (f) maintenance of machinery;
   (g) factory manager's salary;
   (h) supervisory personnel;
   (i) royalty payments.

2.15 Which of the following costs are likely to be controllable by the head of the production department?

   (a) price paid for materials;
   (b) charge for floor space;
   (c) raw materials used;
   (d) electricity used for machinery;
   (e) machinery depreciation;
   (f) direct labour;
   (g) insurance on machinery;
   (h) share of cost of industrial relations department.

2.16 A direct cost is a cost that:

   A is incurred as a direct consequence of a decision;
   B can be economically identified with the item being costed;
   C cannot be economically identified with the item being costed;
   D is immediately controllable;
   E is the responsibility of the board of directors.

2.17 Which of the following would be classed as indirect labour?

   A assembly workers in a company manufacturing televisions;
   B a stores assistant in a factory store;
   C plasterers in a construction company;
   D an audit clerk in a firm of auditors.

2.18 Fixed costs are conventionally deemed to be:

   A constant per unit of output;
   B constant in total when production volume changes;
   C outside the control of management;
   D those unaffected by inflation.

2.19 Data

	(£)
Cost of motor car	5500
Trade-in price after 2 years or 60 000 miles is expected to be	1500
Maintenance – 6-monthly service costing	60
Spares/replacement parts, per 1000 miles	20
Vehicle licence, per annum	80
Insurance, per annum	150
Tyre replacements after 25 000 miles, four at £37.50 each	
Petrol, per gallon	1.90
Average mileage from one gallon is 25 miles.	

(a) From the above data you are required:

    (i) To prepare a schedule to be presented to management showing for the mileages of 5000, 10 000, 15 000 and 30 000 miles per annum:

        (1) total variable cost

        (2) total fixed cost

        (3) total cost

        (4) variable cost per mile (in pence to nearest penny)

        (5) fixed cost per mile (in pence to nearest penny)

        (6) total cost per mile (in pence to nearest penny)

        If, in classifying the costs, you consider that some can be treated as either variable or fixed, state the assumption(s) on which your answer is based together with brief supporting reason(s).

    (ii) On graph paper, to plot the information given in your answer to (i) above for the costs listed against (1), (2), (3) and (6).

    (iii) To read off from your graph(s) in (ii) and state the approximate total costs applicable to 18 000 miles and 25 000 miles and the total cost per mile at these two mileages.

(b) 'The more miles you travel, the cheaper it becomes.' Comment briefly on this statement.

(25 marks)

2.20 Sunk and opportunity costs for decision-making

Mrs Johnston has taken out a lease on a shop for a down payment of £5000. Additionally, the rent under the lease amounts to £5000 per annum. If the lease is cancelled, the initial payment of £5000 is forfeit. Mrs Johnston plans to use the shop for the sale of clothing, and has estimated operations for the next 12 months as follows:

	(£)	(£)
Sales	115 000	
Less Value-added tax (VAT)	15 000	
Sales less VAT		100 000
Cost of goods sold	50 000	
Wages and wage-related costs	12 000	
Rent including the down payment	10 000	
Rates, heating, lighting and insurance	13 000	
Audit, legal and general expenses	2 000	
		87 000
Net profit before tax		13 000

In the figures no provision has been made for the cost of Mrs Johnston but it is estimated that one half of her time will be devoted to the business. She is undecided whether to continue with her plans because she knows that she can sublet the shop to a friend for a monthly rent of £550 if she does not use the shop herself.

You are required to:

(a) explain and identify the 'sunk' and 'opportunity' costs in the situation depicted above;

(b) state what decision Mrs Johnston should make according to the information given, supporting your conclusion with a financial statement.

(11 marks)

CHAPTER 3
COST–VOLUME–PROFIT ANALYSIS

LEARNING OBJECTIVES

After studying this chapter you should be able to:

- **justify the use of linear cost and revenue functions;**
- **apply the numerical approach to answer questions similar to those listed in Example 3.1;**
- **construct break-even, contribution and profit–volume graphs;**
- **apply cost–volume–profit analysis in a multi-product setting;**
- **explain the meaning of operating leverage and describe how it influences profits;**
- **identify and explain the assumptions on which cost–volume–profit analysis is based.**

In this chapter we shall look at how management accounting information can be of assistance in providing answers to questions about the consequences of following particular courses of action. Such questions might include:

- How many units must be sold to break-even?
- What would be the effect on profits if we reduce our selling price and sell more units?
- What sales volume is required to meet the additional fixed charges arising from an advertising campaign?
- Should we pay our sales people on the basis of a salary only, or on the basis of a commission only, or by a combination of the two?

These and other questions can be answered using cost–volume–profit (CVP) analysis.

CVP analysis examines the relationship between changes in activity (i.e. output) and changes in total sales revenue, costs and net profit. The objective is to establish what will happen to the financial results if a specified level of activity or volume fluctuates. This information is vital to management, since one of the most important variables influencing total sales revenue, total costs and profits is output or volume. For this reason output is given special attention, because knowledge of this relationship will enable management to identify critical output levels, such as the level at which neither a profit nor a loss will occur (i.e. the **break-even point**).

CVP analysis is based on the relationship between volume and sales revenue, costs and profit in the short run, the short run normally being a period of one year, or less, in which the output of a firm is likely to be restricted to that available from the current operating capacity. In the short run some inputs can be increased, but others cannot. Additional supplies of materials and unskilled labour may be obtained at short notice, but operating capacity cannot be significantly changed. For example, it is not possible for a hospital to expand its facilities in the short run in order to increase the number of hospital beds. Similarly, a hotel cannot increase the number of rooms in the short run to increase the number of guests. Also, most of the costs and prices of a firm's products or services will already have been predetermined over a short-run period, and the major area of uncertainty will be sales volume. Short-run profitability will therefore be most sensitive to sales volume. CVP analysis thus highlights the effects of changes in sales volume on the level of profits in the short run.

The term 'volume' is used within CVP analysis but this has multiple meanings. Different measures can be used to represent the term. For example, sales revenue is a generic term that can be used by most organizations. However, units of output, or activity, tend to be the most widely used terms. This raises the question of what constitutes a unit of output or activity. For a manufacturing organization, such as a car manufacturer, determining units of output is straightforward. It is the number of cars produced. For a computer manufacturer it is the number of computers produced. Service organizations face a more difficult choice. Hotels may define units as the number of guest nights, leisure centres may use the number of visitors as a measure of output/activity and airlines might use the number of passenger miles.

CURVILINEAR CVP RELATIONSHIPS

A diagram showing CVP behaviour is presented in Figure 3.1. You will see that the total revenue and total cost lines are curvilinear. The total revenue line (0E) initially resembles a straight line but then begins to rise less steeply and eventually starts to decline. This arises because the firm is only able to sell increasing quantities of output by reducing the selling price per unit; thus the total revenue line does not increase proportionately with output. To increase the quantity of sales, it is necessary to reduce the unit selling price, which results in the total revenue line rising less steeply, and eventually beginning to decline. The

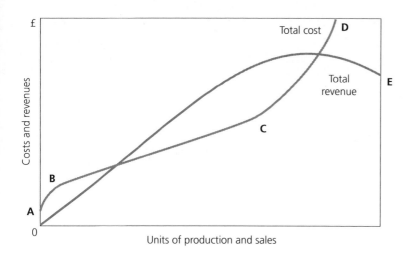

FIGURE 3.1
*Curvilinear CVP
relationships*

decline occurs because the adverse effect of price reductions outweighs the benefits of increased sales volume.

The total cost line (AD) illustrates cost behaviour in a manufacturing firm but similar cost behaviour also applies in non-manufacturing firms. Between points A and B, total costs rise steeply at first as the firm operates at the lower levels of the volume range. This reflects the difficulties of efficiently using manufacturing facilities designed for much larger volume levels. Between points B and C, the total cost line begins to level out and rise less steeply because the firm is now able to operate its manufacturing facilities within the efficient operating range and can take advantage of economies of scale (e.g. specialization of labour and smooth production schedules). Economists describe this situation as **increasing returns to scale**. In the upper portion of the volume range the total cost line between points C and D rises more steeply as the cost per unit increases. This is because manufacturing facilities are being operated beyond their capacity. Bottlenecks develop, production schedules become more complex and equipment breakdowns begin to occur. The overall effect is that the cost per unit of output increases and causes the total cost line to rise steeply. Economists describe this situation as **decreasing returns to scale**.

It is also clear from Figure 3.1 that the shape of the total revenue line is such that it crosses the total cost line at two points. In other words, there are two output levels at which the total costs are equal to the total revenues; or, more simply, there are two break-even points.

LINEAR CVP RELATIONSHIPS

In Figure 3.2 the blue total cost line XY and the red total revenue line 0V assume that variable cost and selling price are constant per unit of output. This results in a linear relationship (i.e. a straight line) for total revenue and total cost as output/volume changes. If you look at these two lines you will see that a linear relationship results in only one break-even point. Also the profit area (i.e. the difference between the total revenue line 0V and the total cost line XY) widens as volume increases. For comparative purposes the curvilinear relationships shown in Figure 3.1 are also reproduced in Figure 3.2 (with blue line AD and red line 0E showing, respectively, curvilinear total cost and total revenue relationships).

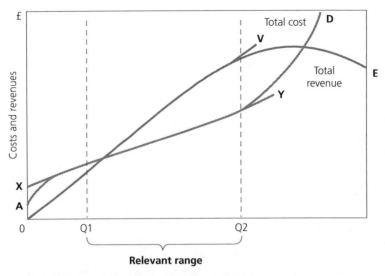

FIGURE 3.2

*Linear CVP
relationships*

Management accounting assumes linear CVP relationships when applying CVP analysis to short-run business problems. Curvilinear relationships appear to be more realistic of cost and revenue behaviour, so how can we justify CVP analysis based on the assumption of linear relationships? The answers are provided in the following sections.

Relevant range

Linear relationships are not intended to provide an accurate representation of total cost and total revenue throughout all ranges of output. The objective is to represent the behaviour of total cost and revenue over the range of output at which a firm expects to be operating within a short-term planning horizon. This range of output is represented by the output range between points Q1 and Q2 in Figure 3.2. The term **relevant range** is used to refer to the output range at which the firm expects to be operating within a short-term planning horizon. This relevant range also broadly represents the output levels that the firm has had experience of operating in the past and for which cost information is available.

It is clear from Figure 3.2 that, between points Q1 and Q2, the cost and revenue relationships are more or less linear. It would be unwise, however, to make this assumption for output levels outside the relevant range. CVP analysis should therefore only be applied within the relevant range. If the relevant range changes, different fixed and variable costs and selling prices must be used.

Fixed cost function

Figure 3.2 indicates that at zero output level fixed costs equivalent to 0X would be incurred. This fixed cost level of 0X is assumed to be applicable to activity level Q1 to Q2, shown in Figure 3.3. If there were to be a prolonged economic recession then output might fall below Q1, and this could result in redundancies and shutdowns. Therefore fixed costs may be reduced to 0B if there is a prolonged and a significant decline in sales demand. Alternatively, additional fixed costs will be incurred if long-term sales volume is expected to be greater than Q2. Over a longer-term time horizon, the fixed cost line will consist of a

FIGURE 3.3
*Fixed costs applicable within
the relevant range*

series of step functions as shown in Figure 3.3. However, since within its short term planning horizon the firm expects to be operating between output levels Q1 and Q2 (i.e. the relevant range), it will be committed, in the short term, to fixed costs of 0X. Thus the fixed cost of ØX shown in Figures 3.2 and 3.3 represent the fixed costs that would be incurred only for the relevant range.

Total revenue function

Linear CVP relationships assume that selling price is constant over the relevant range of output, and therefore the total revenue line is a straight line. This is a realistic assumption in those firms that operate in industries where selling prices tend to be fixed in the short term. Also, beyond the relevant range, increases in output may only be possible by offering substantial reductions in price. As it is not the intention of firms to operate outside the relevant range it is appropriate to assume constant selling prices.

A NUMERICAL APPROACH TO COST–VOLUME–PROFIT ANALYSIS

As an alternative to using diagrams for CVP analysis we can also use a numerical approach. We shall see that diagrams are useful for presenting the outcomes in a more visual form to non-accounting managers. The numerical approach, however, is often a quicker and more flexible method than the graphical approach for producing the appropriate information. Indeed, it is possible to express CVP relationships in a simple mathematical equation format so that they can form an input for computer financial models. To keep things simple we shall avoid mathematical formulae and use a simple numerical approach.

In the previous sections it has been pointed out that CVP analysis is based on the assumption that selling price and variable cost are constant per unit of output. In contrast, you will remember from Chapter 2 that over a short-run period fixed costs are a constant total amount whereas unit cost changes with output levels. As a result, profit per unit also changes with volume. For example, if fixed costs are £10 000 for a period and output is 10 000 units, the fixed cost will be £1 per unit. Alternatively, if output is 5000 units, the fixed cost will be £2 per unit. Profit per unit will not therefore be constant over varying output levels and it is incorrect to unitize fixed costs for CVP decisions.

EXAMPLE 3.1

Norvik Enterprises operates in the leisure and entertainment industry and one of its activities is to promote concerts at locations throughout Europe. The company is examining the viability of a concert in Stockholm. Estimated fixed costs are £60 000. These include the fees paid to performers, the hire of the venue and advertising costs. Variable costs consist of the cost of a pre-packed buffet that will be provided by a firm of caterers at a price, which is currently being negotiated, but it is likely to be in the region of £10 per ticket sold. The proposed price for the sale of a ticket is £20. The management of Norvik have requested the following information:

1 The number of tickets that must be sold to break even (that is, the point at which there is neither a profit nor loss).

2 How many tickets must be sold to earn £30 000 target profit?

3 What profit would result if 8000 tickets were sold?

4 What selling price would have to be charged to give a profit of £30 000 on sales of 8000 tickets, fixed costs of £60 000 and variable costs of £10 per ticket?

5 How many additional tickets must be sold to cover the extra cost of television advertising of £8000?

Instead of using profit per unit we shall use contribution margins to apply the numerical approach. **Contribution margin** is equal to sales revenue minus variable expenses. Because the variable cost per unit and the selling price per unit are assumed to be constant the contribution margin per unit is also assumed to be constant. Example 3.1 will be used to illustrate the application of the numerical approach to CVP analysis. Let us now provide the information requested in Example 3.1.

Example 3.1 calculations

1. Break-even point in units (i.e. number of tickets sold)

You will see from Example 3.1 that each ticket sold generates a contribution of £10 (£20 selling price – £10 variable cost), which is available to cover fixed costs and, after they are covered, to contribute to profit. When we have obtained sufficient total contribution to cover fixed costs, the break-even point is achieved, and so

$$\text{Break-even point in units} = \frac{\text{Fixed costs (£60 000)}}{\text{Contribution per unit (£10)}}$$
$$= 6000 \text{ tickets}$$

2. Units to be sold to obtain a £30 000 profit

To achieve a profit we must obtain sufficient contribution to cover the fixed costs (i.e. the break-even point). If the total contribution is not sufficient to cover the fixed costs then a loss will occur. Once a sufficient total contribution has been achieved any excess contribution represents profit. Thus to determine the total contribution to obtain a target profit simply add the target profit to the fixed costs so that

$$\text{Units sold for the target profit} = \frac{\text{Fixed costs (£60 000) + Target profit (£30 000)}}{\text{Contribution per unit (£10)}}$$

$$= 9000 \text{ tickets}$$

3. Profit from the sale of 8000 tickets

The total contribution from the sale of 8000 tickets is £80 000 (8000 × £10). To ascertain the profit we deduct the fixed costs of £60 000 giving a net profit of £20 000. Let us now assume that we wish to ascertain the impact on profit if a further 1000 tickets are sold so that sales volume increases from 8000 to 9000 tickets. Assuming that fixed costs remain unchanged, the impact on a firm's profits resulting from a change in the number of units sold can be determined by multiplying the unit contribution margin by the change in units sold. Therefore the increase in profits will be £10 000 (1000 units times a unit contribution margin of £10).

4. Selling price to be charged to show a profit of £30 000 on sales of 8000 tickets

First we must determine the total required revenue to obtain a profit of £30 000. This is £170 000, which is derived from the sum of the fixed costs (£60 000), variable costs (8000 × £10) and the target profit (£30 000). Dividing the required sales revenues of £170 000 by the sales volume (8000 tickets) gives a selling price of £21.25.

5. Additional sales volume to meet £8000 additional fixed advertisement charges

The contribution per unit is £10 and fixed costs will increase by £8000. Therefore an extra 800 tickets must be sold to cover the additional fixed costs of £8000.

THE PROFIT-VOLUME RATIO

The **profit–volume ratio** (also known as the **contribution margin ratio**) is the contribution divided by sales. It represents the proportion of each £1 of sales available to cover fixed costs and provide for profit. In Example 3.1 the contribution is £10 per unit and the selling price is £20 per unit; the profit–volume ratio is 0.5. This means that for each £1 sale a contribution of £0.50 is earned. Because we assume that selling price and contribution per unit are constant, the profit–volume ratio is also assumed to be constant. Therefore the profit–volume ratio can be computed using either unit figures or total figures. Given an estimate of total sales revenue, it is possible to use the profit–volume ratio to estimate total contribution. For example, if total sales revenue is estimated to be £200 000, the total contribution will be £100 000 (£200 000 × 0.5). To calculate the profit, we deduct fixed costs of £60 000; thus a profit of £40 000 will be obtained from total sales revenue of £200 000.

The above computation can be expressed in equation form:

Profit = (Sales revenue × PV ratio) – Fixed costs

Rearranging the above equation:

Profit + Fixed costs = Sales revenue × PV ratio

Therefore the break-even sales revenue (where profit = 0) = Fixed costs/PV ratio.

Applying this approach to example 3.1, the break-even sales revenue is £120 000 (£60 000 fixed costs/0.5 PV ratio).

RELEVANT RANGE

It is vital to remember that CVP analysis can only be used for decisions that result in outcomes within the relevant range. Outside this range the unit selling price and the variable cost are no longer deemed to be constant per unit, and any results obtained from the formulae that fall outside the relevant range will be incorrect. The concept of the relevant range is more appropriate for production settings but it can apply within non-production settings. Returning to Norvic Enterprises in Example 3.1, let us assume that the caterers' charges will be higher per ticket if ticket sales are below 4000 but lower if sales exceed 12 000 tickets. Thus, the £10 variable cost relates only to a sales volume within a range of 4000 to 12 000 tickets. Outside this range other costs apply. Also the number of seats made available at the venue is flexible and the hire cost will be reduced for sales of less than 4000 tickets and increased for sales beyond 12 000 tickets. In other words, we will assume that the relevant range is a sales volume of 4000 to 12 000 tickets and outside this range the results of our CVP analysis do not apply.

MARGIN OF SAFETY

The **margin of safety** indicates by how much sales may decrease before a loss occurs. Using Example 3.1, where unit selling price and variable cost were £20 and £10 respectively and fixed costs were £60 000, we noted that the break-even point was 6000 tickets or £120 000 sales value. If sales are expected to be 8000 tickets or £160 000, the margin of safety will be 2000 tickets or £40 000. Alternatively, we can express the margin of safety in a percentage form based on the following ratio:

$$\text{Percentage margin of safety} = \frac{\text{Expected sales} - \text{Break-even sales}}{\text{Expected sales}}$$
$$= \frac{£160\,000 - £120\,000}{£160\,000} = 25\%$$

CONSTRUCTING THE BREAK-EVEN CHART

Managers may obtain a clearer understanding of CVP behaviour if the information is presented in graphical format. Using the data in Example 3.1 we can construct the **break-even chart** for Norvik Enterprises (Figure 3.4). Note that activity/output is plotted on the horizontal axis and monetary amounts for total costs, total revenues and total profits (or loss) are recorded on the vertical axis. In constructing the graph, the fixed costs are plotted as a single horizontal line at the £60 000 level. Variable costs at the rate of £10 per unit of volume are added to the fixed costs to enable the total cost line to be plotted. Two

REAL WORLD VIEWS 3.1

To mine or not to mine?

This is the question faced on a regular basis by exploration and mining companies when they find oil, gas, ores and minerals. The viability of any find must be thoroughly assessed before any investment is made. Thus, while finds may be frequent, commercially viable finds are less frequent. To be commercially viable any find must be examined in terms of volumes accessible, costs of extraction and the sale price.

Conroy Diamonds and Gold plc (listed on London's Alternative Investment Market) provides a clear example. In July 2008 the company reported what could be the biggest gold find ever in the UK and Ireland. It reported a find of over one million ounces of gold having test-drilled only 20 per cent of a site at Clontibret, County Monaghan in the Republic of Ireland. The company chairman, Professor Richard Conroy, stated to the press that the company now had to examine the technical and financial aspects to ensure the viability of the find. He projected this would take two to three years. The price of gold, currently at approximately $900 per ounce, will be a determinant of the viability of the mine. Professor Conroy said: 'Two-thirds of that price would be accounted for in operating costs and building a mine.' Further costs would include remediation costs once the mine was

exhausted. Thus, the market price of gold will be a major determinant in the viability of the find. Should the gold price decrease, the viability may be in question.

Discussion points

1 Do you think it is possible to estimate accurately the costs of operating a mine over its life?
2 How important is it to determine at an early stage the volumes that can be extracted from a mine?

References

Irish Times, 2 July 2008 (from www. irishtimes.com).
London Stock Exchange (www.londonstockexchange. com).

points are required to insert the total cost line. At zero sales volume total cost will be equal to the fixed costs of £60 000. At 12 000 units sales volume total costs will be £180 000 consisting of £120 000 variable costs plus £60 000 fixed costs. The total revenue line is plotted at the rate of £20 per unit of volume. At zero output total sales are zero and at 12 000 units total sales revenue is £240 000. The total revenues for these two points are plotted on the graph and a straight line is drawn that joins these points. The constraints of the relevant range consisting of two vertical lines are then added to the graph; beyond these lines we have little assurance that the CVP relationships are valid.

The point at which the total sales revenue line cuts the total cost line is the point where the concert makes neither a profit nor a loss. This is the break-even point and is 6000 tickets or £120 000 total sales revenue. The distance between the total sales revenue line and the total cost line at a volume below the break-even point represents losses that will occur for various sales levels below 6000 tickets. Similarly, if the company operates at a sales volume above the break-even point, the difference between the total revenue and the total cost lines represents the profit that results from sales levels above 6000 tickets.

ALTERNATIVE PRESENTATION OF COST–VOLUME–PROFIT ANALYSIS

Contribution graph

In Figure 3.4 the fixed cost line is drawn parallel to the horizontal axis, and the variable cost is the difference between the total cost line and the fixed cost line. An alternative to Figure 3.4 for the data contained in Example 3.1 is illustrated in Figure 3.5. This alternative presentation is called a **contribution graph**. In Figure 3.5 the variable cost line is drawn first at £10 per unit of volume. The fixed costs are represented by the difference between the total cost line and the variable cost line. Because fixed costs are assumed to be a constant sum throughout the entire output range, a constant sum of £60 000 for fixed costs is added to the variable cost line, which results in the total cost line being drawn parallel to the variable cost line. The advantage of this form of presentation is that the total contribution is emphasized in the graph, and is represented by the difference between the total sales revenue line and the total variable cost line.

Profit–volume graph

The break-even and contribution charts do not highlight the profit or loss at different volume levels. To ascertain the profit or loss figures from a break-even chart, it is necessary to determine the difference between the total cost and total revenue lines. The **profit–volume graph** is a more convenient method of showing the impact of changes in volume on profit. Such a graph is illustrated in Figure 3.6. The horizontal axis represents the various levels of sales volume, and the profits and losses for the period are recorded on

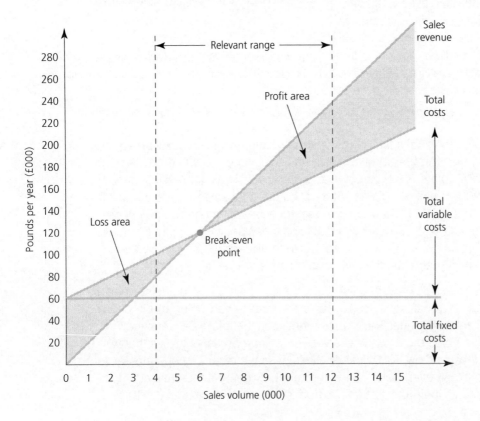

FIGURE 3.4

Break-even chart for Example 3.1

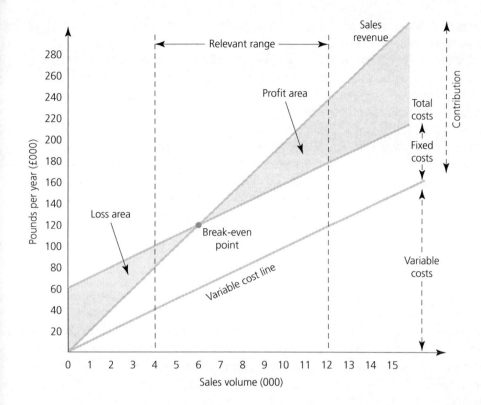

FIGURE 3.5

Contribution chart for Example 3.1

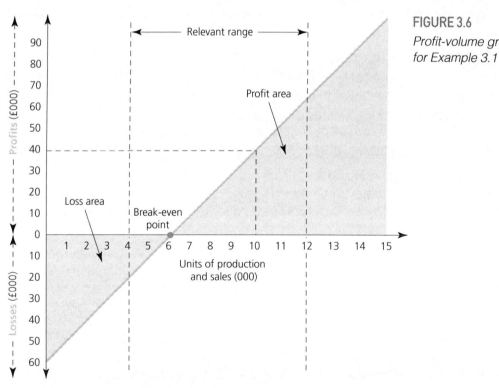

FIGURE 3.6

Profit-volume graph for Example 3.1

the vertical scale. You will see from Figure 3.6 that profits or losses are plotted for each of the various sales levels, and these points are connected by a profit line. Two points are required to plot the profit line. When units sold are zero a loss equal to the amount of fixed costs (£60 000) will be reported. At the break-even point (zero profits) sales volume is 6000 units. Therefore the break-even point is plotted at the point where the profit line intersects the horizontal line at a sales volume of 6000 tickets. The profit line is drawn between the two points. With each unit sold, a contribution of £10 is obtained towards the fixed costs, and the break-even point is at 6000 tickets, when the total contribution exactly equals the total of the fixed costs. With each additional unit sold beyond 6000 tickets, a surplus of £10 per ticket is obtained. If 10 000 tickets are sold, the profit will be £40 000 (4000 tickets at £10 contribution). You can see this relationship between sales and profit at 10 000 tickets from the dotted lines in Figure 3.6.

MULTI-PRODUCT COST–VOLUME–PROFIT ANALYSIS

Our analysis so far has assumed a single-product setting. However, most firms produce and sell many products or services. In this section we shall consider how we can adapt the analysis used for a single-product setting to a multi-product setting. Consider the situation presented in Example 3.2. You will see that the company sells two products so that there are two unit contribution margins. We can apply the same approach as that used for a single product if all of the fixed costs are directly attributable to products (i.e. there are no common fixed costs). We simply apply the analysis separately to each product as follows:

> De-luxe washing machine break-even point
> = Direct fixed costs (£90 000)/Unit contribution (£150)
> = 600 units

> Standard washing machine break-even point
> = Direct fixed costs (£27 000)/Unit contribution (£90)
> = 300 units

However, selling 600 de-luxe and 300 standard washing machines will generate a contribution that only covers direct fixed costs; the common fixed costs will not be covered. A loss equal to the common fixed costs will be reported. The break-even point for the firm as a whole has not been ascertained.

You may think that the break-even point for the firm as a whole can be derived if we allocate the common fixed costs to each individual product but this approach is inappropriate because the allocation will be arbitrary. The common fixed costs cannot be specifically identified with either of the products since they can only be avoided if *both* products are not sold. The solution to our problem is to convert the sales volume measure of the individual products into standard batches of products based on the planned sales mix. You will from see from Example 3.2 that Super Bright plans to sell 1200 de-luxe and 600 standard machines giving a sales mix of 1200:600. Reducing this sales mix to the smallest whole number gives a mix of 2:1. In other words, for the sale of every two de-luxe machines one standard machine is expected to be sold. We therefore define our standard batch of products as comprising two de-luxe and one standard machine giving a contribution of

EXAMPLE 3.2

The Super Bright Company sells two types of washing machines – a de-luxe model and a standard model. The financial controller has prepared the following information based on the sales forecast for the period:

	De-luxe machine 1200 (£)	Standard machine 600 (£)	Total (£)
Sales volume (units)			
Unit selling price	300	200	
Unit variable cost	150	110	
Unit contribution	150	90	
Total sales revenues	360 000	120 000	480 000
Less: Total variable cost	180 000	66 000	246 000
Contribution to direct and common fixed costs[a]	180 000	54 000	234 000
Less: Direct avoidable fixed costs	90 000	27 000	117 000
Contribution to common fixed costs[a]	90 000	27 000	117 000
Less common (indirect) fixed costs			39 000
Operating profit			78 000

The common fixed costs relate to the costs of common facilities and can only be avoided if neither of the products is sold. The managing director is concerned that sales may be less than forecast and has requested information relating to the break-even point for the activities for the period.

Note

[a]Contribution was defined earlier in this chapter as sales less variable costs. Where fixed costs are divided into direct and common (indirect) fixed costs it is possible to identify two separate contribution categories. The first is described as contribution to direct and common fixed costs and this is identical to the conventional definition, being equivalent to sales less variable costs. The second is after a further deduction of direct fixed costs and is described as 'Contribution to common or indirect fixed costs'.

£390 per batch (two de-luxe machines at a contribution of £150 per unit sold plus one standard machine at a contribution of £90).

The break-even point in standard batches can be calculated by using the same break-even equation that we used for a single product, so that:

Break-even number of batches = Total fixed costs (£156 000)/Contribution margin per
batch (£390)
= 400 batches

The sales mix used to define a standard batch (2:1) can now be used to convert the break-even point (measured in standard batches) into a break-even point expressed in terms of the required combination of individual products sold. Thus, 800 de-luxe machines (2 × 400) and 400 (1 × 400) standard machines must be sold to break even. The following profit statement verifies this outcome:

Operating leverage captures relationships

Operating leverage can tell investors a lot about a company's risk profile, and although high operating leverage can often benefit companies, firms with high operating leverage are also vulnerable to sharp economic and business cycle swings. In good times, high operating leverage can supercharge profit. But companies with a lot of costs tied up in machinery, plants, real estate and distribution networks cannot easily cut expenses to adjust to a change in demand. So, if there is a downturn in the economy, earnings do not just fall, they can plummet.

Consider the software developer Inktomi. During the 1990s investors marvelled at the nature of its software business. The company spent tens of millions of dollars to develop each of its digital delivery and storage software programs. But thanks to the internet, Inktomi's software could be distributed to customers at almost no cost. In other words, the company had close to zero cost of goods sold. After its fixed development costs were recovered, each additional sale was almost pure profit.

After the collapse of dotcom technology market demand in 2000, Inktomi suffered the dark side of operating leverage. As sales took a nosedive, profits swung dramatically to a staggering $58 million loss in Q1 of 2001 – plunging down from the $1 million

profit the company had enjoyed in Q1 of 2000. The high leverage involved in counting on sales to repay fixed costs can put companies and their shareholders at risk. High operating leverage during a downturn can be an Achilles heel, putting pressure on profit margins and making a contraction in earnings unavoidable.

Indeed, companies such as Inktomi with high operating leverage typically have larger volatility in their operating earnings and share prices. As a result, investors need to treat these companies with caution.

© LEE TORRENS/DREAMSTIME.COM

Discussion point

1. Provide examples of other companies that have high and low degrees of operating leverage.

	De-luxe machine	Standard machine	
	800	400	Total
Units sold	(£)	(£)	(£)
Unit contribution margin	150	90	
Contribution to direct and common fixed costs	120 000	36 000	156 000
Less: Direct fixed costs	90 000	27 000	117 000
Contribution to common fixed costs	30 000	9 000	39 000
Less: Common fixed costs			39 000
Operating profit			0

Let us now assume that the actual sales volume for the period was 1200 units, the same total volume as the break-even volume, but consisting of a sales mix of 600 units of each machine. Thus, the actual sales mix is 1:1 compared with a planned sales mix of 2:1. The total contribution to direct and common fixed costs will be £144 000 ([£150 × 600 for de-luxe] + [£90 × 600 for standard]) and a loss of £12 000 (£144 000 contribution – £156 000 total fixed costs) will occur. It should now be apparent to you that *the break-even point (or the sales volumes required to achieve a target profit) is not a unique number: it varies depending upon the composition of the sales mix.* Because the actual sales mix differs from the planned sales mix, the sales mix used to define a standard batch has changed from 2:1 to 1:1 so that the contribution per batch changes from £390 to £240 ([1 × £150] + [1 × £90]). Therefore the revised break-even point will be 650 batches (£156 000 total fixed costs/£240 contribution per batch), which converts to a sales volume of 650 units of each machine based on a 1:1 sales mix. Generally, an increase in the proportion of sales of higher contribution margin products will decrease the break-even point whereas increases in sales of the lower margin products will increase the break-even point.

OPERATING LEVERAGE

Companies can sometimes influence the proportion of fixed and variable expenses in their cost structures. For example, they may choose to either rely heavily on automated facilities (involving high fixed and low variable costs) or on manual systems (involving high variable costs and low fixed costs). The chosen cost structure can have a significant impact on profits. Consider the situation presented in Exhibit 3.1 where the managers of an airline company are considering an investment in automated ticketing equipment.

You will see from Exhibit 3.1 that it is unclear which system should be chosen. If periodic sales exceed £960 000 the automated system will result in higher profits. Automation enables the company to lower its variable costs by increasing fixed costs. This cost structure results in a greater increases in profits as sales increase compared with the manual system. Unfortunately, it is also true that a high fixed cost and lower variable cost structure will result in a greater reduction in profits as sales decrease. The term **operating leverage** is used as a measure of the sensitivity of profits to changes in sales. The greater the degree of operating leverage, the more that changes in sales activity will affect profits. The **degree of operating leverage** can be measured for a given level of sales by the following formula:

Degree of operating leverage = Contribution margin/Profit

The degree of operating leverage in Exhibit 3.1 for sales of £1 million is 7 (£700 000/£100 000) for the automated system and 2.5 (£200 000/£80 000) for the manual system. This means that profits change by seven times more than the change in sales for the automated system and 2.5 times for the manual system. Thus, for a 10 per cent increase in sales from £1 million to £1.1 million profits increase by 70 per cent for the automated system (from £100 000 to £170 000) and by 25 per cent for the manual system (from £80 000 to £100 000). In contrast, you will see in Exhibit 3.1 that if sales decline by 10 per cent from £1 million to £0.9 million profits decrease by 70 per cent (from £100 000 to £30 000) for the automated system and by 25 per cent from (£80 000 to £60 000) for the manual system.

The degree of operating leverage provides useful information for the airline company in choosing between the two systems. Higher degrees of operating leverage can provide significantly greater profits when sales are increasing but higher percentage decreases will also occur when sales are declining. Higher operating leverage also results in a greater volatility in profits. The manual system has a break-even point of £600 000 sales (£120 000 fixed expenses/PV ratio of 0.2) whereas the break-even point for the automated

EXHIBIT 3.1

Sensitivity of profits arising from changes in sales for an automated and manual system

An airline company is considering investing in automated ticketing equipment. The estimated sales revenues and costs for the current manual system and the proposed automated system for a typical period are as follows:

	Automated system £	Manual system £
Sales revenue	1 000 000	1 000 000
Less: Variable expenses	300 000	800 000
Contribution	700 000 (70%)	200 000 (20%)
Less: Fixed expenses	600 000	120 000
Profit	100 000	80 000

The above cost structure suggests that the automated system yields the higher profits. However, if sales decline by 10 per cent the following calculations show that the manual system will result in the higher profits:

	Automated system £	Manual system £
Sales revenue	900 000	900 000
Less: Variable expenses	270 000	720 000
Contribution	630 000 (70%)	180 000 (20%)
Less: Fixed expenses	600 000	120 000
Profit	30 000	60 000

What will happen if sales are 10 per cent higher than the predicted sales for the period?

	Automated system £	Manual system £
Sales revenue	1 100 000	1 100 000
Less: Variable expenses	330 000	880 000
Contribution	770 000 (70%)	220 000 (20%)
Less: Fixed expenses	600 000	120 000
Profit	170 000	100 000

The sales revenue where both systems result in the same profits is £960 000. The automated system yields higher profits when periodic sales revenue exceeds £960 000 whereas the manual system gives higher profits when sales revenue is below £960 000.[a]

	Automated system £	Manual system £
Sales revenue	960 000	960 000
Less: Variable expenses	288 000	768 000
Contribution	672 000 (70%)	192 000 (20%)
Less: Fixed expenses	600 000	120 000
Profit	72 000	72 000

Note

[a]The profit–volume ratio is 0.7 for the automated system and 0.2 for the manual system. Let x = periodic sales revenue: the indifference point is where $0.7x - £600 000 = 0.2x - £120 000$, so $x = £960 000$.

system is £857 143 (£600 000 fixed expenses/PV ratio of 0.7). Thus, the automated system has a lower margin of safety. High operating leverage leads to higher risk arising from the greater volatility of profits and higher break-even point. On the other hand, the increase in risk provides the potential for higher profit levels (as long as sales exceed £960 000). We can conclude that if management is confident that sales will exceed £960 000 the automated system is preferable.

It is apparent from the above discussion that labour intensive organizations, such as McDonald's and Pizza Hut have high variable costs and low fixed costs, and thus have low operating leverage. These companies can continue to report profits even when they experience wide fluctuations in sales levels. Conversely, organizations that are highly capital intensive, such as easyJet and Volkswagen, have high operating leverage. These companies must generate high sales volumes to cover fixed costs, but sales above the break-even point produce high profits. In general, these companies tend to be more vulnerable to sharp economic and business cycle swings.

COST–VOLUME–PROFIT ANALYSIS ASSUMPTIONS

It is essential that anyone preparing or interpreting CVP information is aware of the underlying assumptions on which the information has been prepared. If these assumptions are not recognized, or the analysis modified, errors may result and incorrect conclusions may be drawn from the analysis. We shall now consider these important assumptions. They are as follows:

1 All other variables remain constant.
2 A single product or constant sales mix.
3 Total costs and total revenue are linear functions of output.
4 The analysis applies only to the relevant range.
5 The analysis applies only to a short-term time horizon.

1 All other variables remain constant

It has been assumed that all variables other than the particular one under consideration have remained constant throughout the analysis. In other words, it is assumed that volume is the only factor that will cause costs and revenues to change. However, changes in other variables such as production efficiency, sales mix and price levels can have an important influence on sales revenue and costs. If significant changes in these other variables occur the CVP analysis presentation will be incorrect.

2 Single product or constant sales mix

CVP analysis assumes that either a single product is sold or, if a range of products is sold, that sales will be in accordance with a predetermined sales mix. When a predetermined sales mix is used, it can be depicted in the CVP analysis by measuring sales volume using standard batch sizes based on a planned sales mix. Any CVP analysis must be interpreted carefully if the initial product mix assumptions do not hold.

3 Total costs and total revenue are linear functions of output

The analysis assumes that unit variable cost and selling price are constant. This assumption is only likely to be valid within the relevant range of production described earlier in this chapter.

4 Analysis applies only to the relevant range

Earlier in this chapter we noted that CVP analysis is appropriate only for decisions taken within the relevant production range, and that it is incorrect to project cost and revenue figures beyond the relevant range.

5 Analysis applies only to a short-term time horizon

CVP analysis is based on the relationship between volume and sales revenue, costs and profit in the short run, the short run typically being a period of one year in which the output of a firm is likely to be restricted to that available from the current operating capacity. During this period significant changes cannot be made to selling prices and fixed and variable costs. CVP analysis thus examines the effects of changes in sales volume on the level of profits in the short run. It is inappropriate to extend the analysis to long-term decision-making.

THE IMPACT OF INFORMATION TECHNOLOGY

The output from a CVP model is only as good as the input. The analysis will include assumptions about sales mix, production efficiency, price levels, total fixed costs, variable costs and selling price per unit. Obviously, estimates regarding these variables will be subject to varying degrees of uncertainty.

Sensitivity analysis is one approach for coping with changes in the values of the variables. Sensitivity analysis focuses on how a result will be changed if the original estimates or the underlying assumptions change. With regard to CVP analysis, sensitivity analysis answers questions such as the following:

1 What will the profit be if the sales mix changes from that originally predicted?
2 What will the profit be if fixed costs increase by 10 per cent and variable costs decline by 5 per cent?

Developments in information technology have enabled management accountants to build CVP computerized models. Managers can now consider alternative plans by keying the information into a computer, which can quickly show changes both graphically and numerically. Thus managers can study various combinations of changes in selling prices, fixed costs, variable costs and product mix, and can react quickly without waiting for formal reports from the management accountant.

SEPARATION OF COSTS INTO THEIR FIXED AND VARIABLE ELEMENTS

CVP analysis assumes that costs can be accurately analysed into their fixed and variable elements, and mathematical techniques can be used to separate costs in this way. For a discussion of these techniques you should refer to Drury (2008, Chapter 23). However, first-year cost and management accounting courses sometimes require you to separate fixed and variable costs using a more simplistic non-mathematical technique called the **high–low method**.

The high–low method consists of examining past costs and activity, selecting the highest and lowest activity levels and comparing the changes in costs that result from the two levels. Assume that the following activity levels and costs are extracted:

	Volume of production (units)	Indirect costs (£)
Lowest activity	5 000	22 000
Highest activity	10 000	32 000

If variable costs are constant per unit and the fixed costs remain unchanged the increase in costs will be due entirely to an increase in variable costs. The variable cost per unit is therefore calculated as follows:

$$\frac{\text{Difference in cost}}{\text{Difference in activity}} = \frac{£10\,000}{5000}$$
$$= £2 \text{ variable cost per unit of activity}$$

The fixed cost can be estimated at any level of activity by subtracting the variable cost portion from the total cost. At an activity level of 5000 units the total cost is £22 000 and the total variable cost is £10 000 (5000 units at £2 per unit). The balance of £12 000 is assumed to represent the fixed cost.

SUMMARY

The following items relate to the learning objectives listed at the beginning of the chapter.

● **Justify the use of linear cost and revenue functions**. Within the relevant range it is generally assumed that cost and revenue functions are approximately linear. Outside the relevant range linearity is unlikely to apply. Care is therefore required in interpreting CVP relationships outside the relevant range.

● **Apply the numerical approach to answer questions similar to those listed in Example 3.1**. In Example 3.1, the break-even point was derived by dividing fixed costs by the contribution per unit. To ascertain the number of units sold to achieve a target profit the sum of the fixed costs and the target profit is divided by the contribution per unit.

● **Construct break-even, contribution and profit–volume graphs**. Managers may obtain a clearer understanding of CVP behaviour if the information is presented in graphical format. With the break-even chart the fixed costs are plotted as a single horizontal line. The total cost line is plotted by adding variable costs to fixed costs. The reverse situation applies with a contribution graph. The variable costs are plotted first and the fixed costs are added to variable costs to plot the total cost line. Because fixed costs are assumed to be a constant sum throughout the output range, the total cost line is drawn parallel to the variable cost line. The break-even and contribution graphs do not highlight the profit or loss at different output levels and must be ascertained by comparing the differences between the total cost and total revenue lines. The profit–volume graph shows the impact of changes in volume on profits. The profits and losses are plotted for each of the various sales levels and these are connected by a profit line. You should refer to Figures 3.4–3.6 for an illustration of the graphs.

● **Apply cost–volume–profit analysis in a multi-product setting**. Multi-product CVP analysis requires that an assumption is made concerning the expected sales mix. The approach that is used is to convert the multi-product CVP analysis into a single product analysis based on the assumption that output consists of standard batches of the multiple products based on the expected sales mix. However, you should note that the answers change as the sales mix changes.

● **Explain the meaning of operating leverage and describe how it influences profits**. Operating leverage measures the sensitivity of profits in relation to fluctuations in sales. It is measured by dividing total contribution by total profit. An operating leverage of four indicates that profits change by four times more than the change in sales. Therefore if sales increase/decrease by 10 per cent profits will increase/decrease by 40 per cent. High levels of operating leverage lead to higher risk arising from highly volatile profits but the increase in risk also provides the potential for higher profit levels when sales are expanding.

● **Identify and explain the assumptions on which cost–volume–profit analysis is based**. Cost–volume–profit analysis is based on the following assumptions: (a) all variables, other than volume, remain constant; (b) the sales mix remains constant; (c) total costs and revenues are linear functions of output; (d) the analysis applies only to the relevant range; and (e) the analysis applies only to a short-term horizon.

KEY TERMS AND CONCEPTS

break-even chart (p. 50)
break-even point (p. 44)
contribution graph (p. 52)
contribution margin (p. 48)
contribution margin ratio (p. 49)
decreasing returns to scale (p. 45)
degree of operating leverage (p. 57)
high–low method (p. 61)

increasing returns to scale (p. 45)
margin of safety (p. 50)
operating leverage (p.57)
profit–volume graph (p. 52)
profit–volume ratio (p. 49)
relevant range (p. 46)
sensitivity analysis (p. 60)

ASSESSMENT MATERIAL

The review questions are short questions that enable you to assess your understanding of the main topics included in the chapter. The page numbers in parentheses provide you with the page numbers to refer to if you cannot answer a specific question.

The review problems are more complex and require you to relate and apply the content to various business problems. Solutions to review problems are provided in a separate section at the end of the book. Additional review problems can be accessed by lecturers and students on the website (www.drury-online.com). Solutions to these problems are provided for lecturers in the Instructors' Manual. This is available on the lecturers' password-protected section of the website.

The website also includes over 30 case study problems. A list of these cases is provided on pages 389–392. Several cases are relevant to the content of this chapter. Examples include Dumbellow Ltd, Hardhat Ltd and Merrion Products Ltd.

REVIEW QUESTIONS

3.1 Provide examples of how cost–volume–profit analysis can be used for decision-making. *(p. 43)*

3.2 Explain what is meant by the term 'relevant range'. *(p. 46)*

3.3 Define the term 'contribution margin'. *(p. 48)*

3.4 Define the term 'profit–volume ratio' and explain how it can be used for cost–volume–profit analysis. *(p. 48)*

3.5 Describe and distinguish between the three different approaches to presenting cost–volume–profit relationships in graphical format. *(pp. 50–54)*

3.6 How can a company with multiple products use cost–volume–profit analysis? *(pp. 54–57)*

3.7 Explain why the break-even point changes when there is a change in sales mix. *(pp. 54–57)*

3.8 Describe the assumptions underlying cost–volume–profit analysis. *(pp. 59–60)*

3.9 Define the term 'operating leverage' and explain how the degree of operating leverage can influence future profits. *(p. 57–59)*

3.10 How can sensitivity analysis be used in conjunction with cost–volume–profit analysis? *(p. 60)*

REVIEW PROBLEMS

3.11 A company has established a budgeted sales revenue for the forthcoming period of £500 000 with an associated contribution of £275 000. Fixed production costs are £137 500 and fixed selling costs are £27 500.

What is the break-even sales revenue?

A	£75 625
B	£90 750
C	£250 000
D	£300 000

3.12 H Limited manufactures and sells two products, J and K. Annual sales are expected to be in the ratio of J:1, K:3. Total annual sales are planned to be £420 000. Product J has a contribution to sales ratio of 40 per cent, whereas that of product K is 50 per cent. Annual fixed costs are estimated to be £120 000.

What is the budgeted break-even sales value (to the nearest £1000)?

A	£196 000
B	£200 000
C	£253 000
D	£255 000
E	cannot be determined from the above data.

3.13 The following details relate to product R:

Level of activity (units)	1000	2000
	(£/unit)	(£/unit)
Direct materials	4.00	4.00
Direct labour	3.00	3.00
Production overhead	3.50	2.50
Selling overhead	1.00	0.50
	11.50	10.00

What are the total fixed cost and variable cost per unit?

	Total fixed cost (£)	Variable cost per unit (£)
A	2000	1.50
B	2000	7.00
C	2000	8.50
D	3000	7.00
E	3000	8.50

3.14 Z plc currently sells products Aye, Bee and Cee in equal quantities and at the same selling price per unit. The contribution to sales ratio for product Aye is 40 per cent; for product Bee it is 50 per cent; and the total is 48 per cent. If fixed costs are unaffected by mix and are currently 20 per cent of sales, the effect of changing the product mix to:

Aye	40%
Bee	25%
Cee	35%

is that the total contribution/total sales ratio changes to:

A	27.4%
B	45.3%
C	47.4%
D	48.4%
E	68.4%

3.15 For the forthcoming year the variable costs of E plc are budgeted to be 60 per cent of sales value and fixed costs are budgeted to be 10 per cent of sales value.

If E plc increases its selling prices by 10 per cent, but if fixed costs, variable costs per unit and sales volume remain unchanged, the effect on E plc's contribution would be:

A a decrease of 2%
B an increase of 5%
C an increase of 10%
D an increase of 25%
E an increase of 66²/₃%

3.16 A Ltd has fixed costs of £60 000 per annum. It manufactures a single product which it sells for £20 per unit. Its contribution to sales ratio is 40 per cent.

A Ltd's break-even point in units is:

A 1200
B 1800
C 3000
D 5000
E 7500

3.17 Z plc makes a single product which it sells for £16 per unit. Fixed costs are £76 800 per month and the product has a contribution to sales ratio of 40 per cent.

In a period when actual sales were £224 000, Z plc's margin of safety, in units, was:

A 2 000
B 6 000
C 8 000
D 12 000
E 14 000

3.18 A break-even chart is shown below for Windhurst Ltd.

You are required:

(i) to identify the components of the break-even chart labelled *p, q, r, s, t, u, v, w, x* and *y*;

(5 marks)

(ii) to suggest what events are represented at the values of *x* that are labelled *m* and *n* on the chart;

(3 marks)

(iii) to assess the usefulness of break-even analysis to senior management of a small company.

(7 marks)

3.19 Preparation of break-even and profit–volume graphs

ZED plc manufactures one standard product, which sells at £10. You are required to:

(a) prepare, from the data given below, a break-even and profit–volume graph showing the results for the six months ending 30 April and to determine:
   (i) the fixed costs;
   (ii) the variable cost per unit;
   (iii) the profit–volume ratio;
   (iv) the break-even point;
   (v) the margin of safety;

Month	Sales (units)	Profit/(loss) (£)
November	30 000	40 000
December	35 000	60 000
January	15 000	(20 000)
February	24 000	16 000
March	26 000	24 000
April	18 000	(8 000)

(b) discuss the limitations of such a graph;
(c) explain the use of the relevant range in such a graph.

(20 marks)

3.20 Preparation of a break-even chart with step fixed costs

Toowumba manufactures various products and uses CVP analysis to establish the minimum level of production to ensure profitability.

Fixed costs of £50 000 have been allocated to a specific product but are expected to increase to £100 000 once production exceeds 30 000 units, as a new factory will need to be rented in order to produce the extra units. Variable costs per unit are stable at £5 per unit over all levels of activity. Revenue from this product will be £7.50 per unit.

Required:

a   Formulate the equations for the total cost at:
   (i) less than or equal to 30 000 units;
   (ii) more than 30 000 units.

(2 marks)

b   Prepare a break-even chart and clearly identify the break-even point or points.

(6 marks)

c   Discuss the implications of the results from your graph in (b) with regard to Toowomba's production plans.

(2 marks)

3.21 Non-graphical CVP analysis

The summarized profit and loss statement for Exewye plc for the last year is as follows:

	(£000)	(£000)
Sale (50 000 units)		1000
Direct materials	350	
Direct wages	200	
Fixed production overhead	200	
Variable production overhead	50	
Administration overhead	180	
Selling and distribution overhead	120	
		1100
Profit/(loss)		(100)

At a recent board meeting the directors discussed the year's results, following which the chairman asked for suggestions to improve the situation.

You are required as management accountant, to evaluate the following alternative proposals and to comment briefly on each:

(a) Pay salesmen a commission of 10 per cent of sales and thus increase sales to achieve break-even point.

(5 marks)

(b) Reduce selling price by 10 per cent, which it is estimated would increase sales volume by 30 per cent.

(3 marks)

(c) Increase direct wage rates by 25 per cent per hour, as part of a productivity/pay deal. It is hoped that this would increase production and sales by 20 per cent, but advertising costs would increase by £50 000.

(4 marks)

(d) Increase sales by additional advertising of £300 000, with an increased selling price of 20 per cent, setting a profit margin of 10 per cent.

(8 marks)
(Total 20 marks)

3.22 Operating leverage

The profit statements for two different companies in the same industry are as follows:

	Company A (£000)	Company B (£000)
Sales	10 000	10 000
Less: Variable costs	8 000	4 000
Contribution margin	2 000	6 000
Less: Fixed costs	1 000	5 000
Profit	1 000	1 000

Required:

(a) Compute the degree of operating leverage for each company.
(b) Compute the break-even point for each company. Explain why the break-even point for Company B is higher.
(c) Assume that both companies experience a 50 per cent increase in sales revenues. Explain why the percentage increase in Company B's profits is significantly larger than that of Company A.

3.23 Non-graphical CVP behaviour

Tweed Ltd is a company engaged solely in the manufacture of jumpers, which are bought mainly for sporting activities. Present sales are direct to retailers, but in recent years there has been a steady decline in output because of increased foreign competition. In the last trading year (2008) the accounting report indicated that the company produced the lowest profit for 10 years. The forecast for 2009 indicates that the present deterioration in profits is likely to continue. The company considers that a profit of £80 000 should be achieved to provide an adequate return on capital. The managing director has asked that a review be made of the present pricing and marketing policies. The marketing director has completed this review, and passes the proposals on to you for evaluation and recommendation, together with the profit and loss account for the year ending 31 December 2008.

Tweed Ltd profit and loss account for year ending 31 December 2008

	(£)	(£)	(£)
Sales revenue			
(100 000 jumpers at £10)			1 000 000
Factory cost of goods sold:			
Direct materials	100 000		
Direct labour	350 000		
Variable factory overheads	60 000		
Fixed factory overheads	220 000	730 000	
Administration overhead		140 000	
Selling and distribution overhead			
Sales commission (2% of sales)	20 000		
Delivery costs (variable per unit sold)	50 000		
Fixed costs	40 000	110 000	980 000
Profit			20 000

The information to be submitted to the managing director includes the following three proposals:

(i) To proceed on the basis of analyses of market research studies that indicate that the demand for the jumpers is such that a 10 per cent reduction in selling price would increase demand by 40 per cent.

(ii) To proceed with an enquiry that the marketing director has had from a mail order company about the possibility of purchasing 50 000 units annually if the selling price is right. The mail order company would transport the jumpers from Tweed Ltd to its own warehouse, and no sales commission would be paid on these sales by Tweed Ltd. However, if an acceptable price can be negotiated, Tweed Ltd would be expected to contribute £60 000 per annum towards the cost of producing the mail order catalogue. It would also be necessary for Tweed Ltd to provide special additional packaging at a cost of £0.50 per jumper. The marketing director considers that in 2009 the sales from existing business would remain unchanged at 100 000 units, based on a selling price of £10 if the mail order contract is undertaken.

(iii) To proceed on the basis of a view held by the marketing director that a 10 per cent price reduction, together with a national advertising campaign costing £30 000, may increase sales to the maximum capacity of 160 000 jumpers.

Required:

(a) The calculation of break-even sales value based on the 2008 accounts.

(b) A financial evaluation of proposal (i) and a calculation of the number of units Tweed Ltd would require to sell at £9 each to earn the target profit of £80 000.

(c) A calculation of the minimum prices that would have to be quoted to the mail order company, first, to ensure that Tweed Ltd would at least break even on the mail order contract, secondly, to ensure that the same overall profit is earned as proposal (i) and, thirdly, to ensure that the overall target profit is earned.

(d) A financial evaluation of proposal (iii).

CHAPTER 4
MEASURING RELEVANT COSTS AND REVENUES FOR DECISION-MAKING

LEARNING OBJECTIVES

After studying this chapter you should be able to:

- **distinguish between relevant and irrelevant costs and revenues;**
- **explain the importance of qualitative factors;**
- **distinguish between the relevant and irrelevant costs and revenues for the five decision-making problems described;**
- **describe the key concept that should be applied for presenting information for product mix decisions when capacity constraints apply;**
- **explain why the book value of equipment is irrelevant when making equipment replacement decisions;**
- **describe the opportunity cost concept;**
- **explain the misconceptions relating to relevant costs and revenues.**

The provision of relevant information for decision-making is one of the most important functions of management accounting. Decision-making involves choosing between alternatives. For example, managers are faced with decisions as to whether to discontinue a product or a channel of distribution, make a component within the company or buy from an outside supplier, introduce a new product or service, and/or replace existing equipment. A distinguishing feature of these decisions is that they are not routinely made at frequent intervals. They require **special studies** to be undertaken only when a decision needs to be made.

Making decisions requires that only those costs and revenues that are relevant to the alternatives are considered. The inclusion of irrelevant cost and revenue data may result in making wrong decisions. Identifying and comparing relevant costs and revenues is crucial to decision-making. It is therefore essential to identify the relevant costs and revenues that are applicable to the alternatives being considered. The purpose of this chapter is to enable you to distinguish between relevant costs and revenues for various decision-making situations.

Special studies focus on whatever planning time horizon the decision-maker considers appropriate for a given situation. However, it is important not to focus excessively on the short term, because the objective is to maximize long-term benefits. We begin by explaining the concept of relevant cost and applying this principle to special studies relating to the following:

1 special selling price decisions;

2 product mix decisions when capacity constraints exist;

3 decisions on replacement of equipment;

4 outsourcing (make or buy) decisions;

5 discontinuation decisions.

IDENTIFYING RELEVANT COSTS AND REVENUES

The **relevant costs** and **revenues** required for decision-making are only those that will be affected by the decision. Costs and revenues that are independent of a decision are obviously not relevant and need not be considered when making that decision. The relevant financial inputs for decision-making purposes are therefore future cash flows, which will differ between the various alternatives being considered. In other words, only **differential** (or **incremental**) **cash flows** should be taken into account, and cash flows that will be the same for all alternatives are irrelevant. To keep things simple we shall focus on relevant costs based on the understanding that the same principles also apply to relevant revenues.

Because decision-making is concerned with choosing between future alternative courses of action, and nothing can be done to alter the past, then past costs (also known as sunk costs) are not relevant for decision-making. In Chapter 2 it was pointed out that **sunk costs** have already been incurred and cannot be avoided regardless of the alternatives being considered.

Allocated common fixed costs are also irrelevant for decision-making. **Facility sustaining costs** such as general administrative and property costs are examples of common costs. They are incurred to support the organization as a whole and generally will not change whichever alternative is chosen. They will only change if there is a dramatic change in organizational activity resulting in an expansion or contraction in the business facilities. We shall see that for various reasons such costs may be allocated (i.e. apportioned) to cost objects but they should be disregarded for decision-making. This is because decisions merely lead to a redistribution of the same sunk cost between cost objects – they do not affect the level of cost to the company as a whole.

To illustrate the identification of relevant costs in a non-business setting, consider a situation where an individual is uncertain as to whether he or she should purchase a monthly rail ticket to travel to work or use their car. Assuming that the individual already owns and will keep the car, whether or not he or she travels to work by train, the cost of the road fund licence and insurance will be irrelevant. They are sunk costs and will remain the same irrespective of the mode of travel. The cost of fuel will, however, be relevant, because this is a future cost that will differ depending on which alternative method of transport is chosen.

The following general principles can therefore be applied in identifying relevant and irrelevant costs:

1 relevant costs are future costs that differ between alternatives;

2 irrelevant costs consist of sunk costs, allocated costs and future costs that do not differ between alternatives.

IMPORTANCE OF QUALITATIVE FACTORS

In many situations it is difficult to quantify in monetary terms all the important elements of a decision. Those factors that cannot be expressed in monetary terms are classified as **qualitative factors**. A decline in employee morale that results from redundancies arising from a closure decision is an example of a qualitative factor. It is essential that qualitative factors be brought to the attention of management during the decision-making process, because otherwise there may be a danger that a wrong decision will be made. For example, the cost of manufacturing a component internally may be more expensive than purchasing from an outside supplier. However, the decision to purchase from an outside supplier could result in the closing down of the company's facilities for manufacturing the component. The effect of such a decision might lead to redundancies and a decline in employee morale, which could affect future output. In addition, the company will now be at the mercy of the supplier who might seek to increase prices on subsequent contracts and/ or may not always deliver on time. The company may not then be in a position to meet customers' requirements. In turn, this could result in a loss of customer goodwill and a decline in future sales.

The above qualitative factors must be taken into account in the decision-making process. Management must consider the availability of future supplies and the likely effect on customer goodwill if there is a delay in meeting orders. If the component can be obtained from many suppliers and repeat orders for the company's products from customers are unlikely, then the company may give little weighting to these qualitative factors. Alternatively, if the component can be obtained from only one supplier and the company relies heavily on repeat sales to existing customers, then the qualitative factors will be of considerable importance. In the latter situation the company may consider that the quantifiable cost savings from purchasing the component from an outside supplier are insufficient to cover the risk of the qualitative factors occurring.

Let us now move on to apply the relevant cost approach to a variety of decision-making problems. We shall concentrate on measuring the financial outcomes but do remember that they do not always provide the full story. Qualitative factors should also be taken into account in the decision-making process.

SPECIAL PRICING DECISIONS

Special pricing decisions relate to pricing decisions outside the main market. Typically they involve one-time only orders or orders at a price below the prevailing market price. Consider the information presented in Example 4.1.

EXAMPLE 4.1

The Caledonian Company is a manufacturer of clothing that sells its output directly to clothing retailers in the UK. One of its departments manufactures sweaters. The department has a production capacity of 50 000 sweaters per month. Because of the liquidation of one of its major customers the company has excess capacity. For the next quarter, current monthly production and sales volume is expected to be 35 000 sweaters at a selling price of £40 per sweater. Expected *monthly* costs and revenues for an activity level of 35 000 sweaters are as follows:

	(£)	(£ per unit)
Direct labour	420 000	12
Direct materials	280 000	8
Variable manufacturing overheads	70 000	2
Manufacturing fixed (non-variable) overheads	280 000	8
Marketing and distribution fixed (non-variable) costs	105 000	3
Total costs	1 155 000	33
Sales	1 400 000	40
Profit	245 000	7

Caledonian is expecting an upsurge in demand and considers that the excess capacity is temporary. Therefore, even though there is sufficient direct labour capacity to produce 50 000 sweaters, Caledonian intends to retain the temporary excess supply of direct labour for the expected upsurge in demand. A company located overseas has offered to buy 15 000 sweaters each month for the next three months at a price of £20 per sweater. The company would pay for the transportation costs and thus no additional marketing and distribution costs will be incurred. No subsequent sales to this customer are anticipated. The company would require its company logo inserting on the sweater and Caledonian has predicted that this will cost £1 per sweater. Should Caledonian accept the offer from the company?

At first glance it looks as if the order should be rejected since the proposed selling price of £20 is less than the total unit cost of £33. A study of the cost estimates, however, indicates that for the next quarter direct labour will remain unchanged. Therefore it is a fixed cost for the period under consideration. Manufacturing fixed overheads and the marketing and distribution costs are also fixed costs for the period under consideration. These costs will thus remain the same irrespective of whether or not the order is accepted. Hence they are irrelevant for this decision. All of the variable costs (i.e. the direct material costs, variable manufacturing overheads and the cost of adding the leisure company's logo) will be different if the order is accepted. Therefore they are relevant costs for making the decision. The relevant revenue and costs per unit for the decision are:

Selling price		20
Less: Direct materials	8	
Variable overheads	2	
Inserting company logo	1	11
Contribution to fixed costs and profit		9

For sales of 15 000 sweaters Caledonian will obtain an additional contribution of £135 000 per month (15 000 × £9). In Example 4.1 none of the fixed costs are relevant for the decision. It is appropriate to unitize variable costs because they are constant per unit but fixed costs should not be unitized since (you will recall from Chapter 2) they are not constant per unit of output. You should present unit relevant costs and revenues (as shown above) only when all fixed costs are irrelevant for decision-making. In most circumstances you are likely to be faced with situations where fixed costs are relevant. Therefore it is recommended that you avoid using unit costs for decision-making and instead adopt the approach presented in Exhibit 4.1.

Note from Exhibit 4.1 that in columns (1) and (2) both relevant and irrelevant *total* costs are shown for all alternatives under consideration. If this approach is adopted the *same* amounts for the irrelevant items (i.e. those items that remain unchanged as a result of the decision, which are direct labour, and manufacturing and marketing non-variable overheads) are included for all alternatives, thus making them irrelevant for decision-making. Alternatively, you can omit the irrelevant costs in columns (1) and (2) because they are the same for both alternatives. Instead of adopting either of these approaches you can present only the relevant (i.e. differential) costs and revenues. This approach is shown in column (3) of Exhibit 4.1. Note that column (3) represents the difference between columns (1) and (2). You will see that a comparison of columns (1) and (2), or presenting only the relevant items in column (3), shows that the company is better off by £135 000 per month if the order is accepted.

Four important factors must be considered before recommending acceptance of the order. Most of them relate to the assumption that there are no long-run implications from accepting the offer at a selling price of £20 per sweater. First, it is assumed that the future selling price will not be affected by selling some of the output at a price below the going market price. If this assumption is incorrect then competitors may engage in similar practices of reducing their selling prices in an attempt to unload spare capacity. This may lead to a fall in the market price, which in turn would lead to a fall in profits from future sales. The loss of future profits may be greater than the short-term gain obtained from accepting special orders at prices below the existing market price. Given that Caledonian has found a customer in a different market from its normal market it is unlikely that the market price would be affected. However, if the customer had been within Caledonian's normal retail market there would be a real danger that the market price would be affected. Secondly, the

EXHIBIT 4.1
Evaluation of the three-month order from the overseas company

Monthly sales and production in units	(1) Do not accept order 35 000 (£)	(2) Accept the order 50 000 (£)	(3) Difference in relevant costs/(revenues) 15 000 (£)
Direct labour	420 000	420 000	—
Direct materials	280 000	400 000	120 000
Variable manufacturing overheads	70 000	100 000	30 000
Manufacturing non-variable overheads	280 000	280 000	—
Inserting company logo		15 000	15 000
Marketing and distribution costs	105 000	105 000	—
Total costs	1 155 000	1 320 000	165 000
Sales revenues	1 400 000	1 700 000	(300 000)
Profit per month	245 000	380 000	135 000
Difference in favour of accepting the order		135 000	

decision to accept the order prevents the company from accepting other orders that may be obtained during the period at the going price. In other words, it is assumed that no better opportunities will present themselves during the period. Thirdly, it is assumed that the company has unused resources that have no alternative uses that will yield a contribution to profits in excess of £135 000 *per month*. Finally, it is assumed that the fixed costs are unavoidable for the period under consideration. In other words, we assume that the direct labour force and the fixed overheads cannot be reduced in the short term, or that they are to be retained for an upsurge in demand, which is expected to occur in the longer term.

Evaluation of a longer-term order

In Example 4.1 we focused on a short-term time horizon of three months. Capacity could not easily be altered in the short term and therefore direct labour and fixed costs were irrelevant costs with respect to the short-term decision. In the longer term, however, it may be possible to reduce capacity and spending on fixed costs and direct labour. Example 4.2 uses the same cost data as Example 4.1 but presents a revised scenario of a longer time horizon so that some of the costs that were fixed in the short term in Example 4.1 can now be changed in the longer term. You will see from Example 4.2 that Caledonian is faced with the following two alternatives:

1 do not accept the overseas order and reduce monthly capacity from 50 000 to 35 000 sweaters;

2 accept the overseas order of 15 000 sweaters per month and retain capacity at 50 000 sweaters per month.

The appropriate financial data for the analysis is shown in Exhibit 4.2. Note from this exhibit that column (1) incorporates the reduction in direct labour and fixed costs if capacity is reduced from 50 000 to 35 000 sweaters. A comparison of the monthly outcomes reported in columns (1) and (2) of Exhibit 4.2 indicates that the company is better off by £31 000 per month if it reduces capacity to 35 000 sweaters, assuming that there are no qualitative factors. Instead of presenting the data in columns (1) and (2), only the differential (relevant) costs and revenues are shown in column (3). This approach also indicates that the company is better off by £31 000 per month.

Note that the entry in column (3) of £25 000 is the lost revenues from the rent of the unutilized capacity if the company accepts the orders. This represents the opportunity cost of accepting the orders. In Chapter 2 it was pointed out that where the choice of one course of action requires that an alternative course of action is given up, the financial benefits that are foregone or sacrificed are known as **opportunity costs**. In other words, opportunity costs represent the lost contribution to profits arising from the best use of the alternative foregone. Opportunity costs only arise when resources are scarce and have alternative uses. Thus, in our illustration the capacity allocated to producing 15 000 sweaters results in an opportunity cost (i.e. the lost revenues from the rent of the capacity) of £25 000 per month.

In Exhibit 4.2 all of the costs and revenues are relevant to the decision because some of the costs that were fixed in the short term could be changed in the longer term. Therefore, whether or not a cost is relevant often depends on the time horizon under consideration. Thus it is important that the information presented for decision-making relates to the appropriate time horizon. If inappropriate time horizons are selected there is a danger that misleading information will be presented. Remember that our aim should always be to maximize *long-term* net cash inflows.

EXAMPLE 4.2

Assume that the department within Caledonian Company has a *monthly* production capacity of 50 000 sweaters. Liquidation of a major customer has resulted in expected future demand being 35 000 sweaters per *month*. Caledonian has not been able to find any customers for the excess capacity of 15 000 sweaters apart from a company located overseas that would be prepared to enter into a contractual agreement for a three-year period for a supply of 15 000 sweaters per month at an agreed price of £25 per sweater. The company would require that a motif be added to each sweater and Caledonian has predicted that will cost £1 per sweater. The company would pay for the transportation costs and thus no additional marketing and distribution costs will be incurred.

Direct materials and variable overheads are predicted to be £8 and £2, respectively, per sweater (the same as Example 4.1) and fixed manufacturing (£280 000), marketing and distribution costs (£105 000) and direct labour (£420 000) are also currently the same as the costs used in Example 4.1. However, if Caledonian does not enter into a contractual agreement it will reduce the direct labour force by 30 per cent (to reflect a capacity reduction from 50 000 to 35 000 sweaters). Therefore monthly direct labour costs will decline by 30 per cent, from £420 000 to £294 000. Further investigations indicate that manufacturing non-variable costs of £70 000 per month could be saved if a decision was made to reduce capacity by 15 000 sweaters per month. For example, the rental contracts for some of the machinery will not be renewed. Also some savings will be made in supervisory labour and support costs. Savings in marketing and distribution costs would be £20 000 per month. Assume also that if the capacity was reduced, factory rearrangements would result in part of the facilities being rented out at £25 000 per month. Should Caledonian accept the offer from the overseas company?

Monthly sales and production in units	(1) Do not accept order 35 000 (£)	(2) Accept the order 50 000 (£)	(3) Difference in relevant costs/ (revenues) 15 000 (£)
Direct labour	294 000	420 000	126 000
Direct materials	280 000	400 000	120 000
Variable manufacturing overheads	70 000	100 000	30 000
Manufacturing non-variable overheads	210 000	280 000	70 000
Inserting motif		15 000	15 000
Marketing and distribution costs	85 000	105 000	20 000
Total costs	939 000	1 320 000	381 000
Revenues from rental of facilities	25 000		25 000
Sales revenues	1 400 000	1 775 000	(375 000)
Profit per month	486 000	455 000	31 000
Difference in favour of rejecting the order		31 000	

EXHIBIT 4.2

Evaluation of orders for the unutilized capacity over a three-year time horizon

SOURCE: ADAPTED FROM GARDNER, S.C.; MEASURES OF PRODUCT ATTRACTIVENESS AND THE THEORY OF CONSTRAINTS. *INTERNATIONAL JOURNAL OF RETAIL AND DISTRIBUTION*.

REAL WORLD VIEWS 4.1

Measures of product attractiveness in retail operations

Shelf space limits the quantity and variety of products offered by a retail operation. The visibility of a particular stock-keeping unit (SKU) and probability of a stock-out are related to the space allocated to the SKU. Total contribution for the retail operation is influenced by how shelf space is allocated to the SKUs. For retailers, shelf space 'is their life blood – and it's very limited and expensive'. Shelf space, accordingly, can be treated as a constraint in retailing operations. The most attractive SKU is the SKU that generates the greatest contribution per unit of space (square foot or cubic foot). To calculate contribution, all incremental expenses are deducted from incremental revenue. Incremental revenues include retail price and other direct revenue such as deals, allowances, forward-buy and prompt-payment discounts. Incremental expenses include any money paid out as a result of selling one unit of a particular item. Included in the incremental expenses would be the invoice unit cost and other invoiced amounts (shipping charges, for example) that can be traced directly to the sale of the particular item. Incremental revenues and expenses are found by dividing case values by the number of units per case.

If capacity is not changed, then the relevant costs are the incremental costs rather than full costs. The choice of low direct product cost items (i.e. a full product cost including a share of the fixed warehouse, transport and storage costs) over high direct product cost items is essentially a choice to use less of the capacity that has already been paid for. If the costs of capacity are fixed, then using less capacity will not save money. Like the product mix problem, the answer to the space management problem is how to allocate existing capacity so that profit is maximized. To maximize profits where profits are constrained by space limitations, capacity should be allocated on the basis of the SKU that generates the greatest contribution per unit of space.

Discussion point

What are the relevant costs and revenues applicable to retail operations?

© SUHARJOTO/DREAMSTIME.COM

PRODUCT MIX DECISIONS WHEN CAPACITY CONSTRAINTS EXIST

In the short term sales demand may be in excess of current productive capacity. For example, output may be restricted by a shortage of skilled labour, materials, equipment or space. When sales demand is in excess of a company's productive capacity, the resources responsible for limiting the output should be identified. These scarce resources are known as **limiting factors**. Within a short-term time period it is unlikely that constraints can be removed and additional resources acquired. Where limiting factors apply, profit is maximized when the greatest possible contribution to profit is obtained each time the scarce or limiting factor is used. Consider Example 4.3.

In this situation the farmer's ability to increase output and profits/net cash inflows is limited in the short term by the availability of land for growing crops. You may think, when first looking at the available information, that the farmer should give top priority to producing maize, since this yields the highest contribution per tonne sold, but this assumption would be incorrect. To produce a tonne of maize, 80 scarce m² are required, whereas potatoes, barley and wheat require only 32m², 24m² and 16m² respectively of scarce land. By concentrating on growing potatoes, barley and wheat, the farmer can sell 3000 tonnes of each crop and still have some land left to grow maize. If the farmer concentrates on growing maize it will only be possible to meet the maximum sales demand of maize, and there will be no land available to grow the remaining crops. The way in which you should determine the optimum output to maximize profits is to calculate the contribution per limiting factor for each crop and then to rank the crops in order of profitability based on this calculation.

Using the figures in the present example the result would be as follows:

	Maize	Potatoes	Barley	Wheat
Contribution per tonne of output	$160	$112	$96	$80
m² required per tonne of output	80	32	24	16
Contribution per m²	$2	$3.50	$4	$5
Ranking	4	3	2	1

The farmer can now allocate the 240 000m² of land in accordance with the above rankings. The first choice should be to produce as much wheat as possible. The maximum sales are 3000 tonnes, and production of this quantity will result in 48 000m² of land being used. The second choice should be to grow barley and the maximum sales demand of 3000 tonnes will result in a further 72 000m² of land being used. The third choice is to grow potatoes. To meet the maximum sales demand for potatoes a further 96 000m² of land will be required. Growing 3000 tonnes of wheat, barley and potatoes requires 216 000m² of land, leaving a balance of 24 000m² for growing maize, which will enable 300 tonnes of maize to be grown.

We can now summarize the allocation of the 240 000m² of land:

Production	m² of land used	Balance of unused land (m²)
3000 tonnes of wheat	48 000	192 000
3000 tonnes of barley	72 000	120 000
3000 tonnes of potatoes	96 000	24 000
300 tonnes of maize	24 000	—

The above allocation results in the following total contribution:

	$
3000 tonnes of wheat at $80 per tonne contribution	240 000
3000 tonnes of barley at $96 per tonne contribution	288 000
3000 tonnes of potatoes at $112 per tonne contribution	336 000
300 tonnes of maize at $160 per tonne contribution	48 000
Total contribution	912 000

Contrast the above contribution with the contribution that would have been obtained if the farmer had ranked crop profitability by their contributions per tonne of output. This would have resulted in maize being ranked as the most profitable crop and all of the available land would have been used to grow 3000 tonnes of maize, giving a total contribution of $480 000 (3000 tonnes × $160).

EXAMPLE 4.3

A farmer in Ruritania has 240 000 square metres (m²) of land on which he grows maize, barley, potatoes and wheat. He is planning his production for the next growing season. The following information is provided relating to the anticipated demand and productive capacity for the next season:

	Maize	Potatoes	Barley	Wheat
Contribution per tonne of output in Ruritanian dollars	$160	$112	$96	$80
m² required per tonne of output	80	32	24	16
Estimated sales demand (tonnes)	3000	3000	3000	3000
Required area to meet sales demand (m²)	240 000	96 000	72 000	48 000

It is not possible in the short run to increase the area of land beyond 240 000m² for growing the above crops. You have been asked to advise on the mix of crops that should be produced during the period.

Always remember that it is necessary to consider other qualitative factors before the final production programme is determined. For example, customer goodwill may be lost causing a fall in future sales if the farmer is unable to supply all four crops to, say, 50 of its regular customers. Difficulties may arise in applying this procedure when there is more than one scarce resource. It could not be applied if, for example, labour hours were also scarce and the contribution per labour hour resulted in maize having the highest contribution per scarce labour hour. In this type of situation, where more than one resource is scarce, it is necessary to resort to linear programming methods in order to determine the optimal production programme. For an explanation of how linear programming can be applied when there is more than one scarce resource you should refer to Drury (2008, Chapter 25).

Finally, it is important that you remember that the approach outlined in this section applies only to those situations where capacity constraints cannot be removed in the short term. In the longer term additional resources should be acquired if the contribution from the extra capacity exceeds the cost of acquisition.

REPLACEMENT OF EQUIPMENT – THE IRRELEVANCE OF PAST COSTS

Replacement of equipment is a capital investment or long-term decision that requires the use of discounted cash flow procedures. These procedures are discussed in detail in Chapter 6, but one aspect of asset replacement decisions that we will consider at this stage is how to deal with the book value (i.e. the **written down value**) of old equipment. This is a problem that has been known to cause difficulty, but the correct approach is to apply relevant cost principles (i.e. past or sunk costs are irrelevant for decision-making). We shall now use Example 4.4 to illustrate the irrelevance of the book value of old equipment in a replacement decision.

EXAMPLE 4.4

Three years ago the Anytime Bank purchased a cheque sorting machine for £120 000. Depreciation using the straight line basis, assuming a life of six years and no salvage value, has been recorded each year in the financial accounts. The present written down value of the machine is £60 000 and it has a remaining life of three years. Recently a new sorting and imaging machine has been marketed that will cost £50 000 and have an expected life of three years with no scrap value. It is estimated that the new machine will reduce variable operating costs from £50 000 to £30 000 per annum. The current sales value of the old machine is £5000 and will be zero in three years' time.

You will see from an examination of Example 4.4 that the total costs over a period of three years for each of the alternatives are as follows:

	(1) Retain present machine (£)	(2) Buy replacement machine (£)	(3) Difference relevant costs/ (benefits) (£)
Variable/incremental operating costs:			
£50 000 for 3 years	150 000		
£30 000 for 3 years		90 000	(60 000)
Old machine book value:			
3-year annual depreciation charge	60 000		
Lump sum write-off		60 000	
Old machine disposal value		(5000)	(5000)
Initial purchase price of new machine		50 000	50 000
Total cost	210 000	195 000	(15 000)

You can see from the above analysis that the £60 000 book value of the old machine is irrelevant to the decision. Book values are not relevant costs because they are past or sunk costs and are therefore the same for all potential courses of action. If the present machine is retained, three years' depreciation at £20 000 per annum will be written off annually whereas if the new machine is purchased the £60 000 will be written off as a lump sum if it is replaced. Note that depreciation charges for the new machine are not included in the analysis since the cost of purchasing the machine is already included in the analysis. The sum of the annual depreciation charges are equivalent to the purchase cost. Thus, including both items would amount to double counting.

The above analysis shows that the costs of operating the replacement machine are £15 000 less than the costs of operating the existing machine over the three-year period. Again there are several different methods of presenting the information. They all show a £15 000 advantage in favour of replacing the machine. You can present the information shown in columns (1) and (2) above, as long as you ensure that the same amount for the irrelevant items is included for all alternatives. Instead, you can present columns (1) and (2) with the irrelevant item (i.e. the £60 000) omitted or you can present the differential items listed in column (3). However, if you adopt the latter approach you will probably find it more meaningful to restate column (3) as follows:

	£
Savings on variable operating costs (3 years)	60 000
Sale proceeds of existing machine	5000
	65 000
Less purchase cost of replacement machine	50 000
Savings on purchasing replacement machine	15 000

OUTSOURCING AND MAKE OR BUY DECISIONS

Outsourcing is the process of obtaining goods or services from outside suppliers instead of producing the same goods or providing the same services within the organization.

REAL WORLD VIEWS 4.2

Outsourcing at IBM

Krakow, Poland is a location used by many global firms to locate outsourced activities like software development, technical support or billing and accounts receivable. The city has over 150 000 students, who provide a suitable skill base for employers. Another location often used is Bangalore, India where labour costs are cheaper still. Since Poland joined the European Union in 2004, labour costs have steadily increased (7 per cent per annum on average) towards Western European levels, perhaps making Krakow a less attractive location for outsourced activities.

Not so according to IBM. IBM has outsourced activities in both Krakow and Bangalore. It realized that no one location can provide everything and it is not just about cost. In Krakow, for example, the local universities generate a ready supply of graduates – just what IBM needs to staff its software lab. Graduates are also readily available with expertise in US accounting and legal disciplines. The idea is to develop 'centres of competence' less vulnerable to competition based on labour costs alone. 'Even if you're a very well-organized company, it takes time to build a team with experienced people,' says Aleksandra Lichon, human resources director for IBM business consulting services in Krakow. Moreover, IBM needs to challenge its employees to retain them in an increasingly competitive job market. Polish workers do not want to be seen as cheap labour, but as full members of the team.

In addition to IBM, Krakow also hosts outsourced operations of organizations like KPMG and Motorola, and outsourcing specialists like Cap Gemini, one of the world's leading outsourcing vendors. It seems the availability of well-educated staff outweighs the higher labour cost.

© DIRECTPHOTO.ORG/ALAMY

Discussion points

1 Other than those mentioned, what kind of business activities would be best suited to outsourcing?
2 Strategically, do you think outsourcing is a good idea? Does it deliver value financially, operationally and strategically?

References:

Spiegel Online International, 26 September 2007 (http://www.spiegel.de/international/business/0,1518,508014,00.html).

Decisions on whether to produce components or provide services within the organization or to acquire them from outside suppliers are called outsourcing or 'make or buy' decisions. Many organizations outsource some of their activities such as their payroll and purchasing functions or the purchase of speciality components. Increasingly, municipal local services such as waste disposal, highways and property maintenance are being outsourced. Consider the information presented in Example 4.5 (Case A).

At first glance it appears that the component should be outsourced since the purchase price of £30 is less than the current total unit cost of manufacturing. However, the unit costs include some costs that will be unchanged whether or not the components are

EXAMPLE 4.5

Case A

One of the divisions within Rhine Autos is currently negotiating with another supplier regarding outsourcing component A that it manufactures. The division currently manufactures 10 000 units per annum of the component. The costs currently assigned to the components are as follows:

	Total costs of producing 10 000 components (£)	Unit cost (£)
Direct materials AB	120 000	12
Direct labour	100 000	10
Variable manufacturing overhead costs (power and utilities)	10 000	1
Fixed manufacturing overhead costs	80 000	8
Share of non-manufacturing overheads	50 000	5
Total costs	360 000	36

The above costs are expected to remain unchanged in the foreseeable future if the Rhine Autos division continues to manufacture the components. The supplier has offered to supply 10 000 components per annum at a price of £30 per unit guaranteed for a minimum of three years. If Rhine Autos outsources component A the direct labour force currently employed in producing the components will be made redundant. No redundancy costs will be incurred. Direct materials and variable overheads are avoidable if component A is outsourced. Fixed manufacturing overhead costs would be reduced by £10 000 per annum but non-manufacturing costs would remain unchanged. Assume initially that the capacity that is required for component A has no alternative use. Should the division of Rhine Autos make or buy the component?

Case B

Assume now that the extra capacity that will be made available from outsourcing component A can be used to manufacture and sell 10 000 units of component Z at a price of £34 per unit. All of the labour force required to manufacture component A would be used to make component Z. The variable manufacturing overheads, the fixed manufacturing overheads and non-manufacturing overheads would be the same as the costs incurred for manufacturing component A. Materials AB required to manufacture component A would not be required but additional materials XY required for making component Z would cost £13 per unit. Should Rhine Autos outsource component A?

outsourced. These costs are therefore not relevant to the decision. Assume also that there are no alternative uses of the released capacity if the components are outsourced. The appropriate cost information is presented in Exhibit 4.3 (Section A). Alternative approaches to presenting relevant cost and revenue information are presented. In columns (1) and (2) of Exhibit 4.3 cost information is presented that includes both relevant and irrelevant costs for both alternatives under consideration. The same amount for non-manufacturing over-heads, which are irrelevant, is included for both alternatives. By including the same amount in both columns the cost is made irrelevant. Alternatively, you can present cost information in columns (1) and (2) that excludes any irrelevant costs and revenues because they are identical for both alternatives. Adopting either approach will result in a difference of £60 000 in favour of making component A.

The third approach is to list only the relevant costs, cost savings and any relevant revenues. This approach is shown in column (3) of Exhibit 4.3 (Section A). This column represents the differential costs or revenues and it is derived from the differences between

EXHIBIT 4.3

*Evaluating a make
or buy decision*

Section A – Assuming there is no alternative use of the released capacity

	Total cost of continuing to make 10 000 components (1) (£ per annum)	Total cost of buying 10 000 components (2) (£ per annum)	Difference = Extra costs/ (savings) of buying (3) (£ per annum)
Direct materials AB	120 000		(120 000)
Direct labour	100 000		(100 000)
Variable manufacturing overhead costs (power and utilities)	10 000		(10 000)
Fixed manufacturing overhead costs	80 000	70 000	(10 000)
Non-manufacturing overheads	50 000	50 000	
Outside purchase cost incurred/(saved)		300 000	300 000
Total costs incurred/(saved) per annum	360 000	420 000	60 000

Extra costs of buying = 60 000

Section B – Assuming the released capacity can be used to make component Z

	Make component A and do not make component Z (1) (£ per annum)	Buy component A and make component Z (2) (£ per annum)	Difference = Extra costs/ (benefits) of buying component A (3) (£ per annum)
Direct materials XY		130 000	130 000
Direct materials AB	120 000		(120 000)
Direct labour	100 000	100 000	
Variable manufacturing overhead costs	10 000	10 000	
Fixed manufacturing overhead costs	80 000	80 000	
Non-manufacturing overheads	50 000	50 000	
Outside purchase cost incurred		300 000	300 000
Revenue from sales of component Z		(340 000)	(340 000)
Total net costs	360 000	330 000	(30 000)

Extra benefits from buying component A and using the released capacity to make component Z = £30 000 columns (1) and (2). In column (3) only the information that is relevant to the decision is presented. You will see that this approach compares the relevant costs of making directly against outsourcing. It indicates that the additional costs of buying component A are £300 000 but this enables costs of £240 000 associated with making component A to be saved. Therefore the company incurs an extra cost of £60 000 if it buys component A from the outside supplier.

Let us now re-examine the situation when the extra capacity created from not producing component A has an alternative use. Consider the information presented in Example 4.5 (Case B). The management of Rhine Autos now should consider the following alternatives:

1 make component A and do not make component Z;

2 outsource component A and make and sell component Z.

It is assumed that there is insufficient capacity to make both components A and Z. The appropriate financial information is shown in Exhibit 4.3 (Section B). You will see that the same costs will be incurred for both alternatives for direct labour and all of the overhead costs. Therefore these items are irrelevant and the same amount can be entered in columns (1) and (2) or they can be omitted from both columns. Note that direct materials AB (£120 000) will be incurred only if the company makes component A so an entry of £120 000 is shown in column (1) and no entry is made in column (2). However, if component A is bought from the supplier the capacity will be used to produce component Z and this will result in a purchase cost of £130 000 being incurred for materials XY. Thus £130 000 is entered in column (2) and no entry is made in column (1) in respect of materials XY. Also note that the sales revenue arising from the sale of component Z is shown in parentheses in column (2). A comparison of the totals of columns (1) and (2) indicates that that there is a net benefit of £30 000 from buying component A if the released capacity is used to make component Z.

Instead of presenting the information in columns (1) and (2) you can present the relevant costs and benefits as shown by the differential items in column (3). This column indicates that the extra costs of buying component A and using the released capacity to make component Z are:

	£
Outside purchase cost incurred	300 000
Purchase of materials XY for component Z	130 000
	430 000

The extra benefits are:

	£
Revenues from the sale of component Z	340 000
Savings from not purchasing materials AB	120 000
	460 000

The above alternative analysis also shows that there is a net benefit of £30 000 from buying component A if the released capacity is used to make component Z.

DISCONTINUATION DECISIONS

Most organizations periodically analyse profits by one or more cost objects, such as products or services, customers and locations. Periodic profitability analysis provides attention-directing information that highlights those unprofitable activities that require a more detailed appraisal (sometimes referred to as a special study) to ascertain whether or not they should be discontinued. In this section we shall illustrate how the principle of relevant costs can be applied to discontinuation decisions. Consider Example 4.6. You will see that it focuses on a decision whether to discontinue operating a sales territory, but the same principles can also be applied to discontinuing products, services or customers.

In Example 4.6 Euro Company analyses profits by locations. Profits are analysed by regions which are then further analysed by sales territories within each region. It is apparent from Example 4.6 that the Scandinavian region is profitable (showing a budgeted quarterly profit of £202 000) but the profitability analysis suggests that the Helsinki sales territory is unprofitable. A more detailed study is required to ascertain whether it should be discontinued. Let us assume that this study indicates that:

1 Discontinuing the Helsinki sales territory will eliminate cost of goods sold, salespersons' salaries and sales office rent.

2 Discontinuing the Helsinki sales territory will have no effect on depreciation of sales office equipment, warehouse rent, depreciation of warehouse equipment and regional and headquarters expenses. The same costs will be incurred by the company for all of these items even if the sales territory is discontinued.

Note that in the event of discontinuation the sales office will not be required and the rental will be eliminated whereas the warehouse rent relates to the warehouse for the region as a whole and, unless the company moves to a smaller warehouse, the rental will remain

EXAMPLE 4.6

The Euro Company is a wholesaler that sells its products to retailers throughout Europe. Euro's headquarters is in Brussels. The company has adopted a regional structure with each region consisting of 3–5 sales territories. Each region has its own regional office and a warehouse that distributes the goods directly to the customers. Each sales territory also has an office where the marketing staff are located. The Scandinavian region consists of three sales territories with offices located in Stockholm, Oslo and Helsinki. The budgeted results for the next quarter are as follows:

	Stockholm (£000)	Oslo (£000)	Helsinki (£000)	Total (£000)
Cost of goods sold	920	1002	1186	3108
Salespersons' salaries	160	200	240	600
Sales office rent	60	90	120	270
Depreciation of sales office equipment	20	30	40	90
Apportionment of warehouse rent	24	24	24	72
Depreciation of warehouse equipment	20	16	22	58
Regional and headquarters costs	360	400	340	1100
Total costs assigned to each location	1564	1762	1972	5298
Reported profit/(loss)	236	238	(272)	202
Sales	1800	2000	1700	5500

Assuming that the above results are likely to be typical of future quarterly performance, should the Helsinki territory be discontinued?

EXHIBIT 4.4

Relevant cost analysis relating to the discontinuation of the Helsinki territory

Total costs and revenues to be assigned	(1) Keep Helsinki territory open (£000)	(2) Discontinue Helsinki territory (£000)	(3) Difference in incremental costs and revenues (£000)
Cost of goods sold	3108	1922	1186
Salespersons' salaries	600	360	240
Sales office rent	270	150	120
Depreciation of sales office equipment	90	90	
Apportionment of warehouse rent	72	72	
Depreciation of warehouse equipment	58	58	
Regional and headquarters costs	1100	1100	
Total costs to be assigned	5298	3752	1546
Reported profit	202	48	154
Sales	5500	3800	1700

unchanged. It is therefore not a relevant cost. Discontinuation will result in the creation of additional space and if the extra space remains unused there are no financial consequences to take into account. However, if the additional space can be sublet to generate rental income the income would be incorporated as an opportunity cost for the alternative of keeping the Helsinki territory.

Exhibit 4.4 shows the relevant cost and revenue computations. Column (1) shows the costs incurred and revenues derived by the company if the sales territory is kept open (i.e. the items listed in the final column of Example 4.6) and column (2) shows the costs and revenues that will occur if a decision is taken to drop the sales territory. Therefore in column (2) only those costs that would be eliminated (i.e. those in item (1) on our list) are deducted from column (1). For example, Example 4.6 specifies that £240 000 salespersons' salaries will be eliminated if the Helsinki territory is closed so the entry in column (2) is £360 000 (£600 000 – £240 000).

You can see that the company will continue to incur some of the costs (i.e. those in item (2) on our list) even if the Helsinki territory is closed and these costs are therefore irrelevant to the decision. Again you can either include, or exclude, the irrelevant costs in columns (1) and (2) as long as you ensure that the same amount of irrelevant costs is included for both alternatives if you adopt the first approach. Both approaches will show that future profits will decline by £154 000 if the Helsinki territory is closed. Alternatively, you can present just the relevant costs and revenues shown in column (3). This approach indicates that keeping the sales territory open results in additional sales revenues of £1 700 000 but additional costs of £1 546 000 are incurred giving a contribution of £154 000 towards fixed costs and profits. We can conclude that the Helsinki sales territory should not be closed.

DETERMINING THE RELEVANT COSTS OF DIRECT MATERIALS

So far in this chapter we have assumed, when considering various decisions, that any materials required would not be taken from existing stocks but would be purchased at a later date, and so the estimated purchase price would be the relevant material cost. Where materials are taken from existing stock do remember that the original purchase price represents a past or sunk cost and is therefore irrelevant for decision-making. If the materials are to be replaced then using the materials for a particular activity will necessitate their replacement. Thus, the decision to use the materials on an activity will result in additional acquisition costs compared with the situation if the materials were not used on that particular activity. Therefore the future **replacement cost** represents the relevant cost of the materials.

Consider now the situation where the materials have no further use apart from being used on a particular activity. If the materials have some realizable value, the use of the materials will result in lost sales revenues, and this lost sales revenue will represent an opportunity cost that must be assigned to the activity. Alternatively, if the materials have no realizable value the relevant cost of the materials will be zero.

DETERMINING THE RELEVANT COSTS OF DIRECT LABOUR

Determining the direct labour costs that are relevant to short-term decisions depends on the circumstances. Where a company has temporary spare capacity and the labour force is to be maintained in the short term, the direct labour cost incurred will remain the same for all alternative decisions. The direct labour cost will therefore be irrelevant for short-term decision-making purposes. Consider now a situation where casual labour is used and where workers can be hired on a daily basis; a company may then adjust the employment of labour to exactly the amount required to meet the production requirements. The labour cost will increase if the company accepts additional work, and will decrease if production is reduced. In this situation the labour cost will be a relevant cost for decision-making purposes.

In a situation where full capacity exists and additional labour supplies are unavailable in the short term, and where no further overtime working is possible, the only way that labour resources could then be obtained for a specific order would be to reduce existing production. This would release labour for the order, but the reduced production would result in a lost contribution, and this lost contribution must be taken into account when ascertaining the relevant cost for the specific order. The relevant labour cost per hour where full capacity exists is therefore the hourly labour rate plus an opportunity cost consisting of the contribution per hour that is lost by accepting the order. For a more detailed illustration explaining why this is the appropriate cost you should refer to Learning note 4.1 on the open access website (see Preface for details).

SUMMARY

The following items relate to the learning objectives listed at the beginning of the chapter.

● **Distinguish between relevant and irrelevant costs and revenues**. Relevant costs/ revenues represent those future costs/revenues that will be changed by a particular decision, whereas irrelevant costs/revenues will not be affected by that decision. In the short term total profits will be increased (or total losses decreased) if a course of action is chosen where relevant revenues are in excess of relevant costs.

● **Explain the importance of qualitative factors**. Quantitative factors refer to outcomes that can be measured in numerical terms. In many situations it is difficult to quantify all the important elements of a decision. Those factors that cannot be expressed in numerical terms are called qualitative factors. Examples of qualitative factors include changes in employee morale and the impact of being at the mercy of a supplier when a decision is made to close a company's facilities and sub-contract components. Although qualitative factors cannot be quantified it is essential that they are taken into account in the decision-making process.

● **Distinguish between the relevant and irrelevant costs and revenues for the five decision-making problems described**. The five decision-making problems described were: (a) special selling price decisions; (b) product mix decisions when capacity constraints apply; (c) decisions on the replacement of equipment; (d) outsourcing (make or buy) decisions; and (e) discontinuation decisions. Different approaches can be used for presenting relevant cost and revenue information. Information can be presented that includes both relevant and irrelevant items for all alternatives under consideration. If this approach is adopted the same amount for the irrelevant items (i.e. those items that remain unchanged as a result of the decision) are included for all alternatives, thus making them irrelevant for the decision. Alternatively, information can be presented that lists only the relevant costs for the alternatives under consideration. Where only two alternatives are being considered a third approach is to present only the relevant (differential) items. You can adopt either approach. It is a matter of personal preference. All three approaches were illustrated for the five decision-making problems.

● **Describe the key concept that should be applied for presenting information for product mix decisions when capacity constraints apply**. The information presented should rank the products by the contribution per unit of the constraining or limiting factor (i.e. the scarce resource). The capacity of the scarce resource should be allocated according to this ranking.

● **Explain why the book value of equipment is irrelevant when making equipment replacement decisions**. The book value of equipment is a past (sunk) cost that cannot be changed for any alternative under consideration. Only future costs or revenues that will differ between alternatives are relevant for replacement decisions.

● **Describe the opportunity cost concept**. Where the choice of one course of action requires that an alternative course of action be given up the financial benefits that are foregone or sacrificed are known as opportunity costs. Opportunity costs thus represent the lost contribution to profits arising from the best alternative foregone. They arise only when the resources are scarce and have alternative uses. Opportunity costs must therefore be included in the analysis when presenting relevant information for decision-making.

● **Explain the misconceptions relating to relevant costs and revenues**. The main misconception relates to the assumption that only sales revenues and variable costs are relevant and that fixed costs are irrelevant for decision-making. Sometimes variable costs are irrelevant. For example, they are irrelevant when they are the same for all alternatives under consideration. Fixed costs are also relevant when they differ among the alternatives. For a more detailed discussion explaining the misconceptions relating to relevant costs and revenues you should refer to Learning note 4.2 on the open access website (see Preface for details).

KEY TERMS AND CONCEPTS

differential cash flow (p. 72)
facility sustaining costs (p. 72)
incremental cash flow (p. 72)
limiting factor (p. 78)
opportunity cost (p. 76)
outsourcing (p. 82)

qualitative factors (p. 73)
relevant costs and revenues (p. 72)
replacement cost (p. 88)
special studies (p. 71)
sunk costs (p. 72)
written down value (p. 80)

ASSESSMENT MATERIAL

The review questions are short questions that enable you to assess your understanding of the main topics included in the chapter. The page numbers in parentheses provide you with the page numbers to refer to if you cannot answer a specific question.

The review problems are more complex and require you to relate and apply the content to various business problems. Solutions to review problems are provided in a separate section at the end of the book. Additional review problems can be accessed by lecturers and students on the website www.drury-online.com. Solutions to these problems are provided for lecturers in the *Instructors' Manual*. This is available on the lecturers' password-protected section of the website.

The website also includes over 30 case study problems. A list of these cases is provided on pages 389–392. Several cases are relevant to the content of this chapter. Examples include Fleet Ltd and High Street Reproduction Furniture Ltd.

REVIEW QUESTIONS

4.1 What is a relevant cost? *(pp. 72–73)*

4.2 Why is it important to recognize qualitative factors when presenting information for decision-making? Provide examples of qualitative factors. *(p. 73)*

4.3 What underlying principle should be followed in determining relevant costs for decision-making? *(p. 73)*

4.4 Explain what is meant by special pricing decisions. *(pp. 73–74)*

4.5 Describe the important factors that must be taken into account when making special pricing decisions. *(pp. 75–76)*

4.6 Describe the dangers involved in focusing excessively on a short-run decision-making time horizon. *(p. 76)*

4.7 Define limiting factors. *(p. 78)*

4.8 How should a company determine its optimal product mix when a limiting factor exists? *(pp. 79–80)*

4.9 Why is the written down value and depreciation of an asset being considered for replacement irrelevant when making replacement decisions? *(pp. 80–81)*

4.10 Explain the importance of opportunity costs for decision-making. *(p. 76)*

4.11 Explain the circumstances when the original purchase price of materials are irrelevant for decision-making. *(p. 88)*

4.12 Why does the relevant cost of labour differ depending upon the circumstances? *(p. 88)*

REVIEW PROBLEMS

4.13 A company produces three products that have the following details:

	i Per unit	ii Per unit	iii Per unit
Direct materials (at £5/kg)	8 kg	5 kg	6 kg
Contribution per unit	£35	£25	£48
Contribution per kg of material	£4.375	£5	£8
Demand (excluding special contract) (units)	3000	5000	2000

The company must produce 1000 units of Product (i) for a special contract before meeting normal demand. Unfortunately there are only 35 000 kg of material available.

What is the optimal production plan?

	i	ii	iii
A	1000	4600	2000
B	1000	3000	2000
C	2875	—	2000
D	3000	2200	—

4.14 Your company regularly uses material X and currently has in stock 600 kg, for which it paid £1500 two weeks ago. If this were to be sold as raw material it could be sold today for £2.00 per kg. You are aware that the material can be bought on the open market for £3.25 per kg, but it must be purchased in quantities of 1000 kg.

You have been asked to determine the relevant cost of 600 kg of material X to be used in a job for a customer. The relevant cost of the 600 kg is:

(a) £1200
(b) £1325
(c) £1825
(d) £1950
(e) £3250

4.15 Q plc makes two products – Quone and Qutwo – from the same raw material. The selling price and cost details of these products are as shown below:

	Quone (£)	Qutwo (£)
Selling price	20.00	18.00
Direct material (£2.00/kg)	6.00	5.00
Direct labour	4.00	3.00
Variable overhead unit	2.00	1.50
	12.00	9.50
Contribution per unit	8.00	8.50

The maximum demand for these products is:

Quone   500 units per week
Qutwo   unlimited number of units per week

If materials were limited to 2000 kg per week, the shadow price (opportunity cost) of these materials would be:

(a) nil;
(b) £2.00 per kg;
(c) £2.66 per kg;
(d) £3.40 per kg;
(e) none of these.

4.16 BB Limited makes three components: S, T and U. The following costs have been recorded:

	Component S Unit cost (£)	Component T Unit cost (£)	Component U Unit cost (£)
Variable cost	2.50	8.00	5.00
Fixed cost	2.00	8.30	3.75
Total cost	4.50	16.30	8.75

Another company has offered to supply the components to BB Limited at the following prices:

	Component S	Component T	Component U
Price each	£4	£7	£5.50

Which component(s), if any, should BB Limited consider buying in?

(a) Buy in all three components.
(b) Do not buy any.
(c) Buy in S and U.
(d) Buy in T only.

4.17 A company is considering accepting a one-year contract that will require four skilled employees. The four skilled employees could be recruited on a one-year contract at a cost of £40 000 per employee. The employees would be supervised by an existing manager who earns £60 000 per annum. It is expected that supervision of the contract would take 10 per cent of the manager's time.

Instead of recruiting new employees, the company could retrain some existing employees who currently earn £30 000 per year. The training would cost £15 000 in total. If these employees were used they would need to be replaced at a total cost of £100 000.

The relevant labour cost of the contract is:

A £100 000
B £115 000
C £135 000
D £141 000
E £166 000

4.18 A company is considering the costs for a special order. The order would require 1250 kg of material D. This material is readily available and regularly used by the company. There are 265 kg of material D in stock, which cost £795 last week. The current market price is £3.24 per kg.

Material D is normally used to make product X. Each unit of X requires 3 kg of material D and, if material D is costed at £3 per kg, each unit of X yields a contribution of £15.

The cost of material D to be included in the costing of the special order is nearest to

A £3990   B £4050   C £10 000   D £10 300

4.19 Camden has three divisions. Information for the year ended 30 September is as follows:

	Division A £000	Division B £000	Division C £000	Total £000
Sales	350	420	150	920
Variable costs	280	210	120	610
Contribution	70	210	30	310
Fixed costs				262.5
Net profit				47.5

General fixed overheads are allocated to each division on the basis of sales revenue; 60 per cent of the total fixed costs incurred by the company are specific to each division being split equally between them.

Using relevant costing techniques, which divisions should remain open if Camden wishes to maximize profits?

A   A, B and C
B   A and B only
C   B only
D   B and C only

4.20 Decision on which of two mutually exclusive contracts to accept

A company in the civil engineering industry with headquarters located 22 miles from London undertakes contracts anywhere in the United Kingdom.

The company has had its tender for a job in north-east England accepted at £288 000 and work is due to begin in March. However, the company has also been asked to undertake a contract on the south coast of England. The price offered for this contract is £352 000. Both of the contracts cannot be taken simultaneously because of constraints on staff site management personnel and on plant available. An escape clause enables the company to withdraw from the contract in the north-east, provided notice is given before the end of November and an agreed penalty of £28 000 is paid.

The following estimates have been submitted by the company's quantity surveyor:

Cost estimates	North-east (£)	South coast (£)
Materials:		
In stock at original cost, Material X	21 600	
In stock at original cost, Material Y		24 800
Firm orders placed at original cost, Material X	30 400	
Not yet ordered – current cost, Material X	60 000	
Not yet ordered – current cost, Material Z		71 200
Labour – hired locally	86 000	110 000
Site management	34 000	34 000
Staff accommodation and travel for site management	6 800	5 600
Plant on site – depreciation	9 600	12 800
Interest on capital, 8%	5 120	6 400
Total local contract costs	253 520	264 800
Headquarters costs allocated at rate of 5% on total contract costs	12 676	13 240
	266 196	278 040
Contract price	288 000	352 000
Estimated profit	21 804	73 960

Notes:

1   X, Y and Z are three building materials. Material X is not in common use and would not realize much money if resold; however, it could be used on other contracts but only as a substitute for another material currently quoted at 10 per cent less than the original cost of X. The price of Y, a material in common use, has doubled since it was purchased; its net realizable value if resold would be its new price less 15 per cent to cover disposal costs. Alternatively it could be kept for use on other contracts in the following financial year.

2   With the construction industry not yet recovered from the recent recession, the company is confident that manual labour, both skilled and unskilled, could be hired locally on a sub-contracting basis to meet the needs of each of the contracts.

3   The plant which would be needed for the south coast contract has been owned for some years and £12 800 is the year's depreciation on a straight line basis. If the north-east contract is undertaken, less plant will be required but the surplus plant will be hired out for the period of the contract at a rental of £6000.

4   It is the company's policy to charge all contracts with notional interest at 8 per cent on estimated working capital involved in contracts. Progress payments would be receivable from the contractee.

5   Salaries and general costs of operating the small headquarters amount to about £108 000 each year. There are usually ten contracts being supervised at the same time.

6   Each of the two contracts is expected to last from March to February which, coincidentally, is the company's financial year.

7   Site management is treated as a fixed cost.

You are required, as the management accountant to the company,

(a)   to present comparative statements to show the net benefit to the company of undertaking the more advantageous of the two contracts;

(12 marks)

(b)   to explain the reasoning behind the inclusion in (or omission from) your comparative financial statements, of each item given in the cost estimates and the notes relating thereto.

(13 marks)
(Total 25 marks)

4.21 Deletion of a product

Blackarm Ltd makes three products and is reviewing the profitability of its product line. You are given the following budgeted data about the firm for the coming year.

Product	A	B	C
Sales (in units)	100 000	120 000	80 000
	(£)	(£)	(£)
Revenue	1 500 000	1 440 000	880 000
Costs:			
Material	500 000	480 000	240 000
Labour	400 000	320 000	160 000
Overhead	650 000	600 000	360 000
	1 550 000	1 400 000	760 000
Profit/(Loss)	(50 000)	40 000	120 000

The company is concerned about the loss on product A. It is considering ceasing production of it and switching the spare capacity of 100 000 units to Product C.

You are told:

(i)   All production is sold.

(ii)   25 per cent of the labour cost for each product is fixed in nature.

(iii) Fixed administration overheads of £900 000 in total have been apportioned to each product on the basis of units sold and are included in the overhead costs above. All other overhead costs are variable in nature.

(iv)   Ceasing production of product A would eliminate the fixed labour charge associated with it and one-sixth of the fixed administration overhead apportioned to product A.

(v)   Increasing the production of product C by 100 000 units would mean that the fixed labour cost associated with product C would double, the variable labour cost would rise by 20 per cent and its selling price would have to be decreased by £1.50 in order to achieve the increased sales.

Required:

(a)   Prepare a marginal cost statement for a unit of each product on the basis of:
       (i)   the original budget;
       (ii)   if product A is deleted.

(12 marks)

(b)   Prepare a statement showing the total contribution and profit for each product group on the basis of:
       (i)   the original budget;
       (ii)   if product A is deleted.

(8 marks)

(c)   Using your results from (a) and (b) advise whether product A should be deleted from the product range, giving reasons for your decision.

(5 marks)
(Total 25 marks)

4.22 Alternative uses of obsolete materials

Brown Ltd is a company that has in stock some materials of type XY that cost £75 000 but that are now obsolete and have a scrap value of only £21 000. Other than selling the material for scrap, there are only two alternative uses for them.

Alternative 1: Converting the obsolete materials into a specialized product, which would require the following additional work and materials:

Material A	600 units
Material B	1 000 units
Direct labour:	
5000 hours unskilled	
5000 hours semi-skilled	
5000 hours highly skilled	15 000 hours
Extra selling and delivery expenses	£27 000
Extra advertising	£18 000

The conversion would produce 900 units of saleable product, and these could be sold for £400 per unit.

Material A is already in stock and is widely used within the firm. Although present stocks together with orders already planned will be sufficient to facilitate normal activity, any extra material used by adopting this alternative will necessitate such materials being replaced immediately. Material B is also in stock, but it is unlikely that any additional supplies can be obtained for some considerable time because of an industrial dispute. At the present time material B is normally used in the production of product Z, which sells at £390 per unit and incurs total variable cost (excluding material B) of £210 per unit. Each unit of product Z uses four units of material B.

The details of materials A and B are as follows:

	Material A (£)	Material B (£)
Acquisition cost at time of purchase	100 per unit	10 per unit
Net realizable value	85 per unit	18 per unit
Replacement cost	90 per unit	—

Alternative 2: Adapting the obsolete materials for use as a substitute for a sub-assembly that is regularly used within the firm. Details of the extra work and materials required are as follows:

Material C	1000 units
Direct labour:	
4000 hours unskilled	
1000 hours semi-skilled	
4000 hours highly skilled	9000 hours

1200 units of the sub-assembly are regularly used per quarter, at a cost of £900 per unit. The adaptation of material XY would reduce the quantity of the sub-assembly purchased from outside the firm to 900 units for the next quarter only. However, since the volume purchased would be reduced, some discount would be lost, and the price of those purchased from outside would increase to £950 per unit for that quarter.

Material C is not available externally, but is manufactured by Brown Ltd. The 1000 units required would be available from stocks, but would be produced as extra production. The standard cost per unit of material C would be as follows:

	(£)
Direct labour, 6 hours unskilled labour	36
Raw materials	13
Variable overhead, 6 hours at £1	6
Fixed overhead, 6 hours at £3	18
	73

The wage rates and overhead recovery rates for Brown Ltd are:

Variable overhead	£1 per direct labour hour
Fixed overhead	£3 per direct labour hour
Unskilled labour	£6 per direct labour hour
Semi-skilled labour	£8 per direct labour hour
Highly skilled labour	£10 per direct labour hour

The unskilled labour is employed on a casual basis and sufficient labour can be acquired to exactly meet the production requirements. Semi-skilled labour is part of the permanent labour force, but the company has temporary excess supply of this type of labour at the present time. Highly skilled labour is in short supply and cannot be increased significantly in the short term; this labour is presently engaged in meeting the demand for product L, which requires 4 hours of highly skilled labour. The contribution (sales less direct labour and material costs and variable overheads) from the sale of one unit of product L is £24.

Given this information, you are required to present cost information advising whether the stocks of material XY should be sold, converted into a specialized product (alternative 1) or adapted for use as a substitute for a sub-assembly (alternative 2).

4.23 Limiting factors and optimal production programme

A market gardener is planning his production for next season, and he has asked you as a cost accountant, to recommend the optimal mix of vegetable production for the coming year. He has given you the following data relating to the current year.

	Potatoes	Turnips	Parsnips	Carrots
Area occupied (acres)	25	20	30	25
Yield per acre (tonnes)	10	8	9	12
Selling price per tonne (£)	100	125	150	135
Variable cost per acre (£):				
Fertilizers	30	25	45	40
Seeds	15	20	30	25
Pesticides	25	15	20	25
Direct wages	400	450	500	570

Fixed overhead per annum £54 000

The land that is being used for the production of carrots and parsnips can be used for either crop, but not for potatoes or turnips. The land being used for potatoes and turnips can be used for either crop, but not for carrots or parsnips. In order to provide an adequate market service, the gardener must produce each year at least 40 tonnes each of potatoes and turnips and 36 tonnes each of parsnips and carrots.

(a) You are required to present a statement to show:
   (i) the profit for the current year;
   (ii) the profit for the production mix that you would recommend.

(b) Assuming that the land could be cultivated in such a way that any of the above crops could be produced and there was no market commitment, you are required to:
   (i) advise the market gardener on which crop he should concentrate his production;
   (ii) calculate the profit if he were to do so;
   (iii) calculate in sterling the break-even point of sales.

(25 marks)

CHAPTER 5
PRICING DECISIONS AND PROFITABILITY ANALYSIS

LEARNING OBJECTIVES

After studying this chapter you should be able to:

- **explain the relevant cost information that should be presented in price-setting firms for both short-term and long-term decisions;**
- **describe product and customer profitability analysis and the information that should be included for managing the product and customer mix;**
- **describe the target costing approach to pricing;**
- **describe the different cost-plus pricing methods for deriving selling prices;**
- **explain the limitations of cost-plus pricing;**
- **justify why cost-plus pricing is widely used;**
- **identify and describe the different pricing policies.**

Accounting information is often an important input to pricing decisions. Organizations that sell products or services that are highly customized or differentiated from each other by special features, or who are market leaders, have some discretion in setting selling prices. In these organizations the pricing decision will be influenced by the cost of the product. The cost information that is accumulated and presented is therefore important for pricing decisions. In other organizations prices are set by overall market and supply and demand forces and they have little influence over the selling prices of their products and services. Nevertheless, cost information is still of considerable importance in these organizations for determining the relative profitability of different products and services so that management can determine the target product mix to which its marketing effort should be directed.

In this chapter we shall focus on both of the above situations. We shall consider the role that accounting information plays in determining the selling price by a price setting firm. Where prices are set by the market our emphasis will be on examining the cost information that is required for product mix decisions. In particular, we shall focus on both product and customer profitability analysis. The same approaches, however, can be applied to the provision of services such as financial or legal.

The theoretical solution to pricing decisions is derived from economic theory, which explains how the optimal selling price is determined. A knowledge of economic theory is not essential for understanding the content of this chapter but it does provide a theoretical background for the principles influencing pricing decisions. For a discussion of economic theory relating to pricing decisions you should refer to Learning note 5.1 on the dedicated open access website (see Preface for details).

THE ROLE OF COST INFORMATION IN PRICING DECISIONS

Most organizations need to make decisions about setting or accepting selling prices for their products or services. In some firms prices are set by overall market supply and demand forces and the firm has little or no influence over the selling prices of its products or services. This situation is likely to occur where there are many firms in an industry and there is little to distinguish their products from each other. No one firm can influence prices significantly by its own actions. For example, in commodity markets such as wheat, coffee, rice and sugar, prices are set for the market as a whole based on the forces of supply and demand. Also, small firms operating in an industry where prices are set by the dominant market leaders will have little influence over the price of their products or services. Firms that have little or no influence over the prices of their products or services are described as **price takers**.

In contrast firms selling products or services that are highly customized or differentiated from each other by special features, or who are market leaders, have some discretion in setting prices. Here the pricing decision will be influenced by the cost of the product, the actions of competitors and the extent to which customers value the product. We shall describe those firms that have some discretion over setting the selling price of their products or services as **price setters**. In practice, firms may be price setters for some of their products and price takers for others.

Where firms are price setters cost information is often an important input into the pricing decision. Cost information is also of vital importance to price takers in deciding on the output and mix of products and services to which their marketing effort should be directed, given their market prices. For both price takers and price setters the decision time horizon determines the cost information that is relevant for product pricing or output mix decisions. We shall therefore consider the following four different situations:

1 a price-setting firm facing short-run pricing decisions;
2 a price-setting firm facing long-run pricing decisions;
3 a price-taking firm facing short-run product mix decisions;
4 a price-taking firm facing long-run product mix decisions.

REAL WORLD VIEWS 5.1

Pricing in the steel industry

Increasing demand for building materials such as steel has been driven by growing economies like China. Commodities like steel typically increase in price as demand outstrips supply. In recent years, the cost of energy has risen dramatically, which in turn increased the costs of steel producers like German firm Thyssen-Krupp.

In June 2008, Ekkehard Schulz, CEO of Thyssen-Krupp, forecast continuing sharp hikes in steel prices. With rising iron ore prices and increasing energy costs, which combined make up 70–80 per cent of the price of a tonne of steel, Schulz declared, 'We are not driving the price hike. We are being driven by it.' Many customers of Thyssen-Krupp protect themselves against price hikes in the short term by signing fixed-term price agreements for one year. Typically large powerful customers, like the automobile industry, will resist price increases. Schulz noted how price hikes, while unwelcome, will not cripple the automobile manufacturers. They often spend more on advertising per car than on steel per car.

Steel production may thus be an example of a price-setting industry. The market price is determined by the producers. Their price in turn, as mentioned, is driven by the costs of iron ore and energy. Increased competition from producers in China and India may affect the price in Europe. Schulz does not appear troubled by such competition as he argues the German steel industry has differentiated itself by having the most efficient steel production systems. Surprisingly, he explained, the efficiencies resulted from compliance with strict environmental regulations in Europe: 'Because of laws and regulations, the costs of exhaust filters, wastewater treatment, noise protection and other things are, in some cases, twice as high for us in Germany as they are for our European competitors. But as a result we also have the most efficient systems, which are now in demand around the world. So-called green technology is a strongly growing market, offering incredible opportunities for German industry.'

© VARIO IMAGES GMBH & CO.KG/ALAMY

Discussion points

1 What might cause a commodity price to decrease?
2 If a commodity price decreased, how to do think a company like Thyssen-Krupp would react? Would it immediately pass the price decrease to customers?

References

Spiegel Online International, 16 June 2008 (http://www.spiegel.de/international/germany/0,1518,566257,00.html).

A PRICE-SETTING FIRM FACING SHORT-RUN PRICING DECISIONS

Companies can encounter situations where they have temporary unutilized capacity and are faced with the opportunity of bidding for a one-time special order in competition with other suppliers. In this situation only the incremental costs of undertaking the order should be taken into account. It is likely that most of the resources required to fill the order will have already been acquired and the cost of these resources will be incurred whether or not the bid is accepted by the customer. Typically, the incremental costs are likely to consist of:

- extra materials that are required to fulfil the order;
- any extra part-time labour, overtime or other labour costs;
- the extra energy and maintenance costs for the machinery and equipment required to complete the order.

The incremental costs of one-off special orders in service companies are likely to be minimal. For example, the incremental cost of accepting one-off special business for a hotel may consist of only the cost of additional meals, laundering and bathroom facilities.

Bids should be made at prices that exceed incremental costs. Any excess of revenues over incremental costs will provide a contribution to committed fixed costs that would not otherwise have been obtained. Given the short-term nature of the decision long-term considerations are likely to be non-existent and, apart from the consideration of bids by competitors, cost data are likely to be the dominant factor in determining the bid price.

Any bid for one-time special orders that is based on covering only short-term incremental costs must meet all of the following conditions:

- Sufficient capacity is available for all resources that are required to fulfil the order. If some resources are fully utilized, opportunity costs (see Chapter 4 for an illustration) of the scarce resources must be covered by the bid price.
- The bid price will not affect the future selling prices and the customer will not expect repeat business to be priced to cover short-term incremental costs.
- The order will utilize unused capacity for only a short period and capacity will be released for use on more profitable opportunities. If more profitable opportunities do not exist and a short-term focus is always adopted to utilize unused capacity then the effect of pricing a series of special orders over several periods to cover incremental costs constitutes a long-term decision. Thus, the situation arises whereby the decision to reduce capacity is continually deferred and short-term incremental costs are used for long-term decisions.

A PRICE-SETTING FIRM FACING LONG-RUN PRICING DECISIONS

In this section we shall focus on three approaches that are relevant to a price-setting firm facing long-run pricing decisions. They are:

1 pricing customized products/services;

2 pricing non-customized products/services;

3 target costing for pricing non-customized products/services.

Pricing customized products/services

Customized products or services relate to situations where products or services tend to be unique so that no comparable market prices exist for them. Since sales revenues must cover costs for a firm to make a profit, many companies use product costs as an input to establish selling prices. Product costs are calculated and a desired profit margin is added to determine the selling price. This approach is called **cost-plus pricing**. For example, garages undertaking vehicle repairs establish the prices charged to customers using cost-plus pricing. Similarly, firms of accountants use cost-plus pricing to determine the price for the accountancy services that they have provided for their customers. Companies use different cost bases and mark-ups (i.e. the desired profit margin) to determine their selling prices. Consider the following information:

Cost base		Mark-up percentage (£)	Cost-plus selling price (£)
(1) Direct variable costs	200	150	500
(2) Direct fixed (non-variable) costs	100		
(3) Total direct costs	300	70	510
(4) Indirect (overhead) costs	80		
(5) Total cost	380	35	513

In the above illustration three different cost bases are used resulting in three different selling prices. In row (1) only direct variable costs are assigned to products for cost-plus pricing and a high percentage mark-up (150 per cent) is added to cover direct fixed costs and indirect costs and also provide a contribution towards profit. The second cost base is row (3). Here a smaller percentage margin (70 per cent) is added to cover indirect costs and a profit contribution. The final cost base shown in row (5) includes the assignment of a share of company overheads to each product, and when this is added to direct costs a total product cost is computed. This cost (also known as **full cost** or **long-run cost**) is the estimated sum of all those resources that are committed to a product in the long run. It represents an attempt to allocate a share of all costs to products to ensure that all costs are covered in the cost base. The lowest percentage mark-up (35 per cent) is therefore added since the aim is to provide only a profit contribution. We shall focus on cost assignment and the different cost bases in Chapters 7 and 8.

The above illustration is applicable to both manufacturing and non-manufacturing organizations. However, manufacturing organizations generally divide overhead costs (row 4) into manufacturing and non-manufacturing overheads. For example, if the overheads of £80 consist of £60 manufacturing and £20 non-manufacturing then £60 would be added to row (3) above to produce a total manufacturing cost of £360. Assuming that a profit margin of 40 per cent is added to the total manufacturing cost the selling price would be £504.

Mark-ups are related to the demand for a product. A firm is able to command a higher mark-up for a product that has a high demand. Mark-ups are also likely to decrease when competition is intensive. Target mark-up percentages tend to vary from product line to product line to correspond with well-established differences in custom, competitive position and likely demand. For example, luxury goods with a low sales turnover may attract high profit margins whereas non-luxury goods with a high sales turnover may attract low profit margins.

Note that once the target selling price has been calculated, it is rarely adopted without amendment. The price is adjusted upwards or downwards depending on such factors as the future capacity that is available, the extent of competition from other firms, and management's general knowledge of the market. For example, if the price calculation is much lower than that which management considers the customer will be prepared to pay, the price may be increased.

We may ask ourselves the question, 'Why should cost-based pricing formulae be used when the final price is likely to be altered by management?' The answer is that cost-based pricing formulae provide an initial approximation of the selling price. It is a target price and is important information, although by no means the only information that should be used when the final pricing decision is made. Management should use this information, together with their knowledge of the market and their intended pricing strategies, before the final price is set.

Pricing non-customized products/services

With highly customized products or services sales are likely to be to a single customer with the pricing decision being based on direct negotiations with the customer for a known quantity. In contrast, a market leader must make a pricing decision, normally for large and unknown volumes, of a single product that is sold to thousands of different customers. To apply cost-plus pricing in this situation an estimate is required of sales volume to determine a unit cost, which will determine the cost-plus selling price. This circular process occurs because we are now faced with two unknowns that have a cause-and-effect relationship, namely selling price and sales volume. In this situation it is recommended that cost-plus selling prices are estimated for a range of potential sales volumes. Consider the information presented in Example 5.1 (Case A).

You will see that the Auckland Company has produced estimates of total costs for a range of activity levels. Instead of adding a percentage profit margin the Auckland Company has added a fixed lump sum target profit contribution of £2 million.

The information presented indicates to management the sales volumes, and their accompanying selling prices, that are required to generate the required profit contribution. The unit cost calculation indicates the break-even selling price at each sales volume that is required to cover the cost of the resources committed at that particular volume. Management must assess the likelihood of selling the specified volumes at the designated prices and choose the price that they consider has the highest probability of generating at least the specified sales volume. If none of the sales volumes are likely to be achieved at the designated selling prices management must consider how demand can be stimulated and/or costs reduced to make the product viable. If neither of these, or other strategies, are successful the product should not be launched. The final decision must be based on management judgement and knowledge of the market.

The situation presented in Example 5.1 represents the most extreme example of the lack of market data for making a pricing decision. If we reconsider the pricing decision faced by the company it is likely that similar products are already marketed and

EXAMPLE 5.1

Case A

The Auckland Company is launching a new product. Sales volume will be dependent on the selling price and customer acceptance but because the product differs substantially from other products within the same product category it has not been possible to obtain any meaningful estimates of price/demand relationships. The best estimate is that demand is likely to range between 100 000 and 200 000 units provided that the selling price is less than £100. Based on this information the company has produced the following cost estimates and selling prices required to generate a target profit contribution of £2 million from the product.

Sales volume (000s)	100	120	140	160	180	200
Total cost (£000s)	10 000	10 800	11 200	11 600	12 600	13 000
Required profit contribution (£000s)	2 000	2 000	2 000	2 000	2 000	2 000
Required sales revenues (£000s)	12 000	12 800	13 200	13 600	14 600	15 000
Required selling price to achieve target profit contribution (£)	120.00	106.67	94.29	85.00	81.11	75.00
Unit cost (£)	100.00	90.00	80.00	72.50	70.00	65.00

Case B

Assume now an alternative scenario for the product in Case A. The same cost schedule applies but the £2 million minimum contribution no longer applies. In addition, Auckland now undertakes market research. Based on this research, and comparisons with similar product types and their current selling prices and sales volumes, estimates of sales demand at different selling prices have been made. These estimates, together with the estimates of total costs obtained in Case A are shown below:

	£100	£90	£80	£70	£60
Potential selling price					
Estimated sales volume at the potential selling price (000s)	120	140	180	190	200
Estimated total sales revenue (£000s)	12 000	12 600	14 400	13 300	12 000
Estimated total cost (£000s)	10 800	11 200	12 600	12 800	13 000
Estimated profit (loss) contribution (£000s)	1 200	1 400	1 800	500	(1 000)

information may be available relating to their market shares and sales volumes. Assuming that Auckland's product is differentiated from other similar products, a relative comparison should be possible of its strengths and weaknesses and whether customers would be prepared to pay a price in excess of the prices of similar products. It is therefore possible that Auckland may be able to undertake market research to obtain rough approximations of demand levels at a range of potential selling prices. Let us assume that Auckland adopts this approach, and apart from this, the facts are the same as those given in Example 5.1 (Case A).

Now look at Case B in Example 5.1. The demand estimates are given for a range of selling prices. In addition the projected costs, sales revenues and profit contribution are shown. You can see that profits are maximized at a selling price of £80. The information also shows the effect of pursuing other pricing policies. For example, a lower selling price of £70 might be selected to discourage competition and ensure that a larger share of the market is obtained in the future.

Pricing non-customized products/services using target costing

Instead of using the cost-plus pricing approach described in Example 5.1 (Case A) whereby cost is used as the starting point to determine the selling price, **target costing** is the reverse of this process. With target costing the starting point is the determination of the target selling price. Next a standard or desired profit margin is deducted to get a target cost for the product. The aim is to ensure that the future cost will not be higher than the target cost. The stages involved in target costing can be summarized as follows:

Stage 1: determine the target price that customers will be prepared to pay for the product;

Stage 2: deduct a target profit margin from the target price to determine the target cost;

Stage 3: estimate the actual cost of the product;

Stage 4: if estimated actual cost exceeds the target cost investigate ways of driving down the actual cost to the target cost.

The first stage requires market research to determine the customers' perceived value of the product, its differentiation value relative to competing products and the price of competing products. The target profit margin depends on the planned return on investment for the organization as a whole and profit as a percentage of sales. This is then decomposed into a target profit for each product that is then deducted from the target price to give the target cost. The target cost is compared with the predicted actual cost. If the predicted actual cost is above the target cost intensive efforts are made to close the gap. Product designers focus on modifying the design of the product so that it becomes cheaper to produce. Manufacturing engineers also concentrate on methods of improving production processes and efficiencies.

The aim is to drive the predicted actual cost down to the target cost but if the target cost cannot be achieved at the pre-production stage the product may still be launched if management are confident that the process of continuous improvement will enable the target cost to be achieved early in the product's life. If this is not possible the product will not be launched.

The major attraction of target costing is that marketing factors and customer research provide the basis for determining selling price whereas cost tends to be the dominant factor with cost-plus pricing. A further attraction is that the approach requires the collaboration of product designers, production engineers, marketing and finance staff whose focus is on managing costs at the product design stage. At this stage costs can be most effectively managed because a decision committing the firm to incur costs will not have been made.

Target costing is most suited for setting prices for non-customized and high sales volume products. It is also an important mechanism for managing the cost of future products. We shall therefore look at target costing in more detail when we focus on cost management in Chapter 14.

A PRICE-TAKING FIRM FACING SHORT-RUN PRODUCT MIX DECISIONS

Price-taking firms with a temporary excess capacity may be faced with opportunities of taking on short-term business at a market-determined selling price. In this situation the cost information that is required is no different from that of a price-setting firm making a short-run pricing decision. In other words, accepting short-term business where the incremental sales revenues exceed incremental short-run costs will provide a contribution towards committed fixed costs that would not otherwise have been obtained. However, such business is acceptable only if the same conditions as those specified for a price-setting firm apply. You should remember that these conditions are:

- sufficient capacity is available for all resources that are required from undertaking the business (if some resources are fully utilized, opportunity costs of the scarce resources must be covered by the selling price);
- the company will not commit itself to repeat longer-term business that is priced to cover only short-term incremental costs;
- the order will utilize unused capacity for only a short period and capacity will be released for use on more profitable opportunities.

A PRICE-TAKING FIRM FACING LONG-RUN PRODUCT MIX DECISIONS

When prices are set by the market a firm has to decide which products or services to sell given their market prices. In the longer term a firm can adjust the supply of resources committed to a product. Therefore the sales revenue from a product should exceed the cost of all the resources that are committed to it. Hence there is a need to undertake periodic profitability analysis to distinguish between profitable and unprofitable products in order to ensure that only profitable products are sold. Exhibit 5.1 presents an illustration of hierarchical profitability analysis for a company that has three product lines and three individual products within each product line. For example, product line A has three individual products called A1, A2 and A3 within its product line. A similar format has been applied to product lines B and C. A product line consists of a group of similar products. For example, banks have product lines such as savings accounts, lending services, currency services, insurance services and brokering services. Each product line contains individual product variants. The savings product line would include low balance/low interest savings accounts, high balance/high interest accounts, postal and internet savings accounts and other product variants. The lending services product line would include personal loans, house mortgage loans, business loans and other product variants within the product line.

You will see in Exhibit 5.1 that three different hierarchical levels have been identified. In row (3) the contribution to product line fixed costs is derived for each individual product by deducting direct variable and direct fixed costs (e.g. advertising for a specific individual product) from sales revenue. Next, in row (4) avoidable fixed costs that can be directly traced to each product line, but not the individual products, are deducted to derive the total contribution for each product line that is reported in row (5). Finally, in row (6) the costs of sustaining the business that cannot be specifically identified with individual products or product lines are deducted from the sum of the product line contributions to compute the profit for the company as a whole. Business sustaining costs, such as general administrative and property costs, are incurred to support the organization as a whole and cannot be directly attributed to individual products or product lines.

To illustrate how profitability analysis can be used, look at product B2. It provides a negative contribution of £50 000 to product line fixed costs. The analysis indicates that the contribution of product line B2 will increase by £50 000 if product B2 is discontinued. However, periodic profitability analysis as illustrated in Exhibit 5.1 should not be used directly for decision-making. Instead, the profitability analysis represents a periodical strategic review of the costs and profitability of a firm's products/services (or other cost objects, such as customers and sales outlets). In particular, profitability analysis should be used to highlight those products or services that require more detailed special studies.

Before discontinuing product B2 other alternatives or considerations must be taken into account at the special study stage. In some situations it is important to maintain a full product line for marketing reasons. For example, if customers are not offered a full product line to choose from they may migrate to competitors who offer a wider choice. By reporting individual product profitability the cost of maintaining a full product line, being the sum of unprofitable products within the product line, is highlighted. Where maintaining a full product line is not required managers should consider other options before dropping unprofitable products. They should consider re-engineering or redesigning the products to reduce their resource consumption.

You will see from the profitability analysis shown in Exhibit 5.1 that product C1 generates a very small contribution margin (£20 000) relative to other products within the product line. This low contribution margin might trigger the need to undertake a special study. Such a study might reveal that although none of product line C direct fixed costs of £500 000 are traceable to individual products a decision to discontinue product C1 would enable the product line fixed costs to be reduced by £50 000. Thus discontinuing product C1 would result in the product line contribution (shown in row (5)) and total company profits increasing by £20 000 (£50 000 – £30 000).

The profitability analysis shown in Exhibit 5.1 is based on **direct costing** principles whereby all costs can be specifically identified with a cost objective at a particular level within the hierarchy of reported profits. Those fixed costs (row 4) that cannot be specifically identified with individual products, but which can be identified with product lines, are only assigned at the product line level. Similarly those fixed costs (row 6) that cannot be specifically identified with individual products or product lines are assigned at the overall company level. Therefore none of the costs are categorized as indirect within the profit reporting hierarchy. An alternative costing system, known as **absorption costing**, is used by many companies whereby the product line fixed costs (row 4) and the business/facility sustaining fixed costs (row 6) are allocated to the individual products, often on an arbitrary basis. Where absorption costing principles are used such costs represent indirect costs at the individual product level. At this stage the aim is to highlight the role of profitability analysis within price-taking firms and not to focus on the different cost assignment methods. We shall look at the mechanisms for assigning costs to cost objects in Chapters 7 and 8.

EXHIBIT 5.1

An illustration of hierarchical profitability analysis

| | Product line A | | | | Product line B | | | | Product line C | | | | Company total |
	A1 (£000s)	A2 (£000s)	A3 (£000s)	Total £000s	B1 £000s	B2 £000s	B3 £000s	Total £000s	C1 £000s	C2 £000s	C3 £000s	Total £000s	£000s
(1) Sales	100	200	300	600	400	500	600	1500	700	800	900	2400	
(2) Less direct variable and fixed costs	20	60	120	200	200	550	360	1110	680	240	600	1520	
(3) Contribution to product line	80	140	180	400	200	(50)	240	390	20	560	300	880	1670
(4) Fixed costs directly attributable to the product line				350				300				500	1150
(5) Contribution to business sustaining fixed costs				50				90				380	520
(6) Business/facility sustaining fixed costs													200
(7) Overall company profit													320

Finally, you should note that in practice firms may have hundreds of products and many individual product lines. It will not be feasible to present a product profitability analysis, similar to that shown in Exhibit 5.1, in hard copy format. Instead, the necessary information will be maintained on a database. With hundreds of products, managers will seek to avoid information overload and may extract the relevant information that they require only when they are examining the profitability of a particular product line. In addition, the database may be designed so that periodically only individual loss-making products are routinely reported. Managers can then decide whether they need to initiate more detailed studies to ascertain if such products are viable in the long run.

SURVEYS OF PRACTICE RELATING TO PRICING DECISIONS

Generally companies should concentrate on long-run pricing decisions and short-run decisions should be viewed as representing abnormal situations. In the previous sections cost-plus pricing and periodic profitability analysis were examined for price-setting and price-taking firms facing long-run pricing and product mix decisions. To what extent are these approaches used in practice? Exhibit 5.2 summarizes surveys that have been undertaken relating to pricing practices and profitability analysis. A survey of 186 UK companies by Drury and Tayles (2006) reported that 91 per cent of respondents used periodic profitability analysis to monitor the profitability of products, services or customers. The study also indicated that 60 per cent of the respondents used cost-plus pricing even though this practice has been widely criticized. In the following sections the criticisms of cost-plus pricing and the reasons for its widespread use are examined.

EXHIBIT 5.2

Surveys of practice

A survey of 187 UK organizations by Drury and Tayles (2006) indicated that 91 per cent of respondents analysed profits at least on an annual basis and that 60 per cent used cost-plus pricing. Most of the organizations that used cost-plus pricing indicated that it was applied selectively. It accounted for less than 10 per cent of total sales revenues for 26 per cent of the respondents and more than 50 per cent for 39 per cent of the organizations. Most of the firms (85 per cent) used full cost and the remaining 15 per cent used direct cost as the pricing base. The survey also indicated that 74 per cent analysed profits either by customers or customer categories. In terms of factors influencing the importance of cost-plus pricing a survey of UK and Australian companies by Guilding *et al.* (2005) reported that the intensity of competition was positively related to the importance of cost-plus pricing.

An earlier UK study by Innes and Mitchell (1995a) reported that 50 per cent of respondents had used customer profitability analysis and a further 12 per cent planned to do so in the future. Of those respondents that ranked customer profitability, 60 per cent indicated that the Pareto 80/20 rule broadly applied (that, is 20 per cent of the customers were generating 80 per cent of the profits).

Dekker and Smidt (2003b) undertook a survey of 32 Dutch firms on the use of costing practices that resembled the Japanese target costing concept. They reported that 19 out of the 32 firms used these practices, although they used different names for them. Adoption was highest among assembling firms and was related to a competitive and unpredictable environment.

LIMITATIONS OF COST-PLUS PRICING

The main criticism that has been made against cost-plus pricing is that demand is ignored. The price is set by adding a mark-up to cost, and this may bear no relationship to the price–demand relationship. It is assumed that prices should depend solely on costs. For example, a cost-plus formula may suggest a price of £20 for a product where the demand is 100 000 units, whereas at a price of £25 the demand might be 80 000 units. Assuming that the variable cost for each unit sold is £15, the total contribution will be £500 000 at a selling price of £20, compared with a total contribution of £800 000 at a selling price of £25. Thus cost-plus pricing formulae might lead to incorrect decisions.

It is often claimed that cost-based pricing formulae serve as a pricing 'floor' shielding the seller from a loss. This argument, however, is incorrect since it is quite possible for a firm to lose money even though every product is priced higher than the estimated unit cost. The reason for this is that if sales demand falls below the activity level that was used to calculate the fixed cost per unit, the total sales revenue may be insufficient to cover the total fixed costs. Cost-plus pricing will only ensure that all the costs will be met, and the target profits earned, if the sales volume is equal to, or more than, the activity level that was used to estimate total unit costs.

Consider a hypothetical situation where all of the costs attributable to a product are fixed in the short term and amount to £1 million. Assume that the cost per unit is £100 derived from an estimated volume of 10 000 units. The selling price is set at £130 using the cost-plus method and a mark-up of 30 per cent. If actual sales volume is 7000 units, sales revenues will be £910 000 compared with total costs of £1 million. Therefore the product will incur a loss of £90 000 even though it is priced above full cost.

REASONS FOR USING COST-PLUS PRICING

Considering the limitations of cost-plus pricing, why is it that these techniques are frequently used in practice? Baxter and Oxenfeldt (1961) suggest the following reasons:

> They offer a means by which plausible prices can be found with ease and speed, no matter how many products the firm handles. Moreover, its imposing computations look factual and precise, and its prices may well seem more defensible on moral grounds than prices established by other means. Thus a monopolist threatened by a public inquiry might reasonably feel that he is safeguarding his case by cost-plus pricing.

Another major reason for the widespread use of cost-plus pricing methods is that they may help a firm to predict the prices of other firms. For example, if a firm has been operating in an industry where average mark-ups have been 40 per cent in the past, it may be possible to predict that competitors will be adding a 40 per cent mark-up to their costs. Assuming that all the firms in the industry have similar cost structures, it will be possible to predict the price range within which competitors may price their products. If all the firms in an industry price their products in this way, it may encourage price stability.

In response to the main objection that cost-based pricing formulae ignore demand, we have noted that the actual price that is calculated by the formula is rarely adopted without

REAL WORLD VIEWS 5.2

The use of cost information in pricing decisions

The following comments were derived from interviews with UK management accountants relating to the use of cost information in pricing decisions:

> *If we're taking decisions about pricing, generally speaking we would be looking to the market-place to see where our products fit in the market-place ..., costing would only be used to see what kind of profit margins we'd get from those prices. The costing system would not be the primary reason for making decisions.*

(A respondent from a price-taking firm)

> *We have our estimating system, it produces the estimated costs for 1000 boxes. ... And we then add the haulage cost which is based on where the customer happens to be ... And we then have margins. The system actually calculates a guestimated margin for you based on a number of factors: type of box, type of glue, type of business, etc., and it then says I think your margin should be 25.36 per cent. You then sit there and say ... does that make sense in relation to all the other products that we sell to that customer or does it make sense in relation to another box very similar to that we sell to somebody else. It is initially a cost-plus price, but the percentage is very variable.*

(An illustration of the use of cost-plus pricing by a price-setting firm)

> *We tend to do the costing with the historic mark-up to set the base price point and then really leave it to the salesmen to negotiate around that. Sometimes they'll get better, sometimes they won't get as much, but what we tend to do is give them a minimum price. We also tend to differentiate between certain of our market sectors. Dress club business, which is less sort of fashion or sporting oriented, we tend to put a lower margin rate on because we know the market will not take that sort of level. In some of the premium sports customers and certainly some of the premium brands that we work with we find that because some of their products have a high price we tend*

> *to put a high mark-up on. It's the play in the market: to some extent we leave a lot to the sales director and his team to put the best they can on it. ... It gives a little bit of a guide between one market area and another knowing that they will inevitably get better prices in certain areas than in others. Sometimes there will be different prices for exactly the same product with different customers.*

(The use of cost-plus pricing by a price-setting firm)

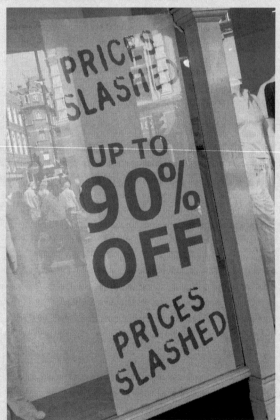

> *If we can't meet the retail price that is demanded by the marketing department we'd have to think again. You'd work it back down the other way to see how much you could do and then you'd use that product cost. You'd say that's what we were thinking of, if you go for a cheaper bottle, if you go for a cheaper carton, you don't put this in, you don't put that in, then you can have what you want*

and you come to some sort of compromise half way through.
(An illustration of a simplistic target costing approach)

More and more, certainly with the larger customers, it's what they're prepared to pay us. The market drives it. We do our estimate of what we estimate to get from it and all that does is to say that if we accept their price we're going to make a profit or loss. Then we'll look at the price they're prepared to give us. ... We'll look at our estimate and then we'll look at how we can reduce the costs. Then we may work with the customer to substitute materials.
(A simplistic form of target costing used by a price taker)

Discussion point

Why do the above organizations place different emphasis on the extent to which cost information influences pricing decisions?

References

Brealey, J. A. (2006) The calculation of product costs and their use in decision-making in British Manufacturing Industry, PhD dissertation, University of Huddersfield.

amendments. The price is adjusted upwards or downwards after taking account of the number of sales orders on hand, the extent of competition from other firms, the importance of the customer in terms of future sales, and the policy relating to customer relations. Therefore it is argued that management attempts to adjust the mark-up based on the state of sales demand and other factors that are of vital importance in the pricing decision.

PRICING POLICIES

Cost information is only one of many variables that must be considered in the pricing decision. The final price that is selected will depend upon the pricing policy of the company. A price-skimming or penetration pricing policy might be selected.

A **price-skimming policy** is an attempt to exploit those sections of the market that are relatively insensitive to price changes. For example, high initial prices may be charged to take advantage of the novelty appeal of a new product when demand is not very sensitive to price changes. A skimming pricing policy offers a safeguard against unexpected future increases in costs, or a large fall in demand after the novelty appeal has declined. Once the market becomes saturated, the price can be reduced to attract that part of the market that has not yet been exploited. A skimming pricing policy should not be adopted when a number of close substitutes are already being marketed. Here demand is likely to be very sensitive to price changes, and any price in excess of that being charged for a substitute product by a competitor is likely to lead to a large reduction in sales.

A **penetration pricing policy** is based on the concept of charging low prices initially with the intention of gaining rapid acceptance of the product. Such a policy is appropriate when close substitutes are available or when the market is easy to enter. The low price discourages potential competitors from entering the market and enables a company to establish a large share of the market. This can be achieved more easily when the product is new, than later on when buying habits have become established.

Many products have a **product life cycle** consisting of four stages: introductory, growth, maturity and decline. At the introductory stage the product is launched and there is minimal awareness and acceptance of it. Sales begin to expand rapidly at the growth stage because of introductory promotions and greater customer awareness, but this begins to taper off at the maturity stage as potential new customers are exhausted. At the decline stage sales diminish as the product is gradually replaced with new and better versions.

Sizer (1989) suggests that in the introductory stage it may be appropriate to shade upwards or downwards the price found by normal analysis to create a more favourable demand in future years. For example, he suggests that limited production capacity may rule out low prices. Therefore a higher initial price than that suggested by normal analysis may be set and progressively reduced, if and when (a) price elasticity of demand increases or (b) additional capacity becomes available. Alternatively if there is no production capacity constraint, a lower price than that suggested by normal analysis may be preferred. Such a price may result in a higher sales volume and a slow competitive reaction, which will enable the company to establish a large market share and to earn higher profits in the long term.

At the maturity stage a firm will be less concerned with the future effects of current selling prices and should adopt a selling price that maximizes short-run profits.

CUSTOMER PROFITABILITY ANALYSIS

In the past, management accounting reports have tended to concentrate on analysing profits by products. Increasing attention is now being given to analysing profits by customers using an activity-based costing approach. **Customer profitability analysis** provides important information that can be used to determine which classes of customers should be emphasized or de-emphasized and the price to charge for customer services. Let us now look at an illustration of customer profitability analysis. Consider the information presented in Example 5.2. Note that the cost driver rate referred to in Example 5.2 represents the costing rates that have been computed by the company for the different activities. An explanation of how these rates are derived will be provided in Chapter 8. The profitability analysis in respect of the four customers is as follows:

	A	B	Y	Z
Customer attributable costs:				
Sales order processing	60 000	30 000	15 000	9 000
Sales visits	4 000	2 000	1 000	1 000
Normal deliveries	30 000	10 000	2 500	1 250
Special (urgent) deliveries	10 000	2 500	0	0
Credit collection[a]	24 658	8 220	1 370	5 480
	128 658	52 720	19 870	16 730
Operating profit contribution	90 000	120 000	70 000	200 000
Contribution to higher level sustaining expenses	(38 658)	67 280	50 130	183 270

Note
[a](Annual sales revenue × 10%) × (Average collection period/365)

You can see from the above analysis that A and B are high cost to serve whereas Y and Z are low cost to serve customers. Customer A provides a positive operating profit contribution but is unprofitable when customer attributable costs are taken into account. This is because customer A requires more sales orders, sales visits, and normal and urgent deliveries than the other customers. In addition, the customer is slow to pay and has higher delivery costs than the other customers. Customer profitability analysis identifies the characteristics of high cost and low cost to serve customers and shows how customer profitability can be increased. The information should be used to persuade high cost to serve customers to modify their buying behaviour away from placing numerous small orders and/or purchasing non-standard items that are costly to make. For example, customer A can be made profitable if action is taken to persuade the customer to place a smaller number of larger quantity orders, avoid special deliveries and reduce the credit period. If unprofitable customers cannot be persuaded to change their buying behaviour selling prices should be increased (or discounts on list prices reduced) to cover the extra resources consumed.

Customer profitability analysis can also be used to rank customers by order of profitability using **Pareto analysis**. This type of analysis is based on observations by Pareto that a very small proportion of items usually account for the majority of the value. For example, the Darwin Company might find that 20 per cent of customers account for 80 per cent of profits. Special attention can then be given to enhancing the relationships with the most profitable customers to ensure that they do not migrate to other competitors. In addition greater emphasis can be given to attracting new customers that have the same attributes as the most profitable customers.

EXAMPLE 5.2

The Darwin Company has recently adopted customer profitability analysis. It has undertaken a customer profitability review for the past 12 months. Details of the activities and the cost driver rates relating to those expenses that can be attributed to customers are as follows:

Activity	Cost driver rate
Sales order processing	£300 per sales order
Sales visits	£200 per sales visit
Normal delivery costs	£1 per delivery kilometre travelled
Special (urgent) deliveries	£500 per special delivery
Credit collection costs	10% per annum on average payment time

Details relating to four of the firm's customers are as follows:

Customer	A	B	Y	Z
Number of sales orders	200	100	50	30
Number of sales visits	20	10	5	5
Kilometres per delivery	300	200	100	50
Number of deliveries	100	50	25	25
Total delivery kilometres	30 000	10 000	2 500	1 250
Special (urgent deliveries)	20	5	0	0
Average collection period (days)	90	30	10	10
Annual sales	£1 million	£1 million	£0.5 million	£2 million
Annual operating profit contribution[a]	£90 000	£120 000	£70 000	£200 000

Note
[a] Consists of sales revenues less variable cost of sales.

Organizations, such as banks, often with a large customer base in excess of one million customers cannot apply customer profitability analysis at the individual customer level. Instead, they concentrate on customer segment profitability analysis by combining groups of customers into meaningful segments. This enables profitable segments to be highlighted where customer retention is particularly important and provides an input for determining the appropriate marketing strategies for attracting the new customers that have the most profit potential. Segment groupings that are used by banks include income classes, age bands, socio-economic categories and family units.

SUMMARY

The following items relate to the learning objectives listed at the beginning of the chapter.

- **Explain the relevant cost information that should be presented in price-setting firms for both short-term and long-term decisions**. For short-term decisions the incremental costs of accepting an order should be presented. Bids should then be made at prices that exceed incremental costs. For short-term decisions many costs are likely to be fixed and irrelevant. Short-term pricing decisions should meet the following conditions: (a) spare capacity should be available for all of the resources that are required to fulfil an order; (b) the bid price should represent a one-off price that will not be repeated for future orders; and (c) the order will utilize unused capacity for only a short period and capacity will be released for use on more profitable opportunities. For long-term decisions a firm can adjust the supply of virtually all of the resources. Therefore, cost information should be presented providing details of all of the resources that are committed to a product or service. Since business facility sustaining costs should be covered in the long term by sales revenues there are strong arguments for allocating such costs for long-run pricing decisions. To determine an appropriate selling price a mark-up is added to the total cost of the resources assigned to the product/service to provide a contribution to profits. If facility sustaining costs are not allocated, the mark-up must be sufficient to provide a contribution to covering facility sustaining costs and a contribution to profit.

- **Describe product and customer profitability analysis and the information that should be included for managing the product and customer mix**. Price-taking firms have to decide which products to sell, given their market prices. A mechanism is therefore required that ascertains whether or not the sales revenues from a product/ service (or customer) exceeds the cost of resources that are committed to it. Periodic profitability analysis meets this requirement. Ideally, hierarchical profitability analysis should be used that categorizes costs according to their variability at different hierarchical levels to report different hierarchical contribution levels. The aim of the hierarchical analysis should be to directly assign all organizational expenses to the particular hierarchical or organizational level where they become avoidable, so that arbitrary apportionments are avoided. The approach is illustrated in Exhibit 5.1.

- **Describe the target costing approach to pricing**. Target costing is the reverse of cost-plus pricing. With target costing the starting point is the determination of the target selling price – the price that customers are willing to pay for the product (or service). Next a target profit margin is deducted to derive a target cost. The target cost represents the estimated long-run cost of the product (or service) that enables the target profit to be achieved. Predicted actual costs are compared with the target cost and, where the predicted actual cost exceeds the target cost, intensive efforts are made through value engineering methods to achieve the target cost. If the target cost is not achieved the product/service is unlikely to be launched.

● **Describe the different cost-plus pricing methods for deriving selling prices.** Different cost bases can be used for cost-plus pricing. Bases include direct variable costs, total direct costs and total cost based on an assignment of a share of all organizational costs to the product or service. Different percentage profit margins are added depending on the cost base that is used. If direct variable cost is used as the cost base, a high percentage margin will be added to provide a contribution to cover a share of all of those costs that are not included in the cost base plus profits. Alternatively if total cost is used as the cost base a lower percentage margin will be added to provide only a contribution to profits.

● **Explain the limitations of cost-plus pricing.** Cost-plus pricing has three major limitations. First, demand is ignored. Secondly, the approach requires that some assumption be made about future volume prior to ascertaining the cost and calculating the cost-plus selling prices. This can lead to an increase in the derived cost-plus selling price when demand is falling and vice-versa. Thirdly, there is no guarantee that total sales revenue will be in excess of total costs even when each product is priced above 'cost'.

● **Justify why cost-plus pricing is widely used.** There are several reasons why cost-plus pricing is widely used. First, it offers a means by which prices can be determined with ease and speed in organizations that produce hundreds of products. Cost-plus pricing is likely to be particularly applicable to those products that generate relatively minor revenues that are not critical to an organization's success. A second justification is that cost-based pricing methods may encourage price stability by enabling firms to predict the prices of their competitors. Also, target mark-ups can be adjusted upwards or downwards according to expected demand, thus ensuring that demand is indirectly taken into account.

● **Identify and describe the different pricing policies.** Cost information is only one of the many variables that must be considered in the pricing decision. The final price that is selected will depend upon the pricing policy of a company. A price-skimming policy or a penetration pricing policy might be selected. A price-skimming policy attempts to charge high initial prices to exploit those sections of the market where demand is initially insensitive to pricing changes. In contrast, a penetration pricing policy is based on the concept of charging low prices, initially with the intention of gaining rapid acceptance of the product (or service).

KEY TERMS AND CONCEPTS

absorption costing (p. 108)
cost-plus pricing (p. 103)
customer profitability analysis (p. 114)
direct costing (p. 108)
full cost (p. 103)
long-run cost (p. 103)
Pareto analysis (p. 115)

penetration pricing policy (p. 113)
price setters (p. 100)
price-skimming policy (p. 113)
price takers (p. 100)
product life cycle (p. 113)
target costing (p. 106)

ASSESSMENT MATERIAL

The review questions are short questions that enable you to assess your understanding of the main topics included in the chapter. The page numbers in parentheses provide you with the page numbers to refer to if you cannot answer a specific question.

The review problems are more complex and require you to relate and apply the content to various business problems. Solutions to review problems are provided in a separate section at the end of the book. Additional review problems can be accessed by lecturers and students on the website (www.drury-online.com). Solutions to these problems are provided for lecturers in the *Instructors' Manual*. This is available on the lecturers' password-protected section of the website.

The website also includes over 30 case study problems. A list of these cases is provided on pages 389–392. Several cases are relevant to the content of this chapter. Examples include Lynch Printers and Reichard Maschinen.

REVIEW QUESTIONS

5.1 Distinguish between a price taker and a price setter. *(p. 100)*

5.2 What costs are likely to be relevant for (a) a short-run pricing decision, and (b) a long-run pricing decision? *(pp. 102–104)*

5.3 What is meant by the term 'full cost'? *(p. 103)*

5.4 What is meant by cost-plus pricing? *(pp. 103–104, pp. 111–113)*

5.5 Distinguish between cost-plus pricing and target costing. *(pp. 106–117)*

5.6 Describe the four stages involved with target costing. *(p. 106)*

5.7 What role does cost information play in price-taking firms? *(p. 107)*

5.8 Describe the alternative cost bases that can be used with cost-plus pricing. *(p. 103)*

5.9 What are the limitations of cost-plus pricing? *(p. 111)*

5.10 Why is cost-plus pricing frequently used in practice? *(pp. 111–113)*

5.11 Describe the different kinds of pricing policies that an organization can apply. *(pp. 113–114)*

5.12 Why is customer profitability analysis important? *(pp. 114–116)*

REVIEW PROBLEMS

5.13 ABC plc is about to launch a new product. Facilities will allow the company to produce up to 20 units per week. The marketing department has estimated that at a price of £8000 no units will be sold, but for each £150 reduction in price one additional unit per week will be sold.

Fixed costs associated with manufacture are expected to be £12 000 per week.

Variable costs are expected to be £4000 per unit for each of the first 10 units; thereafter each unit will cost £400 more than the preceding one.

The most profitable level of output per week for the new product is

A   10 units
B   11 units
C   13 units
D   14 units
E   20 units

(3 marks)

5.14 Calculation of different cost-plus prices

Albany has recently spent some time on researching and developing a new product for which they are trying to establish a suitable price. Previously they have used cost plus 20 per cent to set the selling price.

The standard cost per unit has been estimated as follows:

	£	
Direct materials		
Material 1	10	(4 kg at £2.50/kg)
Material 2	7	(1 kg at £7/kg)
Direct labour	13	(2 hours at £6.50/hour)
Fixed overheads	7	(2 hours at £3.50/hour)
	37	

Required:

(a)   Using the standard costs calculate two different cost-plus prices using two different bases and explain an advantage and disadvantage of each method.

(6 marks)

(b)   Give two other possible pricing strategies that could be adopted and describe the impact of each one on the price of the product.

(4 marks)
(Total 10 marks)

5.15 Calculation of cost-plus selling price and an evaluation of pricing decisions

Note: This question requires knowledge of some of the material covered in chapter 7.

A firm manufactures two products EXE and WYE in departments dedicated exclusively to them. There are also three service departments – stores, maintenance and administration. No stocks are held as the products deteriorate rapidly.

Direct costs of the products, which are variable in the context of the whole business, are identified to each department. The step-wise apportionment of service department costs to the manufacturing departments is based on estimates of the usage of the service provided. These are expressed as percentages and assumed to be reliable over the current capacity range. The general factory overheads of £3.6 million, which are fixed, are apportioned based on floor space occupied. The company establishes product costs based on budgeted volume and marks up these costs by 25 per cent in order to set target selling prices.

Extracts from the budgets for the forthcoming year are provided below:

	Annual volume (units)	
	EXE	WYE
Max capacity	200 000	100 000
Budget	150 000	70 000

	EXE	WYE	Stores	Maintenance	Admin
Costs (£m)					
Material	1.8	0.7	0.1	0.1	
Other variable	0.8	0.5	0.1	0.2	0.2
Departmental usage (%)					
Maintenance	50	25	25		
Administration	40	30	20	10	
Stores	60	40			
Floor space (sq m)	640	480	240	80	160

Required:

Workings may be £000 with unit prices to the nearest penny.

(a) Calculate the budgeted selling price of one unit of EXE and WYE based on the usual mark-up.

(5 marks)

(b) Discuss how the company may respond to each of the following independent events, which represent additional business opportunities:

(i) An enquiry from an overseas customer for 3000 units only of WYE where a price of £35 per unit is offered.

(ii) An enquiry for 50 000 units of WYE to be supplied in full at regular intervals during the forthcoming year at a price that is equivalent to full cost plus 10 per cent.

In both cases support your discussion with calculations and comment on any assumptions or matters on which you would seek clarification.

(11 marks)
(Total 16 marks)

5.16 Preparation of full cost and variable cost information

A small company is engaged in the production of plastic tools for the garden.

Sub-totals on the spreadsheet of budgeted overheads for a year reveal:

	Moulding department	Finishing department	General factory overhead
Variable overhead (£000)	1600	500	1050
Fixed overhead (£000)	2500	850	1750
Budgeted activity			
Machine hours (000)	800	600	
Practical capacity			
Machine hours (000)	1200	800	

For the purposes of reallocation of general factory overhead it is agreed that the variable overheads accrue in line with the machine hours worked in each department. General factory fixed overhead is to be reallocated on the basis of the practical machine hour capacity of the two departments.

It has been a longstanding company practice to establish selling prices by applying a mark-up on full manufacturing cost of between 25 per cent and 35 per cent.

A possible price is sought for one new product that is in a final development stage. The total market for this product is estimated at 200 000 units per annum. Market research indicates that the company could expect to obtain and hold about 10 per cent of the market. It is hoped the product will offer some improvement over competitors' products, which are currently marketed at between £90 and £100 each.

The product development department have determined that the direct material content is £9 per unit. Each unit of the product will take one labour hour (four machine hours) in the moulding department and two labour hours (three machine hours) in finishing. Hourly labour rates are £10 and £8.25 respectively.

Management estimate that the annual fixed costs that would be specifically incurred in relation to the product are: supervision £20 000, depreciation of a recently acquired machine £120 000 and advertising £27 000. It may be assumed that these costs are included in the budget given above. Given the state of development of this new product, management do not consider it necessary to make revisions to the budgeted activity levels given above, for any possible extra machine hours involved in its manufacture.

Required:

(a) Briefly explain the role of costs in pricing.

(6 marks)

(b) Prepare full cost and variable cost information that may help with the pricing decision.
(9 marks)

(c) Comment on the cost information and suggest a price range that should be considered.

(5 marks)
(Total 20 marks)

CHAPTER 6
CAPITAL INVESTMENT DECISIONS: APPRAISAL METHODS

LEARNING OBJECTIVES

After studying this chapter you should be able to:

- **explain the opportunity cost of an investment;**
- **distinguish between compounding and discounting;**
- **explain the concepts of net present value (NPV), internal rate of return (IRR), payback method and accounting rate of return (ARR);**
- **calculate NPV, IRR, the payback period and ARR;**
- **justify the superiority of NPV over the IRR;**
- **explain the limitations of payback and ARR;**
- **justify why the payback and ARR methods are widely used in practice;**
- **describe the effect of performance measurement on capital investment decisions.**

Capital investment decisions are those decisions that involve current outlays in return for a stream of benefits in future years. It is true to say that all of a firm's expenditures are made in expectation of realizing future benefits. The distinguishing feature between short-term decisions and capital investment (long-term) decisions is time. Generally, we can classify short-term decisions as those that involve a relatively short time horizon, say one year, from the commitment of funds to the receipt of the benefits. On the other hand, capital investment decisions are those decisions where a significant period of time elapses between the outlay and the recoupment of the investment. We shall see that this commitment of funds for a significant period of time involves an interest cost, which must be brought into the analysis. With short-term decisions, funds are committed only for short periods of time, and the interest cost is normally so small that it can be ignored.

Capital investment decisions normally represent the most important decisions that an organization makes, since they commit a substantial proportion of a firm's resources to actions that are likely to be irreversible. Such decisions are applicable to all sectors of society. Business firms' investment decisions include investments in plant and machinery, research and development, advertising and warehouse facilities. Investment decisions in the public sector include new roads, schools and airports. Individuals' investment decisions include house-buying and the purchase of consumer durables. In this chapter we shall examine the economic evaluation of the desirability of investment proposals. We shall concentrate on the investment decisions of business firms, but the same principles, with modifications, apply to individuals, and the public sector.

For most of this chapter we shall assume that the investments appraised are in firms that are all equity financed. In other words, projects are financed by the issue of new ordinary shares or from retained earnings. Later in the chapter we shall relax this assumption and assume that projects are financed by a combination of debt (i.e. borrowed funds) and equity capital. You will find throughout the chapter that mathematical formulae and simple arithmetic are used to compute the values that are used to evaluate investments. You can use either approach. If you have an aversion to mathematical formulae you should ignore the formulae calculations. All of the calculations are repeated using non-formulae approaches.

THE OPPORTUNITY COST OF AN INVESTMENT

Investors can invest in securities traded in financial markets. If you prefer to avoid risk, you can invest in government securities, which will yield a *fixed* return. On the other hand, you may prefer to invest in *risky* securities such as the ordinary shares of companies quoted on the stock exchange. If you invest in the ordinary shares of a company, you will find that the return will vary from year to year, depending on the performance of the company and its future expectations. Investors normally prefer to avoid risk if possible, and will generally invest in risky securities only if they believe that they will obtain a greater return for the increased risk. Suppose that **risk-free gilt-edged securities** issued by the government yield a return of 10 per cent. Currently government securities yield a return that is significantly less than 10 per cent but we shall use 10 per cent in order to simplify the calculations. With a return available of 10 per cent on government securities you should only be prepared to invest in ordinary shares if you expect a return in excess of 10 per cent; let us assume that you require an *expected* return of 15 per cent to induce you to invest in ordinary shares in preference to a risk-free security. Note that expected return means the estimated average future return. You would expect to earn, on average, 15 per cent, but in some years you might earn more and in others considerably less.

Suppose you invest in company X ordinary shares. Would you want company X to invest your money in a capital project that gives less than 15 per cent? Surely not,

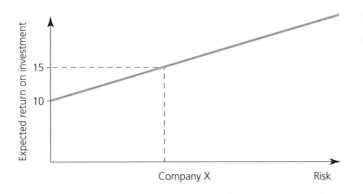

FIGURE 6.1
Risk–return trade-off

assuming the project has the same risk as the alternative investments in shares of other companies that are yielding a return of 15 per cent. You would prefer company X to invest in other companies' ordinary shares at 15 per cent or, alternatively, to repay your investment so that you could invest yourself at 15 per cent.

The rates of return that are available from investments in securities in financial markets such as ordinary shares and government gilt-edged securities represent the **opportunity cost of an investment** in capital projects; that is, if cash is invested in the capital project, it cannot be invested elsewhere to earn a return. A firm should therefore invest in capital projects only if they yield a return in excess of the opportunity cost of the investment. The opportunity cost of the investment is also known as the **minimum required rate of return**, **cost of capital**, **discount rate** or **interest rate**.

The return on securities traded in financial markets provides us with the opportunity costs, that is the required rates of return available on securities. The expected returns that investors require from the ordinary shares of different companies vary because some companies' shares are more risky than others. The greater the risk, the greater the expected returns. Consider Figure 6.1. You can see that as the risk of a security increases the return that investors require to compensate for the extra risk increases. Consequently, investors will expect to receive a return in excess of 15 per cent if they invest in securities that have a higher risk than company X ordinary shares. If this return was not forthcoming, investors would not purchase high-risk securities. It is therefore important that companies investing in high-risk capital projects earn higher returns to compensate investors for this risk. You can also see that a risk-free security such as a gilt-edged government security yields the lowest return, i.e. 10 per cent. Consequently, if a firm invests in a project with zero risk, it should earn a return in excess of 10 per cent. If the project does not yield this return and no other projects are available then the funds earmarked for the project should be repaid to shareholders as dividends. The shareholders could then invest the funds themselves at 10 per cent.

COMPOUNDING AND DISCOUNTING

Our objective is to calculate and compare returns on an investment in a capital project with an alternative equal risk investment in securities traded in the financial markets. This comparison is made using a technique called **discounted cash flow (DCF)** analysis. Because a DCF analysis is the opposite of the concept of **compounding interest**, we shall initially focus on compound interest calculations.

Suppose you are investing £100 000 in a risk-free security yielding a return of 10 per cent payable at the end of each year. Exhibit 6.1 shows that if the interest is reinvested, your investment will accumulate to £146 410 by the end of year 4. Period 0 in the first column of Exhibit 6.1 means that no time has elapsed or the time is *now*, period 1 means one year later, and so on. The values in Exhibit 6.1 can also be obtained by using the formula:

$$FV_n = V_0 (1 + K)^n \qquad (6.1)$$

where FV_n denotes the future value of an investment in n years, V_0 denotes the amount invested at the beginning of the period (year 0), K denotes the rate of return on the investment and n denotes the number of years for which the money is invested. The calculation for £100 000 invested at 10 per cent for two years is

$$FV_2 = £100\,000\,(1 + 0.10)^2 = £121\,000$$

In Exhibit 6.1 all of the year-end values are equal as far as the time value of money is concerned. For example, £121 000 received at the end of year 2 is equivalent to £100 000 received today and invested at 10 per cent. Similarly, £133 100 received at the end of year 3 is equivalent to £121 000 received at the end of year 2, because £121 000 can be invested at the end of year 2 to accumulate to £133 100. Unfortunately, none of the amounts are directly comparable at any single moment in time, because each amount is expressed at a different point in time.

When making capital investment decisions, we must convert cash inflows and outflows for different years into a common value. This is achieved by converting the cash flows into their respective values at the same point in time. Mathematically, any point in time can be chosen, since all four figures in Exhibit 6.1 are equal to £100 000 at year 0, £110 000 at year 1, £121 000 at year 2, and so on. However, it is preferable to choose the point in time at which the decision is taken, and this is the present time or year 0. All of the values in Exhibit 6.1 can therefore be expressed in values at the present time (i.e. **present value**) of £100 000.

The process of converting cash to be received in the future into a value at the present time by the use of an interest rate is termed **discounting** and the resulting present value is the **discounted present value**. Compounding is the opposite of discounting, because it is the future value of present value cash flows. Equation (6.1) for calculating future values can be rearranged to produce the present value formula:

$$V_0 \text{ (Present value)} = \frac{FV_n}{(1 + K)^n} \qquad (6.2)$$

EXHIBIT 6.1

The value of £100 000 invested at 10 per cent, compounded annually, for four years

End of year	Interest earned (£)	Total investment (£)
0		100 000
	0.10 × 100 000	10 000
1		110 000
	0.10 × 110 000	11 000
2		121 000
	0.10 × 121 000	12 100
3		133 100
	0.10 × 133 100	13 310
4		146 410

By applying this equation, the calculation for £121 000 received at the end of year 2 can be expressed as

$$\text{Present value} = \frac{\pounds121\,000}{(1 + 0.10)^2} = \pounds100\,000$$

You should now be aware that £1 received today is not equal to £1 received one year from today. No rational person will be equally satisfied with receiving £1 a year from now as opposed to receiving it today, because money received today can be used to earn interest over the ensuing year. Thus one year from now an investor can have the original £1 plus one year's interest on it. For example, if the interest rate is 10 per cent each £1 invested now will yield £1.10 one year from now. That is, £1 received today is equal to £1.10 one year from today at 10 per cent interest. Alternatively, £1 one year from today is equal to £0.9091 today, its present value because £0.9091, plus 10 per cent interest for one year amounts to £1. The concept that £1 received in the future is not equal to £1 received today is known as the **time value of money**.

We shall now consider four different methods of appraising capital investments: the net present value, internal rate of return, accounting rate of return and payback methods. We shall see that the first two methods take into account the time value of money whereas the accounting rate of return and payback methods ignore this factor.

THE CONCEPT OF NET PRESENT VALUE

By using discounted cash flow techniques and calculating present values, we can compare the return on an investment in capital projects with an alternative equal risk investment in securities traded in the financial market. Suppose a firm is considering four projects (all of which are risk-free) as shown in Exhibit 6.2. You can see that each of the projects is identical with the investment in the risk-free security shown in Exhibit 6.1 because you can cash in this investment for £110 000 in year 1, £121 000 in year 2, £133 100 in year 3 and £146 410 in year 4. In other words your potential cash receipts from the risk-free security are identical to the net cash flows for projects A, B, C and D shown in Exhibit 6.2. Consequently, the firm should be indifferent as to whether it uses the funds to invest in the projects or invests the funds in securities of identical risk traded in the financial markets.

The most straightforward way of determining whether a project yields a return in excess of the alternative equal risk investment in traded securities is to calculate the **net present value (NPV)**. This is the present value of the net cash inflows less the project's initial investment outlay. If the rate of return from the project is greater than the return from an equivalent risk investment in securities traded in the financial market, the NPV will be positive. Alternatively, if the rate of return is lower, the NPV will be negative. A positive NPV therefore indicates that an investment should be accepted, while a negative value indicates that it should be rejected. A zero NPV calculation indicates that the firm should be indifferent to whether the project is accepted or rejected.

You can see that the present value of each of the projects shown in Exhibit 6.2 is £100 000. You should now deduct the investment cost of £100 000 to calculate the project's NPV. The NPV for each project is zero. The firm should therefore be indifferent to whether it accepts any of the projects or invests the funds in an equivalent risk-free

EXHIBIT 6.2

Evaluation of four risk-free projects

	A (£)	B (£)	C (£)	D (£)
Project investment outlay	100 000	100 000	100 000	100 000
End of year cash flows:				
Year 1	110 000	0	0	0
2	0	121 000	0	0
3	0	0	133 100	0
4	0	0	0	146 410
present value =	$\dfrac{110\,000}{1.10}$	$\dfrac{121\,000}{(1.10)^2}$	$\dfrac{133\,100}{(1.10)^3}$	$\dfrac{146\,410}{(1.10)^4}$
	= 100 000	= 100 000	= 100 000	= 100 000

security. This was our conclusion when we compared the cash flows of the projects with the investment in a risk-free security shown in Exhibit 6.1.

You can see that it is better for the firm to invest in any of the projects shown in Exhibit 6.2 if their initial investment outlays are less than £100 000. This is because we have to pay £100 000 to obtain an equivalent stream of cash flows from a security traded in the financial markets. Conversely, we should reject the investment in the projects if their initial investment outlays are greater than £100 000. You should now see that the NPV rule leads to a direct comparison of a project with an equivalent risk security traded in the financial market. Given that the present value of the net cash inflows for each project is £100 000, their NPVs will be positive (thus signifying acceptance) if the initial investment outlay is less than £100 000 and negative (thus signifying rejection) if the initial outlay is greater than £100 000.

CALCULATING NET PRESENT VALUES

You should now have an intuitive understanding of the NPV rule. We shall now learn how to calculate NPVs. The NPV can be expressed as:

$$NPV = \frac{FV_1}{1 + K} + \frac{FV_2}{(1 + K)^2} + \frac{FV_3}{(1 + K)^3} + \ldots + \frac{FV_n}{(1 + K)^n} - I_0 \tag{6.3}$$

where I_0 represents the investment outlay and FV represents the future values received in years 1 to n. The rate of return K used is the return available on an equivalent risk security in the financial market. Consider the situation in Example 6.1.

The net present value calculation for Project A is:

$$NPV = \frac{£300\,000}{(1.10)} + \frac{£1\,000\,000}{(1.10)^2} + \frac{£400\,000}{(1.10)^3} - £1\,000\,000 = +£399\,700$$

Alternatively, the net present value can be calculated by referring to a published table of present values. You will find examples of such a table if you refer to Appendix A (see pages 397–398). To use the table, simply find the discount factors by referring to each year of the cash flows and the appropriate interest rate.

For example, if you refer to year 1 in Appendix A, and the 10 per cent column, this will show a discount factor of 0.909. For years 2 and 3 the discount factors are 0.826 and

0.751. You then multiply the cash flows by the discount factors to find the present value of the cash flows. The calculation is as follows:

Year	Amount (£000)	Discount factor	Present value (£)
1	300	0.9091	272 730
2	1000	0.8264	826 400
3	400	0.7513	300 520
			1 399 650
		Less initial outlay	1 000 000
		Net present value	399 650

In order to reconcile the NPV calculations derived from formula 6.3 and the discount tables, the discount factors used in this chapter are based on four decimal places. Normally the factors given in Appendix A based on three decimal places will suffice. The difference between the two calculations shown above is due to rounding differences.

Note that the discount factors in the present value table shown in Appendix A are based on £1 received in *n* years time calculated according to the present value formula (equation 6.2). For example, £1 received in years 1, 2 and 3 when the interest rate is 10 per cent is calculated (based on four decimal places) as follows:

$$\text{Year 1} = £1/1.10 = 0.9091$$

$$\text{Year 2} = £1(1.10)^2 = 0.8264$$

$$\text{Year 3} = £1(1.10)^3 = 0.7513$$

The positive net present value represents the potential increase in present consumption that the project makes available to the ordinary shareholders, after any funds used have been repaid with interest. For example, assume that the firm finances the investment of £1 million in Example 6.1 by borrowing £1 399 700 at 10 per cent and repays the loan and interest out of the project's proceeds as they occur. You can see from the repayment schedule in Exhibit 6.3 that £399 700 received from the loan is available for current consumption, and the remaining £1 000 000 can be invested in the project. The cash flows from the project are just sufficient to repay the loan. Therefore acceptance of the project enables the ordinary shareholders' present consumption to be increased by the net present value of £399 700. Hence

EXAMPLE 6.1

The Bothnia Company is evaluating two projects with an expected life of three years and an investment outlay of £1 million. The estimated net cash inflows for each project are as follows:

	Project A (£)	Project B (£)
Year 1	300 000	600 000
Year 2	1 000 000	600 000
Year 3	400 000	600 000

The opportunity cost of capital for both projects is 10 per cent. You are required to calculate the net present value for each project.

EXHIBIT 6.3

The pattern of cash flows assuming that the loan is repaid out of the proceeds of the project

Year	Loan outstanding at start of year (1) (£)	Interest at 10% (2) (£)	Total amount owed before repayment (3) = (1) + (2) (£)	Proceeds from project (4) (£)	Loan outstanding at year end (5) = (3) – (4) (£)
1	1 399 700	139 970	1 539 670	300 000	1 239 670
2	1 239 670	123 967	1 363 637	1 000 000	363 637
3	363 637	36 363	400 000	400 000	0

the acceptance of all available projects with a positive net present value should lead to the maximization of shareholders' wealth.

Let us now calculate the net present value for Project B shown in Example 6.1. The cash flows for project B represent an **annuity**. An annuity is an asset that pays a fixed sum each period for a specific number of periods. You can see for project B that the cash flows are £600,000 per annum for three years. When the annual cash flows are equivalent to an annuity, the calculation of net present value is simplified. The discount factors for an annuity are set out in Appendix B (see pages 399–400). We need to find the discount factor for 10 per cent for three years. If you refer to Appendix B, you will see that it is 2.487. The NPV is calculated as follows:

Annual cash inflow	Discount factor	Present value (£)
£600 000	2.487	1 492 200
	Less investment cost	1 000 000
	Net present value	492 200

You will see that the total present value for the period is calculated by multiplying the cash inflow by the discount factor. It is important to note that the annuity tables shown in Appendix B can only be applied when the annual cash flows are the same each year. Annuities are also based on the assumption that cash flows for the first period are received at the end of the period, and not at the start of the period, and that all subsequent cash flows are received at the end of each period. Sometimes, to simplify the calculations, examination questions are set based on the assumption that constant cash flows occur into perpetuity. In this situation the present value is determined by dividing the cash flow by the discount rate. For example, the present value of a cash flow of £100 per annum into perpetuity at a discount rate of 10 per cent is £1000 (£100/0.10). Again the present value calculation is based on the assumption that the first cash flow is received one period hence.

INTERNAL RATE OF RETURN

The **internal rate of return (IRR)** is an alternative technique for use in making capital investment decisions that also takes into account the time value of money. The internal rate of return represents the true interest rate earned on an investment over the course of its economic life. This measure is sometimes referred to as the **discounted rate of return**. The internal rate of return is the interest rate K that when used to discount all cash flows resulting from an investment, will equate the present value of the cash receipts to the present value of the cash outlays. In other words, it is the discount rate that will cause the net present value of an investment to be zero. Alternatively, the internal rate of return can be described as the maximum cost of capital that can be applied to finance a project without causing harm to the shareholders. The internal rate of return is found by solving for the value of K from the following formula:

$$I_0 = \frac{FV_1}{1 + K} + \frac{FV_2}{(1 + K)^2} + \frac{FV_3}{(1 + K)^3} + ... + \frac{FV_n}{(1 + K)^n} \qquad (6.4)$$

It is easier, however, to use the discount tables. Let us now calculate the internal rate of return (using discount factors based on four decimal places) for Project A in Example 6.1.

The IRR can be found by trial and error by using a number of discount factors until the NPV equals zero. For example, if we use a 25 per cent discount factor, we get a positive NPV of £84 800. We must therefore try a higher figure. Applying 35 per cent gives a negative NPV of £66 530. We know then that the NPV will be zero somewhere between 25 per cent and 35 per cent. In fact, the IRR is between 30 per cent and 31 per cent but closest to 30 per cent, as indicated by the following calculation:

Year	Net cash flow (£)	Discount factor (30%)	Present value of cash flow (£)
1	300 000	0.7692	230 760
2	1 000 000	0.5917	591 700
3	400 000	0.4552	182 080
		Net present value	1 004 540
		Less initial outlay	1 000 000
		Net present value	4 540

The decision rule is that if the IRR is greater than the opportunity cost of capital, the investment is profitable and will yield a positive NPV. Alternatively, if the IRR is less than the cost of capital, the investment is unprofitable and will result in a negative NPV. The calculation of the IRR is illustrated in Figure 6.2.

FIGURE 6.2

Interpretation of the internal rate of return

The dots in the graph represent the NPV at different discount rates. The point where the line joining the dots cuts the horizontal axis indicates the IRR (the point at which the NPV is zero). Figure 6.2 indicates that the IRR is approximately 30 per cent, and you can see from this diagram that the interpolation method can be used to calculate the IRR without carrying out trial and error calculations. When we use interpolation, we infer the missing term (in this case the discount rate at which NPV is zero) from a known series of numbers. For example, at a discount rate of 25 per cent the NPV is +£84 800 and for a discount rate of 35 per cent the NPV is –£66 530. The total distance between these points is £151 330 (+£84 800 and –£66 530). The calculation for the approximate IRR is therefore:

$$25\% + \frac{84\,800}{151\,330} \times (35\% - 25\%) = 30.60\%$$

In other words, if you move down line A in Figure 6.2 from a discount rate of 25 per cent by £84 800, you will reach the point at which NPV is zero. The distance between the two points on line A is £151 330, and we are given the discount rates of 25 per cent and 35 per cent for these points. Therefore 84 800/151 330 represents the distance that we must move between these two points for the NPV to be zero. This distance in terms of the discount rate is 5.60 per cent [(84 800/151 330) × 10 per cent], which, when added to the starting point of 25 per cent, produces an IRR of 30.60 per cent. The formula using the interpolation method is as follows:

$$A + \frac{C}{C-D}(B-A) \qquad\qquad (6.5)$$

where A is the discount rate of the low trial, B is the discount rate of the high trial, C is the NPV of cash inflow of the low trial and D is the NPV of cash inflow of the high trial. Thus

$$25\% + \left[\frac{84\,800}{84\,800 - (-66\,530)} \times 10\%\right]$$

$$= 25\% + \left[\frac{84\,800}{151\,330} \times 10\%\right]$$

$$= 30.60\%$$

Note that the interpolation method only gives an approximation of the IRR. The greater the distance between any two points that have a positive and a negative NPV, the less accurate is the IRR calculation using interpolation. Consider line B in Figure 6.2. The point where it cuts the horizontal axis is approximately 33 per cent, whereas the actual IRR is 30.60 per cent.

The calculation of the IRR is easier when the cash flows are of a constant amount each year. Let us now calculate the internal rate of return for Project B in Example 6.1. Because the cash flows are equal each year, we can use the annuity table in Appendix B. When the cash flows are discounted at the IRR, the NPV will be zero. The IRR will therefore be at the point where

$$[\text{Annual cash flow}] \times \left[\begin{array}{c}\text{Discount factor for number of years}\\ \text{for which cash flow is received}\end{array}\right] - \left[\begin{array}{c}\text{Investment}\\ \text{cost}\end{array}\right] = 0$$

Rearranging this formula, the internal rate of return will be at the point where

$$\text{Discount factor} = \frac{\text{Investment cost}}{\text{Annual cash flow}}$$

Substituting the figures for Project B in Example 6.1,

$$\text{Discount factor} = \frac{£1\,000\,000}{£600\,000} = 1.666$$

We now examine the entries for the year 3 row in Appendix B to find the figures closest to 1.666. They are 1.673 (entered in the 36 per cent column) and 1.652 (entered in the 37 per cent column). We can therefore conclude that the IRR is between 36 per cent and 37 per cent. However, because the cost of capital is 10 per cent, an accurate calculation is unnecessary; the IRR is far in excess of the cost of capital.

The calculation of the IRR can be rather tedious (as the cited examples show), but the trial-and-error approach can be programmed for fast and accurate solution by a computer or calculator. The calculation problems are no longer a justification for preferring the NPV method of investment appraisal. Nevertheless, there are theoretical justifications, which we shall discuss later in this chapter, that support the NPV method.

RELEVANT CASH FLOWS

Investment decisions, like all other decisions, should be analysed in terms of the cash flows that can be directly attributable to them. These cash flows should include the incremental cash flows that will occur in the future following acceptance of the investment. The cash flows will include cash inflows and outflows, or the inflows may be represented by savings in cash outflows. For example, a decision to purchase new machinery may generate cash savings in the form of reduced out-of-pocket operating costs. For all practical purposes such cost savings are equivalent to cash receipts.

It is important to note that depreciation is not included in the cash flow estimates for capital investment decisions, since it is a non-cash expense. This is because the capital investment cost of the asset to be depreciated is included as a cash outflow at the start of the project, and depreciation is merely a financial accounting method for allocating past capital costs to future accounting periods. Any inclusion of depreciation will lead to double counting.

TIMING OF CASH FLOWS

To simplify the presentation our calculations have been based on the assumption that any cash flows in future years will occur in one lump sum at the year-end. Obviously, this is an unrealistic assumption, since cash flows are likely to occur at various times throughout the year, and a more realistic assumption is to assume that cash flows occur at the end of each month and use monthly discount rates. Typically, discount and interest rates are quoted as rates per annum using the term **annual percentage rate (APR)**. If you wish to use monthly discount rates it is necessary to convert annual discount rates to monthly rates. An approximation of the monthly discount rate can be obtained by dividing the annual rate by 12. However, this simplified calculation ignores the compounding effect whereby each monthly interest payment is reinvested to earn more interest each month. To convert the annual discount rate to a monthly discount rate that takes into account the compounding effect we must use the following formula:

$$\text{Monthly discount rate} = (\sqrt[12]{1 + \text{APR}}) - 1 \qquad (6.6)$$

Assume that the annual percentage discount rate is 12.68 per cent. Applying formula 6.6 gives a monthly discount rate of:

$$(\sqrt[12]{1.1268}) - 1 = 1.01 - 1 = .01 \text{ (i.e. 1 per cent per month)}.$$

Therefore the monthly cash flows would be discounted at 1 per cent. In other words, 1 per cent compounded monthly is equivalent to 12.68 per cent compounded annually. Note that the monthly discount rates can also be converted to annual percentage rates using the formula:

$$(1 + k)^{12} - 1 \text{ (where } k = \text{the monthly discount rate)} \qquad (6.7)$$

Assuming a monthly rate of 1 per cent the annual rate is $(1.01)^{12} - 1 = 0.1268$ (i.e. 12.68 per cent per annum). Instead of using formulae (6.6) and (6.7) you can divide the annual percentage rate by 12 to obtain an approximation of the monthly discount rate or multiply the monthly discount rate by 12 to approximate the annual percentage rate.

COMPARISON OF NET PRESENT VALUE AND INTERNAL RATE OF RETURN

In many situations the internal rate of return method will result in the same decision as the net present value method. In the case of conventional projects (in which an initial cash outflow is followed by a series of cash inflows) that are independent of each other (i.e. where the selection of a particular project does not preclude the choice of the other), both NPV and IRR rules will lead to the same accept/reject decisions. However, there are also situations where the IRR method may lead to different decisions being made from those that would follow the adoption of the NPV procedure.

Mutually exclusive projects

Where projects are **mutually exclusive**, it is possible for the NPV and the IRR methods to suggest different rankings as to which project should be given priority. Mutually exclusive projects exist where the acceptance of one project excludes the acceptance of another project, for example the choice of one of several possible factory locations, or the choice of one of many different possible machines. When evaluating mutually exclusive projects, the IRR method can incorrectly rank projects, because of its reinvestment assumptions, and in these circumstances it is recommended that the NPV method is used.

Percentage returns

Another problem with the IRR rule is that it expresses the result as a percentage rather than in monetary terms. Comparison of percentage returns can be misleading; for example, compare an investment of £10 000 that yields a return of 50 per cent with an investment of £100 000 that yields a return of 25 per cent. If only one of the investments can be undertaken, the first investment will yield £5000 but the second will yield £25 000. If we assume that the cost of capital is 10 per cent, and that no other suitable investments are available, any surplus funds will be invested at the cost of capital (i.e. the returns available from equal risk securities traded in financial markets). Choosing the first investment will leave a further £90 000 to be invested, but this can only be invested at 10 per cent, yielding a return of £9000. Adding this to the return of £5000 from the £10 000 investment gives a total return of £14 000. Clearly, the second investment, which yields a return of £25 000, is preferable. Thus, NPV provides the correct measure.

Reinvestment assumptions

The assumption concerning the reinvestment of interim cash flows from the acceptance of projects provides another reason for supporting the superiority of the NPV method. The implicit assumption if the NPV method is adopted is that the cash flows generated from an investment will be reinvested immediately at the cost of capital (i.e. the returns available from equal risk securities traded in financial markets). However, the IRR method makes a different implicit assumption about the reinvestment of the cash flows. It assumes that all the proceeds from a project can be reinvested immediately to earn a return equal to the IRR of the original project. This assumption is likely to be unrealistic because a firm should have accepted all projects that offer a return in excess of the cost of capital, and any other funds that become available can only be reinvested at the cost of capital. This is the assumption that is implicit in the NPV rule.

Unconventional cash flows

Where a project has unconventional cash flows, the IRR has a technical shortcoming. Most projects have conventional cash flows that consist of an initial negative cash flow followed by positive cash inflows in later years. In this situation the algebraic sign changes, being negative at the start and positive in all future periods. If the sign of the net cash flows changes in successive periods, it is possible for the calculations to produce as many internal rates of return as there are sign changes. While multiple rates of return are mathematically possible, only one rate of return is economically significant in determining whether or not the investment is profitable.

Fortunately, the majority of investment decisions consist of conventional cash flows that produce a single IRR calculation. However, the problem cannot be ignored, since unconventional cash flows are possible and, if the decision-maker is unaware of the situation, serious errors may occur at the decision-making stage.

In addition to those methods that take into account the time value of money two other methods that ignore this factor are frequently used in practice. These are the payback method and the accounting rate of return method. Methods that ignore the time value of money are theoretically weak, and they will not necessarily lead to the maximization of the net present value. Nevertheless, the fact that they are frequently used in practice means that we should be aware of these techniques and their limitations.

REAL WORLD VIEWS 6.1

Investing in technology is the norm for mobile phone operators

Consumers are always seeking the latest technology, and in the past decade mobile telecommunications services have improved vastly. Consequently, the ownership level of mobile phones is high – approximately 85 per cent in the UK.[1]

For mobile network operators like Vodafone and O2, investing in the latest technology may be a matter of survival. The most recent technology in mobile networks is commonly referred to as 3G. It enables network operators to offer users a wider range of more advanced services and greater network capacity. Thus services such as video messaging, mobile broadband and video calls are now possible.

The capital investment required in 3G is high. In a much publicized auction for 3G operating licences in 2001, the UK government raised £22 billion. Vodafone paid approximately £14 billion for its licence. By 2004, the Vodafone investment in the UK alone topped £20 billion,[2] with €150 billion invested across Europe. With such large investment a good return would be expected, but returns to date have fallen short of expectations. Initially, availability of good quality handsets resulted in low demand. Low demand and high licence costs implied poorer than expected revenues for all operators, which in turn saw share prices decline. This prompted operators to rethink their investment strategy. In 2006, for example, Vodafone put its investment in 3G in the Czech Republic on hold.[3]

As newer handsets (such as the iPhone) come to the market, the demand for 3G services has started to increase. Mobile broadband in particular is in demand. However, as investment in the 3G networks was so costly for operators, many have not provided extensive coverage. Coverage indoors and in rural areas is particularly poor. Operators now have a dilemma – demand is increasing, so do we invest or not? Smaller, less powerful base stations in smaller areas, like public spaces, offices and even homes, may improve coverage in more specific locations without a huge capital investment.[4]

OLEKSIY MAKSYMENKO/ALAMY

Discussion points

1 How might a mobile phone operator estimate the likely uptake of new services?
2 How would a 3G network operator calculate a reasonable value for the purchase of an operating licence?

References

1 *Sunday Times*, 21 May 2006 (http://technology.times-online.co.uk/tol/news/tech_and_web/article722629.ece).
2 *Sunday Times*, 7 November 2004 (http://business.timesonline.co.uk/tol/business/article503620.ece).
3 http://www.infoworld.com/article/06/07/21/HNvodafone3gczech_1.html?3G
4 http://www.networkworld.com/news/2008/050708-poor-indoor-coverage-holding-back.html

PAYBACK METHOD

The **payback method** is one of the simplest and most frequently used methods of capital investment appraisal. It is defined as the length of time that is required for a stream of cash proceeds from an investment to recover the original cash outlay required by the investment. If the stream of cash flows from the investment is constant each year, the payback period can be calculated by dividing the total initial cash outlay by the amount of the expected annual cash proceeds. Therefore if an investment requires an initial outlay of £60 000 and is expected to produce annual cash inflows of £20 000 per year for five years, the payback period will be £60 000 divided by £20 000, or three years. If the stream of expected proceeds is not constant from year to year, the payback period is determined by adding up the cash inflows expected in successive years until the total is equal to the original outlay. Example 6.2 illustrates two projects, A and B, that require the same initial outlay of £50 000 but that display different time profiles of benefits.

In Example 6.2 project A pays back its initial investment cost in three years, whereas project B pays back its initial cost in four years. Therefore project A would be ranked in preference to project B because it has the fastest payback period. However, project B has a higher NPV, and the payback method incorrectly ranks project A in preference to project B. Two obvious deficiencies are apparent from these calculations. First, the payback method does not take into account cash flows that are earned after the payback period and, secondly, it fails to take into account the differences in the timing of the proceeds which are earned before the payback period. Payback computations ignore the important fact that future cash receipts cannot be validly compared with an initial outlay until they are discounted to their present values.

Not only does the payback period incorrectly rank project A in preference to project B, but the method can also result in the acceptance of projects that have a negative NPV. Consider the cash flows for project C in Example 6.3.

EXAMPLE 6.2

The cash flows and NPV calculations for two projects are as follows:

	Project A		Project B	
	(£)	(£)	(£)	(£)
Initial cost				
Net cash inflows		50 000		50 000
Year 1	10 000		10 000	
Year 2	20 000		10 000	
Year 3	20 000		10 000	
Year 4	20 000		20 000	
Year 5	10 000		30 000	
Year 6	–		30 000	
Year 7	–	80 000	30 000	140 000
NPV at a 10% cost of capital		10 500		39 460

EXAMPLE 6.3

The cash flows and NPV calculation for project C are as follows:

	(£)	(£)
Initial cost		
Net cash inflows		50 000
Year 1	10 000	
Year 2	20 000	
Year 3	20 000	
Year 4	3 500	
Year 5	3 500	
Year 6	3 500	
Year 7	3 500	64 000
NPV (at 10% cost of capital)		(–1 036)

The payback period for project C is three years, and if this was within the time limit set by management, the project would be accepted in spite of its negative NPV. Note also that the payback method would rank project C in preference to project B in Example 6.2, despite the fact that B would yield a positive NPV.

The payback period can only be a valid indicator of the time that an investment requires to pay for itself if all cash flows are first discounted to their present values and the discounted values are then used to calculate the payback period. This adjustment gives rise to what is known as the adjusted or **discounted payback method**. Even when such an adjustment is made, the adjusted payback method cannot be a complete measure of an investment's profitability. It can estimate whether an investment is likely to be profitable, but it cannot estimate how profitable the investment will be.

Despite the theoretical limitations of the payback method it is the method most widely used in practice (see Exhibit 6.4). Why, then, is payback the most widely applied formal investment appraisal technique? It is a particularly useful approach for ranking projects where a firm faces liquidity constraints and requires a fast repayment of investments. The payback method may also be appropriate in situations where risky investments are made in uncertain markets that are subject to fast design and product changes or where future cash flows are extremely difficult to predict. The payback method assumes that risk is time-related: the longer the period, the greater the chance of failure. By concentrating on the early cash flows, payback uses data in which managers have greater confidence. Thus, the payback period can be used as a rough measure of risk, based on the assumption that the longer it takes for a project to pay for itself, the riskier it is. Managers may also choose projects with quick payback periods because of self-interest. If a manager's performance is measured using short-term criteria, such as net profits, there is a danger that he or she may choose projects with quick paybacks to show improved net profits as soon as possible. The payback method is also frequently used in conjunction with the NPV or IRR methods. It serves as a simple first-level screening device that identifies those projects that should be subject to more rigorous investigation. A further attraction of payback is that it is easily understood by all levels of management and provides an important summary measure:

EXHIBIT 6.4
Surveys of practice

Surveys conducted by Pike (1996) relating to the investment appraisal techniques used by 100 large UK companies between 1975 and 1992 provide an indication of the changing trends in practice in large UK companies. Pike's findings relating to the percentage of firms using different appraisal methods are as follows:

	1975 %	1981 %	1986 %	1992 %
Payback	73	81	92	94
Accounting rate of return	51	49	56	50
DCF methods (IRR or NPV)	58	68	84	88
Internal rate of return (IRR)	44	57	75	81
Net present value (NPV)	32	39	68	74

Source: Pike (1996).

A study of 300 UK manufacturing organizations by Drury *et al.* (1993) sought to ascertain the extent to which particular techniques were used. The figures below indicate the percentage of firms that often or always used a particular technique:

	All organizations %	Smallest organizations %	Largest organizations %
Payback (unadjusted)	63	56	55
Discounted payback	42	30	48
Accounting rate of return	41	35	53
Internal rate of return	57	30	85
Net present value	43	23	80

More recently a UK study by Arnold and Hatzopoulos (2000) reported that NPV has overtaken IRR as the most widely used method by larger firms. They reported that 97 per cent of large firms use NPV compared with 84 per cent employing IRR.

A survey by Brounen *et al.* (2004) in mainland Europe reported that the usage of the payback method was 65 per cent in the Netherlands, 50 per cent in Germany and 51 per cent in France. NPV was used by 70 per cent of German respondents compared with 56 per cent using IRR. Usage of IRR exceeded that of NPV in the Netherlands and France.

how quickly will the project recover its initial outlay? Ideally, the payback method should be used in conjunction with the NPV method, and the cash flows discounted before the payback period is calculated.

It is apparent from the surveys shown in Exhibit 6.4 that firms use a combination of appraisal methods. The studies by Pike indicate a trend in the increasing usage of discount rates. The Drury *et al.* study suggests that larger organizations use net present value and internal rate of return to a greater extent than smaller organizations. The Drury *et al.* study also asked respondents to rank the appraisal methods in order of importance for evaluating major projects. The larger organizations ranked internal rate of return first, followed by payback and net present value, whereas smaller organizations ranked payback first, internal rate of return second and intuitive management judgement third.

ACCOUNTING RATE OF RETURN

The **accounting rate of return** (also known as the **return on investment** and **return on capital employed**) is calculated by dividing the average annual profits from a project into the average investment cost. It differs from other methods in that profits rather than cash flows are used. Note that profits are not equal to cash flows because financial accounting profit measurement is based on the accruals concept. Assuming that depreciation represents the only non-cash expense, profit is equivalent to cash flows less depreciation. The use of accounting rate of return can be attributed to the wide use of the return on investment measure in financial statement analysis.

When the average annual net profits are calculated, only additional revenues and costs that follow from the investment are included in the calculation. The average annual net profit is therefore calculated by dividing the difference between incremental revenues and costs by the estimated life of the investment. The incremental costs include either the *net* investment cost or the total depreciation charges, these figures being identical. The average investment figure that is used in the calculation depends on the method employed to calculate depreciation. If straight line depreciation is used, it is presumed that investment will decline in a linear fashion as the asset ages. The average investment under this assumption is one-half of the amount of the initial investment plus one-half of the scrap value at the end of the project's life.[1]

For example, the three projects described in Examples 6.2 and 6.3 for which the payback period was computed required an initial outlay of £50 000. If we assume that the projects have no scrap values and that straight line depreciation is used, the average investment for each project will be £25 000. The calculation of the accounting rate of return for each of these projects is as follows:

$$\text{Accounting rate of return} = \frac{\text{Average annual profits}}{\text{Average investment}}$$

$$\text{project A} = \frac{6\,000}{25\,000} = 24\%$$

$$\text{project B} = \frac{12\,857}{25\,000} = 51\%$$

$$\text{project C} = \frac{2\,000}{25\,000} = 8\%$$

For project A the total profit over its five-year life is £30 000 (£80 000 – £50 000), giving an average annual profit of £6000. The average annual profits for projects B and C are calculated in a similar manner.

It follows that the accounting rate of return is superior to the payback method in one respect; that is, it allows for differences in the useful lives of the assets being compared. For example, the calculations set out above reflect the high earnings of project B over the whole life of the project, and consequently it is ranked in preference to project A. Also, projects A and C have the same payback periods, but the accounting rate of return correctly indicates that project A is preferable to project C.

However, the accounting rate of return suffers from the serious defect that it ignores the time value of money. When the method is used in relation to a project where the cash inflows

REAL WORLD VIEWS 6.2

Investment appraisal at Cyto Technologies

Cyto Technologies[1] is a rapidly growing biotechnology company in the USA that manufactures and sells hundreds of products. In the past, the project selection process at Cyto lacked a structured approach. Projects were selected with just sketchy ideas about financial numbers and rough ideas of payback periods. Increasing competition and the higher cost of capital have forced Cyto to change its approach. A project approval team was set up to provide structure for the project development and evaluation process. It consists of five constant members (the heads of manufacturing, quality assurance, finance, marketing, and research and development). The team oversees the allocation of resources to new projects in alignment with the company's objectives.

The new project development and evaluation process consists of four phases. Phase 1 consists of two stages: idea generation and investigation. In the generation stage any R&D scientist with an idea for a new product or technique is granted a small sum of money to undertake initial research. The idea is documented in an idea evaluation report and screened by marketing and R&D. If the idea appears promising, it enters the investigation stage, which results in a proposal, and the project is reviewed by members of the project approval team.

Phase 2, product design, consists of a feasibility study. The study results in a report on the final definition of the product – image, specifications, marketing potential and initial estimates of the return on investment and IRR. Once again the report is reviewed by the project appraisal team and a favourable review moves the project to the next phase.

Phase 3, product development, consists of two stages: specifications and final optimization. In the specifications stage production cost estimates are established and marketing personnel determine the final sales forecasts. Final appraisal estimates of the payback period, NPV and IRR are computed. At this point the project evaluation team once again review the project, which if approved, enters the final optimization stage. Financial performance is one of nine criteria used by the project evaluation team to evaluate projects, so a project may be approved even if it performs relatively poorly on that test. Examples of non-financial criteria include the potential for spin-off products, strategic fit within the planned and existing activities and the impact on long-term corporate positioning. During the optimization stage the first batch is made, quality assurance specifications are detailed, regulatory compliances are met, and the final design is demonstrated. The marketing personnel are involved in planning product promotion and advertising campaigns. Finally, in phase 4, the product is launched.

© ISTOCKPHOTO.COM/RICHARD MIRRO

Discussion point

Why are investment decisions not based purely on financial criteria?

Note

1 The company name has been changed at the request of management.

Source: Kalagnanam, S. and Schimdt, S.K. (1996) Analyzing capital investments in new products, *Management Accounting* (USA), January, pp. 31–36.

do not occur until near the end of its life, it will show the same accounting rate of return as it would for a project where the cash inflows occur early in its life, providing that the average cash inflows are the same. For this reason the accounting rate of return cannot be recommended. Nevertheless, the accounting rate of return is widely employed in practice (see Exhibit 6.4). This is probably due to the fact that the annual accounting rate of return is frequently used to measure the managerial performance of different business units within a company. Therefore, managers are likely to be interested in how any new investment contributes to the business unit's overall accounting rate of return.

THE EFFECT OF PERFORMANCE MEASUREMENT ON CAPITAL INVESTMENT DECISIONS

The way that the performance of a manager is measured is likely to have a profound effect on the decisions he or she will make. There is a danger that, because of the way performance is measured, a manager may be motivated to take the wrong decision and not follow the NPV rule. Consider the information presented in Exhibit 6.5 in respect of the net cash inflows and the annual reported profits or losses for projects J and K. The figures without the parentheses refer to the cash inflows whereas the figures within parentheses refer to annual reported profit. You will see that the total cash inflows over the five-year lives for projects J and K are £11 million and £5 million respectively. Both projects require an initial outlay of £5 million. Assuming a cost of capital of 10 per cent, without undertaking any calculations it is clear that project J will have a positive NPV and project K will have a negative NPV.

If the straight line method of depreciation is used the annual depreciation for both projects will be £1 million (£5 million investment cost/5 years). Therefore the reported profits (shown in parentheses) are derived from deducting the annual depreciation charge from the annual net cash inflows. For decision-making the focus is on the entire life of the projects. Our objective is to ascertain whether the present value of the cash inflows exceeds the present value of the cash outflows over the entire life of a project, and not allocate the NPV to different accounting periods as indicated by the dashed vertical lines

EXHIBIT 6.5

Annual net cash inflows (profits/ losses) for two projects, each with an initial outlay of £5 million

+£0.5m (−£0.5m)	+£0.5m (−£0.5m)	+£2m (+£1m)	+£3m (+£2m)	Project J (+NPV) +£5m (+£4m)
+£2m (+£1m)	+£1.5m (+£0.5m)	+£0.5m (−£0.5m)	+£0.5m (−£0.5m)	Project K (−NPV) +£0.5m (−£0.5m)
Year 1	Year 2	Year 3	Year 4	Year 5

in Exhibit 6.5. In other words we require an answer to the question will the project add value?

In contrast, a company is required to report on its performance externally at annual intervals and managerial performance is also often evaluated on an annual or more frequent basis. Evaluating managerial performance at the end of the five-year project lives is clearly too long a timescale because managers are unlikely to remain in the same job for such lengthy periods. Therefore, if a manager's performance is measured using short-term criteria, such as annual profits, he or she may choose projects that have a favourable impact on short-term financial performance. Because project J will have a negative impact on performance in its early years (i.e. it contributes losses) there is a danger that a manager who is anxious to improve his or her short-term performance might reject project J even though it has a positive impact on the performance measure in the long term.

The reverse may happen with project K. This has a favourable impact on the short-term profit performance measure in years one and two but a negative impact in the longer term, so the manager might accept the project to improve his or her short-term performance measure.

It is thus important to avoid an excessive focus on short-term profitability measures because this can have a negative impact on long-term profitability. Emphasis should also be given to measuring a manager's contribution to an organization's long-term objectives. These issues are discussed in Chapter 12 when we look at performance measurement in more detail. However, at this point you should note that the way in which managerial performance is measured will influence managers' decisions and may motivate them to work in their own best interests, even when this is not in the best interests of the organization.

QUALITATIVE FACTORS

Not all investment projects can be described completely in terms of monetary costs and benefits (e.g. a new cafeteria for the employees or the installation of safety equipment). Nevertheless, the procedures described in this chapter may be useful by making the value placed by management on quantitative factors explicit. For example, if the present value of the cash outlays for a project is £100 000 and the benefits from the project are difficult to quantify, management must make a value judgement as to whether or not the benefits are in excess of £100 000. In the case of capital expenditure on facilities for employees, or expenditure to avoid unpleasant environmental effects from the company's manufacturing process, one can take the view that the present value of the cash outlays represents the cost to shareholders of the pursuit of goals other than the maximization of shareholders' funds.

WEIGHTED AVERAGE COST OF CAPITAL

So far we have assumed that firms are financed only by equity finance (i.e. ordinary share capital and retained earnings). However, most companies are likely to be financed by a combination of debt (i.e. borrowed funds) and equity capital. These companies aim to maintain target proportions of debt and equity.

The cost of *new* debt (i.e borrowed funds) capital is simply the after-tax interest cost of raising new debt. Assume that the after-tax cost of new debt capital is 6 per cent and the required rate of return on equity capital is 14 per cent and that the company intends to maintain a capital structure of 50 per cent debt and 50 per cent equity. The overall cost of capital for the company is calculated as follows:

$$= \begin{pmatrix} \text{proportion of debt capital} \\ \times \text{ cost of debt capital} \\ (0.5 \times 6\%) \end{pmatrix} + \begin{pmatrix} \text{proportion of equity capital} \\ \times \text{ cost of equity capital} \\ (0. \times 14\%) \end{pmatrix} = 10\%$$

The overall cost of capital is also called the **weighted average cost of capital**. Can we use the weighted average cost of capital as the discount rate to calculate a project's NPV? The answer is yes, provided that the project is of equivalent risk to the firm's existing assets and the firm intends to maintain its target capital structure of 50 per cent debt and 50 per cent equity.

We have now established how to calculate the discount rate for projects that are of similar risk to the firm's existing assets and to incorporate the financing aspects. It is the weighted average cost of equity and debt capital.

TAXATION AND INVESTMENT DECISIONS

In our discussion so far we have ignored the impact of taxation. Generally, in most countries net cash inflows are subject to taxation but taxation allowances that enable the amount of taxation payable to be reduced are available on investment outlays. A knowledge of the impact of taxation on capital investment appraisal is unlikely to be a requirement of non-specialist management accounting courses. You can, however, refer to Learning note 6.1 on the open access website (see Preface for details) for an explanation of the impact of taxation on investment appraisal.

SUMMARY

The following items relate to the learning objectives listed at the beginning of the chapter.

● **Explain the opportunity cost of an investment**. The rates of return that are available from investments in financial markets in securities with different levels of risk (e.g. company shares, company and government bonds) represent the opportunity cost of an investment. In other words, if cash is invested in a capital project it cannot be invested elsewhere to earn a return. A firm should therefore only invest in projects that yield a return in excess of the opportunity cost of investment.

● **Distinguish between compounding and discounting**. The process of converting cash invested today at a specific interest rate into a future value is known as compounding. Discounting is the opposite of compounding and refers to the process of converting cash to be received in the future into the value at the present time. The resulting present value is called the discounted present value.

● **Explain the concepts of net present value (NPV), internal rate of return (IRR), payback method and accounting rate of return (ARR)**. Both NPV and IRR are methods of determining whether a project yields a return in excess of an equal risk investment in traded financial securities. A positive NPV provides an absolute value of the amount by which an investment exceeds the return available from an alternative investment in financial securities of equal risk. Conversely, a negative value indicates the amount by which an investment fails to match an equal risk investment in financial securities. In contrast, the IRR indicates the true percentage return from an investment after taking into account the time value of money. To ascertain whether an investment should be undertaken, the percentage internal rate of return on investment should be compared with the returns available from investing in equal risk in financial securities. Investing in all projects that have positive NPVs or IRRs in excess of the opportunity cost of capital should maximize net cash flow. The payback method is the length of time that is required for a stream of cash proceeds from an investment to recover the original cash outflow required by the investment. The ARR expresses the annual average profits arising from a project as a percentage return on the average investment required for the project.

● **Calculate NPV, IRR, the payback period and ARR.** The NPV is calculated by discounting the net cash inflows from a project and deducting the investment outlay. The IRR is calculated by ascertaining the discount rate that will cause the NPV of a project to be zero. The payback period is calculated by adding up the cash flows expected in successive years until the total is equal to the original outlay. The ARR is calculated by dividing the average annual profits estimated from a project by the average investment cost. The calculation of NPV and IRR was illustrated using Example 6.1, while Examples 6.2 and 6.3 were used to illustrate the calculations of the payback period and the ARR.

● **Justify the superiority of NPV over the IRR.** NPV is considered to be theoretically superior to IRR because: (a) unlike the NPV method the IRR method cannot be guaranteed to rank mutually exclusive projects correctly; (b) the percentage returns generated by the IRR method can be misleading when choosing between alternatives; (c) the IRR method makes incorrect reinvestment assumptions by assuming that the interim cash flows can be reinvested at the IRR rather than the cost of capital; and (d) where unconventional cash flows occur multiple IRRs are possible.

● **Explain the limitations of payback and ARR.** The major limitations of the payback method are that it ignores the time value of money and it does not take into account the cash flows that are earned after the payback period. The ARR also fails to take into account the time value of money and relies on a percentage return rather than an absolute value.

● **Justify why the payback and ARR methods are widely used in practice.** The payback method is frequently used in practice because (a) it is considered useful when firms face liquidity constraints and require a fast repayment of their investments; (b) it serves as a simple first-level screening device that identifies those projects that should be subject to more rigorous investigations; and (c) it provides a rough measure of risk, based on the assumption that the longer it takes for a project to pay for itself, the riskier it is. The ARR is a widely used financial accounting measure of managerial and company performance. Therefore, managers are likely to be interested in how any new investment contributes to the business unit's overall accounting rate of return.

● **Describe the effect of performance measurement on capital investment decisions.** Managerial and company performance is normally evaluated using short-term financial criteria whereas investment appraisal decisions should be based on the cash flows over the whole life of the projects. Thus, the way that performance is evaluated can have a profound influence on investment decisions and there is a danger that managers will make decisions on the basis of an investment's impact on the short-term financial performance evaluation criteria rather than using the NPV decision rule.

KEY TERMS AND CONCEPTS

accounting rate of return (p. 140)
annual percentage rate (APR) (p. 133)
annuity (p. 130)
compounding interest (p. 125)
cost of capital (p. 125)
discounted cash flow (DCF) (p. 125)
discounted payback method (p. 138)
discounted present value (p. 126)
discounted rate of return (p. 130)
discounting (p. 126)
discount rate (p. 125)
interest rate (p. 125)

internal rate of return (p. 130)
minimum required rate of return (p. 125)
mutually exclusive projects (p. 134)
net present value (NPV) (p. 127)
opportunity cost of an investment (p. 125)
payback method (p. 137)
present value (p. 126)
return on capital employed (p. 140)
return on investment (p. 140)
risk-free gilt-edged securities (p. 124)
time value of money (p. 127)
weighted average cost of capital (p. 144)

Note

1 Consider a project that costs £10 000 and has a life of four years and an estimated scrap value of £2000. The following diagram (using straight line depreciation to calculate the written down values) illustrates why the project's scrap value is added to the initial outlay to calculate the average capital employed. You can see that at the mid-point of the project's life the capital employed is equal to £6000 (i.e. ½ (10 000 + £2000)).

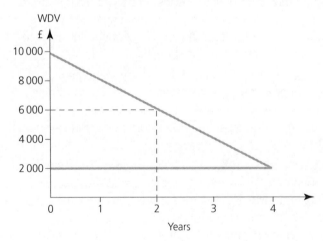

ASSESSMENT MATERIAL

The review questions are short questions that enable you to assess your understanding of the main topics included in the chapter. The page numbers in parentheses provide you with the page numbers to refer to if you cannot answer a specific question.

The review problems are more complex and require you to relate and apply the content to various business problems. Solutions to review problems are provided in a separate section at the end of the book. Additional review problems can be accessed by lecturers and students on the website www.drury-online.com. Solutions to these problems are provided for lecturers in the *Instructors' Manual*. This is available on the lecturers' password-protected section of the website.

The website also includes over 30 case study problems. A list of these cases is provided on pages 389–392. Several cases are relevant to the content of this chapter, including Rawhide Development Company.

REVIEW QUESTIONS

6.1 What is meant by the opportunity cost of an investment? What role does it play in capital investment decisions? *(p. 124)*

6.2 Distinguish between compounding and discounting. *(pp. 125–127)*

6.3 Explain what is meant by the term 'time value of money'. *(p. 127)*

6.4 Describe the concept of net present value (NPV). *(pp. 127–28)*

6.5 Explain what is meant by the internal rate of return (IRR). *(pp. 130–31)*

6.6 Distinguish between independent and mutually exclusive projects. *(p. 134)*

6.7 Explain the theoretical arguments for preferring NPV to IRR when choosing among mutually exclusive projects. *(pp. 134–35)*

6.8 Why might managers choose to use IRR in preference to NPV? *(pp. 131–132)*

6.9 Describe the payback method. What are its main strengths and weaknesses? *(pp. 137–39)*

6.10 Describe the accounting rate of return. What are its main strengths and weaknesses? *(pp. 140–42)*

6.11 Distinguish between the payback method and discounted payback method. *(pp. 138)*

6.12 What impact can the way in which a manager's performance is measured have on capital investment decisions? *(pp. 142–43)*

REVIEW PROBLEMS

6.13 Dalby is currently considering an investment that gives a positive net present value of £3664 at 15 per cent. At a discount rate of 20 per cent it has a negative net present value of £21 451.

What is the internal rate of return of this investment?

A   15.7%
B   16.0%
C   19.3%
D   19.9%.

6.14 Ayr is planning on paying £300 into a fund on a monthly basis, starting 3 months from now, for 12 months. The interest earned will be at a rate of 3 per cent per month.

Note that the annuity factor for 12 periods at 3 per cent is 9.954 and the discount factors for periods 1, 2 and 3 are respectively 0.9709, 0.9426 and 0.9151.

What is the present value of these payments?

A   £2816
B   £2733
C   £2541
D   £2986.

6.15 An investment has the following cash inflows and cash outflows:

	Cash flow per annum
Time	£000
0	(20 000)
1–4	3 000
5–8	7 000
10	(10 000)

What is the net present value of the investment at a discount rate of 8 per cent?

A   (£2416)
B   (£7046)
C   £6981
D   £2351

6.16 Sydney is considering making a monthly investment for her son who will be five years old on his next birthday. She wishes to make payments until his 18th birthday and intends to pay £50 per month into an account yielding an APR of 12.68 per cent. She plans to start making payments into the account the month after her son's fifth birthday.

How much will be in the account immediately after the final payment has been made?

A   £18 847
B   £18 377
C   £17 606
D   £18 610.

6.17 Sydney wishes to make an investment on a monthly basis starting next month for five years. The payments into the fund would be made on the first day of each month.

The interest rate will be 0.5 per cent per month. Sydney needs a terminal value of £7000.

What should be the monthly payments into the fund to the nearest £?

A £75
B £86
C £100
D £117

6.18 Augustine wishes to take out a loan of £2000. The interest rate on this loan would be 10 per cent per annum and Augustine wishes to make equal monthly repayments, comprising interest and principal, over three years starting one month after the loan is taken out.

What would be the monthly repayment on the loan (to the nearest £)?

A £56
B £64
C £66
D £67

6.19 Calculation of payback, ARR and NPV

The following data are supplied relating to two investment projects, only one of which may be selected:

	Project A (£)	Project B (£)
Initial capital expenditure	50 000	50 000
Profit (loss) year 1	25 000	10 000
2	20 000	10 000
3	15 000	14 000
4	10 000	26 000
Estimated resale value at end of year 4	10 000	10 000

Notes
1 Profit is calculated after deducting straight line depreciation.
2 The cost of capital is 10 per cent.

Required:

(a) Calculate for each project:
  (i) average annual rate of return on average capital invested;
  (ii) payback period;
  (iii) net present value.

(12 marks)

(b) Briefly discuss the relative merits of the three methods of evaluation mentioned in (a) above.

(10 marks)

(c) Explain which project you would recommend for acceptance.

(3 marks)

(Total 25 marks)

6.20 A machine with a purchase price of £14 000 is estimated to eliminate manual operations costing £4000 per year. The machine will last five years and have no residual value at the end of its life.

You are required to calculate:

(a) the internal rate of return (IRR);

(b) the level of annual saving necessary to achieve a 12 per cent IRR;

(c) the net present value if the cost of capital is 10 per cent.

6.21 Calculation of payback, ARR and NPV

Stadler is an ambitious young executive who has recently been appointed to the position of financial director of Paradis plc, a small listed company. Stadler regards this appointment as a temporary one, enabling him to gain experience before moving to a larger organization. His intention is to leave Paradis plc in three years' time, with its share price standing high. As a consequence, he is particularly concerned that the reported profits of Paradis plc should be as high as possible in his third and final year with the company.

Paradis plc has recently raised £350 000, and the directors are considering three ways of using these funds. Three projects (A, B and C) are being considered, each involving the immediate purchase of equipment costing £350 000. One project only can be undertaken, and the equipment for each project will have a useful life equal to that of the project, with no scrap value. Stadler favours project C because it is expected to show the highest accounting profit in the third year. However, he does not wish to reveal his real reasons for favouring project C, and so, in his report to the chairman, he recommends project C because it shows the highest internal rate of return. The following summary is taken from his report:

| | Net cash flows (£000) | | | | | | | | |
| | | | Years | | | | | | Internal rate |
Project %	0	1	2	3	4	5	6	7	8	of return
A	−350	100	110	104	112	138	160	180	–	27.5
B	−350	40	100	210	260	160	–	–	–	26.4
C	−350	200	150	240	40	–	–	–	–	33.0

The chairman of the company is accustomed to projects being appraised in terms of payback and accounting rate of return, and he is consequently suspicious of the use of internal rate of return as a method of project selection. Accordingly, the chairman has asked for an independent report on the choice of project. The company's cost of capital is 20 per cent and a policy of straight line depreciation is used to write off the cost of equipment in the financial statements.

Requirements:

(a) Calculate the payback period for each project.

(3 marks)

(b) Calculate the accounting rate of return for each project.

(5 marks)

(c) Prepare a report for the chairman with supporting calculations indicating which project should be preferred by the ordinary shareholders of Paradis plc.

(12 marks)

(d) Discuss the assumptions about the reactions of the stock market that are implicit in Stadler's choice of project C.

(5 marks)

Note: ignore taxation.

(Total 25 marks)

CHAPTER 7
COST ASSIGNMENT

LEARNING OBJECTIVES

After studying this chapter you should be able to:

- **distinguish between direct and absorption costing;**
- **distinguish between cause-and-effect and arbitrary cost allocations;**
- **explain why different cost information is required for different purposes;**
- **describe how cost systems differ in terms of their level of sophistication;**
- **understand the factors influencing the choice of an optimal cost system;**
- **explain why departmental overhead rates should be used in preference to a single blanket overhead rate;**
- **construct an overhead analysis sheet and calculate cost centre allocation rates;**
- **justify why budgeted overhead rates should be used in preference to actual overhead rates;**
- **calculate and explain the accounting treatment of the under-/over-recovery of overheads.**

The aim of this chapter is to provide an understanding of how costs are accumulated and assigned to cost objects. Remember from Chapter 2 that a cost object is anything for which a separate measurement of cost is desired. Typical cost objects include products, services, customers and locations. In this chapter we shall either use the term cost object as a generic term or assume that products are the cost object. However, the same cost assignment approaches can be applied to all cost objects.

Why do we need to assign costs to products or other cost objects? You will remember that in Chapter 5 it was pointed out that cost-plus pricing and product profitability analysis are extensively used by organizations. Cost-plus pricing requires that costs are assigned to each product to ascertain the product cost for adding a profit margin to determine the selling price. With product profitability analysis we need to assign costs to products to distinguish between profitable and unprofitable products in order to ensure that only profitable products are sold.

Costs must also be assigned to products for internal and external profit measurement and inventory valuation. Profit measurement requires that the costs incurred for a period should be allocated between cost of goods sold and inventories. The cost of goods sold that is deducted from sales revenues to compute the profit for the period is derived by summing the manufacturing costs that have been assigned to all those individual products that have been sold during the period. The inventory (stock) valuation is derived from the sum of the costs assigned to all of the partly completed products (i.e. work in progress) and unsold finished products. Inventory valuation, however, is not an issue for many service organizations. They do not carry inventories and therefore a costing system is required mainly for providing relevant decision-making information for cost-plus pricing and for distinguishing between profitable and unprofitable activities.

We begin with a brief description of the two different types of costing systems (i.e. direct and absorption costing) that are used to assign costs to cost objects.

DIRECT AND ABSORPTION COSTING SYSTEMS

Two different types of costing system can be used for cost assignment. They are direct and absorption costing systems. **Direct costing** systems only assign direct costs to cost objects. Because they do not assign indirect costs to cost objects they only report contributions to indirect costs. Proponents of direct costing argue that only direct costs can be accurately traced to cost objects because they can be specifically and exclusively traced to a particular cost object whereas indirect costs cannot. Therefore they advocate that indirect costs should not be assigned to cost objects. They also argue that direct costs tend to be avoidable and therefore direct costing reports only those costs that are relevant for decision-making. Cost assignment with a direct costing system is a simplistic process. It merely involves the implementation of suitable data processing procedures that identify and record those resources that can be specifically and exclusively identified with a particular cost object.

With **absorption costing** systems, both direct and indirect costs are assigned to cost objects. Indirect costs (also known as **overheads**) cannot be directly traced to a cost object because they are usually common to several cost objects. Indirect costs are therefore assigned to cost objects using cost allocations. A **cost allocation** is the process of assigning costs when a direct measure does not exist for the quantity of resources consumed by a particular cost object. Cost allocations involve the use of surrogate rather than direct measures to estimate the amount of indirect costs that are assigned to cost objects. The proponents of absorption costing argue that costs assigned to products (or other cost objects) should represent the estimated sum of all those resources that are committed to a product in the long run. In other words, cost assignment should represent an attempt to allocate a share of all costs to products to ensure that all costs are covered in the cost base.

In summary, a direct costing system represents a partial costing system since only direct costs are assigned to cost objects, whereas absorption costing systems are also called full costing systems because they assign both direct and indirect costs to cost objects. Direct costs can be accurately assigned to cost objects but indirect costs rely on cost allocations, some of which may be on an arbitrary basis. Where direct costs represent a very large proportion of an organization's cost structure there are strong arguments for adopting direct costing systems because most of an organization's costs will be assigned to cost objects. Absorption costing systems, however, are likely to be preferable where indirect costs are a large proportion of total costs. You should also note that external financial accounting requirements require that both direct and indirect manufacturing costs should be assigned to products for profit measurement and inventory valuation requirements. Therefore manufacturing companies must use absorption costing for inventory valuations. Which costing system do firms actually use? A survey of 153 UK manufacturing and non-manufacturing companies by Al-Omiri and Drury (2007) reported that 23 per cent of respondents used direct costing systems and the remainder used absorption costing systems. In the remainder of this chapter we shall examine the cost assignment process for an absorption costing system.

AN OVERVIEW OF THE COST ASSIGNMENT PROCESS FOR AN ABSORPTION COSTING SYSTEM

Figure 7.1 provides an overview of the cost assignment process for an absorption costing system. The term **cost tracing** is used in Figure 7.1 to denote the fact that direct costs can be specifically and exclusively identified with a particular cost object. Cost assignment merely involves the implementation of suitable data processing procedures that identify and record those resources that can be specifically and exclusively identified with a particular cost object. Figure 7.1 also shows that indirect costs are assigned to cost objects using cost allocations. To illustrate a cost allocation, consider an activity such as receiving incoming materials. Assuming that the cost of receiving materials is strongly influenced by the number of receipts, then costs can be allocated to products (i.e. the cost object) based on the number of material receipts each product requires. If 20 per cent of the total number of receipts for a period were required for a particular product then 20 per cent of the total costs of receiving incoming materials would be allocated to that product. Assuming that the product was discontinued, and not replaced, we would expect action to be taken to reduce the resources required for receiving materials by 20 per cent.

In the above illustration the **allocation base** is assumed to be a significant determinant of the cost of receiving incoming materials. Where allocation bases are significant determinants of the costs we shall describe them as **cause-and-effect allocations**. Where a cost allocation base is used that is not a significant determinant of its cost the term arbitrary allocation will be used. An example of an **arbitrary allocation** would be if direct labour hours were used as the allocation base to allocate the costs of materials receiving. If a labour-intensive product required a large proportion of direct labour hours (say 30 per cent) but few material receipts it would be allocated with a large proportion of the costs of material receiving. The allocation would be an inaccurate assignment of the resources consumed by the product. Furthermore, if the product were discontinued, and not replaced, the cost of the material receiving activity would not decline by 30 per cent because the allocation base is not a significant determinant of the costs of the materials

FIGURE 7.1
Cost allocations and cost tracing

receiving activity. Arbitrary allocations are therefore likely to result in inaccurate allocations of indirect costs to cost objects. For the accurate assignment of indirect costs, cause-and-effect allocations should be used.

Figure 7.1 identifies two types of absorption costing systems that can be used to assign indirect costs to cost objects. They are **traditional costing systems** and **activity-based costing (ABC) systems**. Traditional costing systems were developed in the early 1900s and are still widely used today. They rely extensively on arbitrary cost allocations. ABC systems only emerged in the late 1980s. One of the major aims of ABC systems is to use only cause-and-effect cost allocations. Both cost systems adopt identical approaches to assigning direct costs to cost objects. We shall focus mainly on traditional costing systems in this chapter and ABC systems will be explained in detail in the next chapter.

DIFFERENT COSTS FOR DIFFERENT PURPOSES

Earlier in this chapter it was pointed out that manufacturing organizations assign costs to products for two purposes: first, for internal profit measurement and external financial accounting requirements in order to allocate the manufacturing costs incurred during a period between cost of goods sold and inventories; and, secondly, to provide useful information for managerial decision-making requirements. In order to meet financial accounting requirements, it may not be necessary to accurately assign costs to *individual* products. Consider a situation where a firm produces 1000 different products and the costs incurred during a period are £10 million. A well-designed product costing system should accurately analyse the £10 million costs incurred between cost of sales and inventories. Let us assume the true figures are £7 million and £3 million. Approximate but inaccurate *individual* product costs may provide a reasonable approximation of how much of the £10 million should be attributed to cost of sales and inventories. Some product costs may be overstated and others may be understated, but this would not matter for financial accounting purposes as long as the *total* of the individual product costs assigned to cost of sales and inventories was approximately £7 million and £3 million.

For decision-making purposes, however, more accurate product costs are required so that we can distinguish between profitable and unprofitable products. By more accurately measuring the resources consumed by products, or other cost objects, a firm can identify its sources of profits and losses. If the cost system does not capture sufficiently accurately the consumption of resources by products, the reported product costs will be distorted, and there is a danger that managers may drop profitable products or continue production of unprofitable products.

Besides different levels of accuracy, different cost information is required for different purposes. For meeting external financial accounting requirements, financial accounting regulations and legal requirements in most countries require that inventories should be valued at manufacturing cost. Therefore only manufacturing costs are assigned to products for meeting external financial accounting requirements. For decision-making, non-manufacturing costs must be taken into account and assigned to products. Not all costs, however, may be relevant for decision-making. For example, depreciation of plant and machinery will not be affected by a decision to discontinue a product. Such costs were described in the previous chapter as irrelevant and sunk for decision-making. Thus depreciation of plant must be assigned to products for inventory valuation but it should not be assigned for discontinuation decisions.

COST–BENEFIT ISSUES AND COST SYSTEM DESIGN

Until the late 1980s most organizations were relying on costing systems that had been designed primarily for meeting external financial accounting requirements. These systems were designed decades ago when information processing costs were high and precluded the use of more sophisticated methods of assigning indirect costs to products. Such systems are still widely used today. They rely extensively on arbitrary cost allocations, which may be sufficiently accurate for meeting external financial accounting requirements but not for meeting decision-making requirements.

In the late 1980s ABC systems were promoted as a mechanism for more accurately assigning indirect costs to cost objects. Surveys in many countries suggest that between 20 and 30 per cent of the surveyed organizations currently use ABC systems. The majority of organizations therefore continue to operate traditional systems. Both traditional and ABC systems vary in their level of sophistication but, as a general rule, traditional systems tend to be simplistic whereas ABC systems tend to be sophisticated. What determines the chosen level of sophistication of a costing system? The answer is that the choice should be made on costs versus benefits criteria. Simplistic systems are inexpensive to operate, but they are likely to result in inaccurate cost assignments and the reporting of inaccurate costs. Managers using cost information extracted from simplistic systems are more likely to make important mistakes arising from using inaccurate cost information. The end result may be a high cost of errors. Conversely, sophisticated systems are more expensive to operate but they minimize the cost of errors.

Figure 7.2 illustrates the above points with costing systems ranging from simplistic to sophisticated. Highly simplistic costing systems are located on the extreme left. Common features of such systems are that they are inexpensive to operate, make extensive use of arbitrary allocations of indirect costs and normally result in low levels of accuracy and a high cost of errors. On the extreme right are highly sophisticated systems. These systems use only cause-and-effect allocations, are more expensive to operate, have high levels of accuracy and minimize the cost of errors. Cost systems in most organizations are not located at either of these extreme points. Instead, they are located at different points within the range shown in Figure 7.2.

The optimal cost system is different for different organizations. For example, the optimal costing system will be located towards the extreme left for an organization whose indirect

Simplistic systems		Highly sophisticated systems
• Inexpensive to operate • Extensive use of arbitrary cost allocations • Low levels of accuracy • High cost of errors	Level of sophistication ◄──────────────►	• Expensive to operate • Extensive use of cause-and-effect cost allocations • High levels of accuracy • Low cost of errors

FIGURE 7.2

Absorption costing systems – varying levels of sophistication for cost assignment

REAL WORLD VIEWS 7.1

Identifying and managing costs in hospitals

The identification and allocation of costs in hospitals and healthcare facilities is not an easy task. If a hospital is to make best use of available funding or maximize income it, like any other business, must have full cost information.

Hospitals and other healthcare providers may follow a four-stage process in developing and improving their cost accounting. The first stage is to calculate costs for patients in similar diagnostic groups (e.g. pulmonary, cardiac, paediatric). Costs of each patient treatment must be tracked accurately, thus requiring a good patient accounting system that can track all tests, procedures and resources used per patient. This stage also involves identifying cost centres (e.g. radiology) and their direct and indirect costs. Service centres, such as a laboratory, are also identified and charged out to cost centres. With a good knowledge of costs, the second stage is to make more strategic decisions on the utilization of resources. Separating fixed and variable costs at this stage permits hospital managers to select relevant costs for short and long-term decisions.

The next stage in the process is to use the information developed to control costs and resource usage. Often, cost drivers may be identified at this stage, for example case mix, case volume or resources per case. Thus, this stage often represents a move from traditional full costing to activity-based costing. Responsibility for costs in each cost centre is also more formalized at this stage, with cost centre

managers held accountable for cost overruns. The final stage is to ensure that efficient administrative systems are in place to support cost centres rather than increase cost centre overhead. For example, if patient information is collected upon admission and is subsequently passed to patient accounts, there should be no need to request more information or retain duplicate data in other systems.

© IAN FRANCIS/DREAMSTIME.COM

Discussion points

1 Is cost the only factor that must be considered when deciding on treatment?
2 Do you think it is always possible to collect accurate cost data for each patient treatment?

References

Young, D. (1993) *Managing the Stages of Hospital Cost Accounting*, Healthcare Financial Management.

costs are a low percentage of total costs and that also has a fairly standardized product range, all consuming organizational resources in similar proportions. In these circumstances simplistic systems may not result in the reporting of inaccurate costs. In contrast, the optimal costing system for organizations with a high proportion of indirect costs, whose products consume organizational resources in different proportions, will be located towards the extreme right. More sophisticated costing systems are required to capture the diversity of consumption of organizational resources and accurately assign the high level of indirect costs to different cost objects.

PLANT-WIDE (BLANKET) OVERHEAD RATES

The most simplistic traditional costing system assigns indirect costs (overheads) to cost objects using a single overhead rate for the organization as a whole. Such a costing system would be located at the extreme left of the level of sophistication shown in Figure 7.2. The terms **blanket overhead rate** or **plant-wide rate** are used to describe a single overhead rate that is established for the organization as a whole. Let us assume that the total manufacturing overheads for the manufacturing plant of Arcadia are £900 000 and that the company has selected direct labour hours as the allocation base for assigning overheads to products. Assuming that the total number of direct labour hours are 60 000 for the period, the plant-wide overhead rate for Arcadia is £15 per direct labour hour (£900 000/60 000 direct labour hours). This calculation consists of two stages. First, overheads are accumulated in one single plant-wide pool for a period. Second, a plant-wide rate is computed by dividing the total amount of overheads accumulated (£900 000) by the selected allocation base (60 000 direct labour hours). The overhead costs are assigned to products by multiplying the plant-wide rate by the units of the selected allocation base (direct labour hours) used by each product.

Assume now that Arcadia is considering establishing separate overheads for each of its three production departments. Further investigations reveal that the products made by the company require different operations and some products do not pass through all three departments. These investigations also indicate that the £900 000 total manufacturing overheads and 60 000 direct labour hours can be analyzed as follows:

	Department A	Department B	Department C	Total
Overheads	£200 000	£600 000	£100 000	£900 000
Direct labour hours	20 000	20 000	20 000	60 000
Overhead rate per direct labour hour	£10	£30	£5	£15

Consider now a situation where product Z requires 20 direct labour hours in department C but does not pass through departments A and B. If a plant-wide overhead rate is used then overheads of £300 (20 hours at £15 per hour) will be allocated to product Z. On the other hand, if a **departmental overhead rate** is used, only £100 (20 hours at £5 per hour) would be allocated to product Z. Which method should be used? The logical answer must be to establish separate departmental overhead rates, since product Z only consumes overheads in department C. If the plant-wide overhead rate were applied, all the factory overhead rates would be averaged out and product Z would be indirectly allocated with some of the overheads of department B. This would not be satisfactory, since product Z does not consume any of the resources and this department incurs a large amount of the overhead expenditure.

Where some departments are more 'overhead-intensive' than others, products spending more time in the overhead-intensive departments should be assigned more overhead costs than those spending less time. Departmental rates capture these possible effects but plant-wide rates do not, because of the averaging process. We can conclude that a plant-wide rate will generally result in the reporting of inaccurate product costs. A plant-wide rate can only be justified when all products consume departmental overheads in approximately the same proportions. In the above illustration each department accounts for one-third of the total direct labour hours. If all products spend approximately one-third of their time in each department, a plant-wide overhead rate can be used. Consider a situation where product X spends one hour in each department and product Y spends five hours in each department. Overheads of £45 and £225 respectively would be allocated to products X and Y using either a plant-wide rate (3 hours at £15 and 15 hours at £15) or separate departmental overhead rates. If a diverse product range is produced with products spending different proportions of time in each department, separate departmental overhead rates should be established.

Recent surveys indicate that less than 5 per cent of the surveyed organizations use a single plant-wide overhead rate. In Scandinavia only 5 per cent of Finnish companies (Lukka and Granlund, 1996), one Norwegian company (Bjornenak, 1997b) and none of the Swedish companies sampled (Ask *et al.*, 1996) used a single plant-wide rate. Zero usage of plant-wide rates was also reported from a survey of Greek companies (Ballas and Venieris, 1996). In a more recent study of UK organizations Al-Omiri and Drury (2007) reported that a plant-wide rate was used by 4 per cent of the surveyed organizations.

THE TWO-STAGE ALLOCATION PROCESS

It is apparent from the previous section that separate departmental overhead rates should normally be established. To establish departmental overhead rates an approach, known as the two-stage allocation process, is used. This process applies to assigning costs to other cost objects, besides products, and is applicable to all organizations that assign indirect costs to cost objects.

The two-stage allocation process is illustrated in Figure 7.3. You can see that in the first stage overheads are assigned to cost centres (also called cost pools). The terms **cost centres** or **cost pools** are used to describe a location to which overhead costs are initially assigned. Normally cost centres consist of departments, but in some cases they consist of smaller segments such as separate work centres within a department. In the second stage the costs accumulated in the cost centres are allocated to cost objects using selected allocation bases (note that allocation bases are also called **cost drivers**). Traditional costing systems tend to use a small number of second stage allocation bases, typically direct labour hours or machine hours. In other words, traditional systems assume that direct labour or machine hours have a significant influence in the long term on the level of overhead expenditure. Other allocation bases used to a lesser extent by traditional systems are direct labour cost, direct materials cost and units of output.

How many cost centres should a firm establish? If only a small number of cost centres are established it is likely that activities within a cost centre will not be homogeneous and, if the consumption of the activities by products/services within the cost centres varies, activity resource consumption will not be accurately measured. Therefore, in most situations, increasing the number of cost centres increases the accuracy of measuring the

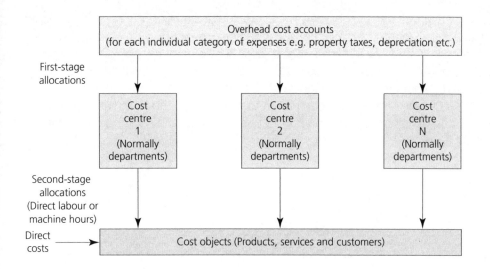

FIGURE 7.3

An illustration of the two-stage allocation process for traditional absorption costing systems

EXHIBIT 7.1

Surveys of practice

A survey of 170 companies by Drury and Tayles (2005) reported the following details in terms of the number of cost centres and number of different types of second-stage allocation bases/cost drivers used:

Number of cost centres	Number of different types of cost drivers
14% used less than 6 cost centres	34% used 1 cost driver
21% used 6–10 cost centres	25% used 2 cost drivers
29% used 11–20 cost centres	31% used 3–10 cost drivers
36% used more than 20 cost centres	10% used more than 10 cost drivers

The percentages below indicate how frequently different cost allocation bases/cost drivers are used. Note that the reported percentages exceed 100 per cent because many companies used more than one allocation base.

	Norway[a]	Holland[b]	Ireland[c]	Australia[d]	Japan[d]	UK[e]	UK[e]
Direct labour hours/cost	65%	20%	52%	57%	57%	68%	73%
Machine hours	29	9	19	19	12	49	26
Direct material costs	26	6	10	12	11	30	19
Units of output	40	30	28	20	16	42	31
Prime cost				1	21		
Other	23	35	9				
ABC cost drivers						9	7

Notes
[a] Bjornenak (1997b)
[b] Boons *et al.* (1994)
[c] Clarke (1995)
[d] Blayney and Yokoyama (1991)
[e] Drury *et al.* (1993) – The first column relates to the responses for automated and the second to non-automated production centres

indirect costs consumed by cost objects. The choice of the number of cost centres should be based on cost–benefit criteria using the principles described on pages 157–159. Exhibit 7.1 (first section) shows the number of cost centres and second-stage cost allocation bases reported by Drury and Tayles (2005) in a survey of 170 UK organizations. It can be seen that 35 per cent of the organizations used less than 11 cost centres whereas 36 per cent used more than 20 cost centres. In terms of the number of different types of second-stage cost drivers/allocation bases, 59 per cent of the responding organizations used less than three.

AN ILLUSTRATION OF THE TWO-STAGE PROCESS FOR A TRADITIONAL COSTING SYSTEM

We shall now use Example 7.1 to provide a more detailed illustration of the two-stage allocation process for a traditional absorption costing system. To keep the illustration manageable it is assumed that the company has only five cost centres – machine departments X and Y, an assembly department, and materials handling and general factory support cost centres. The illustration focuses on manufacturing costs but we shall look at non-manufacturing costs later in the chapter. Applying the two-stage allocation process requires the following four steps:

1 assigning all manufacturing overheads to production and service cost centres;
2 reallocating the costs assigned to service cost centres to production cost centres;
3 computing separate overhead rates for each production cost centre;
4 assigning cost centre overheads to products or other chosen cost objects.

Steps 1 and 2 comprise stage one and steps 3 and 4 relate to the second stage of the two-stage allocation process. Let us now consider each of these steps in detail.

Step 1 – Assigning all manufacturing overheads to production and service cost centres

Using the information given in Example 7.1 our initial objective is to assign all manufacturing overheads to production and service cost centres. To do this requires the preparation of an **overhead analysis sheet**. This document is shown in Exhibit 7.2. In most organizations it will exist only in computer form.

If you look at Example 7.1 you will see that the indirect labour and indirect material costs have been directly traced to cost centres. Although these items cannot be directly assigned to products they can be directly assigned to the cost centres. In other words, they are indirect costs when products are the cost objects and direct costs when cost centres are the cost object. Therefore they are traced directly to the cost centres shown in the overhead analysis sheet in Exhibit 7.2. The remaining costs shown in Example 7.1 cannot be traced directly to the cost centres and must be allocated to the cost centre using appropriate allocation bases. The term **first-stage allocation bases** is used to describe allocations at this point. The following list summarizes commonly used first stage allocation bases:

EXAMPLE 7.1

The annual overhead costs for the Enterprise Company, which has three production centres (two machine centres and one assembly centre) and two service centres (materials procurement and general factory support), are as follows:

	(£)	(£)
Indirect wages and supervision		
Machine centres: X	1 000 000	
Y	1 000 000	
Assembly	1 500 000	
Materials procurement	1 100 000	
General factory support	1 480 000	6 080 000
Indirect materials		
Machine centres: X	500 000	
Y	805 000	
Assembly	105 000	
Materials procurement	0	
General factory support	10 000	1 420 000
Lighting and heating	500 000	
Property taxes	1 000 000	
Insurance of machinery	150 000	
Depreciation of machinery	1 500 000	
Insurance of buildings	250 000	
Salaries of works management	800 000	4 200 000
		11 700 000

The following information is also available:

	Book value of machinery (£)	Area occupied (sq. metres)	Number of employees	Direct labour hours	Machine hours
Machine shop: X	8 000 000	10 000	300	1 000 000	2 000 000
Y	5 000 000	5 000	200	1 000 000	1 000 000
Assembly	1 000 000	15 000	300	2 000 000	
Stores	500 000	15 000	100		
Maintenance	500 000	5 000	100		
	15 000 000	50 000	1000		

Details of total materials issues (i.e. direct and indirect materials) to the production centres are as follows:

	£
Machine shop X	4 000 000
Machine shop Y	3 000 000
Assembly	1 000 000
	8 000 000

To allocate the overheads listed above to the production and service centres we must prepare an overhead analysis sheet, as shown in Exhibit 7.2.

Cost	Basis of allocation
Property taxes, lighting and heating	Area
Employee-related expenditure:	
works management, works canteen, payroll office	Number of employees
Depreciation and insurance of plant and machinery	Value of items of plant and machinery

Applying the allocation bases to the data given in respect of the Enterprise Company in Example 7.1 it is assumed that property taxes, lighting and heating, and insurance of buildings are related to the total floor area of the buildings, and the benefit obtained by each cost centre can therefore be ascertained according to the proportion of floor area that it occupies. The total floor area of the factory shown in Example 7.1 is 50 000 square metres; machine centre X occupies 20 per cent of this and machine centre Y a further 10 per cent. Therefore, if you refer to the overhead analysis sheet in Exhibit 7.2 you will see that 20 per cent of property taxes, lighting and heating and insurance of buildings are allocated to machine centre X, and 10 per cent are allocated to machine centre Y.

The insurance premium paid and depreciation of machinery are generally regarded as being related to the book value of the machinery. Because the book value of machinery for machine centre X is 8/15 of the total book value and machine centre Y is 5/15 of the total book value then 8/15 and 5/15 of the insurance and depreciation of machinery is allocated to machine centres X and Y.

EXHIBIT 7.2

Overhead analysis sheet

			Production centres			Service centres	
Item of expenditure	Basis of allocation	Total (£)	Machine centre X (£)	Machine centre Y (£)	Assembly (£)	Materials procurement (£)	General factory support (£)
Indirect wage and supervision	Direct	6 080 000	1 000 000	1 000 000	1 500 000	1 100 000	1 480 000
Indirect materials	Direct	1 420 000	500 000	805 000	105 000		10 000
Lighting and heating	Area	500 000	100 000	50 000	150 000	150 000	50 000
Property taxes	Area	1 000 000	200 000	100 000	300 000	300 000	100 000
Insurance of machinery	Book value of machinery	150 000	80 000	50 000	10 000	5 000	5 000
Depreciation of machinery	Book value of machinery	1 500 000	800 000	500 000	100 000	50 000	50 000
Insurance of buildings	Area	250 000	50 000	25 000	75 000	75 000	25 000
Salaries of works management	Number of employees	800 000	240 000	160 000	240 000	80 000	80 000
(1)		11 700 000	2 970 000	2 690 000	2 480 000	1 760 000	1 800 000
Reallocation of service centre costs							
Materials procurement	Value of materials issued	—	880 000	660 000	220 000	1 760 000	
General factory support	Direct labour hours	—	450 000	450 000	900 000		1 800 000
(2)		11 700 000	4 300 000	3 800 000	3 600 000	—	—
Machine hours and direct labour hours			2 000 000	1 000 000	2 000 000		
Machine hour overhead rate			£2.15	£3.80			
Direct labour hour overhead rate					£1.80		

It is assumed that the amount of time that works management devotes to each cost centre is related to the number of employees in each centre; since 30 per cent of the total employees are employed in machine centre X, 30 per cent of the salaries of works management will be allocated to this centre.

If you now look at the overhead analysis sheet shown in Exhibit 7.2, you will see in the row labelled '(1)' that all manufacturing overheads for the Enterprise Company have been assigned to the three production and two service cost centres.

Step 2 – Reallocating the costs assigned to service cost centres to production cost centres

The next step is to reallocate the costs that have been assigned to service cost centres to production cost centres. **Service departments** (i.e. service cost centres) are those departments that exist to provide services of various kinds to other units within the organization. They are sometimes called **support departments**. The Enterprise Company has two service centres. They are materials procurement and general factory support, which includes activities such as production scheduling and machine maintenance. These service centres render essential services that support the production process, but they do not deal directly with the products. Therefore it is not possible to allocate service centre costs to products passing through these centres. To assign costs to products, traditional costing systems reallocate service centre costs to production centres that actually work on the product. The method that is chosen to allocate service centre costs to production centres should be related to the benefits that the production centres derive from the service rendered.

We shall assume that the value of materials issued (shown in Example 7.1) provides a suitable approximation of the benefit that each of the production centres receives from materials procurement. Therefore 50 per cent of the value of materials is issued to machine centre X, resulting in 50 per cent of the total costs of materials procurement being allocated to this centre. If you refer to Exhibit 7.2 you will see that £880 000 (50 per cent of material procurement costs of £1 760 000) has been reallocated to machine centre X. It is also assumed that direct labour hours provides an approximation of the benefits received by the production centres from general factory support resulting in the total costs for this centre being reallocated to the production centres proportionate to direct labour hours. Therefore, since machine centre X consumes 25 per cent of the direct labour hours, £450 000 (25 per cent of the total costs of £1 800 000 assigned to general factory support) has been reallocated to machine centre X. You will see in the row labelled '(2)' in Exhibit 7.2 that all manufacturing costs have now been assigned to the three production centres. This completes the first stage of the two-stage allocation process.

Step 3 – Computing separate overhead rates for each production cost centre

The second stage of the two-stage process is to allocate overheads of each production centre to products passing through that centre. The most frequently used allocation bases employed by traditional costing systems are based on the amount of time products spend in each production centre – for example direct labour hours, machine hours and direct wages. In respect of non-machine centres, direct labour hours is the most frequently used allocation base. This implies that the overheads incurred by a production centre are closely related to direct labour hours worked. In the case of machine centres a machine hour overhead rate is preferable because most of the overheads (e.g. depreciation) are likely to be more closely related to machine hours. We shall assume that the Enterprise Company uses a **machine hour rate** for the machine production centres and a **direct labour hour rate** for the assembly centre. The overhead rates are calculated by applying the following formula:

$$\frac{\text{Cost centre overheads}}{\text{Cost centre direct labour hours or machine hours}}$$

The calculations using the information given in Exhibit 7.2 are as follows:

$$\text{Machine centre X} = \frac{£4\,300\,000}{2\,000\,000 \text{ machine hours}} = £2.15 \text{ per machine hour}$$

$$\text{Machine centre Y} = \frac{£3\,800\,000}{1\,000\,000 \text{ machine hours}} = £3.80 \text{ per machine hour}$$

$$\text{Assembly department} = \frac{£3\,600\,000}{2\,000\,000 \text{ direct labour hours}} = £1.80 \text{ per direct labour hour}$$

Step 4 – Assigning cost centre overheads to products or other chosen cost objects

The final step is to allocate the overheads to products passing through the production centres. Therefore if a product spends 10 hours in machine cost centre A overheads of £21.50 (10 × £2.15) will be allocated to the product. We shall compute the manufacturing costs of two products. Product A is a low sales volume product with direct costs of £100. It is manufactured in batches of 100 units and each unit requires 5 hours in machine centre A, 10 hours in machine centre B and 10 hours in the assembly centre. Product B is a high sales volume product thus enabling it to be manufactured in larger batches. It is manufactured in batches of 200 units and each unit requires 10 hours in machine centre A, 20 hours in machine centre B and 20 hours in the assembly centre. Direct costs of £200 have been assigned to product B. The calculations of the manufacturing costs assigned to the products are as follows:

Product A	£
Direct costs (100 units × £100)	10 000
Overhead allocations	
Machine centre A (100 units × 5 machine hours × £2.15)	1 075
Machine centre B (100 units × 10 machine hours × £3.80)	3 800
Assembly (100 units × 10 direct labour hours × £1.80)	1 800
Total cost	16 675
Cost per unit (£16 675/100 units) = £166.75	

Product B	£
Direct costs (200 units × £200)	40 000
Overhead allocations	
Machine centre A (200 units × 10 machine hours × £2.15)	4 300
Machine centre B (200 units × 20 machine hours × £3.80)	15 200
Assembly (200 units × 20 direct labour hours × £1.80)	7 200
Total cost	66 700
Cost per unit (£66 700/200 units) = £333.50	

The overhead allocation procedure is more complicated where service cost centres serve each other. In Example 7.1 it was assumed that materials procurement does not provide any services for general factory support and that general factory support does not provide any services for materials procurement. An understanding of situations where service cost centres do serve each other is not, however, necessary for a general understanding of the overhead procedure, and the problem of service centre reciprocal cost allocations is therefore not covered in this book. For an explanation of how to deal with service centre reciprocal cost allocations you should refer to Drury (2008, Chapter 3).

EXTRACTING RELEVANT COSTS FOR DECISION-MAKING

The cost computations relating to the Enterprise Company for products A and B represent the costs that should be generated for meeting stock valuation and profit measurement requirements. For decision-making, non-manufacturing costs should also be taken into account. In addition, some of the costs that have been assigned to the products may not be relevant for certain decisions. For example, if you look at the overhead analysis sheet in Exhibit 7.2 you will see that property taxes, depreciation of machinery and insurance of buildings and machinery have been assigned to cost centres, and thus included in the costs assigned to products. If these costs are unaffected by a decision to discontinue a product they should not be assigned to products when undertaking product discontinuation reviews. However, if cost information is used to determine selling prices such costs may need to be assigned to products to ensure that the selling price of a customer's order covers a fair share of all organizational costs. It is therefore necessary to ensure that the costs incorporated in the overhead analysis are suitably coded so that different overhead rates can be extracted for different combinations of costs. This will enable relevant cost information to be extracted from the database for meeting different requirements. For an illustration of this approach, see the answer to Review problem 7.19.

BUDGETED OVERHEAD RATES

Our discussion in this chapter has assumed that the *actual* overheads for an accounting period have been allocated to the products. However, the calculation of overhead rates based on the *actual* overheads incurred during an accounting period causes a number of problems. First, the product cost calculations have to be delayed until the end of the accounting period, because the overhead rate calculations cannot be obtained before this date, but information on product costs is required quickly if it is to be used for monthly profit calculations and inventory valuations or as a basis for setting selling prices. Secondly, one may argue that the timing problem can be resolved by calculating actual overhead rates at more frequent intervals, say on a monthly basis, but the objection to this proposal is that a large amount of overhead expenditure is fixed in the short term whereas activity will vary from month to month, giving large fluctuations in the overhead rates. Consider Example 7.2.

The monthly overhead rates of £2 and £5 per hour computed in Example 7.2 are not representative of typical, normal production conditions. Management has committed itself to a specific level of fixed costs in the light of foreseeable needs for beyond one month.

Thus, where production fluctuates, monthly overhead rates may be volatile. Furthermore, some costs such as repairs, maintenance and heating are not incurred evenly throughout the year. Therefore, if monthly overhead rates are used, these costs will not be allocated fairly to units of output. For example, heating costs would be charged only to winter production so that products produced in winter would be more expensive than those produced in summer.

An average, annualized rate based on the relationship of total annual overhead to total annual activity is more representative of typical relationships between total costs and volume than a monthly rate. What is required is a normal product cost based on average long-term production rather than an actual product cost, which is affected by month-to-month fluctuations in production volume. Taking these factors into consideration, it is

REAL WORLD VIEWS 7.2

Product diversity and costing system design choice

Two Australian firms, one with three divisions (HC1, HC2 and HC3), and the second with two divisions (FT1 and FT2) were studied. HC1 and FT1 had the simplest costing systems with all of the overheads accumulated into a single cost pool. In other words, a plant-wide overhead rate was used. HC2 and HC3 established separate 'work centre cost pools' that reflect manufacturing processes (e.g. HC2 had three cost pools and HC3 two cost pools). Overheads such as power were directly traced to the work centres. The remaining overheads were allocated to the work centres based on their levels of direct labour hours (DLHs) usage. The work centre overhead was then determined by dividing the work centre cost pool by the number of DLHs and allocating the costs to the product according to the consumption of DLHs in each of the work centres.

FT2 was the only research site that had a highly sophisticated costing system consisting of many different cost pools. The overheads for each cost pool were allocated to products on the basis of two cost drivers, namely direct labour hours and machine hours. The overheads allocated based on DLHs included indirect labour associated with materials handling, packers and factory foremen. Overheads allocated on the basis of machine hours include costs that vary with machine hours (e.g. power and electricity) as well as fixed costs such as factory management and depreciation.

HC1, HC2 and FT1 all had low product diversity (i.e. products consumed organizational resources in similar proportions) and users were satisfied with the information provided by the costing system. Both HC3 and FT2 had high levels of product diversity. FT2 had a relatively sophisticated costing system while HC3 maintained a simplistic system. The users of the costing system at FT2 were very satisfied with the system whereas there was much dissatisfaction with HC3's system. Costing information at HC3 was particularly important for determining product costs. However, management believed that the costs were highly inaccurate and were inadequate for setting prices. Overheads were large and product diversity was high creating the need for a relatively sophisticated costing system. However, a simplistic costing system was implemented. This absence of 'fit' was a major dissatisfaction with the existing costing system. In contrast, there was a 'fit' between the costing systems and the level of product diversity in the four other business units and a general satisfaction with the costing systems.

Discussion points

1 Why might increasing the number of cost centres (pools) result in the reporting of more accurate product costs?
2 What other factors, besides product diversity, might enable a simplistic product costing system to report reasonably accurate product costs?

SOURCE: ADAPTED FROM ABERNETHY, M.A. ET AL. PRODUCT DIVERSITY AND COSTING SYSTEM DESIGN CHOICE: FIELD STUDY EVIDENCE. MANAGEMENT ACCOUNTING RESEARCH, 2001, 12, PP261–279.

EXAMPLE 7.2

The fixed overheads for Euro are £24 million per annum, and monthly production varies from 400 000 to 1 million direct labour hours. The monthly overhead rate for fixed overhead will therefore fluctuate as follows:

Monthly overhead	£2 000 000	£2 000 000
Monthly production	400 000 hours	1 000 000 hours
Monthly overhead rate	£5 per hour	£2 per hour

Overhead expenditure that is fixed in the short term remains constant each month, but monthly production fluctuates because of holiday periods and seasonal variations in demand. Consequently the overhead rate varies from £2 to £5 per hour. It would be unreasonable for a product worked on in one month to be allocated overheads at a rate of £5 per hour and an identical product worked on in another month allocated at a rate of only £2 per hour.

preferable to establish a **budgeted overhead rate** based on annual *estimated* overhead expenditure and activity.

UNDER- AND OVER-RECOVERY OF OVERHEADS

The effect of calculating overhead rates based on budgeted annual overhead expenditure and activity is that it will be most unlikely that the overhead allocated to products manufactured during the period will be the same as the actual overhead incurred. Consider a situation where the estimated annual fixed overheads are £2 000 000 and the estimated annual activity is 1 000 000 direct labour hours. The estimated fixed overhead rate will be £2 per hour. Assume that actual overheads are £2 000 000 and are therefore identical with the estimate, but that actual activity is 900 000 direct labour hours instead of the estimated 1 000 000 hours. In this situation only £1 800 000 will be charged to production. This calculation is based on 900 000 direct labour hours at £2 per hour, giving an under-recovery of overheads of £200 000.

Consider an alternative situation where the actual overheads are £1 950 000 instead of the estimated £2 000 000, and actual activity is 1 000 000 direct labour hours, which is identical to the original estimate. In this situation 1 000 000 direct labour hours at £2 per hour will be charged to production giving an over-recovery of £50 000. This example illustrates that there will be an **under- or over-recovery of overheads** whenever actual activity or overhead expenditure is different from the budgeted overheads and activity used to estimate the budgeted overhead rate. This under- or over-recovery of fixed overheads is also called a **volume variance**.

Accounting regulations in most countries recommend that the under- or over-recovery of overheads should be regarded as a period cost adjustment (see Chapter 2 for an explanation of period costs). The accounting procedure is illustrated in Figure 7.4. Note that any under- or over-recovery of overhead is not allocated to products. Also note that the under-recovery is recorded as an expense in the current accounting period whereas an over-recovery is recorded as a reduction in the expenses for the period. Finally you should note

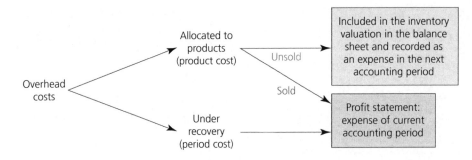

FIGURE 7.4

Illustration of under-recovery of factory overheads

that our discussion here is concerned with how to treat any under- or over-recovery for the purpose of financial accounting and its impact on inventory valuation and profit measurement.

NON-MANUFACTURING OVERHEADS

In respect of financial accounting, only manufacturing costs are allocated to products. Non-manufacturing overheads are regarded as period costs and are disposed of in exactly the same way as the under- or over-recovery of manufacturing overheads outlined in Figure 7.4. For external reporting it is therefore unnecessary to allocate non-manufacturing overheads to products. However, for decision-making non-manufacturing costs should be assigned to products. For example, in many organizations it is not uncommon for selling prices to be based on estimates of total cost or even actual cost. Housing contractors and garages often charge for their services by adding a percentage profit margin to actual cost.

Some non-manufacturing costs may be a direct cost of the product. Delivery costs, salesmen's salaries and travelling expenses may be directly identifiable with the product, but it is likely that many non-manufacturing overheads cannot be allocated directly to specific products. On what basis should we allocate non-manufacturing overheads? The answer is that we should select an allocation base/cost driver that corresponds most closely to non-manufacturing overheads. The problem is that cause-and-effect allocation bases often cannot be established for non-manufacturing overheads. Therefore traditional systems tend to use arbitrary, rather than cause-and-effect allocation bases, to allocate non-manufacturing overheads to products. The most widely used approach is to allocate

EXAMPLE 7.3

The estimated non-manufacturing and manufacturing costs of a company for the year ending 31 December are £500 000 and £1 million respectively. The non-manufacturing overhead absorption rate is calculated as follows:

$$\frac{\text{Estimated non-manufacturing overhead}}{\text{Estimated manufacturing cost}}$$

In percentage terms each product will be allocated with non-manufacturing overheads at a rate of 50 per cent of its total manufacturing cost.

non-manufacturing overheads on the ability of the products to bear such costs. This approach can be implemented by allocating non-manufacturing costs to products on the basis of their manufacturing costs, and this procedure is illustrated in Example 7.3.

SUMMARY

The following items relate to the learning objectives listed at the beginning of the chapter.

● **Distinguish between direct and absorption costing**. A direct costing system represents a partial costing system since only direct costs are assigned to cost objects whereas absorption costing systems are also called full costing systems because they assign both direct and indirect costs to cost objects. Advocates of direct costing argue that only direct costs can be accurately traced to cost objexts, whereas indirect costs must be assigned using arbitrary cost apportionments. They also argue that direct costing provides better information for decision-making because only avoidable costs are assigned to products. Proponents of absorption costing argue that costs assigned to products should represent the estimated sum of all those resources that are committed to a product in the long run.

● **Distinguish between cause-and-effect and arbitrary allocations**. Allocation bases which are significant determinants of costs that are being allocated are described as cause-and-effect allocations whereas arbitrary allocations refer to allocation bases that are not the significant determinants of the costs. To accurately measure the cost of resources used by cost objects cause-and-effect allocations should be used.

● **Explain why different cost information is required for different purposes**. Manufacturing organizations assign costs to products for two purposes: first for external (financial accounting) profit measurement and inventory valuation purposes in order to allocate manufacturing costs incurred during a period to cost of goods sold and inventories; secondly to provide useful information for managerial decision-making requirements. Financial accounting regulations specify that only manufacturing costs should be assigned to products for meeting inventory and profit measurement requirements. Both manufacturing and non-manufacturing costs, however, may be relevant for decision-making. In addition, not all costs that are assigned to products for inventory valuation and profit measurement are relevant for decision-making. For example, costs that will not be affected by a decision (e.g. depreciation) are normally not relevant for decision-making.

● **Describe how cost systems differ in terms of their level of sophistication**. Cost systems range from simplistic to sophisticated. Simplistic systems are inexpensive to operate, involve extensive use of arbitrary allocations, have a high likelihood of reporting inaccurate product costs and generally result in a high cost of errors. Sophisticated costing systems are more expensive to operate, rely more extensively on cause-and-effect allocations, generally report more accurate product costs and have a low cost of errors.

● **Understand the factors influencing the choice of an optimal costing system**. The optimal costing system is different for different organizations and should be determined on a costs versus benefits basis. Simplistic costing systems are appropriate in organizations whose indirect costs are a low percentage of total costs and which also have a fairly standardized product range, all consuming organizational resources in similar proportions. Under these circumstances simplistic costing systems may report costs that are sufficiently accurate for decision-making purposes. Conversely, organizations with a high proportion of indirect costs, whose products consume organizational resources in different proportions, are likely to require sophisticated costing systems.

● **Explain why departmental overhead rates should be used in preference to a single blanket overhead rate.** A blanket (also known as plant-wide) overhead rate establishes a single overhead rate for the organization as a whole whereas departmental rates involve indirect costs being accumulated by different departments and a separate overhead rate being established for each department. A blanket overhead rate can only be justified when all products or services consume departmental overheads in approximately the same proportions. Such circumstances are unlikely to be applicable to most organizations resulting in blanket overheads generally reporting inaccurate product/service costs.

● **Construct an overhead analysis sheet and calculate cost centre allocation rates.** Cost centre overhead allocation rates are established and assigned to cost objects using the two-stage allocation overhead procedure. In the first stage, an overhead analysis sheet is used to (a) allocate overheads to production and service centres or departments and (b) to reallocate the total service department overheads to production departments. The second stage involves (a) the calculation of appropriate departmental overhead rates and (b) the allocation of overheads to products passing through each department. These steps were illustrated using data presented in Example 7.1.

● **Justify why budgeted overhead rates should be used in preference to actual overhead rates.** Because the uses of actual overhead rates causes a delay in the calculation of product or service costs, and the use of monthly rates causes fluctuations in the overhead rates throughout the year, it is recommended that annual budgeted overhead rates should be used.

● **Calculate and explain the treatment of the under-/over-recovery of overheads.** The use of annual budgeted overhead rates gives an under- or over-recovery of overheads whenever actual overhead expenditure or activity is different from budget. Any under- or over-recovery is generally regarded as a period cost adjustment and written off to the profit and loss statement and thus not allocated to products.

KEY TERMS AND CONCEPTS

absorption costing (p.154)

activity-based costing (ABC) systems (p. 156)

allocation base (p. 155)

arbitrary allocation (p. 155)

blanket overhead rate (p. 159)

budgeted overhead rates (p. 169)

cause-and-effect allocations (p. 155)

cost allocation (p. 154)

cost centre (p. 160)

cost driver (p. 160)

cost pool (p. 160)

cost tracing (p. 155)

department overhead rate (p.159)

direct costing (p. 154)

direct labour hour rate (p. 166)

first-stage allocation bases (p. 162)

machine hour rate (p. 166)

overhead analysis sheet (p. 162)

overheads (p. 154)

plant-wide rate (p. 159)

service departments (p. 165)

support departments (p. 165)

traditional costing systems (p. 156)

under- or over-recovery of overheads (p. 169)

volume variance (p. 169)

ASSESSMENT MATERIAL

The review questions are short questions that enable you to assess your understanding of the main topics included in the chapter. The page numbers in parentheses provide you with the page numbers to refer to if you cannot answer a specific question.

The review problems are more complex and require you to relate and apply the content to various business problems. Solutions to review problems are provided in a separate section at the end of the book. Additional review problems can be accessed by lecturers and students on the website (www.drury-online.com). Solutions to these problems are provided for lecturers in the Instructors' Manual. This is available on the lecturers' password-protected section of the website.

The website also includes over 30 case study problems. A list of these cases is provided on pages 389–392. Oak City is a case that is relevant to the content of this chapter.

REVIEW QUESTIONS

7.1 Why are indirect costs not directly traced to cost objects in the same way as direct costs? *(p. 155)*

7.2 Define cost tracing, cost allocation, allocation base and cost driver. *(pp. 155, 160)*

7.3 Distinguish between arbitrary and cause-and-effect allocations. *(p. 155)*

7.4 Explain how cost information differs for profit measurement/inventory valuation requirements compared with decision-making requirements. *(pp. 156–57)*

7.5 Explain why cost systems should differ in terms of their level of sophistication. *(pp. 157–59)*

7.6 Why are separate departmental or cost centre overhead rates preferred to a plant-wide (blanket) overhead rate? *(pp. 159–60)*

7.7 Describe the two-stage overhead allocation procedure. *(pp. 160–62)*

7.8 Why are some overhead costs sometimes not relevant for decision-making purposes? *(p. 167)*

7.9 Why are budgeted overhead rates preferred to actual overhead rates? *(pp. 167–68)*

7.10 Give two reasons for the under- or over-recovery of overheads at the end of the accounting period. *(p. 169)*

REVIEW PROBLEMS

7.11 A company uses a predetermined overhead recovery rate based on machine hours. Budgeted factory overhead for a year amounted to £720 000, but actual factory overhead incurred was £738 000. During the year, the company absorbed £714 000 of factory overhead on 119 000 actual machine hours.

What was the company's budgeted level of machine hours for the year?

A	116 098
B	119 000
C	120 000
D	123 000

7.12 A company absorbs overheads on machine hours which were budgeted at 11 250 with overheads of £258 750. Actual results were 10 980 hours with overheads of £254 692.

Overheads were:

A	under-absorbed by £2152
B	over-absorbed by £4058
C	under-absorbed by £4058
D	over-absorbed by £2152

7.13 The following data are to be used for sub-questions (i) and (ii) below:

Budgeted labour hours	8 500
Budgeted overheads	£148 750
Actual labour hours	7 928
Actual overheads	£146 200

(i) Based on the data given above, what is the labour hour overhead absorption rate?

A	£17.50 per hour
B	£17.20 per hour
C	£18.44 per hour
D	£18.76 per hour

(ii) Based on the data given above, what is the amount of overhead under/over-absorbed?

A	£2550 under-absorbed
B	£2529 over-absorbed
C	£2550 over-absorbed
D	£7460 under-absorbed

7.14 A firm makes special assemblies to customers' orders and uses job costing. The data for a period are:

	Job no. AA10 (£)	Job no. BB15 (£)	Job no. CC20 (£)
Opening WIP	26 800	42 790	—
Material added in period	17 275	—	18 500
Labour for period	14 500	3 500	24 600

The budgeted overheads for the period were £126 000.

(i) What overhead should be added to job number CC20 for the period?

A	£24 600
B	£65 157
C	£72 761
D	£126 000

(ii) Job no. BB15 was completed and delivered during the period and the firm wishes to earn $33\frac{1}{3}$ per cent profit on sales.

What is the selling price of job number BB15?

A	£69 435
B	£75 521

    C   £84 963

    D   £138 870

(iii) What was the approximate value of closing work in progress at the end of the period?

    A   £58 575

    B   £101 675

    C   £147 965

    D   £217 323

7.15 A company absorbs overheads on machine hours. In a period, actual machine hours were 17 285, actual overheads were £496 500 and there was under-absorption of £12 520.

What was the budgeted level of overheads?

    A   £483 980

    B   £496 500

    C   £509 020

    D   It cannot be calculated from the information provided.

7.16 Canberra has established the following information regarding fixed overheads for the coming month:

Budgeted information:

Fixed overheads	£180 000
Labour hours	3 000
Machine hours	10 000
Units of production	5 000

Actual fixed costs for the last month were £160 000.

Canberra produces many different products using highly automated manufacturing processes and absorbs overheads on the most appropriate basis.

What will be the predetermined overhead absorption rate?

    A   £16

    B   £18

    C   £36

    D   £60

7.17 Overhead analysis and calculation of product costs

A furniture-making business manufactures quality furniture to customers' orders. It has three production departments and two service departments. Budgeted overhead costs for the coming year are as follows:

	Total (£)
Rent and rates	12 800
Machine insurance	6 000
Telephone charges	3 200
Depreciation	18 000
Production supervisor's salaries	24 000
Heating/Lighting	6 400
	70 400

The three production departments – A, B and C, and the two service departments – X and Y, are housed in the new premises, the details of which, together with other statistics and information, are given below.

	Departments				
	A	B	C	X	Y
Floor area occupied (sq. metres)	3000	1800	600	600	400
Machine value (£000)	24	10	8	4	2
Direct labour hrs budgeted	3200	1800	1000		
Labour rates per hour	£8.80	£8.50	£8.40	£7.50	£7.50
Allocated overheads:					
Specific to each department (£000)	2.8	1.7	1.2	0.8	0.6
Service department X's costs apportioned	50%	25%	25%		
Service department Y's costs apportioned	20%	30%	50%		

Required:

(a) Prepare a statement showing the overhead cost budgeted for each department, showing the basis of apportionment used. Also calculate suitable overhead absorption rates.

(9 marks)

(b) Two pieces of furniture are to be manufactured for customers. Direct costs are as follows:

	Job 123	Job 124
Direct material	£125	£79.70
Direct labour	10 hours Dept A	8 hours Dept A
	6 hours Dept B	5 hours Dept B
	5 hours Dept C	7 hours Dept C

Calculate the total costs of each job.

(5 marks)

(c) If the firm quotes prices to customers that reflect a required profit of 25 per cent on selling price, calculate the quoted selling price for each job.

(2 marks)
(Total 16 marks)

7.18 Calculation of product overhead costs

Bookdon plc manufactures three products in two production departments, a machine shop and a fitting section; it also has two service departments, a canteen and a machine maintenance section. Shown below are next year's budgeted production data and manufacturing costs for the company.

	Product X	Product Y	Product Z
Production	4200 units	6900 units	1700 units
Prime cost:			
Direct materials	£11 per unit	£14 per unit	£17 per unit
Direct labour:			
Machine shop	£6 per unit	£4 per unit	£2 per unit
Fitting section	£12 per unit	£3 per unit	£21 per unit
Machine hours per unit	6 hours per unit	3 hours per unit	4 hours per unit

	Machine shop	Fitting section	Canteen	Machine maintenance section	Total
Budgeted overheads (£):					
Allocated overheads	27 660	19 470	16 600	26 650	90 380
Rent, rates, heat and light					17 000
Depreciation and insurance of equipment					25 000
Additional data:					
Gross book value of equipment (£)	150 000	75 000	30 000	45 000	
Number of employees	18	14	4	4	
Floor space occupied (square metres)	3 600	1 400	1 000	800	

It has been estimated that approximately 70 per cent of the machine maintenance section's costs are incurred servicing the machine shop and the remainder incurred servicing the fitting section.

Required:

(a) (i) Calculate the following budgeted overhead absorption rates:
   A machine hour rate for the machine shop.

   A rate expressed as a percentage of direct wages for the fitting section.

   All workings and assumptions should be clearly shown.

   (12 marks)

(ii) Calculate the budgeted manufacturing overhead cost per unit of product X.

   (2 marks)

(b) The production director of Bookdon plc has suggested that 'as the actual overheads incurred and units produced are usually different from the budgeted and as a consequence profits of each month-end are distorted by over-/under-absorbed overheads, it would be more accurate to calculate the actual overhead cost per unit each month-end by dividing the total number of all units actually produced during the month into the actual overheads incurred.'
   Critically examine the production director's suggestion.

   (8 marks)
   (Total 22 marks)

7.19 Make or buy decision

Shown below is next year's budget for the forming and finishing departments of Tooton Ltd. The departments manufacture three different types of component, which are incorporated into the output of the firm's finished products.

	Component		
	A	B	C
Production (units)	14 000	10 000	6 000
Prime cost (£ per unit):			
Direct materials			
Forming dept	8	7	9
Direct labour			
Forming dept	6	9	12
Finishing dept	10	15	8
	24	31	29
Manufacturing times (hours per unit):			
Machining			
Forming dept	4	3	2
Direct labour			
Forming dept	2	3	4
Finishing dept	3	10	2

	Forming department (£)	Finishing department (£)
Variable overheads	200 900	115 500
Fixed overheads	401 800	231 000
	£602 700	£346 500
Machine time required and available	98 000 hours	—
Labour hours required and available	82 000 hours	154 000 hours

The forming department is mechanized and employs only one grade of labour; the finishing department employs several grades of labour with differing hourly rates of pay.

Required:

(a) Calculate suitable overhead absorption rates for the forming and finishing departments for the next year and include a brief explanation for your choice of rates.

(6 marks)

(b) Another firm has offered to supply next year's budgeted quantities of the above components at the following prices:

Component A £30   Component B £65
Component C £60

Advise management whether it would be more economical to purchase any of the above components from the outside supplier. You must show your workings and, considering cost criteria only, clearly state any assumptions made or any aspects that may require further investigation.

(8 marks)

(c) Critically consider the purpose of calculating production overheads absorption rates.

(8 marks)

(Total 22 marks)

CHAPTER 8
ACTIVITY-BASED COSTING

LEARNING OBJECTIVES

After studying this chapter you should be able to:

● **describe the differences between activity-based and traditional costing systems;**
● **explain why traditional costing systems can provide misleading information for decision-making;**
● **compute product costs using an activity-based costing system;**
● **identify and explain each of the four stages involved in designing ABC systems;**
● **describe the ABC cost hierarchy.**

In the previous chapter the cost assignment process for a traditional costing system was described. During the 1980s the limitations of traditional product costing systems began to be widely publicized. These systems were designed decades ago when most companies marketed a narrow range of products. Indirect costs were relatively small, and the distortions arising from inappropriate overhead allocations were not significant. Information processing costs were high and it was therefore difficult to justify more sophisticated methods of assigning indirect costs to cost objects.

By the 1980s companies were marketing a wide range of products, indirect costs were no longer relatively unimportant and information costs had ceased to be a barrier to introducing more sophisticated systems. Furthermore, the intense global competition of the 1980s resulted in decision errors from poor cost information becoming more probable and more costly. It is against this background that a new, and more sophisticated costing system, called activity-based costing (ABC) emerged in the late 1980s.

In this chapter we focus on ABC systems – in particular, the measurement of indirect costs for decision-making using ABC techniques. The major aims of the chapter are to explain how an ABC system operates and provide a conceptual understanding of ABC. You should note that ABC can also be used for managing and controlling costs. These aspects are considered in Chapter 14.

Unless otherwise stated, we will assume that products are the cost objects, but the techniques used and the principles established can be applied to other cost objects such as customers, services and locations. We begin with a comparison of traditional and ABC systems.

COMPARISON OF TRADITIONAL AND ABC SYSTEMS

Figure 8.1 illustrates the major differences between traditional and ABC systems. The upper panel of this diagram is identical to Figure 7.3 used in the previous chapter to describe a traditional costing system. Both systems use a two-stage allocation process. In the first stage a traditional system allocates overheads to production and service departments and then reallocates service department costs to the production departments. An ABC system assigns overheads to each major activity (rather than departments). With ABC systems, many activity-based cost centres (alternatively known as activity cost pools) are established, whereas with traditional systems overheads tend to be pooled by departments, although they are normally described as cost centres.

Activities consist of the aggregation of many different tasks and are described by verbs associated with objects. Typical support activities include: schedule production, set up machines, move materials, purchase materials, inspect items, process supplier records, expedite and process customer orders. Production process activities include machine products and assemble products. Within the production process, activity cost centres are often identical to the cost centres used by traditional cost systems. Support activities are also sometimes identical to cost centres used by traditional systems, such as when the purchasing department and activity are both treated as cost centres. Overall, however, ABC systems will normally have a greater number of cost centres.

The second-stage of the two-stage allocation process allocates costs from cost centres (pools) to products or other chosen cost objects. Traditional costing systems trace overheads to products using a small number of second-stage allocation bases (normally described as overhead allocation rates), which vary directly with the volume produced. Instead of using the terms 'allocation bases' or 'overhead allocation rates' the term '**cost driver**' is used by ABC systems. Direct labour and machine hours are the allocation bases that are normally used by traditional costing systems. In contrast, ABC systems use many different types of second-stage cost drivers, including non-volume-based drivers, such as the number of production runs for production scheduling and the number of purchase orders for the purchasing activity.

Therefore the major distinguishing features of ABC systems are that within the two-stage allocation process they rely on:

1 a greater number of cost centres;
2 a greater number and variety of second-stage cost drivers.

(a) Traditional costing systems

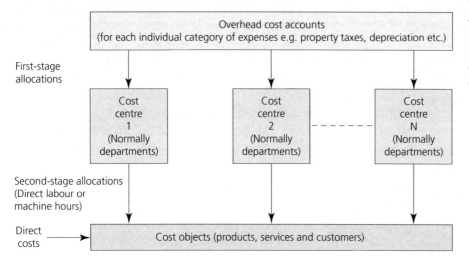

FIGURE 8.1

An illustration of the two-stage allocation for traditional and activity-based costing systems

(b) Activity-based costing systems

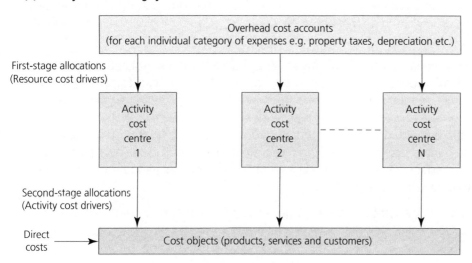

By using a greater number of cost centres and different types of cost drivers that cause activity resource consumption, and assigning activity costs to cost objects on the basis of cost driver usage, ABC systems can more accurately measure the resources consumed by cost objects. Traditional cost systems tend to report less accurate costs because they use cost drivers where no cause-and-effect relationships exist to assign support costs to cost objects.

VOLUME-BASED AND NON-VOLUME-BASED COST DRIVERS

Our comparison of ABC systems with traditional costing systems indicated that ABC systems rely on a greater number and variety of second-stage cost drivers. The term 'variety of cost drivers' refers to the fact that ABC systems use both volume-based and non-volume-based cost drivers. In contrast, traditional systems use only volume-based cost drivers. **Volume-based cost drivers** assume that a product's consumption of overhead resources is directly related to units produced. In other words, they assume that the overhead consumed by products is highly correlated with the number of units produced. Typical volume-based cost drivers used by traditional systems are units of output, direct labour hours and machine hours. These cost drivers are appropriate for measuring the consumption of expenses such as machine energy costs, indirect labour employed in production centres and inspection costs where each item produced is subject to final inspection. For example, machine hours are an appropriate cost driver for energy costs since if volume is increased by 10 per cent, machine hours are likely to increase by 10 per cent, thus causing 10 per cent more energy costs to be consumed.

Volume-based drivers are appropriate in the above circumstances because activities are performed each time a unit of the product or service is produced. In contrast, non-volume-related activities are not performed each time a unit of the product or service is produced. Consider, for example, the activity of setting up a machine. Set-up resources are consumed each time a machine is changed from one product to another. It costs the same to set up a machine for 10 or 5000 items. As more set-ups are done more set-up resources are consumed. The number of set-ups, rather than the number of units produced, is a more appropriate measure of the consumption of the set-up activity. A **non-volume-based cost driver**, such as number of set-ups, is needed for the accurate assignment of the costs of this activity.

Using only volume-based cost drivers to assign non-volume-related overhead costs can result in the reporting of distorted product costs. The extent of distortion depends on what proportion of total overhead costs the non-volume-based overheads represent and the level of product diversity. If a large proportion of an organization's costs are unrelated to volume there is a danger that inaccurate product costs will be reported. Conversely, if non-volume-related overhead costs are only a small proportion of total overhead costs, the distortion of product costs will not be significant. In these circumstances traditional product costing systems are likely to be acceptable.

Product diversity applies when products consume different overhead activities in dissimilar proportions. Differences in product size, product complexity, sizes of batches and set-up times cause product diversity. If all products consume overhead resources in similar proportions product diversity will be low and products will consume non-volume-related activities in the same proportion as volume-related activities. Hence, product cost distortion will not occur with traditional product costing systems. Two conditions are therefore necessary for product cost distortion:

- non-volume-related overhead costs are a large proportion of total overhead costs; and
- product diversity applies.

Where these two conditions exist, traditional product costing systems can result in the overcosting of high-volume products and undercosting of low-volume products. Consider the information presented in Example 8.1. The reported product costs and profits for the two products are as follows:

	Traditional system		ABC system	
	Product HV (£)	Product LV (£)	Product HV (£)	Product LV (£)
Direct costs	310 000	40 000	310 000	40 000
Overheads allocated[a]	300 000 (30%)	50 000 (5%)	150 000 (15%)	150 000 (15%)
Reported profits/(losses)	(10 000)	60 000	140 000	(40 000)
Sales revenues	600 000	150 000	600 000	150 000

Note

[a]Allocation of £1 million overheads using direct labour hours as the allocation base for the traditional system and number of batches processed as the cost driver for the ABC system.

Because product HV is a high-volume product that consumes 30 per cent of the direct labour hours whereas product LV, the low-volume product, consumes only 5 per cent, the traditional system that uses direct labour hours as the allocation base allocates six times more overheads to product HV. However, ABC systems recognize that overheads are caused by other factors, besides volume. In our example, all of the overheads are assumed to be volume unrelated. They are caused by the number of batches processed and the ABC system establishes a cause-and-effect allocation relationship by using the number of batches processed as the cost driver. Both products require 15 per cent of the total number of batches so they are allocated with an equal amount of overheads.

It is apparent from the consumption ratios of the two products that the traditional system based on direct labour hours will overcost high-volume products and undercost low-volume products. **Consumption ratios** represent the proportion of each activity consumed by a product. The consumption ratios if direct labour hours are used as the cost driver are 0.30 for product HV and 0.05 for product LV so that six times more overheads will be assigned to product HV. When the number of batches processed are used as the cost driver the consumption ratios are 0.15 for each product and an equal amount of overhead will be assigned to each product. Distorted product costs are reported with the traditional costing system that uses the volume-based cost driver because the two conditions specified above apply:

1 non-volume related overheads are a large proportion of total overheads, being 100 per cent in our example;

2 product diversity exists because the product consumption ratios for the two identified cost drivers are significantly different.

Our illustration shows that if the consumption ratios for batches processed had been the same as the ratios for direct labour, the traditional and ABC systems would report identical product costs.

With the traditional costing system, misleading information is reported. A small loss is reported for product HV and if it were discontinued the costing system mistakenly gives the impression that overheads will decline in the longer term by £300 000. In contrast, the ABC system allocates overheads on a cause-and-effect basis and more accurately measures the relatively high level of overhead resources consumed by product LV. The message from the profitability analysis is the opposite from the traditional system; that is, product HV is profitable and product LV is unprofitable. If product LV is discontinued, and assuming that the cost driver is the cause of all the overheads then a decision to discontinue product LV should result in the reduction in resource spending on overheads by £150 000.

EXAMPLE 8.1

Assume that the Balearic company has only one overhead cost centre or cost pool. It currently operates a traditional costing system using direct labour hours to allocate overheads to products. The company produces several products, two of which are products HV and LV. Product HV is made in high volumes whereas product LV is made in low volumes. Product HV consumes 30 per cent of the direct labour hours and product LV consumes only 5 per cent. Because of the high-volume production product HV can be made in large production batches but the irregular and low level of demand for product LV requires it to be made in small batches. A detailed investigation indicates that the number of batches processed causes the demand for overhead resources. The traditional system is therefore replaced with an ABC system using the number of batches processed as the cost driver. You ascertain that each product accounts for 15 per cent of the batches processed during the period and the overheads assigned to the cost centre that fluctuate in the long term according to the demand for them amount to £1 million. The direct costs and sales revenues assigned to the products are as follows:

	Product HV (£)	Product LV (£)
Direct costs	310 000	40 000
Sales revenues	600 000	150 000

Show the product profitability analysis for products HV and LV using the traditional and ABC systems.

Example 8.1 is very simplistic. It is assumed that the organization has established only a single cost centre or cost pool, when in reality many will be established with a traditional system, and even more with an ABC system. Furthermore, the data have been deliberately biased to show the superiority of ABC. The aim of the illustration has been to highlight the potential cost of errors that can occur when information extracted from simplistic and inaccurate cost systems is used for decision-making.

AN ILLUSTRATION OF THE TWO-STAGE ALLOCATION PROCESS FOR ABC

Earlier in this chapter Figure 8.1 was used to contrast the general features of ABC systems with traditional costing systems. It was pointed out that ABC systems differ from traditional systems by having a greater number of cost centres in the first stage, and a greater number, and variety, of cost drivers/allocation bases in the second stage of the two-stage allocation process. We will now look at ABC systems in more detail.

You will see from Figure 8.1 that another major distinguishing feature of ABC is that overheads are assigned to each major activity, rather than departments, which normally represent cost centres with traditional systems. When costs are accumulated by activities they are known as **activity cost centres**. Production process activities include machine products and assemble products. Thus within the production process, activity cost centres may be identical to the cost centres used by traditional cost systems. In contrast, support department cost centres are established for traditional systems, whereas these centres are often decomposed into many different activity centres with an ABC system.

We shall now use the data presented in Example 7.1 (the Enterprise Company) from the previous chapter to illustrate ABC in more detail. This example was used to compute the product costs shown in Exhibit 7.2 for a traditional costing system. To refresh your memory you should now refer back to Example 7.1 in the previous chapter and also read pages 162–67 relating to steps 1–4 of the two-stage allocation process.

You will see from Exhibit 7.2 that in step 1 total overheads of £11 700 000 are assigned to production and cost centres. Row 1 shows that costs are assigned as follows:

	£
Machine centre X	2 970 000
Machine centre Y	2 690 000
Assembly	2 480 000
Materials procurement	1 760 000
General factory support	1 800 000
	11 700 000

ABC systems have a greater number of cost centres, but to keep things simple we shall assume that the three production centres (i.e. the two machining centres and the assembly cost centre) established for the traditional costing system have also been identified as activity cost centres with the ABC system. Therefore the production activity cost centres are identical to the cost centres used by traditional cost systems. However, we shall assume that three activity centres have been established for each of the two support functions. For materials procurement the following activity centres have been established:

Activity	£	Activity cost driver
Purchasing materials	960 000	Number of purchase orders
Receiving materials	600 000	Number of material receipts
Disburse materials	200 000	Number of production runs
	1 760 000	

You can see that the total costs assigned to the purchase, receiving and disburse materials activities total £1 760 000, the same as the total allocated to the materials procurement cost centre by the traditional costing system. The process of allocating the costs to the three activity cost centres is the same as that used to allocate the costs of £1 760 000 to the materials procurement cost centre with the traditional costing system. To simplify the presentation these cost assignments are not shown. To emphasize the point that ABC systems use cause-and-effect second-stage allocations, the term cost driver tends to be used instead of allocation base. Cost drivers should be significant determinants of the cost of activities. For example, it is assumed for the Enterprise Company that the cost of processing purchase orders is determined by the number of purchase orders that each product generates, so the number of purchase orders is used to represent the cost driver for the purchasing materials activity. The number of receipts for receiving materials and the number of production runs for the disbursement of materials have been identified as cost drivers for the receipt of materials and disbursement of materials activities.

For the second support department (i.e. general factory support) used as a cost centre with the traditional costing system we shall assume that the following three activity cost centres have been identified:

Activity	£	Activity cost driver
Production scheduling	1 000 000	Number of production runs
Set up machines	600 000	Number of set-up hours
Quality inspection	200 000	Number of first item inspections
	1 800 000	

You can see that the total costs assigned to the production scheduling, set up machines and quality inspection activities total £1 800 000, the same as the total allocated to the general factory support cost centre with the traditional costing system.

Exhibit 8.1 shows the product cost calculations for the ABC system. You will see from columns 1 and 3 in the upper section of Exhibit 8.1 that the Enterprise Company has established nine activity cost centres and seven different second-stage drivers. Note that the production activity cost centres and the cost drivers that have been identified for the ABC system are the same as those used for the traditional costing system. In column 5 in the first section of Exhibit 8.1 cost driver rates are computed by dividing the activity centre cost (column 2) by the quantity of the cost driver used (column 4).

Activity centre costs are assigned to products by multiplying the cost driver rate by the quantity of the cost driver used by products. These calculations are shown in the second section of Exhibit 8.1 You will see from the first section in Exhibit 8.1 that the costs assigned to the purchasing activity are £960 000 for processing 10 000 purchasing orders resulting in a cost driver rate of £96 per purchasing order. The second section shows that a batch of 100 units of product A, and 200 units of product B, each require one purchased component and thus one purchase order. Therefore purchase order costs of £96 are allocated to each batch. Now look at the production scheduling row in the upper section of Exhibit 8.1. You will see that £1 000 000 has been assigned to this activity for 2000 production runs resulting in a cost driver rate of £500 per production run. The second section shows that for a batch of 100 units of product A five production runs are required whereas a batch of 200 units of product B requires one production run. Therefore production scheduling activity costs of £2500 (5 × £500) are allocated to a batch of product A and £500 to a batch of product B. The same approach is used to allocate the costs of the remaining activities shown in Exhibit 8.1. You should now work through Exhibit 8.1 and study the product cost calculations.

The costs assigned to products using each costing system are as follows:

	Traditional costing system £	ABC system £
Product A	166.75	205.88
Product B	333.50	301.03

Note that for the traditional system the calculation of the above product costs is shown on page 166 of the previous chapter and the product costs for the ABC system have been derived from Exhibit 8.1. Compared with the ABC system the traditional system undercosts product A and overcosts product B. By reallocating the service centre costs to the production centres and allocating the costs to products on the basis of either machine hours or direct labour hours the traditional system incorrectly assumes that these allocation bases are the cause of the costs of the support activities. Compared with product A, product B consumes twice as many machine and direct labour hours per unit of output. Therefore, relative to product A, the traditional costing system allocates twice the amount of support costs to product B.

EXHIBIT 8.1

An illustration of cost assignment with an ABC system

(1) Activity	(2) Activity cost £	(3) Activity cost driver	(4) Quantity of activity cost driver	(5) Activity cost driver rate (Col. 2/Col.4)
Production activities:				
Machining: activity centre A	2 970 000	Number of machine hours	2 000 000 machine hours	£1.485 per hour
Machining: activity centre B	2 690 000	Number of machine hours	1 000 000 machine hours	£2.69 per hour
Assembly	2 480 000	Number of direct labour hours	2 000 000 direct lab. hours	£1.24 per hour
	8 140 000			
Materials procurement activities:				
Purchasing components/materials	960 000	Number of purchase orders	10 000 purchase orders	£96 per order
Receiving components/materials	600 000	Number of material receipts	5 000 receipts	£120 per receipt
Disburse materials/components	200 000	Number of production runs	2 000 production runs	£100 per production run
	1 760 000			
General factory support activities:				
Production scheduling	1 000 000	Number of production runs	2 000 production runs	£500 per production run
Set up machines	600 000	Number of set-up hours	12 000 set-up hours	£50 per set-up hour
Quality inspection	200 000	Number of first item inspections	1 000 inspections	£200 per inspection
	1 800 000			
Total cost of all manufacturing activities	11 700 000			

Computation of product costs

(1) Activity	(2) Activity cost driver rate (derived from Col. 5 above)	(3) Quantity of cost driver used by 100 units of product A	(4) Quantity of cost driver used by 200 units of product B	(5) Activity cost assigned to product A (Col. 2 × Col. 3)	(6) Activity cost assigned to product B (Col. 2 × Col. 4)
Machining: activity centre A	£1.485 per hour	500 hours	2 000 hours	742.50	2 970.00
Machining: activity centre B	£2.69 per hour	1 000 hours	4 000 hours	2 690.00	10 760.00
Assembly	£1.24 per hour	1 000 hours	4 000 hours	1 240.00	4 960.00
Purchasing components	£96 per order	1 component	1 component	96.00	96.00
Receiving components	£120 per receipt	1 component	1 component	120.00	120.00
Disburse materials	£100 per production run	5 production runs[a]	1 production run	500.00	100.00
Production scheduling	£500 per production run	5 production runs[a]	1 production run	2 500.00	500.00
Set up machines	£50 per set-up hour	50 set-up hours	10 set-up hours	2 500.00	500.00
Quality inspection	£200 per inspection	1 inspection	1 inspection	200.00	200.00
Total overhead cost				10 588.50	20 206.00
Units produced				100 units	200 units
Overhead cost *per unit*				£105.88	£101.03
Direct costs *per unit* as specified in Chapter 7 (p.166)				100.00	200.00
Total cost *per unit* of output				205.88	301.03

Note
[a] Five production runs are required to machine several unique components before they can be assembled into a final product.

In contrast, ABC systems create separate cost centres for each major support activity and allocate costs to products using cost drivers that are the significant determinants of the cost of the activities. The ABC system recognizes that a batch of both products consume the same quantity of purchasing, receiving and inspection activities and, for these activities, allocates the same costs to both products. Because product B is manufactured in batches of 200 units, and product A in batches of 100 units, the cost per unit of output for product B is half the amount of product A for these activities. Product A also has five unique machined components, whereas product B has only one, resulting in a batch of product A requiring five production runs whereas a batch of product B only requires one. Therefore, relative to product B, the ABC system assigns five times more costs to product A for the production scheduling and disbursement of materials activities (see columns 5 and 6 in the lower part of Exhibit 8.1). Because product A is a more complex product it requires relatively more support activity resources and the cost of this complexity is captured by the ABC system.

DESIGNING ABC SYSTEMS

The discussion so far has provided a broad overview of ABC. We shall now examine ABC in more detail by looking at the design of ABC systems. Four steps are involved. They are:

1 identifying the major activities that take place in an organization;
2 assigning costs to cost pools/cost centres for each activity;
3 determining the cost driver for each major activity;
4 assigning the cost of activities to products according to the product's demand for activities.

The first two steps relate to the first stage, and the final two steps to the second stage, of the two-stage allocation process shown in Figure 8.1. Let us now consider each of these stages in more detail.

Step 1: Identifying activities

Activities are composed of the aggregation of units of work or tasks and are described by verbs associated with tasks. For example, purchasing of materials might be identified as a separate activity. This activity consists of the aggregation of many different tasks, such as receiving a purchase request, identifying suppliers, preparing purchase orders, mailing purchase orders and performing follow-ups.

The activities chosen should be at a reasonable level of aggregation based on costs versus benefits criteria. For example, rather than classifying purchasing of materials as an activity, each of its constituent tasks could be classified as separate activities. However, this level of decomposition would involve the collection of a vast amount of data and is likely to be too costly for product costing purposes. Alternatively, the purchasing activity might be merged with the materials receiving, storage and issuing activities to form a single materials procurement and handling activity. This is likely to represent too high a level of aggregation because a single cost driver is unlikely to provide a satisfactory determinant of the cost of the activity. For example, selecting the number of purchase orders as a cost driver may provide a good explanation of purchasing costs but may be entirely inappropriate for explaining costs relating to receiving and issuing. Therefore, instead of establishing materials procurement and handling as a single activity it may be preferable to decompose it into three separate activities; namely purchasing, receiving and issuing activities, and to establish separate cost drivers for each activity.

Recent studies suggest that between 20 and 30 activity centres tend to be the norm. The final choice of activities must be a matter of judgement but it is likely to be influenced by factors such as the total cost of the activity centre (it must be of significance to justify separate treatment) and the ability of a single driver to provide a satisfactory determinant of the cost of the activity. Where the latter is not possible further decomposition of the activity will be necessary.

Step 2: Assigning costs to activity cost centres

After the activities have been identified the cost of resources consumed over a specified period must be assigned to each activity. The aim is to determine how much the organization is spending on each of its activities. Many of the resources will be directly attributable to specific activity centres but others (such as labour and lighting and heating costs) may be indirect and jointly shared by several activities. These costs should be assigned to activities on the basis of cause-and-effect cost drivers, or interviews with staff who can provide reasonable estimates of the resources consumed by different activities. Arbitrary allocations should not be used. The greater the amount of costs traced to activity centres by cost apportionments at this stage the more arbitrary and less reliable will be the product cost information generated by ABC systems. Cause-and-effect cost drivers used at this stage to allocate shared resources to individual activities are called **resource cost drivers**.

Step 3: Selecting appropriate cost drivers for assigning the cost of activities to cost objects

In order to assign the costs attached to each activity cost centre to products, a cost driver must be selected for each activity centre. Cost drivers used at this stage are called **activity cost drivers**. Several factors must be borne in mind when selecting a suitable cost driver. First, it should provide a good explanation of costs in each activity cost centre. Secondly, a cost driver should be easily measurable, the data should be relatively easy to obtain and be identifiable with products.

Activity cost drivers consist of transaction and duration drivers. **Transaction drivers**, such as the number of purchase orders processed, number of customer orders processed, number of inspections performed and the number of set-ups undertaken, all count the number of times an activity is performed. Transaction drivers are the least expensive type of cost driver but they are also likely to be the least accurate because they assume that the same quantity of resources is required every time an activity is performed. However, if the variation in the amount of resources required by individual cost objects is not great, transaction drivers will provide a reasonably accurate measurement of activity resources consumed. If this condition does not apply then duration cost drivers should be used.

Duration drivers represent the amount of time required to perform an activity. Examples of duration drivers include set-up hours and inspection hours. For example, if one product requires a short set-up time and another requires a long time then using set-up hours as the cost driver will more accurately measure activity resource consumption than the transaction driver (number of set-ups) which assumes that an equal amount of activity resources are consumed by both products. Using the number of set-ups will result in the product that requires a long set-up time being undercosted whereas the product that requires a short set-up will be overcosted. This problem can be overcome by using set-up hours as the cost driver, but this will increase the measurement costs.

Step 4: Assigning the cost of the activities to products

The final stage involves applying the cost driver rates to products. Therefore the cost driver must be measurable in a way that enables it to be identified with individual products. Thus, if set-up hours are selected as a cost driver, there must be a mechanism for

REAL WORLD VIEWS 8.1

ABC at DHL

DHL, part of the Deutsche Post World Net (DPWN) group, is a global leader in the air express industry. The DPWN group posted turnover of €63 billion in 2007, employed more than 500 000 people and operated in 220 countries and territories.

Despite having what might seem like a small number of standardized services (e.g., Same Day, Time Definite and Day Definite), DHL realized back in 1988 that increasing competition and removal of border controls in the European Union could affect its business. In 1988, DHL implemented activity-based costing (ABC) throughout the organization. It used a spreadsheet-based system to calculate product costs. Initial benefits were gained from the system in the form of supporting pricing policy. Over time, the organization increased its package and mail business. However, the ABC system proved inadequate when the business changed. Between 1994 and 1997 an improved ABC model was deployed in Europe, but this still failed to meet the requirements of a business dealing with 5 million shipments of varying sizes to 200 countries on a daily basis. The deployment of the model in Europe did reveal that differing customer profiles and behaviours had an impact on cost, but not all these drivers could be consistently identified. Thus, the drivers that could be measured contributed to a further revision of the ABC model. From this, DHL was able to launch a strategic customer review initiative, that identified problematic customer interfaces contributing to increasing costs. The company also defined a customer negotiation strategy and customer profitability indicators, both of which became cornerstones of the business. Thus from its

ABC system, DHL not only developed a reliable costing system, but also a set of tools that can support the pricing of large global tenders.

Discussion points

1 Do you think it is easy to identify the cost drivers of a business?
2 Would it be beneficial for a management accountant to have an extensive knowledge of business operations if he or she were to be involved in implementing an ABC system? Why or why not?

COURTESY OF DEUTSCHE POST AG

References:

1 Bellis-Jones Hill Group, customer case: 'DHL – customer profitability in action' (www.bellisjoneshill.com).
2 DHL *Annual Report* 2007 (available at www.dhl.com).

measuring the set-up hours consumed by each product. Alternatively, if the number of set-ups is selected as the cost driver, measurements by products are not required since all products that require a set-up are charged with a constant set-up cost. The ease and cost of obtaining data on cost driver consumption by products is therefore a factor that must be considered during the third stage when an appropriate cost driver is being selected.

ACTIVITY HIERARCHIES

Manufacturing activities can be classified along a cost hierarchy dimension consisting of:

1 unit-level activities;
2 batch-level activities;
3 product sustaining activities;
4 facility sustaining activities.

Unit-level activities (also known as volume-related activities) are performed each time a unit of the product or service is produced. Expenses in this category include direct labour, direct materials, energy costs and expenses that are consumed in proportion to machine processing time (such as maintenance). Unit-level activities consume resources in proportion to the number of units of production and sales volume. For example, if a firm produces 10 per cent more units it will consume 10 per cent more labour cost, 10 per cent more machine hours and 10 per cent more energy costs. Typical cost drivers for unit-level activities include labour hours, machine hours and the quantity of materials processed. These cost drivers are also used by traditional costing systems. Traditional systems are therefore also appropriate for assigning the costs of unit-level activities to cost objects.

Batch-related activities, such as setting up a machine or processing a purchase order, are performed each time a batch of goods is produced. The cost of batch-related activities varies with the number of batches made, but is common (or fixed) for all units within the batch. For example, set-up resources are consumed when a machine is changed from one product to another. As more batches are produced, more set-up resources are consumed. It costs the same to set up a machine for 10 or 5000 items. Thus the demands for the set-up resources are independent of the number of units produced after completing the set-up. Similarly, purchasing resources are consumed each time a purchasing order is processed, but the resources consumed are independent of the number of units included in the purchase order. Other examples of batch-related costs include resources devoted to production scheduling, first-item inspection and materials movement. Traditional costing systems treat batch-related expenses as fixed costs, whereas ABC systems assume that batch-related expenses vary with the number of batches processed.

Product sustaining activities or **service sustaining activities** are performed to enable the production and sale of individual products (or services). Examples of product sustaining activities provided by Kaplan and Cooper (1998) include maintaining and updating product specifications and the technical support provided for individual products and services. Other examples are the resources to prepare and implement engineering change notices (ECNs), to design processes and test routines for individual products, and to perform product enhancements. The costs of product sustaining activities are incurred irrespective of the number of units of output or the number of batches processed and their expenses will tend to increase as the number of products manufactured is increased. ABC uses product-level bases such as number of active part numbers and number of ECNs to assign these costs to products. Kaplan and Cooper (1998) have extended their ideas to situations where customers are the cost objects with the equivalent term for product sustaining being **customer sustaining activities**. Customer market research and support for an individual customer, or groups of customers if they represent the cost object, are examples of customer sustaining activities.

The final activity category is **facility sustaining** (or **business sustaining**) **activities**. They are performed to support the facility's general manufacturing process and include general administrative staff, plant management and property costs. They are incurred to support the organization as a whole and are common and joint to all products manufactured in the plant. There would have to be a dramatic change in activity, resulting in an expansion or contraction in the size of the plant, for facility sustaining costs to change. Such events are most unlikely in most organizations. Therefore the ABC literature advocates that these costs should not be assigned to products since they are unavoidable and irrelevant for most decisions. Instead, they are regarded as common costs to *all* products made in the plant and deducted as a lump sum from the total of the operating margins from *all* products.

COST VERSUS BENEFIT CONSIDERATIONS

In the previous chapter it was pointed out that the design of a cost system should be based on cost versus benefit considerations. A sophisticated ABC system should generate the most accurate product costs. However, the cost of implementing and operating an ABC system is significantly more expensive than operating a direct costing or a traditional costing system. In particular, the training and software requirements may prohibit its adoption by small organizations. The partial costs reported by direct costing systems, and the distorted costs reported by traditional systems, may result in significant mistakes in decisions (such as selling unprofitable products or dropping profitable products) arising from the use of this information. If the cost of errors arising from using partial or distorted information generated from using these systems exceeds the additional costs of implementing and operating an ABC system then an ABC system ought to be implemented.

The optimal costing system is different for different organizations. A simplistic traditional costing system may report reasonably accurate product costs in organizations that have the following characteristics:

1 low levels of competition;
2 non-volume-related indirect costs that are a low proportion of total indirect costs;
3 a fairly standardized product range all consuming organizational resources in similar proportions (i.e. low product diversity).

In contrast, a sophisticated ABC system may be optimal for organizations having the following characteristics:

1 intensive competition;
2 non-volume-related indirect costs that are a high proportion of total indirect costs;
3 a diverse range of products, all consuming organizational resources in significantly different proportions (i.e. high product diversity).

ABC IN SERVICE ORGANIZATIONS

Kaplan and Cooper (1998) suggest that service companies are ideal candidates for ABC, even more than manufacturing companies. Their justification for this statement is that most of the costs in service organizations are indirect. In contrast, manufacturing companies can trace important components (such as direct materials and direct labour) of costs to individual products. Therefore indirect costs are likely to be a much smaller proportion of total costs.

A UK survey by Drury and Tayles (2005) suggests that service organizations are more likely to implement ABC systems. They reported that 51 per cent of the financial and service organizations surveyed, compared with 15 per cent of manufacturing organizations, had implemented ABC. Kaplan and Cooper (1998) illustrate how ABC was applied in The Co-operative Bank, a medium sized UK bank. ABC was used for product and customer profitability analysis. The following are some of the activities and cost drivers that were identified:

	Activity	Cost driver
Provide ATM services		Number of ATM transactions
Clear debit items		Number of debits processed
Clear credit items		Number of credits processed
Issue chequebooks		Number of chequebooks issued
Computer processing		Number of computer transactions
Prepare statements of account transactions		Number of statements issued
Administer mortgages		Number of mortgages maintained

EXHIBIT 8.2

Surveys of company practice

Surveys of UK companies indicate that approximately 15 per cent of the surveyed companies had implemented ABC (Drury and Tayles, 2005; Innes *et al.*, 2000). Similar adoption rates of 10 per cent were found in Ireland (Clarke, 1992) and 14 per cent in Canada (Armitage and Nicholson, 1993). Reported usage rates for mainland Europe were 19 per cent in Belgium (Bruggerman *et al.*,, 1996) and 6 per cent in Finland in 1992, 11 per cent in 1993 and 24 per cent in 1995 (Virtanen *et al.*, 1996). Low usage rates have been reported in Denmark (Israelsen *et al.*, 1996), Sweden (Ask *et al.*, 1996) and Germany (Scherrer, 1996). Activity-based techniques do not appear to have been adopted in Greece (Ballas and Venieris, 1996), Italy (Barbato *et al.*, 1996) or Spain (Saez-Torrecilla *et al.*, 1996).

The UK study by Drury and Tayles indicated that company size and business sector had a significant impact on ABC adoption rates. The adoption rates were 45 per cent for the largest organizations (annual sales in excess of £300 million) and 51 per cent for financial and service organizations. Although the ABC adopters used significantly more cost pools and cost drivers than the non-adopters most adopters used fewer cost pools and drivers compared with what is recommended in the literature. Approximately 50 per cent of the ABC adopters used less than 50 cost centres and less than ten separate types of cost driver rates. Other studies have examined the applications of ABC. Innes and Mitchell (1995b) found that cost reduction was the most widely used application. Other widely used applications included product/service pricing, cost modelling and performance measurement/improvement.

Friedman and Lynne's (1995; 1999) case study research of 12 UK companies cited top management support as a significant factor influencing the success or failure of ABC systems. Implementation problems identified included the amount of work in setting up the system and data collection, difficulties in identifying activities and selecting cost drivers, lack of resources and inadequate computer software. The benefits reported included more accurate cost information for product pricing, more accurate profitability analysis, improved cost control and a better understanding of cost causation.

Activity costs were allocated to the different savings and loans products based on their demand for the activities using the cost drivers as a measure of resource consumption. Some expenses, such as finance and human resource management, were not assigned to products because they were considered to be for the benefit of the organization as a whole and not attributable to individual products. These business sustaining costs represented approximately 15 per cent of total operating expenses. Profitability analysis was extended to customer segments within product groups. The study revealed that approximately half of the current accounts, particularly those with low balances and high transactions were unprofitable. By identifying the profitable customer segments the marketing function was able to direct its effort to attracting more new customers, and enhancing relationships with those existing customers whose behaviour would be profitable to the bank.

ABC COST MANAGEMENT APPLICATIONS

Our aim in this chapter has been to look at how ABC can be used to provide information for decision-making by more accurately assigning costs to cost objects, such as products, customers and locations. In addition, ABC can be used for a range of cost management applications. They include cost reduction, activity-based budgeting, performance measurement, benchmarking of activities and business process re-engineering.

The decision to implement ABC should not, therefore, be based only on its ability to produce more accurate and relevant decision-making information. Indeed, surveys by Innes and Mitchell (1995a) and Innes *et al.* (2000) on ABC applications suggest that the cost management applications tend to outweigh the product costing applications that were central to ABC's initial development. We shall examine ABC applications to cost management in Chapter 14.

SUMMARY

The following items relate to the learning objectives listed at the beginning of the chapter.

● **Describe the differences between activity-based and traditional costing systems**. The major differences relate to the two-stage allocation process. In the first stage, traditional systems allocate indirect costs to cost centres (normally departments) whereas activity-based systems allocate indirect costs to cost centres based on activities rather than departments. Since there are many more activities than departments a distinguishing feature is that activity-based systems will have a greater number of cost centres in the first stage of the allocation process. In the second stage, traditional systems use a limited number of different types of second-stage volume-based allocation bases (cost drivers) whereas activity-based systems use many different types of volume-based and non-volume-based cause-and-effect second-stage drivers.

● **Explain why traditional costing systems can provide misleading information for decision-making**. Traditional systems often tend to rely on arbitrary allocations of indirect costs. In particular, they rely extensively on volume-based allocations. Many indirect costs are not volume-based but, if volume-based allocation bases are used, high-volume products are likely to be assigned with a greater proportion of indirect costs than they have consumed whereas low-volume products will be assigned a lower proportion. In these circumstances traditional systems will overcost high-volume products and undercost low-volume products. In contrast, ABC systems recognize that many indirect costs vary in proportion to changes other than production volume. By identifying the cost drivers that cause the costs to change and assigning costs to cost objects on the basis of cost driver usage, costs can be more accurately traced. It is claimed that this cause-and-effect relationship provides a superior way of determining relevant costs.

● **Compute product costs using an activity-based costing system.** The computation of product costs was illustrated in Exhibit 8.1 using data derived from Example 7.1 in the previous chapter.

● **Identify and explain each of the four stages involved in designing ABC systems.** The design of ABC systems involves the following four stages: (a) identify the major activities that take place in the organization; (b) create a cost centre/cost pool for each activity; (c) determine the cost driver for each major activity; and (d) trace the cost of activities to the product according to a product's demand (using cost drivers as a measure of demand) for activities.

● **Describe the ABC cost hierarchy.** ABC systems classify activities along a cost hierarchy consisting of unit-level, batch-level, product sustaining and facility sustaining activities. Unit-level activities are performed each time a unit of the product or service is produced. Examples include direct labour and energy costs. Batch-level activities are performed each time a batch is produced. Examples include setting up a machine or processing a purchase order. Product sustaining activities are performed to enable the production and sale of individual products. Examples include the technical support provided for individual products and the resources required performing product enhancements. Facility sustaining activities are performed to support the facility's general manufacturing process. They include general administrative staff and property support costs.

KEY TERMS AND CONCEPTS

activities (p. 180)
activity cost centres (p. 184)
activity cost drivers (p. 189)
batch-related activities (p. 191)
business sustaining activities (p. 192)
consumption ratios (p. 183)
cost drivers (p. 180)
customer sustaining activities (p. 191)
duration drivers (p. 189)

facility sustaining activities (p. 192)
non-volume-based cost drivers (p. 182)
product sustaining activities (p. 191)
resource cost drivers (p. 189)
service sustaining activities (p. 191)
transaction drivers (p. 189)
unit-level activities (p. 191)
volume-based cost drivers (p. 182)

ASSESSMENT MATERIAL

The review questions are short questions that enable you to assess your understanding of the main topics included in the chapter. The page numbers in parentheses provide you with the page numbers to refer to if you cannot answer a specific question.

The review problems are more complex and require you to relate and apply the content to various business problems. Solutions to review problems are provided in a separate section at the end of the book. Additional review problems can be accessed by lecturers and students on the website (www.drury-online.com). Solutions to these problems are provided for lecturers in the *Instructors' Manual*. This is available on the lecturers' password-protected section of the website.

The website also includes over 30 case study problems. A list of these cases is provided on pages 389–392.

REVIEW QUESTIONS

8.1 What are the fundamental differences between a traditional and an ABC system? *(pp. 180–81)*

8.2 Define activities and cost drivers. *(p. 180)*

8.3 What factors led to the emergence of ABC systems? *(p. 179)*

8.4 Distinguish between volume-based and non-volume-based cost drivers. *(pp. 181–82)*

8.5 Describe the circumstances when traditional costing systems are likely to report distorted costs. *(p. 182)*

8.6 Explain how low-volume products can be undercosted and high-volume products overcosted when traditional costing systems are used. *(pp. 182–83)*

8.7 What is meant by 'product diversity' and why is it important for product costing? *(p.182)*

8.8 Describe each of the four stages involved in designing ABC systems. *(pp. 188–90)*

8.9 Distinguish between resource cost drivers and activity cost drivers. *(p. 189)*

8.10 Distinguish between transaction and duration cost drivers. *(p. 189)*

8.11 Describe the ABC manufacturing cost hierarchy. *(pp. 191–192)*

8.12 Explain the circumstances when ABC is likely to be preferred to traditional costing systems. *(p. 192)*

8.13 Provide examples of how ABC can be used in service organizations. *(pp. 192–194)*

REVIEW PROBLEMS

8.14 CJD Ltd manufactures plastic components for the car industry. The following budgeted information is available for three of its key plastic components:

	W £ per unit	X £ per unit	Y £ per unit
Selling price	200	183	175
Direct material	50	40	35
Direct labour	30	35	30
Units produced and sold	10 000	15 000	18 000

The total number of activities for each of the three products for the period is as follows:

Number of purchase requisitions	1200	1800	2000
Number of set-ups	240	260	300

Overhead costs have been analyzed as follows:

Receiving/inspecting quality assurance	£1 400 000
Production scheduling/machine set-up	£1 200 000

Calculate the budgeted profit per unit for each of the three products using activity-based budgeting.

(4 marks)

8.15 S Ltd manufactures components for the aircraft industry. The following annual information regarding three of its key customers is available:

	W	X	Y
Gross margin	£1 100 000	£1 750 000	£1 200 000
General administration costs	£40 000	£80 000	£30 000
Units sold	1 750	2 000	1 500
Orders placed	1 000	1 000	1 500
Sales visits	110	100	170
Invoices raised	900	1 200	1 500

The company uses an activity-based costing system and the analysis of customer-related costs is as follows:

Sales visits	£500 per visit
Order processing	£100 per order placed
Despatch costs	£100 per order placed
Billing and collections	£175 per invoice raised

Using customer profitability analysis, the ranking of the customers would be:

	W	X	Y
A	1st	2nd	3rd
B	1st	3rd	2nd
C	2nd	1st	3rd
D	2nd	3rd	1st
E	3rd	2nd	1st

(4 marks)

8.16 DRP Limited has recently introduced an activity-based costing system. It manufactures three products, details of which are set out below:

	Product D	Product R	Product P
Budgeted annual production (units)	100 000	100 000	50 000
Batch size (units)	100	50	25
Machine set-ups per batch	3	4	6
Purchase orders per batch	2	1	1
Processing time per unit (minutes)	2	3	3

Three cost pools have been identified. Their budgeted costs for the year ending 30 June 2008 are as follows:

Machine set-up costs	£150 000
Purchasing of materials	£70 000
Processing	£80 000

The budgeted machine set-up cost per unit of product R is nearest to

A £0.52   B £0.60   C £6.52   D £26.09

(3 marks)

8.17 *It is now fairly widely accepted that conventional cost accounting distorts management's view of business through unrepresentative overhead allocation and inappropriate product costing.*

This is because the traditional approach usually absorbs overhead costs across products and orders solely on the basis of the direct labour involved in their manufacture. And as direct labour as a proportion of total manufacturing cost continues to fall, this leads to more and more distortion and misrepresentation of the impact of particular products on total overhead costs.

(From an article in the *Financial Times*)

You are required to discuss the above and to suggest what approaches are being adopted by management accountants to overcome such criticism.

(15 marks)

8.18 Large service organizations, such as banks and hospitals, used to be noted for their lack of standard costing systems, and their relatively unsophisticated budgeting and control systems compared with large manufacturing organizations. But this is changing and many large service organizations are now revising their use of management accounting techniques.

Requirements:

(a) Explain which features of large-scale service organizations encourage the application of activity-based approaches to the analysis of cost information.

(6 marks)

(b) Explain which features of service organizations may create problems for the application of activity-based costing.

(4 marks)

(c) Explain the uses for activity-based cost information in service industries.

(4 marks)

(d) Many large service organizations were at one time state-owned, but have been privatized. Examples in some countries include electricity supply and telecommunications. They are often regulated. Similar systems of regulation of prices by an independent authority exist in many countries, and are designed to act as a surrogate for market competition in industries where it is difficult to ensure a genuinely competitive market.

Explain which aspects of cost information and systems in service organizations would particularly interest a regulator, and why these features would be of interest.

(6 marks)
(Total 20 marks)

8.19 Computation of product costs for traditional and ABC systems

The following information provides details of the costs, volume and cost drivers for a particular period in respect of ABC plc, a hypothetical company:

		Product X	Product Y	Product Z	Total
1.	Production and sales (units)	30 000	20 000	8 000	
2.	Raw material usage (units)	5	5	11	
3.	Direct material cost	£25	£20	£11	£1 238 000
4.	Direct labour hours	1⅓	2	1	88 000
5.	Machine hours	1⅓	1	2	76 000
6.	Direct labour cost	£8	£12	£6	
7.	Number of production runs	3	7	20	30
8.	Number of deliveries	9	3	20	32
9.	Number of receipts (2 × 7)[a]	15	35	220	270
10.	Number of production orders	15	10	25	50
11.	Overhead costs:				
	Set-up	30 000			
	Machines	760 000			
	Receiving	435 000			
	Packing	250 000			
	Engineering	373 000			
		£1 848 000			

[a]The company operates a just-in-time inventory policy, and receives each component once per production run.

In the past the company has allocated overheads to products on the basis of direct labour hours.

However, the majority of overheads are more closely related to machine hours than direct labour hours.

The company has recently redesigned its cost system by recovering overheads using two volume-related bases: machine hours and a materials handling overhead rate for recovering overheads of the receiving department. Both the current and the previous cost system reported low profit margins for product X, which is the company's highest-selling product. The management accountant has recently attended a conference on activity-based costing, and the overhead costs for the last period have been analysed by the major activities in order to compute activity-based costs.

From the above information you are required to:

(a) Compute the product costs using a traditional volume-related costing system based on the assumptions that:
  (i) all overheads are recovered on the basis of direct labour hours (i.e. the company's past product costing system);
  (ii) the overheads of the receiving department are recovered by a materials handling overhead rate and the remaining overheads are recovered using a machine hour rate (i.e. the company's current costing system).
(b) Compute product costs using an activity-based costing system.
(c) Briefly explain the differences between the product cost computations in (a) and (b).

8.20 Preparation of conventional costing and ABC profit statements

The following budgeted information relates to Brunti plc for the forthcoming period:

	Products		
	XYI (000)	YZT (000)	ABW (000)
Sales and production (units)	50	40	30
	(£)	(£)	(£)
Selling price (per unit)	45	95	73
Prime cost (per unit)	32	84	65
	Hours	Hours	Hours
Machine department (machine hours per unit)	2	5	4
Assembly department (direct labour hours per unit)	7	3	2

Overheads allocated and apportioned to production departments (including service cost centre costs) were to be recovered in product costs as follows:

Machine department at
£1.20 per machine hour
Assembly department at
£0.825 per direct labour hour

You ascertain that the above overheads could be re-analysed into 'cost pools' as follows:

Cost pool	£000	Cost driver	Quantity for the period
Machining services	357	Machine hours	420 000
Assembly services	318	Direct labour hours	530 000
Set-up costs	26	Set-ups	520
Order processing	156	Customer orders	32 000
Purchasing	84	Suppliers orders	11 200
	941		

You have also been provided with the following estimates for the period:

	Products		
	XYI	YZT	ABW
Number of set-ups	120	200	200
Customer orders	8 000	8 000	16 000
Suppliers' orders	3 000	4 000	4 200

Required:

(a) Prepare and present profit statements using:
  (i) conventional absorption costing;

(5 marks)

  (ii) activity-based costing.

(10 marks)

(b) Comment on why activity-based costing is considered to present a fairer valuation of the product cost per unit.

(5 marks)
(Total 20 marks)

CHAPTER 9
THE BUDGETING PROCESS

LEARNING OBJECTIVES

After studying this chapter you should be able to:

- **explain how budgeting fits into the overall strategic planning and control framework;**
- **identify and describe the six different purposes of budgeting;**
- **identify and describe the various stages in the budget process;**
- **prepare functional and master budgets;**
- **describe the use of computer-based financial models for budgeting;**
- **describe the limitations of incremental budgeting;**
- **describe activity-based budgeting;**
- **describe zero-base budgeting (ZBB);**
- **describe the criticisms relating to traditional budgeting.**

In the previous chapters we have considered how management accounting can assist managers in making decisions. The actions that follow managerial decisions normally involve several aspects of the business, such as the marketing, production, purchasing and finance functions, and it is important that management should coordinate these various interrelated aspects of decision-making. If they fail to do this, there is a danger that managers may individually make decisions that they believe are in the best interests of the organization when, in fact, taken together they are not; for example, the marketing department may introduce a promotional campaign that is designed to increase sales demand to a level beyond that which the production department can handle. The various activities within a company should be coordinated by the preparation of plans of actions for future periods. These detailed plans are usually referred to as budgets. Our objective in this chapter is to focus on the planning process within a business organization and to consider the role of budgeting within this process.

THE STRATEGIC PLANNING, BUDGETING AND CONTROL PROCESS

To help you understand the budgetary process we shall begin by looking at how it fits into an overall general framework of planning and control. The framework outlined in Figure 9.1 provides an overview of an organization's planning and control process. The first stage involves establishing the objectives of the organization within the strategic planning process.

Strategic planning process

Before the budgeting process begins an organization should have prepared a long-term plan (also known as a strategic plan). Strategic planning begins with the specification of objectives towards which future operations should be directed. Johnson and Scholes (2005) identify a hierarchy of objectives – the mission of an organization, corporate objectives and unit objectives.

The mission of an organization describes in very general terms the broad purpose and reason for an organization's existence, the nature of the business(es) it is in and the customers it seeks to serve and satisfy. It is a visionary projection of the central and overriding concepts on which the organization is based. Corporate objectives relate to the organization as a whole. Objectives tend to be more specific, and represent desired states or results to be achieved. They are normally measurable and are expressed in financial terms such as desired profits or sales levels, return on capital employed, rates of growth or market share. Objectives must also be developed for the different parts of an organization. Unit objectives relate to the specific objectives of individual units within the organization, such as a division or one company within a holding company. Corporate objectives are normally set for the organization as a whole and are then translated into unit objectives, which become the targets for the individual units. It is important that senior managers in an organization understand clearly where their company is going, and why and how their own role contributes to the attainment of corporate objectives. The strategic planning process should also specify how the objectives of the organization will be achieved.

Creation of long-term plan

The term strategy is used to describe the courses of action that need to be taken to achieve the objectives set. When management has identified those strategic options that have the greatest potential for achieving the company's objectives, long-term plans should be created to implement the strategies. A long-term plan is a statement of the preliminary targets and activities required by an organization to achieve its strategic plan together with a broad estimate for each year of the resources required and revenues expected. Because long-term planning involves 'looking into the future' for several years ahead (typically at least five years) the plans tend to be uncertain, general in nature, imprecise and subject to change.

Preparation of the annual budget within the context of the long-term plan

Budgeting is concerned with the implementation of the long-term plan for the year ahead. Because of the shorter planning horizon budgets are more precise and detailed. Budgets

REAL WORLD VIEWS 9.1

EasyJet mission statement

'To provide our customers with safe, good value, point-to-point air services. To effect and to offer a consistent and reliable product and fares appealing to leisure and business markets on a range of European routes. To achieve this we will develop our people and establish lasting relationships with our suppliers.'

COURTESY OF EASYJET AIRLINE COMPANY LTD

are a clear indication of what is expected to be achieved during the budget period whereas long-term plans represent the broad directions that top management intend to follow.

The budget is not something that originates 'from nothing' each year – it is developed within the context of ongoing business and is ruled by previous decisions that have been taken within the long-term planning process. When the activities are initially approved for inclusion in the long-term plan, they are based on uncertain estimates that are projected for several years. These proposals must be reviewed and revised in the light of more recent information. This review and revision process frequently takes place as part of the annual budgeting process, and it may result in important decisions being taken on possible activity adjustments within the current budget period. The budgeting process cannot therefore be viewed as being purely concerned with the current year – it must be considered as an integrated part of the long-term planning process.

Monitor actual outcomes and respond to deviations from planned outcomes

The final stages in the strategic planning, budgeting and control process outlined in Figure 9.1 are to compare the actual and the planned outcomes, and to respond to any deviations from the plan. These stages represent the control process of budgeting. Planning and control are closely linked. Planning involves looking ahead to determine the actions required to achieve the objectives of the organization. Control involves looking back to ascertain what actually happened and comparing it with the planned outcomes. Effective control requires that corrective action is taken so that actual outcomes conform to planned outcomes. Alternatively, the plans may require modification if the comparisons indicate that the plans are no longer attainable. The corrective action is indicated by the arrowed lines in Figure 9.1 linking stages 5 and 2 and 5 and 3. These arrowed lines represent feedback loops. They signify that the process is dynamic and stress the interdependencies between the various stages in the process. The feedback loops between the

FIGURE 9.1

Strategic planning, budgeting and control process

stages indicate that the plans should be regularly reviewed, and if they are no longer attainable then alternative courses of action must be considered for achieving the organization's objectives. The loop between stages 5 and 3 also stresses the corrective action that may be taken so that actual outcomes conform to planned outcomes.

A detailed discussion of the control process will be deferred until the next chapter. Let us now consider the short-term budgeting process in more detail.

THE MULTIPLE FUNCTIONS OF BUDGETS

Budgets serve a number of useful purposes. They include:

1 *planning* annual operations;
2 *coordinating* the activities of the various parts of the organization and ensuring that the parts are in harmony with each other;
3 *communicating* plans to the various responsibility centre managers;
4 *motivating* managers to strive to achieve the organizational goals;
5 *controlling* activities;
6 *evaluating* the performance of managers.

Let us now examine each of these six factors.

Planning

The major planning decisions will already have been made as part of the long-term planning process. However, the annual budgeting process leads to the refinement of those plans, since managers must produce detailed plans for the implementation of the long-range plan. Without the annual budgeting process, the pressures of day-to-day operating problems may tempt managers not to plan for future operations. The budgeting process ensures that managers do plan for future operations, and that they consider how conditions in the next year might change and what steps they should take now to respond to these changed conditions. This process encourages managers to anticipate problems before they arise, so that hasty decisions that are made on the spur of the moment, based on expediency rather than reasoned judgement, will be minimized.

Coordination

The budget serves as a vehicle through which the actions of the different parts of an organization can be brought together and reconciled into a common plan. Without any guidance, managers may each make their own decisions, believing that they are working in the best interests of the organization. For example, the purchasing manager may prefer to place large orders so as to obtain large discounts; the production manager will be concerned with avoiding high stock levels; and the accountant will be concerned with the impact of the decision on the cash resources of the business. It is the aim of budgeting to reconcile these differences for the good of the organization as a whole, rather than for the benefit of any individual area. Budgeting therefore compels managers to examine the relationship between their own operations and those of other departments, and, in the process, to identify and resolve conflicts.

Communication

If an organization is to function effectively, there must be definite lines of communication so that all the parts will be kept fully informed of the plans and the policies, and constraints, to which the organization is expected to conform. Everyone in the organization should have a clear understanding of the part they are expected to play in achieving the annual budget. This process will ensure that the appropriate individuals are made accountable for implementing the budget. Through the budget, top management communicates its expectations to lower level management, so that all members of the organization may understand these expectations and can coordinate their activities to attain them. It is not just the budget itself that facilitates communication – much vital information is communicated in the actual act of preparing it.

Motivation

The budget can be a useful device for influencing managerial behaviour and motivating managers to perform in line with the organizational objectives. A budget provides a standard that, under certain circumstances, a manager may be motivated to strive to achieve. However, budgets can also encourage inefficiency and conflict between managers. If individuals have actively participated in preparing the budget, and it is used as a tool to assist managers in managing their departments, it can act as a strong motivational device by providing a challenge. Alternatively, if the budget is dictated from above, and imposes a threat rather than a challenge, it may be resisted and do more harm than good. We shall discuss the dysfunctional motivational consequences of budgets in the next chapter.

Control

A budget assists managers in managing and controlling the activities for which they are responsible. By comparing the actual results with the budgeted amounts for different categories of expenses, managers can ascertain which costs do not conform to the original plan and thus require their attention. This process enables management to operate a system of **management by exception**, which means that a manager's attention and effort can be concentrated on significant deviations from the expected results. By investigating the reasons for the deviations, managers may be able to identify inefficiencies such as the purchase of inferior quality materials. When the reasons for the inefficiencies have been found, appropriate control action should be taken to remedy the situation.

Performance evaluation

A manager's performance is often evaluated by measuring his or her success in meeting the budgets. In some companies bonuses are awarded on the basis of an employee's ability to achieve the targets specified in the periodic budgets, or promotion may be partly dependent upon a manager's budget record. In addition, the manager may wish to evaluate his or her own performance. The budget thus provides a useful means of informing managers of how well they are performing in meeting targets that they have previously helped to set. The use of budgets as a method of performance evaluation also influences human behaviour, and for this reason we shall consider the behavioural aspects of performance evaluation in Chapter 10.

CONFLICTING ROLES OF BUDGETS

Because a single budget system is normally used to serve several purposes there is a danger that they may conflict with each other. For instance the planning and motivation roles may be in conflict with each other. Demanding budgets that may not be achieved may be appropriate to motivate maximum performance, but they are unsuitable for planning purposes. For these a budget should be set based on easier targets that are expected to be met.

There is also a conflict between the planning and performance evaluation roles. For planning purposes budgets are set in advance of the budget period based on an anticipated set of circumstances or environment. Performance evaluation should be based on a comparison of actual performance with an adjusted budget to reflect the circumstances under which managers actually operated. In practice, many firms compare actual performance with the original budget (adjusted to the actual level of activity, i.e. a flexible budget), but if the circumstances envisaged when the original budget was set have changed then there will be a planning and evaluation conflict.

THE BUDGET PERIOD

The conventional approach is that once per year the manager of each budget centre prepares a detailed budget for one year. The budget is divided into either 12 monthly or 13 four-weekly periods for control purposes. The preparation of budgets on an annual basis has been strongly criticized on the grounds that it is too rigid and ties a company to a 12-month commitment, which can be risky because the budget is based on uncertain forecasts.

An alternative approach is for the annual budget to be broken down by months for the first three months, and by quarters for the remaining nine months.The quarterly budgets are then developed on a monthly basis as the year proceeds. For example, during the first quarter, the monthly budgets for the second quarter will be prepared; and during the second quarter, the monthly budgets for the third quarter will be prepared. The quarterly budgets may also be reviewed as the year unfolds. For example, during the first quarter, the budget for the next three quarters may be changed as new information becomes available. A new budget for a fifth quarter will also be prepared. This process is known as continuous or rolling budgeting, and ensures that a 12-month budget is always available by adding a quarter in the future as the quarter just ended is dropped. Contrast this with a budget prepared once per year. As the year goes by, the period for which a budget is available will shorten until the budget for next year is prepared. Rolling budgets also ensure that planning is not something that takes place once a year when the budget is being formulated. Instead, budgeting is a continuous process, and managers are encouraged to constantly look ahead and review future plans. Furthermore, it is likely that actual performance will be compared with a more realistic target, because budgets are being constantly reviewed and updated. The main disadvantage of a rolling budget is that it can create uncertainty for managers because the budget is constantly being changed.

Irrespective of whether the budget is prepared on an annual or a continuous basis, monthly or four-weekly budgets are normally used for *control* purposes.

ADMINISTRATION OF THE BUDGETING PROCESS

It is important that suitable administration procedures be introduced to ensure that the budget process works effectively. In practice, the procedures should be tailor-made to the requirements of the organization, but as a general rule a firm should ensure that procedures are established for approving the budgets and that the appropriate staff support is available for assisting managers in preparing their budgets.

The budget committee

The budget committee should consist of high-level executives who represent the major segments of the business. Its major task is to ensure that budgets are realistically established and that they are coordinated satisfactorily. The normal procedure is for the functional heads to present their budget to the committee for approval. If the budget does not reflect a reasonable level of performance, it will not be approved and the functional head will be required to adjust the budget and resubmit it for approval. It is important that the person whose performance is being measured should agree that the revised budget can be achieved; otherwise, if it is considered to be impossible to achieve, it will not act as a motivational device. If budget revisions are made, the budgetees should at least feel that they were given a fair hearing by the committee. We shall discuss budget negotiation in more detail later in this chapter.

The budget committee should appoint a budget officer, who will normally be the accountant. The role of the budget officer is to coordinate the individual budgets into a

REAL WORLD VIEWS 9.2

Budgeting in the movie industry

Preparing a budget, and sticking to it, is quite important in the movie industry. While the large sums of money received by movie stars often make for interesting reading, there are many more costs to be considered when making a movie. Production staff, sets and location costs, to name but a few, are often complicated by multiple locations, currencies and languages. With movies like *Spiderman 3* (released 2007) having a budget of $258 million, cost control and tracking are important.

For the past decade, MovieMagic budgeting software by Entertainment Partners has been the accepted standard budgeting software in the movie industry. The software is used by producers, production managers and production accountants who want easily and accurately to create documentary, film, music video and television budgets. MovieMagic allows the user to create multiple budget scenarios for a single project and can incorporate subgroups such as locations and personnel. It also comes pre-loaded with the most common expense categories in the industry and 25 standard forms covering movies, television and videos. These can ease the budget preparation process. It also integrates closely with other software used in the movie industry, such as production scheduling software.

Movie budgets tend to increase from the initial concept once production begins. For example, the 1997 movie *Titanic* was 100 per cent over budget. Even with large earnings, the return on such an investment diminishes with such poor budgeting and cost control. Perhaps the use of software like MovieMagic could help avoid such overruns.

Discussion points

1 Do you think costs to make a movie are more uncontrollable than in other businesses?
2 Can you think of an example of differing cost scenarios that might form part of a movie budget in software like MovieMagic?

References

1 http://www.the-numbers.com/movies/records/allbudgets.php
2 http://www.entertainmentpartners.com
3 Studios still fighting battle of the bulging budget, *Los Angeles Times*, 13 January 1998 (http://articles.latimes.com/1998/jan/13/business/fi-7705).

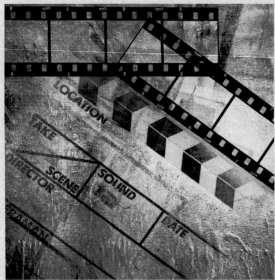

© ALEXANDER VASILYEV/DEAMSTIME.COM

budget for the whole organization, so that the budget committee and budgetees can see the impact of an individual budget on the organization as a whole.

Accounting staff

The accounting staff will normally assist managers in the preparation of their budgets; they will, for example, circulate and advise on the instructions about budget preparation, provide past information that may be useful for preparing the present budget, and ensure that managers submit their budgets on time. The accounting staff do not determine the content of the various budgets, but they do provide a valuable advisory service for line managers.

Budget manual

A budget manual should be prepared by the accountant. It will describe the objectives and procedures involved in the budgeting process and will provide a useful reference source for managers responsible for budget preparation. In addition, the manual may include a timetable specifying the order in which the budgets should be prepared and the dates when they should be presented to the budget committee. The manual should be circulated to all individuals who are responsible for preparing budgets.

STAGES IN THE BUDGETING PROCESS

The important stages are as follows:

1 communicating details of budget policy and guidelines to those people responsible for the preparation of budgets;
2 determining the factor that restricts output;
3 preparation of the sales budget;
4 initial preparation of various budgets;
5 negotiation of budgets with superiors;
6 coordination and review of budgets;
7 final acceptance of budgets;
8 ongoing review of budgets.

Let us now consider each of these stages in more detail.

Communicating details of the budget policy

Many decisions affecting the budget year will have been taken previously as part of the long-term planning process. The long-range plan is therefore the starting point for the preparation of the annual budget. Thus top management must communicate the policy effects of the long-term plan to those responsible for preparing the current year's budgets. Policy effects might include planned changes in sales mix, or the expansion or contraction of certain activities. In addition, other important guidelines that are to govern the preparation of the budget should be specified – for example the allowances that are to be made for price and wage increases, and the expected changes in productivity. Also, any expected changes in industry demand and output should be communicated by top management to the managers responsible for budget preparation. It is essential that all managers be made aware of the policy of top management for implementing the long-term plan in the current year's budget so that common guidelines can be established. The process also indicates to the managers responsible for preparing the budgets how they should respond to any expected environmental changes.

Determining the factor that restricts performance

In every organization there is some factor that restricts performance for a given period. In the majority of organizations this factor is sales demand. However, it is possible for production capacity to restrict performance when sales demand is in excess of available capacity. Prior to the preparation of the budgets, it is necessary for top management to determine the factor that restricts performance, since this factor determines the point at which the annual budgeting process should begin.

Preparation of the sales budget

The volume of sales and the sales mix determine the level of a company's operations when sales demand is the factor that restricts output. For this reason, the sales budget is the most important plan in the annual budgeting process. This budget is also the most difficult plan to produce, because total sales revenue depends on the actions of customers. In addition, sales demand may be influenced by the state of the economy or the actions of competitors.

Initial preparation of budgets

The managers who are responsible for meeting the budgeted performance should prepare the budget for those areas for which they are responsible. The preparation of the budget should be a 'bottom-up' process. This means that the budget should originate at the lowest levels of management and be refined and coordinated at higher levels. The justification for this approach is that it enables managers to participate in the preparation of their budgets and increases the probability that they will accept the budget and strive to achieve the budget targets.

There is no single way in which the appropriate quantity for a particular budget item is determined. Past data may be used as the starting point for producing the budgets, but this does not mean that budgeting is based on the assumption that what has happened in the past will occur in the future. Changes in future conditions must be taken into account, but past information may provide useful guidance for the future. In addition, managers may look to the guidelines provided by top management for determining the content of their budgets. For example, the guidelines may provide specific instructions as to the content of their budgets and the permitted changes that can be made in the prices of purchases of materials and services. For production activities standard costs (see Chapter 11) may be used as the basis for costing activity volumes that are planned in the budget.

Negotiation of budgets

To implement a participative approach to budgeting, the budget should be originated at the lowest level of management. The managers at this level should submit their budget to their superiors for approval. The superior should then incorporate this budget with other budgets for which he or she is responsible and then submit this budget for approval to his or her superior. The manager who is the superior then becomes the budgetee at the next higher level. The process is illustrated in Figure 9.2. Sizer (1989) describes this approach as a two-way process of a top-down statement of objectives and strategies, bottom-up budget preparation and top-down approval by senior management.

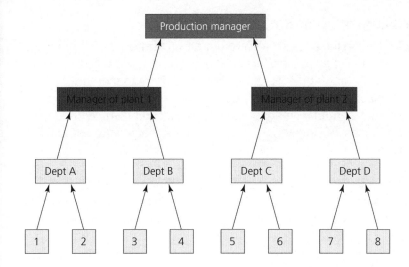

FIGURE 9.2

An illustration of budgets moving up the organization

The lower-level managers are represented by boxes 1–8. Managers 1 and 2 will prepare their budgets in accordance with the budget policy and the guidelines laid down by top management. The managers will submit their budget to their supervisor, who is in charge of the whole department (department A). Once these budgets have been agreed by the manager of department A, they will be combined by the departmental manager, who will then present this budget to his or her superior (manager of plant 1) for approval. The manager of plant 1 is also responsible for department B, and will combine the agreed budgets for departments A and B before presenting the combined budget to his or her supervisor (the production manager). The production manager will merge the budget for plants 1 and 2, and this final budget will represent the production budget that will be presented to the budget committee for approval.

At each of these stages the budgets will be negotiated between the budgetees and their superiors, and eventually they will be agreed by both parties. Hence the figures that are included in the budget are the result of a bargaining process between a manager and his or her superior. It is important that the budgetees should participate in arriving at the final budget and that the superior does not revise the budget without giving full consideration to the subordinates' arguments for including any of the budgeted items. Otherwise, real participation will not be taking place, and it is unlikely that the subordinate will be motivated to achieve a budget that he or she did not accept.

It is also necessary to be watchful that budgetees do not deliberately attempt to obtain approval for easily attainable budgets, or attempt to deliberately understate budgets in the hope that the budget that is finally agreed will represent an easily attainable target. It is equally unsatisfactory for a superior to impose difficult targets in the hope that an authoritarian approach will produce the desired results. The desired results may be achieved in the short term, but only at the cost of a loss of morale and increased labour turnover in the future.

The negotiation process is of vital importance in the budgeting process, and can determine whether the budget becomes a really effective management tool or just a routine to follow. If managers are successful in establishing a position of trust and confidence with their subordinates, the negotiation process will produce a meaningful improvement in the budgetary process and outcomes for the period.

Coordination and review of budgets

As the individual budgets move up the organizational hierarchy in the negotiation process, they must be examined in relation to each other. This examination may indicate that some budgets are out of balance with other budgets and need modifying so that they will be compatible with other conditions, constraints and plans that are beyond a manager's knowledge or control. For example, a plant manager may include equipment replacement in his or her budget when funds are simply not available. The accountant must identify such inconsistencies and bring them to the attention of the appropriate manager. Any changes in the budgets should be made by the responsible managers, and this may require that the budgets be recycled from the bottom to the top for a second or even a third time until all the budgets are coordinated and are acceptable to all the parties involved. During the coordination process, a budgeted profit and loss account, a balance sheet and a cash flow statement should be prepared to ensure that all the parts combine to produce an acceptable whole. Otherwise, further adjustments and budget recycling will be necessary until the budgeted profit and loss account, the balance sheet and the cash flow statement prove to be acceptable.

Final acceptance of budgets

When all the budgets are in harmony with each other, they are summarized into a **master budget** consisting of a budgeted profit and loss account, a balance sheet and a cash flow statement. After the master budget has been approved, the budgets are then passed down through the organization to the appropriate responsibility centres. The approval of the master budget is the authority for the manager of each responsibility centre to carry out the plans contained in each budget.

Budget review

The budget process should not stop when the budgets have been agreed. Periodically, the actual results should be compared with the budgeted results. These comparisons should normally be made on a monthly basis and a report should be available online in the first week of the following month, so that it has the maximum motivational impact. This will enable management to identify the items that are not proceeding according to plan and to investigate the reasons for the differences. If these differences are within the control of management, corrective action can be taken to avoid similar inefficiencies occurring again in the future.

During the budget year, the budget committee should periodically evaluate the actual performance and reappraise the company's future plans. If there are any changes in the actual conditions from those originally expected, this will normally mean that the budget plans should be adjusted. This revised budget then represents a revised statement of formal operating plans for the remaining portion of the budget period. The important point to note is that the budgetary process does not end for the current year once the budget has begun; budgeting should be seen as a continuous and dynamic process.

A DETAILED ILLUSTRATION

Let us now look at an illustration of the procedure for constructing budgets in a manufacturing company, using the information contained in Example 9.1. Note that the level of detail included here is much less than that which would be presented in practice. A truly realistic illustration would fill many pages, with detailed budgets being analysed in various ways. We shall consider an annual budget, whereas a realistic illustration would analyse the annual budget into 12 monthly periods. Monthly analysis would considerably increase the size of the illustration, but would not give any further insight into the basic concepts or procedures. In addition, we shall assume in this example that the budgets are prepared for only two responsibility centres (namely departments 1 and 2). In practice, many responsibility centres are likely to exist.

Sales budget

The sales budget shows the quantities of each product that the company plans to sell and the intended selling price. It provides the predictions of total revenue from which cash receipts from customers will be estimated, and it also supplies the basic data for constructing budgets for production costs, and for selling, distribution and administrative expenses. The sales budget is therefore the foundation of all other budgets, since all expenditure is ultimately dependent on the volume of sales. If the sales budget is not accurate, the other budget estimates will be unreliable. We will assume that the Enterprise Company has completed a marketing analysis and that the following annual sales budget is based on the result:

		Schedule 1 – Sales budget for year ending 200X		
Product	Units sold	Selling price (£)	Total revenue (£)
Alpha	8 500	400	3 400 000
Sigma	1 600	560	896 000
			4 296 000

Schedule 1 represents the *total* sales budget for the year. In practice, the *total* sales budget will be supported by detailed *subsidiary* sales budgets where sales are analysed by areas of responsibility, such as sales territories, and into monthly periods analysed by products.

Production budget and budgeted stock levels

When the sales budget has been completed, the next stage is to prepare the production budget. This budget is expressed in *quantities only* and is the responsibility of the production manager. The objective is to ensure that production is sufficient to meet sales demand and that economic stock levels are maintained. The production budget (schedule 2) for the year will be as follows:

Schedule 2 – Annual production budget	Department 1 (alpha)	Department 2 (sigma)
Units to be sold	8 500	1 600
Planned closing stock	1 870	90
Total units required for sales and stocks	10 370	1 690
Less planned opening stocks	170	85
Units to be produced	10 200	1 605

The total production for each department should also be analysed on a monthly basis.

EXAMPLE 9.1

The Enterprise Company manufactures two products, known as alpha and sigma. Alpha is produced in department 1 and sigma in department 2. The following information is available for 200X.
Standard material and labour costs:

	(£)
Material X	7.20 per unit
Material Y	16.00 per unit
Direct labour	12.00 per hour

Overhead is recovered on a direct labour hour basis.
The standard material and labour usage for each product is as follows:

	Model alpha	Model sigma
Material X	10 units	8 units
Material Y	5 units	9 units
Direct labour	10 hours	15 hours

The balance sheet for the previous year end 200X was as follows:

	(£)	(£)	(£)
Fixed assets:			
Land		170 000	
Buildings and equipment	1 292 000		
Less depreciation	255 000	1 037 000	1 207 000
Current assets:			
Stocks, finished goods	99 076		
raw materials	189 200		
Debtors	289 000		
Cash	34 000		
	611 276		
Less current liabilities			
Creditors	248 800		362 476
Net assets			1 569 476
Represented by shareholders' interest:			
1 200 000 ordinary shares of £1 each		1 200 000	
Reserves		369 476	
			1 569 476

Other relevant data is as follows for the year 200X:

	Finished product	
	Model alpha	Model sigma
Forecast sales (units)	8500	1600
Selling price per unit	£400	£560
Ending inventory required (units)	1870	90
Beginning inventory (units)	170	85

	Direct material	
	Material X	Material Y
Beginning inventory (units)	8 500	8 000
Ending inventory required (units)	10 200	1 700

	Department 1 (£)	Department 2 (£)
Budgeted variable overhead rates (per direct labour hour):		
Indirect materials	1.20	0.80
Indirect labour	1.20	1.20
Power (variable portion)	0.60	0.40
Maintenance (variable portion)	0.20	0.40
Budgeted fixed overheads		
Depreciation	100 000	80 000
Supervision	100 000	40 000
Power (fixed portion)	40 000	2 000
Maintenance (fixed portion)	45 600	3 196

	(£)
Estimated non-manufacturing overheads:	
Stationery etc. (Administration)	4 000
Salaries	
Sales	74 000
Office	28 000
Commissions	60 000
Car expenses (Sales)	22 000
Advertising	80 000
Miscellaneous (Office)	8 000
	276 000

Budgeted cash flows are as follows:

	Quarter 1 (£)	Quarter 2 (£)	Quarter 3 (£)	Quarter 4 (£)
Receipts from customers	1 000 000	1 200 000	1 120 000	985 000
Payments:				
Materials	400 000	480 000	440 000	547 984
Payments for wages	400 000	440 000	480 000	646 188
Other costs and expenses	120 000	100 000	72 016	13 642

You are required to prepare a master budget for the year 200X and the following budgets:

1 sales budget;
2 production budget;
3 direct materials usage budget;
4 direct materials purchase budget;
5 direct labour budget;
6 factory overhead budget;
7 selling and administration budget;
8 cash budget.

Direct materials usage budget

The supervisors of departments 1 and 2 will prepare estimates of the materials required to meet the production budget. The materials usage budget for the year will be as follows:

Schedule 3 – Annual direct material usage budget

	Department 1			Department 2					
	Units	Unit price (£)	Total (£)	Units	Unit price (£)	Total (£)	Total units	Total unit price (£)	Total (£)
Material X	102 000[a]	7.20	734 400	12 840[c]	7.20	92 448	114 840	7.20	826 848
Material Y	51 000[b]	16.00	816 000	14 445[d]	16.00	231 120	65 445	16.00	1 047 120
			1 550 400			323 568			1 873 968

[a]10 200 units production at 10 units per unit of production.
[b]10 200 units production at 5 units per unit of production.
[c]1605 units production at 8 units per unit of production.
[d]1605 units production at 9 units per unit of production.

Direct materials purchase budget

The direct materials purchase budget is the responsibility of the purchasing manager, since it will be he or she who is responsible for obtaining the planned quantities of raw materials to meet the production requirements. The objective is to purchase these materials at the right time at the planned purchase price. In addition, it is necessary to take into account the planned raw material stock levels. The annual materials purchase budget for the year will be as follows:

Schedule 4 – Direct materials purchase budget

	Material X (units)	Material Y (units)
Quantity necessary to meet production requirements as per material usage budget	114 840	65 445
Planned closing stock	10 200	1 700
	125 040	67 145
Less planned opening stock	8 500	8 000
Total units to be purchased	116 540	59 145
Planned unit purchase price	£7.20	£16
Total purchases	£839 088	£946 320

Note that this budget is a summary budget for the year, but for detailed planning and control it will be necessary to analyse the annual budget on a monthly basis.

Direct labour budget

The direct labour budget is the responsibility of the respective managers of departments 1 and 2. They will prepare estimates of the departments' labour hours required to meet the planned production. Where different grades of labour exist, these should be specified separately in the budget. The budget rate per hour should be determined by the industrial relations department. The direct labour budget will be as follows:

Schedule 5 – Annual direct labour budget

	Department 1	Department 2	Total
Budgeted production (units)	10 200	1 605	
Hours per unit	10	15	
Total budgeted hours	102 000	24 075	126 075
Budgeted wage rate per hour	£12	£12	
Total wages	£1 224 000	£288 900	£1 512 900

Factory overhead budget

The factory overhead budget is also the responsibility of the respective production department managers. The total of the overhead budget will depend on the behaviour of the costs of the individual overhead items in relation to the anticipated level of production. The overheads must also be analysed according to whether they are controllable or non-controllable for the purpose of cost control. The factory overhead budget will be as follows:

Schedule 6 – Annual factory overhead budget
Anticipated activity – 102 000 direct labour hours (department 1)
24 075 direct labour hours (department 2)

	Variable overhead rate per direct labour hour		Overheads		Total
	Department 1 (£)	Department 2 (£)	Department 1 (£)	Department 2 (£)	(£)
Controllable overheads:					
Indirect material	1.20	0.80	122 400	19 260	
Indirect labour	1.20	1.20	122 400	28 890	
Power (variable portion)	0.60	0.40	61 200	9 630	
Maintenance (variable portion)	0.20	0.40	20 400	9 630	
			326 400	67 410	393 810
Non-controllable overheads:					
Depreciation			100 000	80 000	
Supervision			100 000	40 000	
Power (fixed portion)			40 000	2 000	
Maintenance (fixed portion)			45 600	3 196	
			285 600	125 196	410 796
Total overhead			612 000	192 606	804 606
Budgeted departmental overhead rate			£6.00[a]	8.00[b]	

[a] £612 000 total overheads divided by 102 000 direct labour hours.
[b] £192 606 total overheads divided by 24 075 direct labour hours.

The budgeted expenditure for the variable overhead items is determined by multiplying the budgeted direct labour hours for each department by the budgeted variable overhead rate per hour. It is assumed that all variable overheads vary in relation to direct labour hours.

Selling and administration budget

The selling and administration budgets have been combined here to simplify the presentation. In practice, separate budgets should be prepared: the sales manager will be responsible for the selling budget, the distribution manager will be responsible for the distribution expenses and the chief administrative officer will be responsible for the administration budget.

Schedule 7 – Annual selling and administration budget

	(£)	(£)
Selling:		
Salaries	74 000	
Commission	60 000	
Car expenses	22 000	
Advertising	80 000	236 000
Administration:		
Stationery	4 000	
Salaries	28 000	
Miscellaneous	8 000	40 000
		276 000

Departmental budgets

For cost control the direct labour budget, materials usage budget and factory overhead budget are combined into separate departmental budgets. These budgets are normally broken down into 12 separate monthly budgets, and the actual monthly expenditure is compared with the budgeted amounts for each of the items concerned. This comparison is used for judging how effective managers are in controlling the expenditure for which they are responsible. The departmental budget for department 1 will be as follows:

Department 1 – Annual departmental operating budget

	(£)	Budget (£)	Actual (£)
Direct labour (from schedule 5):			
102 000 hours at £12		1 224 000	
Direct materials (from schedule 3):			
102 000 units of material X at £7.20 per unit	734 400		
51 000 units of material Y at £16 per unit	816 000	1 550 400	
Controllable overheads (from schedule 6):			
Indirect materials	122 400		
Indirect labour	122 400		
Power (variable portion)	61 200		
Maintenance (variable portion)	20 400	326 400	
Uncontrollable overheads (from schedule 6):			
Depreciation	100 000		
Supervision	100 000		
Power (fixed portion)	40 000		
Maintenance (fixed portion)	45 600	285 600	
		3 386 400	

Master budget

When all the budgets have been prepared, the budgeted profit and loss account and balance sheet provide the overall picture of the planned performance for the budget period.

Budgeted profit and loss account for the year ending 200X

	(£)	(£)
Sales (schedule 1)		4 296 000
Opening stock of raw materials	189 200	
(from opening balance sheet)		
Purchases (schedule 4)	1 785 408[a]	
	1 974 608	
Less closing stock of raw materials (schedule 4)	100 640[b]	
Cost of raw materials consumed	1 873 968	
Direct labour (schedule 5)	1 512 900	
Factory overheads (schedule 6)	804 606	
Total manufacturing cost	4 191 474	
Add opening stock of finished goods	99 076	
(from opening balance sheet)		
Less closing stock of finished goods	665 984[c]	
		(566 908)
Cost of sales		3 624 566
Gross profit		671 434
Selling and administration expenses (schedule 7)		276 000
Budgeted operating profit for the year		395 434

[a] £839 088 (X) + £946 320 (Y) from schedule 4.
[b] 10 200 units at £7.20 plus 1700 units at £16 from schedule 4.
[c] 1870 units of alpha valued at £332 per unit, 90 units of sigma valued at £501.60 per unit. The product unit costs are calculated as follows:

	Alpha		Sigma	
	Units	(£)	Units	(£)
Direct materials				
X	10	72.00	8	57.60
Y	5	80.00	9	144.00
Direct labour	10	120.00	15	180.00
Factory overheads:				
Department 1	10	60.00	—	—
Department 2	—	—	15	120.00
		332.00		501.60

Budgeted balance sheet as at 31 December

	(£)	(£)
Fixed assets:		
Land		170 000
Building and equipment	1 292 000	
Less depreciation[a]	435 000	857 000
		1 027 000
Current assets:		
Raw material stock	100 640	
Finished good stock	665 984	
Debtors[b]	280 000	
Cash[c]	199 170	
	1 245 794	
Current liabilities:		
Creditors[d]	307 884	937 910
		1 964 910

Represented by shareholders' interest:

1 200 000 ordinary shares of £1 each	1 200 000	
Reserves	369 476	
Profit and loss account	395 434	1 964 910

[a]£255 000 + £180 000 (schedule 6) = £435 000.
[b]£289 000 opening balance + £4 296 000 sales − £4 305 000 cash.
[c]Closing balance as per cash budget.
[d]£248 800 opening balance + £1 785 408 purchases + £141 660 indirect materials − £1 876 984 cash.

Cash budgets

The objective of the **cash budget** is to ensure that sufficient cash is available at all times to meet the level of operations that are outlined in the various budgets. The cash budget for Example 9.1 is presented below and is analysed by quarters, but in practice monthly or weekly budgets will be necessary. Because cash budgeting is subject to uncertainty, it is necessary to provide for more than the minimum amount required to allow for some margin of error in planning. Cash budgets can help a firm to avoid cash balances that are surplus to its requirements by enabling management to take steps in advance to invest the surplus cash in short-term investments. Alternatively, cash deficiencies can be identified in advance, and steps can be taken to ensure that bank loans will be available to meet any temporary cash deficiencies. For example, by looking at the cash budget for the Enterprise Company, management may consider that the cash balances are higher than necessary in the second and third quarters of the year, and they may invest part of the cash balance in short-term investments.

The overall aim should be to manage the cash of the firm to attain maximum cash availability and maximum interest income on any idle funds.

Cash budget for year ending 200X

	Quarter 1 (£)	Quarter 2 (£)	Quarter 3 (£)	Quarter 4 (£)	Total (£)
Opening balance	34 000	114 000	294 000	421 984	34 000
Receipts from debtors	1 000 000	1 200 000	1 120 000	985 000	4 305 000
	1 034 000	1 314 000	1 414 000	1 406 984	4 339 000
Payments:					
Purchase of materials	400 000	480 000	440 000	547 984	1 867 984
Payment of wages	400 000	440 000	480 000	646 188	1 966 188
Other costs and expenses	120 000	100 000	72 016	13 642	305 658
	920 000	1 020 000	992 016	1 207 814	4 139 830
Closing balance	114 000	294 000	421 984	199 170	199 170

Final review

The budgeted profit and loss account, the balance sheet and the cash budget will be submitted by the accountant to the budget committee, together with a number of budgeted financial ratios such as the return on capital employed, working capital, liquidity and gearing ratios. If these ratios prove to be acceptable, the budgets will be approved. In Example 9.1 the return on capital employed is approximately 20 per cent, but the working capital ratio (current assets:current liabilities) is over 4:1, so management should consider alternative ways of reducing investment in working capital before finally approving the budgets.

COMPUTERIZED BUDGETING

In the past, budgeting was a task dreaded by many management accountants. You will have noted from Example 9.1 that many numerical manipulations are necessary to prepare the budget. In the real world the process is far more complex, and, as the budget is being formulated, it is altered many times because some budgets are found to be out of balance with each other or the master budget proves to be unacceptable.

In today's world, the budgeting process is computerized, and instead of being primarily concerned with numerical manipulations, the accounting staff can now become more involved in the real planning process. Computer-based financial models normally consist of mathematical statements of inputs and outputs. By simply altering the mathematical statements budgets can be quickly revised with little effort. However, the major advantage of computerized budgeting is that management can evaluate many different options before the budget is finally agreed. Establishing a model enables 'what-if?' analysis to be employed. For example, answers to the following questions can be displayed in the form

REAL WORLD VIEWS 9.3

Using web technology for the budget process

An e-budgeting solution completely automates the development of an organization's budget and forecast. From anywhere in the world, at all times, participants in the process can log through the internet to access their budget and any pertinent related information so they can work on their plans. Web-based enterprise budgeting systems offer a centrally administered system that provides easy-to-use flexible tools for the end-users who are responsible for budgeting. The web functionality of these applications allows constant monitoring, updates and modelling.

E-budgeting provides the flexibility demanded by modern organizations. For example, the finance department can request across-the-board reallocations of expenditures and model the result immediately. No longer do management accountants have to go back and forth with other managers reinputing data and retallying results. E-budgeting can eliminate the cumbersome accounting tasks of pulling numbers from disparate files, cutting and pasting, entering and uploading, and constantly performing reconciliation.

Also, a web-based budgeting application lets managers access data from office or home – wherever they happen to be working. It broadens the system's availability to the user community.

When executives at Toronto-Dominion Bank were searching for a new solution capable of handling the bank's enterprise budgeting and planning function, they turned to the internet. The company selected Clarus Corporation's web-deployed, enterprise Clarus™ Budget solution. Its accountant stated 'in the past, we have compiled our business plan using hundreds of spreadsheets, and our analysts have spent a disproportionate amount of their time compiling and verifying data from multiple sources. Implementing a web-based, enterprise-wide budgeting solution will help us to develop our business plans and allow our analysts to be proactive in monitoring quarterly results.'

Discussion point

What impact does e-budgeting have on the management accounting function?

of a master budget: What if sales increase or decrease by 10 per cent? What if unit costs increase or decrease by 5 per cent? What if the credit terms for sales were reduced from 30 to 20 days?

In addition, computerized models can incorporate actual results, period by period, and carry out the necessary calculations to produce budgetary *control* reports. It is also possible to adjust the budgets for the remainder of the year when it is clear that the circumstances on which the budget was originally set have changed.

ACTIVITY-BASED BUDGETING

The conventional approach to budgeting that was illustrated using Example 9.1 is appropriate for unit-level activities (see Chapter 8), such as the direct labour and direct materials budgets, where the consumption of resources varies proportionately with the volume of final output of products or services. However, for those indirect costs and support activities where there are no clearly identified input–output relationships, conventional budgets merely serve as authorization levels for the budgeted level of spending for each item of expense. They can only indicate whether the budget has been exceeded and thus provide little relevant information for managing the costs of the support activities.

With conventional budgeting indirect costs and support activities are prepared on an incremental basis. This means that existing operations and the current budgeted allowance for existing activities are taken as the starting point for preparing the next annual budget. The base is then adjusted for changes (such as changes in product mix, volumes and prices) which are expected to occur during the new budget period. This approach is called incremental budgeting, since the budget process is concerned mainly with the increment in operations or expenditure that will occur during the forthcoming budget period. For example, the allowance for budgeted expenses may be based on the previous budgeted allowance plus an increase to cover higher prices caused by inflation. The major disadvantage of the incremental approach is that the majority of expenditure, which is associated with the 'base level' of activity, remains unchanged. Thus, the cost of the support activities become fixed and past inefficiencies and waste inherent in the current way of doing things are perpetuated.

To manage costs more effectively organizations that have implemented activity-based costing (ABC) have also adopted activity-based budgeting (ABB). The aim of ABB is to authorize the supply of only those resources that are needed to perform activities required to meet the budgeted production and sales volume. ABB involves the following stages:

1 estimate the production and sales volume by individual products and customers;
2 estimate the demand for organizational activities;
3 determine the resources that are required to perform organizational activities;
4 estimate for each resource the quantity that must be supplied to meet the demand;
5 take action to adjust the capacity of resources to match the projected supply.

The *first stage* is identical to conventional budgeting. Details of budgeted production and sales volumes for individual products and customer types will be contained in the sales and production budgets. Next, ABC extends conventional budgeting to support activities such as ordering, receiving, scheduling production and processing customers' orders. To implement ABB a knowledge of the activities that are necessary to produce and sell the products and services is essential. In the *second stage*, estimates of the quantity of activity cost drivers must be derived for each activity. For example, the number of purchase orders, the number of receipts, the number of set-ups and the number of customer orders processed are estimated using the same approach as that used by conventional budgeting to determine the quantity of direct labour and materials that are incorporated into the direct labour and materials purchase budgets.

The *third stage* is to estimate the resources that are required for performing the quantity of activity drivers demanded. In particular, estimates are required of each type of resource, and their quantities required, to meet the demanded quantity of activities. For example, if the number of customer orders to be processed is estimated to be 5000 and each order takes 30 minutes processing time then 2500 labour hours of the customer processing activity must be supplied.

In the *fourth stage* the resources demanded (derived from the third stage) are converted into an estimate of the total resources that must be supplied for each type of resource used by an activity. The quantity of resources supplied depends on the cost behaviour of the resource. For flexible resources where the supply can be matched exactly to meet demand, the quantity of resources supplied will be identical to the quantity demanded. For example, if customer processing were a flexible resource exactly 2500 hours would be purchased. However, a more likely assumption is that customer processing labour will be a step cost function in relation to the volume of the activity (see Chapter 2 for a description of step cost functions). Assuming that each person employed is contracted to work 1500 hours per year then 1.67 persons (2500/1500) represents the quantity of resources required, but because resources must be acquired in whole amounts, two persons must be employed. For other resources, such as equipment, resources will tend to be fixed and committed over a very wide range of volume for the activity. As long as demand is less than the capacity supplied by the committed resource no additional spending will be required.

The *final stage* is to compare the estimates of the quantity of resources to be supplied for each resource with the quantity of resources that are currently committed. If the estimated demand for a resource exceeds the current capacity additional spending must be authorized within the budgeting process to acquire additional resources. Alternatively, if the demand for resources is less than the projected supply, the budgeting process should result in management taking action to either redeploy or reduce those resources that are no longer required.

Exhibit 9.1 illustrates an activity-based budget for an order receiving process or department. You will see that the budget is presented in a matrix format with the major activities being shown for each of the columns and the resource inputs listed by rows. The cost driver activity levels are also highlighted. A major feature of ABB is the enhanced visibility arising from highlighting the cost of activities and showing the outcomes, in terms of cost drivers, from the budgeted expenditure. This information is particularly useful for planning and estimating future expenditure.

EXHIBIT 9.1

Activity-based budget for an order receiving process

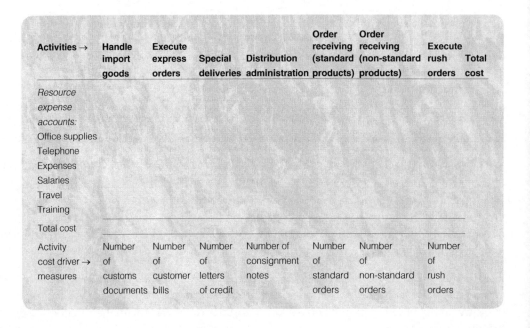

Activities →	Handle import goods	Execute express orders	Special deliveries	Distribution administration	Order receiving (standard products)	Order receiving (non-standard products)	Execute rush orders	Total cost
Resource expense accounts:								
Office supplies								
Telephone								
Expenses								
Salaries								
Travel								
Training								
Total cost								
Activity cost driver → measures	Number of customs documents	Number of customer bills	Number of letters of credit	Number of consignment notes	Number of standard orders	Number of non-standard orders	Number of rush orders	

ZERO-BASED BUDGETING

Zero-based budgeting (also known as **priority-based budgeting**) emerged in the late 1960s in municipal government organizations as an attempt to overcome the limitations of **incremental budgets**. This approach requires that all activities are justified and prioritized before decisions are taken relating to the amount of resources allocated to each activity. Besides adopting a 'zero-based' approach, zero-base budgeting (ZBB) also focuses on programmes or activities instead of functional departments which is a feature of traditional budgeting. Programmes normally relate to various activities undertaken by municipal or government organizations. Examples include extending childcare facilities, improvement of healthcare for senior citizens and the extension of nursing facilities.

ZBB works from the premise that projected expenditure for existing programmes should start from base zero, with each year's budgets being compiled as if the programmes were being launched for the first time. The budgetees should present their requirements for appropriations in such a fashion that all funds can be allocated on the basis of cost–benefit or some similar kind of evaluative analysis. The cost–benefit approach is an attempt to ensure 'value for money'; it questions long-standing assumptions and serves as a tool for systematically examining and perhaps abandoning any unproductive projects.

ZBB is best suited to discretionary costs and support activities. With **discretionary costs** management has some discretion as to the amount it will budget for the particular activity in question. Examples of discretionary costs include advertising, research and development and training costs. There is no optimum relationship between inputs (as measured by the costs) and outputs (measured by revenues or some other objective function) for these costs. Furthermore, they are not predetermined by some previous commitment. In effect, management can determine what quantity of service it wishes to purchase and there is no established method for determining the appropriate amount to be spent in particular periods. ZBB has mostly been applied in municipal and government organizations where the predominant costs are of a discretionary nature.

ZBB involves the following three stages:

● a description of each organizational activity in a decision package;
● the evaluation and ranking of decision packages in order of priority;
● allocation of resources based on order of priority up to the spending cut-off level.

Decision packages are identified for each decision unit. Decision units represent separate programmes or groups of activities that an organization undertakes. A decision package represents the operation of a particular programme with incremental packages reflecting different levels of effort that may be expended on a specific function. One package is usually prepared at the 'base' level for each programme. This package represents the minimum level of service or support consistent with the organization's objectives. Service or support higher than the base level is described in one or more incremental packages. For example, managers might be asked to specify the base package in terms of level of service that can be provided at 70 per cent of the current cost level and incremental packages identify higher activity or cost levels.

Once the decision packages have been completed, management is ready to start to review the process. To determine how much to spend and where to spend it, management will rank all packages in order of decreasing benefits to the organization. Theoretically, once management has set the budgeted level of spending, the packages should be accepted down to the spending level based on cost–benefit principles.

The benefits of ZBB over traditional methods of budgeting are claimed to be as follows:

1 Traditional budgeting tends to extrapolate the past by adding a percentage increase to the current year. ZBB avoids the deficiencies of incremental budgeting and represents a move towards the allocation of resources by need or benefit. Thus, unlike traditional budgeting the level of funding is not taken for granted.
2 ZBB creates a questioning attitude rather than one that assumes that current practice represents value for money.
3 ZBB focuses attention on outputs in relation to value for money.

ZBB was first applied in Texas Instruments in 1969. It quickly became one of the fashionable management tools of the 1970s and, according to Phyrr (1976), there were 100 users in the USA in the early 1970s. ZBB never achieved the widespread adoption that its proponents envisaged. The major reason for its lack of success would appear to be that it is too costly and time-consuming. The process of identifying decision packages and determining their purpose, cost and benefits is extremely time-consuming. Furthermore, there are often too many decision packages to evaluate and there is frequently insufficient information to enable them to be ranked.

Research suggests that many organizations tend to approximate the principles of ZBB rather than applying the full-scale approach outlined in the literature. For example, it does not have to be applied throughout the organization. It can be applied selectively to those areas about which management is most concerned and used as a one-off cost reduction programme. Some of the benefits of ZBB can be captured by using priority-based incremental budgets. Priority incremental budgets require managers to specify what incremental activities or changes would occur if their budgets were increased or decreased by a specified percentage (say 10 per cent). Budget allocations are made by comparing the change in costs with the change in benefits. Priority incremental budgets thus represent an economical compromise between ZBB and incremental budgeting.

CRITICISMS OF BUDGETING

In recent years criticisms of traditional budgeting have attracted much publicity. Ekholm and Wallin (2000) and Dugdale and Lyne (2006) have reviewed the literature relating to annual budgets. They have identified the following criticisms relating to the annual budgeting process:

- encouraging rigid planning and incremental thinking;
- being time-consuming;
- ignoring key drivers of shareholder value by focusing too much attention on short-term financial numbers;
- being a yearly rigid ritual;
- tying the company to a 12-month commitment, which is risky since it is based on uncertain forecasts;
- meeting only the lowest targets and not attempting to beat the targets;
- spending what is in the budget even if this is not necessary in order to guard against next year's budget being reduced;
- achieving the budget even if this results in undesirable actions.

The term **beyond budgeting** is used by Hope and Fraser (2003) to relate to alternative approaches that should be used instead of annual budgeting. Rolling forecasts, produced on a monthly or quarterly basis, are suggested as the main alternative to the annual budget. Such rolling forecasts should embrace key performance indicators based on balanced scorecards (see Chapter 15). Rolling forecasts are advocated because they do not have the same compulsory and stifling image when compared with the annual budget.

Because of the criticisms of budgeting, and the beyond budgeting movement, Dugdale and Lyne (2006) surveyed financial and non-financial managers in 40 UK companies. Their main conclusion was that budgeting is alive and well. All of the companies surveyed used budgets and, generally, both financial and non-financial managers thought they were important for planning, control, performance measurement, coordination and communication. To find out how problematic the respondents viewed their budgets, they were asked whether they agreed with 20 critical propositions. The respondents tended to disagree with the propositions.

SUMMARY

The following items relate to the learning objectives listed at the beginning of the chapter.

- **Explain how budgeting fits into the overall strategic planning and control framework.** The annual budget should be set within the context of longer-term plans, which are likely to exist even if they have not been made explicit. A long-term plan is a statement of the preliminary targets and activities required by an organization to achieve its strategic plans together with a broad estimate for each year of the resources required. Because long-term planning involves 'looking into the future' for several years, the plans tend to be uncertain, general in nature, imprecise and subject to change. Annual budgeting is concerned with the detailed implementation of the long-term plan for the year ahead.

- **Identify and describe the six different purposes of budgeting.** Budgets are used for the following purposes: (a) planning annual operations; (b) coordinating the activities of the various parts of the organization and ensuring that the parts are in harmony with each other; (c) communicating the plans to the managers of the various responsibility centres; (d) motivating managers to strive to achieve organizational goals; (e) controlling activities; and (f) evaluating the performance of managers.

- **Identify and describe the various stages in the budget process.** The important stages are as follows: (a) communicating details of the budget policy and guidelines to those people responsible for the preparation of the budgets; (b) determining the factor that restricts output (normally sales volume); (c) preparation of the sales budget (assuming that sales demand is the factor that restricts output); (d) initial preparation of the various budgets; (e) negotiation of budgets with superiors; (f) coordination and review of budgets; (g) final acceptance of budgets; and (h) ongoing review of budgets. Each of the above stages is described in the chapter.

- **Prepare functional and master budgets.** When all of the budgets have been prepared they are summarized into a master budget consisting in a budgeted profit and loss account, a balance sheet and a cash budget statement. The preparation of functional and master budgets was illustrated using Example 9.1.

- **Describe the use of computer-based financial models for budgeting.** Computer-based financial models are mathematical statements of the inputs and output relationships that affect the budget. These models allow management to conduct sensitivity analysis to ascertain the effects on the master budget of changes in the original predicted data or changes in the assumptions that were used to prepare the budgets.

- **Describe the limitations of incremental budgeting.** With incremental, budgeting, indirect costs and support activities are prepared on an incremental basis. This means that existing operations and the current budgeted allowance for existing activities are taken as the starting point for preparing the next annual budget. The base is then adjusted for changes (such as changes in product mix, volumes and prices) which are expected to occur during the new budget period. When this approach is adopted the concern is mainly with the increment in operations or expenditure that will occur during the forthcoming budget period. The major disadvantage of the incremental approach is that the majority of expenditure, which is associated with the 'base level' of activity, remains unchanged. Thus, past inefficiencies and waste inherent in the current way of doing things are perpetuated.

● **Describe activity-based budgeting.** With conventional budgeting the budgeted expenses for the forthcoming budget for support activities are normally based on the previous year's budget plus an adjustment for inflation. Support costs are therefore considered to be fixed in relation to activity volume. Activity-based budgeting (ABB) aims to manage costs more effectively by authorizing the supply of only those resources that are needed to perform activities required to meet the budgeted production and sales volume. Whereas ABC assigns resource expenses to activities and then uses activity cost drivers to assign activity costs to cost objects (such as products, services or customers) ABB is the reverse of this process. Cost objects are the starting point. Their budgeted output determines the necessary activities that are then used to estimate the resources required for the budget period. ABB involves the following stages: (a) estimate the production and sales volume by individual products and customers; (b) estimate the demand for organizational activities; (c) determine the resources that are required to perform organizational activities; (d) estimate for each resource the quantity that must be supplied to meet the demand; and (e) take action to adjust the capacity of resources to match the projected supply.

● **Describe zero-base budgeting (ZBB).** ZBB is a method of budgeting that is mainly used in non-profit organizations but it can also be applied to discretionary costs and support activities in profit organizations. It seeks to overcome the deficiencies of incremental budgeting. ZBB works from the premise that projected expenditure for existing programmes should start from base zero, with each year's budgets being compiled as if the programmes were being launched for the first time. The budgetees should present their requirements for appropriations in such a fashion that all funds can be allocated on the basis of cost–benefit or some similar kind of evaluative analysis. The cost–benefit approach is an attempt to ensure 'value for money'; it questions long-standing assumptions and serves as a tool for systematically examining and perhaps abandoning any unproductive projects.

● **Describe the criticisms relating to traditional budgeting.** Criticisms relating to traditional budgeting include encouraging rigid planning and incremental thinking, being time-consuming, a failure to encourage continuous improvement, achieving the target even if this results in undesirable actions and being a yearly rigid ritual. The beyond budgeting movement advocates that budgeting should be replaced with rolling forecasts that embrace key performance indicators and also incorporate exception-based monitoring and benchmarking.

KEY TERMS AND CONCEPTS

activity-based budgeting (ABB) (p. 222)
beyond budgeting (p. 226)
budgeting (p. 202)
budgets (p. 201)
cash budgets (p. 220)
continuous budgeting (p. 207)
control process (p. 203)

corporate objectives (p. 202)
decision package (p. 225)
discretionary costs (p. 224)
feedback loops (p. 203)
incremental budgeting (p. 222)
incremental budgets (p. 224)
long-term plan (p. 202)

management by exception (p. 206)
master budget (p. 212)
mission (p. 202)
priority-based budgets (p. 224)
priority-based incremental budgets (p. 225)

rolling budgeting (p. 207)
strategic plan (p. 202)
strategy (p. 202)
unit objectives (p. 202)
zero-based budgeting (p. 224)

ASSESSMENT MATERIAL

The review questions are short questions that enable you to assess your understanding of the main topics included in the chapter. The page numbers in parentheses provide you with the page numbers to refer to if you cannot answer a specific question.

The review problems are more complex and require you to relate and apply the content to various business problems. Solutions to review problems are provided in a separate section at the end of the book. Additional review problems can be accessed by lecturers and students on the website (www.drury-online.com). Solutions to these problems are provided for lecturers in the *Instructors' Manual*. This is available on the lecturers' password-protected section of the website.

The website also includes over 30 case study problems. A list of these cases is provided on pages 389–392. Several cases are relevant to the content of this chapter. Examples include Endeavour Twoplise Ltd, Global Ltd and Integrated Technology Services (UK) Ltd.

REVIEW QUESTIONS

9.1 Define the term 'budget'. How are budgets used in planning? *(pp. 202–4)*

9.2 Describe the different stages in the planning and control process. *(pp. 202–4)*

9.3 Distinguish between budgeting and long-range planning. How are they related? *(pp. 202–4)*

9.4 Describe the different purposes of budgeting. *(pp. 204–6)*

9.5 Explain what is meant by the term 'management by exception'. *(pp. 206)*

9.6 Describe how the different roles of budgets can conflict with each other. *(p. 206)*

9.7 Distinguish between continuous and rolling budgets. *(p. 207)*

9.8 Describe the different stages in the budgeting process. *(pp. 209–12)*

9.9 All budgets depend on the sales budget. Do you agree? Explain. *(p. 213)*

9.10 What is a master budget? *(p. 219)*

9.11 Define incremental budgeting. *(p. 222)*

9.12 What are the distinguishing features of activity-based budgeting? *(pp. 222–24)*

9.13 Describe the five different stages that are involved with activity-based budgeting. *(pp. 222–24)*

9.14 How does zero-based budgeting differ from traditional budgeting? *(pp. 224–25)*

9.15 What are discretionary costs? *(pp. 224–25)*

9.16 Distinguish between zero-based budgeting and priority-based incremental budgeting. *(pp. 225–26)*

REVIEW PROBLEMS

9.17 When preparing a production budget, the quantity to be produced equals

A   sales quantity + opening stock + closing stock
B   sales quantity − opening stock + closing stock
C   sales quantity − opening stock − closing stock
D   sales quantity + opening stock − closing stock
E   sales quantity

9.18 BDL plc is currently preparing its cash budget for the year to 31 December 2009.
An extract from its sales budget for the same year shows the following sales values:

	£
March	60 000
April	70 000
May	55 000
June	65 000

40 per cent of its sales are expected to be for cash. Of its credit sales, 70 per cent
are expected to pay in the month after sale and take a 2 per cent discount; 27 per
cent are expected to pay in the second month after the sale, and the remaining 3
per cent are expected to be bad debts.

The value of sales receipts to be shown in the cash budget for May 2009 is:

A   £38 532
B   £39 120
C   £60 532
D   £64 220
E   £65 200

9.19 The following data is to be used to answer questions (a) and (b) below

A division of PLR plc operates a small private aircraft that carries passengers and
small parcels for other divisions.

In the year ended 31 March 2008, it carried 1024 passengers and 24 250 kg of
small parcels. It incurred costs of £924 400.

The division has found that 70 per cent of its total costs are variable, and that 60 per
cent of these vary with the number of passengers and the remainder varies with the
weight of the parcels.

The company is now preparing its budget for the three months ending 30
September 2008 using an incremental budgeting approach. In this period it
expects:

- all prices to be 3 per cent higher than the average paid in the year ended
  31 March 2008;
- efficiency levels to be unchanged;
- activity levels to be:
  - 209 passengers;
  - 7200 kg of small parcels.

(a) The budgeted passenger-related cost (to the nearest £100) for the **three months** ending 30 September 2008 is

A   £81 600
B   £97 100
C   £100 000
D   £138 700

(2 marks)

(b) The budgeted small parcel-related cost (to the nearest £100) for the **three months** ending 30 September 2008 is

A   £64 700
B   £66 600
C   £79 200
D   £95 213

(2 marks)

9.20 Preparation of functional budgets

Wollongong wishes to calculate an operating budget for the forthcoming period. Information regarding products, costs and sales levels is as follows:

Product	A	B
Materials required		
X (kg)	2	3
Y (litres)	1	4
Labour hours required		
Skilled (hours)	4	2
Semi-skilled (hours)	2	5
Sales level (units)	2000	1500
Opening stocks (units)	100	200

Closing stock of materials and finished goods will be sufficient to meet 10 per cent of demand. Opening stock of material X was 300 kg and for material Y was 1000 litres. Material prices are £10 per kg for material X and £7 per litre for material Y. Labour costs are £12 per hour for the skilled workers and £8 per hour for the semi-skilled workers.

Required:

Produce the following budgets:

(a) production (units);
(b) materials usage (kg and litres);
(c) materials purchases (kg, litres and £); and
(d) labour (hours and £).

(10 marks)

9.21 Budget preparation and comments on sales forecasting methods

You have recently been appointed as the management accountant to Alderley Ltd, a small company manufacturing two products, the Elgar and the Holst. Both products use the same type of material and labour but in different proportions. In the past, the company has had poor control over its working capital. To remedy this, you have recommended to the directors that a budgetary control system be introduced. This proposal has, now, been agreed.

Because Alderley Ltd's production and sales are spread evenly over the year, it was agreed that the annual budget should be broken down into four periods, each of 13 weeks, and commencing with the 13 weeks ending 4 April. To help you in this task, the sales and production directors have provided you with the following information:

1   Marketing and production data

	Elgar	Holst
Budgeted sales for 13 weeks (units)	845	1235
Material content per unit (kilograms)	7	8
Labour per unit (standard hours)	8	5

2   Production labour
    The 24 production employees work a 37-hour, five-day week and are paid £8 per hour. Any hours in excess of this involve Alderley in paying an overtime premium of 25 per cent. Because of technical problems, which will continue over the next 13 weeks, employees are only able to work at 95 per cent efficiency compared to standard.

3   Purchasing and opening stocks
    The production director believes that raw materials will cost £12 per kilogram over the budget period. He also plans to revise the amount of stock being kept. He estimates that the stock levels at the commencement of the budget period will be as follows:

Raw materials	Elgar	Holst
2328 kilograms	163 units	361 units

4   Closing stocks
    At the end of the 13-week period closing stocks are planned to change. On the assumption that production and sales volumes for the second budget period will be similar to those in the first period:

- raw materials stocks should be sufficient for 13 days' production;
- finished stocks of the Elgar should be equivalent to 6 days' sales volume;
- finished stocks of the Holst should be equivalent to 14 days' sales volume.

Task 1

Prepare in the form of a statement the following information for the 13-week period to 4 April:

(a)   the production budget in units for the Elgar and Holst;
(b)   the purchasing budget for Alderley Ltd in units;
(c)   the cost of purchases for the period;
(d)   the production labour budget for Alderley Ltd in hours;
(e)   the cost of production labour for the period.

Note: Assume a five-day week for both sales and production.

The managing director of Alderley Ltd, Alan Dunn, has also only recently been appointed. He is keen to develop the company and has already agreed to two new products being developed. These will be launched in 18 months' time. While talking to you about the budget, he mentions that the quality of sales forecasting will need to improve if the company is to grow rapidly. Currently, the budgeted sales figure is found by initially adding 5 per cent to the previous year's sales volume and then revising the figure following discussions with the marketing director. He believes this approach is increasingly inadequate and now requires a more systematic approach.

A few days later, Alan Dunn sends you a memo. In that memo, he identifies three possible strategies for increasing sales volume. They are:

- more sales to existing customers;
- the development of new markets;
- the development of new products.

He asks for your help in forecasting likely sales volumes from these sources.

Task 2

Write a brief memo to Alan Dunn. Your memo should:

(a) identify *four* ways of forecasting future sales volume;

(b) show how each of your four ways of forecasting can be applied to *one* of the sales strategies identified by Alan Dunn, and justify your choice;

(c) give *two* reasons why forecasting methods might not prove to be accurate.

9.22 Preparation of cash budgets

The management of Beck plc have been informed that the union representing the direct production workers at one of their factories, where a standard product is produced, intends to call a strike. The accountant has been asked to advise the management of the effect the strike will have on cash flow.

The following data has been made available:

	Week 1	Week 2	Week 3
Budgeted sales	400 units	500 units	400 units
Budgeted production	600 units	400 units	Nil

The strike will commence at the beginning of week 3 and it should be assumed that it will continue for at least four weeks. Sales at 400 units per week will continue to be made during the period of the strike until stocks of finished goods are exhausted. Production will stop at the end of week 2. The current stock level of finished goods is 600 units. Stocks of work in progress are not carried.

The selling price of the product is £60 and the budgeted manufacturing cost is made up as follows:

	(£)
Direct materials	15
Direct wages	7
Variable overheads	8
Fixed overheads	18
Total	£48

Direct wages are regarded as a variable cost. The company operates a full absorption costing system and the fixed overhead absorption rate is based upon a budgeted fixed overhead of £9000 per week. Included in the total fixed overheads is £700 per week for depreciation of equipment. During the period of the strike direct wages and variable overheads would not be incurred and the cash expended on fixed overheads would be reduced by £1500 per week.

The current stock of raw materials are worth £7500; it is intended that these stocks should increase to £11 000 by the end of week 1 and then remain at this level during the period of the strike. *All direct materials are paid for one week after they have been received. Direct wages are paid one week in arrears. It should be assumed that all relevant overheads are paid for immediately the expense is incurred.* All sales are on credit, 70 per cent of the sales value is received in cash from the debtors at the end of the first week after the sales have been made and the balance at the end of the second week.

The current amount outstanding to material suppliers is £8000 and direct wage accruals amount to £3200. Both of these will be paid in week 1. The current balance owing from debtors is £31 200, of which £24 000 will be received during week 1 and the remainder during week 2. The current balance of cash at the bank and in hand is £1000.

Required:

(a) (i) Prepare a cash budget for weeks 1 to 6 showing the balance of cash at the end of each week together with a suitable analysis of the receipts and payments during each week.

(13 marks)

(ii) Comment upon any matters arising from the cash budget which you consider should be brought to management's attention.

(4 marks)

(b) Explain why the reported profit figure for a period does not normally represent the amount of cash generated in that period.

(5 marks)

(Total 22 marks)

9.23 You are the management accountant of a group of companies and your managing director has asked you to explore the possibilities of introducing a zero-based budgeting system experimentally in one of the operating companies in place of its existing orthodox system. You are required to prepare notes for a paper for submission to the board that sets out:

(a) how zero-based budgeting would work within the company chosen;

(6 marks)

(b) what advantages it might offer over the existing system;

(5 marks)

(c) what problems might be faced in introducing a zero-based budgeting scheme;

(5 marks)

(d) the features you would look for in selecting the operating company for the introduction in order to obtain the most beneficial results from the experiment.

(4 marks)

(Total 20 marks)

9.24 Traditional budgeting systems are incremental in nature and tend to focus on cost centres. Activity-based budgeting links strategic planning to overall performance measurement aiming at continuous improvement.

(a) Explain the weaknesses of an incremental budgeting system.

(5 marks)

(b) Describe the main features of an activity-based budgeting system and comment on the advantages claimed for its use.

(10 marks)

(Total 15 marks)

9.25 Budgeting has been criticized as:

- a cumbersome process that occupies considerable management time;
- concentrating unduly on short-term financial control;
- having undesirable effects on the motivation of managers;
- emphasizing formal organization structure.

Requirements:

(a) Explain these criticisms.

(8 marks)

(b) Explain what changes can be made in response to these criticisms to improve the budgeting process.

(12 marks)
(Total 20 marks)

CHAPTER 10
MANAGEMENT CONTROL
SYSTEMS

LEARNING OBJECTIVES

After studying this chapter you should be able to:

- describe the three different types of controls used in organizations;
- distinguish between feedback and feed-forward controls;
- explain the potential harmful side-effects of results controls;
- define the four different types of responsibility centres;
- explain the different elements of management accounting control systems;
- describe the controllability principle and the methods of implementing it;
- describe the different approaches that can be used to determine financial performance targets and discuss the impact of their level of difficulty on motivation and performance;
- describe the influence of participation in the budgeting process.

Control is the process of ensuring that a firm's activities conform to its plan and that its objectives are achieved. There can be no control without objectives and plans, since these predetermine and specify the desirable behaviour and set out the procedures that should be followed by members of the organization to ensure that a firm is operated in a desired manner.

Drucker (1964) distinguishes between 'controls' and 'control'. Controls are measurement and information, whereas control means direction. In other words, 'controls' are purely a means to an end; the end is control. 'Control' is the function that makes sure that actual work is done to fulfil the original intention, and 'controls' are used to provide information to assist in determining the control action to be taken. For example, material costs may be greater than budget. 'Controls' will indicate that costs exceed budget and that this may be because the purchase of inferior quality materials causes excessive wastage. 'Control' is the action that is taken to purchase the correct quality materials in the future to reduce excessive wastage.

'Controls' encompasses all the methods and procedures that direct employees towards achieving the organization objectives. Many different control mechanisms are used in organizations and the management accounting control system represents only one aspect of the various control mechanisms that companies use to control their managers and employees. To fully understand the role that management accounting control systems play in the control process, it is necessary to be aware of how they relate to the entire array of control mechanisms used by organizations. Note that the term **management control system** is used to refer to the entire array of controls used by an organization

This chapter begins by describing the different types of controls that are used by companies. The elements of management accounting control systems will then be described within the context of the overall control process.

DIFFERENT TYPES OF CONTROLS

Companies use many different control mechanisms to cope with the problem of organizational control. To make sense of the vast number of controls that are used we shall classify them into three categories using approaches that have been adopted by Ouchi (1979) and Merchant (1998). They are:

1 action (or behavioural) controls;
2 personnel, cultural and social controls;
3 results (or output) controls.

You should note that management accounting systems are normally synonymous with output controls whereas management control systems encompass all of the above categories of controls.

Action or behavioural controls

Behavioural controls (also known as **action controls**) involve observing the actions of individuals as they go about their work. They are appropriate where cause-and-effect relationships are well understood, so that if the correct means are followed, the desired outcomes will occur. Under these circumstances effective control can be achieved by having superiors watch and guide the actions of subordinates. For example, if the supervisor watches the workers on the assembly line and ensures that the work is done exactly as prescribed then the expected quality and quantity of work should ensue. Forms of action controls described by Merchant include behavioural constraints, preaction reviews and action accountability.

The aim of *behavioural constraints* is to prevent people from doing things that should not be done. They include physical constraints, such as computer passwords that restrict accessing or updating information sources to authorized personnel, and administrative constraints, such as ceilings on the amount of capital expenditure that managers may authorize.

Preaction reviews involve the scrutiny and approval of action plans of the individuals being controlled before they can undertake a course of action. Examples include the approval by municipal authorities of plans for the construction of properties prior to building commencing or the approval by a tutor of a dissertation plan prior to the student being authorized to embark on the dissertation.

Action accountability involves defining actions that are acceptable or unacceptable, observing the actions and rewarding acceptable or punishing unacceptable actions. Examples of action accountability include establishing work rules and procedures and company codes of conduct that employees must follow. Budgets are another form of action accountability whereby an upper limit on an expense category is given for the budget period. If managers exceed these limits they are held accountable and are required to justify their actions.

Personnel, cultural and social controls

Social controls involve the selection of people who have already been socialized into adopting particular norms and patterns of behaviour to perform particular tasks. For example, if the only staff promoted to managerial level are those who display a high commitment to the firm's objectives then the need for other forms of controls can be reduced, provided that the managers are committed to achieving the 'right' objectives.

Personnel controls involve helping employees do a good job by building on employees' natural tendencies to control themselves. In particular, they ensure that the employees have the capabilities (in terms of intelligence, qualifications and experience) and the resources needed to do a good job. Merchant identifies three major methods of implementing personnel controls. They are selection and placement, training and job design and the provision of the necessary resources. Selection and placement involves finding the right people to do a specified job. Training can be used to ensure that employees know how to perform the assigned tasks and to make them fully aware of the results and actions that are expected from them. Job design entails designing jobs in such a way that enables employees to undertake their tasks with a high degree of success. This requires that jobs are not made too complex, onerous or badly defined such that employees do not know what is expected of them.

Cultural controls represent a set of values, social norms and beliefs that are shared by members of the organization and that influence their actions. Cultural controls are exercised by individuals over one another – for example, procedures used by groups within an organization to regulate performance of their own members and to bring them into line when they deviate from group norms. It is apparent from the above description that cultural controls are virtually the same as social controls.

Results or output controls

Output or results controls involve collecting and reporting information about the outcomes of work effort. The major advantage of results controls is that senior managers do not have to be knowledgeable about the means required to achieve the desired results or be involved in directly observing the actions of subordinates. They merely rely on output reports to ascertain whether or not the desired outcomes have been achieved. Management accounting control systems can be described as a form of output controls. They are mostly defined in monetary terms such as revenues, costs, profits and ratios (e.g. return on investment). Results measures also include non-accounting measures such as the number of units of defective production, the number of loan applications processed or ratio measures such as the number of customer deliveries on time as a percentage of total deliveries.

Results controls involve the following stages:

1 establishing results (i.e. performance) measures that minimize undesirable behaviour;

2 establishing performance targets;

3 measuring performance;

4 providing rewards or punishment.

Ideally, desirable behaviour should improve the performance measure and undesirable behaviour should have a detrimental effect on the measure. A performance measure that is not a good indicator of what is desirable to achieve the organization's objectives might actually encourage employees to take actions that are detrimental to the organization. The term 'What you measure is what you get' can apply whereby employees concentrate on improving the performance measures even when they are aware that their actions are not in the firm's best interests. For example, a divisional manager whose current return on investment (ROI) is 30 per cent might reject a project that yields an ROI of 25 per cent because it will lower the division's average ROI, even though the project has a positive NPV, and acceptance is in the best interests of the organization.

Without the *second-stage* requirement of a pre-set performance target individuals do not know what to aim for. It is also difficult for employees or their superiors to interpret performance unless actual performance can be compared against predetermined standards.

The *third stage* specified above relates to measuring performance. Ability to measure some outputs effectively constrains the use of results measures. Consider a personnel department. The accomplishments of the department can be difficult to measure and other forms of control are likely to be preferable.

The *final stage* of results controls involves encouraging employees to achieve organizational goals by having rewards (or punishments) linked to their success (or failure) in achieving the results measures. Organizational rewards include salary increases, bonuses, promotions and recognition. Employees can also derive intrinsic rewards through a sense of accomplishment and achievement. Punishments include demotions, failure to obtain the rewards and possibly the loss of one's job.

FEEDBACK AND FEED-FORWARD CONTROLS

Feedback control involves monitoring outputs achieved against desired outputs and taking whatever corrective action is necessary if a deviation exists. In feed-forward control, instead of actual outputs being compared against desired outputs, predictions are made of what outputs are expected to be at some future time. If these expectations differ from what is desired, control actions are taken that will minimize these differences. The objective is for control to be achieved before any deviations from desired outputs actually occur. In other words, with feed-forward controls likely errors can be anticipated and steps taken to avoid them, whereas with feedback controls actual errors are identified after the event and corrective action is taken to implement future actions to achieve the desired outputs.

A major limitation of feedback control is that errors are allowed to occur. This is not a significant problem when there is a short time lag between the occurrence of an error and the identification and implementation of corrective action. Feed-forward control is therefore preferable when a significant time lag occurs. The budgeting process is a feed-forward control system. To the extent that outcomes fall short of what is desired, alternatives are considered until a budget is produced that is expected to achieve what is desired. The comparison of actual results with budget, in identifying variances and taking remedial action to ensure that future outcomes will conform with budgeted outcomes is an illustration of a feedback control system. Thus accounting control systems consist of both feedback and feed-forward controls.

HARMFUL SIDE-EFFECTS OF CONTROLS

Harmful side-effects occur when the controls motivate employees to engage in behaviour that is not organizationally desirable. In this situation the control system leads to a lack of goal congruence. Alternatively, when controls motivate behaviour that is organizationally desirable they are described as encouraging goal congruence.

Results controls can lead to a lack of goal congruence if the results that are required can only be partially specified. Here there is a danger that employees will concentrate only on what is monitored by the control system, regardless of whether or not it is organizationally desirable. In other words, they will seek to maximize their individual performance according to the rules of the control system irrespective of whether their actions contribute to the organization's objectives. In addition, they may ignore other important areas, if they are not monitored by the control system. The term 'What you measure is what you get' applies in these circumstances.

Figure 10.1, derived from Otley (1987), illustrates the problems that can arise when the required results can only be partially specified. You will see that those aspects of behaviour on which subordinates are likely to concentrate to achieve their personal goals (circle B) do not necessarily correspond with those necessary for achieving the wider organizational goals (circle A). In an ideal system the measured behaviour (represented by circle C) should completely cover the area of desired behaviour (represented by circle A). Therefore if a manager maximizes the performance measure, he or she will also maximize his or her contribution to the goals of the organization. In other words, the performance measures encourage goal congruence. In practice, it is unlikely that perfect performance measures can be constructed that measure all desirable organizational behaviour, and so it is unlikely that all of circle C will cover circle A. Assuming that managers desire the rewards offered by circle C, their actual behaviour (represented by circle B) will be altered to include more of circle C and, to the extent that C coincides with A, more of circle A.

However, organizational performance will be improved only to the extent that the performance measure is a good indicator of what is desirable to achieve the firm's goals.

REAL WORLD VIEWS 10.1

Crime-fighting targets lead to 'dysfunctional' policing says police chief

Government crime-fighting targets are a shambles and should be scrapped, claims Chief Superintendent Ian Johnston. Mr Johnston was speaking ahead of the Police Superintendents' Association's 2007 annual conference, when he will ask the police minister to scrap the current targets regime.

'I believe we should abolish the performance framework in its entirety,' Mr Johnston said. 'It sounds radical, but it would be very warmly welcomed by the police service and would allow us, the professionals, to make judgements. We want to reclaim policing for the police.' He added: 'Centrally imposed targets are preventing senior police officers from delivering the policing that the public wants and deserves. We need to restore discretion to senior police officers enabling them to make decisions that relate to local policing issues, ensuring that we deliver a high standard of quality policing.'

In May 2007, the leaders of rank-and-file police officers made a similar demand to reverse the target-driven culture that has forced them to make 'ludicrous' decisions such as a case in Kent where a child was arrested for throwing cream buns at a bus. The Police Federation said judging officers purely on how many arrests, cautions or on-the-spot fines they can deliver was making a mockery of the criminal justice system. The drive to meet Whitehall performance targets was compelling officers to criminalize middle England, they added.

The organization published a dossier of ridiculous cases they claimed resulted from Home Office targets placed on beat bobbies. The cases included a Cheshire man who was cautioned by police for being found in possession of an egg with intent to throw, and a West Midlands woman arrested on her wedding day for criminal damage to a car park barrier when her foot slipped on her accelerator.

Today, Mr Johnston said, 'current Home Office targets have made some senior officers seriously ill from the stress of managing a wide range of competing demands. More than 70 per cent of basic command unit commanders believe national targets have had a negative impact on service delivery. We are obliged to count everything and in order to account for our performance we are not addressing a lot of the issues that the public see as far more important.' He added: 'The time has come for someone to say that the performance framework and the red tape and the bureaucracy have got to go. The government's focus on volume crime targets is skewing all police activity in a way that our members see as increasingly dysfunctional.'

Discussion point

How might the dysfunctional effects of the performance system in the police force be minimized?

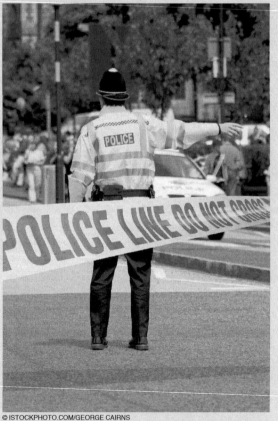

© ISTOCKPHOTO.COM/GEORGE CAIRNS

SOURCE: DAILY MAIL, 7 SEPTEMBER 2007 (WWW.DAILYMAIL.CO.UK/NEWS/ARTICLE-480296).

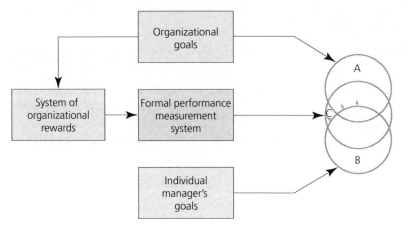

FIGURE 10.1

The measurement and reward process with imperfect measures

A Behaviour necessary to achieve organizational goals
B Behaviour actually engaged in by an individual manager
C Behaviour formally measured by control systems

Unfortunately, performance measures are not perfect, and ideal measures of overall performance are unlikely to exist. Some measures may encourage goal congruence or organizationally desirable behaviour (the part of circle C that coincides with A), but other measures will not encourage goal congruence (the part of circle C that does not coincide with A). Consequently, there is a danger that subordinates will concentrate only on what is measured, regardless of whether or not it is organizationally desirable. Furthermore, actual behaviour may be modified so that desired results appear to be obtained, although they may have been achieved in an undesirable manner that is detrimental to the firm.

MANAGEMENT ACCOUNTING CONTROL SYSTEMS

Although output controls predominantly consist of management accounting controls, the latter have not been examined in detail. To enable you to understand the role that management accounting control systems play within the overall control process this chapter has initially adopted a broad approach to describing management control systems. We shall now concentrate on management accounting control systems, which represent the predominant controls in most organizations.

Why are accounting controls the predominant controls? There are several reasons. First, all organizations need to express and aggregate the results of a wide range of dissimilar activities using a common measure. The monetary measure meets this requirement. Secondly, profitability and liquidity are essential to the success of all organizations and financial measures relating to these and other areas are closely monitored by stakeholders. It is therefore natural that managers will wish to monitor performance in monetary terms. Thirdly, financial measures also enable a common decision rule to be applied by all managers when considering alternative courses of action. That is, a course of action will normally benefit a firm only if it results in an improvement in its financial performance. Finally, measuring results in financial terms enables managers to be given more autonomy. Focusing on the outcomes of managerial actions, summarized in financial terms, gives managers the freedom to take whatever actions they consider to be appropriate to achieve the desired results.

RESPONSIBILITY CENTRES

The complex environment in which most businesses operate today makes it virtually impossible for most firms to be controlled centrally. This is because it is not possible for central management to have all the relevant information and time to determine the detailed plans for all the organization. Some degree of decentralization is essential for all but the smallest firms. Organizations decentralize by creating responsibility centres. A **responsibility centre** may be defined as a unit of a firm where an individual manager is held responsible for the unit's performance. There are four types of responsibility centre. They are:

1 cost or expense centres;
2 revenue centres;
3 profit centres;
4 investment centres.

The creation of responsibility centres is a fundamental part of management accounting control systems. It is therefore important that you can distinguish between the various forms of responsibility centres.

Cost or expense centres

Cost or **expense centres** are responsibility centres whose managers are normally accountable for only those costs that are under their control. We can distinguish between two types of cost centres – standard cost centres and discretionary cost centres. The main features of **standard cost centres** are that output can be measured and the input required to produce each unit of output can be specified. Control is exercised by comparing the standard cost (that is, the cost of the inputs that *should* have been consumed in producing the output) with the cost that was *actually* incurred. The difference between the actual cost and the standard cost is described as the variance. Standard cost centres and variance analysis will be discussed extensively in the next chapter.

Discretionary expense centres are those responsibility cost centres where output cannot be measured in financial terms and there are no clearly observable relationships between inputs (the resources consumed) and the outputs (the results achieved). Control normally takes the form of ensuring that actual expenditure adheres to budgeted expenditure for each expense category and also ensuring that the tasks assigned to each centre have been successfully accomplished. Examples of discretionary centres include advertising and publicity and research and development departments. One of the major problems arising in discretionary expense centres is measuring the effectiveness of expenditures. For example, the marketing support department may not have exceeded an advertising budget but this does not mean that the advertising expenditure has been effective. The advertising may have been incorrectly timed, it may have been directed to the wrong audience, or it may have contained the wrong message. Determining the effectiveness and efficiency of discretionary expense centres is one of the most difficult areas of management control.

Revenue centres

Revenue centres are responsibility centres where managers are mainly accountable for financial outputs in the form of generating sales revenues. Typical examples of revenue centres are where regional sales managers are accountable for sales within their regions. Revenue centre managers may also be held accountable for selling expenses, such as salesperson salaries, commissions and order-getting costs. They are not, however, made accountable for the cost of the goods and services that they sell.

Profit centres

Both cost and revenue centre managers have limited decision-making authority. Cost centre managers are accountable only for managing inputs of their centres and decisions relating to outputs are made by other units within the firm. Revenue centres are accountable for selling the products or services but they have no control over their manufacture. A significant increase in managerial autonomy occurs when unit managers are given responsibility for both production and sales. In this situation managers are normally free to set selling prices, choose which markets to sell in, make product mix and output decisions and select suppliers. Units within an organization whose managers are accountable for both revenues and costs are called profit centres.

Investment centres

Investment centres are responsibility centres whose managers are responsible for both sales revenues and costs and, in addition, have responsibility and authority to make working capital and capital investment decisions. Typical investment centre performance measures include return on investment and economic value added. These measures are influenced by revenues, costs and assets employed and thus reflect the responsibility that managers have for both generating profits and managing the investment base. Investment centres represent the highest level of managerial autonomy. They include the company as a whole, operating subsidiaries, operating groups and divisions. Investment and profit centres will be discussed extensively in Chapter 12.

THE NATURE OF MANAGEMENT ACCOUNTING CONTROL SYSTEMS

Management accounting control systems have two core elements. The first is the formal planning processes such as budgeting and long-term planning that were described in the previous chapter. These processes are used for establishing performance expectations for evaluating performance. The second is responsibility accounting, which involves the creation of responsibility centres. Responsibility centres enable accountability for financial results and outcomes to be allocated to individuals throughout the organization. The objective of responsibility accounting is to accumulate costs and revenues for each individual responsibility centre so that the deviations from a performance target (typically the budget) can be attributed to the individual who is accountable for the responsibility centre. For each responsibility centre the process involves setting a performance target, measuring performance, comparing performance against the target, analysing the variances and taking action where significant variances exist between actual and target performance.

Responsibility accounting is implemented by issuing performance reports at frequent intervals (normally monthly) that inform responsibility centre managers of the deviations

EXHIBIT 10.1

Responsibility accounting monthly performance reports

Performance report to managing director		Budget		Variance[a] F (A)	
		Current month (£)	Year to date (£)	This month (£)	Year to date (£)
Managing director	▶Factory A	453 900	6 386 640	80 000(A)	98 000(A)
	Factory B	X	X	X	X
	Factory C	X	X	X	X
	Administration costs	X	X	X	X
	Selling costs	X	X	X	X
	Distribution costs	X	X	X	X
		2 500 000	30 000 000	400 000(A)	600 000(A)
Performance report to production manager of factory A					
Production manager	Works manager's office	X	X	X	X
	▶Machining department 1	165 600	717 600	32 760(A)	89 180(A)
	Machining department 2	X	X	X	X
	Assembly department	X	X	X	X
	Finishing department	X	X	X	X
		453 900	6 386 640	80 000(A)	98 000(A)
Performance report to head of responsibility centre					
Head of responsibility centre	Direct materials	X	X	X	X
	Direct labour	X	X	X	X
	Indirect labour	X	X	X	X
	Indirect materials	X	X	X	X
	Power	X	X	X	X
	Maintenance	X	X	X	X
	Idle time	X	X	X	X
	Other	X	X	X	X
		165 600	717 600	32 760(A)	89 180(A)

[a] F indicates a favourable variance (actual cost less than budgeted cost) and (A) indicates an adverse budget (actual cost greater than budget cost). Note that, at the lowest level of reporting, the responsibility centre head's performance report contains detailed information on operating costs. At successively higher levels of management less detail is reported. For example, the managing director's information on the control of activities consists of examining those variances that represent significant departures from the budget for each factory and functional area of the business and requesting explanations from the appropriate managers.

from budgets for which they are accountable and are required to take action. An example of a performance report issued to a cost centre manager is presented in the lower section of Exhibit 10.1. You should note that at successively higher levels of management less detailed information is reported. You can see from the upper sections of Exhibit 10.1 that the information is condensed and summarized as the results relating to the responsibility centre are reported at higher levels. Exhibit 10.1 only includes financial information. In addition, non-financial measures such as those relating to quality and timeliness may be reported. We shall look at non-financial measures in more detail in Chapter 15.

Responsibility accounting involves:

● distinguishing between those items that managers can control and for which they should be held accountable and those items over which they have no control and for which they are not held accountable (i.e. applying the controllability principle);

- setting financial performance targets and determining how challenging the financial targets should be;
- determining how much influence managers should have in the setting of financial targets.

We shall now examine each of these items in detail.

THE CONTROLLABILITY PRINCIPLE

Responsibility accounting is based on the application of the controllability principle, which means that it is appropriate to charge to an area of responsibility only those costs that are significantly influenced by the manager of that responsibility centre. The controllability principle can be implemented by either eliminating the uncontrollable items from the areas for which managers are held accountable or calculating their effects so that the reports distinguish between controllable and uncontrollable items.

Applying the controllability principle is difficult in practice because many areas do not fit neatly into either controllable or uncontrollable categories. Instead, they are partially controllable. For example, even when outcomes may be affected by occurrences outside a manager's control – such as competitors' actions, price changes and supply shortages – managers can take action to reduce their adverse effects. They can substitute alternative materials where the prices of raw materials change or they can monitor and respond to competitors' actions. If these factors are categorized as uncontrollables managers will be motivated not to try and influence them.

Dealing with the distorting effects of uncontrollable factors before the measurement period

Management can attempt to deal with the distorting effects of uncontrollables by making adjustments either before or after the measurement period. Uncontrollable and controllable factors can be determined prior to the measurement period by specifying which budget line items are to be regarded as controllable and uncontrollable. Uncontrollable items can either be excluded from performance reports or shown in a separate section within the performance report so that they are clearly distinguishable from controllable items. The latter approach has the advantage of drawing managerial attention to those costs that a company incurs to support their activities. Managers may be able to indirectly influence these costs if they are made aware of the sums involved.

How do we distinguish between controllable and uncontrollable items? Merchant suggests that the following general rule should be applied to all employees – 'Hold employees accountable for the performance areas you want them to pay attention to.' Applying this rule explains why some organizations assign the costs of shared resource pools, such as administrative costs relating to personnel and data processing departments, to responsibility centres. Assigning these costs authorizes managers of the user responsibility centres to question the amount of the costs and the quantity and quality of services supplied. In addition, responsibility centres are discouraged from making unnecessary requests for the use of these services when they are aware that increases in costs will be assigned to the users of the services.

Dealing with the distorting effects of uncontrollable factors after the measurement period

Merchant identifies four methods of removing the effects of uncontrollable factors from the results measures after the measurement period and before the rewards are assigned. They are:

1 variance analysis;
2 flexible performance standards;
3 relative performance evaluations;
4 subjective performance evaluations.

Variance analysis seeks to analyse the factors that cause the actual results to differ from pre-determined budgeted targets. In particular, variance analysis helps to distinguish between controllable and uncontrollable items and identify those individuals who are accountable for the variances. For example, variances analysed by each type of cost, and by their price and quantity effects, enables variances to be traced to accountable individuals and also to isolate those variances that are due to uncontrollable factors. Variance analysis will be discussed extensively in the next chapter.

Flexible performance standards apply when targets are adjusted to reflect variations in uncontrollable factors arising from the circumstances not envisaged when the targets were set. The most widely used flexible performance standard is to use flexible budgets whereby the uncontrollable volume effects on cost behaviour are removed from the manager's performance reports. Because some costs vary with changes in the level of activity, it is essential when applying the controllability principle to take into account the variability of costs. For example, if the actual level of activity is greater than the budgeted level of activity then those costs that vary with activity will be greater than the budgeted costs purely because of changes in activity. Let us consider the simplified situation presented in Example 10.1.

Assuming that the increase in activity was due to an increase in sales volume greater than that anticipated when the budget was set then the increases in costs arising from the volume change are beyond the control of the responsibility centre manager. It is clearly inappropriate to compare actual *variable* costs of £105 000 from an activity level of 24 000 units with budgeted *variable* costs of £100 000 from an activity level of 20 000 units. This would incorrectly suggest an overspending of £5000. If managers are to be made responsible for their costs, it is essential that they are responsible for performance under the conditions in which they worked, and not for a performance based on conditions when the budget was drawn up. In other words, it is misleading to compare actual costs at one level of activity with budgeted costs at another level of activity. At the end of the period the original budget must be adjusted to the actual level of activity to take into account the impact of the uncontrollable volume change on costs. This procedure is called flexible budgeting. In Example 10.1 the performance report should be as follows:

Budgeted expenditure	Actual expenditure
(flexed to 24 000 units)	(24 000 units)
£120 000	£105 000

The budget is adjusted to reflect what the costs should have been for an actual activity of 24 000 units. This indicates that the manager has incurred £15 000 less expenditure than

EXAMPLE 10.1

An item of expense that is included in the budget for a responsibility centre varies directly in relation to activity at an estimated cost of £5 per unit of output. The budgeted monthly level of activity was 20 000 units and the actual level of activity was 24 000 units at a cost of £105 000.

would have been expected for the actual level of activity, and a favourable variance of £15 000 should be recorded on the performance report, not an adverse variance of £5000, which would have been recorded if the original budget had not been adjusted.

In Example 10.1 it was assumed that there was only one variable item of expense, but in practice the budget will include many different expenses including fixed, semi-variable and variable expenses. You should note that fixed expenses do not vary in the short term with activity and therefore the budget should remain unchanged for these expenses. The budget should be flexed only for variable and semi-variable expenses.

Budgets may also be adjusted to reflect other uncontrollable factors besides volume changes. Budgets are normally set based on the environment that is anticipated during the budget setting process. If the budget targets are then used throughout the duration of the annual budget period for performance evaluation the managers will be held accountable for uncontrollable factors arising from forecasting errors. To remove the managerial exposure to uncontrollable risks arising from forecasting errors ex post budget adjustments can be made whereby the budget is adjusted to the environmental and economic conditions that the manager's actually faced during the period.

Relative performance evaluation relates to the situations where the performance of a responsibility centre is evaluated relative to the performance of similar centres within the same company or to similar units outside the organization. To be effective responsibility centres must perform similar tasks and face similar environmental and business conditions with the units that they are being benchmarked against. Such relative comparisons with units facing similar environmental conditions neutralizes the uncontrollable factors because they are in effect held constant when making the relative comparisons. The major difficulty relating to relative performance evaluations is finding benchmark units that face similar conditions and uncertainties.

Instead of making the formal and quantitative adjustments that are a feature of the methods that have been described so far, subjective judgements can be made in the evaluation process based on the knowledge of the outcome measures and the circumstances faced by the responsibility centre heads. The major advantage of subjective evaluations is that they can alleviate some of the defects of the measures used by accounting control systems. The disadvantages of subjective evaluations are that they are not objective, they tend not to provide the person being evaluated with a clear indication of how performance has been evaluated, they can create conflict with superiors resulting in a loss of morale and a decline in motivation and they are expensive in terms of management time.

REAL WORLD VIEWS 10.2

SOURCE: ADAPTED FROM Z. JUN LIN AND Z. YU (2002). RESPONSIBILITY COST CONTROL SYSTEM IN CHINA: A CASE OF MANAGEMENT ACCOUNTING

Responsibility cost control systems in China

Because of the previous lack of effective control of expenditure by the Han Dan Company a system of responsibility accounting and standard costing was introduced in 1990. The basic principles underlying the responsibility cost control system included: (1) setting cost and profit targets (responsibility standards) that take into account market pressures; (2) assigning target costs to various levels of responsibility centre; (3) evaluating performance based on fulfilment of the responsibility targets; and (4) implementing a reward scheme with built-in incentive mechanisms. In order to facilitate performance measurement and evaluation, non-controllable common costs were excluded from the responsibility costs decomposed within primary production factories. Responsibility contracts between factory managers and managers at lower levels must also be signed. Breakdown of the aggregated responsibility targets to all profit centres and their subordinates are conducted by the Department of Finance and Accounting. In addition, the department is responsible for monthly and yearly reporting of the execution results of the responsibility cost control system. It also reports and analyses the variances between actual outcomes and responsibility targets, and determines the necessary bonus rewards (or penalty) for each responsibility centre in terms of the fulfilment of the cost and profit targets signed by managers. If a responsibility centre or individual worker fails to meet the cost targets specified in the responsibility contracts, all bonus and other benefits relating to the responsibility unit or worker will be forfeited.

© FLEYEING/DREAMSTIME.COM

Discussion point

What are the limitations of linking bonuses to meeting cost targets?

Guidelines for applying the controllability principle

Dealing with uncontrollables represents one of the most difficult areas for the design and operation of management accounting control systems. The following guidelines published by the Report of the Committee of Cost Concepts and Standards in the United States in 1956 still continues to provide useful guidance:

1 If a manager *can control the quantity and price paid* for a service then the manager is responsible for all the expenditure incurred for the service.

2 If the manager *can control the quantity of the service but not the price paid* for the service then only that amount of difference between actual and budgeted expenditure that is due to usage should be identified with the manager.

3 If the manager *cannot control either the quantity or the price paid* for the service then the expenditure is uncontrollable and should not be identified with the manager.

An example of the latter situation is when the costs of an industrial relations department are apportioned to a department on some arbitrary basis; such arbitrary apportionments are likely to result in an allocation of expenses that the managers of responsibility centres may not be able to influence. In addition to the above guidelines Merchants's general rule should also be used as a guide – 'Hold employees accountable for the performance areas you want them to pay attention to.'

SETTING FINANCIAL PERFORMANCE TARGETS AND DETERMINING HOW CHALLENGING THEY SHOULD BE

There are three approaches that can be used to set financial targets. They are targets derived from engineering studies of input–output relationships, targets derived from historical data and targets derived from negotiations between superiors and subordinates.

Engineered targets can be used when there are clearly defined and stable input–output relationships such that the inputs required can be estimated directly from product specifications. For example, in a fast-food restaurant for a given output of hamburgers it is possible to estimate the inputs required because there is a physical relationship between the ingredients such as meats, buns, condiments and packaging and the number of hamburgers made. Input–output relationships can also be established for labour by closely observing the processes to determine the quantity of labour that will be required for a given output.

Where clearly defined input–output relationships do not exist other approaches must be used to set financial targets. One approach is to use historical targets derived directly from the results of previous periods. Previous results plus an increase for expected price changes may form the basis for setting the targets or an improvement factor may be incorporated into the estimate, such as previous period costs less a reduction of 10 per cent. The disadvantage of using historical targets is that they may include past inefficiencies or may encourage employees to underperform if the outcome of efficient performance in a previous period is used as a basis for setting a more demanding target in the next period.

Negotiated targets are set based on negotiations between superiors and subordinates. The major advantage of negotiated targets is that they address the information asymmetry gap that can exist between superior and subordinate. This gap arises because subordinates have more information than their superiors on the relationships between outputs and inputs and the constraints that exist at the operating level, whereas superiors have a broader view of the organization as a whole and the resource constraints that apply. You should refer back to the previous chapter for a more detailed discussion of the negotiation process.

The effect of the level of budget difficulty on motivation and performance

The fact that a financial target represents a specific quantitative goal gives it a strong motivational potential, but the targets set must be accepted if managers are to be motivated to achieve higher levels of performance. Unfortunately, it is not possible to specify exactly the optimal degree of difficulty for financial targets, since task uncertainty and cultural, organizational and personality factors all affect an individual manager's reaction to a financial target.

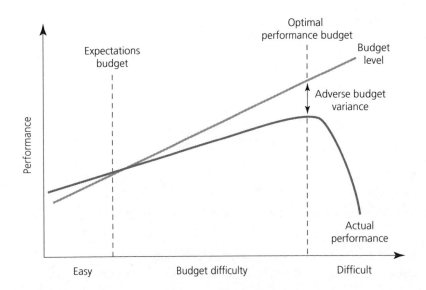

FIGURE 10.2
The effect of budget difficulty on performance

Figure 10.2, derived from Otley (1987), shows the theoretical relationship between budget difficulty, aspiration levels and performance. In Figure 10.2 it is assumed that performance and aspiration levels are identical. Note that the aspiration level relates to the personal goal of the budgetee (that is, the person who is responsible for the budget). In other words, it is the level of performance that they hope to attain. You will see from Figure 10.2 that as the level of budget difficulty is increased both the budgetees' aspiration level and performance increases. However, there comes a point where the budget is perceived as impossible to achieve and the aspiration level and performance decline dramatically. It can be seen from Figure 10.2 that the budget level that motivates the best level of performance may not be achievable. In contrast, the budget that is expected to be achieved (that is, the expectations budget in Figure 10.2) motivates a lower level of performance.

To motivate the best level of actual performance, demanding budgets should be set and small adverse variances should be regarded as a healthy sign and not as something to be avoided. If budgets are always achieved with no adverse variances, this indicates that the standards are too loose to motivate the best possible results.

Arguments in favour of setting highly achievable budgets

It appears from our previous discussion that tight budgets should be established to motivate maximum performance, although this may mean that the budget has a high probability of not being achieved. However, budgets are not used purely as a motivational device to maximize performance. They are also used for planning purposes and it is most unlikely that tight budgets will be suitable for planning purposes. Why? Tight budgets that have a high probability of not being achieved are most unsuitable for cash budgeting and for harmonizing the company plans in the form of a master budget. Most companies use the same budgets for planning and motivational purposes (Umapathy, 1987). If only one set of budgets is used it is most unlikely that one set can, at the same time, perfectly meet both the planning and the motivational requirements.

Budgets with a high probability of being achieved are widely used in practice. They provide managers with a sense of achievement and self-esteem that can be beneficial to the organization in terms of increased levels of commitment and aspirations. Rewards such as bonuses, promotions and job security are normally linked to budget achievement so that the costs of failing to meet budget targets can be high. The greater the probability of the failure to meet budget targets the greater is the probability that managers will be motivated to distort their performance by engaging in behaviour that will result in the harmful side-effects described earlier in this chapter.

PARTICIPATION IN THE BUDGETING AND TARGET SETTING PROCESS

Participation relates to the extent that subordinates or budgetees are able to influence the figures that are incorporated in their budgets or targets. Participation is sometimes referred to as bottom-up budget setting whereas a non-participatory approach whereby subordinates have little influence on the target setting process is sometimes called top-down budget setting.

Allowing individuals to participate in the setting of performance targets has several advantages. First, individuals are more likely to accept the targets and be committed to achieving them if they have been involved in the target setting process. Secondly, participation can reduce the information asymmetry gap that applies when standards are imposed from above. Earlier in this chapter it was pointed out that subordinates have more information than their superiors on the relationships between outputs and inputs and the constraints that exist at the operating level whereas the superiors have a broader view of the organization as a whole and the resource constraints that apply. This information-sharing process enables more effective targets to be set that attempt to deal with both operational and organizational constraints. Finally, imposed standards can encourage negative attitudes and result in demotivation and alienation. This in turn can lead to a rejection of the targets and poor performance.

Participation has been advocated by many writers as a means of making tasks more challenging and giving individuals a greater sense of responsibility. For many years participation in decision-making was thought to be a panacea for effective organizational effort but this school of thought was later challenged. The debate has never been resolved. The believers have never been able to demonstrate that participation really does have a positive effect on productivity and the sceptics have never been able to prove the opposite (Macintosh, 1985).

Because of the conflicting findings relating to the effectiveness of participation, research has tended to concentrate on studying how various factors influence the effectiveness of participation. If participation is used selectively and in the right circumstances it has an enormous potential for encouraging the commitment to organizational goals, improving attitudes towards the budgeting system and increasing subsequent performance. Note, however, at this stage that there are some limitations on the positive effects of participation in standard setting and circumstances where top-down budget setting is preferable. They are:

1 Performance is measured by precisely the same standard that the budgetee has been involved in setting. This gives the budgetee the opportunity to negotiate lower targets that increase the probability of target achievement and the accompanying rewards. Therefore an improvement in performance – in terms of comparison with the budget – may result merely from a lowering of the standard.

2 Participation by itself is not adequate in ensuring commitment to standards. The manager must also believe that he or she can significantly influence the results and be given the necessary feedback about them.

3 A top-down approach to budget setting is likely to be preferable where a process is highly programmable, and there are clear and stable input–output relationships, so that engineered studies can be used to set the targets. Here there is no need to negotiate targets using a bottom-up process.

SUMMARY

The following items relate to the learning objectives listed at the beginning of the chapter.

● **Describe the three different types of controls used in organizations**. Three different categories of controls are used – action/behavioural controls, personnel/ cultural controls and results/output controls. With action controls the actions themselves are the focus of controls. Personnel controls help employees do a good job by building on employees' natural tendencies to control themselves. They include selection and placement, training and job design. Cultural controls represent a set of values, social norms and beliefs that are shared by members of the organization and that influence their actions. Output or results controls involve collecting and reporting information about the outcomes of work effort.

● **Distinguish between feedback and feed-forward controls**. Feedback control involves monitoring outputs achieved against desired outputs and taking whatever corrective action is necessary if a deviation exists. In feed-forward control, instead of actual outputs being compared against desired outputs, predictions are made of what outputs are expected to be at some future time. If these expectations differ from what is desired, control actions are taken that will minimize these differences. The objective is for control to be achieved before any deviations from desired outputs actually occur. The budgeting process is a feed-forward control system. The comparison of actual results with budget, in identifying variances and taking remedial action to ensure future outcomes will conform with budgeted outcomes, is an illustration of a feedback control system.

● **Explain the potential harmful side-effects of results controls**. Results controls can promote a number of harmful side-effects. They can lead to a lack of goal congruence when employees seek to achieve the performance targets in a way that is not organizationally desirable. They can also lead to data manipulation and negative attitudes, which can result in a decline in morale and a lack of motivation.

● **Define the four different types of responsibility centres**. A responsibility centre may be defined as a unit of a firm where an individual manager is held accountable for the unit's performance. There are four types of responsibility centres – cost or expense centres, revenue centres, profit centres and investment centres. Cost or expense centres are responsibility centres whose managers are normally accountable for only those costs that are under their control. Revenue centres are responsibility centres where managers are accountable only for financial outputs in the form of generating sales revenues. A significant increase in managerial autonomy occurs when unit managers are given responsibility for both production and sales. Units within an organization whose managers are accountable for both revenues and costs are called profit centres. Investment centres are responsibility centres whose managers are responsible for both sales revenues and costs and, in addition, have responsibility and authority to make working capital and capital investment decisions.

● **Explain the different elements of management accounting control systems.** Management accounting control systems have two core elements. The first is the formal planning processes such as budgeting and long-term planning. These processes are used for establishing performance expectations for evaluating performance. The second is responsibility accounting, which involves the creation of responsibility centres. Responsibility centres enable accountability for financial results/outcomes to be allocated to individuals throughout the organization. Responsibility accounting involves: (a) distinguishing between those items that managers can control and for which they should be held accountable and those items over which they have no control and for which they are not held accountable; (b) determining how challenging the financial targets should be; and (c) determining how much influence managers should have in the setting of financial targets.

● **Describe the controllability principle and the methods of implementing it.** The controllability principle states that it is appropriate to charge to an area of responsibility only those costs that are significantly influenced by the manager of that responsibility centre. The controllability principle can be implemented by either eliminating the uncontrollable items from the areas that managers are held accountable for or calculating their effects so that the reports distinguish between controllable and uncontrollable items.

● **Describe the different approaches that can be used to determine financial performance targets and discuss the impact of their level of difficulty on motivation and performance.** There are three approaches that can be used to set financial targets. They involve targets derived from engineering studies of input/output relationships, targets derived from historical data and targets derived from negotiations between superiors and subordinates. Different types of financial performance targets can be set ranging from easily achievable to difficult to achieve. Targets that are considered moderately difficult to achieve (called highly achievable targets) are recommended because they can be used for planning purposes and they also have a motivational impact.

● **Describe the influence of participation in the budgeting process.** Participation relates to the extent that budgetees are able to influence the figures that are incorporated in their budgets or targets. Allowing individuals to participate in the setting of performance targets has the following advantages: (a) individuals are more likely to accept the targets and be committed to achieving them if they have been involved in the target setting process; (b) participation can reduce the information asymmetry gap that applies when standards are imposed from above; and (c) imposed standards can encourage negative attitudes and result in demotivation and alienation. Participation, however, is subject to the following limitations: (a) performance is measured by precisely the same standard that the budgetee has been involved in setting; and (b) a top-down approach to budget setting is likely to be preferable where a process is highly programmable. Participation must be used selectively; but if it is used in the right circumstances, it has an enormous potential for encouraging the commitment to organizational goals.

KEY TERMS AND CONCEPTS

action controls (p. 238)
aspiration level (p. 256)
behavioural controls (p. 238)
bottom-up budget setting (p. 253)
control (p. 237)
controllability principle (p. 247)
controls (p. 237)
cost centres (p. 245)
cultural controls (p. 239)
discretionary expense centres (p. 244)
engineered targets (p. 251)
expense centres (p. 244)
ex post budget adjustments (p. 249)
feedback control (p. 240)
feed-forward control (p. 240)
flexible budgets (p. 248)
goal congruence (p. 241)
historical targets (p. 251)

investment centres (p. 245)
management control systems (p. 238)
negotiated targets (p. 251)
output controls (p. 239)
participation (p. 253)
personnel controls (p. 239)
profit centres (p. 245)
relative performance evaluation (p. 249)
responsibility accounting (p. 245)
responsibility centre (p. 244)
results controls (p. 239)
revenue centres (p. 244)
social controls (p. 239)
standard cost centres (p. 244)
subjective judgements (p. 249)
top-down budget setting (p. 253)
variance analysis (p. 248)

ASSESSMENT MATERIAL

The review questions are short questions that enable you to assess your understanding of the main topics included in the chapter. The page numbers in parentheses provide you with the page numbers to refer to if you cannot answer a specific question.

The review problems are more complex and require you to relate and apply the content to various business problems. Solutions to review problems are provided in a separate section at the end of the book. Additional review problems can be accessed by lecturers and students on the website www.drury-online.com. Solutions to these problems are provided for lecturers in the *Instructors' Manual*. This is available on the lecturers' password-protected section of the website.

The website also includes over 30 case study problems. A list of these cases is provided on pages 389–392. Several cases are relevant to the content of this chapter. Examples include Airport Complex and Integrated Technology Services (UK) Ltd.

REVIEW QUESTIONS

10.1 Distinguish between 'controls' and 'control'. *(pp. 237–38)*

10.2 Identify and describe three different types of control mechanisms used by companies. *(pp. 238–40)*

10.3 Provide examples of behavioural, action, social, personnel and cultural controls. *(pp. 238–40)*

10.4 Describe the different stages that are involved with output/results controls. *(p. 240)*

10.5 Distinguish between feedback and feed-forward controls. Provide an example of each type of control. *(pp. 240–41)*

10.6 Describe some of the harmful side-effects that can occur with output/results controls. *(pp. 241–42*

10.7 Describe the four different types of responsibility centres. *(pp. 244–45)*

10.8 Explain what is meant by the term 'responsibility accounting'. *(pp. 245–47)*

10.9 What factors must be taken into account when operating a responsibility accounting system? *(p. 245–47)*

10.10 What is the 'controllability principle'? Describe the different ways in which the principle can be applied. *(pp. 247–51)*

10.11 What are flexible budgets? Why are they preferred to fixed (static) budgets? *(pp. 248–49)*

10.12 What is meant by the term 'aspiration level'? *(p. 252)*

10.13 Describe the effect of the level of budget difficulty on motivation and performance. *(pp. 251–52)*

10.14 Distinguish between participation and top-down budget setting. *(pp. 253–54)*

10.15 Describe the factors influencing the effectiveness of participation in the budget process. *(p. 253)*

10.16 What are the limitations of participation in the budget process? *(pp. 253–54)*

REVIEW PROBLEMS

10.17   Preparation of a flexible budget performance report

The Viking Smelting Company established a division, called the reclamation division, two years ago, to extract silver from jewellers' waste materials. The waste materials are processed in a furnace, enabling silver to be recovered. The silver is then further processed into finished products by three other divisions within the company.

A performance report is prepared each month for the reclamation division which is then discussed by the management team. Sharon Houghton, the newly appointed financial controller of the reclamation division, has recently prepared her first report for the four weeks to 31 May. This is shown below:

Performance Report Reclamation Division
4 weeks to 31 May

	Actual	Budget	Variance	Comments
Production (tonnes)	200	250	50 (F)[a]	
	(£)	(£)	(£)	
Wages and social security costs	46 133	45 586	547 (A)	Overspend
Fuel	15 500	18 750	3 250 (F)	
Consumables	2 100 .	2 500	400 (F)	
Power	1 590	1 750	160 (F)	
Divisional overheads	21 000	20 000	1 000 (A)	Overspend
Plant maintenance	6 900	5 950	950 (A)	Overspend
Central services	7 300	6 850	450 (A)	Overspend
Total	100 523	101 386	863 (F)	

[a](A) = adverse, (F) = favourable

In preparing the budgeted figures, the following assumptions were made for May:

- the reclamation division was to employ four teams of six production employees;
- each employee was to work a basic 42-hour week and be paid £7.50 per hour for the four weeks of May;
- social security and other employment costs were estimated at 40 per cent of basic wages;
- a bonus, shared amongst the production employees, was payable if production exceeded 150 tonnes. This varied depending on the output achieved, as follows:
  1. if output was between 150 and 199 tonnes, the bonus was £3 per tonne produced;
  2. if output was between 200 and 249 tonnes, the bonus was £8 per tonne produced;
  3. if output exceeded 249 tonnes the bonus was £13 per tonne produced;
- the cost of fuel was £75 per tonne;
- consumables were £10 per tonne;
- power comprised a fixed charge of £500 per four weeks plus £5 per tonne for every tonne produced;
- overheads directly attributable to the division were £20 000;

- plant maintenance was to be apportioned to divisions on the basis of the capital values of each division;
- the cost of Viking's central services was to be shared equally by all four divisions.

You are the deputy financial controller of the reclamation division. After attending her first monthly meeting with the board of the reclamation division, Sharon Houghton arranges a meeting with you. She is concerned about a number of issues, one of them being that the current report does not clearly identify those expenses and variances that are the direct responsibility of the reclamation division.

Task 1

Sharon Houghton asks you to prepare a flexible budget report for the reclamation division for May in a form consistent with responsibility accounting.

On receiving your revised report. Sharon tells you about the other questions raised at the management meeting when the original report was presented. These are summarized below:

(i)   Why are the budget figures based on two-year-old data taken from the proposal recommending the establishment of the reclamation division?
(ii) Should the budget data be based on what we were proposing to do or what we actually did do?
(iii) is it true that the less we produce the more favourable our variances will be?
(iv) Why is there so much maintenance in a new division with modern equipment and why should we be charged with the actual costs of the maintenance department even when they overspend?
(v)   Could the comments, explaining the variances, be improved?
(vi) Should all the variances be investigated?
(vii) Does showing the cost of central services on the divisional performance report help control these costs and motivate the divisional managers?

Task 2

Prepare a memo for the management of the reclamation division. Your memo should answer their queries and justify their comments.

10.18 Comments on a performance report

The Victorial Hospital is located in a holiday resort that attracts visitors to such an extent that the population of the area is trebled for the summer months of June, July and August. From past experience, this influx of visitors doubles the activity of the hospital during these months. The annual budget for the hospital's laundry department is broken down into four quarters, namely April–June, July–September, October–December and January–March, by dividing the annual budgeted figures by four. The budgeting work has been done for the current year by the secretary of the hospital using the previous year's figures and adding 3 per cent for inflation. It is realized by the Hospital Authority that management information for control purposes needs to be improved, and you have been recruited to help to introduce a system of responsibility accounting.

You are required, from the information given, to:

(a) comment on the way in which the quarterly budgets have been prepared and to suggest improvements that could be introduced when preparing the budgets for 2009–10;

(b) state what information you would like to flow from the actual against budget comparison (note that calculated figures are not required);

(c) state the amendments that would be needed to the current practice of budgeting and reporting to enable the report shown below to be used as a measure of the efficiency of the laundry manager.

Victorial Hospital – Laundry Department
Report for quarter ended 30 September 2008

	Budget	Actual
Patients days	9 000	12 000
Weight processed (kg)	180 000	240 000
	(£)	(£)
Costs:		
Wages	8 800	12 320
Overtime premium	1 400	2 100
Detergents and other supplies	1 800	2 700
Water, water softening and heating	2 000	2 500
Maintenance	1 000	1 500
Depreciation of plant	2 000	2 000
Manager's salary	1 250	1 500
Overhead, apportioned:		
for occupancy	4 000	4 250
for administration	5 000	5 750

(15 marks)

10.19 Flexible budgets and the motivational role of budgets

Club Atlantic is an all-weather holiday complex providing holidays throughout the year. The fee charged to guests is fully inclusive of accommodation and all meals. However, because the holiday industry is so competitive, Club Atlantic is only able to generate profits by maintaining strict financial control of all activities.

The club's restaurant is one area where there is a constant need to monitor costs. Susan Green is the manager of the restaurant. At the beginning of each year she is given an annual budget which is then broken down into months. Each month she receives a statement monitoring actual costs against the annual budget and highlighting any variances. The statement for the month ended 31 October is reproduced below along with a list of assumptions:

Club Atlantic Restaurant Performance Statement
Month to 31 October

	Actual	Budget	Variance (over)/ under
Number of guest days	11 160	9 600	(1 560)
	(£)	(£)	(£)
Food	20 500	20 160	(340)
Cleaning materials	2 232	1 920	(312)
Heat, light and power	2 050	2 400	350
Catering wages	8 400	7 200	(1 200)
Rent rates, insurance and depreciation	1 860	1 800	(60)
	35 042	33 480	(1 562)

Assumptions:

(a) The budget has been calculated on the basis of a 30-day calendar month with the cost of rents, insurance and depreciation being an apportionment of the fixed annual charge.

(b) The budgeted catering wages assume that:

   (i) there is one member of the catering staff for every 40 guests staying at the complex;

   (ii) the daily cost of a member of the catering staff is £30.

(c) All other budgeted costs are variable costs based on the number of guest days.

Task 1

Using the data above, prepare a revised performance statement using flexible budgeting. Your statement should show both the revised budget and the revised variances. Club Atlantic uses the existing budgets and performance statements to motivate its managers as well as for financial control. If managers keep expenses below budget they receive a bonus in addition to their salaries. A colleague of Susan is Brian Hilton. Brian is in charge of the swimming pool and golf course, both of which have high levels of fixed costs. Each month he manages to keep expenses below budget and in return enjoys regular bonuses. Under the current reporting system, Susan Green only rarely receives a bonus.

At a recent meeting with Club Atlantic's directors Susan Green expressed concern that the performance statement was not a valid reflection of her management of the restaurant. You are currently employed by Hall and Co., the club's auditors, and the directors of Club Atlantic have asked you to advise them whether there is any justification for Susan Green's concern.

At the meeting with the Club's directors, you were asked the following questions:

(a) Do budgets motivate managers to achieve objectives?

(b) Does motivating managers lead to improved performance?

(c) Does the current method of reporting performance motivate Susan Green and Brian Hilton to be more efficient?

Task 2

Write a *brief* letter to the directors of Club Atlantic addressing their question and justifying your answers.

Note: You should make use of the data given in this task plus your findings in Task 1.

10.20 Recommendations for improvements to a performance report and a review of the management control system

Your firm has been consulted by the managing director of Inzone plc, which owns a chain of retail stores. Each store has departments selling furniture, tableware and kitchenware. Departmental managers are responsible to a store manager, who is in turn responsible to head office (HO).

All goods for sale are ordered centrally and stores sell at prices fixed by HO. Store managers (aided by departmental managers) order stocks from HO and stores are charged interest based on month-end stock levels. HO appoints all permanent staff and sets all pay levels. Store managers can engage or dismiss temporary workers, and are responsible for store running expenses.

The introduction to Inzone plc's management accounting manual states:

Budgeting starts three months before the budget year, with product sales projections which are developed by HO buyers in consultation with each store's departmental managers. Expense budgets, adjusted for expected inflation, are then prepared by HO for each store. Inzone plc's accounting year is divided into 13 four-weekly control periods, and the budgeted sales and expenses are assigned to periods with due regard to seasonal factors. The budgets are completed one month before the year begins on 1 January.

All HO expenses are recharged to stores in order to give the clearest indication of the 'bottom line' profit of each store. These HO costs are mainly buying expenses, which are recharged to stores according to their square footage.

Store reports comparing actual results with budgets are on the desks of HO and store management one week after the end of each control period. Significant variations in performance are then investigated, and appropriate action taken.

Ms Lewis is manager of an Inzone plc store. She is eligible for a bonus equal to 5 per cent of the amount by which her store's 'bottom-line' profit exceeds the year's budget. However, Ms Lewis sees no chance of a bonus this year, because major roadworks near the store are disrupting trade. Her store report for the four weeks ending 21 June is as follows:

	Actual (£)	Budget (£)
Sales	98 850	110 000
Costs:		
Cost of goods (including stock losses)	63 100	70 200
Wages and salaries	5 300	5 500
Rent	11 000	11 000
Depreciation of store fittings	500	500
Distribution costs	4 220	4 500
Other store running expenses	1 970	2 000
Interest charge on stocks	3 410	3 500
Store's share of HO costs	2 050	2 000
Store profit	7 300	10 800
	98 850	110 000
Stocks held at end of period	341 000	350 000
Store fittings at written down value	58 000	58 000

Requirements:

(a) Make recommendations for the improvement of Inzone plc's store report, briefly justifying each recommendation.

(11 marks)

(b) Prepare a report for the managing director of Inzone plc reviewing the company's responsibility delegation, identifying the major strengths and weaknesses of Inzone plc's management control system, and recommending any changes you consider appropriate.

(14 marks)
(Total 25 marks)

10.21 You are required to:

(i) discuss the factors that are likely to cause managers to submit budget estimates of sales and costs that do not represent their best estimates or expectations of what will actually occur;

(8 marks)

(ii) suggest, as a budget accountant, what procedures you would advise in order to minimize the likelihood of such biased estimates arising.

(4 marks)

10.22 (a) Identify and explain the essential elements of an effective cost control system.

(13 marks)

(b) Outline possible problems that may be encountered as a result of the introduction of a system of cost control into an organization.

(4 marks)
(Total 17 marks)

10.23 You are required, within the context of budgetary control, to:

(a) explain the specific roles of planning, motivation and evaluation;

(7 marks)

(b) describe how these roles may conflict with each other;

(7 marks)

(c) give *three* examples of ways by which the management accountant may resolve the conflict described in (b).

(6 marks)

10.24 (a) Explain the ways in which the attitudes and behaviour of managers in a company are liable to pose more threat to the success of its budgetary control system than are minor technical inadequacies that may be in the system.

(15 marks)

(b) Explain briefly what the management accountant can do to minimize the disruptive effects of such attitudes and behaviour.

(5 marks)

10.25 What are the behavioural aspects that should be borne in mind by those who are designing and operating standard costing and budgetary control systems?

(20 marks)

10.26 In his study of 'The Impact of Budgets on People', C. Argyris reported *inter alia* the following comment by a financial controller on the practice of participation in the setting of budgets in his company:

'We bring in the supervisors of budget areas, we tell them that we want their frank opinion, but most of them just sit there and nod their heads. We know they're not coming out with exactly how they feel. I guess budgets scare them.'

You are required to suggest reasons why managers may be reluctant to participate fully in setting budgets, and to suggest also unwanted side-effects that may arise from the imposition of budgets by senior management.

(13 marks)

10.27 The typical budgetary control system in practice does not encourage *goal congruence*, contains *budgetary slack*, ignores the *aspiration levels* of participants and attempts to control operations by *feedback*, when *feed-forward* is likely to be more effective; in summary the typical budgetary control system is likely to have dysfunctional effects.

 You are required to

(a) explain briefly *each* of the terms in italics;

(6 marks)

(b) describe how the major dysfunctional effects of budgeting could be avoided.

(11 marks)
(Total 17 marks)

CHAPTER 11
STANDARD COSTING AND VARIANCE ANALYSIS

LEARNING OBJECTIVES

After studying this chapter you should be able to:

- **explain how a standard costing system operates;**
- **explain how standard costs are set;**
- **explain the meaning of standard hours produced;**
- **identify and describe the purposes of a standard costing system;**
- **calculate labour, material, overhead and sales margin variances and reconcile actual profit with budgeted profit;**
- **identify the causes of labour, material, overhead and sales margin variances.**

In the previous chapter the major features of management accounting control systems were examined. The different types of controls used by companies were explained so that the elements of management accounting control systems could be described within the context of the overall control process. A broad approach to control was adopted and the detailed procedures of financial controls were not examined. In this chapter we shall focus on the detailed financial controls that are used by organizations.

We shall consider a financial control system that enables the deviations from budget to be analysed in detail, thus enabling costs to be controlled more effectively. This system of control is called standard costing. In particular, we shall examine how a standard costing system operates and how the variances are calculated. Standard costing systems are applied in cost centres where the output can be measured and the input required to produce each unit of output can be specified. Therefore standard costing is generally applied to manufacturing activities, and non-manufacturing activities are not incorporated within the standard costing system. In addition, the sales variances that are described in this chapter can also be applied in revenue centres.

Standard costs are predetermined costs; they are target costs that should be incurred under efficient operating conditions. They are not the same as budgeted costs. A budget relates to an entire activity or operation; a standard presents the same information on a per unit basis. A standard therefore provides cost expectations per unit of activity and a budget provides the cost expectation for the total activity. If the budget output for a product is for 10 000 units and the standard cost is £3 per unit, budgeted cost will be £30 000. We shall see that establishing standard costs for each unit produced enables a detailed analysis to be made of the difference between the budgeted cost and the actual cost so that costs can be controlled more effectively.

OPERATION OF A STANDARD COSTING SYSTEM

Standard costing is most suited to an organization whose activities consist of a series of *common* or *repetitive* operations and the input required to produce each unit of output can be specified. It is therefore relevant in manufacturing companies, since the processes involved are often of a repetitive nature. Standard costing procedures can also be applied in service industries such as units within banks, where output can be measured in terms of the number of cheques or the number of loan applications processed, and there are also well-defined input–output relationships. Standard costing cannot, however, be applied to activities of a non-repetitive nature, since there is no basis for observing repetitive operations and consequently standards cannot be set.

A standard costing system can be applied to organizations that produce many different products, as long as production consists of a series of common operations. For example, if the output from a factory is the result of five common operations, it is possible to produce many different product variations from these operations. It is therefore possible that a large product range may result from a small number of common operations. Thus standard costs should be developed for repetitive operations and product standard costs are derived simply by combining the standard costs from the operations that are necessary to make the product. This process is illustrated in Exhibit 11.1.

It is assumed that the standard costs are £20, £30, £40 and £50 for each of the operations 1 to 4. The standard cost for *product* 100 is therefore £110, which consists of £20 for operation 1, plus £40 and £50 for operations 3 and 4. The standard costs for each of the other products are calculated in a similar manner. In addition, the total standard cost for the total output of each operation for the period has been calculated. For example, six items of operation number 1 have been completed, giving a total standard cost of £120 for this operation (six items at £20 each). Three items of operation 2 have been completed, giving a total standard cost of £90, and so on.

Variances allocated to responsibility centres

You can see from Exhibit 11.1 that different responsibility centres are responsible for each operation. For example, responsibility centre A is responsible for operation 1, responsibility

EXHIBIT 11.1

Standard costs analysed by operations and products

Responsibility centre	Operation no. and standard cost		Products							Total standard cost	Actual cost
	No.	(£)	100	101	102	103	104	105	106	(£)	
A	1	20	✓	✓		✓	✓	✓	✓	120	
B	2	30		✓		✓		✓		90	
C	3	40	✓		✓		✓			120	
D	4	50	✓	✓	✓				✓	200	
Standard product cost			£110	£100	£90	£50	£60	£50	£70	530	

FIGURE 11.1

An overview of a standard costing system

centre B for operation 2, and so on. Consequently, there is no point in comparing the actual cost of *product* 100 with the standard cost of £110 for the purposes of control, since responsibility centres A, C and D are responsible for the variance. None of the responsibility centres is solely answerable for the variance. Cost control requires that responsibility centres be identified with the standard cost for the output achieved. Therefore if the actual costs for responsibility centre A are compared with the standard cost of £120 for the production of the six items (see first row of Exhibit 11.1), the manager of this responsibility centre will be answerable for the full amount of the variance. Only by comparing total actual costs with total standard costs *for each operation or responsibility centre* for a period can control be effectively achieved. A comparison of standard *product* costs (i.e. the columns in Exhibit 11.1) with actual costs that involves several different responsibility centres is clearly inappropriate.

Figure 11.1 provides an overview of the operation of a standard costing system. You will see that the standard costs for the actual output for a particular period are traced to the managers of responsibility centres who are responsible for the various operations. The actual costs for the same period are also charged to the responsibility centres. Standard and actual costs are compared and the variance is reported. For example, if the actual cost for the output of the six items produced in responsibility centre A during the period is £220 and the standard cost is £120 (Exhibit 11.1), a variance of £100 will be reported.

Detailed analysis of variances

The box below the first arrow in Figure 11.1 indicates that the operation of a standard costing system also enables a detailed analysis of the variances to be reported. For example, variances for each responsibility centre can be identified by each element of cost and analysed according to the price and quantity content. The accountant assists managers by pinpointing where the variances have arisen and the responsibility managers can undertake to carry out the appropriate investigations to identify the reasons for the variance. For example, the accountant might identify the reason for a direct materials variance as being excessive usage of a certain material in a particular process, but the responsibility centre manager must investigate this process and identify the reasons for the excessive usage. Such an investigation should result in appropriate remedial action being taken or, if it is found that the variance is due to a permanent change in the standard, the standard should be changed.

Actual product costs are not required

It is questionable whether the allocation of actual costs to products serves any useful purpose. Because standard costs represent *future* target costs, they are preferable to actual *past* costs for decision-making. Also, the external financial accounting regulations in most countries specify that if standard product costs provide a reasonable approximation of actual product costs, they are acceptable for inventory valuation calculations for external reporting.

There are therefore strong arguments for not producing actual *product* costs when a standard costing system exists, since this will lead to a large reduction in information processing costs. However, it must be stressed that actual costs must be accumulated periodically for each operation or responsibility centre, so that comparisons can be made with standard costs. Nevertheless, there will be considerably fewer responsibility centres than products, and the accumulation of actual costs is therefore much less time-consuming.

ESTABLISHING COST STANDARDS

Control over costs is best effected through action at the point where the costs are incurred. Hence the standards should be set for the quantities of material, labour and services to be consumed in performing an *operation*, rather than the complete *product* cost standards. Variances from these standards should be reported to show causes and responsibilities for deviations from standard. Product cost standards are derived by listing and adding the standard costs of operations required to produce a particular product. For example, if you refer to Exhibit 11.1 you will see that the standard cost of product 100 is £110 and is derived from the sum of the standard costs of operations 1, 3 and 4.

There are two approaches that can be used to set standard costs. First, past historical records can be used to estimate labour and material usage. Secondly, standards can be set based on **engineering studies**. With engineering studies a detailed study of each operation is undertaken based on careful specifications of materials, labour and equipment and on controlled observations of operations. If historical records are used to set standards, there is a danger that the latter will include past inefficiencies. With this approach, standards are set based on average past performance for the same or similar operations.

The disadvantage of this method is that, unlike the engineering method, it does not focus attention on finding the best combination of resources, production methods and product quality. Nevertheless, standards derived from average historical usage do appear to be widely used in practice. (See Exhibit 11.3.)

Let us now consider how standards are established for each operation for direct labour, direct materials and overheads using the engineering studies approach. Note that the standard cost for each operation is derived from multiplying the quantity of input that should be used per unit of output (i.e. the quantity standard) by the amount that should be paid for each unit of input (i.e. the price standard).

Direct material standards

These are based on product specifications derived from an intensive study of the input *quantity* necessary for each operation. This study should establish the most suitable materials for each operation, based on product design and quality policy, and also the optimal quantity that should be used after taking into account any wastage or loss that is considered inevitable in the production process. Material quantity standards are usually recorded on a bill of materials. This describes and states the required quantity of materials for each operation to complete the product. A separate bill of materials is maintained for each product. The standard material product cost is then found by multiplying the standard quantities by the appropriate standard prices.

The standard *prices* are obtained from the purchasing department. The standard material prices are based on the assumption that the purchasing department has carried out a suitable search of alternative suppliers and has selected suppliers who can provide the required quantity of sound quality materials at the most competitive price. Standard prices then provide a suitable base against which actual prices paid for materials can be evaluated.

Direct labour standards

To set labour standards, activities should be analysed by the different operations. Each operation is studied and an allowed time computed. The normal procedure for such a study is to analyse each operation to eliminate any unnecessary elements and to determine the most efficient production method. The most efficient methods of production, equipment and operating conditions are then standardized. This is followed by time measurements that are made to determine the number of standard hours required by an average worker to complete the job. Unavoidable delays such as machine breakdowns and routine maintenance are included in the standard time. The wage rates are applied to the standard time allowed to determine the standard labour cost for each operation.

Overhead standards

The procedure for establishing standard manufacturing overhead rates for a standard costing system is the same as that which is used for establishing *predetermined* overhead rates as described in Chapter 7. Separate rates for fixed and variable overheads are essential for planning and control. With traditional costing systems the standard overhead rate will be based on a rate per direct labour hour or machine hour of input.

EXHIBIT 11.2

An illustration of a standard cost card

Date standard set ....   Product: sigma

Direct materials

Operation no.	Item code	Quantity (kg)	Standard price (£)	Department				Totals (£)
				A	B	C	D	
1	5.001	5	3	£15				
2	7.003	4	4		£16			
								31

Direct labour

Operation no.	Standard hours	Standard rate (£)				
1	7	9	£63			
2	8	9		£72		
						135

Factory overhead

Operation no.	Standard hours	Standard rate (£)			
1	7	3	£21		
2	8	4		£32	
					53
Total manufacturing cost per unit (£)					219

Fixed overheads are largely independent of changes in activity, and remain constant over wide ranges of activity in the short term. It is therefore inappropriate for short-term cost control purposes to unitize fixed overheads to derive a fixed overhead rate per unit of activity. However, in order to meet the external financial reporting stock valuation requirements, fixed manufacturing overheads must be traced to products. It is therefore necessary to unitize fixed overheads for stock valuation purposes.

The main difference with the treatment of overheads under a standard costing system as opposed to a non-standard costing system is that the product overhead cost is based on the hourly overhead rates multiplied by the *standard hours* (that is, hours that should have been used) rather than the *actual hours* used.

A standard cost card should be maintained for each product and operation. It reveals the quantity of each unit of input that should be used to produce one unit of output. A typical product standard cost card is illustrated in Exhibit 11.2. In most organizations standard cost cards are now in computerized format. Standards should be continuously reviewed, and, where significant changes in production methods or input prices occur, they should be changed in order to ensure that standards reflect current targets.

Standard hours produced

It is not possible to measure *output* in terms of units produced for a department making several different products or operations. For example, if a department produces 100 units of product X, 200 units of product Y and 300 units of product Z, it is not possible to add the production of these items together, since they are not homogeneous. This problem can be overcome by ascertaining the amount of time, working under efficient conditions, it should take to make each product. This time calculation is called standard hours produced. In other words, standard hours are an *output* measure that can act as a common denominator for adding together the production of unlike items.

The effect of standards on product and service quality

Setting standards in an organization may be primarily to assist in the calculation of a standard cost for the product or service for management accounting purposes. Standards are also relevant for operational and customer service managers as they may affect the manufacture of the product or the quality of the service.

Take McDonald's, Burger King or Coca-Cola for example. All three companies produce products that adhere to standard ingredients, albeit with some minimal regional variation. A BigMac or Whopper for example, will contain a beef pattie that is manufactured to an exact uncooked weight. Similarly, every bottle or Coca-Cola will contain a similar amount of cola concentrate. As the ingredients are standardized according to 'recipes', a standard cost can be readily calculated and used for cost control and performance reporting. Perhaps more importantly, the customer is confident of getting a similar product on each purchase.

In comparison, consider a car-hire company like Hertz or a bank like HSBC. Most service organizations will have a customer care (HSBC) or reservations (Hertz) call centre. Staff at these centres will have a standard customer handling time to adhere to – perhaps three minutes. It is not always possible to deal with customer issues or make a sale in the allotted time. Exceeding the standard handling time ultimately increases cost as more staff may be needed to handle customer call volume. On the other hand, by strictly adhering to a standard handling time, customer satisfaction and quality of service may be reduced. Thus, in a service company scenario, a fine balance between standards and quality must be achieved to ensure customer satisfaction in the longer term.

© PETER HORREE/ALAMY

Discussion points

1 Do you think it is plausible to set standards for delivery of a service, which are primarily dictated by cost?
2 Is it possible to measure the delivery of a service (e.g. a mortgage application) against a set standard?

Let us assume that the following standard times are established for the production of one unit of each product:

Product X	5 standard hours
Product Y	2 standard hours
Product Z	3 standard hours

This means that it should take five hours to produce one unit of product X under efficient production conditions. Similar comments apply to products Y and Z. The production for the department will be calculated in standard hours as follows:

Product	Standard time per unit produced (hours)	Actual output (units)	Standard hours produced
X	5	100	500
Y	2	200	400
Z	3	300	900
			1800

Remember that standard hours produced is an output measure, and flexible budget allowances should be based on this. In the illustration we should expect the *output* of 1800 standard hours to take 1800 direct labour hours of *input* if the department works at the prescribed level of efficiency. The department will be inefficient if 1800 standard hours of output are produced using, say, 2000 direct labour hours of input. The flexible budget allowance should therefore be based on 1800 standard hours produced to ensure that no extra allowance is given for the 200 excess hours of input. Otherwise, a manager will obtain a higher budget allowance through being inefficient.

PURPOSES OF STANDARD COSTING

Standard costing systems are widely used because they provide cost information for many different purposes, such as the following:

- Providing a prediction of future costs that can be used for *decision-making purposes.* Standard costs can be derived from either traditional or activity-based costing systems. Because standard costs represent *future* target costs based on the elimination of avoidable inefficiencies they are preferable to estimates based on adjusted past costs which may incorporate inefficiencies. For example, in markets where competitive prices do not exist products may be priced on a bid basis. In these situations standard costs provide more appropriate information because efficient competitors will seek to eliminate avoidable costs. It is therefore unwise to assume that inefficiencies are recoverable within the bid price.

- Providing a *challenging target* that individuals are motivated to achieve. For example, research evidence suggests that the existence of a defined quantitative goal or target is likely to motivate higher levels of performance than would be achieved if no such target was set.

- Assisting in *setting budgets* and evaluating managerial performance. Standard costs are particularly valuable for budgeting because a reliable and convenient source of data is provided for converting budgeted production into physical and monetary resource requirements. Budgetary preparation time is considerably reduced if standard costs are available because the standard costs of operations and products can be readily built up into total costs of any budgeted volume and product mix.

- Acting as a *control device* by highlighting those activities that do not conform to plan and thus alerting managers to those situations that may be 'out of control' and in need of corrective action. With a standard costing system variances are analysed in great detail such as by element of cost, and price and quantity elements. Useful feedback is therefore provided in pinpointing the areas where variances have arisen.

EXHIBIT 11.3
*Surveys of
company practice*

Since its introduction in the early 1900s standard costing has flourished and is now one of the most widely used management accounting techniques. Three independently conducted surveys of USA practice indicate highly consistent figures in terms of adopting standard costing systems. Cress and Pettijohn (1985) and Schwarzbach (1985) report an 85 per cent adoption rate, while Cornick *et al.* (1988) found that 86 per cent of the surveyed firms used a standard costing system. A Japanese survey by Scarborough *et al.* (1991) reported a 65 per cent adoption rate. Surveys of UK companies by Drury *et al.* (1993) and New Zealand companies by Guilding *et al.* (1998) reported adoption rates of 76 per cent and 73 per cent respectively.

A CIMA sponsored study of 41 UK manufacturing organizations by Dugdale *et al.* (2006) reported that 30 of the firms employed standard costing. The majority of these firms (26) set standard costs for materials and labour and a smaller majority (20) also set standard overhead costs. They conclude that despite the huge changes in the manufacturing environment standard costing is alive and well.

In relation to the methods to set labour and material standards Drury *et al.* reported the following usage rates:

	Extent of use (%)				
	Never	Rarely	Sometimes	Often	Always
Standards based on design/ engineering studies	18	11	19	31	21
Observations based on trial runs	18	16	36	25	5
Work study techniques	21	18	19	21	21
Average of historic usage	22	11	23	35	9

In the USA Lauderman and Schaeberle (1983) reported that 43 per cent of the respondents used average historic usage, 67 per cent used engineering studies, 11 per cent used trial runs under controlled conditions and 15 per cent used other methods. The results add up to more than 100 per cent because some companies used more than one method.

● Simplifying the task of tracing costs to products for *profit measurement and inventory valuation* purposes. Besides preparing annual financial accounting profit statements most organizations also prepare monthly internal profit statements. If actual costs are used a considerable amount of time is required in tracking costs so that monthly costs can be allocated between cost of sales and inventories. A data processing system is required that can track monthly costs in

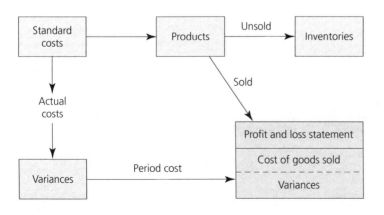

FIGURE 11.2
*Standard costs for
inventory valuation
and profit
measurement*

a resource efficient manner. Standard costing systems meet this requirement. You will see from Figure 11.2 that product costs are maintained at standard cost. Inventories and cost of goods sold are recorded at standard cost and a conversion to actual cost is made by writing off all variances arising during the period as a period cost. Note that the variances from standard cost are extracted by comparing actual with standard costs at the responsibility centre level, and not at the product level, so that actual costs are not assigned to individual products.

VARIANCE ANALYSIS

It is possible to compute variances simply by committing to memory a series of variance formulae. If you adopt this approach, however, it will not help you to understand what a variance is intended to depict and what the relevant variables represent. In our discussion of each variance we shall therefore concentrate on the fundamental meaning of the variance, so that you can logically deduce the variance formulae as we go along.

All of the variances presented in this chapter are illustrated from the information contained in Example 11.1. Note that the level of detail presented is highly simplified. A truly realistic situation would involve many products, operations and responsibility centres but would not give any further insights into the basic concepts or procedures.

Figure 11.3 shows the breakdown of the profit variance (the difference between budgeted and actual profit) into the component cost and revenue variances that can be calculated for a standard variable costing system. We shall now calculate the variances set out in Figure 11.3 using the data presented in Example 11.1.

FIGURE 11.3

Variance analysis for a variable costing system

aSelling and distribution cost variances are not presented in this chapter. If activities are of a repetitive nature, standards can be established and variances can be calculated in a similar manner to production cost variances. If standards cannot be established, costs should be controlled by comparing budgeted and actual costs.

EXAMPLE 11.1

Alpha manufacturing company produces a single product, which is known as sigma. The product requires a single operation, and the standard cost for this operation is presented in the following standard cost card:

Standard cost card for product sigma	(£)
Direct materials:	
2 kg of A at £10 per kg	20.00
1 kg of B at £15 per kg	15.00
Direct labour (3 hours at £9 per hour)	27.00
Variable overhead (3 hours at £2 per direct labour hour)	6.00
Total standard variable cost	68.00
Standard contribution margin	20.00
Standard selling price	88.00

Alpha Ltd plans to produce 10 000 units of sigma in the month of April, and the budgeted costs based on the information contained in the standard cost card are as follows:

Budget based on the above standard costs and an output of 10 000 units	(£)	(£)	(£)
Sales (10 000 units of sigma at £88 per unit)			880 000
Direct materials:			
A: 20 000 kg at £10 per kg	200 000		
B: 10 000 kg at £15 per kg	150 000	350 000	
Direct labour (30 000 hours at £9 per hour)		270 000	
Variable overheads (30 000 hours at £2 per direct labour hour)		60 000	680 000
Budgeted contribution			200 000
Fixed overheads			120 000
Budgeted profit			80 000

Annual budgeted fixed overheads are £1 440 000 and are assumed to be incurred evenly throughout the year. The company uses a variable costing system for internal profit measurement purposes.
    The actual results for April are:

	(£)	(£)
Sales (9000 units at £90)		810 000
Direct materials:		
A: 19 000 kg at £11 per kg	209 000	
B: 10 100 kg at £14 per kg	141 400	
Direct labour (28 500 hours at £9.60 per hour)	273 600	
Variable overheads	52 000	676 000
Contribution		134 000
Fixed overheads		116 000
Profit		18 000

Manufacturing overheads are charged to production on the basis of direct labour hours. Actual production and sales for the period were 9000 units.

MATERIAL VARIANCES

The costs of the materials used in a manufactured product are determined by two basic factors: the price paid for the materials, and the quantity of materials used in production. This gives rise to the possibility that the actual cost will differ from the standard cost because the *actual quantity* of materials used will be different from the *standard quantity* and/or that the *actual price* paid will be different from the *standard price*. We can therefore calculate a material usage and a material price variance.

MATERIAL PRICE VARIANCES

The starting point for calculating this variance is simply to compare the standard price per unit of materials with the actual price per unit. You should now read Example 11.1. You will see that the standard price for material A is £10 per kg, but the actual price paid was £11 per kg. The price variance is £1 per kg. This is of little consequence if the excess purchase price has been paid only for a small number of units or purchases. But the consequences are important if the excess purchase price has been paid for a large number of units, since the effect of the variance will be greater.

The difference between the standard material price and the actual price per unit should therefore be multiplied by the quantity of materials purchased. For material A the price variance is £1 per unit; but since 19 000 kg were purchased, the excess price was paid out 19 000 times. Hence the total material price variance is £19 000 adverse. The formula for the material price variance now follows logically:

the **material price variance** is equal to the difference between the standard price (SP) and the actual price (AP) per unit of materials multiplied by the quantity of materials purchased (QP):

$$(SP - AP) \times QP$$

Now refer to material B in Example 11.1. The standard price is £15, compared with an actual price of £14 giving a £1 saving per kg. As 10 100 kg were purchased, the total price variance will be £10 100 (10 100 kg at £1). The variance for material B is favourable and that for material A is adverse. The normal procedure is to present the amount of the variances followed by symbols A or F to indicate either adverse or favourable variances.

It is incorrect to assume that the material price variance will always indicate the efficiency of the purchasing department. Actual prices may exceed standard prices because of a change in market conditions that causes a general price increase for the type of materials used. The price variance might therefore be beyond the control of the purchasing department. Alternatively, an adverse price variance may reflect a failure by the purchasing department to seek the most advantageous sources of supply. A favourable price variance might be due to the purchase of inferior quality materials, which may lead to inferior product quality or more wastage. For example, the price variance for material B is favourable, but we shall see in the next section that this is offset by excess usage. If the reason for this excess usage is the purchase of inferior quality materials then the material usage variance should be charged to the purchasing department.

Calculation on quantity purchased or quantity used

It is important that variances be reported as quickly as possible so that any inefficiencies can be identified and remedial action taken. A problem occurs, however, with material purchases in that the time of purchase and the time of usage may not be the same: materials may be purchased in one period and used in a subsequent period. For example, if 10 000 units of a material are purchased in period 1 at a price of £1 per unit over standard and 2000 units are used in each of periods 1 to 5, the following alternatives are available for calculating the price variance:

1 The full amount of the price variance of £10 000 is reported in *period 1* with quantity being defined as the *quantity purchased*.

2 The price variance is calculated with quantity being defined as the *quantity used*. The unit price variance of £1 is multiplied by the quantity used (i.e. 2000 units), which means that a price variance of £2000 will be reported for each of *periods 1 to 5*.

Method 1 is recommended, because the price variance can be reported in the period in which it is incurred, and reporting of the total variance is not delayed until months later when the materials are used. Also, adopting this approach enables corrective action to be taken earlier. For the sake of simplicity we shall assume in Example 11.1 that the actual purchases are identical with the actual usage.

MATERIAL USAGE VARIANCE

The starting point for calculating this quantity variance is simply to compare the standard quantity that should have been used with the actual quantity that has been used. Refer again to Example 11.1. You will see that the standard usage for the production of one unit of sigma is 2 kg for material A. As 9000 units of sigma are produced, 18 000 kg of material A should have been used; however, 19 000 kg are actually used, which means there has been an excess usage of 1000 kg.

The importance of this excess usage depends on the price of the materials. For example, if the price is £0.01 per kg then an excess usage of 1000 kg will not be very significant, but if the price is £10 per unit then an excess usage of 1000 kg will be very significant. It follows that to assess the importance of the excess usage, the variance should be expressed in monetary terms.

Should the standard material price per kg or the actual material price per kg be used to calculate the variance? The answer is the standard price. If the *actual* material price is used, the usage variance will be affected by the efficiency of the purchasing department, since any excess purchase price will be assigned to the excess usage. It is therefore necessary to remove the price effects from the usage variance calculation, and this is achieved by valuing the variance at the standard price. Hence the 1000 kg excess usage of material A is multiplied by the standard price of £10 per unit, which gives an adverse usage variance of £10 000. The formula for the variance is:

the **material usage variance** is equal to the difference between the standard quantity (SQ) required for actual production and the actual quantity (AQ) used multiplied by the standard material price (SP):

$$(SQ - AQ) \times SP$$

For material B you will see from Example 11.1 that the standard quantity is 9000 kg (9000 units × 1 kg), but 10 100 kg have been used. The excess usage of 1100 kg is multiplied by the standard price of £15 per kg, which gives an adverse variance of £16 500. Note that the principles of flexible budgeting described in the previous chapter also apply here, with *standard quantity being based on actual production and not budgeted production.* This ensures that a manager is evaluated under the conditions in which he or she actually worked and not those envisaged at the time the budget was prepared.

The material usage variance is normally controllable by the manager of the appropriate production responsibility centre. Common causes of material usage variances include the careless handling of materials by production personnel, the purchase of inferior quality materials, pilferage, changes in quality control requirements, or changes in methods of production. Separate material usage variances should be calculated for each type of material used and allocated to each responsibility centre.

TOTAL MATERIAL VARIANCE

From Figure 11.3 you will see that this variance is the total variance before it is analysed into the price and usage elements. The formula for the variance is:

the **total material variance** is the difference between the standard material cost (SC) for the actual production and the actual cost (AC):

$$SC - AC$$

To compute the total material variance we need to determine what the standard cost of materials should be for the actual production. For material A the standard material cost is £20 per unit (see Example 11.1), giving a total standard material cost of £180 000 (9000 units × £20). The actual cost is £209 000, and therefore the variance is £29 000 adverse. The price variance of £19 000 plus the usage variance of £10 000 agrees with the total material variance. Similarly, the total material variance for material B is £6400, consisting of a favourable price variance of £10 100 and an adverse usage variance of £16 500.

Note that if the price variance is calculated on the actual quantity *purchased* instead of the actual quantity *used*, the price variance plus the usage variance will agree with the total variance only when the quantity purchased is equal to the quantity that is used in the particular accounting period. Reconciling the price and usage variance with the total variance is merely a reconciliation exercise, and you should not be concerned if reconciliation of the sub-variances with the total variance is not possible.

WAGE RATE VARIANCE

The cost of labour is determined by the price paid for labour and the quantity of labour used. Thus a price and quantity variance will also arise for labour. The price (wage rate) variance is calculated by comparing the standard price per hour with the actual price paid per hour. In Example 11.1 the standard wage rate per hour is £9 and the actual wage rate is £9.60 per hour, giving a wage rate variance of £0.60 per hour. To determine the importance of the variance, it is necessary to ascertain how many times the excess payment of £0.60 per hour is paid. As 28 500 labour hours are used (see Example 11.1), we multiply

28 500 hours by £0.60. This gives an adverse wage rate variance of £17 100. The formula for the wage rate variance is:

the **wage rate variance** is equal to the difference between the standard wage rate per hour (SR) and the actual wage rate (AR) multiplied by the actual number of hours worked (AH):

$$(SR - AR) \times AH$$

Note the similarity between this variance and the material price variance. Both variances multiply the difference between the standard price and the actual price paid for a unit of a resource by the actual quantity of resources used.

The wage rate variance is probably the one that is least subject to control by management. In most cases the variance is due to wage rate standards not being kept in line with changes in actual wage rates, and for this reason it is not normally controllable by departmental managers.

LABOUR EFFICIENCY VARIANCE

The labour efficiency variance represents the quantity variance for direct labour. The quantity of labour that should be used for the actual output is expressed in terms of *standard hours produced*. In Example 11.1 the standard time for the production of one unit of sigma is three hours. Thus a production level of 9000 units results in an output of 27 000 standard hours. In other words, working at the prescribed level of efficiency, it should take 27 000 hours to produce 9000 units. However, 28 500 direct labour hours are actually required to produce this output, which means that 1500 excess direct labour hours are used. We multiply the excess direct labour hours by the *standard* wage rate of £9 per hour to calculate the variance. This gives an adverse variance of £13 500. The formula for calculating the labour efficiency variance is:

the **labour efficiency variance** is equal to the difference between the standard labour hours for actual production (SH) and the actual labour hours worked (AH) during the period multiplied by the standard wage rate per hour (SR):

$$(SH - AH) \times SR$$

This variance is similar to the material usage variance. Both variances multiply the difference between the standard quantity and actual quantity of resources consumed by the standard price.

The labour efficiency variance is normally controllable by the manager of the appropriate production responsibility centre and may be due to a variety of reasons. For example, the use of inferior quality materials, different grades of labour, failure to maintain machinery in proper condition, the introduction of new equipment or tools and changes in the production processes will all affect the efficiency of labour. An efficiency variance may not always be controllable by the production supervisors; it may be due, for example, to poor production scheduling by the planning department, or to a change in quality control standards.

TOTAL LABOUR VARIANCE

From Figure 11.3 you will see that this variance represents the total variance before analysis into the price and quantity elements. The formula for the variance is:

the **total labour variance** is the difference between the standard labour cost (SC) for the actual production and the actual labour cost (AC):

$$SC - AC$$

In Example 11.1 the actual production was 9000 units, and, with a standard labour cost of £27 per unit, the standard cost is £243 000 (9000 × £27). The actual cost is £273 600, which gives an adverse variance of £30 600. This consists of a wage rate variance of £17 100 and a labour efficiency variance of £13 500.

VARIABLE OVERHEAD VARIANCES

A total variable overhead variance is calculated in the same way as the total direct labour and material variances. In Example 11.1 the output is 9000 units and the standard variable overhead cost is £6 *per unit* produced. The standard cost for the production of 9000 units for variable overheads is thus £54 000. The actual variable overheads incurred are £52 000, giving a favourable variance of £2000. The formula for the variance is:

the **total variable overhead variance** is the difference between the standard variable overheads charged to production (SC) and the actual variable overheads incurred (AC):

$$SC - AC$$

Where variable overheads vary with direct labour or machine hours of *input* the total variable overhead variance will be due to one or both of the following:

1 A *price* variance arising from actual expenditure being different from budgeted expenditure.
2 A *quantity* variance arising from actual direct labour or machine hours of input being different from the hours of input, which *should* have been used.

These reasons give rise to the two sub-variances, which are shown in Figure 11.3: the variable overhead expenditure variance and the variable overhead efficiency variance.

Variable overhead expenditure variance

To compare the actual overhead expenditure with the budgeted expenditure, it is necessary to flex the budget. Because it is assumed in Example 11.1 that variable overheads will vary with direct labour hours of *input* the budget is flexed on this basis. Actual variable overhead expenditure is £52 000, resulting from 28 500 direct labour hours of input. For this level of activity variable overheads of £57 000, which consist of 28 500 input hours at £2 per hour, should have been spent. Spending was £5000 less than it should have been, and the result is a favourable variance.

If we compare the budgeted and the actual overhead costs for 28 500 direct labour hours of input, we shall ensure that any efficiency content is removed from the variance.

This means that any difference must be due to actual variable overhead spending being different from the budgeted variable overhead spending. The formula for the variance is:

the **variable overhead expenditure variance** is equal to the difference between the budgeted flexed variable overheads (BFVO) for the actual direct labour hours of input and the actual variable overhead costs incurred (AVO):

$$BFVO - AVO$$

Variable overhead represents the aggregation of a large number of individual items, such as indirect labour, indirect materials, electricity, maintenance and so on. The variable overhead variance can arise because the prices of individual items have changed. Alternatively, the variance can also be affected by how efficiently the individual variable overhead items are used. Waste or inefficiency, such as using more kilowatt-hours of power than should have been used will increase the cost of power and, thus, the total cost of variable overhead. The variable overhead expenditure on its own is therefore not very informative. Any meaningful analysis of this variance requires a comparison of the actual expenditure for each individual item of variable overhead expenditure against the budget.

Variable overhead efficiency variance

In Example 11.1 it is assumed that variable overheads vary with direct labour hours of input. The variable overhead efficiency variance arises because 28 500 direct labour hours of input were required to produce 9000 units. Working at the prescribed level of efficiency (3 hours per unit of output), it should take 27 000 hours to produce 9000 units of output. Therefore an extra 1500 direct labour hours of input were required. Because variable overheads are assumed to vary with direct labour hours of input, an additional £3000 (1500 hours at £2) variable overheads will be incurred. The formula for the variance is:

the **variable overhead efficiency variance** is the difference between the standard hours of output (SH) and the actual hours of input (AH) for the period multiplied by the standard variable overhead rate (SR):

$$(SH - AH) \times SR$$

You should note that if it is assumed that variable overheads vary with direct labour hours of input, this variance is identical to the labour efficiency variance. Consequently, the reasons for the variance are the same as those described previously for the labour efficiency variance. If you refer again to Figure 11.3, you will see that the variable overhead expenditure variance (£5000 favourable) plus the variable efficiency variance (£3000 adverse) add up to the total variable overhead variance of £2000 favourable.

SIMILARITIES BETWEEN MATERIALS, LABOUR AND OVERHEAD VARIANCES

So far, we have calculated price and quantity variances for direct material, direct labour and variable overheads. You will have noted the similarities between the computations of the three quantity and price variances. For example, we calculated the quantity variances (i.e. material usage, labour efficiency and variable overhead efficiency variances) by multiplying the difference between the standard quantity (SQ) of resources consumed for the actual production and the actual quantity (AQ) of resources consumed by the standard price (SP) per unit of the resource. Thus, the three quantity variances can be formulated as:

$$(SQ - AQ) \times SP$$

Note that the standard quantity is derived from determining the quantity that should be used *for the actual production* for the period so that the principles of flexible budgeting are applied.

The price variances (i.e. material price, wage rate and variable overhead expenditure variances) were calculated by multiplying the difference between the standard price (SP) and the actual price (AP) per unit of a resource by the actual quantity (AQ) of resources acquired/used. The price variances can be formulated as:

$$(SP - AP) \times AQ$$

This can be re-expressed as:

$$(AQ \times SP) - (AQ \times AP)$$

Note that the first term in this formula (with AQ representing actual hours) is equivalent to the budgeted flexed variable overheads that we used to calculate the variable overhead expenditure variance. The last term represents the actual cost of the resources consumed.

We can therefore calculate all the price and quantity variances illustrated so far in this chapter by applying the two formulae outlined above.

FIXED OVERHEAD EXPENDITURE OR SPENDING VARIANCE

The final production variance shown in Figure 11.3 is the fixed overhead expenditure variance. With a direct costing system, fixed manufacturing overheads are not unitized and allocated to products. Instead, the total fixed overheads for the period are charged as an expense to the period in which they are incurred. Fixed overheads are assumed to remain unchanged in the short term in response to changes in the level of activity, but they may change in response to other factors. For example, price increases may cause expenditure on fixed overheads to increase. The fixed overhead expenditure variance therefore explains the difference between budgeted fixed overheads and the actual fixed overheads incurred. The formula for the **fixed overhead expenditure variance** is the difference between the budgeted fixed overheads (BFO) and the actual fixed overhead (AFO) spending:

$$BFO - AFO$$

In Example 11.1 budgeted fixed overhead expenditure is £120 000 and actual fixed overhead spending £116 000. Therefore the fixed overhead expenditure variance is £4000. Whenever the actual fixed overheads are less than the budgeted fixed overheads, the variance will be favourable. The total of the fixed overhead expenditure variance on its own is not particularly informative. Any meaningful analysis of this variance requires a comparison of the actual expenditure for each individual item of fixed overhead expenditure

EXAMPLE 11.2

The budgeted sales for a company are £110 000 consisting of 10 000 units at £11 per unit. The standard cost per unit is £7. Actual sales are £120 000 (12 000 units at £10 per unit) and the actual cost per unit is £7.

against the budget. The difference may be due to a variety of causes, such as changes in salaries paid to supervisors, or the appointment of additional supervisors. Only by comparing individual items of expenditure and ascertaining the reasons for the variances, can one determine whether the variance is controllable or uncontrollable. Generally, this variance is likely to be uncontrollable in the short term.

SALES VARIANCES

Sales variances can be used to analyse the performance of the sales function or revenue centres on broadly similar terms to those for manufacturing costs. The most significant feature of sales variance calculations is that they are calculated in terms of profit contribution margins rather than sales values. Consider Example 11.2.

You will see that when the variances are calculated on the basis of sales *value*, it is necessary to compare the budgeted sales *value* of £110 000 with the actual sales of £120 000. This gives a favourable variance of £10 000. This calculation, however, ignores the impact of the sales effort on profit. The budgeted profit contribution is £40 000, which consists of 10 000 units at £4 per unit, but the actual impact of the sales effort in terms of profit margins indicates a profit contribution of £36 000, which consists of 12 000 units at £3 per unit, indicating an adverse variance of £4000. If we examine Example 11.2, we can see that compared with the budget the selling prices have been reduced, and that this has led not only to an increase in the total sales revenue but also to a reduction in total profits. The objective of the selling function is to influence favourably total profits. Thus a more meaningful performance measure will be obtained by comparing the results of the sales function in terms of profit contribution margins rather than sales revenues. Let us now calculate the sales variances from the information contained in Example 11.1.

Total sales margin variance

The total sales margin variance seeks to identify the influence of the sales function on the difference between budget and actual profit contribution. In Example 11.1 the budgeted profit contribution is £200 000, which consists of budgeted sales of 10 000 units at a contribution of £20 per unit. This is compared with a contribution derived from the actual sales volume of 9000 units. Because the sales function is responsible for the sales volume and the unit selling price, but not the unit manufacturing costs, the standard cost of sales and not the actual cost of sales is deducted from the actual sales revenue. The calculation of the contribution for ascertaining the total sales margin variance will therefore be as follows:

	(£)
Actual sales revenue (9000 units at £90)	810 000
Standard variable cost of sales for actual sales volume (9000 units at £68)	612 000
Profit contribution margin	198 000

To calculate the total sales margin variance we deduct the budgeted contribution for the period of £200 000 from the above profit contribution of £198 000. This gives an adverse variance of £2000 because the above contribution derived from the actual sales is less than the budgeted profit contribution.

The formula for calculating the variance is as follows:

the **total sales margin variance** is the difference between actual sales revenue (ASR) less the standard variable cost of sales (SCOS) and the budgeted contribution (BC):

$$(ASR - SCOS) - BC$$

Using the standard cost of sales in the above formula and calculation ensures that production variances do not distort the calculation of the sales variances. Therefore sales variances arise only because of changes in those variables controlled by the sales function (i.e. selling prices and sales quantity). Figure 11.3 indicates that it is possible to analyse the total sales margin variance into two sub-variances – a sales margin price variance and a sales margin volume variance.

Sales margin price variance

In Example 11.1 the actual selling price is £90 and the standard selling price is £88. In order to ensures that production variances do not distort the calculation of the sales margin price variance the standard unit variable cost of £68 should be deducted from both the actual and the standard selling prices. This gives a contribution of £22 that is derived from the actual selling price and a contribution of £20 derived from the standard selling price. Because the actual sales volume is 9000 units, the increase in selling price means that the increase in contribution of £2 per unit is obtained 9000 times giving a favourable sales margin variance of £18 000. In formula terms the variance is calculated as follows:

[(Actual selling price – Standard variable cost) – (Standard selling price – Standard variable cost)] × Actual sales volume

Note that the standard variable cost is deducted from both the actual and standard selling price. Therefore the above formula can be simplified by omitting standard variable cost so that:

the **sales margin price variance** is the difference between the actual selling price (ASP) and the standard selling price (SSP) multiplied by the actual sales volume (AV):

$$(ASP - SSP) \times AV$$

Sales margin volume variance

To ascertain the effect of changes in the sales volume on the difference between the budgeted and the actual contribution, we must compare the budgeted sales volume with the actual sales volume. You will see from Example 11.1 that the budgeted sales are 10 000 units but the actual sales are 9000 units, and to enable us to determine the impact of this reduction in sales volume on profit, we must multiply the 1000 units by the standard contribution margin of £20. This gives an adverse variance of £20 000.

The use of the standard margin (standard selling price less standard cost) ensures that the standard selling price is used in the calculation, and the volume variance will not be affected by any *changes* in the actual selling prices. The formula for calculating the variance is:

the **sales margin volume variance** is the difference between the actual sales volume (AV) and the budgeted volume (BV) multiplied by the standard contribution margin (SM):

$$(AV - BV) \times SM$$

Difficulties in interpreting sales margin variances

The favourable sales margin price variance of £18 000 plus the adverse volume variance of £20 000 add up to the total adverse sales margin variance of £2000. It may be argued that it is not very meaningful to analyse the total sales margin variance into price and volume components, since changes in selling prices are likely to affect sales volume. Consequently, a favourable price variance will tend to be associated with an adverse volume variance, and vice versa. It may be unrealistic to sell more than the budgeted volume when selling prices have increased.

A further problem with sales variances is that the variances may arise from external factors and may not be controllable by management. For example, changes in selling prices may be the result of a response to changes in selling prices of competitors. Alternatively, a reduction in both selling prices and sales volume may be the result of an economic recession that was not foreseen when the budget was prepared. For control and performance appraisal it may be preferable to compare actual market share with target market share for each product. In addition, the trend in market shares should be monitored and selling prices should be compared with competitors' prices.

	(£)	(£)	(£)
Budgeted net profit			80 000
Sales variances:			
Sales margin price	18 000F		
Sales margin volume	20 000A	2 000A	
Direct cost variances:			
Material: Price	8 900A		
Usage	26 500A	35 400A	
Labour: Rate	17 100A		
Efficiency	13 500A	30 600A	
Manufacturing overhead variances:			
Fixed overhead expenditure	4 000F		
Variable overhead expenditure	5 000F		
Variable overhead efficiency	3 000A	6 000F	62000A
Actual profit			18 000

EXHIBIT 11.4

Reconciliation of budgeted and actual profits for a standard variable costing system

RECONCILING BUDGETED PROFIT AND ACTUAL PROFIT

Top management will be interested in the reason for the actual profit being different from the budgeted profit. By adding the favourable production and sales variances to the budgeted profit and deducting the adverse variances, the reconciliation of budgeted and actual profit shown in Exhibit 11.4 can be presented in respect of Example 11.1.

Example 11.1 assumes that Alpha Ltd produces a single product consisting of a single operation and that the activities are performed by one responsibility centre. In practice, most companies make many products, which require operations to be carried out in different responsibility centres. A reconciliation statement such as that presented in Exhibit 11.4 will therefore normally represent a summary of the variances for many responsibility centres. The reconciliation statement thus represents a broad picture to top management that explains the major reasons for any difference between the budgeted and actual profits.

SUMMARY

The following items relate to the learning objectives listed at the beginning of the chapter.

- **Explain how a standard costing system operates.** Standard costing is most suited to an organization whose activities consist of a series of repetitive operations and the input required to produce each unit of output can be specified. A standard costing system involves the following: (a) the standard costs for the actual output are recorded for each operation for each responsibility centre; (b) actual costs for each operation are traced to each responsibility centre; (c) the standard and actual costs are compared; (d) variances are investigated and corrective action is taken where appropriate; and (e) standards are monitored and adjusted to reflect changes in standard usage and/or prices.

- **Explain how standard costs are set.** Standards should be set for the quantities and prices of materials, labour and services to be consumed in performing each operation associated with a product. Product standard costs are derived by listing and adding the standard costs of operations required to produce a particular product. Two approaches are used for setting standard costs. First, past historical records can be used to estimate labour and material usage. Secondly, standards can be set based on engineering studies. With engineering studies a detailed study of each operation is undertaken under controlled conditions, based on high levels of efficiency, to ascertain the quantities of labour and materials required. Target prices are then applied to ascertain the standard costs.

- **Explain the meaning of standard hours produced.** It is not possible to measure output in terms of units produced for a department making several different products or operations. This problem is overcome by ascertaining the amount of time, working under efficient operating conditions, it should take to make each product. This time calculation is called standard hours produced. Standard hours thus represents an

EXHIBIT 11.5
*Summary of the
formulae for the
computation of
variances*

The following variances are reported for both variable and absorption costing systems:

Materials and labour

1 Material price variance = (Standard price per unit of material – Actual price) × Quantity of materials purchased

2 Material usage variance = (Standard quantity of materials for actual production – Actual quantity used) × Standard price per unit

3 Total materials cost variance = (Actual production × Standard material cost per unit of production) – Actual materials cost

4 Wage rate variance = (Standard wage rate per hour – Actual wage rate) × Actual labour hours worked

5 Labour efficiency variance = (Standard quantity of labour hours for actual production – Actual labour hours) × Standard wage rate

6 Total labour cost variance = (Actual production × Standard labour cost per unit of production) – Actual labour cost

Fixed production overhead

7 Fixed overhead expenditure = Budgeted fixed overheads – Actual fixed overheads

Variable production overhead

8 Variable overhead expenditure variance = (Budgeted variable overheads for actual input volume – Actual variable overhead cost)

9 Variable overhead efficiency variance = (Standard quantity of input hours for actual production – Actual input hours) × Variable overhead rate

10 Total variable overhead variance = (Actual production × Standard variable overhead rate per unit) – Actual variable overhead cost

Sales margins

11 Sales margin price variance = (Actual selling price – Standard selling price) × Actual sales volume

12 Sales margin volume variance = (Actual sales volume – Budgeted sales volume) × Standard contribution margin

13 Total sales margin variance = (Actual sales revenue – Standard variable cost of sales) – Total budgeted contribution

output measure that acts as a common denominator for adding together the production of unlike items.

● **Identify and describe the purposes of a standard costing system.** Standard costing systems can be used for the following purposes: (a) providing a prediction of future costs that can be used for decision-making; (b) providing a challenging target that individuals are motivated to achieve; (c) providing a reliable and convenient source of data for budget preparation; (d) acting as a control device by highlighting those activities that do not conform to plan and thus alerting managers to those situations that may be 'out of control' and in need of corrective action; and (e) simplifying the task of tracing costs to products for profit measurement and inventory valuation purpose.

● **Calculate labour, material, overhead and sales margin variances and reconcile actual profit with budgeted profit.** To reconcile actual profit with budget profit the favourable variances are added to the budgeted profit and adverse variances are deducted. The end result should be the actual profit. A summary of the formulae for the computation of the variances is presented in Exhibit 11.5. In each case the formula is presented so that so that a positive variance is favourable and a negative variance unfavourable.

● **Identify the causes of labour, material, overhead and sales margin variances.** Quantities cost variances arise because the actual quantity of resources consumed exceeds actual usage. Examples include excess usage of materials and labour arising from the usage of inferior materials, careless handling of materials and failure to maintain machinery in proper condition. Price variances arise when the actual prices paid for resources exceed the standard prices. Examples include the failure of the purchasing function to seek the most efficient sources of supply or the use of a different grade of labour to that incorporated in the standard costs.

KEY TERMS AND CONCEPTS

bill of materials (p. 269)
budgeted costs (p. 266)
engineering studies (p. 268)
fixed overhead expenditure variance (p. 282)
labour efficiency variance (p. 279)
material price variance (p. 276)
material usage variance (p. 277)
sales margin price variance (p. 284)
sales margin volume variance (p. 285)
standard costs (p. 266)

standard hours (p. 270)
standard hours produced (p. 270)
total labour variance (p. 280)
total material variance (p. 278)
total sales margin variance (p. 284)
total variable overhead variance (p. 280)
variable overhead efficiency variance (p. 281)
variable overhead expenditure variance (p. 281)
wage rate variance (p. 279).

ASSESSMENT MATERIAL

The review questions are short questions that enable you to assess your understanding of the main topics included in the chapter. The page numbers in parentheses provide you with the page numbers to refer to if you cannot answer a specific question.

The review problems are more complex and require you to relate and apply the content to various business problems. Solutions to review problems are provided in a separate section at the end of the book. Additional review problems can be accessed by lecturers and students on the website www.drury-online.com. Solutions to these problems are provided for lecturers in the *Instructors' Manual*. This is available on the lecturers' password-protected section of the website.

The website also includes over 30 case study problems. A list of these cases is provided on pages 389–392. Several cases are relevant to the content of this chapter. Examples include Anjo Ltd, Boston Creamery and Berkshire Toy Company.

REVIEW QUESTIONS

11.1 Describe the difference between budgeted and standard costs. *(p. 266)*

11.2 Explain how a standard costing system operates. *(pp. 266–68)*

11.3 Describe how standard costs are established using engineering studies. *(pp. 268–69)*

11.4 What are standard hours produced? What purpose do they serve? *(pp. 270–72)*

11.5 Describe the different purposes of a standard costing system. *(pp. 272–74)*

11.6 What are the possible causes of (a) material price and (b) material usage variances? *(pp. 276, 278)*

11.7 Explain why it is preferable for the material price variance to be computed at the point of purchase rather than the point of issue. *(p. 286)*

11.8 What are the possible causes of (a) wage rate and (b) labour efficiency variances? *(p. 279)*

11.9 Explain how variable overhead efficiency and expenditure variances are computed. What are the possible causes of each of these variances? *(pp. 280–81)*

11.10 Why are sales variances based on contribution margins rather than sales revenues? *(p. 283)*

REVIEW PROBLEMS

11.11 During a period, 17 500 labour hours were worked at a standard cost of £6.50 per hour. The labour efficiency variance was £7800 favourable.

How many standard hours were produced?

A   1200

B 16 300
C 17 500
D 18 700

11.12 T plc uses a standard costing system, which is material stock account being maintained at standard costs. The following details have been extracted from the standard cost card in respect of direct materials:

> 8 kg at £0.80/kg = £6.40 per unit
> Budgeted production in April was 850 units.

The following details relate to actual materials purchased and issued to production during April, when actual production was 870 units:

Materials purchased	8200 kg costing £6888
Materials issued to production	7150 kg

Which of the following correctly states the material price and usage variance to be reported?

	Price	Usage
A	£286 (A)	£152 (A)
B	£286 (A)	£280 (A)
C	£286 (A)	£294 (A)
D	£328 (A)	£152 (A)
E	£328 (A)	£280 (A)

11.13 PQ Limited operates a standard costing system for its only product. The standard cost card is as follows:

Direct material (4 kg at £2/kg)	£8.00
Direct labour (4 hours at £8/hour)	£32.00
Variable overhead (4 hours at £3/hour)	£12.00
Fixed overhead (4 hours at £5/hour)	£20.00

Fixed overheads are absorbed on the basis of labour hours. Fixed overhead costs are budgeted at £120 000 per annum, arising at a constant rate during the year.

Activity in period 3 is budgeted to be 10 per cent of total activity for the year. Actual production during period 3 was 500 units, with actual fixed overhead costs incurred being £9800 and actual hours worked being 1970.

The fixed overhead expenditure variance for period 3 was:

A £2200 (F)
B £200 (F)
C £50 (F)
D £200 (A)
E £2200 (A)

11.14 J Limited operates a standard cost accounting system. The following information has been extracted from its standard cost card and budgets:

Budgeted sales volume	5000 units
Budgeted selling price	£10.00 per unit
Standard variable cost	£5.60 per unit
Standard total cost	£7.50 per unit

If it used a standard marginal cost accounting system and its actual sales were 4500 units at a selling price of £12.00, its sales volume variance would be:

A   £1250 adverse
B   £2200 adverse
C   £2250 adverse
D   £3200 adverse
E   £5000 adverse

11.15 Variance analysis and reconciliation of actual and budgeted profit

BS Limited manufactures one standard product and operates a system of variance accounting using a fixed budget. As assistant management accountant, you are responsible for preparing the monthly operating statements. Data from the budget, the standard product cost and actual data for the month ended 31 October are given below.

Using the data given, you are required to prepare the operating statement for the month ended 31 October to show the budgeted profit; the variances for direct materials, direct wages, overhead and sales, each analysed into causes; and actual profit.

Budgeted and standard cost data:

Budgeted sales and production for the month: 10 000 units
 Standard cost for each unit of product:
 Direct material: X: 10 kg at £1 per kg
                           Y: 5 kg at £5 per kg
 Direct wages: 5 hours at £8 per hour
 Budgeted fixed overheads are £300 000

Budgeted sales price has been calculated to give a contribution of 50 per cent of the selling price.

Actual data for the month ended 31 October:

Production: 9500 units sold at a price of £160
Direct materials consumed:
  X: 96 000 kg at £1.20 per kg
  Y: 48 000 kg at £4.70 per kg
Direct wages incurred 46 000 hours at £8.20 per hour
Fixed production overhead incurred £290 000

(30 marks)

11.16 Calculation of actual input data working back from variances

The following data relate to actual output, costs and variances for the four-weekly accounting period number 4 of a company that makes only one product. Opening and closing work in progress figures were the same.

	(£000)
Actual production of product XY	18 000 units
Actual costs incurred:	
Direct materials purchased and used (150 000 kg)	210
Direct wages for 32 000 hours	264
Variable production overhead	38

	(£000)
Variances:	
Direct materials price	15 F
Direct materials usage	9 A
Direct labour rate	8 A
Direct labour efficiency	32 F

| Variable production overhead expenditure | 6 A |
| Variable production overhead efficiency | 4 F |

Variable production overhead varies with labour hours worked.
A standard marginal costing system is operated.

You are required to:

(a) present a standard product cost sheet for one unit of product XY;

(16 marks)

(b) describe briefly *three* types of standard that can be used for a standard costing system, stating which is usually preferred in practice and why.

(9 marks)
(Total 25 marks)

11.17 Reconciliation of budgeted and actual contribution

JK plc operates a chain of fast-food restaurants. The company uses a standard marginal costing system to monitor the costs incurred in its outlets. The standard cost of one of its most popular meals is as follows:

		£ per meal
Ingredients	(1.08 units)	1.18
Labour	(1.5 minutes)	0.15
Variable conversion costs	(1.5 minutes)	0.06
The standard selling price of this meal is		1.99

In one of its outlets, which has budgeted sales and production activity level of 50 000 such meals, the number of such meals that were produced and sold during April was 49 700. The actual cost data was as follows:

		£
Ingredients	(55 000 units)	58 450
Labour	(1 200 hours)	6 800
Variable conversion costs	(1 200 hours)	3 250
The actual revenue from the sale of the meals was		96 480

Required:

(a) Calculate
  (i) the total budgeted contribution for April;
  (ii) the total actual contribution for April.

(3 marks)

(b) Present a statement that reconciles the budgeted and actual contribution for April. Show all variances to the nearest £1 and in as much detail as possible.

(17 marks)
(Total 20 marks)

11.18 Calculation of labour variances and actual material inputs working backwards from variances

A company manufactures two components in one of its factories. Material A is one of several materials used in the manufacture of both components.

The standard direct labour hours per unit of production and budgeted production quantities for a 13-week period were:

	Standard direct labour hours	Budgeted production quantities
Component X	0.40 hours	36 000 units
Component Y	0.56 hours	22 000 units

The standard wage rate for all direct workers was £9.00 per hour. Throughout the 13-week period 53 direct workers were employed, working a standard 40-hour week.

The following actual information for the 13-week period is available:

Production:
    Component X, 35 000 units
    Component Y, 25 000 units
Direct wages paid, £248 740
Material A purchases, 47 000 kilos costing £85 110
Material A price variance, £430 F
Material A usage (component X), 33 426 kilos
Material A usage variance (component X), £320.32 A

Required:

(a) Calculate the direct labour variances for the period.

(5 marks)

(b) Calculate the standard purchase price for material A for the period and the standard usage of material A per unit of production of component X.

(8 marks)

(c) Describe the steps, and information, required to establish the material purchase quantity budget for material A for a period.

(7 marks)
(Total 20 marks)

CHAPTER 12
DIVISIONAL FINANCIAL
PERFORMANCE MEASURES

LEARNING OBJECTIVES

After studying this chapter you should be able to:

- **distinguish between non-divisionalized and divisionalized organizational structures;**
- **explain why it is preferable to distinguish between managerial and economic performance;**
- **explain the factors that should be considered in designing financial performance measures for evaluating divisional managers;**
- **explain the meaning of return on investment, residual income and economic value added (EVA$^{(TM)}$);**
- **compute economic value added (EVA$^{(TM)}$);**
- **identify and explain the approaches that can be used to reduce the dysfunctional consequences of short-term financial measures.**

Large companies produce and sell a wide variety of products throughout the world. Because of the complexity of their operations, it is difficult for top management to directly control operations. It may therefore be appropriate to divide a company into separate self-contained segments or divisions and to allow divisional managers to operate with a great deal of independence. A divisional manager has responsibility for both the production and marketing activities of the division. The danger in creating autonomous divisions is that divisional managers might not pursue goals that are in the best interests of the company as a whole. The objective of this chapter is to consider financial performance measures that aim to motivate divisional managers to pursue those goals that will best benefit the company as a whole. In other words, the objective is to develop performance measures that will achieve goal congruence.

In this chapter we shall focus on financial measures of divisional performance. However, financial measures cannot adequately measure all those factors that are critical to the success of a division. Emphasis should also be given to reporting key non-financial measures relating to such areas as competitiveness, product leadership, quality, delivery performance, innovation and flexibility to respond to changes in demand. In particular, performance measures should be developed that support the objectives and competitive strategies of the organization. Divisional financial performance measures should therefore be seen as one of a range of measures that should be used to measure and control divisional performance.

DIVISIONAL ORGANIZATIONAL STRUCTURES

Figure 12.1 shows a simplified **divisionalized organizational structure**, which is split up into divisions in accordance with the products that are made. You will see from the diagram that each divisional manager is responsible for all of the operations relating to his or her particular product. To reflect this greater autonomy each division is either an investment centre or a profit centre. To simplify the presentation it is assumed that all of the divisions in Figure 12.1 are investment centres (we shall discuss the factors influencing the choice of investment or profit centres later in the chapter). Note that within each division there are multiple cost and revenue centres at lower management levels within each division. The controls described in the two previous chapters should be applied to the cost and revenue centres. Also, in practice only parts of a company may be divisionalized. For example, activities such as research and development, industrial relations and general administration may be structured centrally with a responsibility for providing services to all of the divisions. Figure 12.1 also shows that each divisional manager reports to a chief executive or top management team that will normally be located at corporate headquarters who are responsible for the activities of all of the divisions. In this chapter we shall focus on financial measures and controls at the profit or investment centre (i.e. divisional) level.

Generally, a divisionalized organizational structure will lead to decentralization of the decision-making process. For example, divisional managers will normally be free to set selling prices, choose which market to sell in, make product mix and output decisions, and select suppliers (this may include buying from other divisions within the company or from other companies). In non-divisionalized organizations pricing, product mix and output decisions will be made by central management. Consequently, managers in non-divisionalized organizations will have far less independence than divisional managers. Thus divisional managers have profit responsibility whereas managers in non-divisionalized companies do not have profit responsibility.

Profit centres and investment centres

The creation of separate divisions may lead to the delegation of different degrees of authority; for example, in some organizations a divisional manager may also have responsibility for making capital investment decisions. Where this situation occurs, the division is known as an **investment centre**. Alternatively, where a manager cannot control the investment and is responsible only for the profits obtained from operating the assets assigned to him or her by corporate headquarters, the segment is referred to as a **profit**

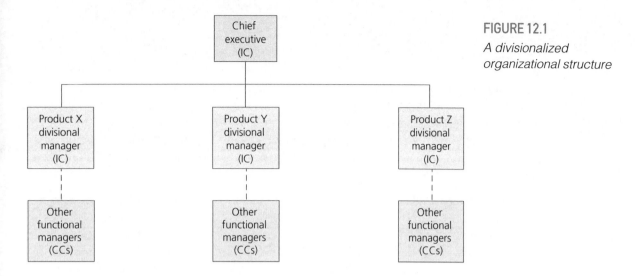

FIGURE 12.1

A divisionalized organizational structure

IC = Investment centres, CC = Cost centres.

centre. In contrast, the term **cost centre** is used to describe a responsibility centre where a manager is responsible for costs but not profits.

ADVANTAGES AND DISADVANTAGES OF DIVISIONALIZATION

Divisionalization can improve the decision-making process both from the point of view of the quality of the decision and the speed of the decision. The quality of the decisions should be improved because decisions can be made by the person who is familiar with the situation and who should therefore be able to make more informed judgements than central management who cannot be intimately acquainted with all the activities of the various segments of the business. Speedier decisions should also occur because information does not have to pass along the chain of command to and from top management. Decisions can be made on the spot by those who are familiar with the product lines and production processes and who can react to changes in local conditions in a speedy and efficient manner. In addition, delegation of responsibility to divisional managers provides them with greater freedom, thus making their activities more challenging and providing the opportunity to achieve self-fulfilment. This process should mean that motivation will be increased not just at the divisional manager level but throughout the whole division.

The major potential disadvantage of divisionalization is that there is a danger that divisions may compete with each other excessively and that divisional managers may be encouraged to take action that will increase their own profits at the expense of the profits of other divisions and the company as a whole. This may adversely affect cooperation between the divisions and lead to a lack of harmony in achieving the overall organizational goals of the company.

PREREQUISITES FOR SUCCESSFUL DIVISIONALIZATION

A divisionalized structure is most suited to companies engaged in several dissimilar activities. The reason is that it is difficult for top management to be intimately acquainted with all the diverse activities of the various segments of the business. On the other hand, when the major activities of a company are closely related, these activities should be carefully coordinated, and this coordination is more easily achieved in a centralized organizational structure.

For successful divisionalization it is important that the activities of a division be as independent as possible of other activities. However, Solomons (1965) argues that even though substantial independence of divisions from each other is a necessary condition for divisionalization, if carried to the limit it would destroy the very idea that such divisions are an integral part of any single business. Divisions should be more than investments – they should contribute not only to the success of the company but to the success of each other.

DISTINGUISHING BETWEEN THE MANAGERIAL AND ECONOMIC PERFORMANCE OF THE DIVISION

Before discussing the factors to be considered in determining how divisional profitability should be measured, we must decide whether the primary purpose is to measure the performance of the division or that of the divisional manager. The messages transmitted from these two measures may be quite different. For example, a manager may be assigned to an ailing division to improve performance, and might succeed in substantially improving the performance of the division. However, the division might still be unprofitable because of industry factors, such as overcapacity and a declining market. The future of the division might be uncertain, but the divisional manager may well be promoted as a result of the outstanding managerial performance. Conversely, a division might report significant profits but, because of management deficiencies, the performance may be unsatisfactory when the favourable economic environment is taken into account.

If the purpose is to evaluate the divisional manager then only those items directly controllable by the manager should be included in the profitability measure. Thus all allocations of indirect costs, such as central service and central administration costs, which cannot be influenced by divisional managers, ought not to be included in the profitability measure. Such costs can only be controlled where they are incurred; which means that central service managers should be held accountable for them.

Corporate headquarters, however, will also be interested in evaluating a division's economic performance for decision-making purposes, such as expansion, contraction and divestment decisions. In this situation a measure that includes only those amounts directly controllable by the divisional manager would overstate the economic performance of the division. Therefore, to measure the economic performance of the division many items that the divisional manager cannot influence, such as interest expenses, taxes and the allocation of some central administrative staff expenses, should be included in the profitability measure.

ALTERNATIVE DIVISIONAL PROFIT MEASURES

There are strong arguments for two measures of divisional profitability – one to evaluate managerial performance and the other to evaluate the economic performance of the division. In this chapter we shall focus on both measures. Exhibit 12.1 presents a divisional profit statement that contains three different measures that we can use to measure divisional performance. For measuring *managerial performance* the application of the controllability principle (see Chapter 10) suggests that controllable profit is the most appropriate measure. This is computed by deducting from divisional revenues all those costs that are controllable by a divisional manager. Controllable profit provides a measure of divisional managerial performance based on their ability to use only those resources under their control effectively. It should not be interpreted in isolation if it is used to evaluate the performance of a divisional manager. Instead, it should be evaluated relative to a budgeted performance, so that market conditions and size (in terms of assets employed) are taken into account.

Controllable profit provides an incomplete measure of the *economic performance* of a division, since it does not include those costs that are attributable to the division but which are not controllable by the divisional manager. For example, depreciation of divisional assets, and head office finance and legal staff who are assigned to providing services for specific divisions, would fall into this category. These expenses would be avoidable if a decision were taken to close the division. Those non-controllable expenses that are attributable to a division, and which would be avoidable if the division was closed, are deducted from controllable profit to derive the divisional profit contribution. This is clearly a useful figure for evaluating the *economic contribution* of the division, since it represents the contribution that a division is making to corporate profits and overheads. It should not be used, however, to evaluate managerial performance, because it includes costs that are not controllable by divisional managers.

Many companies allocate all corporate general and administrative expenses to divisions to derive a divisional net profit before taxes. From a theoretical point of view, it is difficult to justify such allocations since they tend to be arbitrary and do not have any connection with the manner in which divisional activities influence the level of these corporate expenses. Divisional profit contribution would therefore seem to be the most appropriate measure of the *economic* performance of divisions, because it is not distorted by arbitrary allocations. We have noted, however, that corporate headquarters may wish to compare a division's economic performance with that of comparable firms operating in the same industry. The divisional profit contribution would overstate the performance of the division, because if the division were independent, it would have to incur the costs of those services performed by head office. The apportioned head office costs are an

	£
Total sales revenues	xxx
Less controllable costs	xxx
1 *Controllable profit*	xxx
Less non-controllable avoidable costs	xxx
2 *Divisional profit contribution*	xxx
Less allocated corporate expenses	xxx
3 *Divisional net profit before taxes*	xxx

EXHIBIT 12.1

Alternative divisional profit measures

approximation of the costs that the division would have to incur if it traded as a separate company. Consequently, companies may prefer to use divisional net profit when comparing the economic performance of a division with similar companies.

SURVEYS OF PRACTICE

Despite the many theoretical arguments against divisional net profit, survey evidence indicates that this measure is used widely to evaluate both divisional economic and managerial performance (Reece and Cool, 1978; Fremgen and Liao, 1981; Ramadan, 1989; Skinner, 1990; Drury *et al.*, 1993; Drury and El-Shishini, 2005). The UK study by Drury and El-Shishini (2005) asked the respondents to rank in order of importance the factors influencing organizations to allocate the cost of shared corporate resources to divisions. In rank order the highest rankings were attributed to the following factors:

1 to show divisional managers the total costs of operating their divisions;
2 to make divisional managers aware that such costs exist and must be covered by divisional profits;
3 divisional managers would incur such costs if they were independent units.

The counter-argument to item 2 above is that if central management wishes to inform managers that divisions must be profitable enough to cover not only their own operations but corporate expenses as well, it is preferable to set a high budgeted controllable profit target that takes account of these factors. Divisional managers can then concentrate on increasing controllable profit by focusing on those costs and revenues that are under their control, and not be concerned with costs that they cannot control.

There is also some evidence to suggest that companies hold managers accountable for divisional net profit because this is equivalent to the measure that financial markets focus on to evaluate the performance of the company as a whole (Joseph *et al.*, 1996). Top management therefore require their divisional managers to concentrate on the same measures as those used by financial markets. A further reason to justify the use of divisional net profit as a managerial performance measure is that it represents the application of the controllability principle by the use of relative performance evaluations that were described in Chapter 10. You should remember from Chapter 10 that with relative performance evaluations the performance of a responsibility centre is evaluated relative to the performance of similar centres within the same company or to similar units outside the organization.

RETURN ON INVESTMENT

Instead of focusing purely on the absolute size of a division's profits most organizations focus on the return on investment (ROI) of a division. Note that ROI is also referred to as return on capital employed or accounting rate of return. ROI expresses divisional profit as a percentage of the assets employed in a division. Any three of the alternative divisional profit measures described earlier (i.e. divisional controllable profit, divisional profit contribution and net profit before taxes) can be used as the measure of divisional profit, while assets employed can be defined as assets controllable by the divisional manager, total divisional assets or net assets.

ROI is the most widely used financial measure of divisional performance. Why? Consider a situation where division A earns a profit of £1 million and division B a profit of £2 million. Can we conclude that division B is more profitable than division A? The answer is no, since we should consider whether the divisions are returning a sufficiently high return on the capital invested in the division. Assume that £4 million capital is invested in division A and £20 million in division B. Division A's ROI is 25 per cent (£1 million/£4 million) whereas the return for division B is 10 per cent (£2 million/£20 million). Capital invested has alternative uses, and corporate management will wish to ascertain whether the returns being earned on the capital invested in a particular division exceed the division's opportunity cost of capital (i.e. the returns available from the alternative use of the capital). If, in the above illustration, the return available on similar investments to that in division B is 15 per cent then the economic viability of division B is questionable if profitability cannot be improved. In contrast, the ROI measure suggests that division A is very profitable.

Another feature of ROI is that because it is a ratio measure it can be used as a common denominator for comparing the returns of dissimilar businesses, such as other divisions within the group or outside competitors.

Despite the widespread use of ROI, a number of problems exist when this measure is used to evaluate the performance of divisional managers. For example, it is possible that divisional ROI can be increased by actions that will make the company as a whole worse off, and conversely, actions that decrease the divisional ROI may make the company as a whole better off. In other words, evaluating divisional managers on the basis of ROI may not encourage goal congruence. Consider the following example:

	Division X	Division Y
Investment project available	£10 million	£10 million
Controllable profit	£2 million	£1.3 million
Return on the proposed project	20%	13%
ROI of divisions at present	25%	9%

It is assumed that neither project will result in any changes in non-controllable costs and that the overall cost of capital for the company is 15 per cent. The manager of division X would be reluctant to invest the additional £10 million because the return on the proposed project is 20 per cent, and this would reduce the existing overall ROI of 25 per cent. On the other hand, the manager of division Y would wish to invest the £10 million because the return on the proposed project of 13 per cent is in excess of the present return of 9 per cent, and it would increase the division's overall ROI. Consequently, the managers of both divisions would make decisions that would not be in the best interests of the company. The company should accept only those projects where the return is in excess of the cost of capital of 15 per cent, but the manager of division X would reject a potential return of 20 per cent and the manager of division Y would accept a potential return of 13 per cent. ROI can therefore lead to a lack of goal congruence.

RESIDUAL INCOME

To overcome some of the dysfunctional consequences of ROI, the residual income approach can be used. For the purpose of evaluating the performance of *divisional managers*, residual income is defined as controllable profit less a cost of capital charge on the investment controllable by the divisional manager. For evaluating the *economic performance* of the division residual income can be defined as divisional profit contribution (see Exhibit 12.1) less a cost of capital charge on the total investment in assets employed by the division. If residual income is used to measure the managerial performance of investment centres, there is a greater probability that managers will be encouraged, when acting in their own best interests, also to act in the best interests of the company. Returning to our previous illustration in respect of the investment decision for divisions X and Y, the residual income calculations are as follows:

	Division X (£)	Division Y (£)
Proposed investment	10 million	10 million
Controllable profit	2 million	1.3 million
Cost of capital charge (15% of the investment cost)	1.5 million	1.5 million
Residual income	0.5 million	– 0.2 million

This calculation indicates that the residual income of division X will increase and that of division Y will decrease if both managers accept the projects. Therefore the manager of division X would invest, whereas the manager of division Y would not. These actions are in the best interests of the company as a whole.

Residual income suffers from the disadvantages of being an absolute measure, which means that it is difficult to compare the performance of a division with that of other divisions or companies of a different size. For example, a large division is more likely to earn a larger residual income than a small division. To overcome this deficiency, targeted or budgeted levels of residual income should be set for each division that are consistent with asset size and the market conditions of the divisions.

Surveys of methods used by companies to evaluate the performance of divisional managers indicate a strong preference for ROI over residual income. For example, the UK survey by Drury *et al.* (1993) reported that the following measures were used:

	(%)
A target ROI set by the group	55
Residual income	20
A target profit before charging interest on investment	61
A target cash flow figure	43

Why is ROI preferred to residual income? Skinner (1990) found evidence to suggest that firms prefer to use ROI because, being a ratio, it can be used for inter-division and inter-firm comparisons. ROI for a division can be compared with the return from other divisions within the group or with whole companies outside the group, whereas absolute monetary measures such as residual income are not appropriate in making such comparisons. A second possible reason for the preference for ROI is that 'outsiders' tend to use ROI as a measure of a company's overall performance. Corporate managers therefore want their divisional managers to focus on ROI so that their performance measure is congruent with outsiders' measure of the company's overall economic performance.

ECONOMIC VALUE ADDED (EVA(™))

During the 1990s residual income was refined and renamed as **economic value added (EVA(™))** by the Stern Stewart consulting organization, and they have registered EVA(™)

as their trademark. *The Economist* (1997) reported that more than 300 firms worldwide had adopted EVA(TM) including Coca-Cola, AT&T, ICL, Boots and the Burton Group. A UK study by El-Shishini and Drury (2005) reported that 23 per cent of the responding organizations used EVA(TM) to evaluate divisional performance.

The EVA(TM) concept extends the traditional residual income measure by incorporating adjustments to the divisional financial performance measure for distortions introduced by conforming to external financial accounting reporting regulations. EVA(TM) can be defined as:

$$\text{EVA}^{(TM)} = \text{Conventional divisional profit} \pm \text{Accounting adjustments} - \text{Cost of capital charge on divisional assets}$$

REAL WORLD VIEWS 12.1

How the use of EVA(TM) analysis transformed Armstrong's financial performance

The financial mission of a company should be to invest and create cash flows in excess of the cost of capital. If an investment is announced that is expected to earn in excess of the cost of capital, then the value of the firm will immediately rise by the present value of that excess – as long as the market understands and believes the available projections. The question is: what is the best way to measure this?

Traditional measures of return, such as ROI, actually could unwittingly motivate and reward managers to shrink the value of the company. Therefore, the concept EVA(TM) was developed. In a nutshell, EVA(TM) is designed to measure the degree to which a company's after-tax operating profits exceed – or fall short of – the cost of capital invested in the business. It makes managers think more about the use of capital and the amount of capital in each business.

Armstrong World Industries Inc. is a multibillion-dollar manufacturer and supplier of floor coverings, insulation products, ceiling and wall systems, and installation products. In 1993 the decision was made to discontinue the ROI concept and use EVA(TM) for strategic planning, performance measurement and compensation. EVA(TM) is computed from straightforward adjustments to convert book values on the income statement and balance sheet to an economic basis. Armstrong used about a dozen adjustments.

Armstrong considered EVA(TM) to be the best financial measure for accurately linking accounting measures to stock market value and performance, making it ideal for setting financial targets. Changes in behaviour have become focused on three basic actions: (1) improving profit without more capital; (2) investing in projects earning above the cost of capital; and (3) eliminating operations unable to earn above the cost of capital.

On a higher strategic level, EVA(TM) allowed Armstrong to step back to see where the company was losing value. In what the company called its 'sunken ship' chart it was clear that businesses earning above the cost of capital were providing huge amounts of EVA(TM). However, the ship was being dragged down because of negative EVA(TM) businesses and corporate overhead. By selling or combining negative EVA(TM) businesses and by growing and further reducing costs in its positive EVA(TM) businesses, the company provided the potential to more than double its EVA(TM).

Discussion points

1 Can you provide examples of accounting adjustments required to compute EVA(TM)?
2 Why is EVA(TM) preferred to ROI?

Our earlier discussion relating to which of the conventional alternative divisional profit measures listed in Exhibit 12.1 should be used also applies to the calculation of EVA(TM). There are strong theoretical arguments for using controllable profit as the conventional divisional EVA(TM) profit measure for managerial performance and divisional profit contribution for measuring economic performance. Many companies, however, use divisional net profit (after allocated costs) as an input to the EVA(TM) calculation to evaluate both divisional managerial and economic performance.

Adjustments are made to the chosen conventional divisional profit measure in order to provide more realistic measures of a division's performance. These adjustments result in the capitalization of many discretionary expenditures, such as research and development and marketing and advertising, by spreading these costs over the periods in which the benefits are received. Therefore managers will not bear the full costs of the discretionary expenditures in the period in which they are incurred. Also, by making cost of capital visible managers are made aware that capital has a cost so that they need to generate sufficient income to cover their cost of capital.

Stern Stewart developed EVA(TM) with the aim of producing an overall financial measure that encourages senior managers to concentrate on the delivery of shareholder value. They consider that the aim of managers of companies, whose shares are traded in the stock market, should be to maximize shareholder value. It is therefore important that the key financial measure that is used to measure divisional or company performance should be congruent with shareholder value. Stern Stewart claim that, compared with other financial measures, EVA(TM) is more likely to meet this requirement and also to reduce dysfunctional behaviour.

ADDRESSING THE DYSFUNCTIONAL CONSEQUENCES OF SHORT-TERM FINANCIAL PERFORMANCE MEASURES

Ideally, divisional accounting performance measures should report economic income rather than accounting profit. To calculate economic income all future cash flows should be estimated and discounted to their present value (see Chapter 6 for an explanation of present values). This calculation should be made for a division at the beginning and end of a measurement period. The difference between the beginning and ending values represents economic income. Economic income represents a theoretical ideal since in practice it is extremely difficult to approximate.

Accounting performance measures are used as surrogates for economic income. Their main weaknesses are that they are backward-looking and short-term oriented. The longer the measurement period, the more congruent accounting measures of performance are with economic income. For example, profits over a three-year measurement period are a better indicator of economic income than profits over a six-month period. The disadvantage of lengthening the measurement period is that rewards are often tied to the performance evaluation, and if they are provided a long time after actions are taken, there is a danger that they will lose much of their motivational effects. Also feedback information is required at frequent intervals to enable managers to respond to deviations from plan.

Probably the most widely used approach to mitigate against the dysfunctional consequences that can arise from relying excessively on short-term financial performance measures is to supplement them with non-financial measures that measure those factors that are critical to the long-term success and profits of the organization. These measures focus on areas such as competitiveness, product leadership, productivity, quality, delivery performance, innovation and flexibility in responding to changes in demand. If managers focus excessively on the short term, the benefits from improved short-term financial performance may be counter-balanced by a deterioration in the non-financial measures. Such non-financial measures should provide a broad indication of the contribution of a divisional manager's current actions to the long-term success of the organization.

The incorporation of non-financial measures creates the need to link financial and non-financial measures of performance. The balanced scorecard emerged in the 1990s to meet this requirement. The balanced scorecard will be covered extensively in Chapter 15 but at this stage you should note that the divisional financial performance evaluation measures discussed in this chapter ought to be seen as one of the elements within the balanced scorecard. Divisional performance evaluation should be based on a combination of financial and non-financial measures.

SUMMARY

The following items relate to the learning objectives listed at the beginning of the chapter.

- **Distinguish between non-divisionalized and divisionalized organizational structures**. In non-divisionalized organizations the organization as a whole is an investment centre. With a divisionalized structure, the organization is split up into divisions that consist of either investment centres or profit centres. Thus, the distinguishing feature is that in a non-divisionalized structure only the organization as a whole is an investment centre and below this level a functional structure consisting of cost centres and revenue centres applies throughout. In contrast, in a divisionalized structure the organization is divided into separate profit or investment centres, and a functional structure applies below this level.

- **Explain why it is preferable to distinguish between managerial and economic performance**. Divisional economic performance can be influenced by many factors beyond the control of divisional managers. For example, good or bad economic performance may arise mainly from a favourable or unfavourable economic climate faced by the division rather than the specific contribution of the divisional manager. To evaluate the performance of divisional managers an attempt ought to be made to distinguish between economic and managerial performance.

- **Explain the factors that should be considered in designing financial performance measures for evaluating divisional managers**. To evaluate the performance of a divisional manager only those items directly controllable by the manager should be included in the divisional managerial performance financial measures. Thus, all allocations of indirect costs, such as those central service and administration costs that cannot be influenced by divisional managers, ought not to be included in the performance measure. Such costs can only be controlled where they are incurred, which means those central service managers should be held accountable for them.

- **Explain the meaning of return on investment (ROI), residual income and economic value added (EVA⁽ᵀᴹ⁾).** ROI expresses divisional profit as a percentage of the assets employed in a division. Residual income is defined as divisional profit less a cost of capital charge on divisional investment (e.g. net assets or total assets). During the 1990s, residual income was refined and renamed as EVA™. It extends the traditional residual income measure by incorporating adjustments to the divisional financial performance measure for distortions introduced by using generally accepted accounting principles that are used for external financial reporting. Thus, EVA™ consists of a divisional profit measure plus or minus the accounting adjustments less a cost of capital charge. All three measures can be used either as measures of managerial or economic performance.

- **Compute economic value added (EVA⁽ᵀᴹ⁾).** EVA⁽ᵀᴹ⁾ is computed by starting with a conventional divisional profit measure and (a) adding or deducting adjustments for any distortions to divisional profit measures arising from using generally accepted accounting principles for external reporting, and (b) deducting a cost of capital charge on divisional assets. The measure can be used either as a measure of managerial or economic performance as described above. Typical accounting adjustments include the capitalization of discretionary expenditures, such as research and development expenditure.

- **Identify and explain the approaches that can be used to reduce the dysfunctional consequences of short-term financial measures.** Methods suggested for reducing the dysfunctional consequences include (a) use of improved financial performance measures such as EVA⁽ᵀᴹ⁾ that incorporate accounting adjustments that attempt to overcome the deficiencies of conventional accounting measures; (b) lengthening the performance measurement period; and (c) not relying excessively on accounting measures and incorporating non-financial measures using the balanced scorecard approach described in Chapter 15.

KEY TERMS AND CONCEPTS

accounting rate of return (p. 300)
balanced scorecard (p. 305)
controllable profit (p. 299)
cost centre (p. 296)
divisional profit contribution (p. 299)
divisional net profit before taxes (p. 299)

divisionalized organizational structure (p. 296)
economic value added (EVA⁽ᵀᴹ⁾) (p. 302)
investment centre (p. 296)
profit centre (p. 296)
residual income (p. 301)
return on capital employed (p. 300)
return on investment (ROI) (p. 300)

ASSESSMENT MATERIAL

The review questions are short questions that enable you to assess your understanding of the main topics included in the chapter. The page numbers in parentheses provide you with the page numbers to refer to if you cannot answer a specific question.

The review problems are more complex and require you to relate and apply the content to various business problems. Solutions to review problems are provided in a separate section at the end of the book. Additional review problems can be accessed by lecturers and students on the website (www.drury-online.com). Solutions to these problems are provided for lecturers in the *Instructors' Manual*. This is available on the lecturers' password-protected section of the website.

The website also includes over 30 case study problems. A list of these cases is provided on pages 389–392. For an additional case that is relevant to the content of this chapter see EVA Ault Foods Ltd. (Drury, 2008; pp. 669–680).

REVIEW QUESTIONS

12.1 Distinguish between a divisionalized and a non-divisionalized organizational structure. *(p. 296)*

12.2 Distinguish between profit centres and investment centres. *(pp. 296–7)*

12.3 What are the advantages and disadvantages of divisionalization? *(p. 297)*

12.4 What are the prerequisites for successful divisionalization? *(p. 298)*

12.5 Why might it be appropriate to distinguish between the managerial and economic performance of a division? *(p. 298)*

12.6 Describe three alternative profit measures that can be used to measure divisional performance. Which measures are preferable for (a) measuring divisional managerial performance and (b) measuring divisional economic performance? *(pp. 299–300)*

12.7 Why is it common practice not to distinguish between managerial and economic performance? *(p. 300)*

12.8 Why is it common practice to allocate central costs to measure divisional managerial performance? *(p. 299)*

12.9 Distinguish between return on investment, residual income and economic value added. *(pp. 300–02)*

12.10 How does the use of return on investment as a performance measure lead to bad decisions? How do residual income and economic value added overcome this problem? *(pp. 302–4)*

12.11 Explain how economic value added is calculated. *(pp. 302–4)*

12.12 Explain the approaches that can be used to reduce the dysfunctional consequences of short-term financial measures. *(pp. 304–5)*

REVIEW PROBLEMS

12.13 Bollon uses residual income to appraise its divisions using a cost of capital of 10 per cent. It gives the managers of these divisions considerable autonomy although it retains the cash control function at head office.

The following information was available for one of the divisions:

	Net profit after tax	Profit before interest and tax £000	Divisional net assets £000	Cash/ (overdraft) £000	£000
Division 1	47	69	104	(21)	

What is the residual income for this division based on controllable profit and controllable net assets?

A   £36 600
B   £56 500
C   £58 600
D   £60 700.

12.14 A company has reported annual operating profits for the year of £89.2 million after charging £9.6 million for the full development costs of a new product that is expected to last for the current year and two further years. The cost of capital is 13 per cent per annum. The balance sheet for the company shows fixed assets with a historical cost of £120 million. A note to the balance sheet estimates that the replacement cost of these fixed assets at the beginning of the year is £168 million. The assets have been depreciated at 20 per cent per year.

The company has a working capital of £27.2 million.

Ignore the effects of taxation.

The ecomonic valued added (EVA(TM)) of the company is closest to

A   £64.16 million
B   £70.56 million
C   £83.36 million
D   £100.96 million

12.15 Division L has reported a net profit after tax of £8.6 million for the year ended 30 April 2006. Included in the costs used to calculate this profit are the following items:

- interest payable of £2.3 million;
- development costs of £6.3 million for a new product that was launched in May 2005, and is expected to have a life of three years;
- advertising expenses of £1.6 million that relate to the re-launch of a product in June 2006.

The net assets invested in Division L are £30 million.

The cost of capital for Division L is 13 per cent per year.

Calculate the economic valued added(TM) for Division L for the year ended 30 April 2006.

(3 marks)

12.16 Return on investment and residual income

Southe plc has two divisions, A and B, whose respective performances are under review.

Division A is currently earning a profit of £35 000 and has net assets of £150 000.

Division B currently earns a profit of £70 000 with net assets of £325 000.

South plc has a current cost of capital of 15 per cent.

Required:

a   Using the information above, calculate the return on investment and residual income figures for the two divisions under review and comment on your results.

(5 marks)

b   State which method of performance evaluation (i.e. return on investment or residual income) would be more useful when comparing divisional performance and why.

(2 marks)

c   List three general aspects of performance measures that would be appropriate for a service sector company.

(3 marks)

12.17 Division Q makes a single product. Information for the division for the year just ended is:

Sales	30 000 units
Fixed costs	£487 000
Depreciation	£247 500
Residual income	£47 200
Net assets	£1 250 000

Head Office assesses divisional performance by the residual income achieved. It uses a cost of capital of 12 per cent a year.

Division Q's average contribution per unit was

A   £14.82
B   £22.81
C   £28.06
D   £31.06
E   £32.81

(2 marks)

12.18 Conflict between NPV and performance measurement

Linamix is the chemicals division of a large industrial corporation. George Elton, the divisional general manager, is about to purchase new plant in order to manufacture a new product. He can buy either the Aromatic or the Zoman plant, each of which have the same capacity and expected four-year life, but which differ in their capital costs and expected net cash flows, as shown below:

	Aromatic	Zoman
Initial capital investment	£6 400 000	£5 200 000
Net cash flows (before tax)		
2009	£2 400 000	£2 600 000
2010	£2 400 000	£2 200 000
2011	£2 400 000	£1 500 000
2012	£2 400 000	£1 000 000
Net present value (@ 16% p.a.)	£315 634	£189 615

In the above calculations it has been assumed that the plant will be installed and paid for by the end of December 2008, and that the net cash flows accrue at the end of each calendar year. Neither plant is expected to have a residual value after decommissioning costs.

Like all other divisional managers in the corporation, Elton is expected to generate a before tax return on his divisional investment in excess of 16 per cent p.a., which he is currently just managing to achieve. Anything less than a 16 per cent return would make him ineligible for a performance bonus and may reduce his pension when he retires in early 2011. In calculating divisional returns, divisional assets are valued at net book values at the beginning of the year. Depreciation is charged on a straight line basis.

Requirements:

(a) Explain, with appropriate calculations, why neither return on investment nor residual income would motivate Elton to invest in the process showing the higher net present value. To what extent can the use of alternative accounting techniques assist in reconciling the conflict between using accounting-based performance measures and discounted cash flow investment appraisal techniques?

(12 marks)

(b) Managers tend to use post-tax cash flows to evaluate investment opportunities, but to evaluate divisional and managerial performance on the basis of pre-tax profits. Explain why this is so and discuss the potential problems that can arise, including suggestions as to how such problems can be overcome.

(8 marks)

(c) Discuss what steps can be taken to avoid dysfunctional behaviour which is motivated by accounting-based performance targets.

(5 marks)
(Total 25 marks)

12.19 Computation and discussion of economic value added

The managers of Toutplut Inc were surprised at a recent newspaper article which suggested that the company's performance in the last two years had been poor. The CEO commented that turnover had increased by nearly 17 per cent and pre-tax profit by 25 per cent between the last two financial years, and that the company compared well with others in the same industry.

| | $ million | |
| | Profit and loss account extracts for the year | |
	2007	2008
Turnover	326	380
Pre-tax accounting profit[1]	67	84
Taxation	23	29
Profit after tax	44	55
Dividends	15	18
Retained earnings	29	37

Balance sheet extracts for the year ending

	2007	2008
Fixed assets	120	156
Net current assets	130	160
	250	316
Financed by:		
Shareholders' funds	195	236
Medium- and long-term bank loans	55	80
	250	316

[1]After deduction of the economic depreciation of the company's fixed assets. This is also the depreciation used for tax purposes.

Other information:

(i)   Toutplut had non-capitalized leases valued at $10 million in each year 2006–08.

(ii) Balance sheet capital employed at the end of 2006 was $223 million.

(iii) The company's pre-tax cost of debt was estimated to be 9 per cent in 2007, and 10 per cent in 2008.

(iv) The company's cost of equity was estimated to be 15 per cent in 2007 and 17 per cent in 2008.

(v) The target capital structure is 60 per cent equity, 40 per cent debt.

(vi) The effective tax rate was 35 per cent in both 2007 and 2008.

(vii) Economic depreciation was $30 million in 2007 and $35 million in 2008.

(viii) Other non-cash expenses were $10 million per year in both 2007 and 2008.

(ix) Interest expense was $4 million in 2007 and $6 million in 2008.

Required:

(a) Estimate the economic valued added (EVA(TM)) for Toutplut Inc for both 2007 and 2008. State clearly any assumptions that you make.
Comment upon the performance of the company.

(7 marks)

(b) Briefly discuss the advantages and disadvantages of EVA(TM).

(6 marks)
(Total 13 marks)

12.20 A long-established, highly centralized company has grown to the extent that its chief executive, despite having a good supporting team, is finding difficulty in keeping up with the many decisions of importance in the company.

Consideration is therefore being given to reorganizing the company into profit centres. These would be product divisions, headed by a divisional managing director, who would be responsible for all the divisions' activities relating to its products.

You are required to explain, in outline:

(a) the types of decision areas that should be transferred to the new divisional managing directors if such a reorganization is to achieve its objectives;

(b) the types of decision areas that might reasonably be retained at company head office;

(c) the management accounting problems that might be expected to arise in introducing effective profit centre control.

(20 marks)

12.21 (a) Explain the meaning of each of the undernoted measures that may be used for divisional performance measurement and investment decision-making. Discuss the advantages and problems associated with the use of each.
(i) Return on capital employed.
(ii) Residual income.
(iii) Discounted future earnings.

(9 marks)

(b) Comment on the reasons why the measures listed in (a) above may give conflicting investment decision responses when applied to the same set of data. Use the following figures to illustrate the conflicting responses that may arise:

Additional investment of £60 000 for a six-year life with nil residual value.

Average net profit per year: £9000 (after depreciation).

Cost of capital: 14 per cent.

Existing capital employed: £300 000 with ROCE of 20 per cent.

(8 marks)

(Solutions should ignore taxation implications.)

(Total 17 marks)

12.22 Residual income and return on investment are commonly used measures of performance. However, they are frequently criticized for placing too great an emphasis on the achievement of short-term results, possibly damaging longer-term performance.

You are required to discuss

(a) the issues involved in the long-term–short-term conflict referred to in the above statement;

(11 marks)

(b) suggestions that have been made to reconcile this difference.

(11 marks)
(Total 22 marks)

CHAPTER 13
TRANSFER PRICING IN
DIVISIONALIZED COMPANIES

LEARNING OBJECTIVES

After studying this chapter you should be able to:

● **describe the different purposes of a transfer pricing system;**

● **identify and describe five different transfer pricing methods;**

● **explain why the correct transfer price is the external market price when there is a perfectly competitive market for the intermediate product;**

● **explain why cost-plus transfer prices will not result in the optimum output being achieved;**

● **explain a method of transfer pricing that has been advocated to resolve the conflicts between the decision-making and performance evaluation objectives;**

● **describe the additional factors that must be considered when setting transfer prices for multinational transactions.**

In the previous chapter alternative financial measures for evaluating divisional performance were examined. However, all of the financial measure outcomes will be significantly affected when divisions transfer goods and services to each other. The established transfer price is a cost to the receiving division and revenue to the supplying division, which means that whatever transfer price is set will affect the profitability of each division. In addition, this transfer price will also significantly influence each division's input and output decisions, and thus total company profits.

In this chapter we shall examine the various approaches that can be adopted to arrive at transfer prices between divisions. Although our focus will be on transfer pricing between divisions (i.e. profit or investment centres), transfer pricing can also apply between cost centres (typically support/service centres) or from cost centres to profit/investment centres. The same basic principles apply as those that apply between divisions, the only difference being that there is no need for a profit element to be included in the transfer price to reimburse the supplying cost centre.

PURPOSE OF TRANSFER PRICING

A transfer pricing system can be used to meet the following purposes:

1 To provide information that motivates divisional managers to make good economic decisions. This will happen when actions that divisional managers take to improve the reported profit of their divisions also improves the profit of the company as a whole.

2 To provide information that is useful for evaluating the managerial and economic performance of the divisions.

3 To ensure that divisional autonomy is not undermined.

4 To intentionally move profits between divisions or locations.

Providing information for making good economic decisions

Goods transferred from the supplying division to the receiving division are known as **intermediate products**. The products sold by a receiving division to the outside world are known as **final products**. The objective of the receiving division is to subject the intermediate product to further processing before it is sold as a final product in the outside market. The transfer price of the intermediate product represents a cost to the receiving division and a revenue to the supplying division. Therefore transfer prices are used to determine how much of the intermediate product will be produced by the supplying division and how much will be acquired by the receiving division. In a centralized company the decision as to whether an intermediate product should be sold or processed further is determined by comparing the incremental cost of, and the revenues from, further processing. In a divisionalized organization structure, however, the manager of the receiving division will treat the price at which the intermediate product is transferred as an incremental cost, and this may lead to incorrect decisions being made.

For example, let us assume that the incremental cost of the intermediate product is £100, and the additional further processing costs of the receiving division are £60. The incremental cost of producing the final product will therefore be £160. Let us also assume that the supplying division has a temporary excess capacity, which is being maintained in order to meet an expected resurgence in demand, and that the market price of the final product is £200. To simplify the illustration, we assume there is no market for the intermediate product. The correct short-term decision would be to convert the intermediate product into the final product. In a centralized company this decision would be taken, but in a divisionalized organization structure where the transfer price for the intermediate product is £150 based on full cost plus a profit margin, the incremental cost of the receiving division will be £210 (£150 + £60). The divisional manager would therefore incorrectly decide not to purchase the intermediate product for further processing. This problem can be overcome if the transfer price is set at the incremental cost of the supplying division, which in this example is £100.

Evaluating divisional performance

When goods are transferred from one division to another, the revenue of the supplying division becomes a cost of the receiving division. Consequently, the prices at which goods are transferred can influence each division's reported profits, and there is a danger that an unsound transfer price will result in a misleading performance measure that may cause divisional managers to believe that the transfer price is affecting their performance rather unfairly. This may lead to disagreement and negative motivational consequences.

Conflict of objectives

Unfortunately, no single transfer price is likely to perfectly serve all of the specified purposes. They often conflict and managers are forced to make trade-offs. In particular, the decision-making and the performance evaluation purposes may conflict with each other. For example, in some situations the transfer price that motivates the short-run optimal economic decision is incremental cost. If the supplier in our earlier example has excess capacity, this cost will probably equal variable cost. The supplying division will fail to cover any of its fixed costs when transfers are made at variable cost, and will therefore report a loss. Furthermore, if a transfer price equal to variable cost (£100 in the above example) is imposed on the manager of the supplying division, the concept of divisional autonomy and decentralization is undermined. On the other hand, a transfer price that may be satisfactory for evaluating divisional performance (£150 in the above example) may lead divisions to make suboptimal decisions when viewed from the overall company perspective.

ALTERNATIVE TRANSFER PRICING METHODS

The management accounting literature identifies many different types of transfer prices that companies can use to transfer goods and services. The most notable ones are:

1 market-based transfer prices;
2 cost plus a profit mark-up transfer prices;
3 marginal/variable cost transfer prices;
4 full cost transfer prices;
5 negotiated transfer prices;
6 marginal/variable cost plus opportunity cost transfer prices.

Exhibit 13.1 sets out the results of surveys of the primary transfer pricing methods used in various countries. This exhibit shows that in the USA transfer prices are used by the vast majority of the firms surveyed. It is apparent from all of the surveys that a small minority (less than 10 per cent) transfer at marginal or variable cost. A significant proportion of firms use each of the other methods with the largest proportions transferring goods or services at market prices or either full cost or full cost plus a mark-up. The following sections describe in detail each of the transfer pricing methods.

MARKET-BASED TRANSFER PRICES

In most circumstances, where a **perfectly competitive market** for an intermediate product exists it is optimal for both decision-making and performance evaluation purposes to set

EXHIBIT 13.1

Surveys of company practice

The studies listed below relate to surveys of transfer pricing practices in the UK and USA. It is apparent from these surveys that variable/marginal cost methods are not widely used, whereas full cost or full cost plus a mark-up are used extensively. Market price methods are also widely used. Similar findings have also been reported in surveys undertaken in Canada (Tang, 1992) and Australia (Joye and Blayney, 1991).

UK survey (Abu-Serdaneh, 2004)

A survey based on responses from 170 companies reported the percentage of companies that used particular transfer pricing methods to a considerable extent. The percentage usage was as follows:

	%	%
Prevailing market price	16	
Adjusted market price	15	31
Unit full manufacturing cost	24	
Unit full manufacturing cost plus a profit margin	38	62
Unit variable manufacturing cost	2	
Unit variable manufacturing cost plus a profit margin	6	
Unit variable manufacturing cost plus a fixed fee	1	9
Negotiated transfer price		8

The findings indicated that a minority of companies used more than one transfer price.

USA Survey (Borkowski, 1990)

Number of companies participating	215	
Percentage using transfer prices	89.6%	
Percentage using transfers on following bases		
Market price		
Full market price	20.2	
Adjusted market price	12.5	32.7
Negotiated		
To external price	13.6	
To manufacturing costs	3.0	
With no restrictions	6.0	22.6
Full cost		
Standard	14.3	
Actual	7.1	
Plus profit based on cost	14.9	
Plus fixed profit	2.4	
Other	2.4	41.1
Variable cost		
Standard	2.4	
Actual	0.6	
Plus contribution based on cost	0.6	3.6
Total		100.0

transfer prices at competitive market prices. A perfectly competitive market exists where products sold are identical and no individual buyer or seller can affect market prices.

When transfers are recorded at market prices, divisional performance is more likely to represent the real economic contribution of the division to total company profits. If the supplying division did not exist, the intermediate product would have to be purchased on the outside market at the current market price. Alternatively, if the receiving division did not exist, the intermediate product would have to be sold on the outside market at the current market price. Divisional profits are therefore likely to be similar to the profits that would be calculated if the divisions were separate organizations. Consequently, divisional profitability can be compared directly with the profitability of similar companies operating in the same type of business.

Where the selling costs for internal transfers of the intermediate product are identical with those that arise from sales in the outside market, it will not matter whether the supplying division's output is sold internally or externally. To illustrate this we shall consider two alternatives. First, assume initially that the output of the supplying division is sold *externally* and that the receiving division purchases its requirements *externally*. Now

EXHIBIT 13.2

Profit impact using market-based transfer prices

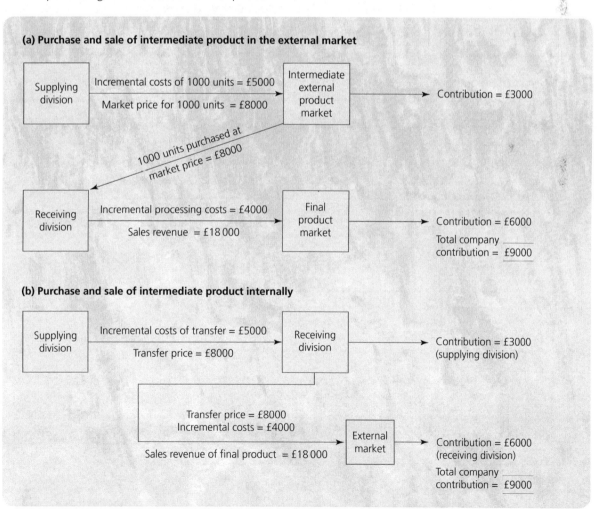

consider a second situation where the output of the intermediate product is transferred *internally* at the market price and is not sold on the outside market. You should now refer to Exhibit 13.2. The aim of this diagram is to show that divisional and total profits are not affected, whichever of these two alternatives is chosen.

Exhibit 13.2 illustrates a situation where the receiving division sells 1000 units of the final product in the external market. The incremental costs of the supplying division for the production of 1000 units of the intermediate product are £5000, with a market price for the output of £8000. The incremental costs of the receiving division for the additional processing of the 1000 units of the intermediate product are £4000. This output can be sold for £18 000. You will see that it does not matter whether the intermediate product is transferred internally or sold externally – profits of each division and total company profits remain unchanged.

COST PLUS A MARK-UP TRANSFER PRICES

Before we discuss different cost-based transfer prices read Example 13.1 and then look at Exhibit 13.3. This exhibit shows the profit for the Baltic Group as a whole using the data given in Example 13.1. The profit maximizing output is 5000 units. The aim of the transfer pricing system should be to motivate both the supplying division (Oslo) and the receiving division (Bergen) to operate at the optimum output level of 5000 units. Assuming that the

EXAMPLE 13.1

The Oslo division and the Bergen division are divisions within the Baltic Group. One of the products manufactured by the Oslo division is an intermediate product for which there is no external market. This intermediate product is transferred to the Bergen division where it is converted into a final product for sale on the external market. One unit of the intermediate product is used in the production of the final product. The expected units of the final product which the Bergen division estimates it can sell at various selling prices are as follows:

Net selling price (£)	Quantity sold (units)
100	1000
90	2000
80	3000
70	4000
60	5000
50	6000

The costs of each division are as follows:

(£)	Oslo (£)	Bergen (£)
Variable cost per unit	11	7
Fixed costs attributable to the products	60 000	90 000

EXHIBIT 13.3

*Profit computations
for the Baltic Group*

Note that the following profit computations for the company as a whole do not incorporate the transfer price since it represents inter-company trading with the transfer pricing revenues of the supplying division cancelling out the transfer pricing costs incurred by the receiving division.

Whole company profit computations

Output level (units)	Total revenues	Company variable costs	Company fixed costs	Company profit/(loss)
1000	100 000	18 000	150 000	(68 000)
2000	180 000	36 000	150 000	(6 000)
3000	240 000	54 000	150 000	36 000
4000	280 000	72 000	150 000	58 000
5000	300 000	90 000	150 000	60 000
6000	300 000	108 000	150 000	42 000

cost base for the cost plus a mark-up transfer price is full cost the fixed costs of the supplying division will be unitized by dividing the fixed costs of £60 000 for the period by the estimated output. The resulting unitized fixed cost will be added to the unit variable cost to derive a full cost per unit of output. A profit mark-up is then added to full cost to derive the transfer price. Let us assume that £35 per unit (or £35 000 per 1000 units) is the full cost plus a mark-up transfer price. At this transfer price the profit computations for each division will be as follows:

Oslo division (Supplying division)

Output level (units)	Transfer price revenues	Variable costs	Fixed costs	Total profit/(loss)
1000	35 000	11 000	60 000	(36 000)
2000	70 000	22 000	60 000	(12 000)
3000	105 000	33 000	60 000	12 000
4000	140 000	44 000	60 000	36 000
5000	175 000	55 000	60 000	60 000
6000	210 000	66 000	60 000	84 000

Bergen division (Receiving division)

Output level (units)	Total revenues	Variable costs	Total cost of transfers	Fixed costs	Total profit/(loss)
1000	100 000	7 000	35 000	90 000	(32 000)
2000	180 000	14 000	70 000	90 000	6 000
3000	240 000	21 000	105 000	90 000	24 000
4000	280 000	28 000	140 000	90 000	22 000
5000	300 000	35 000	175 000	90 000	0
6000	300 000	42 000	210 000	90 000	(42 000)

The supplying division maximizes profits at an output level of 6000 units whereas the receiving division maximizes profits at 3000 units so neither division will be motivated to operate at the optimal output level for the company as a whole of 5000 units. The receiving division will therefore choose to purchase 3000 units from the supplying division. This is because the Bergen division will compare its net marginal revenue with the transfer price and expand output as long as the **net marginal revenue** of the additional output exceeds the transfer price. Note that net marginal revenue is defined as the marginal (incremental) revenue from the sale of an extra unit (or a specified number of incremental units) of the final product less the marginal/incremental conversion costs (excluding the transfer price). The calculations of net marginal revenues are as follows for increments of 1000 units:

Units	Net marginal revenue (£)
1000	93 000 (100 000 − 7000)
2000	73 000 (80 000 − 7000)
3000	53 000 (60 000 − 7000)
4000	33 000 (40 000 − 7000)
5000	13 000 (20 000 − 7000)
6000	−7 000 (0 − 7000)

If you refer to the receiving division (Bergen) in the schedule of profit calculations you will see that expanding output from 1000 to 2000 units results in total revenues increasing from £100 000 to £180 000 so the marginal revenue is £80 000. Also variable conversion costs increase from £7000 to £14 000 so marginal cost is £7000. Therefore net marginal revenue is £73 000 (£80 000 − £7000). Faced with a transfer price of £35 000 per 1000 units the Bergen division will not expand output beyond 3000 units because the transfer price paid for each batch exceeds the net marginal revenue.

MARGINAL/VARIABLE COST TRANSFER PRICES

Marginal cost is a term that is used by economists. It refers to the additional cost of one extra unit of output. Accountants generally assume that marginal cost is the same as variable cost. When the market for the intermediate product is imperfect or non-existent, transfer prices set at the variable/marginal cost of the supplying division can motivate both the supplying and receiving division managers to operate at output levels that will maximize overall company profits. Using the data given in Example 13.1, the variable cost transfer price is £11 per unit or £11 000 for each batch of 1000 units. The receiving division will expand output as long as net marginal revenue exceeds the transfer price. Now look at the net marginal revenue that we calculated for the receiving division in the previous section to illustrate cost plus a mark-up transfer pricing. You will see that the net marginal revenue from expanding output from 4000 to 5000 units is £13 000 and the transfer price that the receiving division must pay to acquire this batch of 1000 units is £11 000. Therefore expanding the output will increase the profits of the receiving division. Will the manager of the receiving division be motivated to expand output from 5000 to 6000 units? The answer is no because the net marginal revenue (−£7000) is less than the transfer price of purchasing the 1000 units.

Setting the transfer price at the unit variable cost of the supplying division will motivate the divisional managers to operate at the optimum output level for the company as a whole provided that the supplying division manager is instructed to meet the demand of the receiving division at this transfer price. Although the variable cost transfer price encourages overall company optimality it is a poor measure of divisional performance. At a variable cost transfer price of £11 per unit the profit computations for each division will be as follows:

Oslo division (Supplying division)

Output level (units)	Transfer price revenues	Variable costs	Fixed costs	Total profit/(loss)
1000	11 000	11 000	60 000	(60 000)
2000	22 000	22 000	60 000	(60 000)
3000	33 000	33 000	60 000	(60 000)
4000	44 000	44 000	60 000	(60 000)
5000	55 000	55 000	60 000	(60 000)
6000	66 000	66 000	60 000	(60 000)

Bergen division (Receiving division)

Output level (units)	Total revenues	Variable costs	Total cost of transfers	Fixed costs	Total profit/(loss)
1000	100 000	7 000	11 000	90 000	(8 000)
2000	180 000	14 000	22 000	90 000	54 000
3000	240 000	21 000	33 000	90 000	96 000
4000	280 000	28 000	44 000	90 000	118 000
5000	300 000	35 000	55 000	90 000	120 000
6000	300 000	42 000	66 000	90 000	102 000

You can see that the supplying division reports a loss equal to £60 000 at all output levels. In the short term fixed costs are unavoidable and therefore the division manager is no worse off since fixed costs will still be incurred. Note also that the Oslo division also produces other products so the overall divisional profit (excluding the inter-divisional transfers with Bergen) may be positive. In contrast, the receiving division maximizes its profits at the optimal output level of 5000 units with a reported profit of £120 000. We can conclude that the variable cost transfer price motivates managers to choose the optimal output level for the company as a whole but it results in a poor measure of divisional performance since the allocation of the £60 000 profits from inter-divisional profits results in the supplying division reporting a loss of £60 000 and the receiving division reporting a profit of £120 000.

FULL COST TRANSFER PRICES WITHOUT A MARK-UP

In Chapter 7 it was pointed out that full costs require that predetermined fixed overhead rates should be established. Let us assume that the 5000 units optimal output level for the company as a whole is used to determine the fixed overhead rate per unit. Therefore the fixed cost per unit for the intermediate product will be £12 per unit (£60 000 fixed costs/5000 units) giving a full cost of £23 (£11 variable cost plus £12 fixed cost). If the transfer price is set at £23 per unit (i.e. £23 000 per 1000 batch) the receiving division manager will expand output as long as net marginal revenue exceeds the transfer price. If you refer to the net marginal revenue schedule shown in the section describing cost plus a mark-up transfer prices you will see that the receiving division manager will choose to purchase 4000 units. The manager will choose not to expand output to the 5000 units optimal level for the company as a whole because the transfer cost of £23 000 exceeds the net marginal revenue of £13 000. Also, at the selected output level of 4000 units the total transfer price revenues of the supplying division will be £92 000 (4000 units at £23), but you will see from the profit calculations shown earlier for the Oslo division that the total costs are £104 000

(£44 000 variable cost + £60 000 fixed cost). Therefore the supplying division will report a loss because all of its fixed costs have not been recovered. Hence the transfer price is suitable for neither performance evaluation nor ensuring that optimal output decisions are made.

NEGOTIATED TRANSFER PRICES

The difficulties encountered in establishing a sound system of transfer pricing have led to suggestions that negotiated transfer prices should be used. Negotiated transfer prices are most appropriate in situations where some market imperfections exist for the intermediate product, such as where there are several different market prices. When there are such imperfections in the market, the respective divisional managers must have the freedom to buy and sell outside the company to enable them to engage in a bargaining process. It is claimed that if this is the case then the friction and bad feeling that may arise from a centrally controlled market transfer price will be eliminated without incurring a mis--allocation of resources.

For negotiation to work effectively it is important that managers have equal bargaining power. If the receiving division has many sourcing possibilities for the intermediate product or service, but the supplying division has limited outlets, the bargaining power of the managers will be unequal. Unequal bargaining power can also occur if the transfers are a relatively small proportion of the business for one of the divisions and a relatively large proportion of the business of the other. Negotiated transfer prices also have other limitations. A further difficulty with negotiation is that it is time-consuming for the managers concerned, particularly where a large number of transactions are involved.

Would the managers of the Baltic Group be able to negotiate a transfer price that meets the decision-making and performance evaluation requirements of a transfer pricing system? If the manager of the supplying division cannot avoid the fixed costs in the short run, he or she will have no bargaining power because there is no external market for the intermediate product. The manager would therefore accept any price as long as it is not below variable cost. Meaningful negotiation is not possible. If the fixed costs are avoidable the manager has some negotiating power since he or she can avoid £60 000 by not producing the intermediate product. The manager will try and negotiate a selling price in excess of full cost. If an output level of 5000 units is used to calculate the full cost the unit cost from our earlier calculations was £23 and the manager will try and negotiate a price in excess of £23. If you examine the net marginal revenue of the receiving division shown on page 318 you will see that the manager of the receiving division will not expand output to 5000 units if the transfer price is set above £23 per unit. As indicated earlier, negotiation is only likely to work when there is an imperfect external market for the intermediate product.

MARGINAL/VARIABLE COST PLUS OPPORTUNITY COST TRANSFER PRICES

Setting transfer prices at the marginal/variable cost of the supplying division per unit transferred plus the opportunity cost per unit of the supplying division is often cited as a general rule that should lead to optimum decisions for the company as a whole. Opportunity cost is defined as the contribution foregone by the supplying division from transferring internally the intermediate product. This rule will result in the transfer price being set at the variable cost per unit when there is no market for the intermediate product. Why? If the facilities are dedicated to the production of the intermediate product they will have no alternative use, so the opportunity cost will be zero. Consider now a situation where there is a perfectly competitive external market for the intermediate product. Assume that the market price for the intermediate product is £20 per unit and the variable cost per unit of output is £5. If the supplying division has no spare capacity the contribution foregone from transferring the intermediate product is £15. Adding this to the variable cost per unit will result in the transfer price being set at the market price of £20 per unit. What is the transfer price if the supplying division has temporary spare capacity? In this situation there will be no foregone contribution and the transfer price will be set at the variable cost per unit of £5.

You should have noted that applying the above general rule leads to the same transfer price as was recommended earlier in this chapter. In other words, if there is a perfectly competitive external market for the intermediate product, the market price is the optimal transfer price. When there is no market for the intermediate product, transfers should be made at the variable cost per unit of output of the intermediate product. Thus, the general rule is merely a restatement of the principles that have been established earlier. The major problem with this general rule is that it is difficult to apply in more complex situations such as when there is an imperfect market for the intermediate product.

COMPARISON OF COST-BASED TRANSFER PRICING METHODS

Figure 13.1 enables us to compare the cost-based transfer pricing methods in terms of whether they result in the optimal output levels for the company as a whole. Note that it is assumed that there is no market for the intermediate product. You will see that the variable cost of the intermediate product is assumed to be constant throughout the entire production range and that the net marginal revenue for the final product declines to reflect the fact that to sell more the price must be lowered. Remember that it was pointed out earlier that term 'net marginal revenue' refers to the marginal revenue of the final product less the marginal/variable conversion costs (excluding the transfer price) incurred by the receiving division. Economic theory indicates that the optimal output for the company as a whole is where the marginal cost of producing the intermediate product is equal to the net marginal revenue from the sale of the final product. That is an output level of Q_2.

If the transfer price is set at the variable cost per unit of the intermediate product the receiving division will purchase the intermediate product up to the point where net marginal revenue equals its marginal/variable costs. It will therefore result in the optimal output from the overall company perspective (Q_2). If a higher transfer price is set (as indicated by the blue line) to cover full cost, or a mark-up is added to full cost, then the supplying division will restrict output to suboptimal levels such as Q_1.

It is apparent from our discussion of the different transfer pricing methods using the data in Example 13.1 and the diagrammatic presentation in Figure 13.1 that the theoretically correct transfer to encourage divisions to choose the optimal output for the company as a whole is the variable/marginal cost of producing the intermediate product. To simplify our analysis we have assumed that there is no market for the intermediate product.

FIGURE 13.1

A comparison of marginal cost and full cost or cost-plus transfer pricing

Transfer pricing becomes even more complex when we introduce an imperfect market for the intermediate product. You should note, however, that where there is an imperfect market for the intermediate product the theoretically correct transfer price is still the variable/marginal cost of producing the intermediate product at the optimal output for the company as a whole (see Drury, 2008, Chapter 20 for a more detailed explanation).

PROPOSALS FOR RESOLVING TRANSFER PRICING CONFLICTS

Our discussion so far has indicated that in the absence of a perfect market for the intermediate product none of the transfer pricing methods can perfectly meet both the decision-making and performance evaluation requirements and also not undermine divisional autonomy. It has been suggested that if the external market for the intermediate product is imperfect or non-existent, transfers at marginal/variable cost should motivate decisions that are optimal from the overall company's perspective. However, transfers at marginal/variable cost are unsuitable for performance evaluation because they do not provide an incentive for the supplying division to transfer goods and services internally. This is because they do not contain a profit margin for the supplying division. Central headquarters intervention may be necessary to instruct the supplying division to meet the receiving division's demand at the marginal cost of the transfers. Thus, divisional autonomy will be undermined. Transferring at cost plus a mark-up creates the opposite conflict. Here the transfer price meets the performance evaluation requirement but will not induce managers to make optimal decisions.

A solution that has been proposed to resolve the above conflicts is to charge all transfers at variable cost and for the supplying division to also charge the receiving division a fixed fee for the privilege of obtaining these transfers at short-run variable cost. This approach is sometimes described as a **two-part transfer pricing system**. With this system, the receiving division acquires additional units of the intermediate product at the variable cost of production. Therefore when it equates its marginal (variable) costs with its net marginal revenues to determine the optimum profit-maximizing output level, it will use the appropriate variable costs of the supplying division. The supplying division can recover its fixed costs and earn a profit on the inter-divisional transfers through the fixed fee charged each period. The fixed fee is intended to compensate the supplying division for tying up some of its fixed capacity for providing products or services that are trans-ferred internally. The fixed fee should cover a share of fixed costs of the supplying division and also provide a return on capital. The advantage of this approach is that transfers will be made at the variable cost of the supplying division, and both divisions should also be able to report profits from inter-divisional trading. Furthermore, the receiving divisions are made aware, and charged for the full cost of obtaining intermediate products from other divisions, through the two components of the two-part transfer pricing system.

If you refer back to Example 13.1 you will see that this proposal would result in a transfer price at a variable cost of £11 per unit for the intermediate product plus a fixed fee lump-sum payment of £60 000 to cover the fixed costs of the capacity allocated to producing the intermediate product. In addition, a fixed sum to reflect the required return on the capital employed would be added to the £60 000. Adopting this approach the receiving division will use the short-run variable cost to equate with its net marginal revenue and choose to purchase the optimal output level for the company as a whole (5000 units). For longer-term decisions the receiving division will be made aware that the revenues must be sufficient to cover the full cost of producing the intermediate product (£11 unit variable cost plus £60 000 fixed costs plus the opportunity cost of capital). When the lump-sum fixed fee is added to the short-run transfer price you will see that the supplying division will report a profit at all output levels. Assume, for example that the fixed fee is £75 000 (£60 000 fixed costs plus £15 000 to provide a satisfactory return on capital). Now refer back to the divisional profit calculations shown on page 321 for the variable cost transfer pricing system. You will see that the supplying division will report a profit of £15 000 (the revenues from the fixed fee of £75 000 less the £60 000 loss equal to the fixed costs). The receiving division's reported profits will be reduced by the £75 000 fixed fee for all output levels but its profits will still be maximized at the optimal output level of 5000 units.

INTERNATIONAL TRANSFER PRICING

The rise of multinational organizations introduces additional issues that must be considered when setting transfer prices. When the supplying and the receiving divisions are located in different countries with different taxation rates, and the taxation rates in one country are much lower than those in the other, it would be in the company's interest if most of the profits were allocated to the division operating in the low taxation country. For example, consider an organization that manufactures products in country A, which has a marginal tax rate of 25 per cent, and sells those products to country B, which has a marginal tax rate of 40 per cent. It is in the company's best interests to locate most of its profits in country A, where the tax rate is lowest. Therefore it will wish to use the highest possible transfer price so that the receiving division operating in country B will have higher costs and report lower profits whereas the supplying division operating in country A will be credited with higher revenues and thus report the higher profits. In many multinational organizations, the taxation issues outweigh other transfer pricing issues and the dominant consideration in the setting of transfer prices is the minimization of global taxes.

In an attempt to provide a worldwide consensus on the pricing of international intra-firm transactions the Organization for Economic Co-operation and Development issued a

REAL WORLD VIEWS 13.1

A guide to transfer pricing from the OECD

Transfer pricing is often driven by taxation issues. Large multinational organizations will endeavour to have a larger proportion of profits realized in the lowest taxation environment. Transfer pricing can deprive governments of a fair share of taxation revenue and expose multinationals to double taxation.

In an effort to avoid issues in transfer pricing, organizations such as the OECD issue guidelines on best practice transfer pricing. The OECD guidelines are based on the 'arm's-length' principle. This simply means pricing between two companies occurs as if the two were completely independent companies. The OECD Transfer Pricing Guidelines provide a framework for settling such matters by providing considerable detail as to how to apply the arm's-length principle in an effort to equally distribute taxation revenue and avoid double taxation. This does assume that tax authorities and multinationals work together. As some multinationals have a turnover greater than the GDP of some countries, this is not always the case. Abuse of transfer pricing may be a particular problem for developing countries, as multinationals might utilize it to get round exchange controls or to repatriate profits in a tax-free form. The OECD provides technical assistance to developing countries to help them implement and administer transfer pricing rules. Providing assistance may also not be easy. For example, the arm's-length principle requires the existence of a comparable product. It may be the case, for example, that a computer chip manufacturer has no comparable manufacturer in a particular country. This obviously creates a problem obtaining an arm's-length value.

Are there any alternatives to transfer pricing? A frequently mentioned alternative is to split all profits of a multinational among its subsidiaries, regardless of location, using a derived formula. This may sound like a simple solution, but it is unlikely that tax authorities would agree easily to a formula. As arm's-length pricing is based on realistic market conditions, it is likely to remain the basis for transfer pricing among tax authorities and multinationals.

Discussion point

If no comparable market price exists to determine an arm's-length price, how might an acceptable transfer price be derived?

References

OECD (2002) Transfer pricing: Keeping it at arm's length, OECD Observer, January (available at http://www.oecdobserver.org/news/fullstory.php/aid/670).

guideline statement in 1995 (OECD, 1995) to ensure that companies do not use transfer prices for taxation manipulation purposes. International transfer pricing is a complex issue and is beyond the scope of this book, but you should note that there are additional considerations that must be taken into account when setting transfer prices within multinational companies.

SUMMARY

The following items relate to the learning objectives listed at the beginning of the chapter.

- **Describe the different purposes of a transfer pricing system.** Transfer pricing can be used for the following purposes: (a) to provide information that motivates divisional managers to make good economic decisions; (b) to provide information that is useful for evaluating the managerial and economic performance of a division; (c) to intentionally move profits between divisions or locations; and (d) to ensure that divisional autonomy is not undermined.

- **Identify and describe five different transfer pricing methods.** The five main transfer pricing methods are (a) market-based transfer prices; (b) marginal cost transfer prices; (c) full cost transfer prices; (d) cost plus a mark-up transfer prices; and (e) negotiated transfer prices.

- **Explain why the correct transfer price is the external market price when there is a perfectly competitive market for the intermediate product.** If there is a perfectly competitive market for the intermediate product, transfers recorded at market prices are likely to represent the real economic contribution to total company profits. If the supplying division did not exist, the intermediate product would have to be purchased on the outside market at the current market price. Alternatively, if the receiving division did not exist, the intermediate product would have to be sold on the outside market at the current market price. Divisional profits are therefore likely to be similar to the profits that would be calculated if the divisions were separate organizations. For decision-making, if the receiving division does not acquire the intermediate product internally it would be able to acquire the product at the competitive external market price. Similarly, if the supplying division does transfer internally it will be able to sell the product at the external market price. Thus, the market price represents the opportunity cost of internal transfers.

- **Explain why cost-plus transfer prices will not result in the optimum output being achieved.** If cost-plus transfer prices are used, the receiving division will determine its optimal output at the point where the marginal cost of its transfers is equal to its net marginal revenue (i.e. marginal revenue less marginal conversion costs, excluding the transfer price). However, the marginal cost of the transfers (i.e. the cost-plus transfer price) will be in excess of the marginal cost of producing the intermediate product for the company as a whole. Thus, marginal cost will be overstated and the receiving division manager will restrict output to the point where net marginal revenue equals the transfer price, rather than the marginal cost to the company of producing the intermediate product.

- **Explain a method of transfer pricing that has been advocated to resolve the conflicts between the decision-making and performance evaluation objectives.** To overcome the decision-making and performance evaluation conflicts that can occur with cost-based transfer pricing a two-part transfer pricing system is recommended. The two-part transfer pricing system involves transfers being made at the variable cost per unit of output of the supplying division plus a lump-sum fixed fee charged by the supplying division to the receiving division for the use of the capacity allocated to the intermediate product. This transfer pricing system should also motivate the receiving division to choose the optimal output level and enable the supplying division to obtain a profit on inter-divisional trading.

● **Describe the additional factors that must be considered when setting transfer prices for multinational transactions.** When divisions operate in different countries, taxation implications can be a dominant influence. The aim is to set transfer prices at levels that will ensure that most of the profits are allocated to divisions operating in low taxation counties. However, taxation authorities in the countries where the divisions are located and the OECD have introduced guidelines and legislation to ensure that companies do not use transfer prices for taxation manipulation purposes.

KEY TERMS AND CONCEPTS

cost plus a mark-up transfer prices (p. 318)

final products (p. 314)

full cost transfer prices (p. 321)

intermediate products (p. 314)

marginal cost transfer prices (p. 320)

marginal/variable cost plus opportunity cost transfer prices (p. 322)

market-based transfer prices (p. 316)

negotiated transfer prices (p. 322)

net marginal revenue (p. 319)

perfectly competitive market (p. 316)

two-part transfer pricing system (p. 324)

variable cost transfer prices (p. 320)

ASSESSMENT MATERIAL

The review questions are short questions that enable you to assess your understanding of the main topics included in the chapter. The page numbers in parentheses provide you with the page numbers to refer to if you cannot answer a specific question.

The review problems are more complex and require you to relate and apply the content to various business problems. Solutions to review problems are provided in a separate section at the end of the book. Additional review problems can be accessed by lecturers and students on the website (www.drury-online.com). Solutions to these problems are provided for lecturers in the *Instructors' Manual*. This is available on the lecturers' password-protected section of the website.

The website also includes over 30 case study problems. A list of these cases is provided on pages 389–392.

REVIEW QUESTIONS

13.1 Distinguish between intermediate products and final products. *(p. 314)*

13.2 Explain the four purposes for which transfer pricing can be used. *(pp. 314–15)*

13.3 Explain why a single transfer pricing method cannot serve all four purposes. *(pp. 314–15)*

13.4 If an external, perfectly competitive market exists for an intermediate product what should be the transfer price? Why? *(pp. 316–18)*

13.5 Define the term 'net marginal revenue'. *(pp. 319-20)*

13.6 If there is no external market for the intermediate product what is the optimal transfer price? Why? *(pp. 323–24)*

13.7 Why are full cost and cost plus a mark-up transfer prices unlikely to result in the optimum output? *(pp. 323–24)*

13.8 Why are marginal cost transfer prices not widely used in practice? *(pp. 320–21)*

13.9 Discuss the advantages and disadvantages of negotiated transfer prices. *(p. 322)*

13.10 What are the circumstances that favour the use of negotiated transfer prices? *(p. 322)*

13.11 Describe a proposal that has been recommended for resolving transfer pricing conflicts. *(pp. 324–25)*

13.12 What are the special considerations that must be taken into account with international transfer pricing? *(pp. 325–26)*

REVIEW PROBLEMS

13.13 X plc, a manufacturing company, has two divisions: division A and division B. Division A produces one type of product, ProdX, which it transfers to division B and also sells externally. Division B has been approached by another company, which has offered to supply 2500 units of ProdX for £35 each.

The following details for division A are available:

	£
Sales revenue	
Sales to division B @ £40 per unit	400 000
External sales @ £45 per unit	270 000
Less:	
Variable cost @ £22 per unit	352 000
Fixed costs	100 000
Profit	218 000

If division B decides to buy from the other company, the impact of the decision on the profits of division A and X plc, assuming external sales of ProdX cannot be increased, will be

	Division A	X plc
A	£12 500 decrease	£12 500 decrease
B	£15 625 decrease	£12 500 increase
C	£32 500 decrease	£32 500 increase
D	£45 000 decrease	£32 500 decrease
E	£45 000 decrease	£45 000 decrease

(3 marks)

13.14 Division A transfers 100 000 units of a component to division B each year.

The market price of the component is £25.

Division A's variable cost is £15 per unit.

Division A's fixed costs are £500 000 each year.

What price would be credited to division A for each component that it transfers to division B under two-part tariff pricing (where the divisions have agreed that the fixed fee will be £200 000)?

A   £15

B   £17

C   £20

(2 marks)

13.15 ZP plc operates two subsidiaries, X and Y. X is a component manufacturing subsidiary and Y is an assembly and final product subsidiary. Both subsidiaries produce one type of output only. Subsidiary Y needs one component from subsidiary X for every unit of product W produced. Subsidiary X transfers to subsidiary Y all of the components needed to produce product W. Subsidiary X also sells components on the external market.

The following budgeted information is available for each subsidiary.

	X	Y
Market price per component	$800	
Market price per unit of W		$1,200
Production costs per component	$600	
Assembly costs per unit of W		$400
Non-production fixed costs	$1.5m	$1.3m
External demand	10 000 units	12 000 units
Capacity	22 000 units	
Taxation rates	25%	30%

The production cost per component is 60 per cent variable. The fixed production costs are absorbed based on budgeted output.

X sets a transfer price at marginal cost plus 70 per cent.

Calculate the post-tax profit generated by each subsidiary.

(4 marks)

13.16 Determining optimal transfer prices for three different scenarios

Manuco Ltd has been offered supplies of special ingredient Z at a transfer price of £15 per kg by Helpco Ltd, which is part of the same group of companies. Helpco Ltd processes and sells special ingredient Z to customers external to the group at £15 per kg. Helpco Ltd bases its transfer price on cost plus 25 per cent profit mark-up. Total cost has been estimated as 75 per cent variable and 25 per cent fixed.

Required:

Discuss the transfer prices at which Helpco Ltd should offer to transfer special ingredient Z to Manuco Ltd in order that group profit maximizing decisions may be taken on financial grounds in each of the following situations:

(i)   Helpco Ltd has an external market for all of its production of special ingredient Z at a selling price of £15 per kg. Internal transfers to Manuco Ltd would enable £1.50 per kg of variable packing cost to be avoided.

(ii) Conditions are as per (i) but Helpco Ltd has production capacity for 3000 kg of special ingredient Z for which no external market is available.

(iii) Conditions are as per (ii) but Helpco Ltd has an alternative use for some of its spare production capacity. This alternative use is equivalent to 2000 kg of special ingredient Z and would earn a contribution of £6000.

(13 marks)

13.17 Impact of cost-plus transfer price on decision-making and divisional profits

Enormous Engineering (EE) plc is a large multi-divisional engineering company having interests in a wide variety of product markets. The industrial products division (IPD) sells component parts to consumer appliance manufacturers, both inside and outside the company. One such part, a motor unit, it sells solely to external customers, but buys the motor itself internally from the electric motor division (EMD). The EMD makes the motor to IPD specifications and it does not expect to be able to sell it to any other customers.

In preparing the 2009 budgets IPD estimated the number of motor units it expects to be able to sell at various prices as follows:

Price (ex works) (£)	Quantity sold (units)
50	1000
40	2000
35	3000
30	4000
25	6000
20	8000

It then sought a quotation from EMD, which offered to supply the motors at £16 each based on the following estimate:

	(£)
Materials and bought-in parts	2
Direct labour costs	4
Factory overhead (150% of direct labour costs)	6
Total factory cost	12
Profit margin (33$\frac{1}{3}$% on factory cost)	4
Quoted price	16

Factory overhead costs are fixed. All other costs are variable.

Although it considered the price quoted to be on the high side, IPD nevertheless believed that it could still sell the completed unit at a profit because it incurred costs of only £4 (material £1 and direct labour £3) on each unit made. It therefore placed an order for the coming year.

On reviewing the budget for 2009 the finance director of EE noted that the projected sales of the motor unit were considerably less than those for the previous year, which was disappointing as both divisions concerned were working well below their capacities. On making enquiries he was told by IPD that the price reduction required to sell more units would reduce rather than increase profit and that the main problem was the high price charged by EMD. EMD stated that they required the high price in order to meet their target profit margin for the year, and that any reduction would erode their pricing policy.

You are required to:

(a) develop tabulations for each division, and for the company as a whole, that indicate the anticipated effect of IPD selling the motor unit at each of the prices listed;

(10 marks)

(b) (i) show the selling price that IPD should select in order to maximize its own divisional profit on the motor unit;

(2 marks)

(ii) show the selling price that would be in the best interest of EE as a whole;

(2 marks)

(iii) explain why this latter price is not selected by IPD;

(1 mark)

(c) state:

(i) what changes you would advise making to the transfer pricing system so that it will motivate divisional managers to make better decisions in future;

(5 marks)

(ii) what transfer price will ensure overall optimality in this situation.

(5 marks)

(Total 25 marks)

13.18 Calculating the effects of a transfer pricing system on divisional and company profits

Division A of a large divisionalized organization manufactures a single standardized product. Some of the output is sold externally while the remainder is transferred to division B where it is a subassembly in the manufacture of that division's product. The unit costs of division A's product are as follows:

	(£)
Direct material	4
Direct labour	2
Direct expense	2
Variable manufacturing overheads	2
Fixed manufacturing overheads	4
Selling and packing expense – variable	1
	15

Annually 10 000 units of the product are sold externally at the standard price of £30.

In addition to the external sales, 5000 units are transferred annually to division B at an internal transfer charge of £29 per unit. This transfer price is obtained by deducting variable selling and packing expense from the external price since this expense is not incurred for internal transfers.

Division B incorporates the transferred-in goods into a more advanced product. The unit costs of this product are as follows:

	(£)
Transferred-in item (from division A)	29
Direct material and components	23
Direct labour	3
Variable overheads	12
Fixed overheads	12
Selling and packing expense – variable	1
	80

Division B's manager disagrees with the basis used to set the transfer price. He argues that the transfers should be made at variable cost plus an agreed (minimal) mark-up since he claims that his division is taking output that division A would be unable to sell at the price of £30.

Partly because of this disagreement, a study of the relationship between selling price and demand has recently been made for each division by the company's sales director. The resulting report contains the following table:

Customer demand at various selling prices:

Division A			
Selling price	£20	£30	£40
Demand	15 000	10 000	5 000
Division B			
Selling price	£80	£90	£100
Demand	7 200	5 000	2 800

The manager of division B claims that this study supports his case. He suggests that a transfer price of £12 would give division A a reasonable contribution to its fixed overheads while allowing division B to earn a reasonable profit. He also believes that it would lead to an increase of output and an improvement in the overall level of company profits.

You are required:

(a) to calculate the effect that the transfer pricing system has had on the company's profits, and

(16 marks)

(b) to establish the likely effect on profits of adopting the suggestion by the manager of division B of a transfer price of £12.

(6 marks)
(Total 22 marks)

13.19 P plc is a multinational conglomerate company with manufacturing divisions, trading in numerous countries across various continents. Trade takes place between a number of the divisions in different countries, with partly completed products being transferred between them. Where a transfer takes place between divisions trading in different countries, it is the policy of the board of P plc to determine centrally the appropriate transfer price without reference to the divisional managers concerned. The board of P plc justifies this policy to divisional managers on the grounds that its objective is to maximize the conglomerate's post-tax profits and that the global position can be monitored effectively only from the head office.

Requirements:

(a) Explain and critically appraise the possible reasoning behind P plc's policy of centrally determining transfer prices for goods traded between divisions operating in different countries.

(10 marks)

(b) Discuss the ethical implications of P plc's policy of imposing transfer prices on its overseas divisions in order to maximize post-tax profits.

(10 marks)
(Total 20 marks)

CHAPTER 14
STRATEGIC COST MANAGEMENT

LEARNING OBJECTIVES

After studying this chapter you should be able to:

- **distinguish between the features of a traditional management accounting control system and strategic cost management;**
- **describe the typical pattern of cost commitment and cost incurrence during the three stages of a product's life cycle;**
- **describe the target costing approach to cost management;**
- **describe tear-down analysis and value analysis;**
- **describe activity-based cost management;**
- **distinguish between value-added and non-value-added activities;**
- **explain the purpose of a cost of quality report;**
- **describe how value chain analysis can be used to increase customer satisfaction and manage costs more effectively;**
- **explain the role of benchmarking within the cost management framework;**
- **outline the main features of a just-in-time philosophy.**

In Chapters 9–11 the major features of traditional management accounting control systems and the mechanisms that can be used to control costs were described. The focus was on comparing actual results against a pre-set standard (typically the budget), identifying and analysing variances and taking remedial action to ensure that future outcomes conform with budgeted outcomes. Traditional cost control systems tend to be based on the preservation of the status quo and the ways of performing existing activities are not reviewed. The emphasis is on cost containment rather than major reductions in an organization's cost base.

Strategic cost management seeks to have a more profound effect on reducing an organization's costs and to provide a competitive advantage. It aims to provide a competitive advantage by creating better or equivalent customer satisfaction at a lower cost than that offered by competitors. In particular, strategic cost management focuses on cost reduction and continuous improvement and changes in the ways that activities and processes are performed, rather than just focusing on cost containment. Whereas traditional cost control systems are routinely applied on a continuous basis, strategic cost management tends to be applied on an ad hoc basis when opportunities for major cost reductions are identified. Also, many of the approaches that are incorporated within the area of strategic cost management do not necessarily involve the use of accounting techniques. In contrast, cost control relies heavily on accounting techniques.

Strategic cost management consists of those actions that are taken by managers to reduce costs, some of which are prioritized on the basis of information extracted from the accounting system. Other actions, however, are initiated without the use of accounting information but cost information is likely to be required to estimate the magnitude of the cost reductions. Typical cost reduction actions involve process improvements, where an opportunity has been identified to perform processes more effectively and efficiently, and which have obvious cost reduction outcomes. It is important that you are aware of all the approaches that can be used to reduce costs even if these methods do not rely on accounting information. You should also note that although strategic cost management seeks to reduce costs, it should not be at the expense of customer satisfaction. Ideally, the aim is to take actions that will both reduce costs and enhance customer satisfaction.

LIFE-CYCLE COST MANAGEMENT

Identifying the costs incurred during the different stages of a product's life cycle provides an insight into understanding and managing the total costs incurred throughout its life cycle. In particular, life-cycle cost management enables management to understand the cost consequences of developing and making a product and to identify areas in which cost reduction efforts are likely to be most effective.

Figure 14.1 illustrates a typical pattern of cost commitment and cost incurrence during the three stages of a product's life cycle – the planning and design stage, the manufacturing stage and the service and abandonment stage. **Committed** or **locked-in costs** are those costs that have not been incurred but that will be incurred in the future on the basis of decisions that have already been made. At this stage costs become committed and broadly determine the future costs that will be incurred during the manufacturing stage. You will see from Figure 14.1 that approximately 80 per cent of a product's costs are committed during the planning and design stage. At this stage product designers determine the product's design and the production process. In contrast, the majority of costs are incurred at the manufacturing stage, but they have already become locked in at the planning and design stage and are difficult to alter.

It is apparent from Figure 14.1 that cost management can be most effectively exercised during the planning and design stage and not at the manufacturing stage when the product design and processes have already been determined and costs have been committed. At this latter stage the focus is more on cost containment than cost management. An understanding of life-cycle costs and how they are committed and incurred at different

FIGURE 14.1
Product life-cycle phases: relationship between costs committed and costs incurred

stages throughout a product's life cycle led to the emergence of **target costing**, a technique that focuses on managing costs during a product's planning and design phase.

TARGET COSTING

In Chapter 5 we briefly looked at target costing as a mechanism for determining selling prices. We now consider how target costing can be used as a cost management tool. Target costing involves the following stages:

Stage 1: Determine the target price that customers will be prepared to pay for the product.

Stage 2: Deduct a target profit margin from the target price to determine the target cost.

Stage 3: Estimate the actual cost of the product.

Stage 4: If estimated actual cost exceeds the target cost, investigate ways of driving down the actual cost to the target cost.

The first stage requires market research to determine the customers' perceived value of the product based on its functions and its attributes (i.e. its functionality), its differentiation value relative to competing products and the price of competing products. A target profit is deducted from the target price to give the target cost. The target cost is compared with the predicted actual cost. If the predicted actual cost is above the target cost, intensive efforts are made to close the gap so that the predicted cost equals the target cost. A major feature of target costing is that a team approach is adopted to achieve the target cost. For example, team members may include designers, engineers, purchasing, manufacturing, marketing and management accounting personnel, and sometimes representatives from suppliers.

The major advantage of adopting target costing is that it is deployed during a product's design and planning stage so that it can have maximum impact in determining the level of the locked-in costs. It is an iterative process with the design team, which ideally should result in the design team continuing with its product and process design attempts until it finds designs that give an expected cost that is equal to or less than the target cost. If the target cost cannot be attained then the product should not be launched. Design teams should not be allowed to achieve target costs by eliminating desirable product functions. Thus, the aim is to design a product with an expected cost that does not exceed target cost and that also meets the target level of functionality. Design teams use tear-down analysis, value analysis and process improvement to achieve the target cost.

Tear-down analysis (also known as **reverse engineering**) involves examining a competitor's product in order to identify opportunities for product improvement and/or cost reduction. The aim is to benchmark provisional product designs with the designs of competitors and to incorporate any observed relative advantages of the competitor's approach to product design.

Value analysis (also known as **value engineering**) attempts to determine the value placed on various product functions by customers. The cost of each function is compared with the benefits perceived by the customers. If the cost of the function exceeds the benefit to the customer, then the function should be either eliminated or modified to reduce its cost. Process improvements relate to cost reductions arising from redesigning the processes used to produce and market the product.

An illustration of target costing

Example 14.1 is used to illustrate the target costing process. You will note from reading the information presented in this example that the projected cost of the product is £700 compared with a target cost of £560. To achieve the target cost the company establishes a project team to undertake an intensive target costing exercise. Example 14.1 indicates that the end result of the target costing exercise is a projected cost of £555, which is marginally below the target cost of £560. Let us now look at how the company has achieved the target cost and also how the costs shown in Example 14.1 have been derived.

In response to the need to reduce the projected cost the project team starts by purchasing similar types of camcorders from its main competitors and undertaking a tear-down analysis. This process involves dismantling the camcorders to provide insights into potential design improvements for the new camcorder that will be launched. Value analysis is also undertaken with the project team working closely with the design engineers. Their objective is to identify new designs that will accomplish the same functions at a lower cost and also to eliminate any functions that are deemed to be unnecessary. This process results in a simplified design, a reduction in the number of parts and the replacement of some customized parts with standard parts. The outcome of the tear-down analysis and value analysis activities is a significant reduction in the projected direct materials, labour and rework costs, but the revised cost estimates still indicate that the projected cost exceeds the target cost.

The team now turn their attention to redesigning the production and support processes. They decide to redesign the ordering and receiving process by reducing the number of suppliers and working closely with a smaller number of suppliers. The suppliers are prepared to enter into contractual arrangements whereby they are periodically given a predetermined production schedule and in return they will inspect the shipments and guarantee quality prior to delivery. In addition, the marketing, distribution and customer after-sales services relating to the product are subject to an intensive review, and process improvements are made that result in further reductions in costs that are attributable to the camcorder. The projected cost after undertaking all of the above activities is £555 compared with the target cost of £560 and at this point the target costing exercise is concluded.

EXAMPLE 14.1

The Digital Electronics Company manufactures cameras and video equipment. It is in the process of introducing the world's smallest and lightest camcorder with HD and SD recording modes. The company has undertaken market research to ascertain the customers' perceived value of the product based on its special features and a comparison with competitors' products. The results of the survey, and a comparison of the new camcorder with competitors' products and market prices, have been used to establish a target selling price and projected lifetime volume. In addition, cost estimates have been prepared based on the proposed product specification. The company has set a target profit margin of 30 per cent on the proposed selling price and this has been deducted from the target selling price to determine the target cost. The following is a summary of the information that has been presented to management:

Projected lifetime sales volume	300 000 units
Target selling price	£800
Target profit margin (30% of selling price)	£240
Target cost (£800 – £240)	£560
Projected cost	£700

The excess of the projected cost over the target cost results in an intensive target costing exercise. After completing the target costing exercise the projected cost is £555 which is marginally below the target cost of £560. The analysis of the projected cost before and after the target costing exercise is as follows:

	Before (£)	(£)	After (£)	(£)
Manufacturing cost				
Direct material (bought in parts)	390		325	
Direct labour	100		80	
Direct machining costs	20		20	
Ordering and receiving	8		2	
Quality assurance	60		50	
Rework	15		6	
Engineering and design	10	603	8	491
Non-manufacturing costs				
Marketing	40		25	
Distribution	30		20	
After-sales service and warranty costs	27	97	19	64
Total cost		700		555

Having described the target costing approach that the Digital Electronics Company has used let us now turn our attention to the derivation of the projected costs shown in Example 14.1. The projected cost for direct materials prior to the target costing exercise is £390 but value engineering has resulted in a reduction in the number of parts that are required to manufacture the camcorder. The elimination of most of the unique parts, and the use of standard parts that the company currently purchases in large volumes, also provides scope for further cost savings. The outcome of the redesign process is a direct material cost of £325.

The simplified product design enables the assembly time to be reduced thus resulting in the reduction of direct labour costs from £100 to £80. The direct machine costs relate to machinery that will be used exclusively for the production of the new product. The estimated cost of acquiring, maintaining and operating the machinery throughout the product's life cycle is £6 million. This is divided by the projected lifetime sales volume of the camera (300 000 units) giving a unit cost of £20. However, it has not been possible to reduce the unit cost because the machinery costs are committed, and fixed, and the target costing exercise has not resulted in a change in the predicted lifetime volume.

Prior to the target costing exercise 80 separate parts were included in the product specification. The estimated number of orders placed for each part throughout the product's life cycle is 150 and the predicted cost per order for the order and receiving activity is £200. Therefore the estimated lifetime costs are £2.4 million (80 parts × 150 orders × £200 per order) giving a unit cost of £8 (£2.4 million/300 000 units). The simplified design, and the parts standardization arising from the value engineering activities, have enabled the number of parts to be reduced to 40. The redesign of the ordering and receiving process has also enabled the number of orders and the ordering cost to be reduced (the former from 150 to 100 and the latter from £200 to £150 per order). Thus the projected lifetime ordering and receiving costs after the target costing exercise are £600 000 (40 parts × 100 orders × £150 per order) giving a revised unit cost of £2 (£600 000/300 000 units).

Quality assurance involves inspecting and testing the camcorders. Prior to the target costing exercise the projected cost was £60 (12 hours at £5 per hour) but the simplified design means that the camcorder will be easier to test resulting in a revised cost of £50 (10 hours at £5 per hour). Rework costs of £15 represent the average rework costs per camcorder. Past experience with manufacturing similar products suggests that 10 per cent of the output will require rework. Applying this rate to the estimated total lifetime volume of 300 000 camcorders results in 30 000 camcorders requiring rework at an estimated average cost of £150 per reworked camcorder. The total lifetime rework cost is therefore predicted to be £4.5 million (30 000 × £150) giving an average cost per unit of good output of £15 (£4.5 million/300 000). Because of the simplified product design the rework rate and the average rework cost will be reduced. The predicted rework rate is now 5 per cent and the average rework cost will be reduced from £150 to £120. Thus, the revised estimate of the total lifetime cost is £1.8 million (15 000 reworked units at £120 per unit) and the projected unit cost is £6 (£1.8 million/300 000 units).

The predicted total lifetime engineering and design costs and other product sustaining costs are predicted to be £3 million giving a unit cost of £10. The simplified design and reduced number of parts enables the lifetime cost to be reduced by 20 per cent, to £2.4 million, and the unit cost to £8. The planned process improvements have also enabled the predicted marketing, distribution and after-sales service costs to be reduced. In addition, the simplified product design and the use of fewer parts has contributed to the reduction in the after-sales warranty costs. However, to keep our example brief the derivation of the non-manufacturing costs will not be presented, other than to note that the company uses an activity-based-costing system. All costs are assigned using cost drivers that are based on established cause-and-effect relationships.

REAL WORLD VIEWS 14.1

*Applying target costing to existing
products at Montclair Papers Division*

It is generally considered that target costing should normally be applied early in the product life cycle, but there is no conceptual reason why it cannot be applied to existing products. Montclair Papers Division of Mohawk Forest Products applied target costing to one of its existing products – Forest Green Carnival. The standard cost of this product was $2900 even though this resulted in a premium selling price with competitors selling at prices below the standard cost. Ajax Papers won a contract over Montclair with a bid of $1466 per ton, thereby setting the prevailing price in the market. The realization that an important competitor could operate under a dramatically different cost structure motivated managers to adopt a target costing approach and remove its standard cost blinders. Based on a target selling price of $1466, and deducting a target profit margin, a target cost of $1162 was derived. The target costing process focused on the four major cost components:

- fibre cost (changing the mix of recycled paper and virgin pulp to reduce raw materials cost);
- paper machine cost (getting on grade faster to improve yields);
- dye costs;
- conversion cost.

Fibre cost. A project team began a series of manufacturing trials showing that the mill could increase the percentage of recycled paper in the raw materials mix above the standard allowance of 22 per cent. Experience proved that recycled percentages ranging up to 75 per cent would not detrimentally affect the quality of the finished sheet if the scrap paper was handled carefully. Using 75 per cent scrap in the raw material mix reduced the fibre cost by 60 per cent with no negative effect on paper quality.

Paper machine cost. Because the product had such poor yields, the mill scheduled a production run only about twice a year. A root cause analysis of the long changeover time revealed that the biggest time loss was getting 'on shade' for a designer-created colour such as Forest Green. A project team tackled this problem by first observing that if the production run could start with a fibre mix closer to the desired shade, there was a dramatically reduced 'off shade' time. That implied starting with green fibre, rather than white. This had never been possible when 80 per cent of the fibre was virgin pulp that can only be purchased in one colour – white. But increasing the percentage of recycled fibre opened the possibility of buying green scrap paper instead of white. Since there was virtually no market demand for green 'broke' (scrap), the mill was able to buy unlimited quantities at low prices. Another project team experimented with Montclair's computerized colour-mixing system. They were able to develop proprietary software that allowed the colour-mixing crew to get 'on shade' in 40 minutes instead of 2 hours by starting with green broke. Reducing changeover time from 2 hours to 40 minutes raised the yield rate to 75 per cent when producing 2 hours of good paper.

Dye costs. Starting the papermaking process with up to 75 per cent green fibre required much less dye to achieve the exact Forest Green shade. The newly developed proprietary software enabled getting on shade with an average dye cost that was an amazing $796 reduction in the cost per ton.

Conversion costs. Another project team tackled this cost component by seriously considering the make-versus-buy option. Each converting department

$303 per ton conversion cost for Forest Green Carnival fell to $240 – a 20 per cent reduction.

By combining the improvements contributed by the four project teams, it was possible to envision lowering the manufacturing cost from $2900 to $1162.

Discussion points

1 How does target costing differ from standard costing?
2 What are the advantages and disadvantages of using target costing instead of standard costing?

was challenged to develop competitive programmes or risk job loss to outsourcing. Over 18 months, the

ACTIVITY-BASED MANAGEMENT

The early adopters of activity-based costing (ABC) used it to produce more accurate product (or service) costs but it soon became apparent to the users that it could be extended beyond purely product costing to a range of cost management applications. The terms **activity-based management (ABM)** or **activity-based cost management (ABCM)** are used to describe the cost management applications of ABC. To implement an ABM system, only the first three of the four stages described in Chapter 8 for designing an activity-based product costing system are required. They are:

1 identifying the major activities that take place in an organization (i.e. activity analysis);
2 assigning costs to cost pools/cost centres for each activity;
3 determining the cost driver for each major activity.

ABM views the business as a set of linked activities that ultimately add value to the customer. It focuses on managing the business on the basis of the activities that make up the organization. ABM is based on the premise that activities consume costs. Therefore by managing activities costs will be managed in the long term. Managing activities requires an understanding of what factors cause activities to be performed and what causes activity costs to change. The goal of ABM is to enable customer needs to be satisfied while making fewer demands on organizational resources (i.e. cost reduction). Besides providing information on what activities are performed, ABM provides information on the cost of activities, why the activities are undertaken, and how well they are performed.

Traditional budget and control reports analyse costs by types of expense for each responsibility centre. In contrast, ABM analyses costs by activities and thus provides management with information on why costs are incurred and the output from the activity (in terms of cost drivers). Exhibit 14.1 illustrates the difference between the conventional analysis and the activity-based analysis in respect of customer order processing. The major differences are that the ABM approach reports by *activities* whereas the traditional analysis is by *departments*. Also ABM reporting is by sub-activities but traditional reporting

EXHIBIT 14.1

*Customer order
processing activity*

	(£000s)
Traditional analysis	
Salaries	320
Stationery	40
Travel	140
Telephone	40
Depreciation of equipment	40
	580
ABM analysis	
Preparing quotations	120
Receiving customer orders	190
Assessing the creditworthiness of customers	100
Expediting	80
Resolving customer problems	90
	580

is by expense categories. Another distinguishing feature of ABM reporting is that it often reports information on activities that cross departmental boundaries. For example, different production departments and the distribution department might undertake customer processing activities. They may resolve customer problems by expediting late deliveries. The finance department may assess customer creditworthiness and the remaining customer processing activities might be undertaken by the customer service department. Therefore the total cost of the customer processing activity could be considerably in excess of the costs that are assigned to the customer service department. However, to simplify the presentation it is assumed in Exhibit 14.1 that the departmental and activity costs are identical but if the cost of the customer order processing activity was found to be, say, three times the amount assigned to the customer service department, this would be important information because it may change the way in which the managers view the activity. For example, the managers may give more attention to reducing the costs of the customer processing activity.

It is apparent from an examination of Exhibit 14.1 that the ABM approach provides more meaningful information. It gives more visibility to the cost of undertaking the activities that make up the organization and may raise issues for management action that are not high-lighted by the traditional analysis. For example, why is £90 000 spent on resolving customer problems? Attention-directing information such as this is important for managing the cost of the activities.

Johnson (1990) suggests that knowing costs by activities is a catalyst that eventually triggers the action necessary to become competitive. Consider a situation where sales-persons, as a result of costing activities, are informed that it costs £50 to process a customer's order. They therefore become aware that it is questionable to pursue orders with a low sales value. By eliminating many small orders, and concentrating on larger value orders, the demand for customer processing activities should decrease, and future spending on this activity should be reduced.

Prior to the introduction of ABM most organizations have been unaware of the cost of undertaking the activities that make up the organization. Knowing the cost of activities enables those activities with the highest cost to be highlighted so that they can be priori-tized for detailed studies to ascertain whether they can be eliminated or performed more

REAL WORLD VIEWS 14.2

The impact of ABC at Insteel Industries

In 1996 Insteel Industries decided to implement ABC at the Andrews, South Carolina plant. The ABC team analysed Andrews' operations and identified 12 business processes involving a total of 146 activities. The ABC study revealed that the 20 most expensive activities accounted for 87 per cent of Andrews' total physical and people resource of $21.4 million. Within the top 20 activities, almost $5 million pertained to quality-related activities such as reactive maintenance, management of by-products and scrap, and preventive maintenance. The analysis also revealed that material-handling costs, including freight costs, consumed $4.6 million. Activities were further classified into value-added and non-value-added. Nearly $4.9 million was spent on non-value-added activities such as reactive maintenance, dealing with scrap, moving materials, reworking products and managing customer complaints. Those activities, within the 20 most expensive, were targeted for cost reduction and process improvement.

Separate teams were formed for managing quality costs, material handling, and preventive maintenance. The company estimates that within a year of the first ABC study, $1.8 million had been saved in quality costs, mainly through a reduction of scrap and reactive maintenance costs. Freight costs were reduced $555,000 in a year in the Andrews' plant alone. Non-value-added activities were reduced from 22 per cent of activity costs to 17 per cent.

Insteel focused on freight because delivering products to customers represented 16 per cent of the total people and physical resources cost at the Andrews' plant. As a part of the ABC study, Insteel started tracking freight cost per pound shipped. This directed attention to ways in which these costs could be reduced. In 1997, by changing the layout of boxes within each truck, the Andrews' plant was able to ship 7400 pounds more per truckload than in 1996. This represented a 20 per cent reduction in freight expense.

When Insteel realized how much they were actually incurring in quality costs, the team probed deeper into understanding better what was causing the quality costs to be incurred and worked on suggesting steps to reduce them. Insteel realized that certain foreign suppliers of rods were lower in price but supplied poorer-quality rods that caused breakdowns in Insteel's manufacturing process. The lower price of those suppliers did not compensate for the quality costs. Insteel switched to higher-quality rod suppliers. Insteel also realized that smaller-diameter wire products were more likely to break and disrupt the manufacturing process. Insteel migrated its product mix to more large-diameter wire products. Such initiatives led to a reduction in quality costs from $6.7 million in 1996 to $4.9 million in 1997.

It is hard to estimate how much of these savings would have been realized had Insteel not conducted an ABC analysis. The activity analysis gave them an appreciation of the scope and quantified the magnitude of the improvement potential, thereby allowing them to prioritize among various process improvement possibilities. Clearly ABC served as a focusing device at Insteel by providing cost data by activity rather than by department, directing attention to the top 20 activities, and by labelling some of them as non-value-added activities.

© ISTOCKPHOTO.COM/MICHAEL UTECH

Discussion points

1 How might activity costs for Insteel differ from departmental costs?
2 What approaches can be used to identify the activities undertaken by Insteel?

SOURCE: ADAPTED FROM NARAYANAN, V.G. AND SARKAR, R.G. THE IMPACT OF ACTIVITY-BASED COSTING ON MANAGERIAL DECISIONS AT INSTEEL INDUSTRIES: A FIELD STUDY. *JOURNAL OF* efficiently. To identify and prioritize the potential for cost reduction many organizations have found it useful to classify activities as either value-added or non-value-added. Definitions of what constitutes value-added and non-value-added activities vary. A common definition is that a **value-added activity** is an activity that customers perceive as adding usefulness to the product or service they purchase. For example, painting a car would be a value-added activity in an organization that manufactures cars. Other definitions are an activity that is being performed as efficiently as possible or an activity that supports the primary objective of producing outputs.

In contrast, a **non-value-added activity** is an activity where there is an opportunity for cost reduction without reducing the product's service potential to the customer. Examples of non-value-added activities include inspecting, storing and moving raw materials. The cost of these activities can be reduced without reducing the value of the products to the customers. Non-value-added activities are essentially those activities that customers should not be expected to pay for. Reporting the cost of non-value-added activities draws management's attention to the vast amount of waste that has been tolerated by the organization. This should prioritize those activities with the greatest potential for cost reduction by eliminating or carrying them out more effectively, such as reducing material movements, improving production flows and taking actions to reduce stock levels. Taking action to reduce or eliminate non-value-added activities is given top priority because by doing so the organization permanently reduces the cost it incurs without reducing the value of the product to the customer.

Our discussion so far has related to the application of ABM during the manufacturing or service phase of a product's life cycle. However, some organizations have used their activity-based costing systems to influence future costs at the design stage within the target costing process. For example, the Tektronix Portable Instruments Division assigned material support expenses using a single cost driver – number of part numbers. The company wanted to encourage design engineers to focus their attention on reducing the number of part numbers, parts and vendors in future generations of products. Product timeliness was seen as a critical success factor and this was facilitated by designs that simplified parts procurement and production processes. The cost system motivated engineers to design simpler products requiring less development time because they had fewer parts and part numbers. The cost system designers knew that most of the material support expenses were not incurred in direct proportion to the single cost driver chosen, but the simplified and imprecise cost system focused attention on factors deemed to be most critical to the division's future success.

BUSINESS PROCESS RE-ENGINEERING

Business process re-engineering involves examining business processes and making substantial changes to how the organization currently operates. It involves the redesign of how work is done through activities. A business process consists of a collection of activities that are linked together in a coordinated manner to achieve a specific objective. For example, material handling might be classed as a business process consisting of separate activities relating to scheduling production, storing materials, processing purchase orders, inspecting materials and paying suppliers.

The aim of business process re-engineering is to improve the key business processes in an organization by focusing on simplification, cost reduction, improved quality and enhanced customer satisfaction. Consider the materials handling process outlined in the above paragraph. The process might be re-engineered by sending the production schedule direct to nominated suppliers and entering into contractual agreements to deliver the materials in accordance with the production schedule and also guaranteeing their quality by inspecting them prior to delivery. The end result might be the elimination, or a permanent reduction, of the storing, purchasing and inspection activities. These activities are non-value-added activities since they represent an opportunity for cost reduction without reducing the products' service potential to customers.

A distinguishing feature of business process re-engineering is that it involves radical and dramatic changes in processes by abandoning current practices and reinventing completely new methods of performing business processes. The focus is on major changes rather than marginal improvements. A further example of business process re-engineering is moving from a traditional functional plant layout to a just-in-time cellular product layout and adopting a just-in-time philosophy. Adopting a just-in-time (JIT) system and philosophy has significant implications for cost management and performance reporting. It is therefore important that you understand the nature of such systems and how they differ from traditional systems, but rather than deviating at this point from our discussion of cost management, the description of a JIT system will be deferred until the end of the chapter.

COST OF QUALITY

To compete successfully in today's global competitive environment companies are becoming 'customer-driven' and making customer satisfaction an overriding priority. Customers are demanding ever-improving levels of service regarding cost, quality, reliability, delivery and the choice of innovative new products. Quality has become one of the key competitive variables in both service and manufacturing organizations and this has created the need for management accountants to become more involved in the provision of information relating to the quality of products and services and activities that produce them. In the UK quality-related costs have been reported to range from 5 per cent to 15 per cent of total company sales revenue (Plunkett *et al.*, 1985). Eliminating inferior quality by implementing quality improvement initiatives can therefore result in substantial cost savings and higher revenues.

Total quality management (TQM), a term used to describe a situation where all business functions are involved in a process of continuous quality improvement, has been adopted by many companies. TQM is a customer-oriented process of continuous improvement that focuses on delivering products or services of consistent high quality in a timely fashion. Companies have found that it is cheaper to produce the items correctly the first time rather than wasting resources by making substandard items that have to be detected, reworked, scrapped or returned by customers.

Management accounting systems can help organizations achieve their quality goals by providing a variety of reports and measures that motivate and evaluate managerial efforts to improve quality. These include financial and non-financial measures. Many companies are currently not aware of how much they are spending on quality because costs are incurred across many different departments and not accumulated as a separate cost object within the costing system. Managers need to know the costs of quality and how they are changing over time. A **cost of quality report** should be prepared to indicate the total cost to the organization of producing products or services that do not conform with quality requirements. Four categories of costs should be reported.

1 **Prevention costs** are the costs incurred in preventing the production of products that do not conform to specification. They include the costs of preventive maintenance, quality planning and training and the extra costs of acquiring higher quality raw materials.

2 **Appraisal costs** are the costs incurred to ensure that materials and products meet quality conformance standards. They include the costs of inspecting purchased parts, work in process and finished goods, quality audits and field tests.

3 **Internal failure costs** are the costs associated with materials and products that fail to meet quality standards. They include costs incurred before the product is despatched to the customer, such as the costs of scrap, repair, downtime and work stoppages caused by defects.

4 **External failure costs** are the costs incurred when products or services fail to conform to requirements or satisfy customer needs after they have been delivered. They include the costs of handling customer complaints, warranty replacement, repairs of returned products and the costs arising from a damaged

	(£000)	% of sales (£100 million)
Prevention costs		
Quality training	1000	
Supplier reviews	300	
Quality engineering	400	
Preventive maintenance	500	
	2 200	2.2
Appraisal costs		
Inspection of materials received	500	
Inspection of WIP and completed units	1000	
Testing equipment	300	
Quality audits	800	
	2 600	2.6
Internal failure costs		
Scrap	800	
Rework	1000	
Downtime due to quality problems	600	
Retesting	400	
	2 800	2.8
External failure costs		
Returns	2000	
Recalls	1000	
Warranty repairs	800	
Handling customer complaints	500	
Foregone contribution from lost sales	3000	
	7 300	7.3
	14 900	14.9

EXHIBIT 14.2
Cost of quality report

company reputation. Costs within this category can have a dramatic impact on future sales.

Exhibit 14.2 presents a typical cost of quality report. By expressing each category of costs as a percentage of sales revenues, comparisons can be made with previous periods, other organizations and divisions within the same group. Such comparisons can highlight problem areas. For example, comparisons of external failure costs with other companies can provide an indication of the current level of customer satisfaction.

The cost of quality report can be used as an attention-directing device to make the top management of a company aware of how much is being spent on quality-related costs. The report can also draw management's attention to the possibility of reducing total quality costs by a wiser allocation of costs among the four quality categories. For example, by spending more on prevention costs, the amount of spending in the internal and external failure categories can be substantially reduced, and therefore total spending can be lowered. Also, by designing quality into the products and processes, appraisal costs can be reduced, since far less inspection is required.

COST MANAGEMENT AND THE VALUE CHAIN

Increasing attention is now being given to **value-chain analysis** as a means of increasing customer satisfaction and managing costs more effectively. The value chain is illustrated in Figure 14.2. It is the linked set of value-creating activities all the way from basic raw material sources for component suppliers through to the ultimate end-use product or service delivered to the customer. A value-chain analysis is used to analyse, coordinate and optimize linkages in the value chain. Coordinating the individual parts of the value chain together creates the conditions to improve customer satisfaction, particularly in terms of cost efficiency, quality and delivery. A firm that performs the value-chain activities more efficiently, and at a lower cost, than its competitors will gain a competitive advantage. Therefore it is necessary to understand how value-chain activities are performed and how they interact with each other. The activities are not just a collection of independent activities but a system of inter-dependent activities in which the performance of one activity affects the performance and cost of other activities.

The linkages in the value chain express the relationships between the performance of one activity and its effects on the performance of another activity. A linkage occurs when interdependence exists between activities and the higher the interdependence between activities the greater is the required coordination. Thus, it is appropriate to view the value chain from the customer's perspective, with each link being seen as the customer of the previous link. If each link in the value chain is designed to meet the needs of its customers, then end-customer satisfaction should ensue. Furthermore, by viewing each link in the value chain as a supplier–customer relationship, the opinions of customers can be used to provide useful feedback information on assessing the quality of service provided by the supplier. Opportunities are thus identified for improving activities throughout the entire value chain.

Shank and Govindarajan (1992) argue that traditional management accounting adopts an internal focus which, in terms of the value chain, starts too late and stops too soon. Starting cost analysis with purchases misses all the opportunities for exploiting linkages with the firm's suppliers and stopping cost analysis at the point of sale eliminates all

FIGURE 14.2

The value chain

opportunities for exploiting linkages with customers. Shank (1989) illustrates how an American automobile company failed to use the value chain approach to exploit links with suppliers and enhance profitability. The company had made significant internal savings from introducing JIT manufacturing techniques (described later in this chapter), but, at the same time, price increases from suppliers more than offset these internal cost savings. A value-chain perspective revealed that 50 per cent of the firm's costs related to purchases from parts suppliers. As the automobile company reduced its own need for buffer stocks, it placed major new strains on the manufacturing responsiveness of suppliers. The increase in the suppliers' manufacturing costs was greater than the decrease in the automobile company's internal costs. Shank states:

> For every dollar of manufacturing cost the assembly plants saved by moving
> towards JIT management concepts, the suppliers' plant spent much more than
> one dollar extra because of schedule instability arising from the introduction of
> JIT. Because of its narrow value added perspective, the auto company had
> ignored the impact of its changes on its suppliers' costs. Management had
> ignored the idea that JIT involves a partnership with suppliers (Shank, 1989: 51).

Similarly, by developing linkages with customers mutually beneficial relationships can be established. For example, Shank and Govindarajan (1992), drawing off research by Hergert and Morris (1989) point out that some container producers in the USA have constructed manufacturing facilities near beer breweries and deliver the containers through overhead conveyers directly onto the customers' assembly lines. This practice results in significant cost reductions for both the container producers and their customers by expediting the transport of empty containers, which are bulky and heavy.

BENCHMARKING

In order to identify the best way of performing activities and business processes organizations are turning their attention to **benchmarking**, which involves comparing key activities with best practices found within and outside the organization. External benchmarking attempts to identify an activity, such as customer order processing, that needs to be improved and finding a non-rival organization that is considered to represent world-class best practice for the activity and studying how it performs the activity. The objective is to find out how the activity can be improved and ensure that the improvements are implemented. In contrast, with internal benchmarking different business units within an organization that perform the same activities are compared. The unit that is considered to represent best practice becomes the target to achieve.

Benchmarking is cost beneficial since an organization can save time and money avoiding mistakes that other companies have made and/or the organization can avoid duplicating the efforts of other companies. The overall aim should be to find and implement best practice.

ENVIRONMENTAL COST MANAGEMENT

Environmental cost management is becoming increasingly important in many organizations. There are several reasons for this. First, environmental costs can be large for some industrial sectors. For example, Ranganathan and Ditz (1996) reported that Amoco's environmental costs at its Yorktown refinery were at least 22 per cent of operating costs. Secondly, regulatory requirements involving huge fines for non-compliance have increased significantly over the past decade. Therefore, selecting the least costly method of compliance has become a major objective. Thirdly, society is demanding that companies focus on becoming more environmentally friendly. Companies are finding that becoming a good social citizen and being environmentally responsible improves their image and enhances their ability to sell their products and services. These developments have created the need for companies to develop a system of measuring, reporting and monitoring environmental costs.

According to Epstein and Roy (1997) many companies cannot identify their total environmental costs and do not recognize that they can be controlled and reduced. In most cost accounting systems, environmental costs are hidden within general overheads and are either not allocated to cost objects, or they are allocated on an arbitrary basis within the allocation of general overheads. Thus, crucial relationships are not identified between environmental costs and the responsible products, processes and underlying activities. For example, Ranganathan and Ditz (1996) point out that the principal environmental issue facing Spectrum Glass, a major manufacturer of specialty sheet glass, is the use and release of cadmium. It discovered that only one product (ruby red glass) was responsible for all of its cadmium emissions but the cost accounting system allocated a portion of this cost to all products. This process resulted in ruby red glass being undercosted and other products being overcosted.

Environmental costs should be accumulated by separate cost pools, analysed by appropriate categories and traced to the products or processes that caused the costs using ABC concepts. Knowledge of the amount and categories of environmental costs, and their causes, provides the information that managers need to not only manage environmental costs more effectively by process redesign but to also reduce the pollutants emitted to the environment.

Hansen and Mendoza (1999) point out that environmental costs are incurred because poor environmental quality exists and thus are similar in nature to quality costs discussed earlier in this chapter. They advocate that an environmental cost report should be periodically produced, based on the principles of a cost of quality report (see Exhibit 14.2) to indicate the total environmental costs to the organization associated with the creation, detection, remedy and prevention of environmental degradation. Adopting a similar classification as that used for quality costs, the following four categories of environmental costs can be reported:

1 **Environmental prevention costs** are the costs of activities undertaken to prevent the production of waste that could cause damage to the environment. Examples include the costs associated with the design and operation of processes to reduce contaminants, training employees, recycling products and obtaining certification relating to meeting the requirements of international and national standards.

2 **Environmental detection costs** are the costs incurred to ensure that a firm's activities, products and processes conform to regulatory laws and voluntary standards. Examples include inspection of products and processes to ensure regulatory compliance, auditing environmental activities and performing contamination tests.

3 **Environmental internal failure costs** are the costs incurred from performing activities that have produced contaminants and waste that have not been discharged into the environment. Such costs are incurred to eliminate or reduce waste to levels that comply with regulatory requirements. Examples include the costs of disposing of toxic materials and recycling scrap.

4 **Environmental external failure costs** are the costs incurred on activities performed after discharging waste into the environment. Examples include the costs of cleaning up contaminated soil, restoring land to its natural state and cleaning up oil spills and waste discharges. Clearly this category of costs has the greatest impact on a company in terms of adverse publicity.

The environmental cost report should be similar in format to the cost of quality report (see Exhibit 14.2) with each category of costs expressed as a percentage of sales revenues (or operating costs) so that comparisons can be made with previous periods, other organizations and divisions within the same group. The environmental cost report should be used as an attention-directing device to make top management aware of how much is being spent on environmental costs and the relative amount in each category. The report also draws management's attention to those areas that have the greatest potential for cost reduction.

Finally, you should note at this point that incorporating an environmental perspective within a balanced scorecard framework has been adopted by some companies to link their environmental strategy to concrete performance measures. The balanced scorecard framework requires that within the scorecard the environmental objectives are clearly specified and that these objectives should be translated into specific performance measures. In addition, within the scorecard, firms should describe the major initiatives for achieving each objective and also establish targets for each performance measure. For feedback reporting, actual performance measures should also be added. The balanced scorecard framework is described in the next chapter.

JUST-IN-TIME SYSTEMS

Earlier in this chapter it was pointed out that reorganizing business processes and adopting a just-in-time (JIT) system was an illustration of business process engineering, but so far a JIT system has not been explained. Given that implementing a JIT system is a mechanism for reducing non-value-added costs and long-run costs it is important that you understand the nature of such a system and its cost management implications.

REAL WORLD VIEWS 14.3

Environmental accounting

Most businesses are concerned with their effect on the environment. Many businesses portray themselves as being friendly to the environment or carbon neutral. Lever Brothers, for example, developed a 'Small & Mighty' detergent range that has half the packaging, uses half the water and needs half the lorries to deliver it.[1] BSkyB, the company behind Sky television, claimed to be a carbon neutral company in 2006.[2] Reporting on environmental performance is even recognized in the UK Companies Act 2006, which increased the narrative reporting requirements of UK companies. Thus, with legal and practical recognition it would seem environmental issues are integral to business strategy.

Management accounting plays an important role in ensuring companies take environmental factors into account when making decisions. According to Gray and Bebbington (2001, p.9)[3], a management accountant's job changes somewhat:

1 planning will include new costs and capital expenditures – for example clean-up or recycling costs;
2 investment appraisal will incorporate environmental costs and benefits;
3 decisions on costs and benefits of environmental improvements will be undertaken;
4 environmental performance reporting will be required;
5 cost analysis and efficiency improvement programmes will consider environmental issues.

At an operational level, management accountants – who are well-trained in information gathering and analysis – are ideally placed to play a role in a number of areas, including: accounting for and controlling energy costs; reducing packaging and waste material; investment analysis; and product life-cycle analysis. Additionally, many governments now issue carbon credits to companies based on national carbon emission targets. Such credits are not free and companies are under pressure to reduce carbon emissions to reduce costs. Here again, management accountants can help analyse business processes to determine operational and cost efficient methods of operating.

Discussion points

1 Do you think environmental costs and benefits can be accurately determined?
2 Do issues such as the environment help management accountants to become more strategically important members of an organization?

References

1 http://www.persil.com/formatsmallandmighty.aspx
2 http://media.corporate-ir.net/media_files/irol/10/104016/SkyCNPressRelease_18052006.pdf
3 Gray, R. and Bebbington, J. (2001) *Accounting for the Environment*, Sage Publications.

The success of Japanese firms in international markets in the 1980s and 1990s generated interest among many Western companies as to how this success was achieved. The implementation of **just-in-time (JIT) production methods** was considered to be one of the major factors contributing to this success. The JIT approach involves a continuous commitment to the pursuit of excellence in all phases of manufacturing systems design and operations. The aims of JIT are to produce the required items, at the required quality and in the required quantities, at the precise time they are required. In particular, JIT seeks to achieve the following goals:

● elimination of non-value-added activities;
● zero inventory;

- zero defects;
- batch sizes of one;
- zero breakdowns;
- a 100 per cent on-time delivery service.

The above goals represent perfection, and are most unlikely to be achieved in practice. They do, however, offer targets, and create a climate for continuous improvement and excellence. Let us now examine the major features of a JIT manufacturing philosophy.

Elimination of non-value-added activities

JIT manufacturing is best described as a philosophy of management dedicated to the elimination of waste. Waste is defined as anything that does not add value to a product. The lead or cycle time involved in manufacturing and selling a product consists of process time, inspection time, move time, queue time and storage time. Of these five steps, only process time actually adds value to the product. All the other activities add cost but no value to the product, and are thus deemed non-value-added processes within the JIT philosophy. According to Berliner and Brimson (1988), process time was less than 10 per cent of total manufacturing lead time in many organizations in the USA in the 1980s. Therefore 90 per cent of the manufacturing lead time associated with a product added costs, but no value, to the product. By adopting a JIT philosophy and focusing on reducing lead times, it is claimed that total costs can be significantly reduced. The ultimate goal of JIT is to convert raw materials to finished products with lead times equal to processing times, thus eliminating all non-value-added activities.

Factory layout

The first stage in implementing JIT manufacturing techniques is to rearrange the production process away from a **batch production functional layout** towards a product layout using flow lines. With a functional plant layout products pass through a number of specialist departments that normally contain a group of similar machines. Products are processed in large batches so as to minimize the set-up times when machine settings are changed between processing batches of different products. Batches move via different and complex routes through the various departments, travelling over much of the factory floor before they are completed. Each process normally involves a considerable amount of waiting time. The consequences of this complex routing process are high work in progress stock levels, long manufacturing cycle times and high material handling costs.

The JIT solution is to reorganize the production process by dividing the many different products that an organization makes into families of similar products or components. All of the products in a particular group will have similar production requirements and routings. Production is rearranged so that each product family is manufactured in a well-defined production cell based on flow line principles. In a **product flow line**, specialist departments containing *similar* machines no longer exist. Instead groups of *dissimilar* machines are organized into product or component family flow lines that function like an assembly line. For each product line the machines are placed close together in the order in which they are required by the group of products to be processed. Items in each product family can now move, one at a time, from process to process more easily, thereby reducing work in progress (WIP) stocks and lead times. The ideal layout of each flow line is normally U-shaped. This layout is called **cellular manufacturing**.

JIT manufacturing aims to produce the right parts at the right time, only when they are needed, and only in the quantity needed. This philosophy has resulted in a **pull manufacturing system**, which means that parts move through the production system based on end-unit demand, focusing on maintaining a constant flow of components rather than batches of WIP. With the pull system, work on components does not commence until specifically requested by the next process. JIT techniques aim to keep the materials moving in a continuous flow with no stoppages and no storage.

The pull system is implemented by monitoring the consumption of parts at each operation stage and using various types of visible signalling systems (known as *Kanbans*) to authorize production and movement of the part to the using location. The producing cell cannot run the parts until authorized to do so. The signalling mechanism usually involves the use of *Kanban* containers. These containers hold materials or parts for movement from one work centre to another. The capacity of *Kanban* containers tends to vary from two to five units. They are just big enough to permit the production line to operate smoothly despite minor interruptions to individual work centres within the cell. To illustrate how the system works consider three machines forming part of a cell where the parts are first processed by machine A before being further processed on machine B and then machine C. The *Kanbans* are located between the machines. As long as the *Kanban* container is not full, the worker at machine A continues to produce parts, placing them in the *Kanban* container. When the container is full the worker stops producing and recommences when a part has been removed from the container by the worker operating machine B. A similar process applies between the operations of machines B and C. This process can result in idle time within certain locations within the cell, but the JIT philosophy considers that it is more beneficial to absorb short-run idle time rather than add to inventory during these periods. During idle time the workers perform preventive maintenance on the machines.

With a pull system, problems arising in any part of the system will immediately halt the production line because work centres at the earlier stages will not receive the pull signal (because the *Kanban* container is full) if a problem arises at a later stage. Alternatively, work centres at a later stage will not have their pull signal answered (because of empty *Kanban* containers) when problems arise with work centres at the earlier stages of the production cycle. Thus attention is drawn immediately to production problems so that appropriate remedial action can be taken. This is deemed to be preferable to the approach adopted in a traditional manufacturing system where large stock levels provide a cushion for production to continue.

In contrast, the traditional manufacturing environment is based on a **push manufacturing system**. With this system, machines are grouped into work centres based on the similarity of their functional capabilities. Each manufactured part has a designated routing, and the preceding process supplies parts to the subsequent process without any consideration being given to whether the next process is ready to work on the parts or not. Hence the use of the term 'push-through system'.

Batch sizes of one

Set-up time is the amount of time required to adjust equipment settings and to retool for a different product. Long set-up and changeover times make the production of batches with a small number of units uneconomic. However, the production of large batches leads to substantial throughput delays and the creation of high inventory levels. Throughput delays arise because several lengthy production runs are required to process larger batches through the factory. A further problem with large batches is that they often have to wait for lengthy periods before they are processed by the next process or before they are sold. The JIT philosophy is to reduce and eventually eliminate set-up times. For example, by investing in advanced manufacturing technologies some machine settings can be adjusted automatically instead of manually.

If set-up times are approaching zero, this implies that there are no advantages in producing in batches. Therefore the optimal batch size can be one. With a batch size of one, the work can flow smoothly to the next stage without the need for storage and to schedule the next machine to accept this item. In many situations set-up times will not be approaching zero, but by significantly reducing set-up times, small batch sizes will be economical. Small batch sizes, combined with short throughput times, also enable a firm to adapt more readily to short-term fluctuations in market demand and respond faster to customer requests, since production is not dependent on long planning lead times.

JIT purchasing arrangements

The JIT philosophy also extends to adopting JIT purchasing techniques, whereby the delivery of materials immediately precedes their use. By arranging with suppliers for more frequent deliveries, stocks can be cut to a minimum. Considerable savings in material handling expenses can be obtained by requiring suppliers to inspect materials before their delivery and guaranteeing their quality. This improved service is obtained by giving more business to fewer suppliers and placing longer-term purchasing orders. Therefore the supplier has an assurance of long-term sales, and can plan to meet this demand. Thus, a critical component of JIT purchasing is that strong relationships are established with suppliers.

Companies that have implemented JIT purchasing techniques claim to have substantially reduced their investment in raw materials and work in progress stocks. Other advantages include a substantial saving in factory space, large quantity discounts, savings in time from negotiating with fewer suppliers and a reduction in paperwork arising from issuing blanket long-term orders to a few suppliers rather than individual purchase orders to many suppliers.

JIT and management accounting

Management accountants in many organizations have been strongly criticized because of their failure to alter the management accounting system to reflect the move from a traditional manufacturing to a just-in-time manufacturing system. Conventional management accounting systems can encourage behaviour that is inconsistent with a JIT manufacturing philosophy. Management accounting must support JIT manufacturing by monitoring, identifying and communicating to decision-makers any delay, error and waste in the system. Modern management accounting systems are now placing greater emphasis on providing information on supplier reliability, set-up times, throughput cycle times, percentage of deliveries that are on time and defect rates. All of these measures are critical to supporting a JIT manufacturing philosophy and are discussed in more detail in the next chapter.

Because JIT manufacturing systems result in the establishment of production cells that are dedicated to the manufacturing of a single product or a family of similar products many of the support activities can be directly traced to the product dedicated cells. Thus, a high proportion of costs can be directly assigned to products. Therefore the benefits from implementing ABC product costing may be lower in JIT organizations.

SUMMARY

The following items relate to the learning objectives listed at the beginning of the chapter.

- **Distinguish between the features of a traditional management accounting control system and strategic cost management.** A traditional management accounting control system tends to be based on the preservation of the status quo and the ways of performing existing activities are not reviewed. The emphasis is on cost containment rather than major cost reductions. Strategic cost management focuses on cost reduction rather than cost containment. Thus, it has a more profound effect on reducing an organization's costs and also provides a competitive advantage. Whereas traditional cost control systems are routinely applied on a continuous basis, strategic cost management tends to be applied on an *ad-hoc* basis when an opportunity for cost reduction is identified.

- **Describe the typical pattern of cost commitment and cost incurrence during the three stages of a product's life cycle.** Three stages of a product's cost life cycle can be identified – the planning and design stage, the manufacturing stage and the service and abandonment stage. Approximately 80 per cent of a product's costs are committed during the planning and design stage. At this stage product designers determine the product's design and the production process. In contrast, the majority of costs are incurred at the manufacturing stage, but they have already become locked in at the planning and design stage and are difficult to alter. Cost management can be most effectively exercised during the planning and design stage and not at the manufacturing stage when the product design and processes have already been determined and costs have been committed.

- **Describe the target costing approach to cost management.** The first stage requires market research to determine the target selling price for a product. Next a standard or desired profit margin is deducted to establish a target cost for the product. The target cost is compared with the predicted actual cost. If the predicted actual cost is above the target cost intensive efforts are made to drive the predicted actual cost down to the target cost. The major advantage of adopting target costing is that it is deployed during a product's design and planning stage so that it can have a maximum impact in determining the level of the locked-in costs.

- **Describe tear-down analysis and value analysis.** Tear-down analysis involves examining a competitor's product in order to identify opportunities for product improvement and/or cost reduction. The aim of value analysis is to achieve the assigned target cost by (a) identifying improved product designs that reduce the product's cost without sacrificing functionality and/or (b) eliminating unnecessary functions that increase the product's costs and for which customers are not prepared to pay extra.

- **Describe activity-based cost management.** Activity-based management (ABM) focuses on managing the business on the basis of the activities that make up the organization. It is based on the premise that activities consume costs. Therefore, by managing activities, costs will be managed in the long term. The goal of ABM is to enable customer needs to be satisfied while making fewer demands on organization resources. Knowing the cost of activities enables those activities with the highest cost to be highlighted so that they can be prioritized for detailed studies to ascertain whether they can be eliminated or performed more efficiently.

● **Distinguish between value-added and non-value-added activities**. To identify and prioritize the potential for cost reduction using ABM, many organizations have found it useful to classify activities as either value-added or non-value added. A value-added activity is an activity that customers perceive as adding usefulness to the product or service they purchase whereas a non-value-added activity is an activity where there is an opportunity for cost reduction without reducing the product's service potential to the customer. Taking action to reduce or eliminate non-value-added activities is given top priority because by doing so the organization permanently reduces the cost it incurs without reducing the value of the product to the customer.

● **Explain the purpose of a cost of quality report**. A cost of quality report indicates the total cost to the organization of producing products or services that do not conform with quality requirements. Quality costs are analysed by four categories for reporting purposes (prevention, appraisal, and internal and external failure costs). The report draws management's attention to the possibility of reducing total quality costs by a wiser allocation of costs among the four quality categories.

● **Describe how value-chain analysis can be used to increase customer satisfaction and manage costs more effectively**. Increasing attention is now being given to value-chain analysis as a means of increasing customer satisfaction and managing costs more effectively. The value chain is the linked set of value-creating activities all the way from basic raw material sources from component suppliers through to the ultimate end-use product or service delivered to the customer. Understanding how value chain activities are performed and how they interact with each other creates the conditions to improve customer satisfaction, particularly in terms of cost efficiency, quality and delivery.

● **Explain the role of benchmarking within the cost management framework**. Benchmarking involves comparing key activities with world-class best practices by identifying an activity that needs to be improved, finding a non-rival organization that is considered to represent world-class best practice for the activity, and studying how it performs the activity. The objective is to establish how the activity can be improved and ensure that the improvements are implemented. The outcome should be reduced costs for the activity or process or performing the activity more effectively, thus increasing customer satisfaction.

● **Outline the main features of a just-in-time philosophy**. Many companies seek to eliminate and/or reduce the costs of non-value-added activities by introducing just-in-time (JIT) systems. The aims of a JIT system are to produce the required items, at the required quality and in the required quantities, at the precise time they are required. In particular, JIT aims to eliminate waste by minimizing inventories and reducing cycle or throughput times (i.e. the time elapsed from when customers place an order until the time when they receive the desired product or service). Adopting a JIT manufacturing system involves moving from a batch production functional layout to a cellular flow line manufacturing system. The JIT philosophy also extends to adopting JIT purchasing techniques, whereby the delivery of materials immediately precedes their use. By arranging with suppliers for more frequent deliveries, stocks can be cut to a minimum.

KEY TERMS AND CONCEPTS

activity-based cost management (ABCM) (p. 342)

activity-based management (ABM) (p. 342)

appraisal costs (p. 347)

batch production functional layout (p. 353)

benchmarking (p. 349)

business process re-engineering (p. 345)

cellular manufacturing (p. 353)

committed costs (p. 336)

cost of quality report (p. 346)

environmental detection costs (p. 351)

environmental external failure costs (p. 351)

environmental internal failure costs (p. 345)

environmental prevention costs (p. 338)

external failure costs (p. 347)

internal failure costs (p. 347)

just-in-time (JIT) production methods (p. 352)

Kanbans (p. 354)

life-cycle cost management (p. 336)

locked in costs (p. 336)

non-value-added activity (p. 345)

prevention costs (p. 347)

product flow line (p. 353)

pull manufacturing system (p. 354)

push manufacturing system (p. 354)

reverse engineering (p. 338)

standard cost blinder (p. 341)

target costing (p. 337)

tear-down analysis (p. 338)

total quality management (p. 346)

value-added activity (p. 351)

value analysis (p. 338)

value-chain analysis (p. 348)

value engineering (p. 338)

ASSESSMENT MATERIAL

The review questions are short questions that enable you to assess your understanding of the main topics included in the chapter. The page numbers in parentheses provide you with the page numbers to refer to if you cannot answer a specific question.

The review problems are more complex and require you to relate and apply the content to various business problems. Solutions to review problems are provided in a separate section at the end of the book. Additional review problems can be accessed by lecturers and students on the website (www.drury-online.com). Solutions to these problems are provided for lecturers in the *Instructors' Manual*. This is available on the lecturers' password-protected section of the website.

The website also includes over 30 case study problems. A list of these cases is provided on pages 389–392.

REVIEW QUESTIONS

14.1   How does cost management differ from traditional management accounting control systems? *(pp. 335–36)*

14.2   What are committed (locked-in) costs? *(p. 336)*

14.3   Explain the features of life-cycle cost management. *(pp. 336–37)*

14.4   Describe the stages involved with target costing. Describe how costs are reduced so that the target cost can be achieved. *(pp. 337–40)*

14.5   What are the distinguishing features of activity-based management? *(pp. 342–45)*

14.6   Distinguish between value-added and non-value-added activities. *(p. 345)*

14.7   What is business process re-engineering? *(pp. 345–46)*

14.8   Identify and discuss the four kinds of quality costs that are included in a cost of quality report. Give examples of costs that fall within each category. *(pp. 346–48)*

14.9   Discuss the value of a cost of quality report. *(pp. 346–48)*

14.10 Explain what is meant by value-chain analysis. Illustrate how value-chain analysis can be applied. *(pp. 348–49)*

14.11 Explain how benchmarking can be used to manage costs and improve activity performance. *(pp. 349–50)*

14.12 What are the major features of a just-in-time manufacturing philosophy? *(pp. 351–55)*

14.13 Distinguish between a pull and push manufacturing system. *(p. 354)*

14.14 What are the essential features of just-in-time purchasing arrangements? *(p. 355)*

REVIEW PROBLEMS

14.15 Cost of quality reporting

Burdoy plc has a dedicated set of production facilities for component X. A just-in-time system is in place such that no stock of materials, work in progress or finished goods are held.

At the beginning of period 1, the planned information relating to the production of component X through the dedicated facilities is as follows:

(i)   Each unit of component X has input materials: 3 units of material A at £18 per unit and 2 units of material B at £9 per unit.

(ii)   Variable cost per unit of component X (excluding materials) is £15 per unit worked on.

(iii) Fixed costs of the dedicated facilities for the period: £162 000.

(iv)   It is anticipated that 10 per cent of the units of X worked on in the process will be defective and will be scrapped.

It is estimated that customers will require replacement (free of charge) of faulty units of component X at the rate of 2 per cent of the quantity invoiced to them in fulfilment of orders.

Burdoy plc is pursuing a total quality management philosophy. Consequently all losses will be treated as abnormal in recognition of a zero defect policy and will be valued at variable cost of production.

Actual statistics for each of periods 1 to 3 for component X are shown in Appendix 1 to this question. No changes have occurred from the planned price levels for materials, variable overhead or fixed overhead costs.

Required:

(a)   Prepare an analysis of the relevant figures provided in Appendix 1 to show that the period 1 actual results were achieved at the planned level in respect of (i) quantities and losses and (ii) unit cost levels for materials and variable costs.

(5 marks)

(b)   Use your analysis from (a) in order to calculate the value of the planned level of each of internal and external failure costs for period 1.

(3 marks)

(c)   Actual free replacements of component X to customers were 170 units and 40 units in periods 2 and 3 respectively. Other data relating to periods 2 and 3 is shown in Appendix 1 to this question.

Burdoy plc authorized additional expenditure during periods 2 and 3 as follows:

Period 2: Equipment accuracy checks of £10 000 and staff training of £5000.

Period 3: Equipment accuracy checks of £10 000 plus £5000 of inspection costs; also staff training costs of £5000 plus £3000 on extra planned maintenance of equipment.

Required:

(i)   Prepare an analysis for *each* of periods 2 and 3 that reconciles the number of components invoiced to customers with those worked on in the production process. The analysis should show the changes from the planned quantity of process losses and changes from the planned quantity of replacement of faulty components in customer hands.

(All relevant working notes should be shown)

(8 marks)

(ii) Prepare a cost analysis for *each* of periods 2 and 3 that shows actual internal failure costs, external failure costs, appraisal costs and prevention costs.

(6 marks)

(iii) Prepare a report explaining the meaning and interrelationship of the figures in Appendix 1 and in the analysis in (a), (b) and (c) (i)/(ii). The report should also give examples of each cost type and comment on their use in the monitoring and progressing of the TQM policy being pursued by Burdoy plc.

(13 marks)
(Total 35 marks)

Appendix 1
Actual statistics for component X

	Period 1	Period 2	Period 3
Invoiced to customers (units)	5 400	5 500	5 450
Worked on in the process (units)	6 120	6 200	5 780
Total costs:			
Materials A and B (£)	440 640	446 400	416 160
Variable cost of production (£)			
(excluding material cost)	91 800	93 000	86 700
Fixed cost (£)	162 000	177 000	185 000

14.16 Traditional and activity-based budget statements and life-cycle costing

The budget for the Production, Planning and Development Department of Obba plc, is currently prepared as part of a traditional budgetary planning and control system. The analysis of costs by expense type for the period ended 30 November 2008 where this system is in use is as follows:

Expense type	Budget %	Actual %
Salaries	60	63
Supplies	6	5
Travel cost	12	12
Technology cost	10	7
Occupancy cost	12	13

The total budget and actual costs for the department for the period ended 30 November 2008 are £1 000 000 and £1 060 000 respectively.

The company now feels that an activity-based budgeting approach should be used. A number of activities have been identified for the Production, Planning and Development Department. An investigation has indicated that total budget and actual costs should be attributed to activities on the following basis:

	Budget %	Actual %
Activities		
1 Routing/scheduling – new products	20	16
2 Routing/scheduling – existing products	40	34
3 Remedial re-routing/scheduling	5	12
4 Special studies – specific orders	10	8
5 Training	10	15
6 Management and administration	15	15

Required:

(a) (i) Prepare *two* budget control statements for the Production Planning and Development Department for the period ended 30 November 2008 which compare budget with actual cost and show variances using

1 a traditional expense-based analysis and
2 an activity-based analysis.

(6 marks)

(ii) Identify and comment on *four* advantages claimed for the use of activity-based budgeting over traditional budgeting using the Production Planning and Development Department example to illustrate your answer.

(12 marks)

(iii) Comment on the use of the information provided in the activity-based statement that you prepared in (i) in activity-based performance measurement and suggest additional information that would assist in such performance measurement.

(8 marks)

(b) Other activities have been identified and the budget quantified for the three months ended 31 March 2009 as follows:

Activities	Cost driver unit basis	Units of cost driver	Cost (£000)
Product design	Design hours	8 000	2000 (see note 1)
Purchasing	Purchase orders	4 000	200
Production	Machine hours	12 000	1500 (see note 2)
Packing	Volume (cu.m.)	20 000	400
Distribution	Weight (kg)	120 000	600

Note 1: this includes all design costs for new products released this period.
Note 2: this includes a depreciation provision of £300 000 of which £8000 applies to 3 months' depreciation on a straight line basis for a new product (NPD). The remainder applies to other products.

New product NPD is included in the above budget. The following additional information applies to NPD:

(i)   Estimated total output over the product life cycle: 5000 units (4 years life cycle).
(ii) Product design requirement: 400 design hours
(iii) Output in quarter ended 31 March 2009: 250 units
(iv) Equivalent batch size per purchase order: 50 units

(v)   Other product unit data: production time 0.75 machine hours: volume 0.4 cu. metres; weight 3 kg.

Required:

Prepare a unit overhead cost for product NPD using an activity-based approach which includes an appropriate share of life-cycle costs using the information provided in (b) above.

(9 marks)
(Total 35 marks)

14.17 The implementation of budgeting in a world-class manufacturing environment may be affected by the impact of (i) a total quality ethos (ii) a just-in-time philosophy and (iii) an activity-based focus.

Briefly describe the principles incorporated in *each* of (i) to (iii) and discuss ways in which each may result in changes in the way in which budgets are prepared as compared to a traditional incremental budgeting system.

(15 marks)

14.18 New techniques are often described as contributing to cost reduction, but when cost reduction is necessary it is not obvious that such new approaches are used in preference to more established approaches. Three examples are:

new technique	compared with	*established approach*
(a) benchmarking		inter-firm comparison
(b) activity-based budgeting		zero-based budgeting
(c) target costing		continuous cost improvement

You are required, for two of the three newer techniques mentioned above:

- to explain its objectives;
- to explain its workings;
- to differentiate it from the related approach identified;
- to explain how it would contribute to a cost reduction programme.

(20 marks)

14.19 'ABC is still at a relatively early stage of its development and its implications for process control may in the final analysis be more important than its product costing implications. It is a good time for every organization to consider whether or not ABC is appropriate to its particular circumstances.'

J. Innes & F. Mitchell, *Activity Based Costing, A Review with Case Studies*, CIMA, 1990.

You are required:

(a)   discuss the factors that might influence organizations to implement ABC systems;

(8 marks)

(b)   to explain in what ways ABC may be used to manage costs, and the limitations of these approaches;

(11 marks)

(c)   to explain and to discuss the use of target costing to control product costs.

(6 marks)
(Total 25 marks)

CHAPTER 15
STRATEGIC PERFORMANCE MANAGEMENT

LEARNING OBJECTIVES

After studying this chapter you should be able to:

- **describe three competitive strategies that a firm can adopt to achieve sustainable competitive advantage and explain how they influence management accounting practices;**
- **describe the balanced scorecard;**
- **explain each of the four perspectives of the balanced scorecard;**
- **provide illustrations of performance measures for each of the four perspectives;**
- **explain how the balanced scorecard links strategy formulation to financial outcomes;**
- **describe the distinguishing characteristics of service organizations that influence performance measurement.**

Increasing emphasis is now being given to the need for management accounting to support an organization's competitive strategies. The emphasis that organizations give to the use of the various accounting techniques that have been described in this book depends on the strategies that they adopt. This chapter describes how management accounting can be used to support and implement the competitive strategies adopted by organizations.

The chapter begins with a description of three generic strategies that firms can use to achieve competitive advantage and the impact that the choice of a particular strategy has on the emphasis given to different accounting techniques. To encourage behaviour that is consistent with an organization's strategy, attention is now being given to an integrated framework of performance measurement that can be used to clarify, communicate and manage strategy. The major aim of this chapter is to describe the recent developments that seek to incorporate performance measurement and management within the strategic management process.

ACCOUNTING IN RELATION TO STRATEGIC POSITIONING

Various classifications of strategic positions that firms may choose have been identified in the strategic management literature. Porter (1985) suggests that a firm has a choice of three generic strategies in order to achieve sustainable competitive advantage. They are:

- A **cost leadership strategy**, whereby an enterprise aims to be the lowest-cost producer within the industry thus enabling it to compete on the basis of lower selling prices rather than providing unique products or services. The source of this competitive advantage may arise from factors such as economies of scale, access to favourable raw materials prices and superior technology (Langfield-Smith, 1997).

- A **differentiation strategy**, whereby the enterprise seeks to offer products or services that are considered by its customers to be superior and unique relative to its competitors. Examples include the quality or dependability of the product, after-sales service, the wide availability of the product and product flexibility (Langfield-Smith, 1997).

- A **focusing strategy**, which involves seeking competitive advantage by focusing on a narrow segment of the market that has special needs that are poorly served by other competitors in the industry. A focusing strategy recognizes that differences can exist within segments (e.g. customers and geographical regions) of the same market. Competitive advantage is based on adopting either a cost leadership or product differentiation strategy within the chosen segment.

In practice firms may choose a combination of the three strategies within the different markets in which they operate. **Strategic positioning** relates to the choice of the optimal mix of the three general strategies. Firms should place more emphasis on particular accounting techniques, depending on which strategic position they adopt. For example, firms pursuing a cost leadership strategy will place more emphasis on the importance of standard costing variance analysis, flexible budgets, using tightly controlled budgets and strategic cost management.

Firms pursuing a differentiation strategy place greater emphasis on seeking ways to differentiate their products and services from those provided by competitors. This frequently results in a greater number of products and services offered and also increased customer segmentation. Companies that pursue a differentiation strategy need more complex product costing systems (e.g. ABC systems) that have the potential to more accurately measure the costs of product and volume diversity that stem from pursuing this strategy. Without such a system they run the risk of not being able to determine whether the higher revenues generated from their products or services exceed the extra costs associated with differentiation.

THE BALANCED SCORECARD

A more recent contribution to management accounting that emphasizes the role of management accounting in formulating and supporting the overall competitive strategy of an organization is the **balanced scorecard**. The balanced scorecard seeks to encourage behaviour that is consistent with an organization's strategy. It comprises an integrated framework of performance measurements that aim to clarify, communicate and manage strategy implementation. The financial performance measures that have been described in Chapters 10–12 tend to be used primarily as a financial control mechanism whereas the balanced scorecard integrates both financial and non-financial measures and incorporates performance measurement within the strategic management process.

Prior to the 1980s management accounting control systems tended to focus mainly on financial measures of performance. The inclusion of only those items that could be expressed in monetary terms motivated managers to focus excessively on cost reduction and ignore other important variables which were necessary to compete in the global competitive environment that emerged during the 1980s. Product quality, delivery, reliability, after-sales service and customer satisfaction became key competitive variables but none of these were given sufficient importance by the traditional management accounting performance measurement system.

During the 1980s much greater emphasis was given to incorporating into the management reporting system those non-financial performance measures that provided feedback on the key variables that are required to compete successfully in a global economic environment. However, a proliferation of performance measures emerged. This resulted in confusion when some of the measures conflicted with each other and it was possible to enhance one measure at the expense of another. It was also not clear to managers how the non-financial measures they were evaluated on contributed to the whole picture of achieving success in financial terms. According to Kaplan and Norton (2001a) previous performance measurement systems that incorporated non-financial measurements used *ad hoc* collections of such measures, more like checklists of measures for managers to keep track of and improve than a comprehensive system of linked measurements.

The need to integrate financial and non-financial measures of performance and identify key performance measures that link measurements to strategy led to the emergence of the balanced scorecard. The balanced scorecard was devised by Kaplan and Norton (1992) and refined in later publications (Kaplan and Norton, 1993, 1996a, 1996b, 2001a, 2001b). Therefore the following discussion is a summary of Kaplan and Norton's writings on this topic. They use the diagram reproduced in Figure 15.1 to illustrate how the balanced scorecard translates strategy into tangible objectives and linked performance measures.

Figure 15.1 emphasizes that the balanced scorecard philosophy creates a strategic focus by translating an organization's vision and strategy into operational objectives and performance measures for the following four perspectives:

1 **Financial perspective** (How do we look to shareholders?)
2 **Customer perspective** (How do customers see us?)
3 **Internal business perspective** (What must we excel at?)
4 **Learning and growth perspective** (Can we continue to improve and create value?)

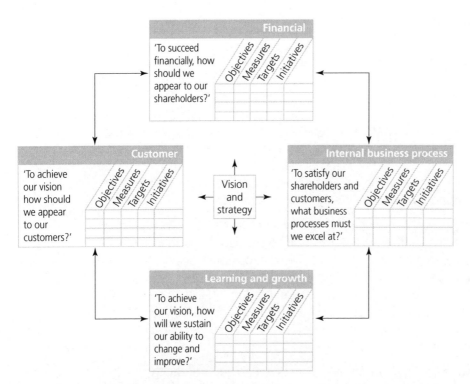

FIGURE 15.1

The balanced scorecard

The balanced scorecard is a strategic management technique for communicating and evaluating the achievement of the mission and strategy of the organization. Kaplan and Norton define strategy as:

> Choosing the market and customer segments the business unit intends to serve, identifying the critical internal and business processes that the unit must excel at to deliver the value propositions to customers in the targeted market segments, and selecting the individual and organizational capabilities required for the internal and financial objectives.

You will see from Figure 15.1 that strategy is implemented by specifying the major objectives for each of the four perspectives and translating them into specific performance measures, targets and initiatives. There may be one or more objectives for each perspective and one or more performance measures linked to each objective. Only the critical performance measures are incorporated in the scorecard. To minimize information overload and avoid a proliferation of measures each perspective ought to comprise four to five separate measures. Thus, the scorecard can provide *top* management with a fast but comprehensive view of the organizational unit (i.e. a division/strategic business unit). Let us now examine each of the four perspectives. The following discussion presents generic core objectives and measures applicable to each perspective. In practice each organization will customize the objectives and performance measures to fit its own specific strategies.

The financial perspective

The financial perspective specifies the financial performance objectives anticipated from pursuing the organization's strategy and also the economic consequences of the outcomes expected from achieving the objectives specified from the other three perspectives. Therefore the objectives and measures from the other perspectives should be selected to

REAL WORLD VIEWS 15.1

How Southwest Airlines developed its balanced scorecard analysis

Southwest Airlines set 'operating efficiency' as its strategic theme. The four perspectives embodied in the balanced scorecard were linked together by a series of relatively simple questions and answers:

Financial: What will drive operating efficiency? *Answer:* More customers on fewer planes.

Customer: How will we get more customers on fewer planes? *Answer:* Attract targeted segments of customers who value price and on-time arrivals.

Internal: What must our internal focus be? *Answer:* Fast aircraft turnaround time.

Learning: How will our people accomplish fast turnaround? *Answer:* Educate and compensate the ground crew regarding how they contribute to the firm's success. Also, use the employee stockholder programme.

The chart below shows how Southwest used this framework to lay out its balanced scorecard model.

© JIM WEST/ALAMY

The first column of the chart contains the 'strategy map' that illustrates the cause-and-effect relationships between strategic objectives. The Objectives column shows what each strategy must achieve and what is critical to its success. The Measurement column shows how success in achieving each strategy will be measured and tracked. The Target column spells out the level of performance or rate of improvement that is needed. The Initiative column contains key action programmes required to achieve objectives. Note that all of the measures, targets and initiatives are all aligned to each objective.

Southwest Airlines' balanced scorecard framework

Strategic theme: Operating efficiency	Objectives	Measurement	Target	Initiative
Financial Profitability Fewer planes More customers	Profitability	Market value	30% CAGR	
	More customers	Seat revenue	20% CAGR	
	Fewer planes	Plane lease cost	5% CAGR	
Customer Flight is on time Lowest prices	Flight is on time	FAA on-time arrival rating	#1	Quality management
	Lowest prices	Customer ranking (market survey)	#1	Customer loyalty programme
Internal Fast ground turnaround	Fast ground turnaround	On ground time	30 minutes	Cycle time optimization
		On-time departure	90%	
Learning Ground crew alignment	Ground crew alignment	% Ground crew trained	Yr. 1 70%	ESOP Ground crew training
		% Ground crew stockholders	Yr. 3 90%	
			Yr. 5 100%	

(Source: Balanced Scorecard Collaborative)

The company extended the effort to the department level, and the degree of development varied between departments. The goal was to identify key performance measures in each segment for the operating personnel. Some of the non-financial metrics that have emerged on a departmental level include: load factor (percentage of seats occupied); utilization factors on aircraft and personnel; on-time performance; available seat miles; denied-boarding rate; lost-bag reports per 10 000 passengers; flight cancellation rate; employee head count; and customer complaints per 10 000 passengers filed with the Department of Transportation.

ensure that the financial outcomes will be achieved. Kaplan and Norton state that they have observed three core financial themes that drive the business strategy: revenue growth and mix, cost reduction and asset utilization.

Generic objectives and possible measures for these themes are shown in Exhibit 15.1. Typical *revenue growth* objectives for a business pursuing a growth strategy include increasing the number of new products, developing new customers and markets, and changing to a more profitable product or service mix. Once the objectives have been determined performance measures should be established that are linked to each objective. Possible measures are listed against each objective in Exhibit 15.1. They are percentage revenues from new products, percentage revenues from new customers/markets and growth of sales in the targeted segments.

The *cost reduction* objectives may include reduction in unit product costs and a reduction in selling and general and administration costs. Thus the percentage reduction in costs per unit of output for the selected cost objects and the percentage to total revenues of selling and administrative costs represent possible performance measures.

Exhibit 15.1 lists the improvement of *asset utilization* as the major objective of the asset utilization theme. Financial performance measures such as return on investment and economic value added that were described in Chapter 12 provide overall outcome measures of success for the overall financial objectives of revenue growth, cost reduction and asset utilization.

EXHIBIT 15.1

Financial perspective objectives and measures

Objectives	Measures
Revenue growth:	
Increase the number of new products	Percentage of revenues from new products
Develop new customers and markets	Percentage of revenues from new customers/markets
Change to a more profitable product (or service) mix	Sales growth percentage for targeted segments
Cost reduction:	
Reduce product/service cost per unit	Percentage reduction in cost per unit
Reduce selling/general administration costs	Percentage to total revenues of selling and administration costs
Asset utilization:	
Improve asset utilization	Return on investment Economic value added

The customer perspective

The customer perspective should identify the customer and market segments in which the business unit will compete. The customer perspective underpins the revenue element for the financial perspective objectives. Therefore the achievement of customer objectives should ensure that target revenues will be generated. Exhibit 15.2 lists five typical core or generic objectives. They are: increasing market share, increasing customer retention, increasing customer acquisition, increasing customer satisfaction and increasing customer profitability. Typical core measures for these objectives (see Exhibit 15.2) are respectively: percentage market share, percentage growth of business with existing customers, number of new customers or total sales to new customers, ratings from customer satisfaction surveys and profitability analysis by customer segments. The first four measures relate to the means required to achieve customer profitability but they do not measure the outcome. Customer profitability measures meet this requirement. In other words, a company does not want just satisfied customers, it also wants profitable customers.

Kaplan and Norton state that there is also a need to focus on **customer value propositions** that represent the attributes that drive core objectives and measures relating to the customer perspective. They identify common product/service attributes as encompassing the functionality of the products/services, their price and quality, and for the customer dimension they identify the delivery time attribute. Focusing on these attributes has the potential to increase customer value and thus have a favourable impact on the core objectives. Typical objectives relating to the above attributes are listed in Exhibit 15.2. They are respectively: improve product functionality, decrease price relative to competitors, improve quality and improve delivery time. Possible measures for these objectives include, respectively, customer survey satisfaction scores relating to product functionality, price relative to competitors, percentage of returns from customers and percentage of on-time deliveries.

The internal business perspective

The internal business perspective requires that managers identify the critical internal processes for which the organization must excel in implementing its strategy. Critical processes should be identified that are required to achieve the organization's customer and financial objectives. Kaplan and Norton identify a generic process value chain that provides guidance for companies applying the internal process perspective. The process value

Objectives	Measures
Core:	
Increase market share	Percentage market share
Increase customer retention	Percentage growth in business from existing customers
Increase customer acquisition	Total sales to new customers
Increase customer satisfaction	Customer survey satisfaction ratings
Increase customer profitability	Customer profitability analysis
Customer value propositions:	
Improve product functionality	Customer survey product functionality rating scores
Decrease price relative to competitors	Price relative to competitors
Improve product/service quality	Percentage returns from customers
Improve delivery time	Percentage on-time deliveries

EXHIBIT 15.2

Customer perspective objectives and measures

chain consists of three processes: the innovation process, the operations process and the post-sales process.

In the *innovation process*, managers research the needs of customers and then create the products or services that will meet those needs. It represents the long wave of value creation in which companies first identify new markets, new customers, and the emerging and latent needs of existing customers. Then continuing on this long wave of value creation companies design and develop new products and services that enable them to reach these new markets and customers. Typical objectives for the innovation process are listed in Exhibit 15.3. They are increasing the number of new products, developing new markets and customers and decreasing the time taken to develop new products. Supporting performance measures are, respectively: percentage of sales from new products (also new product introductions versus competitors), percentage of sales from new markets and development cycle time (e.g. time to the market).

The *operations process* represents the short wave of value creation. It is concerned with producing and delivering existing products and services to customers. Objectives of the operation process listed in Exhibit 15.3 include, increasing process efficiency, increasing process quality, decreasing process cost and decreasing process time. Historically, the operations process has been the major focus of most of an organization's performance measurement system and many possible measures exist. Typical measures associated with each of the objectives for the operations process are listed in Exhibit 15.3.

Process efficiency measures tend to focus on output/input measures such as the **production efficiency ratio** (standard hours of output/actual hours of input). Quality measures include total quality costs as a percentage of sales derived from the cost of quality report (see Chapter 14), and percentage of defective units. Process cost measures include unit cost trend measures relating to key processes and cycle time measures have evolved that support the objective of decreasing process time.

EXHIBIT 15.3

Internal business perspective objectives and measures

Objectives	Measures
Innovation:	
Increase the number of new products	Percentage of sales from new products
	New product introductions versus competitors
Develop new markets and customers	Percentage of sales from new markets
Decrease the time taken to develop new products	Development cycle time (time to the market)
Operations:	
Increase process efficiency	Output/inputs ratios
Increase process quality	Total quality costs as a percentage of sales
	Percentage of defective output
Decrease process cost	Unit cost trends
Decrease process time	Manufacturing cycle efficiency
Post-sales service:	
Increase service quality	Percentage of customer requests that are handled with a single call
Increase service efficiency	Output/inputs ratios
Decrease service time	Cycle time in resolving customer problems
Decrease service cost	Unit cost trends

The total manufacturing cycle time consists of the sum of processing time, inspection time, wait time and move time. Only processing time adds value, and the remaining activities are non-value-added activities. The aim is to reduce the time spent on non-value-added activities and thus minimize manufacturing cycle time. A measure of cycle time that has been adopted is **manufacturing cycle efficiency (MCE)**:

$$MCE = \frac{\text{Processing time}}{\text{Processing time + Inspection time + Wait time + Move time}}$$

The generic performance measures that have been illustrated above relate to manufacturing operations but similar measures can be adopted for service companies. For example, many customers are forced to queue to receive a service. Companies that can eliminate waiting time for a service will find it easier to attract customers. Processing mortgage and loan applications by financial institutions can take a considerable time period involving a considerable amount of non-value-added waiting time. Thus, reducing the time to process the applications enhances customer satisfaction and creates the potential for increasing sales revenues. Therefore service companies should also develop cycle time measures that support their specific customer processing activity objectives.

The *post-sales service process* represents the final item in the process value chain for the operations process perspective. It focuses on how responsive the organization is to customers after the product or service has been delivered. Post-sales services include warranty and repair activities, treatment of defects and returns, and the process and administration of customer payments. Increasing quality, increasing efficiency and decreasing process time and cost are also objectives that apply to the post-sales service. Performance can be measured by some of the time, quality and cost measurements that have been suggested for the operations process. For example, service quality can be measured by first-pass yields defined as the percentage of customer requests that are handled with a single service call, rather than requiring multiple calls to resolve the problem. Increasing efficiency can be measured by appropriate output/input ratios and decreasing process time can be measured by cycle time where the process starts with the receipt of a customer request and ends with the ultimate resolution of the problem. Finally, the trend in unit costs can be used to measure the key post-sale service processes.

The learning and growth perspective

To ensure that an organization will continue to have loyal and satisfied customers in the future and continue to make excellent use of its resources, the organization and its employees must keep learning and developing. Hence there is a need for a perspective that focuses on the capabilities that an organization needs to create long-term growth and improvement. This perspective stresses the importance of organizations investing in their infrastructure (people, systems and organizational procedures) to provide the capabilities that enable the accomplishment of the other three perspectives' objectives. Kaplan and Norton have identified three major enabling factors for this perspective. They are: employee capabilities, information systems capabilities and the organizational climate for motivation, empowerment and alignment. Thus this perspective has three major core objectives: increase employee capabilities, increase information system capabilities and increase motivation, empowerment and alignment. The objectives and associated performance measures for this perspective are listed in Exhibit 15.4.

EXHIBIT 15.4

Learning and growth perspective objectives and measures

Objectives	Measures
Increase employee capabilities	Employee satisfaction survey ratings
	Annual percentage of key staff leaving
	Sales revenue per employee
Increase information system capabilities	Percentage of processes with real-time feedback capabilities
	Percentage of customer-facing employees having online access to customer and product information
Increase motivation, empowerment and alignment	Number of suggested improvements per employee
	Number of suggestions implemented per employee
	Percentage of employees with personal goals aligned to the balanced scorecard
	Percentage of employees who achieve personal goals

Core measures for the *employee capabilities* objective are concerned with employee satisfaction, employee retention and employee productivity. Many companies periodically measure employee satisfaction using surveys to derive employee satisfaction ratings. Employee retention can be measured by the annual percentage of key staff that resigns and many different methods can be used to measure employee productivity. A generic measure of employee productivity that can be applied throughout the organization and compared with different divisions is the sales revenue per employee.

For employees to be effective in today's competitive environment they need accurate and timely information on customers, internal processes and the financial consequences of their decisions. Measures of *strategic information system capabilities* suggested by Kaplan and Norton include percentage of processes with real-time quality, cycle time and cost feedback capabilities available and the percentage of customer-facing employees having online access to customer and product information.

The number of suggested improvements per employee and the number of suggestions implemented per employee are proposed measures relating to the objective having *motivated and empowered employees*. Suggested measures relating to the objective of increasing individual and organizational alignment are the percentage of employees with personal goals aligned to the balanced scorecard and the percentage of employees who achieve personal goals.

Targets and initiatives

Look at Figure 15.1. You will see that, besides objectives and measures, targets and initiatives are also incorporated in the balanced scorecard. Target values should be established for the measures associated with each objective. In addition, the major initiatives for each objective should be described. For feedback reporting actual performance measures can also be added. There is also evidence to indicate that the balanced scorecard approach is linked to incentive compensation schemes. Epstein and Manzoni (1998) reported that 60 per cent of the 100 large USA organizations surveyed linked the balanced scorecard approach to incentive pay for their senior executives. Failure to change the reward system may result in managers continuing to focus on short-term financial performance at the expense of concentrating on the strategic objectives of the scorecard.

Cause-and-effect relationships

A critical assumption of the balanced scorecard is that each performance measure is part of a cause-and-effect relationship involving a linkage from strategy formulation to financial outcomes. Measures of organizational learning and growth are assumed to be the drivers of the internal business processes. The measures of these processes are in turn assumed to be the drivers of measures of customer perspective, while these measures are the driver of the financial perspective. The assumption that there is a cause-and-effect relationship is necessary because it allows the measurements relating to the non-financial perspectives to be used to predict future financial performance. In this context, Kaplan and Norton (1996b) indicate that the chain of cause-and-effect relationships encompasses all four perspectives of the balanced scorecard such that economic value added (see Chapter 12) may be an outcome measure for the financial perspective. The driver of this measure could be an expansion of sales from existing customers. This expansion may be achieved by enhancing customers' loyalty by meeting their preference for on-time delivery. Thus, the improved on-time delivery is expected to lead to higher customer loyalty, which in turn leads to higher financial performance. The on-time delivery is part of the internal process perspective and to achieve it the business needs to achieve short cycle time in operating processes and the short cycle time can be achieved by training the employees, this goal being part of the learning and growth perspective.

The balanced scorecard thus consists of two types of performance measures. The first consists of **lagging measures**. These are the outcome measures that mostly fall within the financial perspective and are the results of past actions. These measures generally do not incorporate the effect of decisions when they are made. Instead, they show the financial impact of the decisions as their impact materializes and this can be long after the decisions were made. The second are **leading measures** that are the drivers of future financial performance. They cause the outcome. These tend to be the non-financial measures relating to the customer, internal business process, and learning and growth perspectives.

Benefits and limitations of the balanced scorecard approach

The following is a summary of the major benefits that can be attributed to the balanced scorecard approach:

1 The scorecard brings together in a single report four different perspectives on a company's performance that relate to many of the disparate elements of the company's competitive agenda such as becoming customer-oriented, shortening response time, improving quality, emphasizing teamwork, reducing new product launch times and managing for the long term. Many organizations collect some performance measures relating to each of the four perspectives but they are typically presented in several different large reports that often prove to be unhelpful because they suffer from information overload.

2 The approach provides a comprehensive framework for translating company's strategic goals into a coherent set of performance measures by developing the major goals for the four perspectives and then translating these goals into specific performance measures.

3 The scorecard helps managers to consider all the important operational measures together. It enables managers to see whether improvements in one area may have been at the expense of another.

4 The approach improves communications within the organization and promotes the active formulation and implementation of organizational strategy by making it highly visible through the linkage of performance measures to business unit strategy.

The balanced scorecard has also been subject to frequent criticisms. Most of them question the assumption of the cause-and-effect relationship on the grounds that they are too ambiguous and lack a theoretical underpinning or empirical support. The empirical studies that have been undertaken have failed to provide evidence on the underlying linkages between non-financial data and future financial performance (American Accounting Association Financial Accounting Standards Committee, 2002). Other criticisms relate to the omission of important perspectives, the most notable being the environmental/

EXHIBIT 15.5

Potential scorecard measures in different business sectors

	Generic	Healthcare	Airlines	Banking
Financial strength (Looking back)	Market share Revenue growth Operating profits Return on equity Stock market performance Growth in margin	Patient census Unit profitability Funds raised for capital improvements Cost per care Per cent of revenue – new programmes	Revenue/cost per available passenger mile Mix of freight Mix of full fare to discounted Average age of fleet Available seat miles and related yields	Outstanding loan balances Deposit balances Non-interest income
Customer service and satisfaction (Looking from the outside in)	Customer satisfaction Customer retention Quality customer service Sales from new products/services	Patient satisfaction survey Patient retention Patient referral rate Admittance or discharge timeliness Medical plan awareness	Lost bag reports per 10 000 passengers Denied boarding rate Flight cancellation rate Customer complaints filed with the DOT	Customer retention Number of new customers Number of products per customer Face time spent between loan officers and customers
Internal operating efficiency (Looking from the inside out)	Delivery time Cost Process quality Error rates on shipments Supplier satisfaction	Weekly patient complaints Patient loads Breakthroughs in treatments and medicines Infection rates Readmission rate Length of stay	Load factors (percentage of seats occupied) Utilization factors on aircraft and personnel On-time performance	Sales calls to potential customers Thank you calls or cards to new and existing customers Cross selling statistics
Learning and growth (Looking ahead)	Employee skill level Training availability Employee satisfaction Job retention Amount of overtime worked Amount of vacation time taken	Training hours per caregiver Number of peer reviewed papers published Number of grants awarded (NIH) Referring MDs Employee turnover rate	Employee absenteeism Worker safety statistics Performance appraisals completed Training programme hours per employee	Test results from training knowledge of product offerings, sales and service Employee satisfaction survey

(*Source*: Learby and Wenteel, 2002)

EXHIBIT 15.6
Surveys of practice relating to balanced scorecard usage

Surveys indicate that even though the balanced scorecard did not emerge until the early 1990s it is now widely used in many countries throughout the world. A USA survey by Silk (1998) estimated that 60 per cent of Fortune 1000 firms have experimented with the balanced scorecard. In the UK a survey of 163 manufacturing companies (annual sales turnover in excess of £50 million) by Zuriekat (2005) reported that 30 per cent had implemented the balanced scorecard. Other studies in mainland Europe indicate significant usage. Pere (1999) reported a 31 per cent usage rate of companies in Finland with a further 30 per cent in the process of implementing it. In Sweden Kald and Nilsson (2000) reported that 27 per cent of major Swedish companies have implemented the approach. Oliveras and Amat (2002) report widespread usage in Spain and and Speckbacher *et al.* (2003) report a usage rate of 24 per cent in German-speaking countries (Germany, Austria and Switzerland). Major companies adopting the balanced scorecard include KPMG Peat Marwick, Allstate Insurance and AT&T (Chow *et al.*, 1997).

In terms of the perspectives used Malmi (2001) conducted a study involving semi-structured interviews in 17 companies in Finland. He found that 15 companies used the four perspectives identified by Kaplan and Norton and two companies added a fifth – an employee's perspective. The UK study by Zuriekat (2005) reported that virtually all of the balanced scorecard respondents used the financial, customer and internal business process perspectives. Other perspectives used were learning and growth, employee, supplier and the environment. The respective percentage usage rates for the balance scorecard adopters were 39 per cent, 45 per cent, 65 per cent and 26 per cent. The study also reported that 35 per cent of the adopters linked their reward systems to the balanced scorecard. A study by Olve *et al.* (2000) found that 15–20 performance measures are customarily used.

impact on society perspective (see Chapter 14) and an employee perspective. It should be noted, however, that Kaplan and Norton presented the four perspectives as a suggested framework rather than a constraining straitjacket. There is nothing to prevent companies adding additional perspectives to meet their own requirements but they must avoid the temptation of creating too many perspectives and performance measures since one of the major benefits of the balanced scorecard is its conciseness and clarity of presentation.

Our discussion relating to the core objectives and measures of the four perspectives has concentrated mainly on the manufacturing organizations. The balance scorecard, however, has been widely adopted in service organizations. Exhibit 15.5 provides an illustration of potential balanced scorecard performance measures for different types of service organizations. You will also find it appropriate at this point to refer to Exhibit 15.6 which summarizes surveys of practice relating to the usage of the balanced scorecard.

PERFORMANCE MEASUREMENT IN SERVICE ORGANIZATIONS

Although Kaplan and Norton (1996b) illustrate how the balanced scorecard can be applied in both the manufacturing and service sectors, much of the performance measurement literature concentrates on the manufacturing sector. To remedy this deficiency this section focuses on performance measurement in the service sector. Based on their

REAL WORLD VIEWS 15.2

Performance management in the public sector

In 2007, a study of over 1000 public sector organizations was conducted to determine the type of performance management and control systems used. The study was sponsored by Actuate Corporation and the Chartered Institute of Public Finance and Accountancy (CIPFA). The report found that organizations that apply the principles of strategic performance management significantly outperformed those that do not.

A number of key insights were highlighted by the study. First, the study found many implementations of performance management systems were too mechanical and too numbers-focused. Secondly, although vast amounts of data were captured, many organizations lacked the analytical skills to extract and use the information to support decision-making. Thirdly, many organizations had no clear strategy to link the performance measures to, thus creating a sense of confusion among staff as to what performance improvement actually entailed. Finally and surprisingly, the survey found that 68 per cent of organizations 'fabricated' performance data. This simply means the system cannot be trusted to support decisions or improve public accountability.

The report author, Bernard Marr of the Advanced Performance Institute, suggests it is the handling of performance management in public sector organizations that makes the difference between a top-performing one and a poor one. Organizations indulging in performance management systems purely to keep external parties (such as central government) 'off their back' are missing an opportunity to assess and improve their operations.

The study also identified ten principles of good performance management. All are not listed here. The most important of the ten were (a) to create clarity and agreement on the strategic aims of the organization and (b) to create a positive culture of learning from performance information. With these two principles in place a strong impact on performance improvement was witnessed. When all 10 were in place, the performance improvement was substantial.

Discussion points

1 What difficulties might be encountered in selecting key performance indicators for public sector bodies?
2 Can you think of any factors that might hinder the implementation of a performance management system in a public sector organization?

References

1 http://www.reuters.com/article/pressRelease/idUS124137+13-May-2008+BW20080513
2 *Strategic Performance Management in Government and Public Sector Organizations*, Bernard Marr, Advanced Performance Institute (available at http://www.actuate.com/download/whitepapers/strategic-performance-management-wp.pdf).

research into the management accounting practices of a range of companies in several different service industries Fitzgerald *et al.* (1989) identified four unique characteristics distinguishing service companies from manufacturing organizations. First, most services are intangible. Fitzgerald *et al.* state:

> In travelling on a particular airline the customer will be influenced by the comfort of the seat, the meals served, the attitudes and confidence of the cabin staff, the boarding process and so on. This makes managing and controlling the operation complex because it is difficult to establish exactly what an individual customer is buying; is it the journey or the treatment? (Fitzgerald et al., 1989, p. 2)

Secondly, service outputs vary from day to day, because services tend to be provided by individuals whose performance is subject to variability that significantly affects the service quality the customer receives. Thirdly, the production and consumption of many services are inseparable such as in taking a rail journey. Fourthly, services are perishable and cannot be stored. Fitzgerald *et al.* illustrate this characteristic with a hotel, which contains a fixed number of rooms. If a room is unoccupied, the sales opportunity is lost for ever and the resource is wasted.

With regard to the control of the intangible aspects, the authors found that companies used the following methods to measure performance:

1 *Measures of satisfaction after the service.* The most common method was the monitoring and analysis of letters of complaint, but some companies interviewed samples of customers or used questionnaires to ascertain the customers' perception of service quality.

2 *Measures during the service.* An approach used by some companies was for management to make unannounced visits, with the aim of observing the quality of service offered. Another mechanism was the use of mystery shoppers, where staff employed by external agencies were sent out to sample the service as customers and formally report back on their findings.

3 *Tangibles as surrogates for intangibles.* The researchers observed that some firms used internal measures of tangible aspects of the service as indicators of how the customers might perceive the service. Some companies measured waiting times and the conditions of the waiting environment as surrogates of customers' satisfaction with the service.

Fitzgerald *et al.* also draw attention to the importance of relating the performance measures to the corporate and marketing strategies of the organizations. For example, if the delivery of high-quality service is seen to be a key strategic variable then quality measures should be the dominant performance measures. On the other hand, if a low cost of the service relative to competitors is seen as the key strategic variable then strict adherence to budgets will be a key feature of the control system. There is also a greater danger in service organizations of focusing excessively on financial performance measures, which can be easily quantified, thus placing an undue emphasis on maximizing short-term performance, even if this conflicts with maximizing long-term performance. Consequently, it is more important in service organizations that a range of non-financial performance indicators be developed providing better predictors for the attainment of long-term profitability goals.

Dimensions of performance measurement

Fitzgerald *et al.* (1991) advocate the measurement of service business performance across six dimensions. They propose that managers of every service organization need to develop their own set of performance measures across the six dimensions to monitor the continued relevance of their competitive strategy. Exhibit 15.7 shows the six dimensions with examples of types of performance measures for each dimension. You should note that the dimensions fall into two conceptually different categories. Competitiveness and financial performance reflect the success of the chosen strategy (i.e. ends or results). The remaining four dimensions (quality, flexibility, resource utilization and innovation) are the drivers or determinants of competitive success. Fitzgerald *et al.* conclude that the design

EXHIBIT 15.7

Performance measures for service organizations

	Dimensions of performance	Types of measures
Results	Competitiveness	Relative market share and position
		Sales growth
		Measures of the customer base
	Financial performance	Profitability
		Liquidity
		Capital structure
		Market ratios
Determinants	Quality of service	Reliability
		Responsiveness
		Aesthetics/appearance
		Cleanliness/tidiness
		Comfort
		Friendliness
		Communication
		Courtesy
		Competence
		Access
		Availability
		Security
	Flexibility	Volume flexibility
		Delivery speed flexibility
		Specification flexibility
	Resource utilization	Productivity
		Efficiency
	Innovation	Performance of the innovation process
		Performance of individual innovations

Source: Fitzgerald *et al.* (1991).

of a balanced range of performance measures should be dependent upon the company's service type, competitive environment and chosen strategy.

Moon and Fitzgerald (1996) point out the similarities between the Fitzgerald *et al.* framework and the balanced scorecard. Both frameworks emphasize the need to link performance measures to corporate strategy, include external (customer type) as well as internal measures, include non-financial as well as financial measures and make explicit the trade-offs between the various measures of performance. In addition, both frameworks distinguish between 'results' of actions taken and the 'drivers' or 'determinants' of future performance. The balanced scorecard complements financial measures with operational measures on customer satisfaction, internal processes, and the organization's innovation and improvement activities that are the drivers of future financial performance (Kaplan and Norton, 1992). The Fitzgerald *et al.* framework specifies that measures of financial performance and competitiveness are the 'results' of actions previously taken and reflect the success of the chosen strategy. The remaining four dimensions (quality, flexibility, resource utilization and innovation) are the factors or drivers that determine competitive success, either now or in the future. The objective of both approaches is to ensure that a balanced set of performance measures is used so that no dimension is overly stressed to the detriment of another.

SUMMARY

The following items relate to the learning objectives listed at the beginning of the chapter.

- **Describe three competitive strategies that a firm can adopt to achieve sustainable competitive advantage and explain how they influence management accounting practices.** Porter suggests that a firm has a choice of three generic strategies to achieve sustainable competitive advantage. A firm adopting a cost leadership strategy seeks to be the lowest-cost producer within the industry, thus enabling it to compete on the basis of lower selling prices. A differentiation strategy applies when a firm seeks to offer products or services that are considered by its customers to be superior and unique relative to its competitors. Finally, a firm can adopt a focus strategy, which involves focusing on a narrow segment of the market that has special needs that are poorly served by other competitors. More emphasis is likely to be given to cost controls (e.g. standard costing) in firms pursuing a low-cost strategy whereas firms following a product differentiation strategy are likely to have a greater need for information about new product innovations, design cycle times and marketing cost analysis.

- **Describe the balanced scorecard.** Recent developments in performance evaluation have sought to integrate financial and non-financial measures and assist in clarifying, communicating and managing strategy. The balanced scorecard attempts to meet these requirements. It requires that managers view the business from the following four different perspectives: (a) customer perspective (how do customers see us?); (b) internal business process perspective (what must we excel at?); (c) learning and growth perspective (can we continue to improve and create value?), and (d) financial perspective (how do we look to shareholders?). Organizations should articulate the major goals for each of the four perspectives and then translate these goals into specific performance measures. Each organization must decide what are its critical performance measures. The choice will vary over time and should be linked to the strategy that the organization is following.

- **Explain each of the four perspectives of the balanced scorecard.** The financial perspective provides objectives and associated performance measures relating to the financial outcomes of past actions. Thus, it provides feedback on the success of pursuing the objectives identified for the other three perspectives. In the customer perspective managers identify the customer and market segments in which the businesses unit will compete. Obectives and performance measures should be developed within this perspective that track a business unit's ability to create satisfied and loyal customers in the targeted segments. They relate to market share, customer retention, new customer acquisition, customer satisfaction and customer profitability. In the internal business perspective, managers identify the critical internal processes for which the organization must excel in implementing its strategy. The internal business process objectives and measures should focus on the internal processes that will have the greatest impact on customer satisfaction and achieving the organization's financial objectives. The principal internal business processes include the innovation processes, operation processes and post-service sales processes. The final perspective on the balanced scorecard identifies the infrastructure that the business must build to create long-term growth and improvement. The following three categories have been identified as falling within this perspective: employee capabilities, information system capabilities and motivation, empowerment and alignment.

● **Provide illustrations of performance measures for each of the four perspectives**. Within the financial perspective examples include economic value added and residual income. Market share and customer satisfaction ratings are generic measures within the customer perspective. Typical internal business perspective measures include percentage of sales from new products (innovation processes), cycle time measures such as manufacturing cycle efficiency (operation processes) and percentage returns from customers (post-service sales processes). Measures of employee satisfaction represent generic measures within the learning and growth perspective.

● **Explain how the balanced scorecard links strategy formulation to financial outcomes**. The balanced scorecard philosophy translates an organization's vision and strategy into operational objectives and performance measures for each of the four perspectives. Each performance measure is part of a cause-and-effect relationship involving a linkage from strategy formulation to financial outcomes. Measures of organizational learning and growth are assumed to be the drivers of the internal business processes. The measures of these processes are in turn assumed to be the drivers of measures of customer perspective, while these measures are the driver of the financial perspective. Measurements relating to the non-financial perspectives are assumed to be predictors of future financial performance.

● **Describe the distinguishing characteristics of service organizations that influence performance measurement**. Four unique characteristics distinguishing service companies from manufacturing organizations can be identified. They are (a) most services are intangible; (b) service outputs vary from day to day, since services tend to be provided by individuals whose performance is subject to variability that significantly affects the service quality the customer receives; (c) the production and consumption of many services are inseparable such as in taking a rail journey; and (d) services are perishable and cannot be stored. For example, a hotel contains a fixed number of rooms. If a room is unoccupied, the sales opportunity is lost forever and the resource is wasted.

KEY TERMS AND CONCEPTS

balanced scorecard (p. 367)
cost leadership strategy (p. 366)
customer perspective (p. 367)
customer value propositions (p. 371)
differentiation strategy (p. 366)
financial perspective (p. 367)
focusing strategy (p. 366)
internal business perspective (p. 367)

lagging measures (p. 375)
leading measures (p. 375)
learning and growth perspective (p. 367)
manufacturing cycle efficiency (MCE) (p. 373)
production efficiency ratio (p. 372)
strategic positioning (p. 366)

ASSESSMENT MATERIAL

The review questions are short questions that enable you to assess your understanding of the main topics included in the chapter. The page numbers in parentheses provide you with the page numbers to refer to if you cannot answer a specific question.

The review problems are more complex and require you to relate and apply the content to various business problems. Solutions to review problems are provided in a separate section at the end of the book. Additional review problems can be accessed by lecturers and students on the website (www.drury-online.com). Solutions to these problems are provided for lecturers in the *Instructors' Manual*. This is available on the lecturers' password-protected section of the website.

The website also includes over 30 case study problems. A list of these cases is provided on pages 389–392. The Kinkead Equipment Ltd case study includes elements of strategic performance measurement.

REVIEW QUESTIONS

15.1 How do different competitive strategies influence the emphasis that is given to particular management accounting techniques? *(p. 366)*

15.2 What is the purpose of a balanced scorecard? *(pp. 367–68)*

15.3 Describe the four perspectives of the balanced scorecard. *(pp. 368–74)*

15.4 Explain the differences between lag measures and lead measures. *(p. 375)*

15.5 Explain what is meant by cause-and-effect relationships within the balanced scorecard. *(p. 375)*

15.6 Discuss the benefits and limitations of the balanced scorecard. *(pp. 375–76)*

15.7 Identify and describe the core objectives of the customer perspective. *(p. 371)*

15.8 Describe the three principal internal business processes that can be included within the internal business perspective. *(pp. 371–73)*

15.9 What is manufacturing cycle efficiency? *(p. 373)*

15.10 Describe three principal categories within the learning and growth perspective. *(pp. 373–74)*

15.11 Provide examples of performance measures within each of the four perspectives of the balanced scorecard. *(pp. 370–74)*

15.12 Describe the four unique characteristics distinguishing service companies from manufacturing organizations. *(pp. 378–79)*

REVIEW PROBLEMS

15.13 Financial and non-financial performance measures

BS Ltd provides consultancy services to small and medium-sized businesses. Three types of consultants are employed offering administrative, data processing and marketing advice respectively. The consultants work partly on the client's premises and partly in BS Ltd premises, where chargeable development work in relation to each client contract will be undertaken. Consultants spend some time negotiating with potential clients, attempting to secure contracts from them. BS Ltd has recently implemented a policy change which allows for a number of follow-up (remedial) hours at the client's premises after completion of the contract in order to eliminate any problems that have arisen in the initial stages of operation of the system. Contract negotiation and remedial work hours are not charged directly to each client. BS Ltd carries out consultancy for new systems and also to offer advice on existing systems that a client may have introduced before BS Ltd became involved. BS Ltd has a policy of retaining its consultancy staff at a level of 60 consultants on an ongoing basis.

Additional information for the year ended 30 April is as follows:

(i) BS Ltd invoices clients £75 per chargeable consultant hour.
(ii) Consultant salaries are budgeted at an average per consultant of £30 000 per annum. Actual salaries include a bonus for hours in excess of budget paid for at the budgeted average rate per hour.
(iii) Sundry operating costs (other than consultant salaries) were budgeted at £3 500 000. Actual was £4 100 000.
(iv) BS Ltd capital employed (start of year) was £6 500 000.
(v) Table 1 shows an analysis of sundry budgeted and actual quantitative data.

Required:

(a) (i) Prepare an analysis of actual consultancy hours for the year ended 30 April which shows the increase or decrease from the standard/allowed non-chargeable hours. This increase or decrease should be analysed to show the extent to which it may be shown to be attributable to a change from standard in:
1. standard chargeable hours; 2. remedial advice hours; 3. contract negotiation hours; 4. other non-chargeable hours.

(13 marks)

(ii) Calculate the total value of each of 1 to 4 in (i) above in terms of chargeable client income per hour.

(4 marks)

(b) BS Ltd measures business performance in a number of ways. For each of the undernoted measures, comment on the performance of BS Ltd using quantitative data from the question and your answer to (a) to assist in illustrating your answer:
(i) financial performance;
(ii) competitive performance;
(iii) quality of service;
(iv) flexibility;
(v) resource utilization;
(vi) innovation.

(18 marks)
(Total 35 marks)

Table 1: BS Ltd sundry statistics for year ended 30 April

	Budget	Actual
Number of consultants:		
Administration	30	23
Data processing	12	20
Marketing	18	17
Consultants' hours analysis:		
contract negotiation hours	4 800	9 240
remedial advice hours	2 400	7 920
other non-chargeable hours	12 000	22 440
general development work hours (chargeable)	12 000	6 600
customer premises contract hours	88 800	85 800
Gross hours	120 000	132 000
Chargeable hours analysis:		
new systems	70%	60%
existing systems advice	30%	40%
Number of client enquiries received:		
new systems	450	600
existing systems advice	400	360
Number of client contracts worked on:		
new systems	180	210
existing systems advice	300	288
Number of client complaints	5	20
Contracts requiring remedial advice	48	75

15.14 Financial and non-financial performance measurement in a service organization

The owners of The Eatwell Restaurant have diversified business interests and operate in a wide range of commercial areas. Since buying the restaurant in 2004 they have carefully recorded the data below.

Recorded data for The Eatwell Restaurant (2005–08)

	2005	2006	2007	2008
Total meals served	3 750	5 100	6 200	6 700
Regular customers attending weekly	5	11	15	26
Number of items on offer per day	4	4	7	9
Reported cases of food poisoning	4	5	7	7
Special theme evenings introduced	0	3	9	13
Annual operating hours with no customers	380	307	187	126
Proposals submitted to cater for special events	10	17	29	38
Contracts won to cater for special events	2	5	15	25
Complimentary letters from satisfied customers	0	4	3	6
Average number of customers at peak times	18	23	37	39
Average service delay at peak time (mins)	32	47	15	35
Maximum seating capacity	25	25	40	40
Weekly opening hours	36	36	40	36
Written complaints received	8	12	14	14

Idle time	570	540	465	187
New meals introduced during the year	16	8	27	11
Financial data	**£**	**£**	**£**	**£**
Average customer spend on wine	3	4	4	7
Total turnover	83 000	124 500	137 000	185 000
Turnover from special events	2 000	13 000	25 000	55 000
Profit	11 600	21 400	43 700	57 200
Value of food wasted in preparation	1 700	1 900	3 600	1 450
Total turnover of all restaurants in locality	895 000	1 234 000	980 000	1 056 000

Required:

(a) Assess the overall performance of the business and submit your comments to the owners. They wish to compare the performance of the restaurant with their other business interests and require your comments to be grouped into the key areas of performance such as those described by Fitzgerald and Moon.

(14 marks)

(b) Identify any additional information that you would consider of assistance in assessing the performance of The Eatwell Restaurant in comparison with another restaurant. Give reasons for your selection and explain how they would relate to the key performance area categories used in (a).

(6 marks)
(Total 20 marks)

15.15 CM Limited was formed 10 years ago to provide business equipment solutions to local businesses. It has separate divisions for research, marketing, product design, technology and communication services, and now manufactures and supplies a wide range of business equipment (copiers, scanners, printers, fax machines and similar items).

To date it has evaluated its performance using monthly financial reports that analyse profitability by type of equipment.

The managing director of CM Limited has recently returned from a course on which it had been suggested that the 'balanced scorecard' could be a useful way of measuring performance.

Required:

(a) Explain the balanced scorecard and how it could be used by CM Limited to measure its performance.

(13 marks)

While on the course, the managing director of CM Limited overheard someone mention how the performance of their company had improved after they introduced 'benchmarking'.

Required:

(b) Explain benchmarking and how it could be used to improve the performance of CM Limited.

(12 marks)
(Total 25 marks)

15.16 The introduction of improved quality into products has been a strategy applied by many organizations to obtain competitive advantage. Some organizations believe it is necessary to improve levels of product quality if competitive advantage is to be preserved or strengthened.

Required:

Discuss how a management accountant can assist an organization to achieve competitive advantage by measuring the increase in added value from improvement in its product quality.

(20 marks)

15.17 Performance measurement in non-profit organizations

   (a) The absence of the profit measure in not-for-profit (NFP) organizations causes problems for the measurement of their efficiency and effectiveness.

      You are required to explain:

      (i) why the absence of the profit measure should be a cause of the problems referred to;

(9 marks)

      (ii) how these problems extend to activities within business entities that have a profit motive. Support your answer with examples.

(4 marks)

   (b) A public health clinic is the subject of a scheme to measure its efficiency and effectiveness. Among a number of factors, the 'quality of care provided' has been included as an aspect of the clinic's service to be measured. Three features of 'quality of care provided' have been listed:

- clinic's adherence to appointment times;
- patients' ability to contact the clinic and make appointments without difficulty;
- the provision of a comprehensive patient health monitoring programme.

      You are required to:

      (i) suggest a set of quantitative measures that can be used to identify the effective level of achievement of each of the features listed;

(9 marks)

      (ii) indicate how these measures could be combined into a single 'quality of care' measure.

(3 marks)
(Total 25 marks)

15.18 ZY is an airline operator. It is implementing a balanced scorecard to measure the success of its strategy to expand its operations. It has identified two perspectives and two associated objectives. They are:

Perspective	Objective
Growth	Fly to new destinations
Internal capabilities	Reduce time between touch down and takeoff

(i)   For the 'growth perspective' of ZY, recommend a performance measure and briefly justify your choice of the measure by explaining how it will reflect the success of the strategy.

(2 marks)

(ii)   For the 'internal capabilities perspective' of ZY, state data that you would gather and explain how this could be used to ensure the objective is met.

(2 marks)

CASE STUDIES

The dedicated website for this book includes over 30 case studies. Both students and lecturers can download these case studies from the open access website. The authors of the cases have provided teaching notes for each case and these can be downloaded only by lecturers from the password-protected lecturers' section of the website.

The cases generally cover the content of several chapters and contain questions to which there is no ideal answer. They are intended to encourage independent thought and initiative and to relate and apply the content of this book to more uncertain situations. They are also intended to develop critical thinking and analytical skills.

Details relating to the cases that are available from the website are listed below.

Airport Complex Peter Nordgaard and Carsten Rhode, Copenhagen Business School
A general case providing material for discussion of several aspects involved in the management control of a service company, which is mainly characterized by mass services.

Anjo Ltd Lin Fitzgerald, Loughborough University Business School
Variance analysis that provides the opportunity to be used as a role playing exercise.

Berkshire Threaded Fasteners Company John Shank, The Amos Tuck School of Business Administration, Dartmouth College
Cost analysis for dropping a product, for pricing, for product mix and product improvement.

Berkshire Toy Company D. Crawford and E.G. Henry, State University of New York (SUNY) at Oswego
Variance analysis, performance evaluation, responsibility accounting and the balanced scorecard.

Blessed Farm Partnership Rona O'Brien, Sheffield Hallam University
Strategic decision-making, evaluation of alternatives, ethics, sources of information.

Boston Creamery John Shank, The Amos Tuck School of Business Administration, Dartmouth College
Management control systems, profit planning, profit variance analysis and flexible budgets.

Brunswick Plastics Anthony Atkinson, University of Waterloo and adapted by John Shank, The Amos Tuck School of Business Administration, Dartmouth College
Relevant cost analysis for a new product, short-run versus strategic considerations, pricing considerations.

Chadwick's Department Store Lewis Gordon, Liverpool John Moores University
The application of budget-building techniques and spreadsheet skills to a retail sector situation.

Company A Mike Tayles, University of Hull Business School and Paul Walley, Warwick Business School
Evaluation of a product costing system and suggested performance measures to support key success factors.

Company B Mike Tayles, University of Hull Business School and Paul Walley, Warwick Business School
The impact of a change in manufacturing strategy and method upon product costing and performance measurement systems.

Danfoss Drives Dan Otzen, Copenhagen Business School
The linkage between operational management and management accounting/control of a company including a discussion of the operational implications of JIT for management accounting.

Dumbellow Ltd Stan Brignall, Aston Business School
Marginal costing versus absorption costing, relevant costs and cost–volume–profit analysis.

Edit 4U Ltd Rona O'Brien, Sheffield Hallam University
The case study explores and evaluates the role of management accounting information in a small business context.

Electronic Boards plc John Innes, University of Dundee and Falconer Mitchell, University of Edinburgh
A general case that may be used at an introductory stage to illustrate the basics of management accounting and the role it can play within a firm.

Endeavour Twoplise Ltd Jayne Ducker, Antony Head, Brenda McDonnell, Sheffield Hallam University and Susan Richardson, Sheffield University
Functional budget and master budget construction, budgetary control and decision-making.

Fleet Ltd Lin Fitzgerald, Loughborough University Business School
Outsourcing decision involving relevant costs and qualitative factors.

Fosters Construction Ltd Deryl Northcott, Auckland University of Technology
Capital investment appraisal, relevant cash flows, taxation, inflation, uncertainty, post-audits.

Global Ltd Susan Richardson, Sheffield University
Cash budgeting, links between cash and profit, pricing/bidding, information system design and behavioural aspects of management control.

Hardhat Ltd Stan Brignall, Aston Business School
Cost–volume–profit analysis.

High Street Reproduction Furniture Ltd Jayne Ducker, Antony Head, Rona O'Brien, Sheffield Hallam University and Sue Richardson, Sheffield University
Relevant costs, strategic decision-making and limiting factors.

Integrated Technology Services (UK) Ltd Mike Johnson, University of Dundee
An examination of the planning and control framework of an information services business which provides outsourced computing support services to large industrial and government organizations.

Kinkead Equipment Ltd John Shank, The Amos Tuck School of Business Administration, Dartmouth College
Profit variance analysis that emphasizes how variance analysis should be redirected to consider strategic issues.

Lynch Printers Peter Clarke, University College Dublin
Cost-plus pricing within the context of correctly forecasting activity for a forthcoming period in order to determine the overhead rates. The case illustrates that a company can make a loss even when an anticipated profit margin is added to all jobs.

Majestic Lodge John Shank, The Amos Tuck School of Business Administration, Dartmouth College
Relevant costs and cost–volume–profit analysis.

Maxcafe Ltd Colin Drury, University of Huddersfield.
Design of management accounting control systems.

Merrion Products Ltd Peter Clarke, University College Dublin
Cost–volume–profit analysis, relevant costs and limiting factors.

Mestral Robin Roslender, Heriot-Watt University, Edinburgh
The different roles and purposes of management accounting.

Moult Hall Jayne Ducker, Antony Head, Brenda McDonnell, Sheffield Hallam University and Susan Richardson, Sheffield University
Organizational objectives, strategic decision-making, evaluation of alternatives, relevant costs, debating the profit ethos, break-even analysis.

Oak City R.W. Ingram, W.C. Parsons, University of Alabama and W.A. Robbins, Attorney, Pearson and Sutton
Cost allocation in a government setting to determine the amount of costs that should be charged to business for municipal services. The case also includes ethical considerations.

Quality Shopping Rona O'Brien, Sheffield Hallam University
Departmental budget construction, credit checking, environmental issues, behavioural issues and management control systems.

Rawhide Development Company Bill Doolin, Deryl Northcott, Auckland University of Technology
Capital investment appraisal involving relevant cash flows, uncertainty, application of spreadsheet tools and social considerations.

Reichard Maschinen, GmbH Professor John Shank, The Amos Tuck School of Business Administration, Dartmouth College
Relevant costs and pricing decisions.

Rogatec Ltd Jayne Ducker, Antony Head, Brenda McDonnell, Sheffield Hallam University and Susan Richardson, Sheffield University
Standard costing and variance analysis, budgets, ethics, sources of information.

Southern Paper Inc – ERP in Spain Martin Quinn, Dublin City University
Control issues faced by internal accounting functions with ERP systems.

The Beta Company Peter Clarke, University College Dublin
Cost estimation involving regression analysis and relevant costs.

Traditions Ltd Jayne Ducker, Antony Head, Brenda McDonnell, Sheffield Hallam University and Susan Richardson, Sheffield University
Relevant cost analysis relating to a discontinuation decision and budgeting.

BIBLIOGRAPHY

Abernethy, M.A., Lillis, A.M., Brownell, P. and Carter, P. (2001) Product diversity and costing system design: field study evidence, *Management Accounting Research*, **12**(3), 261–80.

Abu-Serdaneh, J. (2004) Transfer Pricing in UK Manufacturing Companies, PhD dissertation, University of Huddersfield.

Al-Omiri, M. and Drury, C. (2007), A survey of the factors influencing the choice of product costing systems in UK organizations, *Management Accounting Research,* **18**(4), 399–424.

American Accounting Association (1957) *Accounting and Reporting Standards for Corporate Financial Statements and Preceding Statements and Supplements*, 4.

American Accounting Association (1966) *A Statement of Basic Accounting Theory*, American Accounting Association.

American Accounting Association Financial Accounting Standards Committee (2002), Recommendations on disclosure on non-financial performance disclosures, *Accounting Horizons*, **16**(4), 353–62.

Armitage, H.M. and Nicholson, R. (1993) Activity based costing: a survey of Canadian practice, Issue Paper No. 3, Society of Management Accountants of Canada.

Arnold, G.C. and Hatzopoulos, P.D. (2000) The theory–practice gap in capital budgeting: evidence from the United Kingdom, *Journal of Business Finance and Accounting*, **27**(5) and (6), June/July, 603–26.

Ask, U. and Ax, C. (1992) Trends in the Development of Product Costing Practices and Techniques – A Survey of Swedish Manufacturing Industry, Paper presented at the 15th Annual Congress of the European Accounting Association, Madrid.

Ask, U., Ax, C. and Jonsson, S. (1996) Cost management in Sweden: from modern to post-modern, in Bhimani, A. (ed.) *Management Accounting: European Perspectives*, Oxford, Oxford University Press, 199–217.

Ballas, A. and Venieris, G. (1996) A survey of management accounting practices in Greek firms, in Bhimani, A. (ed.) *Management Accounting: European Perspectives*, Oxford, Oxford University Press, 123–39.

Barbato, M.B., Collini, P. and Quagli, C. (1996) Management accounting in Italy, in Bhimani, A. (ed.) *Management Accounting: European Perspectives*, Oxford, Oxford University Press, 140–63.

Barrett, M.E. and Fraser, L.B. (1977) Conflicting roles in budget operations, *Harvard Business Review*, July–August, 137–46.

Baxter, W.T. and Oxenfeldt, A.R. (1961) Costing and pricing: the cost accountant versus the economist, *Business Horizons*, Winter, 77–90; also in *Studies in Cost Analysis*, 2nd edn (ed. D. Solomons) Sweet and Maxwell (1968), 293–312.

Berliner, C. and Brimson, J.A. (1988) *Cost Management for Today's Advanced Manufacturing*, Harvard Business School Press.

Bjornenak T. (1997a) Diffusion and accounting: the case of ABC in Norway, *Management Accounting Research*, **8**(1), 317.

Bjornenak T. (1997b) Conventional wisdom and accounting practices, *Management Accounting Research*, **8**(4), 367–82.

Blayney, P. and Yokoyama, I. (1991) Comparative Analysis of Japanese and Australian Cost Accounting and Management Practices, Working paper, University of Sydney, Australia.

Boons, A., Roozen, R.A. and Weerd, R.J. de (1994) Kosteninformatie in de Nederlandse Industrie, in *Relevantie methoden en ontwikkelingen* (Rotterdam: Coopers and Lybrand).

Borkowski, S.C. (1990) Environmental and organizational factors affecting transfer pricing: a survey, *Journal of Management Accounting Research*, **2**, 78–99.

Brierley, J.A., Cowton, C.J. and Drury, C. (2001) Research into product costing practice: a European perspective, *The European Accounting Review*, **10**(2), 215–56.

Brounen, D., de Jong, A. and Koedijk, K. (2004) Corporate finance in Europe: confronting theory with practice, *Financial Management*, **33**(4), 71–101.

Bruggerman, W., Slagmulder, R. and Waeytens, D. (1996) Management accounting changes; the Belgian experience, in Bhimani, A. (ed.) *Management Accounting: European Perspectives*, Oxford, Oxford University Press, 1–30.

Burchell, S., Clubb, C., Hopwood, A.G., Hughes, J. and Jahapier, J. (1980) The roles of accounting in organizations and society, *Accounting, Organisations and Society*, **1**, 5–27.

Chenhall, R.H. and Langfield-Smith, K. (1998) Adoption and benefits of management accounting practices: an Australian perspective, *Management Accounting Research*, **9**(1), 120.

Chow, C., Haddad, K. and Williamson, J. (1997) Applying the balanced scorecard to small companies, *Management Accounting*, August, 21–7.

Clarke, P.J. (1992) Management Accounting Practices and Techniques in Irish Manufacturing Firms, The 15th Annual Congress of the European Accounting Association, Madrid, Spain.

Clarke, P. (1995) Management Accounting Practices and Techniques in Irish Manufacturing Companies, Working paper, Trinity College, Dublin.

Cooper, R. (1990a) Cost classifications in unit-based and activity-based manufacturing cost systems, *Journal of Cost Management*, Fall, 4–14.

Cooper, R. (1990b) Explicating the logic of ABC, *Management Accounting*, November, 58–60.

Cooper, R. (1997) Activity-based costing: theory and practice, in Brinker, B.J. (ed.), *Handbook of Cost Management*, Warren, Gorham and Lamont, B1–B33.

Cooper, R. and Kaplan, R.S. (1987) How cost accounting systematically distorts product costs, in *Accounting and Management: Field Study Perspectives* (eds W.J. Bruns and R.S. Kaplan), Harvard Business School Press, Ch. 8.

Cooper, R. and Kaplan, R.S. (1988) Measure costs right: make the right decisions, *Harvard Business Review*, September/October, 96–103.

Cooper, R. and Kaplan, R.S. (1991) *The Design of Cost Management Systems: Text, Cases and Readings*, Prentice-Hall.

Cooper, R. and Kaplan, R.S. (1992) Activity based systems: measuring the costs of resource usage, *Accounting Horizons*, September, 1–13.

Cornick, M., Cooper, W. and Wilson, S. (1988) How do companies analyse overhead?, *Management Accounting*, June, 41–3.

Cress, W. and Pettijohn, J. (1985) A survey of budget-related planning and control policies and procedures, *Journal of Accounting Education*, **3**, Fall, 61–78.

Dekker, H.C. (2003a) Value chain analysis in interfirm relationships: a field study, *Management Accounting Research*, **14**(1), 1–23.

Dekker, H. and Smidt, P. (2003b) A survey of the adoption and use of target costing in Dutch firms, *International Journal of Production Economics*, **84**(3), 293–306.

Drucker, P.F. (1964) Controls, control and management, in *Management Controls: New Directions in Basic Research* (eds C.P. Bonini, R. Jaedicke and H. Wagner), McGraw-Hill.

Drury, C. (2008) *Management and Cost Accounting*, Cengage Learning EMEA.

Drury, C., Braund, S., Osborne, P. and Tayles, M. (1993) A Survey of Management Accounting Practices in UK Manufacturing Companies, ACCA Research Paper, Chartered Association of Certified Accountants.

Drury, C. and El-Shishini, H. (2005) *Divisional Performance Measurement,* Chartered Institute of Management Accountants.

Drury, C. and Tayles, M. (1994) Product costing in UK manufacturing organisations, *The European Accounting Review*, **3**(3), 443–69.

Drury, C. and Tayles, M. (2000) *Cost System Design and Profitability Analysis in UK Companies*, Chartered Institute of Management Accountants.

Drury, C. and Tayles M. (2005) Explicating the design of overhead absorption procedures in UK organizations, *British Accounting Review*, **37**(1), 47–84.

Drury, C. and Tayles, M. (2006) Profitability analysis in UK organizations: An exploratory study, *British Accounting Review*, **38**(4), 405–25.

Dugdale, D., Jones, T.C. and Green, S. (2006) *Contemporary Management Accounting Practices in UK Manufacturing Companies*, Chartered Institute of Management Accountants.

Dugdale, D. and Lyne, S. (2006) Are budgets still needed?, *Financial Management*, November, 32–5.

Ekholm, B-G. and Wallin, J. (2000) Is the annual budget really dead?, *The European Accounting Review*, **9**(4), 519–39.

El-Shishini, H. and Drury, C. (2001) Divisional Performance Measurement in UK Companies, Paper presented to the Annual Congress of the European Accounting Association, Athens.

Epstein, M. and Manzoni, J.F. (1998) Implementing corporate strategy: From tableaux de bord to balanced scorecards, *European Management Journal*, **16**(2), 190–203.

Epstein, M. and Roy, M.J. (1997) Environmental management to improve corporate profitability, *Journal of Cost Management*, November–December, 26–34.

Fitzgerald, L., Johnston, R., Brignall, T.J., Silvestro, R. and Voss, C. (1991) *Performance Measurement in Service Businesses*, Chartered Institute of Management Accountants.

Fitzgerald, L., Johnston, R., Silvestro, R. and Steele, A. (1989) Management control in service industries, *Management Accounting*, April, 44–6.

Fitzgerald, L. and Moon, P. (1996) *Performance Management in Service Industries*, Chartered Institute of Management Accountants.

Fremgen, J.M. and Liao, S.S. (1981) *The Allocation of Corporate Indirect Costs*, National Association of Accountants, New York.

Friedman, A.L. and Lynne, S.R. (1995) *Activity-based Techniques: The Real Life Consequences*, Chartered Institute of Management Accountants.

Friedman, A.L. and Lynne, S.R. (1999) *Success and Failure of Activity-based Techniques: A Long-term Perspective*, Chartered Institute of Management Accountants.

Granlund, M. and Lukka, K. (1998) It's a small world of management accounting practices, *Journal of Management Accounting Research*, **10**, 151–79.

Guilding, C., Drury, C. and Tayles, M. (2005) An empirical investigation of the importance of cost-plus pricing, *Managerial Auditing Journal,* **20** (2), 125–37.

Guilding, C., Lamminmaki, D. and Drury, C. (1998) Budgeting and standard costing practices in New Zealand and the United Kingdom, *The International Journal of Accounting*, **33**(5), 41–60.

Hansen, D.R. and Mendoza, R. (1999) Costos de Impacto Ambiental: Su Medicion, Asignacion, y Control, *INCAE Revista*, Vol. X, No. 2.

Hergert, M. and Morris, D. (1989) Accounting data for value chain analysis, *Strategic Management Journal*, **10**, 175–88.

Hope, J. and Fraser, R. (2003) Who needs budgets?, *Harvard Business Review*, February, 42–8.

Innes, J. and Mitchell, F. (1995a) A survey of activity-based costing in the UK's largest companies, *Management Accounting Research*, June, 137–54.

Innes, J. and Mitchell, F. (1995b) Activity-based costing, in *Issues in Management Accounting* (eds D. Ashton, T. Hopper and R.W. Scapens), Prentice-Hall, 115–36.

Innes, J., Mitchell, F. and Sinclear, D. (2000) Activity-based costing in the UK's largest companies: a comparison of 1994 and 1999 survey results, *Management Accounting Research*, **11**(3), 349–62.

Israelsen, P., Anderson, M., Rohde, C. and Sorensen, P.E. (1996) Management accounting in Denmark: theory and practice, in Bhimani, A. (ed.) *Management Accounting: European Perspectives*, Oxford, Oxford University Press, 31–53.

Johnson, H.T. (1990) Professors, customers and value: bringing a global perspective to management accounting education, in *Performance Excellence in Manufacturing and Services Organizations* (ed. P. Turney), American Accounting Association.

Johnson, H.T. and Kaplan, R.S. (1987) *Relevance Lost: The Rise and Fall of Management Accounting*, Harvard Business School Press.

Johnson, G. and Scholes, K. (2005) *Exploring Corporate Strategy*, Prentice-Hall.

Joseph, N., Turley, S., Burns, J., Lewis, L., Scapens, R.W. and Southworth, A. (1996) External financial reporting and management information: A survey of UK management accountants, *Management Accounting Research* 7(1), 73–94.

Joye, M.P. and Blayney, P.J. (1991) Strategic Management accounting survey, Monograph No. 8, University of Sydney.

Kald, M. and Nilsson, F. (2000) Performance measurement at Nordic companies, *European Management Journal*, 1, 113–27.

Kaplan, R.S. (1994) Management accounting (1984–1994): development of new practice and theory, *Management Accounting Research*, September and December, 247–60.

Kaplan, R.S. and Cooper, R. (1998) *Cost and Effect: Using Integrated Systems to Drive Profitability and Performance*, Harvard Business School Press.

Kaplan, R.S. and Norton, D.P. (1992) The balanced scorecard: measures that drive performance, *Harvard Business Review*, Jan–Feb, 71–9.

Kaplan, R.S. and Norton, D.P. (1993) Putting the balanced scorecard to work, *Harvard Business Review*, September–October, 134–47.

Kaplan, R.S. and Norton, D.P. (1996a) Using the balanced scorecard as a strategic management system, *Harvard Business Review*, Jan–Feb, 75–85.

Kaplan, R.S. and Norton, D.P. (1996b) *The Balanced Scorecard: Translating Strategy Into Action*, Harvard Business School Press.

Kaplan, R.S. and Norton, D.P. (2001a) *The Strategy-focused Organization*, Harvard Business School Press.

Kaplan, R.S. and Norton, D.P. (2001b) Balance without profit, *Financial Management*, January, 23–6.

Kaplan, R.S. and Norton, D.P. (2001c) Transforming the balanced scorecard from performance measurement to strategic management: Part 1, *Accounting Horizons*, March, 87–104.

Kaplan, R.S. and Norton, D.P. (2001d) Transforming the balanced scorecard from performance measurement to strategic management: Part 2, *Accounting Horizons*, June, 147–60.

Langfield-Smith, K. (1997) Management control systems and strategy: a critical review, *Accounting, Organizations and Society*, **22**, 207–32.

Lauderman, M. and Schaeberle, F.W. (1983) The cost accounting practices of firms using standard costs, *Cost and Management* (Canada), July/August, 21–5.

Leauby, B.A. and Wentzel, K. (2002) Know the score: the balanced scorecard approach to strategically assist clients, *Pennsylvania CPA Journal*, Spring, 29–32.

Lukka, K. and Granlund, M. (1996) Cost accounting in Finland: current practice and trends of development, *The European Accounting Review*, **5**(1), 1–28.

Macintosh, N.B. (1985) *The Social Software of Accounting and Information Systems*, Wiley.

Macintosh, N.B. (1994) *Management Accounting and Control Systems: An Organisational and Behavioural Approach*, Wiley.

Malmi, T. (2001) Balanced scorecards in Finnish companies: a research note, *Management Accounting Research*, **12**(2), 207–20.

Merchant, K.A. (1998) *Modern Management Control Systems: Text and Cases*, Prentice-Hall, New Jersey.

Moon, P. and Fitzgerald, L. (1996) *Performance Measurement in Service Industries: Making it Work*, Chartered Institute of Management Accountants, London.

Norreklit, H. (2000) The balance on the balanced scorecard – a critical analysis of some of its assumptions, *Management Accounting Research*, Vol. 11, No. 1, pp 65–88.

Norreklit, H. (2003) The balanced scorecard: what is the score? A rhetorical analysis of the balanced scorecard, *Accounting, Organizations and Society*, **28**, 591–619.

Oliveras, E. and Amat, O. (2002) The Balanced Scorecard Assumptions and the Drivers of Business Growth, Paper presented at the 25th Annual Congress of the European Accounting Association, Copenhagan, Denmark.

Olve, N., Roy, J. and Wetter, M. (2000) *Performance Drivers: A Practical Guide to Using the Balanced Scorecard*, John Wiley & Sons.

Osni, M. (1973) Factor analysis of behavioural variables affecting budgetary stock, *The Accounting Review*, 535–48.

Otley, D.T. (1987) *Accounting Control and Organizational Behaviour*, Heinemann.

Ouchi, W.G. (1979) A conceptual framework for the design of organizational control mechanisms, *Management Science*, 833–48.

Pere, T. (1999) How the Execution of Strategy is Followed in Large Organisations Located in Finland, Masters Thesis (Helsinki School of Economics and Business Administration).

Phyrr, P.A. (1976) Zero-based budgeting – where to use it and how to begin, *S.A.M. Advanced Management Journal*, Summer, 5.

Pike, R.H. (1996) A longitudinal study of capital budgeting practices, *Journal of Business Finance and Accounting*, **23**(1), 79–92.

Plunkett, J.J., Dale, B.G. and Tyrrell, R.W. (1985) *Quality Costs*, London, Department of Trade and Industry.

Porter, M. (1985) *Competitive Advantage*, New York, Free Press.

Ramadan, S.S. (1989) The rationale for cost allocation: A study of UK companies, *Accounting and Business Research*, Winter, 31–7.

Ranganathan, J. and Ditz, D. (1996) Environmental accounting: a tool for better management, *Management Accounting*, February, 38–40.

Reece, J.S. and Cool, W.R. (1978) Measuring investment centre performance, *Harvard Business Review*, May/June 29–49.

Saez-Torrecilla, A., Fernandez-Fernandez, A., Texeira-Quiros, J. and Vaquera-Mosquero, M. (1996) Management accounting in Spain: trends in thought and practice, in Bhimani, A. (ed.) *Management Accounting: European Perspective 3*, Oxford, Oxford University Press, 180–90.

Scarborough, P.A., Nanni, A. and Sakurai, M. (1991) Japanese management accounting practices and the effects of assembly and process automation, *Management Accounting Research*, **2**, 27–46.

Scherrer, G. (1996) Management accounting: a German perspective, in Bhimani, A. (ed.), *Management Accounting: European Perspectives*, Oxford, Oxford University Press, 100–22.

Schwarzbach, H.R. (1985) The impact of automation on accounting for direct costs, *Management Accounting* (USA), **67**(6), 45–50.

Shank, J.K. (1989) Strategic cost management: new wine or just new bottles?, *Journal of Management Accounting Research* (USA), Fall, 47–65.

Shank, J. and Govindarajan, V. (1992) Strategic cost management: the value chain perspective, *Journal of Management Accounting Research*, **4**, 179–97.

Silk, S. (1998) Automating the balanced scorecard, *Management Accounting*, May, 38–44.

Simon, H.A. (1959) Theories of decision making in economics and behavioural science, *The American Economic Review*, June, 233–83.

Sizer, J. (1989) *An Insight into Management Accounting*, Penguin, Chs 11–12.

Skinner, R.C. (1990) The role of profitability in divisional decision making and performance, *Accounting and Business Research*, Spring, 135–41.

Solomons, D. (1965) *Divisional Performance: Measurement and Control*, R.D. Irwin.

Speckbacher, G., Bischof, J. and Pfeiffer, T. (2003) A descriptive analysis on the implementation of balanced scorecards in German-speaking countries, *Management Accounting Research*, **14**(4), 361–88.

Tang, R. (1992) Canadian transfer pricing in the 1990s, *Management Accounting* (USA), February.

Umapathy, S. (1987) *Current Budgeting Practices in U.S. Industry: The State of the Art*, New York, Quorum.

Virtanen, K., Malmi, T., Vaivio, J. and Kasanen, E. (1996) Drivers of management accounting in Finland, in Bhimani, A. (ed.) *Management Accounting: European Perspectives*, Oxford, Oxford University Press, 218–41.

Zuriekat, M. (2005) Performance Measurement Systems: An Examination of the Influence of Contextual Factors and Their Impact on Performance with Specific Emphasis on the Balanced Scorecard Approach, PhD dissertation, University of Huddersfield.

APPENDIX A: PRESENT VALUE OF £1 AFTER n YEARS = $£1/(1+k)^n$

Years hence	1%	2%	4%	6%	8%	10%	12%	14%	15%	16%
1	0.990	0.980	0.962	0.943	0.926	0.909	0.893	0.877	0.870	0.862
2	0.980	0.961	0.925	0.890	0.857	0.826	0.797	0.769	0.756	0.743
3	0.971	0.942	0.889	0.840	0.794	0.751	0.712	0.675	0.658	0.641
4	0.961	0.924	0.855	0.792	0.735	0.683	0.636	0.592	0.572	0.552
5	0.951	0.906	0.822	0.747	0.681	0.621	0.567	0.519	0.497	0.476
6	0.942	0.888	0.790	0.705	0.630	0.564	0.507	0.456	0.432	0.410
7	0.933	0.871	0.760	0.665	0.583	0.513	0.452	0.400	0.376	0.354
8	0.923	0.853	0.731	0.627	0.540	0.467	0.404	0.351	0.327	0.305
9	0.914	0.837	0.703	0.592	0.500	0.424	0.361	0.308	0.284	0.263
10	0.905	0.820	0.676	0.558	0.463	0.386	0.322	0.270	0.247	0.227
11	0.896	0.804	0.650	0.527	0.429	0.350	0.287	0.237	0.215	0.195
12	0.887	0.788	0.625	0.497	0.397	0.319	0.257	0.208	0.187	0.168
13	0.879	0.773	0.601	0.469	0.368	0.290	0.229	0.182	0.163	0.145
14	0.870	0.758	0.577	0.442	0.340	0.263	0.205	0.160	0.141	0.125
15	0.861	0.743	0.555	0.417	0.315	0.239	0.183	0.140	0.123	0.108
16	0.853	0.728	0.534	0.394	0.292	0.218	0.163	0.123	0.107	0.093
17	0.844	0.714	0.513	0.371	0.270	0.198	0.146	0.108	0.093	0.080
18	0.836	0.700	0.494	0.350	0.250	0.180	0.130	0.095	0.081	0.069
19	0.828	0.686	0.475	0.331	0.232	0.164	0.116	0.083	0.070	0.060
20	0.820	0.673	0.456	0.312	0.215	0.149	0.104	0.073	0.061	0.051

Years hence	18%	20%	22%	24%	25%	26%	28%	30%	35%
1	0.847	0.833	0.820	0.806	0.800	0.794	0.781	0.769	0.741
2	0.718	0.694	0.672	0.650	0.640	0.630	0.610	0.592	0.549
3	0.609	0.579	0.551	0.524	0.512	0.500	0.477	0.455	0.406
4	0.516	0.482	0.451	0.423	0.410	0.397	0.373	0.350	0.301
5	0.437	0.402	0.370	0.341	0.328	0.315	0.291	0.269	0.223
6	0.370	0.335	0.303	0.275	0.262	0.250	0.227	0.207	0.165
7	0.314	0.279	0.249	0.222	0.210	0.198	0.178	0.159	0.122
8	0.266	0.233	0.204	0.179	0.168	0.157	0.139	0.123	0.091
9	0.225	0.194	0.167	0.144	0.134	0.125	0.108	0.094	0.067
10	0.191	0.162	0.137	0.116	0.107	0.099	0.085	0.073	0.050
11	0.162	0.135	0.112	0.094	0.086	0.079	0.066	0.056	0.037
12	0.137	0.112	0.092	0.076	0.069	0.062	0.052	0.043	0.027
13	0.116	0.093	0.075	0.061	0.055	0.050	0.040	0.033	0.020
14	0.099	0.078	0.062	0.049	0.044	0.039	0.032	0.025	0.015
15	0.084	0.065	0.051	0.040	0.035	0.031	0.025	0.020	0.011
16	0.071	0.054	0.042	0.032	0.028	0.025	0.019	0.015	0.008
17	0.060	0.045	0.034	0.026	0.023	0.020	0.015	0.012	0.006
18	0.051	0.038	0.028	0.021	0.018	0.016	0.012	0.009	0.005
19	0.043	0.031	0.023	0.017	0.014	0.012	0.009	0.007	0.003
20	0.037	0.026	0.019	0.014	0.012	0.010	0.007	0.005	0.002

APPENDIX B: PRESENT VALUE OF AN ANNUITY OF £1
RECEIVED ANNUALLY FOR n YEARS $= \frac{£1}{K}\left(1-\frac{1}{(1+K)^n}\right)$

Years hence	1%	2%	4%	6%	8%	10%	12%	14%	15%	16%	18%
1	0.990	0.980	0.962	0.943	0.926	0.909	0.893	0.877	0.870	0.862	0.847
2	1.970	1.942	1.886	1.833	1.783	1.736	1.690	1.647	1.626	1.605	1.566
3	2.941	2.884	2.775	2.673	2.577	2.487	2.402	2.322	2.283	2.246	2.174
4	3.902	3.808	3.630	3.465	3.312	3.170	3.037	2.914	2.855	2.798	2.690
5	4.853	4.713	4.452	4.212	3.993	3.791	3.605	3.433	3.352	3.274	3.127
6	5.795	5.601	5.242	4.917	4.623	4.355	4.111	3.889	3.784	3.685	3.498
7	6.728	6.472	6.002	5.582	5.206	4.868	4.564	4.288	4.160	4.039	3.812
8	7.652	7.325	6.733	6.210	5.747	5.335	4.968	4.639	4.487	4.344	4.078
9	8.566	8.162	7.435	6.802	6.247	5.759	5.328	4.946	4.772	4.607	4.303
10	9.471	8.983	8.111	7.360	6.710	6.145	5.650	5.216	5.019	4.833	4.494
11	10.368	9.787	8.760	7.887	7.139	6.495	5.937	5.453	5.234	5.029	4.656
12	11.255	10.575	9.385	8.384	7.536	6.814	6.194	5.660	5.421	5.197	4.793
13	12.134	11.343	9.986	8.853	7.904	7.103	6.424	5.842	5.583	5.342	4.910
14	13.004	12.106	10.563	9.295	8.244	7.367	6.628	6.002	5.724	5.468	5.008
15	13.865	12.849	11.118	9.712	8.559	7.606	6.811	6.142	5.847	5.575	5.092
16	14.718	13.578	11.652	10.106	8.851	7.824	6.974	6.265	5.954	5.669	5.162
17	15.562	14.292	12.166	10.477	9.122	8.022	7.120	6.373	6.047	5.749	5.222
18	16.398	14.992	12.659	10.828	9.372	8.201	7.250	6.467	6.128	5.818	5.273
19	17.226	15.678	13.134	11.815	9.604	8.365	7.366	6.550	6.198	5.877	5.316
20	18.046	16.351	13.590	11.470	9.818	8.514	7.469	6.623	6.259	5.929	5.353

Years hence	20%	22%	24%	25%	26%	28%	30%	35%	36%	37%
1	0.833	0.820	0.806	0.800	0.794	0.781	0.769	0.741	0.735	0.730
2	1.528	1.492	1.457	1.440	1.424	1.392	1.361	1.289	1.276	1.263
3	2.106	2.042	1.981	1.952	1.923	1.868	1.816	1.696	1.673	1.652
4	2.589	2.494	2.404	2.362	2.320	2.241	2.166	1.997	1.966	1.935
5	2.991	2.864	2.745	2.689	2.635	2.532	2.436	2.220	2.181	2.143
6	3.326	3.167	3.020	2.951	2.885	2.759	2.643	2.385	2.339	2.294
7	3.605	3.416	3.242	3.161	3.083	2.937	2.802	2.508	2.455	2.404
8	3.837	3.619	3.421	3.329	3.241	3.076	2.925	2.598	2.540	2.485
9	4.031	3.786	3.566	3.463	3.366	3.184	3.019	2.665	2.603	2.544
10	4.192	3.923	3.682	3.571	3.465	3.269	3.092	2.715	2.649	2.587
11	4.327	4.035	3.776	3.656	3.544	3.335	3.147	2.752	2.683	2.618
12	4.439	4.127	3.851	3.725	3.606	3.387	3.190	2.779	2.708	2.641
13	4.533	4.203	3.912	3.780	3.656	3.427	3.223	2.799	2.727	2.658
14	4.611	4.265	3.962	3.824	3.695	3.459	3.249	2.814	2.740	2.670
15	4.675	4.315	4.001	3.859	3.726	3.483	3.268	2.825	2.750	2.679
16	4.730	4.357	4.033	3.887	3.751	3.503	3.283	2.834	2.757	2.685
17	4.775	4.391	4.059	3.910	3.771	3.518	3.295	2.840	2.763	2.690
18	4.812	4.419	4.080	3.928	3.786	3.529	3.304	2.844	2.767	2.693
19	4.844	4.442	4.097	3.942	3.799	3.539	3.311	2.848	2.770	2.696
20	4.870	4.460	4.110	3.954	3.808	3.546	3.316	2.850	2.772	2.698

ANSWERS TO REVIEW PROBLEMS

Chapter 2

2.14 (a) SV (or variable if direct labour can be matched exactly to output)
(b) F
(c) F
(d) V
(e) F (Advertising is a discretionary cost. See Chapter 9, Zero-based budgeting for an explanation of this cost.)
(f) SV
(g) F
(h) SF
(i) V

2.15 Controllable c, d, f
Non-controllable a, b, e, g, h

2.16 Answer = B

2.17 Answer = B

2.18 Answer = B

2.19 (a) (i) Schedule of annual mileage costs

	5000 miles (£)	10 000 miles (£)	15 000 miles (£)	30 000 miles (£)
Variable costs:				
Spares	100	200	300	600
Petrol	380	760	1140	2280
Total variable cost	480	960	1440	2880
Variable cost per mile	0.096	0.096	0.096	0.096
Fixed costs				
Depreciation[a]	2000	2000	2000	2000
Maintenance	120	120	120	120
Vehicle licence	80	80	80	80
Insurance	150	150	150	150
Tyres[b]	—	—	75	150
	2350	2350	2425	2500
Fixed cost per mile	0.47	0.235	0.162	0.083
Total cost	2830	3310	3865	5380
Total cost per mile	0.566	0.331	0.258	0.179

Notes

[a]Annual depreciation $= \dfrac{\text{£5500 (cost)} - \text{£1500 (trade-in price)}}{2 \text{ years}} = \text{£2000}$

[b]At 15 000 miles per annum tyres will be replaced once during the two-year period at a cost of £150. The average cost per year is £75. At 30 000 miles per annum tyres will be replaced once each year.

Comments

Tyres are a semi-fixed cost. In the above calculations they have been regarded as a step fixed cost. An alternative approach would be to regard the semi-fixed cost as a variable cost by dividing £150 tyre replacement by 25 000 miles. This results in a variable cost per mile of £0.006.

Depreciation and maintenance cost have been classified as fixed costs. They are likely to be semi-variable costs, but in the absence of any additional information they have been classified as fixed costs.

(ii) See Figure 2.19.

(iii) The respective costs can be obtained from the vertical dashed lines in the graph (Figure 2.19).

(b) The *cost per mile* declines as activity increases. This is because the majority of costs are fixed and do not increase when mileage increases. However, *total cost* will increase with increases in mileage.

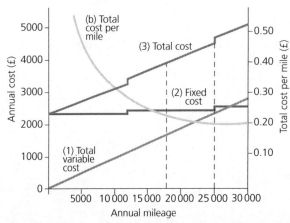

Figure 2.19 *The step increase in fixed cost is assumed to occur at an annual mileage of 12 500 and 25 000 miles, because tyres are assumed to be replaced at this mileage*

2.20 (a) For an explanation of sunk and opportunity costs see Chapter 2. The down payment of £5000 represents a sunk cost. The lost profit from subletting the shop of £1600 p.a. ((£550 × £12) – £5000) is an example of an opportunity cost. Note that only the £5000 additional rental is included in the opportunity cost calculation. (The £5000 sunk cost is excluded from the calculation.)

(b) The relevant information for running the shop is:

	(£)
Net sales	100 000
Costs (£87 000 – £5000 sunk cost)	82 000
	18 000
Less opportunity cost from subletting	1 600
Profit	16 400

The above indicates that £16 400 additional profits will be obtained from using the shop for the sale of clothing. It is assumed that Mrs Johnston will not suffer any other loss of income if she devotes half her time to running the shop.

Chapter 3

3.11 BEP = Fixed costs/PV ratio

PV ratio = Contribution/Sales = £275 000/£500 000 = 0.55

BEP = £165 000/0.55 = £300 000

Answer = D

3.12 Average contribution to sales ratio $= \dfrac{(40\% \times 1) + (50\% \times 3)}{4} = 47.5\%$

Break-even point is at the point where 47.5% of the sales equal the fixed costs (i.e. £120 000/0.475 = £252 632).

In other words, the break-even point $= \dfrac{\text{Fixed costs}}{\text{PV ratio}}$

Answer = C

3.13

	Total cost (1000 units) (£)	Total cost (2000 units) (£)
Production overhead	3500 (£3.50 × 1000)	5000 (£2.50 × 2000)
Selling overhead	1000 (£1 × 1000)	1000 (£0.5 × 2000)

Variable cost per unit $= \dfrac{\text{Change in cost}}{\text{Change in activity}}$

Production overhead = £1500/1000 units = £1.50

Selling overhead = Fixed cost since total costs remain unchanged.

The unit costs of direct materials are constant at both activity levels and are therefore variable.

Production overheads fixed cost element = Total cost (£3500) − Variable cost (1000 × £1.50) = £2000

Total fixed cost = £2000 + £1000 = £3000

Unit variable cost £4 + £3 + £1.50 = £8.50

Answer = E

3.14 Contribution/sales (%) = (0.33 × 40% Aye) + (0.33 × 50% Bee) + (0.33 × ? Cee) = 48%

Cee = 54% (Balancing figure)

The total contribution/sales ratio for the revised sales mix is:

(0.40 × 40% Aye) + (0.25 × 50% Bee) + (0.35 × 54% Cee) = 47.4%

Answer = C

3.15

Sales	100	110 (100 + 10%)
Variable cost	60	60
Contribution	40	50

Increase = 25%

Answer = D

3.16 Contribution per unit = 40% × £20 = £8

Break even point $= \dfrac{\text{Fixed costs (£60 000)}}{\text{Contribution per units (£8)}} = 7500$ units

Answer = E

3.17 Break-even point in sales value   = Fixed costs (£76 800)/ Profit–volume ratio (i.e. contribution/sales ratio)

= £76 800/(0.40)

	= £192 000
Actual sales	= £224 000
Margin of safety	= £32 000 (in sales revenues)
Margin of safety in units	= £2000 (£32 000/£16)
Answer = A	

3.18 (i)

p	=	total sales revenue
q	=	total cost (fixed cost + variable cost)
r	=	total variable cost
s	=	fixed costs at the specific level of activity
t	=	total loss at the specific level of activity
u	=	total profit at that level of activity
v	=	total contribution at the specific level of activity
w	=	total contribution at a lower level of activity
x	=	level of activity of output sales
y	=	monetary value of cost and revenue function for level of activity

(ii) At event m the selling price per *unit* decreases, but it remains constant. Note that p is a straight line, but with a lower gradient above m compared with below m.

At event n there is an increase in fixed costs equal to the dotted line. This is probably due to an increase in capital expenditure in order to expand output beyond this point. Also note that at this point the variable cost per unit declines as reflected by the gradient of the variable cost line. This might be due to more efficient production methods associated with increased investment in capital equipment.

(iii) Break-even analysis is of limited use in a multi-product company, but the analysis can be a useful aid to the management of a small single-product company. The following are some of the main benefits:

(a) Break-even analysis forces management to consider the functional relationship between costs, revenue and activity, and gives an insight into how costs and revenue change with changes in the level of activity.

(b) Break-even analysis forces management to consider the fixed costs at various levels of activity and the selling price that will be required to achieve various levels of output.

You should refer to Chapter 3 for a discussion of more specific issues of break-even analysis. Break-even analysis can be a useful tool, but it is subject to a number of assumptions that restrict its usefulness (see, especially, 'Cost–volume–profit analysis assumptions').

3.19 *Preliminary calculations:*

	Sales (units)	Profit/(loss)
November	30 000	£40 000
December	35 000	£60 000
Increase	5 000	£20 000

An increase in sales of 5000 units increases contribution (profits) by £20 000. Therefore contribution is £4 per unit. Selling price is £10 per unit (given) and variable cost per unit will be £6.

At £30 000 unit sales:

Contribution	minus Fixed costs	= Profit
£120 000	minus ?	= £40 000

∴ Fixed costs = £80 000

The above information can now be plotted on a graph.

A break-even chart or a profit–volume graph could be constructed. A profit–volume graph avoids the need to calculate the profits since the information can be read directly from the graph. (See Figure 3.19a for a break-even chart and Figure 3.19b for a profit–volume graph.)

(a) (i) Fixed costs = £80 000.
(ii) Variable cost per unit = £6.
(iii) Profit–volume =

$$\frac{\text{Contribution per unit (£4)}}{\text{Selling price per unit (£10)}} \times 100 = 40\%$$

(iv) Break-even point = 20 000 units.
(v) The margin of safety represents the difference between actual or expected sales volume and the break-even point. Therefore the margin of safety will be different for each month's sales. For example, the margin of safety in November is 10 000 units (30 000 units – 20 000 units). The margin of safety can be read from Figure 3.19b for various sales levels.

(b) and (c) See the section 'Linear CVP relationships' in Chapter 3 for the answers.

Figure 3.19a *Break-even chart*

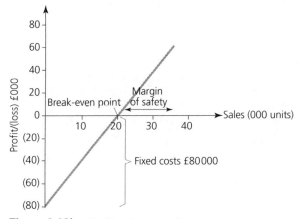

Figure 3.19b *Profit–volume graph*

3.20 a. Let *x* = number of units of output
Total cost for 30 000 units or less = £50 000 + 5*x* (where 5 = variable cost per unit)
Total cost for more than 30 000 units = £100 000 + 5*x*

b.

c. There are two break-even points resulting in the production plan being profitable only between 20 000 and 30 000 units and above 40 000 units. The production plan should be set based on these considerations.

3.21

Workings:	(000)
Sales	1000
Variable costs	600
Contribution	400
Fixed costs	500
Profit/(loss)	(100)

Unit selling price = £20   (£1m/50 000)

Unit variable cost = £12   (£600 000/50 000)

Unit contribution = £8

(a) Sales commission will be £2 per unit, thus reducing the contribution per unit to £6. The break-even point will be 83 333 units (£500 000/£6) or £1 666 666 sales value. This requires an increase of 67 per cent on previous sales and the company must assess whether or not sales can be increased by such a high percentage.

(b) A 10 per cent decrease in selling price will decrease the selling price by £2 per unit and the revised unit contribution will be £6:

	(£)
Revised total contribution (65 000 × £6)	390 000
Less fixed costs	500 000
Profit/(loss)	(110 000)

The estimated loss is worse than last year and the proposal is therefore not recommended.

(c) Wages will increase by 25 per cent – that is, from £200 000 to £250 000 – causing output to increase by 20 per cent.

		(£)
Sales		1 200 000
Direct materials and variable overheads	480 000	
Direct wages	250 000	730 000
Contribution		470 000
Less fixed costs		550 000
Profit/(loss)		(80 000)

This represents an improvement of £20 000 on last year's loss of £100 000.

(d) Revised selling price = £24

$$\text{Let } X = \text{Revised sales volume}$$

∴ sales revenue less (variable costs + fixed costs) = Profit

24X less (12X + 800 000) = 0.1 (24X)

∴ 9.6X = 800 000

∴ X = 83 333 units

Clearly this proposal is preferable since it is the only proposal to yield a profit. However, the probability of increasing sales volume by approximately 67 per cent plus the risk involved from increasing fixed costs by £300 000 must be considered.

3.22 (a) Degree of operating leverage = Contribution margin/profit

Company A = £2000/£1000 = 2

Company B = £6000/£1000 = 6

(b) Break-even point = Fixed costs/PV ratio

Company A = £1000/0.2 = £5000 (expressed in 000s)

Company B = £5000/0.6 = £8333.333 (expressed in 000s)

The break-even point for Company B is higher because its fixed costs are £5 million compared with £1 million for company A. Company A generates a contribution of £0.20 per £1 of sales whereas Company B generates a contribution of £0.60. However, to cover its fixed costs of £5 million Company B mush achieve a higher level of sales (£8.33 million sales at £0.60 per £1 of sales) whereas to cover fixed costs of £1 million Company A only needs to achieve sales of £5 million at a contribution of £0.20 per £1 of sales.

(c) Revised profits for Company A = £15 million sales yielding a contribution of £3 million less fixed costs of £1 million giving a profit of £2 million.

Revised profits for Company B = £15 million sales yielding a contribution of £9 million less fixed costs of £5 million giving a profit of £4 million.

Company A's profits have increased from £1 million to £2 million representing an increase of 100 per cent. In contrast, Company B's profits have increased from £1 million to £4 million representing an increase of 300 per cent. The degree of operating leverage for Company A is 2, which means that an increase in sales of 50 per cent will result in an increase in profits of 100 per cent (50% × 2). In contrast, the degree of operating leverage for Company B is 6 so that an increase in sales of 50 per cent results in an increase in profits of 300 per cent (50% × 6). The degree of operating leverage measures the sensitivity of profits to changes in sales. A degree of operating leverage (DOL) of 2 means that profits change by two times more than the change in sales whereas a DOL of 6 means that profits change by six times more than the change in sales.

3.23 (a) $\text{BEP} = \dfrac{400\ 000 \text{ (fixed costs)} \times £1\ 000\ 000 \text{ (sales)}}{£420\ 000 \text{ (contribution)}}$

= 952 380

(b) (i)

	(£)	(£)
Revised selling price		9.00
Less variable costs:		
Direct materials	1.00	
Direct labour	3.50	
Variable overhead	0.60	
Delivery expenses	0.50	
Sales commission	0.18	
(2% of selling price)		5.78
Contribution per unit		3.22
Number of units sold	140 000	
Total contribution (140 000 × 3.22)	450 800	
Fixed costs	400 000	
Profit from proposal (i)	50 800	

(ii)

Desired contribution	= 480 000
Contribution per unit for present proposal	= 3.22
Required units to earn large profit	= 149 068

(c) (i)   The variable cost of selling to the mail order firm is:

	(£)
Direct material	1.00
Direct labour	3.50
Variable overhead	0.60
Delivery expenses	nil
Sales commission	nil
Additional package cost	0.50
	5.60

To break even, a contribution of £1.20 is required (60 000 fixed cost/50 000 units sold). Therefore selling price to break even is £6.80 (£5.60 + £1.20).

(ii)   To earn £50 800 profit, a contribution of £110 800 (£60 000 + £50 800) is required.

That is, a contribution of £2.22 per unit is required. Therefore required selling price is £7.82 (£5.60 + £2.22).

(iii) To earn the target profit of £80 000, a contribution of £140 000 is required. That is, £2.80 per unit. Therefore required selling price = £8.40 (£5.60 + £2.80).

(d) Contribution per unit is £3.22 per (B)

Unit sold		160 000
Total contribution		£515 200
Fixed costs		£430 000
	Profit	£85 200

Chapter 4

4.13 Based on the contribution per limiting factor (materials) the rankings are products (iii), (ii) and (i). Minimum demand requirements for product (i) = 8000 kg leaving a balance of 27 000 kg to be allocated as follows:

Product (iii) maximum demand = 2000

Product (ii) maximum output from the unallocated materials = 3000 units (15 000kg/5kg)

Answer = B (with a minimum demand of 1000 units for product (i)).

4.14 The material is in regular use and if used will have to be replaced at a cost of £1950 (600 × £3.25). The cash flow consequences are £1950.
Answer = D

4.15 The shadow price is the opportunity cost or contribution per unit of a scarce resource.

	Quone	Qutwo
Contribution per unit	£8	£8.50
Kg per unit	3 (£6/£2)	2.50 (£5/£2)
Contribution per kg	£2.67	£3.40

Scarce materials will be used to make Qutwos and will yield a contribution of £3.40 per kg. Therefore the opportunity cost is £3.40 per kg.

Answer = D

4.16 Assuming that fixed costs will remain unchanged whether or not the company makes or buys the components the relevant cost of manufacture will be the variable cost. Under these circumstances the company should only purchase components if the purchase price is less than the variable cost. Therefore the company should only purchase component T.

Answer = D

4.17 Incremental cost of new employees = £40 000 × 4 = £160 000

Supervision is not an incremental cost.

Incremental costs of retraining

= £15 000 + £100 000 replacement cost = £115 000

Retraining is the cheaper alternative and therefore the relevant cost of the contract is £115 000.

Answer = B

4.18 The material is readily available and the use of the materials will necessitate their replacement. The relevant cost is therefore the replacement cost of £4050 (1250 kg at £3.24).
Answer = B

4.19 Specific (avoidable) fixed overheads per division = £262.5 × 60% = £157.5/3 = £52.5

The specific fixed costs are deducted from the divisional contributions to derive the following contributions (£000s) to general fixed costs:

Division A = £17.5

Division B = £157.5

Division C = –£22.5

Only divisions A and B should remain open since they both provide positive contributions to general fixed costs.

Answer = B

4.20 (a)

	North-east (£)	South coast (£)
Material X from stock (i)	19 440	
Material Y from stock (ii)		49 600
Firm orders of material X (iii)	27 360	
Material X not yet ordered (iv)	60 000	
Material Z not yet ordered (v)		71 200
Labour (vi)	86 000	110 000
Site management (vii)	—	—
Staff accommodation and travel for site management (viii)	6 800	5 600
Plant rental received (ix)	(6000)	—
Penalty clause (x)		28 000
	193 600	264 400
Contract price	288 000	352 000
Net benefit	94 400	87 600

(b) (i) If material X is not used on the north-east contract the most beneficial use is to use it as a substitute material thus avoiding future purchases of £19 440 (0.9 × 21 600). Therefore by using the stock quantity of material X the company will have to spend £19 440 on the other materials.

(ii) Material Y is in common use and the company should not dispose of it. Using the materials on the south coast contract will mean that they will have to be replaced at a cost of £49 600 (£24 800 × 2). Therefore the future cash flow impact of taking on the contract is £49 600.

(iii) It is assumed that with firm orders for materials it is not possible to cancel the purchase. Therefore the cost will occur whatever future alternative is selected. The materials will be used as a substitute material if they are not used on the contract and therefore, based on the same reasoning as note (i) above, the relevant cost is the purchase price of the substitute material (0.9 × £30 400).

(iv) The material has not been ordered and the cost will only be incurred if the contract is undertaken. Therefore additional cash flows of £60 000 will be incurred if the company takes on the north-east contract.

(v) The same principles apply here as were explained in note (iv) and additional cash flows of £71 200 will be incurred only if the company takes on the south coast contract.

(vi) It is assumed that labour is an incremental cost and therefore relevant.

(vii) The site management function is performed by staff at central headquarters. It is assumed that the total company costs in respect of site management will remain unchanged in the short term whatever contracts are taken on. Site management costs are therefore irrelevant.

(viii) The costs would be undertaken only if the contracts are undertaken. Therefore they are relevant costs.

(ix) If the north-east contract is undertaken the company will be able to hire out surplus plant and obtain a £6000 cash inflow.

(x) If the south coast contract is undertaken the company will have to withdraw from the north-east contract and incur a penalty cost of £28 000.

(xi) The headquarters costs will continue whichever alternative is selected and they are not relevant costs.

(xii) It is assumed that there will be no differential cash flows relating to notional interest. However, if the interest costs associated with the contract differ then they would be relevant and should be included in the analysis.

(xiii) Depreciation is a sunk cost and irrelevant for decision-making.

4.21 (a) (i)

Product	A	B	C
	(£)	(£)	(£)
Selling price	15	12	11
Less variable costs:			
Materials	(5)	(4)	(3)
Labour	(3)	(2)	(1.5)
Variable overhead (1)	(3.50)	(2)	(1.5)
Contribution	3.50	4	5

Note:
(1) Fixed overheads are apportioned to products on the basis of sales volume and the remaining overheads are variable with output.

(ii)

Product	B	C
	(£)	(£)
Selling price	12	9.50
Less variable costs:		
Materials	(4)	(3)
Labour	(2)	(1.80)
Variable overhead	(2)	(1.50)
Contribution	4	3.20

(b) (i)

Product	A	B	C	Total
Total contribution	350 000	480 000	400 000	1 230 000
Less fixed costs:				
Labour				(220 000)
Fixed administration				(900 000)
Profit				110 000

(ii)

Product	B	C	Total
Total contribution[a]	480 000	576 000	1 056 000
Less fixed costs:			
Labour[b]			(160 000)
Fixed administration[c]			(850 000)
Profit			46 000

Notes:
[a]B = 120 000 units × £4 contribution,
C = 18 000 units × £3.20 contribution.
[b](25% × £320 000 for B) plus (25% × £160 000 × 2 for C).
[c]Fixed administration costs will decline by $\frac{1}{6}$ of the amount apportioned to Product A (100/300 × £900 000). Therefore fixed overheads will decline from £900 000 to £850 000.

(c) Product A should not be eliminated even though a loss is reported for this product. If product A is eliminated the majority of fixed costs allocated to it will still continue and will be borne by the remaining products. Product A generates a contribution of £350 000 towards fixed costs but the capacity released can be used to obtain an additional contribution from product C of £176 000 (£576 000 – £400 000). This will result in a net loss in contribution of £174 000. However, fixed cost savings of £110 000 (£50 000 administration apportioned to product A plus £100 000 labour for A less an extra £40 000 labour for product C) can be obtained if product A is abandoned. Therefore there will be a net loss in contribution of £64 000 (£174 000 – £110 000) and profits will decline from £110 000 to £64 000.

4.22 The following information represents a comparison of alternatives 1 and 2 with the sale of material XY.

Alternative 1: Conversion versus immediate sale	(£)	(£)	(£)
1. Sales revenue (900 units at £400 per unit			360 000
Less Relevant costs:			
2. Material XY opportunity cost		21 000	
3. Material A (600 units at £90)		54 000	
4. Material B (1000 units at £45)		45 000	
5. Direct labour:			
Unskilled (5000 hrs at £6)	30 000		
Semi-skilled	nil		
Highly skilled (5000 hrs at £17)	85 000	115 000	
6. Variable overheads (15 000 hrs at £1)		15 000	
7. Selling and delivery expenses		27 000	
Advertising		18 000	
8. Fixed overheads		—	295 000
Excess of relevant revenues			65 000

Alternative 2: Adaptation versus immediate sale			
9. Saving on purchase of sub-assembly:			
Normal spending (1200 units at £900)		1 080 000	
Revised spending (900 units at £950)		855 000	225 000
Less relevant costs:			
2. Material XY opportunity cost		21 000	
10. Material C (1000 units at £55)		55 000	
5. Direct labour:			
Unskilled (4000 hrs at £6)	24 000		
Semi-skilled	nil		
Skilled (4000 hrs at £16)	64 000	88 000	
6. Variable overheads (9000 hrs at £1)		9 000	
8. Fixed overheads		nil	173 000
Net relevant savings			52 000

1. There will be additional sales revenue of £360 000 if alternative 1 is chosen.

2. Acceptance of either alternative 1 or 2 will mean a loss of revenue of £21 000 from the sale of the obsolete material XY. This is an opportunity cost, which must be covered whichever alternative is chosen. The original purchase cost of £75 000 for material XY is a sunk cost and is irrelevant.

3. Acceptance of alternative 1 will mean that material A must be replaced at an additional cost of £54 000.

4. Acceptance of alternative 1 will mean that material B will be diverted from the production of product Z. The excess of relevant revenues over relevant cost for product Z is £180 and each unit of product Z uses four units of material. The lost contribution (excluding the cost of material B which is incurred for both alternatives) will therefore be £45 for each unit of material B that is used in converting the raw materials into a specialized product.

5. Unskilled labour can be matched exactly to the company's production requirements. The acceptance of either alternative 1 or 2 will cause the company to incur additional unskilled labour costs of £6 for each hour of unskilled labour that is used. It is assumed that the semi-skilled labour would be retained and that there would be sufficient excess supply for either alternative at no extra cost to the company. In these circumstances semi-skilled labour will not have a relevant cost. Skilled labour is in short supply and can only be obtained by reducing production of product L, resulting in a lost contribution of £24 or £6 per hour of skilled labour. We have already established that the relevant cost for labour that is in short supply is the hourly labour cost plus the lost contribution per hour, so the relevant labour cost here will be £16 per hour.

6. It is assumed that for each direct labour hour of input variable overheads will increase by £1. As each alternative uses additional direct labour hours, variable overheads will increase, giving a relevant cost of £1 per direct labour hour.

7. As advertising selling and distribution expenses will be different if alternative 1 is chosen, these costs are clearly relevant to the decision.

8. The company's fixed overheads will remain the same whichever alternative is chosen, and so fixed overheads are not a relevant cost for either alternative.

9. The cost of purchasing the sub-assembly will be reduced by £225 000 if the second alternative is chosen, and so these savings are relevant to the decision.

10. The company will incur additional variable costs of £55 for each unit of material C that is manufactured, so the fixed overheads for material C are not a relevant cost.
   When considering a problem such as this one, there are many different ways in which the information may be presented. The way in which we have dealt with the problem here is to compare each of the two stated alternatives with the other possibility of selling off material XY for its scrap value of £21 000. The above answer sets out the relevant information, and shows that of the three possibilities alternative 1 is to be preferred.

   An alternative presentation of this information, which you may prefer, is as follows:

	Sale of obsolete materials for scrap	Alternate 1	Alternate 2
Relevant revenues less relevant costs	£21 000	£86 000	£73 000

Difference = £65 000

Difference = £13 000 (£86 000 − £73 000)

We show here *the sale of the obsolete materials as a separate alternative*, and so the opportunity cost of material XY, amounting to £21 000 (see item 2 in the answer) is not included in either alternative 1 or 2, since it is brought into the analysis under the heading 'Sale of obsolete materials for scrap' in the above alternative presentation. Consequently, in both alternatives 1 and 2 the relevant revenues less relevant costs figure is increased by £21 000. The differences between alternative 1 and 2 and the sale of the obsolete materials are still, however, £65 000 and £52 000 respectively, which gives an identical result to that obtained in the above solution.

4.23 (a) *Preliminary calculations*

Variable costs are quoted per acre, but selling prices are quoted per tonne. Therefore, it is necessary to calculate the planned sales revenue per acre. The calculation of the selling price and contribution per acre is as follows:

	Potatoes	Turnips	Parsnips	Carrots
(a) Yield per acre in tonnes	10	8	9	12
(b) Selling price per tonne	£100	£125	£150	£135
(c) Sales revenue per acre, (a) × (b)	£1 000	£1 000	£1 350	£1 620
(d) Variable cost per acre	£470	£510	£595	£660
(e) Contribution per acre	£530	£490	£755	£960

(a) (i)

(i) Profit statement for current year

	Potatoes	Turnips	Parsnips	Carrots	Total
(a) Acres	25	20	30	25	
(b) Contribution per acre	£530	£490	£755	£960	
(c) Total contribution (a × b)	£13 250	£9 800	£22 650	£24 000	£69 700
				Less fixed costs	£54 000
				Profit	£15 700

(ii) Profit statement for recommended mix

	Area A (45 acres)		Area B (55 acres)		
	Potatoes	Turnips	Parsnips	Carrots	Total
(a) Contribution per acre	£530	£490	£755	£960	
(b) Ranking	1	2	2	1	
(c) Minimum sales requirements in acres[a]		5	4		
(d) Acres allocated[b]	40			51	
(e) Recommended mix (acres)	40	5	4	51	
(f) Total contribution, (a) × (e)	£21 200	£2 450	£3 020	£48 960	£75 630
				Less fixed costs	£54 000
				Profit	£21 630

Notes

[a]The minimum sales requirement for turnips is 40 tonnes, and this will require the allocation of 5 acres (40 tonnes/8 tonnes yield per acre). The minimum sales requirement for parsnips is 36 tonnes, requiring the allocation of 4 acres (36 tonnes/9 tonnes yield per acre).

[b]Allocation of available acres to products on basis of a ranking that assumes that acres are the key factor.

(b) (i) Production should be concentrated on carrots, which have the highest contribution per acre (£960).

	(£)
(ii) Contribution from 100 acres of carrots (100 × £960)	96 000
Fixed overhead	54 000
Profit from carrots	42 000

(iii) Break-even point in acres for carrots $= \dfrac{\text{Fixed costs (£54 000)}}{\text{Contribution per acre (£960)}}$

$= 56.25$ acres

Contribution in sales value for carrots

$= £91\ 125$ (56.25 acres at £1620 sales revenue per acre).

Chapter 5

5.13

Units	Total variable costs (£)	Selling price per unit (£)	Total sales revenue (£)	Total contribution (£)
10	40 000	6 500	65 000	25 000
11	44 400	6 350	69 850	25 450
12	49 200	6 200	74 400	25 200
13	54 400	6 050	78 650	24 250

It is apparent from the cost and revenue functions that contribution declines beyond an output of 11 units so there is no need to compute the contribution for 14 and 20 units. The most profitable output is 11 units.

Answer = B

5.14 (a) Variable cost plus 20% = £30 × 1.20 = £36
Total cost plus 20% = £37 × 1.20 = £44.40

Advantages of variable costs include that it avoids arbitrary allocations, identifies short-term relevant costs, simplicity and mark-up can be increased to provide a contribution to fixed costs and profit. The disadvantages are that it represents only a partial cost, it is short-term oriented and ignores price/demand relationships.

Advantages of total cost include that it attempts to include all costs, reduces the possibility that fixed costs will not be covered and simplicity. The disadvantages are that total cost is likely to involve some arbitrary apportionments and the price/demand relationship is ignored.

(b) See 'Pricing policies' in Chapter 5 for the answer to this question. The answer should point out that price skimming is likely to lead to a higher initial price whereas a pricing penetration policy is likely to lead to a lower initial price.

5.15 (a) *Computation of full costs and budgeted cost-plus selling price*

	EXE (£m)	WYE (£m)	Stores (£m)	Maintenance (£m)	Admin (£m)
Material	1.800	0.700	0.100		
Other variable	0.800	0.500	0.100	0.200	0.200
Gen factory	1.440	1.080	0.540	0.180	0.360
					0.560
Admin reallocation	0.224	0.168	0.112	0.056	(0.560)
				0.536	
Maintenance reallocation	0.268	0.134	0.134	(0.536)	
			0.986		
Stores	0.592	0.394	(0.986)		
	5.124	2.976			
Volume	150 000	70 000			
	(£)	(£)			
Full cost	34.16	42.51			
Mark up (25%)	8.54	10.63			
Price	42.70	53.14			

(b) (i) The incremental costs for the order consist of the variable costs. The calculation of the unit variable cost is as follows:

	EXE (£m)	WYE (£m)	Stores (£m)	Maintenance (£m)	Admin (£m)
Material	1.800	0.700	0.100	0.100	
Other variable	0.800	0.500	0.100	0.200	0.200
Admin	0.080	0.060	0.040	0.020	(0.200)
				0.320	
Maintenance	0.160	0.080	0.080	(0.320)	
			0.320		
Stores	0.192	0.128	(0.320)		
	3.032	1.468			
Volume	150 000	70 000			
	(£)	(£)			
Variable cost	20.21	20.97			

The proposed selling price exceeds the incremental cost and provides a contribution towards fixed costs and profits of £14.03 (£35 – £20.97) per unit thus giving a total contribution of £42 090. Given that the company has spare capacity no lost business will be involved and it appears that the order is a one-off short-term special order. Therefore the order is acceptable provided it does not have an impact on the selling price in the existing market or utilize capacity that has alternative uses. Given that the markets are segregated the former would appear to be an unlikely event. However, if the order were to generate further regular business the longer-term cost considerations described in Chapter 5 should be taken into account in determining an acceptable long-run price.

(ii) The proposed selling price is £46.76 (full cost of £42.51 plus 10%). This will generate a contribution of £25.79 (£46.76 – £20.97) per unit. Unutilized capacity is 30 000 units but the order is for 50 000 units. Therefore the order can only be met by reducing existing business by 20 000 units. The financial evaluation is as follows:

Increase in contribution from existing business	
(50 000 units at a contribution of £25.79)	£1 289 500
Lost contribution from existing business	
(20 000 units at a contribution of (£53.14 – £20.97))	643 400
Net increase in contribution	646 100

Before accepting the order the longer-term implications should be considered. The inability to meet the full demand from existing customers may result in a significant reduction in customer goodwill and the lost contribution from future sales to these customers may exceed the short-term gain of £646 100. Also the above analysis has not considered the alternative use of the unutilized capacity of 30 000 units. If the cost savings from reducing the capacity exceed £646 100 for the period under consideration the order will not be worthwhile. The order will also result in the company operating at full capacity and it is possible that the cost structure may change if the company is operating outside its normal production range.

If the company does not rely on customer repeat orders and customer goodwill it is unlikely to be affected and the order would appear to be profitable. It is important, however, that long-term considerations are taken into account when evaluating the order. In particular, consideration should be given to the negotiation of a longer-term contract on both price and volume.

5.16 (a) For the answer to this question you should refer to Chapter 5. In particular the answer should discuss the role of cost information in the following situations:
1 a price-setting firm facing short-run pricing decisions;
2 a price-setting firm facing long-run decisions;
3 a price-taking firm facing short-run product mix decisions;
4 a price-taking firm facing long-run decisions.

(b) *Calculation of variable overhead absorption rates*

	Moulding (£000)	Finishing (£000)	General factory (£000)
Allocated overheads	1600	500	1050
Reallocation of general factory based on machine hours	600	450	(1050)
	2200	950	
Machine hours	800	600	
Variable overhead rate per hour	£2.75	£1.583	

Calculation of fixed overhead absorption rates

	Moulding (£000)	Finishing (£000)	General factory (£000)
Allocated overheads	2500	850	1750
Reallocation of General factory based on machine hours	1050	700	(1750)
	3550	1550	
Machine hours	800	600	
Variable overhead rate per hour	£4.4375	£2.583	

Calculation of full manufacturing cost

		(£)
Direct material		9.00
Direct labour	10.00 (1 × £10)	
	16.50 (2 × £8.25)	26.50
Variable overheads	11.00 (4 × £2.75)	
	4.75 (3 × £1.583)	15.75
Variable manufacturing cost		51.25
Fixed overheads	17.75 (4 × £4.4375)	
	7.75 (3 × £2.583)	25.50
Full manufacturing cost		76.75

Prices based on full manufacturing cost

25% mark up = £95.94

30% mark up = £99.78

35% mark up = £103.61

Minimum prices based on short-term variable cost and incremental cost are as follows:

Variable cost = £51.25

Incremental cost = £59.60 (£51.25 plus specific fixed costs of £8.35)

The specific fixed cost per unit is calculated by dividing the fixed costs of £167 000 by the estimated sales volume (10% × 200 000).

(c) The cost information is more likely to provide a general guide to the pricing decision but the final pricing decision will be influenced by the prices of competitors' products (£90–£100). The full cost prices indicate prices within a range of £96–£104. The variable/incremental price indicates a minimum short-run price that may be appropriate if the company wishes to pursue a price-skimming policy. Given that the product is an improvement on competitors, a price in the region of £100 would seem to be appropriate but the final decision should be based on marketing considerations drawing off the knowledge of the marketing staff. The role of the cost information has been to indicate that a price within this range should provide a reasonable margin and contribution to general fixed costs.

Chapter 6

6.13 Using the interpolation method the IRR is:

$$15\% + \frac{£3664}{(£3664 + £21\,451)} \times (20\% - 15\%) = 15.7\%$$

Answer = A

6.14 Because the same amount is paid each period the cumulative (annuity) discount tables in Appendix B can be used. For 12 periods at 3 per cent the annuity factor is 9.954. The present value 3 months from now will be £2986 (300 × 9.954). Assuming that the first payment is made at the beginning of month 3 this is the equivalent to the end of month 2 for discounting purposes. Therefore it is necessary to discount the present value back two months (periods) to today (time zero). Using the discount factor for 3 per cent and 2 periods the present value at time zero is £2816 (£2986 × 0.9426). Therefore the answer is A.

6.15

Time (£000)	Cash flow at 8%	Discount factor value (£000)	Present
0	(20 000)	1.0	(20 000)
1–4	3 000	3.312	9 936
5–8	7 000	2.435 (5.747 − 3.312)	17 045
10	(10 000)	0.463	(4 630)
		NPV	2 351

Note that the discount factors for periods 1–4 and 5–8 are derived from the annuity tables since the cash flows are constant per period for the time period involved.

Answer = D

6.16 The annual percentage rate (APR) is 12.68 per cent, which is based on annual payments.

Monthly interest rate = $\sqrt[12]{1.1268} - 1 = 0.01$ so that $r = 1\%$

In other words a monthly interest rate compounded for 12 periods at 1 per cent is equivalent to an annual rate of 12.68 per cent. This is derived from using the compound interest formula used in the chapter = $(1 + 0.01)^{12} - 1 = 0.1268 = 12.68\%$

To determine the future value of an annuity where a constant amount is invested each period the future value

$$= A\left[\frac{(1+r)^n - 1}{r}\right] \text{ where } r \text{ is the rate of interest per period}$$

and A is the annuity amount.

$$\text{Future value} = 50 \times \left[\frac{1.01^{13 \times 12} - 1}{.01}\right] = £18\,610$$

Answer = D

6.17 Because the investment is a constant amount each period we can use the annuity future value formula shown in the answer to question 6.16:

$$\text{Future value} = A\left[\frac{(1+r)^n - 1}{r}\right] \text{ where } r \text{ is the rate of interest per period and A is the annuity amount.}$$

$$£7000 = A \times \left[\frac{1.005^{12 \times 5} - 1}{.005}\right]$$

£7000 = 69.77A

A = £100.33

Answer = C

6.18 The loan represents the present value of a series of repayments over a three-year period. Since the payments are constant per period we can use the following annuity present value formula:

$$\text{Present value} = \frac{A}{r}\left[1 - \frac{1}{(1+r)^n}\right]$$

where A is the annuity amount and r is the interest rate per period.

The annual interest rate must be converted to a monthly rate since we are dealing with monthly repayments.

Monthly interest rate $= \sqrt[12]{1.10} - 1 = .0079$ (i.e. 0.79%)

$$\text{Present value (2000)} = \frac{A}{0.0079}\left[1 - \frac{1}{1.0079^{36}}\right]$$

$$2000 = \frac{A}{0.0079}(0.2467)$$

$2000\,(0.0079) = 0.2467A$

$A = 15.8/.2467 = £64.04$

Answer = B

6.19 (a) (i) Average capital invested

$$= \frac{£50\,000 + £10\,000}{2} = £30\,000$$

For an explanation of why the project's scrap value is added to the initial cost to calculate the average capital employed, you should refer to note 1 at the end of Chapter 6.

Note that the mid-point of the project's life is two years and the written down value at the end of year 2 is £30 000.

Average annual profit (Project A)

$$= \frac{£25\,000 + £20\,000 + £15\,000 + £10\,000}{4}$$

$= £17\,500$

Average annual profit (Project B)

$$= \frac{£10\,000 + £10\,000 + £14\,000 + £26\,000}{4}$$

$= £15\,000$

Average annual return:

$$\begin{matrix} A \\ 58.33\% \end{matrix}\left(\frac{£17\,500}{£30\,000} \times 100\right)$$

$$\begin{matrix} B \\ 50\% \end{matrix}\left(\frac{£15\,000}{£30\,000} \times 100\right)$$

(ii) Payback period:

$$\begin{matrix} \text{Project A} \\ \text{1.5 years} \end{matrix}\left(1 + \frac{£15\,000}{£30\,000}\right)$$

$$\begin{matrix} \text{Project B} \\ \text{2.4 years} \end{matrix}\left(2 + \frac{£10\,000}{£24\,000}\right)$$

(iii) Not present value

Year	Project A Cash inflows (W1) (£)	Project B Cash inflows (W1) (£)	Discount factor	Project A PV (£)	Project B PV (£)
1	35 000	20 000	0.909	31 815	18 180
2	30 000	20 000	0.826	24 780	16 520
3	25 000	24 000	0.751	18 775	18 024

4		20 000	36 000	0.683	13 660	24 588
4		10 000	10 000	0.683	6 830	6 830
					95 860	84 142
			Investment cost		(50 000)	(50 000)
			NPV		45 860	34 142

Workings:

(W1) Cash flows = Profit + depreciation.

Note that the estimated resale value is included as a year 4 cash inflow.

(b) See Chapter 6 for the answer to this section of the problem.

(c) Project A is recommended because it has the highest NPV and also the shortest payback period.

6.20 (a) The IRR is where:

annual cash inflows × discount factor = investment cost

i.e. £4000 × discount factor = £14 000

Therefore discount factor = $\dfrac{£14\ 000}{£4\ 000}$

= 3.5

We now work along the five-row table of the cumulative discount tables to find the discount rate with a discount factor closest to 3.5. This is 13 per cent. Therefore the IRR is 13 per cent.

(b) The annual saving necessary to achieve a 12 per cent internal rate of return is where:
annual savings × 12% discount factor = investment cost

i.e. annual savings × 3.605 = £14 000

Therefore annual savings = $\dfrac{£14\ 000}{3.605}$

= £3 883

(c) NPV is calculated as follows:

	(£)
£4000 received annually from years 1–5:	
£4000 × 3.791 discount factor	15 164
Less investment cost	14 000
NPV	1 164

6.21 (a) Project A = 3 years + $\dfrac{350-314}{112}$ = 3.32 years

Project B = 3.0 years

Project C = 2.00 years

(b) Accounting rate of return = average profit/average investment

Project A = 79/175 = 45%

Project B = 84/175 = 48%

Project C = 70/175 = 40%

Note that average profit = (sum of cash flows – investment cost)/project's life.

(c) The report should include:

(i) NPVs of each project (project A = £83 200 (W1), project B = £64 000 (W2), project C = £79 000 (W3). A simple description of NPV should also be provided. For example, the NPV is the amount over and above the cost of the project that could be borrowed, secure in the knowledge that the cash flows from the project will repay the loan.

(ii) The following rankings are based on the different evaluation procedures:

Project	IRR	Payback	ARR	NPV
A	2	3	2	1
B	3	2	1	3
C	1	1	3	2

(iii) A discussion of each of the above evaluation procedures.
(iv) IRR is subject to the following criticisms:
1   Multiple rates of return can occur when a project has unconventional cash flows.
2   It is assumed that the cash flows received from a project are reinvested at the IRR and not the cost of capital.
3   Inability to rank mutually exclusive projects.
4   It cannot deal with different sized projects. For example, it is better to earn a return of 35 per cent on £100 000 than 40 per cent on £10 000.
Note that the above points are explained in detail in Chapter 6.
(v) Payback ignores cash flows outside the payback period, and it also ignores the timing of cash flows within the payback period. For example, the large cash flows for project A are ignored after the payback period. This method may be appropriate for companies experiencing liquidity problems who wish to recover their initial investment quickly.
(vi) Accounting rate of return ignores the timing of cash flows, but it is considered an important measure by those who believe reported profits have a significant impact on share prices.
(vii) NPV is generally believed to be the theoretically correct evaluation procedure. A positive NPV from an investment is supposed to indicate the increase in the market value of shareholders' funds, but this claim depends upon the belief that the share price is the discounted present value of the future dividend stream. If the market uses some other method of valuing shares then a positive NPV may not represent the increase in market value of shareholders' funds. Note that the cash flows have been discounted at the company's cost of capital. It is only suitable to use the company's cost of capital as the discount rate if projects A, B and C are equivalent to the average risk of all the company's existing projects. If they are not of average risk then project risk-adjusted discount rates should be used.
(viii) The projects have unequal lives. It is assumed that the equipment will not be replaced.
(ix) It is recommended that NPV method is used and project A should be selected.
(d) Stadler prefers project C because it produces the highest accounting profit in year 3. Stadler is assuming that share prices are influenced by short-run reported profits. This is in contrast with theory, which assumes that the share price is the discounted present value of the future dividend stream. Stadler is also assuming that the market only has access to reported historical profits and is not aware of the future benefits arising from the projects. The stock market also obtains company information on future prospects from sources other than reported profits. For example, press releases, chairman's report and signals of future prosperity via increased dividend payments.

Workings

(W1) Project A = $(100 \times 0.8333) + (110 \times 0.6944) + (104 \times 0.5787) + (112 \times 0.4823) + (138 \times 0.4019) + (160 \times 0.3349) + (180 \times 0.2791) - £350$

(W2) Project B = $(40 \times 0.8333) + (100 \times 0.6944) + (210 \times 0.5787) + (260 \times 0.4823) + (160 \times 0.4019) - £350$

(W3) Project C = $(200 \times 0.8333) + (150 \times 0.6944) + (240 \times 0.5787) + (40 \times 0.4823) - £350$

Chapter 7

7.11 Overhead absorbed (£714 000) = Actual hours (119 000) × Pre-determined overhead rate.
Pre-determined overhead rate = £714 000/119 000 = £6.

Budgeted overheads (£720 000) = Budgeted machine hours ×
   Budgeted overhead rate (£6).

Budgeted machine hours = £720 000/£6 = 120 000 hours.

Answer = C

7.12 Budgeted overhead rate = £258 750/11 250 hours = £23 per
   machine hour

Overheads absorbed = £23 × 10 980 Actual hours = £252 540

Overheads incurred = £254 692

Overheads absorbed = £252 540

Under-absorbed overheads = £2152

Answer = A

7.13 (i) Budgeted overhead rates and not actual overhead rates should be used as indicated in
Chapter 7.

Overhead rate = £148 750/8500 hours = £17.50 per hour.

Answer = A

(ii)

	(£)
Actual overheads incurred	146 200
Overheads absorbed (7928 × £17.50)	138 740
Under-absorbed overheads	7 460

Answer = D

7.14 (i) It is assumed that labour cost is to be used as the allocation base.
Total labour cost = £14 500 + £3500 + £24 600 = £42 600

Overhead recovery rate = £126 000/£42 600 = £2.9578
  per £1 of labour

Overhead charged to Job CC20 = £24 600 × £2.9578 =
  £72 761

Answer = C

(ii)

	(£)
Opening WIP	42 790
Direct labour	3 500
Overhead (£3500 × £2.9578)	10 352
	56 642
Selling price (£56 642/0.667)	84 921
or £56 642 divided by 2/3 =	£84 963

Answer = C

(iii) Closing WIP = Total cost of AA10 and CC20

	Total (£)	AA10 (£)	CC20 (£)
Opening WIP		26 800	0
Materials in period		17 275	18 500
Labour in period		14 500	24 600
Overheads in period:			
2.9577465 × £14 500		42 887	
2.9577465 × £24 600			72 761
	217 323	101 462	115 861

Answer = D

7.15 Answer = D

7.16 Because production is highly automated it is assumed that overheads will be most closely associated with machine hours. The predetermined overhead rate will therefore be £18 derived from dividing budgeted overheads (£180 000) by the budgeted machine hours (10 000). Therefore the answer is B.

7.17 (a)

	Total (£)	A (£)	B (£)	C (£)	X (£)	Y (£)
Rent and rates[a]	12 800	6 000	3 600	1 200	1200	800
Machine insurance[b]	6 000	3 000	1 250	1 000	500	250
Telephone charges[c]	3 200	1 500	900	300	300	200
Depreciation[b]	18 000	9 000	3 750	3 000	1500	750
Supervisors' salaries[d]	24 000	12 800	7 200	4 000		
Heat and light[a]	6 400	3 000	1 800	600	600	400
	70 400					
Allocated		2 800	1 700	1 200	800	600
		38 100	20 200	11 300	4900	3000
Reapportionment of X		2 450 (50%)	1 225 (25%)	1 225 (25%)	(4900)	
Reapportionment of Y		600 (20%)	900 (30%)	1 500 (50%)		(3000)
		£41 150	£22 325	£14 025		
Budgeted D.L. hours[e]		3 200	1 800	1 000		
Absorption rates		£12.86	£12.40	£14.02		

Notes
[a]Apportioned on the basis of floor area.
[b]Apportioned on the basis of machine value.
[c]Should be apportioned on the basis of the number of telephone points or estimated usage. This information is not given and an alternative arbitrary method of apportionment should be chosen. In the above analysis telephone charges have been apportioned on the basis of floor area.
[d]Apportioned on the basis of direct labour hours.
[e]Machine hours are not given but direct labour hours are. It is assumed that the examiner requires absorption to be on the basis of direct labour hours.

(b)

	Job 123 (£)	Job 124 (£)
Direct material	125.00	79.70
Direct labour:		
Department A	88.00	70.40
Department B	51.00	42.50
Department C	42.00	58.80
Total direct cost	306.00	251.40
Overhead:		
Department A	257.20	205.76
Department B	148.80	124.00
Department C	140.20	196.28
Total cost	852.20	777.44
Profit	284.07	259.15
(c) Listed selling price	1136.27	1036.59

Note
Let SP represent selling price.
Cost + 0.25SP = SP
Job 123: £852.20 + 0.25SP = 1SP
0.75SP = £852.20
Hence SP = £1136.27
For Job 124: 0.75SP = £777.44
Hence SP = £1036.59

7.18 (a) (i) Calculation of budgeted overhead absorption rates:

Apportionment of overheads to production departments

	Machine shop (£)	Fitting section (£)	Canteen (£)	Machine maintenance section (£)	Total (£)
Allocated overheads	27 660	19 470	16 600	26 650	90 380
Rent, rates, heat and light[a]	9 000	3 500	2 500	2 000	17 000
Depreciation and insurance of equipment[a]	12 500	6 250	2 500	3 750	25 000
	49 160	29 220	21 600	32 400	132 380
Service department apportionment					
Canteen[b]	10 800	8 400	(21 600)	2 400	—
Machine maintenance section	24 360	10 440	—	(34 800)	—
	84 320	48 060	—	—	132 380

Calculation of absorption bases

		Machine shop		Fitting section	
Product	Budgeted production	Machine hours per product	Total machine hours	Direct labour cost per product (£)	Total direct wages (£)
X	4200 units	6	25 200	12	50 400
Y	6900 units	3	20 700	3	20 700
Z	1700 units	4	6 800	21	35 700
			52 700		106 800

Budgeted overhead absorption rates

Machine shop

$$\frac{\text{Budgeted overheads}}{\text{Budgeted machine hours}} = \frac{\pounds 84\ 320}{52\ 700}$$

$$= \pounds 1.60 \text{ per machine hour}$$

Fitting section

$$\frac{\text{Budgeted overheads}}{\text{Budgeted direct wages}} = \frac{\pounds 48\ 060}{106\ 800}$$

$$= 45\% \text{ of direct wages}$$

Notes

[a]Rents, rates, heat and light are apportioned on the basis of floor area. Depreciation and insurance of equipment are apportioned on the basis of book value.

[b]Canteen costs are reapportioned according to the number of employees. Machine maintenance section costs are reapportioned according to the percentages given in the question.

(ii) The budgeted manufacturing overhead cost for producing one unit of product X is as follows:

	(£)
Machine shop: 6 hours at £1.60 per hour	9.60
Fittings section: 45% of £12	5.40
	15.00

(b) The answer should discuss the limitations of blanket overhead rates and actual overhead rates. See 'Blanket overhead rates' and 'Budgeted overhead rates' in Chapter 7 for the answer to this question.

7.19 (a) The calculation of the overhead absorption rates are as follows:

Forming department machine hour rate = £6.15 per machine hour (£602 700/98 000 hours)

Finishing department labour hour rate = £2.25 per labour hour (£346 500/154 000 hours)

The forming department is mechanized, and it is likely that a significant proportion of overheads will be incurred as a consequence of employing and running the machines. Therefore a machine hour rate has been used. In the finishing department several grades of labour are used. Consequently the direct wages percentage method is inappropriate, and the direct labour hour method should be used.

(b) The decision should be based on a comparison of the incremental costs with the purchase price of an outside supplier if spare capacity exists. If no spare capacity exists then the lost contribution on displaced work must be considered. The calculation of incremental costs requires that the variable element of the total overhead absorption rate must be calculated. The calculation is:

Forming department variable machine hour rate = £2.05 (£200 900/98 000 hours)

Finishing department variable direct labour hour rate = £0.75 (£115 500/154 000 hours)

The calculation of the variable costs per unit of each component is:

	A (£)	B (£)	C (£)
Prime cost	24.00	31.00	29.00
Variable overheads: Forming	8.20	6.15	4.10
Finishing	2.25	7.50	1.50
Variable unit manufacturing cost	34.45	44.65	34.60
Purchase price	£30	£65	£60

On the basis of the above information, component A should be purchased and components B and C manufactured. This decision is based on the following assumptions:

(i) Variable overheads vary in proportion to machine hours (forming department) and direct labour hours (finishing department).
(ii) Fixed overheads remain unaffected by any changes in activity.
(iii) Spare capacity exists.

For a discussion of make-or-buy decisions see Chapter 4.

(c) Production overhead absorption rates are calculated in order to ascertain costs per unit of output for stock valuation and profit measurement purposes. Such costs are inappropriate for decision-making and cost control. For an explanation of this see the section in Chapter 7 entitled 'Different costs for different purposes'.

Chapter 8

8.14 Cost driver rates are as follows:

Receiving/inspection etc. = £1 400 000/5000 = £280 per requisition

Production scheduling/machine set-up = £1 200 000/800 = £1500 per set-up

	W (£)	X (£)	Y (£)
Direct costs	80.00	75.00	65.00
Receiving/inspection[a]	33.60	33.60	31.11
Production scheduling[a]	36.00	26.00	25.00
Total cost per unit	149.60	134.60	121.11
Selling price	200.00	183.00	175.00
Profit per unit	50.40	48.40	53.89

Notes:
[a](Number of units of activity used by each product × Cost driver rate)/Units produced, e.g. Product W for receiving/inspection = (1200 × £280)/10 000 = £33.60

8.15

	W (£000)	X (£000)	Y (£000)
Gross margin	1100	1750	1200
Less customer related costs:			
Sales visits at £500 per visit	55	50	85
Order processing at £100 per order placed	100	100	150
Despatch costs at £100 per order placed	100	100	150
Billing and collections at £175 per invoice raised	157	210	262
Profit/(loss)	688	1290	553
Ranking	2	1	3

Answer = C

8.16 Budgeted number of batches per product:

D = 1000 (100 000/100)
R = 2000 (100 000/50)
P = 2000 (50 000/25)
      5000

Budgeted machine set-ups:

D =   3 000 (1000 × 3)
R =   8 000 (2000 × 4)
P = 12 000 (2000 × 6)
      23 000

Budgeted cost per set-up = £150 000/23 000 = £6.52

Budgeted set-up cost per unit of R = (£6.52 × 4)/50 = £0.52

Answer = A

8.17 The answer to the question should describe the two-stage overhead allocation process and indicate that most cost systems use direct labour hours in the second stage. In today's production environment direct labour costs have fallen to about 10 per cent of total costs for many firms and it is argued that direct labour is no longer a suitable base for assigning overheads to products. Using direct labour encourages managers to focus on reducing direct labour costs when they represent only a small percentage of total costs.
Approaches that are being adopted include:

(i)   Changing from a direct labour overhead-recovery rate to recovery methods based on machine time. The justification for this is that overheads are caused by machine time rather than direct labour hours and cost.

(ii) Implementing activity-based costing systems that use many different cost drivers in the second stage of the two-stage overhead allocation procedure.

The answer should then go on to describe the benefits of ABC outlined in Chapter 8. Attention should also be drawn to the widespread use of direct labour hours by Japanese companies. According to Hiromoto[1] Japanese companies allocate overhead costs using the direct labour cost/hours to focus design engineers' attention on identifying opportunities to reduce the products' labour content. They use direct labour to encourage designers to make greater use of technology because this frequently improves long-term competitiveness by increasing quality, speed and flexibility of manufacturing.

Notes
[1] Hiromoto, T. (1988) Another hidden edge – Japanese management accounting, *Harvard Business Review*, July/August, pp. 22–6.

8.18 (a) Large-scale service organizations have a number of features that have been identified as being necessary to derive significant benefits from the introduction of ABC:

(i)   they operate in a highly competitive environment;

(ii) they incur a large proportion of indirect costs that cannot be directly assigned to specific cost objects;

     (iii) products and customers differ significantly in terms of consuming overhead resources;

     (iv) they market many different products and services.

Furthermore, many of the constraints imposed on manufacturing organizations, such as also having to meet financial accounting stock valuation requirements, or a reluctance to change or scrap existing systems, do not apply. Many service organizations have only recently implemented cost systems for the first time. This has occurred at the same time as when the weaknesses of existing systems and the benefits of ABC systems were being widely publicized. These conditions have provided a strong incentive for introducing ABC systems.

(b) The following may create problems for the application of ABC:

     (i) Facility sustaining costs (such as property rents etc.) represent a significant proportion of total costs and may only be avoidable if the organization ceases business. It may be impossible to establish appropriate cost drivers.

     (ii) It is often difficult to define products where they are of an intangible nature. Cost objects can therefore be difficult to specify.

     (iii) Many service organizations have not previously had a costing system and much of the information required to set up an ABC system will be non-existent. Therefore introducing ABC is likely to be expensive.

(c) The uses for ABC information for service industries are similar to those for manufacturing organizations:

     (i) It leads to more accurate product costs as a basis for pricing decisions when cost-plus pricing methods are used.

     (ii) It results in more accurate product and customer profitability analysis statements that provide a more appropriate basis for decision-making.

     (iii) ABC attaches costs to activities and identifies the cost drivers that cause the costs. Thus ABC provides a better understanding of what causes costs and highlights ways of performing activities more effectively by reducing cost driver transactions. Costs can therefore be managed more effectively in the long term. Activities can also be analysed into value-added and non-value-added activities and by highlighting the costs of non-value-added activities attention is drawn to areas where there is a potential for cost reduction without reducing the products' service potential to customers.

(d) The following aspects would be of most interest to a regulator:

     (i) The costing method used (e.g. marginal, traditional full cost or ABC). This is of particular importance to verify whether or not reasonable prices are being set and that the organization is not taking advantage of its monopolistic situation. Costing information is also necessary to ascertain whether joint costs are fairly allocated so that cross-subsidization from one service to another does not apply.

     (ii) Consistency in costing methods from period to period so that changes in costing methods are not used to distort pricing and profitability analysis.

     (iii) In many situations a regulator may be interested in the ROI of the different services in order to ensure that excessive returns are not being obtained. A regulator will therefore be interested in the methods and depreciation policy used to value assets and how the costs of assets that are common to several services (e.g. corporate headquarters) are allocated. The methods used will influence the ROI of the different services.

8.19 (a) (i) Direct labour overhead rate

$$= \frac{\text{Total overheads (£1 848 000)}}{\text{Total direct labour hours (88 000)}}$$

$$= \text{£21 per direct labour hour}$$

Product costs

Product	X (£)	Y (£)	Z (£)
Direct labour	8	12	6
Direct materials	25	20	11

Overhead[a]	28	42	21
Total cost	61	74	38

Note
[a]X = $1^1/_3$ hours × £21
   Y = 2 hours × £21
   Z = 1 hour × £21

(ii) Materials handling

Overhead rate

$$= \frac{\text{Receiving department overheads (£435 000)}}{\text{Direct material cost (£1 238 000)}} \times 100$$

= 35.14% of direct material cost

Machine hour overhead rate

$$= \frac{\text{Other overheads (£1 413 000)}}{76\ 000 \text{ machine hours}}$$

= £18.59 per machine hour

Product costs

Product	X (£)	Y (£)	Z (£)
Direct labour	8.00	12.00	6.00
Direct materials	25.00	20.00	11.00
Materials handling overhead	8.78 (£25 × 35.14%)	7.03 (£20 × 35.14%)	3.87 (£11 × 35.14%)
Other overheads[a] (machine hour basis)	24.79	18.59	37.18
Total cost	66.57	57.62	58.05

Note
[a]X = $1^1/_3$ × £18.59
   Y = 1 × £18.59
   Z = 2 × £18.59

(b) The cost per transaction or activity for each of the cost centres is as follows:

Set-up cost

Cost per set-up

$$= \frac{\text{Setup cost (£30 000)}}{\text{Number of production runs (30)}} = £1000$$

Receiving

Cost per receiving order

$$= \frac{\text{Receiving cost (£435 000)}}{\text{Number of orders (270)}} = £1611$$

Packing

Cost per packing order

$$= \frac{\text{Packing cost (£250 000)}}{\text{Number of orders (32)}} = £7812$$

Engineering

Cost per production order

$$= \frac{\text{Engineering cost (£373 000)}}{\text{Number of production orders (50)}} = £7460$$

The total set-up cost for the period was £30 000 and the cost per transaction or activity for the period is £1000 per set-up. Product X required three production runs, and thus £3000 of the set-up cost is traced to the production of product X for the period. Thus the cost per set-up per unit produced for product X is £0.10 (£3000/30 000 units).

Similarly, product Z required 20 set-ups, and so £20 000 is traced to product Z. Hence the cost per set-up for product Z is £2.50 (£20 000/8000 units).

The share of a support department's cost that is traced to each unit of output for each product is therefore calculated as follows:

$$\text{Cost per transaction} \times \frac{\text{Number of transactions per product}}{\text{Number of units produced}}$$

The unit standard costs for products X, Y and Z using an activity-based costing system are

	X	Y	Z
Direct labour	£8.00	£12.00	£6.00
Direct materials	25.00	20.00	11.00
Machine overhead[a]	13.33	10.00	20.00
Set-up costs	0.10	0.35	2.50
Receiving[b]	0.81	2.82	44.30
Packing[c]	2.34	1.17	19.53
Engineering[d]	3.73	3.73	23.31
Total manufacturing cost	53.31	50.07	126.64

Notes

[a]Machine hours × machine overhead rate (£760 000/ 76 000 hrs)

[b]X = (£1611 × 15)/30 000
Y = (£1611× 35)/20 000
Z = (£1611 × 220)/8000

[c]X = (£7812 × 9)/30 000
Y = (£7812 × 3)/20 000
Z = (£7812 × 20)/8000

[d]X = (£7460 × 15)/30 000
Y = (£7460 × 10)/20 000
Z = (£7460 × 25)/8000

(c) The traditional product costing system assumes that products consume resources in relation to volume measures such as direct labour, direct materials or machine hours. The activity-based system recognizes that some overheads are unrelated to production volume, and uses cost drivers that are independent of production volume. For example, the activity-based system assigns the following percentage of costs to product Z, the low-volume product:

Set-up-related costs   66.67%
(20 out of 30 set-ups)

Delivery-related costs   62.5%
(20 out of 32 deliveries)

Receiving costs   81.5%
(220 out of 270 receiving orders)

Engineering-related costs   50%
(25 out of 50 production orders)

In contrast, the current costing system assigns the cost of the above activities according to production volume, measured in machine hours. The total machine hours are

Product X 40 000 (30 000 × $1^1/_3$)

Product Y 20 000 (20 000 × 1)

Product Z 16 000 (8 000 × 2)
        76 000

Therefore 21 per cent (16 000/76 000) of the non-volume-related costs are assigned to product Z if machine hours are used as the allocation base. Hence the traditional system undercosts the low-volume product, and, on applying the above approach, it can be shown that the high-volume product (product X) is overcosted. For example, 53 per cent of the costs (40 000/76 000) are traced to product X with the current system, whereas the activity-based system assigns a much lower proportion of non-volume-related costs to this product.

8.20 (a) (i) *Conventional absorption costing profit statement:*

	XYI	YZT	ABW
(1) Sales volume (000 units)	50	40	30
	£	£	£
(2) Selling price per unit	45	95	73
(3) Prime cost per unit	32	84	65
(4) Contribution per unit	13	11	8
(5) Total contribution in £000s (1 × 4)	650	440	240
(6) Machine department overheads*a*	120	240	144
(7) Assembly department overheads*b*	288.75	99	49.5
Profit (£000)	241.25	101	46.5

Total profit = £388 750

Notes:
*a*XYI = 50 000 × 2 hrs × £1.20, YZT = 40 000 × 5 hrs × £1.20
*b*XYI = 50 000 × 7 hrs × £0.825, YZT = 40 000 × 3 hrs × £0.825

(ii) *Cost pools:*

	Machining services	Assembly services	Set-ups	Order processing	Purchasing
£000	357	318	26	156	84
Cost drivers	420 000 machine hours	530 000 direct labour hours	520 set-ups	32 000 customer orders	11 200 suppliers' orders
Cost driver rates	£0.85 per machine hour	£0.60 per direct labour hour	£50 per set-up	£4.875 per customer order	£7.50 per suppliers' order

ABC profit statement:

	XYI (£000)	YZT (£000)	ABW (£000)
Total contribution	650	440	240
Less overheads:			
Machine department at £0.85 per hour	85	170	102
Assembly at £0.60 per hour	210	72	36
Set-up costs at £50 per set-up	6	10	10
Order processing at £4.875 per order	39	39	78
Purchasing at £7.50 per order	22.5	30	31.5
Profit (Loss)	287.5	119	(17.5)

Total profit = £389 000

(b) See the sections on 'Comparison of traditional and ABC systems' and 'Volume-based and non-volume-based cost drivers' in Chapter 8 for the answer to this question.

Material ordering cost per unit of output:
Product	A (1 × £192)/500	= £0.38
	B (4 × £192)/5000	= £0.15
	C (1 × £192)/600	= £0.32
	D (4 × £192)/7000	= £0.11

Material handling related costs
Cost per material handling = £7580/27 = £280.74
Material handling cost per unit of output:
Product	A (2 × £280.74)/500	= £1.12
	B (10 × £280.74)/5000	= £0.56
	C (3 × £280.74)/600	= £1.40
	D (12 × £280.74)/7000	= £0.48

Spare parts
Cost per part = £8600/12 = £716.67
Administration of spare parts cost per unit of output:

Product	A (2 × £716.67)/500	= £2.87
	B (5 × £716.67)/5000	= £0.72
	C (1 × £716.67)/600	= £1.19
	D (4 × £716.67)/7000	= £0.41

Overhead cost per unit of output

Product	A (£)	B (£)	C (£)	D (£)
ABC overhead cost:				
Machine overheads	0.75	0.75	3.00	4.50
Set-ups	0.51	0.31	0.85	0.29
Material ordering	0.38	0.15	0.32	0.11
Material handling	1.12	0.56	1.40	0.48
Spare parts	2.87	0.72	1.19	0.41
	5.63	2.49	6.76	5.79
Present system	1.20	1.20	4.80	7.20
Difference	+4.43	+1.29	+1.96	−1.41

The present system is based on the assumption that all overhead expenditure is volume-related, measured in terms of machine hours. However, the overheads for the five support activities listed in the question are unlikely to be related to machine hours. Instead, they are related to the factors that influence the spending on support activities (i.e. the cost drivers). The ABC system traces cost to products based on the quantity (cost drivers) of activities consumed. Product D is the high-volume product, and thus the present volume-based system traces a large share of overheads to this product. In contrast, the ABC system recognizes that product D consumes overheads according to activity consumption and traces a lower amount of overhead to this product. The overall effect is that, with the present system, product D is overcosted and the remaining products are undercosted. For a more detailed explanation of the difference in resource consumption between products for an ABC and traditional cost system see 'A comparison of traditional and ABC systems' and 'Volume-based and non-volume-based cost drivers' in Chapter 8 for the answer to this question.

Chapter 9

9.17 Answer = A

9.18

	(£)	(£)
Cash sales		22 000
Credit sales		
April (70% × 0.6 × 0.98 × £70 000)	28 812	
March (27% × 0.6 × £60 000)	9 720	38 532
		60 532

Answer = C

9.19 Total variable costs for year ended March 2008 = £647 080 (£924 400 × 70%)
Analysed by:

	Passengers	Parcels
Variable costs	£388 248 (60%)	258 832 (40%)
Activity for year ended March 2008	1024	24 250 kg
£ per passenger	£379.148	
£ per kg		£10.674
Revised costs based on 3% increase	£390.52	£10.994

	209	7200 kg
Activity for period ending September 2008	209	7200 kg
Budgeted cost (Activity × Revised cost)	£81 619	£79 157

The answer is A for part (a) and C for part (b)

9.20 (a) Production budget

Product	A	B
Sales	2000	1500
Opening stock	(100)	(200)
Closing stock		
(10% × sales level)	200	150
	2100	1450

(b) Materials usage budget

Material type	X kg	Y litres
Usage		
(2100 × 2) + (1450 × 3)	8550	
(2100 × 1) + (1450 × 4)		7900

(c) Materials purchases budget

Usage	8550	7900
Opening stock	(300)	(1000)
Closing stock[a]	850	800
	9100	7700
	× £10	× £7
	£91 000	£53 900

(d) Labour budget

	Skilled hours	Semi-skilled hours
(2100 × 4) + (1450 × 2)	11 300	
(2100 × 2) + (1450 × 5)		11 450
	× £12	× £8
	£135 600	£91 600

Note:
[a]Material closing stock
Material X (2000 × 2 + 1500 × 3) × 10% = 850
Material Y (2000 × 1 + 1500 × 4) × 10% = 850

9.21

Task 1

Alderley Ltd Budget Statements 13 weeks to 4 April

(a) Production budget

	Elgar units	Holst units
Budgeted sales volume	845	1235
Add closing stock[a]	78	1266
Less Opening stock	(163)	(361)
Units of production	760	1140

(b) Material purchases budget

	Elgar kg	Holst kg	Total kg
Material consumed	5320 (760 × 7)	9120 (1140 × 8)	14 440
Add raw material closing stock[b]			2 888
Less raw material opening stock			(2 328)
Purchases (kg)			15 000

(c) Purchases (£) (1500 × £12)   £180 000

(d) Production labour budget

	Elgar hours	Holst hours	Total hours
Standard hours produced[c]	6080	5700	11 780
Productivity adjustment (5/95 × 11 780)			620
Total hours employed			12 400
Normal hours employed[d]			11 544
Overtime hours			856

(e) Labour cost

	£
Normal hours (11 544 × £8)	92 352
Overtime (856 × £8 × 125%)	8 560
Total	100 912

Notes:
[a]Number of days per period = 13 weeks × 5 days = 65
 Stock: Elgar = (6/65) × 845 = 78, Holst = (14/65) × 1235 = 266
[b](13/65) × (5320 + 9120) = 2888
[c]Elgar 760 × 8 hours = 6080, Holst 1140 × 5 hours = 5700
[d]24 employees × 37 hours × 13 weeks = 11 544

Task 2

(a) Four ways of forecasting future sales volume are:
  (i)   Where the number of customers is small it is possible to interview them to ascertain what their likely demand will be over the forecasting period.
  (ii) Produce estimates based on the opinion of executives and sales personnel. For example, sales personnel may be asked to estimate the sales of each product to their customers, or regional sales managers may estimate the total sales for each of their regions.
  (iii) Market research may be necessary where it is intended to develop new products or new markets. This may involve interviews with existing and potential customers in order to estimate potential demand.
  (iv) Estimates involving statistical techniques that incorporate general business and market conditions and past growth in sales.
(b) Interviewing customers and basing estimates on the opinions of sales personnel are likely to be more appropriate for existing products and customers involving repeat sales. Market research is appropriate for new products or markets and where the market is large and anticipated revenues are likely to be sufficient to justify the cost of undertaking the research.
    Statistical estimates derived from past data are likely to be appropriate where conditions are likely to be stable and past demand patterns are likely to be repeated through time. This method is most suited to existing products or markets where sufficient data is available to establish a trend in demand.
(c) The major limitation of interviewing customers is that they may not be prepared to divulge the information if their future plans are commercially sensitive. There is also no guarantee that the orders will be placed with Alderley Ltd. They may place their orders with competitors.

Where estimates are derived from sales personnel there is a danger that they might produce over-optimistic estimates in order to obtain a favourable performance rating at the budget setting stage. Alternatively, if their future performance is judged by their ability to achieve the budgeted sales they may be motivated to underestimate sales demand.

Market research is expensive and may produce unreliable estimates if inexperienced researchers are used. Also small samples are often used which may not be indicative of the population and this can result in inaccurate estimates.

Statistical estimates will produce poor demand estimates where insufficient past data is available, demand is unstable over time and the future environment is likely to be significantly different from the past. Statistical estimates are likely to be inappropriate for new products and new markets where past data is unavailable.

9.22 (a) (i) *Cash budget for weeks 1–6*

	Week 1 (£)	Week 2 (£)	Week 3 (£)	Week 4 (£)	Week 5 (£)	Week 6 (£)
Receipts from debtors[a]	24 000	24 000	28 200	25 800	19 800	5 400
Payments:						
To material suppliers[b]	8 000	12 500	6 000	nil	nil	nil
To direct workers[c]	3 200	4 200	2 800	nil	nil	nil
For variable overheads[d]	4 800	3 200	nil	nil	nil	nil
For fixed overhead[e]	8 300	8 300	6 800	6 800	6 800	6 800
Total payments	24 300	28 200	15 600	6 800	6 800	6 800
Net movement	(300)	(4 200)	12 600	19 000	13 000	(1 400)
Opening balance (week 1 given)	1 000	700	(3 500)	9 100	28 100	41 100
Closing balance	700	(3 500)	9 100	28 100	41 100	39 700

Notes
[a]Debtors:

	Week 1	Week 2	Week 3	Week 4	Week 5	Week 6
Units sold*	400	500	400	300	—	—
Sales (£)	24 000	30 000	24 000	18 000	—	—
Cash received (70%)		16 800	21 000	16 800	12 600	
(30%)			7 200	9 000	7 200	5 400
Given	24 000	7 200				
Total receipts (£)	24 000	24 000	28 200	25 800	19 800	5 400

*Sales in week 4 = opening stock (600 units) + production in weeks 1 and 2 (1000 units) less sales in weeks 1–3 (1300 units) = 300 units.
[b]Creditors:

	Week 1 (£)	Week 2 (£)	Week 3 (£)	Week 4	Week 5	Week 6
Materials consumed at £15	9 000	6 000	—	—	—	—
Increase in stocks	3 500	—				
Materials purchased	12 500	6 000				
Payment to suppliers	8 000 (given)	12 500	6000	nil	nil	nil

[c]Wages:

	Week 1 (£)	Week 2 (£)	Week 3 (£)	Week 4	Week 5	Week 6
Wages consumed at £7	4200	2800	nil	nil	nil	nil
Wages paid	3200 (given)	4200	2800	—	—	—

[d]Variable overhead payment = budgeted production × budgeted cost per unit.
[e]Fixed overhead payments for weeks 1–2 = fixed overhead per week (£9000).
less weekly depreciation (£700).
Fixed overhead payments for weeks 3–6 = £8300 normal payment less £1500 per week.

    (ii) *Comments*

        1. Finance will be required to meet the cash deficit in week 2, but a lowering of the budgeted material stocks at the end of week 1 would reduce the amount of cash to be borrowed at the end of week 2.

        2. The surplus cash after the end of week 2 should be invested on a short-term basis.

        3. After week 6, there will be no cash receipts, but cash outflows will be £6800 per week. The closing balance of £39 700 at the end of week 6 will be sufficient to finance outflows for a further 5 or 6 weeks (£39 700/£6800 per week).

(b) The answer should include a discussion of the matching concept, emphasizing that revenues and expenses may not be attributed to the period when the associated cash inflows and outflows occur. Also, some items of expense do not affect cash outflow (e.g. depreciation).

9.23 (a) See 'Zero-based budgeting' in Chapter 9 for the answer to this question. In particular the answer should stress that the first stage should be to explicitly state the objectives that each part of the organization is trying to achieve. The activities for achieving these objectives should be described in a decision package. A decision package should consist of a base package, which would normally represent a minimum level of activity, plus incremental packages for higher levels of activity and costs. The packages are then evaluated and ranked in order of their decreasing benefits. A cut-off point is determined by the budgeted spending level, and packages are allocated according to their ranking until the budgeted spending level is reached.

(b) For the answer to this question see 'Zero-based budgeting' in Chapter 9.

(c) The problems that might be faced in introducing a zero-based budgeting scheme are:

    (i) Implementation of zero-based budgeting might be resisted by staff. Traditional incremental budgeting tends to protect the empire that a manager has built. Zero-based budgeting challenges this empire, and so there is a strong possibility that managers might resist the introduction of such a system.

    (ii) There is a need to combat a feeling that current operations are efficient.

    (iii) The introduction of zero-based budgeting is time-consuming, and management may lack the necessary expertise.

    (iv) Lack of top-management support.

(d) Beneficial results are likely to be obtained from a company with the following features:

    (i) A large proportion of the expenditure is of a discretionary nature.

    (ii) Management and employees of the company are unlikely to be resistant to change.

    (iii) Suitable output measures can be developed.

    (iv) A senior manager is employed who has some experience from another organization of implementing zero-based budgeting.

9.24 (a) Incremental budgeting uses the previous year's budget as the starting point for the preparation of next year's budget. It is assumed that the basic structure of the budget will remain unchanged and that adjustments will be made to allow for changes in volume, efficiency and price levels. The budget is therefore concerned with increments to operations that will occur during the period and the focus is on existing use of resources rather than considering alternative strategies for the future budget period. Incremental budgeting suffers from the following weaknesses:

    (i) it perpetuates past inefficiencies;

    (ii) there is insufficient focus on improving efficiency and effectiveness;

    (iii) the resource allocation tends to be based on existing strategies rather than considering future strategies;

    (iv) it tends to focus excessively on the short term and often leads to arbitrary cuts being made in order to achieve short-term financial targets.

(b) See 'Activity-based budgeting' in Chapter 9 for the answer to this question. In particular, the answer should stress that:

    (i) the focus is on managing activities;

    (ii) the focus is on the resources that are required for undertaking activities and identifying those activity resources that are unutilized or which are insufficient to meet the requirements specified in the budget;

(iii) attention is given to eliminating non-value-added activities;

(iv) the focus is on the control of the causes of costs (i.e. the cost drivers).

For a more detailed discussion of some of the above points you should also refer to 'Activity-based management' in Chapter 14.

9.25 (a) *Cumbersome process*

The answer to the first comment in the question should include a very brief summary of 'Stages in the budgeting process' in Chapter 9. The process involves detailed negotiations between the budget holders and their superiors and the accountancy staff. Because the process is very time-consuming it must be started well before the start of the budget year. Subsequent changes in the environment, and the fact that the outcomes reflected in the master budget may not meet financial targets, may necessitate budget revisions and a repeat of the negotiation process. The renegotiating stage may well be omitted because of time constraints. Instead, across the board cost reductions may be imposed to meet the budget targets.

Concentration on short-term financial control

Short-term financial targets are normally set for the budget year and the budget is used as the mechanism for achieving the targets. Budget adjustments are made to ensure that the targets are achieved often with little consideration being given to the impact such adjustments will have on the longer-term plans.

Undesirable motivation effects on managers

Managers are often rewarded or punished based on their budget performance in terms of achieving or exceeding the budget. There is a danger that the budget will be viewed as a punitive device rather than as an aid to managers in managing their areas of responsibility. This can result in dysfunctional consequences such as attempting to build slack into the budgeting system by overstating costs and understating revenues. Alternatively, cuts may be made in discretionary expenses, which could have adverse long-term consequences. The overriding aim becomes to achieve the budget, even if this is done in a manner that is not in the organization's best interests.

Emphasizing formal organizational structure

Budgets are normally structured around functional responsibility centres, such as departments and business units. A functional structure is likely to encourage bureaucracy and slow responses to environmental and competitive changes. There is a danger that there will be a lack of goal congruence and that managers may focus on their own departments to the detriment of the organization. Also if budgets are extended to the lower levels of the organization employees will focus excessively on meeting the budget and this may constrain their activities in terms of the flexibility that is required when dealing with customers.

(b) *Cumbersome process*

Managers could be given greater flexibility on how they will meet their targets. For example, top management might agree specific targets with the managers and the managers could be given authority to achieve the targets in their own way. Detailed budgets are not required and the emphasis is placed on managers achieving their overall targets.

Another alternative is to reduce the budget planning period by implementing a system of continuous or rolling budgets.

Concentration on short-term financial control

This might be overcome by placing more stress on a manager's long-term performance and adopting a profit-conscious style of budget evaluation and also placing more emphasis on participative budgeting (see 'Participation in the budget process' in Chapter 9). Attention should also be given to widening the performance measurement system and focusing on key result areas that deal with both short-term and long-term considerations. In particular a balanced scorecard approach (see Chapter 15) might be adopted.

Undesirable motivation effects on managers

The same points as those made above (i.e. profit-conscious style of evaluation, participative budgeting and a broader range of performance measures) also apply here. In addition, the rewards and punishment system must be changed so that it is linked to a range of performance criteria rather than being dominated by short-term financial budget performance. Consideration could also be given to changing the reward system from focusing on responsibility centre performance to rewards being based on overall company performance.

Emphasizing formal organizational structure

Here the answer could discuss activity-based budgeting with the emphasis being on activity centres and business processes, rather than functional responsibility centres that normally consist of departments. For a discussion of these issues you should refer to 'Activity-based budgeting' in Chapter 9 and 'Activity-based cost management' in Chapter 14. Consideration should also given to converting cost centres to profit centres and establishing a system of internal transfer prices. This would encourage managers to focus more widely on profits rather than just costs. Finally, budgets should not be extended to lower levels of the organization and more emphasis should be given to empowering employees to manage their own activities.

Chapter 10

10.17 *Task 1*

Reclamation Division Performance Report – 4 weeks to 31 May:

Original budget   250 tonnes
Actual output   200 tonnes

	Budget based on 200 tonnes	Actual	Variance	Comments
Controllable expenses:				
Wages and social security costs[a]	43 936	46 133	2197A	
Fuel[b]	15 000	15 500	500A	
Consumables[c]	2 000	2 100	100A	
Power[d]	1 500	1 590	90A	
Directly attributable overheads[e]	20 000	21 000	1000A	
	82 436	86 323	3887A	
Non-controllable expenses:				
Plant maintenance[e]	5 950	6 900	950A	
Central services[e]	6 850	7 300	450A	
	12 800	14 200	1400A	
Total	95 236	100 523	5287A	

Notes:
[a]6 employees × 4 teams × 42 hours per week × £7.50 per hour × 4 weeks = £30 240.
[b]200 tonnes × £75
[c]200 tonnes × £10
d£500 + (£5 × 200) = £1500
[e]It is assumed that directly attributable expenses, plant maintenance and central services are non-variable expenses.

Task 2

(a) (i) Past knowledge can provide useful information on future outcomes but ideally budgets ought to be based on the most up-to-date information. Budgeting should be related to the current environment and the use of past information that is two years old can only be justified where the operating conditions and environment are expected to remain unchanged.

(ii) For motivation and planning purposes budgets should represent targets based on what we are proposing to do. For control purposes budgets should be flexed based on what was actually done so that actual costs for actual output can be compared with budgeted costs for the actual output. This ensures that valid comparisons will be made.

(iii) For variable expenses the original budget should be reduced in proportion to reduced output in order to reflect cost behaviour. Fixed costs are not adjusted since they are unaffected in the short term by output changes. Flexible budgeting ensures that like is being compared with like so that reduced output does not increase the probability that favourable cost variances will be reported. However, if less was produced because of actual sales being less than budget this will result in an adverse sales variance and possibly an adverse profit variance.

(iv) Plant maintenance costs are apportioned on the basis of capital values and therefore newer equipment (with higher written down values) will be charged with a higher maintenance cost. Such an approach does not provide a meaningful estimate of maintenance resources consumed by departments since older equipment is likely to be more expensive to maintain. The method of recharging should be reviewed and ideally based on estimated usage according to maintenance records. The charging of the overspending by the maintenance department to user departments is questionable since this masks inefficiencies. Ideally, maintenance department costs should be recharged based on actual usage at budgeted cost and the maintenance department made accountable for the adverse spending (price) variance.

(v) The comments do not explain the causes of the variances and are presented in a negative tone. No comments are made, nor is any praise given, for the favourable variances.

(vi) Not all variances should be investigated. The decision to investigate should depend on both their absolute and relative size and the likely benefits arising from an investigation.

(vii) Central service costs are not controllable by divisional managers. However, even though the divisional manager cannot control these costs there is an argument for including them as non-controllable costs in the performance report. The justification for this is that divisional managers are made aware of central service costs and may put pressure on central service staff to control such costs more effectively. It should be made clear to divisional managers that they are not accountable for any non-controllable expenses that are included in their performance reports.

10.18 (a) (i) Activity varies from month to month, but quarterly budgets are set by dividing total annual expenditure by 4.

(ii) The budget ought to be analysed by shorter intervals (e.g. monthly) and costs estimated in relation to monthly activity.

(iii) For control purposes monthly comparisons and cumulative monthly comparisons of planned and actual expenditure to date should be made.

(iv) The budget holder does not participate in the setting of budgets.

(v) An incremental budget approach is adopted. A zero-based approach would be more appropriate.

(vi) The budget should distinguish between controllable and uncontrollable expenditure.

(b) The information that should flow from a comparison of the actual and budgeted expenditure would consist of the variances for the month and year to date analysed into the following categories:

(i) controllable and uncontrollable items;

(ii) price and quantity variances with price variance analysed by inflationary and non-inflationary effects.

(c) (i) Flexible budgets should be prepared on a monthly basis. Possible measures of activity are number of patient days or expected laundry weight.

(ii) The laundry manager should participate in the budgetary process.

(iii) Costs should be classified into controllable and non-controllable items.

(iv) Variances should be reported and analysed by price and quantity on a monthly and cumulative basis.

(v) Comments should be added explaining possible reasons for the variances.

10.19

Task 1

Performance Statement – Month to 31 October

Number of guest days = Original budget   9 600

Flexed budget   11 160

	Flexed budget (£)	Actual (£)	Variance (£)
Controllable expenses			
Food (1)	23 436	20 500	2936F
Cleaning materials (2)	2 232	2 232	0
Heat, light and power (3)	2 790	2 050	740F
Catering staff wages (4)	8 370	8 400	30A
	36 828	33 182	3646F
Non-controllable expenses			
Rent, rates, insurance and depreciation (5)	1 860	1 860	0

Notes:

(1) £20 160/9600 × 11 160.

(2) £1920/9600 × 11 160.

(3) £2400/9600 × 11 160.

(4) £11 160/40 × £30.

(5) Original fixed budget based on 30 days but October is a 31-day month (£1800/30 × 31).

Task 2

(a) See the sections on the multiple functions of budgets (motivation) in Chapter 9, and 'Setting financial performance targets' in Chapter 10 for the answers to this question.

(b) Motivating managers ought to result in improved performance. However, besides motivation, improved performance is also dependent on managerial ability, training, education and the existence of a favourable environment. Therefore motivating managers is not guaranteed to lead to improved performance.

(c) The use of a fixed budget is unlikely to encourage managers to become more efficient where budgeted expenses are variable with activity. In the original performance report actual expenditure for 11 160 guest days is compared with budgeted expenditure for 9600 days. It is misleading to compare actual costs at one level of activity with budgeted costs at another level of activity. Where the actual level of activity is above the budgeted level adverse variances are likely to be reported for variable cost items. Managers will therefore be motivated to reduce activity so that favourable variances will be reported. Therefore it is not surprising that Susan Green has expressed concern that the performance statement does not reflect a valid reflection of her performance. In contrast, most of Brian Hilton's expenses are fixed and costs will not increase when volume increases. A failure to flex the budget will therefore not distort his performance.

    To motivate, challenging budgets should be set and small adverse variances should normally be regarded as a healthy sign and not something to be avoided. If budgets are always achieved with no adverse variances this may indicate that undemanding budgets may have been set that are unlikely to motivate best possible performance. This situation could apply to Brian Hilton who always appears to report favourable variances.

10.20 (a) Recommendations are as follows:

(i) For cost control and managerial performance evaluation, expenses should be separated into their controllable and non-controllable categories. Two separate profit calculations should be presented: controllable profit, which is appropriate for measuring managerial performance, and a 'bottom-line' net profit, which measures the economic performance of each store rather than the manager.

(ii) The report should be based on an *ex post* basis. In other words, if the environment is different from that when the original budget was set, actual performance should be compared with a budget that reflects any changed conditions. For example, the budget should be adjusted to reflect the effect of the roadworks.

(iii) Actual expenses should be compared with flexed budgets and not the original budget.

(iv) Each store consists of three departments. The report should therefore analyse gross profits by departments. Selling prices and the cost of goods sold are beyond the control of the stores' managers, but each departmental manager can influence sales volume. An analysis of gross profits by departments and a comparison with previous periods should provide useful feedback on sales performance and help in deciding how much space should be allocated to each activity.

(v) Stock losses should be minimized. Such losses are controllable by departmental managers. The cost of stock losses should therefore be monitored and separately reported.

(vi) The budget should include cumulative figures to give an indication of trends, performance to date and the potential annual bonus.

(vii) Any imputed interest charges should be based on economic values of assets and not historic costs.

(b) The report should include a discussion of the following:

(i) *Review of delegation policies:* Head office purchases the goods for sale, fixes selling prices, appoints permanent staff and sets pay levels. Stores managers are responsible for stores' running expenses, employment of temporary staff and control of stocks.

Purchasing is centralized, thus enabling the benefits of specialized buying and bulk purchasing to be obtained. Purchasing policies are coordinated with expected sales by consultation between head office buyers and stores and departmental managers. It is wise to make store managers responsible for controlling stocks because they are in the best position to assess current and future demand.

Managers are responsible for sales volume but they cannot fix selling prices. There are strong arguments for allowing stores to set selling prices, and offer special discounts on certain goods. Central management may wish to retain some overall control by requiring proposed price changes beyond certain limits to be referred to them for approval. There are also strong arguments for allowing the stores' managers to appoint permanent staff. The stores' managers are likely to be in a better position to be able to assess the abilities necessary to be a successful member of their own team.

(ii) *Strengths of the management control system:*

1   Sales targets are set after consultation between head office and the departmental managers.

2   The budgets are prepared well in advance of the start of the budget year, thus giving adequate time for consultation.

3   Performance reports are available one week after the end of the period.

4   Budgets are adjusted for seasonal factors.

5   Significant variations in performance are investigated and appropriate action is taken.

(iii) *Weaknesses of the management control system:*

1   There is no consultation in the setting of expense budgets.

2   Actual costs are compared with a fixed budget and not a flexible budget.

3   Costs are not separated into controllable and non-controllable categories.

4   Budgets are set on an incremental basis with budgets set by taking last year's base and adjusting for inflation.

5   Budgets are not revised for control purposes. Targets set for the original budget before the start of the year may be inappropriate for comparison with actual expenses incurred towards the end of the budget year.

6   Using a budget that does not include *ex post* results and that is not linked to controllable profit is likely to be demotivating, and results in managers having little confidence in the budget system.

(iv) *Recommendations:*
1 Compare actual costs with a flexed budget.
2 The performance report should separate costs into controllable and uncontrollable categories, and controllable profit should be highlighted. Any bonus payments should be related to controllable profit and not 'bottom-line' profits.
3 Introduce monthly or quarterly rolling budgets.
4 Ensure that the store's managers participate in setting the budget and accept the target against which they will be judged.
5 Set targets using a zero-based approach.
6 Consider extending the bonus scheme to departmental managers.

10.21 (i) Budgets are used for a variety of purposes, one of which is to evaluate the performance of budgetees. When budgets form the basis for future performance evaluation, there is a possibility that budgetees will introduce bias into the process for personal gain and self-protection. Factors that are likely to cause managers to submit budget estimates that do not represent their best estimates include:
1 *The reward system:* If managers believe that rewards depend upon budget attainment then they might be encouraged to underestimate sales budgets and overestimate cost budgets.
2 *Past performance:* If recent performance has been poor, managers may submit favourable plans so as to obtain approval from their supervisors. Such an approach represents a trade-off advantage of short-run security and approval against the risk of not being able to meet the more optimistic plans.
3 *Incremental budgeting:* Incremental budgeting involves adding increments to past budgets to reflect expected future changes. Consequently, the current budget will include bias that has been built into previous budgets.
4 *External influences:* If managers believe that their performance is subject to random external influences then, from a self-protection point of view, they might submit budgets that can easily be attained.
5 *Style of performance evaluation:* A budget-constrained style of evaluation might encourage the budgetee to meet the budget at all costs. Consequently, budgetees will be motivated to bias their budget estimates.

(ii) The following procedures should be introduced to minimize the likelihood of biased estimates:
1 Encourage managers to adopt a more flexible profit-conscious style of evaluation.
2 Adopt a system of zero-based budgeting.
3 Key figures in the budget process (e.g. sales estimates) should be checked by using information from different sources.
4 Planning and operating variances should be segregated. Managers might be motivated to submit more genuine estimates if they are aware that an *ex post* budget will be used as a basis for performance appraisal.
5 Participation by the budgetees in the budget process should be encouraged so as to secure a greater commitment to the budget process and improve communication between budgetees, their superior and the budget accountants.

10.22 (a) See Chapter 10 for the answer to this question. In particular, your answer should stress:
(i) The need for a system of responsibility accounting based on a clear definition of a manager's authority and responsibility.
(ii) The production of performance reports at frequent intervals comparing actual and budget costs for individual expense items. Variances should be analysed according to whether they are controllable or non-controllable by the manager.
(iii) The managers should participate in the setting of budgets and standards.
(iv) The system should ensure that variances are investigated, causes found and remedial action is taken.
(v) An effective cost control system must not be used as a punitive device, but should be seen as a system that helps managers to control their costs more effectively.

(b) Possible problems include:
  (i) Difficulties in setting standards for non-repetitive work.
  (ii) Non-acceptance by budgetees if they view the system as a punitive device to judge their performance.
  (iii) Isolating variances where interdependencies exist.

10.23 (a) See 'Planning', 'Motivation' and 'Performance evaluation' in the section on the multiple functions of budgets in Chapter 9 for the answer to this question. The answer should emphasize that the role of motivation is to encourage goal congruence between the company and the employees.

(b) See 'Conflicting roles of budgets' in Chapter 9 for an explanation of how the planning and motivation roles can conflict. Prior to the commencement of the budget period, management should prepare budgets that represent targets to be achieved based upon anticipated environmental variables. It is possible that at the end of the budget period the *actual* environmental variables will be different from those envisaged when the budget was prepared. Therefore actual performance will be determined by the actual environment variables, but the plans reflected in the budget may be based on different environmental variables. It is inappropriate to compare actual performance based on one set of environmental variables with budgeted performance based on another set of environmental variables. Consequently, a budget that is used for planning purposes will be in conflict with one that is used for performance evaluation.

The conflict between motivation and evaluation is described by Barrett and Fraser (1977) as follows:

In many situations the budget that is most effective in the evaluation role might be called an ex-post facto budget. It is one that considers the impact of uncontrollable or unforeseeable events, and it is constructed or adjusted after the fact.

The potential role conflict between the motivation and evaluation roles involves the impact on motivation of using an ex-post facto standard in the evaluation process. Managers are unlikely to be totally committed to achieving the budget's objectives if they know that the performance standards by which they are to be judged may change.

In other words, for evaluation purposes the budget might be adjusted to reflect changes in environmental variables. If a manager expects that the budget will be changed for evaluation purposes, there is a danger that he or she will not be as highly motivated to achieve the original budget.

(c) (i) The planning and motivation conflict might be resolved by setting two budgets. A budget based on most likely outcomes could be set for planning purposes and a separate, more demanding budget could be used for motivation purposes.
  (ii) The planning and evaluation role conflict can be resolved by comparing actual performance with an *ex post* budget (see Chapter 10 for an indication of how this conflict can be resolved).
  (iii) Barrett and Fraser (1977) suggest the following approach for resolving the motivation and evaluation conflict:

The conflict between the motivation and evaluation roles can also be reduced by using 'adjustable budgets'. These are operational budgets whose objectives can be modified under predetermined sets of circumstances. Thus revision is possible during the operating period and the performance standard can be changed.

In one company that uses such a budgeting system, managers commit themselves to a budget with the understanding that, if there are substantial changes in any of five key economic or environmental variables, top management will revise the budget and new performance criteria will be set. This company automatically makes budget revisions whenever there are significant changes in any of these five variables. Naturally, the threshold that triggers a new budget will depend on the relative importance of each variable. With this system, managers know they are expected to meet their budgets. The budget retains its motivating characteristics because it represents objectives that are possible to achieve. Uncontrollable events are not allowed to affect budgeted objectives in such a way that they stand little chance of being met. Yet revisions that are made do not have to adversely affect commitment, since revisions are agreed to in advance and procedures for making them are structured into the overall budgeting system.

A more detailed answer to this question can be found in Barrett and Fraser (1977).

10.24 (a) The answer should include a discussion of the following points:
  (i) Constant pressure from top management for greater production may result in the creation of anti-management work groups and reduced efficiency, so that budgetees can protect themselves against what they consider to be increasingly stringent targets.
  (ii) Non-acceptance of budgets if the budgetees have not been allowed to participate in setting the budgets.
  (iii) Negative attitudes if the budget is considered to be a punitive control device instead of a system to help managers do a better job. The negative attitudes might take the form of reducing cooperation between departments and also with the accounting department. Steps might be taken to ensure that costs do not fall below budget, so that the budget will not be reduced next year. There is a danger that data will be falsified, and more effort will be directed to finding excuses for failing to achieve the budget than trying to control or reduce costs.
  (iv) Managers might try and achieve the budget at all costs even if this results in actions that are not in the best interests of the organization, e.g. delaying maintenance costs.
  (v) Organizational atmosphere may become one of competition and conflict rather than one of cooperation and conciliation.
  (vi) Suspicion and mistrust of top management, resulting in the whole budgeting process being undermined.
  (vii) Belief that the system of evaluation is unjust and widespread worry and tension by the budgetees. Tension might be relieved by falsifying information, blaming others or absenteeism.
  (b) For the answer to this question see 'Dealing with the distorting effects of uncontrollable factors before (and after) the measurement period' in Chapter 10.

10.25 The answer should include a discussion of the following:
  (i) The impact of targets on performance.
  (ii) The use of accounting control techniques for performance evaluation.
  (iii) Participation in the budgeting and standard setting process.
  (iv) Bias in the budget process.
  (v) Management use of budgets and the role of the accountant in the education process.
  See Chapter 10 for a discussion of each of the above items.

10.26 Managers may be reluctant to participate in setting budgets for the following reasons:
  (i) Managers may consider that they do not engage in true participation if they cannot influence the budget. They may consider the process to be one of the senior managers securing formal acceptance of previously determined target levels.
  (ii) Personality of budgetees may result in authoritarian managers having authoritarian expectations of their superiors. Consequently, authoritarian budgetees may be reluctant to participate in the budget process.
  (iii) The degree to which individuals have control over their own destiny appears to influence the desire for participation. Managers may believe that they cannot significantly influence results and thus consider participation to be inappropriate.
  (iv) Bad management/superior relationships.
  (v) Lack of understanding of the budget process or a belief by the budgetees that they will be engaging in a process that will be used in a recriminatory manner by their superiors.

The unwanted side-effects that might arise from the imposition of budgets by senior management include the following:

(i) Non-acceptance of budgets.
(ii) The budgetees might consider the method of performance evaluation to be unjust.
(iii) Creation of anti-management cohesive work groups.
(iv) Reduced efficiency by work groups so as to protect themselves against what they consider to be increasingly stringent targets.
(v) The budget system will be undermined. The real problem is the way management use the system rather than inadequacies of the budget system itself.
(vi) An increase in suspicion and mistrust, so undermining the whole budgeting process.
(vii) Encouraging budgetees to falsify and manipulate information presented to management.
(viii) Organizational atmosphere may become one of competition and conflict rather than one of cooperation and conciliation.
(ix) Managers might try to achieve the budget at all costs even if this results in actions that are not in the best interests of the organization.

10.27 (a) For a discussion of feedback and feed-forward controls see Chapter 10. The remaining terms are also discussed in Chapter 10.
(b) For the answer to this question see 'Dealing with the distorting effects of uncontrollable factors before (and after) the measurement period', 'Participation in the budget and target setting process' and 'Side-effects from using accounting information for performance evaluation' in Chapter 10.

Chapter 11

11.11 A favourable labour efficiency variance indicates that actual hours used were less than the standard hours produced. The favourable variance was £7800. Therefore the standard hours produced were 18 700 (17 500 + £7800/£6.50).

Answer = D

11.12 Materials price variance = (Standard price – Actual price) × Actual quantity
= (Actual quantity × Standard price) – Actual cost
= (8200 × £0.80) – £6888
= £328 Adverse

Material usage variance = (Standard quantity – Actual quantity) × Standard price
= (870 × 8 kg = 6960 – 7150) × £0.80
= £152 Adverse

Answer = D

11.13 Fixed overhead variance = Budgeted cost (not flexed) – Actual cost
= £10 000 per month – £9800
= £200 Favourable

Answer = B

11.14 Sales volume variance = (Actual sales volume – Budgeted sales volume) × Standard contribution margin
= (4500 – 5000) £4.40
= £2200 Adverse

Answer = B

11.15 *Preliminary calculations*

The standard product cost and selling price are calculated as follows:

	(£)
Direct materials	
X (10 kg at £1)	10
Y (5 kg at £5)	25
Direct wages (5 hours × £8)	40
Standard variable cost	75
Profit/contribution margin	75
Selling price	150

The actual profit for the period is calculated as follows:

	(£)	(£)
Sales (9500 at £160)		1 520 000
Direct materials: X	115 200	
Y	225 600	
Direct wages (46 000 × £8.20)	377 200	
Fixed overhead	290 000	1 008 000
Actual profit		512 000

It is assumed that the term 'using a fixed budget' refers to the requirement to reconcile the actual results with the original fixed budget.

	(£)	(£)
Material price variance:		
(Standard price – Actual price) × Actual quantity		
X: (£1 – £1.20) × 96 000	19 200 A	
Y: (£5 – £4.70) × 48 000	14 440 F	4800 A
Material usage variance:		
(Standard quantity – Actual quantity) × Standard price		
X: (9500 × 10 = 95 000 – 96 000) × £1	1 000 A	
Y: (9500 × 5 = 47 500 – 48 000) × £5	2 500 A	3500 A

The actual materials used are in standard proportions. Therefore there is no mix variance.

	(£)	(£)
Wage rate variance:		
(Standard rate – Actual rate) × Actual hours		
(£8 – £8.20) × 46 000	9 200 A	
Labour efficiency variance:		
(Standard hours – Actual hours) × Standard rate		
(9500 × 5 = 47 500 – 46 000) × £8	12 000 F	2 800 F
Fixed overhead expenditure:		
Budgeted fixed overheads – Actual fixed overheads		
(10 000 × £30 = £300 000 – £290 000)		10 000 F
Sales margin price variance:		
(Actual margin – Standard margin) × Actual sales volume (£85 – £75) × 9500	95 000 F	
Sales margin volume variance:		
(Actual sales volume – Budgeted sales volume) × Standard margin		
(9500 – 10 000) × £75	37 500 A	57 500 F
Total variance		62 000 F

	(£)
Budgeted profit contribution	
(10 000 units at £75)	750 000
Less budgeted fixed overheads	300 000
Budgeted profit	450 000
Add favourable variances (see above)	62 000
Actual profit	512 000

11.16 (a) *Standard product cost for one unit of product XY*

	(£)
Direct materials (8 kg (W2) at £1.50 (W1) per kg)	12.00
Direct wages (2 hours (W4) at £4 (W3) per hour)	8.00
Variable overhead (2 hours (W4) at £1 (W5) per hour)	2.00
	22.00

Workings

(W1) Actual quantity of materials purchased at standard price is £225 000 (actual cost plus favourable material price variance).
Therefore standard price = £1.50 (£225 000/150 000 kg).

(W2) Material usage variance = 6000 kg (£9000/£1.50 standard price).
Therefore standard quantity for actual production = 144 000 kg (150 000 – 6000 kg).
Therefore standard quantity per unit = 8 kg (144 000 kg/18 000 units).

(W3) Actual hours worked at standard rate = £256 000 (£264 000 – £8 000).
Therefore standard rate per hour = £8 (£256 000/32 000 hours).

(W4) Labour efficiency variance = 4000 hours (£32 000/£8).
Therefore standard hours for actual production = 36 000 hours (32 000 + 4000).
Therefore standard hours per unit = 2 hours (36 000 hours/18 000 units).

(W5) Actual hours worked at the standard variable overhead rate is £32 000 (£38 000 actual variable overheads less £6000 favourable expenditure variance).
Therefore, standard variable overhead rate = £1 (£32 000/32 000 hours).

(b) See 'Types of cost standards' in Chapter 11 for the answer to this question.

11.17 (a) Budgeted contribution = Standard unit contribution (£1.99 – £1.39 = £0.60) × 50 000 = £30 000
Actual contribution = £96 480 – (£58 450 + £6800 + £3250) = £27 980

(b) Sales margin price = (Actual price – Standard price) × Actual sales volume
= Actual sales (£96 480) – Actual sales volume (49 700) × Standard price (£1.99)

= £2423A (note that the same answer would be obtained using contribution margins in the above formula)

Sales margin volume = (Actual volume – Budgeted volume) × Standard unit contribution

= (49 700 – 50 000) × £0.60 = £180A

Ingredients price = (SP – AP)AQ = (AQ × SP) – (AQ × AP)

= (55 000 × £1.18/1.08 = £60 093) – £58 450 = £1643F

Ingredients usage = (SQ – AQ)SP = (49 700 × 1.08 = 53 676 – 55 000) £1.18/1.08 = £1447A

Wage rate = (SP – AP)AH = (AH × SP) – (AH ×AP)
= (1200 × £6[1] = £7200) – £6800 = £400F

Labour efficiency = (SH – AH)SP = (49 700 × 1.5 minutes = 1242.5 hours – 1200 hours) × £6 = £255F

Variable conversion price = (SP – AP)AH = (AH × SP) – (AH × AP)
= (1200 × £2.40[2] = £2880 – £3250 = £370A

Variable conversion efficiency = (SH – AH)SP = (49 700 × 1.5 minutes = 1242.5 hours – 1200 hours) × £2.40 = £102F

Notes
[1]Actual price paid for labour = £0.15/1.5 minutes = £0.10 per minute = £6 per hour
[2]Actual variable overhead price = £0.06/1.5 minutes = £0.04 per minute = £2.40 per hour

Reconciliation statement

		(£)
Budgeted contribution		30 000
Sales volume contribution variance		180 (A)
Standard contribution on actual sales		29 820
Sales price variance		2 423 (A)
		27 397

Cost variances		A	F
Ingredients:	Price		1643
	Usage	1447	
Labour	Rate		400
	Efficiency		255
Conversion cost	Expenditure	370	
	Efficiency		102	583 (F)
Total		1817	2400	27 980
Actual contribution			

11.18 (a) Wage rate variance = (SP – AP)AH = (SP × AH) – (AP × AH)
= (£9 × 53 workers × 13 weeks × 40 hrs) – £248 740 = £700A

Labour efficiency = (SH – AH)SP

SH (Standard hours) = (35 000 × 0.4 hrs) + (25 000 × 0.56 hrs) = 28 000

AH (Actual hours) = 53 workers × 13 weeks × 40 hrs = 27 560

Variance = (28 000 – 27 560) × £9 = £3960A

(b) Material price variance = (SP – AP)AQ
= (AQ × SP) – (AQ × AP)

£430F (given) = 47 000 SP – £85 110

SP (Standard price) = $\frac{£430 + 85\,110}{47\,000}$

= £1.82

Material usage variance = (SQ – AQ)SP
= (SQ × SP) – (AQ × SP)

£320.32A (given) = £1.82 SQ – (33 426 × £1.82)

– £320.32A = £1.82 SQ – £60 835.32

£1.82 SQ = £60 515

SQ = £60 515/£1.82 = 33 250

Note that SQ = Actual production (35 000 units) × Standard usage

Therefore 35 000 × Standard usage = 33 250

Standard usage = 33 250/35 000

= 0.95 kg per unit of component X

(c) For the answer to this question you should refer to the detailed illustration of the budget process shown in Chapter 9. In particular, the answer should indicate that if sales are the limiting factor the production budget should be linked to the sales budget. Once the production budget has been established for the two components, the production quantity of each component multiplied by the standard usage of material A per unit of component output determines the required quantity of material to meet the production requirements. The budgeted purchase quantity of material A consists of the quantity to meet the production usage requirements plus or minus an adjustment to take account of any planned change in the level of raw material stock.

Chapter 12

12.13 Divisional managers do not control the cash function. Therefore controllable net assets should exclude the cash overdraft so controllable net assets are £125 000 (£101 000 + £24 000).

Controllable residual income	= £69 000 (Profit before interest and tax)	
Less cost of capital	= <u>12 500</u> (10% × 125 000)	
Residual income	= <u>56 500</u>	

Answer = B

12.14

	£m
Profit	89.20
Add back:	
Current depreciation (120 × 20%)	24.00
Development costs ((£9.60 × 2/3)	6.40
Less: Replacement depreciation (£168 × 20%)	33.60
Adjusted profit	86.00
Less: Cost of capital charge (13% × £168)[a]	21.84
EVA	64.16

Note:

[a] 13% × [Fixed assets (£168 − £33.6) + Working capital (£27.2) + Development costs (£6.4)]

Answer = A

12.15

	£m	£m
Net profit after tax		8.6
Add:		
Interest	2.3	
Development costs	6.3	
Advertising	1.6	10.2
Less development costs (1/3)		(2.1)
		16.7
Less cost of capital charge (£30m × 13%)		(3.9)
EVA		12.8

12.16 (a)   Return on investment (ROI)

Division A	£
Profit	35 000
Net assets	150 000

Return on investment = 35 000/150 000 = 23.3%

Division B	£
Profit	70 000
Net assets	325 000

Return on investment = 70 000/325 000% = 21.5%

Residual income (RI)

Division A = £35 000 − (150 000 × 0.15) = £12 500
Division B = £70 000 − (325 000 × 0.15) = £21 250

Division A has a higher ROI but a lower residual income.

(b) Return on investment would be the better measure when comparing divisions as it is a relative measure (i.e. based on percentage returns).

(c) Appropriate aspects of performance include:

- competitiveness;
- financial performance;
- quality of service;
- flexibility;
- innovation;
- resource utilization efficiency.

12.17 Working backwards to derive the divisional contribution:

	£
Cost of capital charge	150 000 (£1.25m × 12%)
Residual income	47 200
Profit	197 200
Depreciation	247 500
Fixed costs	487 000
Total contribution	931 700

Contribution per unit = £31.06 (£931 700/30 000 units)

Answer = D

12.18 (a) The annual ROI and residual income calculations for each plant are as follows:

		2009	2010	2011	2012	Total
Aromatic						
(1)	Net cash flow (£m)	2.4	2.4	2.4	2.4	9.6
(2)	Depreciation	1.6	1.6	1.6	1.6	
(3)	Profit	0.8	0.8	0.8	0.8	3.2
(4)	Cost of capital (16% of 6)	(1.02)	(0.77)	(0.51)	(0.26)	
(5)	Residual income	(0.22)	0.03	0.29	0.54	
(6)	Opening WDV of asset	6.4	4.8	3.2	1.6	
(7)	ROI (Row 3/Row 6)	12.5%	16.67%	25%	50%	
Zoman						
(1)	Net cash flow	2.6	2.2	1.5	1.0	7.3
(2)	Depreciation	1.3	1.3	1.3	1.3	
(3)	Profit	1.3	0.9	0.2	(0.3)	2.1
(4)	Cost of capital (16%)	(0.83)	(0.62)	(0.42)	(0.21)	
(5)	Residual income	0.47	0.28	(0.22)	(0.51)	
(6)	Opening WDV of asset	5.2	3.9	2.6	1.3	
(7)	ROI	25%	23%	7.7%	(23%)	

The answer should indicate:

(i) Over the whole life of the project both ROI and residual income (RI) favour the Aromatic plant. The average ROI and RI figures are 25 per cent and £0.16 million (£0.64m/4) for the Aromatic plant and 20 per cent and £0.005 million (£0.02m/4) for the Zoman plant. The ROI calculations are based on expressing the average profits as a percentage of the average investment (defined as one-half of the initial capital investment).

(ii) An explanation that Mr Elton will favour the Zoman plant because it yields a higher ROI and RI over the first two years. Mr Elton will probably focus on a two-year time horizon because of his personal circumstances, since choosing the Aromatic plant is likely to result in him losing his bonus. Therefore he will choose the plant with the lower NPV and there will be a lack of goal congruence.

(iii) Suggestions as to how alternative accounting techniques can assist in reconciling the conflict between accounting performance measures and DCF techniques:

1 Avoiding short-term evaluations and evaluating performance at the end of the project's life. Thus bonuses would be awarded with hindsight.
2 Use alternative asset valuations other than historic cost (e.g. replacement cost).
3 Choose alternative depreciation methods that are most consistent with NPV calculations (e.g. annuity depreciation).
4 Incorporate a range of variables (both financial and non-financial when evaluating managerial performance) that give a better indication of future results that can be expected from current actions.

(b) Managers may use pre-tax profits to evaluate divisional performance because it is assumed that taxation is non-controllable. Taxation payable is based on total group profits and present and past capital expenditure rather than individual divisional profitability. After-tax cash flows are used to appraise capital investments because the focus is on decision-making and accepting those projects that earn a return in excess of the investors' opportunity cost of capital. To do this IRRs and NPVs should be based on after-tax cash flows.

The following potential problems can arise:

(i) Managers may ignore the taxation impact at the decision-making stage because it is not considered when evaluating their performance.
(ii) Confusion and demotivation can occur when different criteria are used for decision-making and performance evaluation.

Possible solutions include evaluating divisional profitability after taxes or evaluating performance based on a comparison of budgeted and actual cash flows. Adopting the latter approach is an attempt to ensure that the same criteria is used for decision-making and performance evaluation.

(c) Steps that can be taken to avoid dysfunctional behaviour include:

(i) Not placing too much emphasis on short-term performance measures and placing greater emphasis on the long term by adopting a profit-conscious style of evaluation.
(ii) Focusing on controllable residual income or economic value added combined with asset valuations derived from depreciation models that are consistent with NPV calculations. Alternatively, performance evaluation might be based on a comparison of budgeted and actual cash flows. The budgeted cash flows should be based on cash flows that are used to appraise capital investments.
(iii) Supplementing financial performance measures with non-financial measures when evaluating performance (see 'Addressing the dysfunctional consequences of short-term financial measures' in Chapter 12).

12.19 (a) To compute EVA(™), adjustments must be made to the conventional after-tax profit measures of $44 million and $55 million shown in the question. Normally an adjustment is made to convert conventional financial accounting depreciation to an estimate of economic depreciation, but the question indicates that profits have already been computed using economic depreciation. Non-cash expenses are added back since the adjusted profit attempts to approximate cash flow after taking into account economic depreciation. Net interest is also added back because the returns required by the providers of funds will be reflected in the cost of capital deduction. Note that net interest is added back because interest will have been allowed as an expense in determining the taxation payment.

The capital employed used to calculate EVA(™) should be based on adjustments that seek to approximate book economic value at the start of each period. Because insufficient information is given, the book value of shareholders' funds plus medium- and long-term loans at the end of 2007 is used as the starting point to determine economic capital employed at the beginning of 2008.

	2007 ($m)	2008 ($m)
Adjusted profit	56.6 (44 + 10 + (4 × 0.65))	68.9 (55 + 10 + (6 × 0.65))
Capital employed	233 (223 + 10)	260 (250 + 10)

The weighted average cost of capital should be based on the target capital structure. The calculation is as follows:

2007 = (15% × 0.6) + (9% × 0.65 × 0.4) = 11.34%
2008 = (17% × 0.6) + (10% × 0.65 × 0.4) = 12.8%

EVA 2007 = 56.6 − (233 × 0.1134) = $30.18m

EVA 2008 = 68.9 − (260 × 0.128) = $35.62

The EVA$^{(TM)}$ measures indicate that the company has added significant value in both years and achieved a satisfactory level of performance.

(b) Advantages of EVA$^{(TM)}$ include:
1   because some discretionary expenses are capitalized the harmful side-effects of financial measures described in Chapters 10 and 12 are reduced;
2   EVA$^{(TM)}$ is consistent with maximizing shareholders' funds;
3   EVA$^{(TM)}$ is easily understood by managers;
4   EVA$^{(TM)}$ can also be linked to managerial bonus schemes and can motivate managers to take decisions that increase shareholder value.

Disadvantages of EVA$^{(TM)}$ include:
1   the EVA$^{(TM)}$ computation can be complicated when many adjustments are required;
2   EVA$^{(TM)}$ is difficult to use for inter-firm and inter-divisional comparisons because it is not a ratio measure;
3   if economic depreciation is not used, the short-term measure can conflict with the long-term measure;
4   economic depreciation is difficult to estimate and conflicts with generally accepted accounting principles, which may hinder its acceptance by financial managers.

12.20 (a) Examples of the types of decisions that should be transferred to the new divisional managers include:
(i)   Product decisions such as product mix, promotion and pricing.
(ii) Employment decisions, except perhaps for the appointment of senior managers.
(iii) Short-term operating decisions of all kinds. Examples include production scheduling, subcontracting and direction of marketing effort.
(iv) Capital expenditure and disinvestment decisions (with some constraints).
(v)   Short-term financing decisions (with some constraints).
(b) The following decisions might be retained at company head office:
(i)   Strategic investment decisions that are critical to the survival of the company as a whole.
(ii) Certain financing decisions that require that an overall view be taken. For example, borrowing commitments and the level of financial gearing should be determined for the group as a whole.
(iii) Appointment of top management.
(iv) Sourcing decisions such as bulk buying of raw materials if corporate interests are best served by centralized buying.
(v)   Capital expenditure decisions above certain limits.
(vi) Common services that are required by all profit centres. Corporate interests might best be served by operating centralized service departments such as an industrial relations department. Possible benefits include reduced costs and the extra benefits of specialization.
(vii) Arbitration decisions on transfer pricing disputes.
(viii)Decisions on items that benefit the company rather than an individual division, e.g. taxation and computer applications.
(c) The answer to this question should focus on the importance of designing performance reports which encourage goal congruence. For a discussion of this topic see Chapter 12.

12.21 (a) For the answer to this question see 'Return on investment' and 'Residual income' in Chapter 12. Note that discounted future earnings are the equivalent to discounted future profits.

(b) The existing ROCE is 20 per cent and the estimated ROCE on the additional investment is 15 per cent (£9000/£60 000). The divisional manager will therefore reject the additional investment, since adding this to the existing investments will result in a decline in the existing ROCE of 20 per cent.

The residual income on the additional investment is £600 (£9000 average profit for the year less an imputed interest charge of 14% × £6000 = £8400). The manager will accept the additional investment, since it results in an increase in residual income.

If the discounted future earnings method is used, the investment would be accepted, since it will yield a positive figure for the year (that is, £9000 × 3.889 discount factor).

Note that the annual future cash flows are £19 000 (£9000 net profit plus £10 000 depreciation provision). The project has a 6-year life. The annual cash inflow must be in excess of £15 428 (£60 000/3.889 annuity factor – 6 years at 14%) if the investment is to yield a positive NPV. If annual cash flows are £19 000 each year for the next 6 years, the project should be accepted.

The residual income and discounted future earnings methods of evaluation will induce the manager to accept the investment. These methods are consistent with the correct economic evaluation using the NPV method. If ROCE is used to evaluate performance, the manager will incorrectly reject the investment. This is because the manager will only accept projects that yield a return in excess of the current ROCE of 20 per cent.

Note that the above analysis assumes that the cash flows/profits are constant from year to year.

12.22 (a) For cost control and performance measurement purposes it is necessary to measure performance at frequent intervals. Managers tend to be evaluated on short-term (monthly, quarterly or even yearly) performance measures such as residual income (RI) or return on investment (ROI). Such short-term performance measures focus only on the performance for the particular control period. If a great deal of stress is placed on managers meeting short-term performance measure targets, there is a danger that they will take action that will improve short-term performance but that will not maximize long-term profits. For example, by skimping on expenditure on advertising, customer services, maintenance, and training and staff development costs, it is possible to improve short-term performance. However, such actions may not maximize long-term profits.

Ideally, performance measures ought to be based on future results that can be expected from a manager's actions during a period. This would involve a comparison of the present value of future cash flows at the start and end of the period, and a manager's performance would be based on the increase in present value during the period. Such a system is not feasible, given the difficulty in predicting and measuring outcomes from current actions.

ROI and RI represent single summary measures of performance. It is virtually impossible to capture in summary financial measures all the variables that measure the success of a manager. It is therefore important that accountants broaden their reporting systems to include additional non-financial measures of performance that give clues to future outcomes from present actions.

It is probably impossible to design performance measures that will ensure that maximizing the short-run performance measure will also maximize long-term performance. Some steps, however, can be taken to improve the short-term performance measures so that they minimize the potential conflict. For example, during times of rising prices, short-term performance measures can be distorted if no attempt is made to adjust for the changing price levels. ROI has a number of deficiencies. In particular, it encourages managers to accept only those investments that are in excess of the current ROI, and this can lead to the rejection of profitable projects. Such actions can be reduced by replacing ROI with RI as the performance measure. However, merely changing from ROI to RI will not eliminate the short-run versus long-run conflicts.

(b) One suggestion that has been made to overcome the conflict between short-term and long-term measures is for accountants to broaden their reporting systems and include non-financial performance measures in the performance reports. For example, obtaining feedback from customers regarding the quality of service encourages managers not to skimp on reducing the quality of service in order to save costs in the short term. For a discussion of the potential contribution from including non-financial measures in the reporting system see 'Addressing the dysfunctional consequences of short-term financial performance measures' in Chapter 12.

Other suggestions have focused on refining the financial measures so that they will reduce the potential for conflict between actions that improve short-term performance at the expense of long-term performance.

Chapter 13

13.13 The loss of contribution (profits) in division A from lost internal sales of 2500 units at £18 (£40 − £22) is £45 000.

The impact on the whole company is that the external purchase cost is £87 500 (2500 × £35) compared with the incremental cost of manufacture of £55 000 (2500 × £22). Therefore the company will be worse off by £32 500.

Answer = D

13.14 The two-part tariff transfer price per unit is the marginal cost of £15.

Answer = A

13.15 Variable cost of the component = $360 (60% of $600)
Transfer price = (1.7 × $360) = $612

	X($)	Y ($)
External sales (10 000 × $800)	8 000 000	
Internal sales (12 000 × $612)	7 344 000	
External sales (12 000 × $1 200)		14 400 000
Production costs: (22 000 × $600)	(13 200 000)	
Transfer costs (12 000 × $612)		(7 344 000)
Assembly costs (12 000 × $400)		(4 800 000)
Non-production costs	(1 500 000)	(1 300 000)
Profit	644 000	956 000
Tax	(161 000)	(286 800)
Profit after tax	483 000	669 200

13.16
(i) The proposed transfer price of £15 is based on cost plus 25 per cent implying that the total cost is £12. This comprises £9 variable cost (75 per cent) and £3 fixed cost. The general transfer pricing guideline described in Chapter 13 can be applied to this question. That is the transfer price that should be set at marginal cost plus the opportunity cost. It is assumed in the first situation that transferring internally will result in Helpco having a lost contribution of £6 (£15 external market price less £9 variable cost for the external market). The marginal cost of the transfer is £7.50 (£9 external variable cost less £1.50 packaging costs not required for internal sales). Adding the opportunity cost of £6 gives a transfer price of £13.50 per kg. This is equivalent to applying the market price rule where the transfer price is set at the external market price (£15) less selling costs avoided (£1.50) by transferring internally.

(ii) For the 3000 kg where no external market is available the opportunity cost will not apply and transfers should be at the variable cost of £7.50. The remaining output should be transferred at £13.50 as described above.

(iii) The lost contribution for the 2000 kg is £3 per kg (£6000/2000 kg) giving a transfer price of £10.50 (£7.50 variable cost plus £3 opportunity cost). The remaining 1000 kg for which there is no external market should be transferred at £7.50 variable cost and the balance for which there is an external market transferred at £13.50.

13.17 (a) The effects on each division and the company as a whole of selling the motor unit at each possible selling price are presented in the following schedules:

(i) *EM division*

Output level (units)	Total revenues (£)	Variable costs (£)	Total contribution (£)
1000	16 000	6 000	10 000
2000	32 000	12 000	20 000
3000	48 000	18 000	30 000
4000	64 000	24 000	40 000
6000	96 000	36 000	60 000
8000	128 000	48 000	**80 000**

(ii) *IP division*

Output level (units)	Total revenues (£)	Variable costs (£)	Total cost of transfers (£)	Total contribution (£)
1000	50 000	4 000	16 000	30 000
2000	80 000	8 000	32 000	40 000
3000	105 000	12 000	48 000	**45 000**
4000	120 000	16 000	64 000	40 000
6000	150 000	24 000	96 000	30 000
8000	160 000	32 000	128 000	nil

(iii) *Enormous Engineering plc*

Output level (units)	Total revenues (£)	Variable costs (EMD) (£)	Variable costs (IPD) (£)	Total contribution (£)
1000	50 000	6 000	4 000	40 000
2000	80 000	12 000	8 000	60 000
3000	105 000	18 000	12 000	75 000
4000	120 000	24 000	16 000	80 000
6000	150 000	36 000	24 000	**90 000**
8000	160 000	48 000	32 000	80 000

The above schedules indicate that EM division maximizes profits at an output of 8000 units, whereas IP division maximizes profits at an output level of 3000 units. Profits are maximized for the company as a whole at an output level of 6000 units.

(b) (i) Based on the tabulation in (a), IPD should select a selling price of £35 per unit. This selling price produces a maximum divisional contribution of £45 000.

(ii) The company as a whole should select a selling price of £25 per unit. This selling price produces a maximum company contribution of £90 000.

(iii) If IPD selected a selling price of £25 per unit instead of £35 per unit, its overall marginal revenue would increase by £45 000 but its marginal cost would increase by £60 000. Consequently it is not in IPD's interest to lower the price from £35 to £25 when the transfer price of the intermediate product is set at £16.

(c) (i) Presumably profit centres have been established so as to provide a profit incentive for each division and to enable divisional managers to exercise a high degree of divisional autonomy. The maintenance of divisional autonomy and the profitability incentive can lead to suboptimal decisions. The costs of suboptimization may be acceptable to a certain extent in order to preserve the motivational advantages that arise with divisional autonomy.

Within the EE group, EMD has decision-making autonomy with respect to the setting of transfer prices. EMD sets transfer prices on a full cost-plus basis in order to earn a target profit. The resulting transfer price causes IPD to restrict output to 3000 units, which is less than the group optimum. The cost of this suboptimal

454 ANSWERS TO REVIEW PROBLEMS

decision is £15 000 (£90 000 – £75 000). A solution to the problem is to set the transfer price at the variable cost per unit of the supplying division. This transfer price will result in IPD selecting the optimum output level, but will destroy the profit incentive for the EM division. Note that fixed costs will not be covered and there is no external market for the intermediate product.

A possible solution to achieving the motivational and optimality objectives is to operate a two-part transfer pricing system. See Chapter 13 for an explanation.

(ii) Where there is no market for the intermediate product and the supplying division has no capacity constraints, the correct transfer price is the marginal cost of the supplying division for that output at which marginal cost equals the receiving division's net marginal revenue from converting the intermediate product. When unit variable cost is constant and fixed costs remain unchanged, this rule will result in a transfer price which is equal to the supplying division's unit variable cost. Therefore the transfer price will be set at £6 per unit when the variable cost transfer pricing rule is applied. IPD will then be faced with the following marginal cost and net marginal revenue schedule:

Output level (units)	Marginal cost of transfers (£)	Net marginal revenue of IPD (£)
1000		
2000	6 000	26 000
3000	6 000	21 000
4000	6 000	11 000
6000	12 000	22 000
8000	12 000	2 000

IPD will select an output level of 6000 units and will not go beyond this because NMR < marginal cost. This is the optimal output for the group, but the profits from the sale of the motor unit will accrue entirely to the IP division, and the EM division will make a loss equal to the fixed costs.

13.18 (a) The variable costs per unit of output for sales *outside* the company are £11 for the intermediate product and £49 [£10(A) + £39(B)] for the final product. Note that selling and packing expenses are not incurred by the supplying division for the transfer of the intermediate product. It is assumed that the company has sufficient capacity to meet demand at the various selling prices.

Optimal output of intermediate product for sale on external market

Selling price (£)	20	30	40
Unit contribution (£)	9	19	29
Demand (units)	15 000	10 000	5 000
Total contribution (£)	135 000	190 000	145 000

Optimal output is 10 000 units at a selling price of £30.

Optimal output for final product

Selling price (£)	80	90	100
Unit contribution (£)	31	41	51
Demand (units)	7 200	5 000	2 800
Total contribution (£)	223 200	205 000	142 800

Optimal output is 7200 units at a selling price of £80.

Optimal output of Division B based on a transfer price of £29

Division B will regard the transfer price as a variable cost. Therefore total variable cost per unit will be £68 (£29 + £39), and division B will calculate the following contributions:

Selling price (£)	80	90	100
Unit contribution (£)	12	22	32
Demand (units)	7 200	5 000	2 800
Total contribution (£)	86 400	110 000	89 600

The manager of division B will choose an output level of 5000 units at a selling price of £90. This is sub-optimal for the company as a whole. Profits for the *company as a whole* from the sale of the final product are reduced from £223 200 (7200 units) to £205 000 (5000 units). The £205 000 profits would be allocated as follows:

Division A £95 000 [5000 units at (£29 – £10)]

Division B £110 000

(b) At a transfer price of £12, the variable cost per unit produced in division B will be £51 (£12 + £39). Division B will calculate the following contributions:

Selling price (£)	80	90	100
Unit contribution (£)	29	39	49
Demand (units)	7 200	5 000	2 800
Total contribution (£)	208 800	195 000	137 200

The manager of division B will choose an output level of 7200 units and a selling price of £80. This is the optimum output level for the company as a whole. Division A would obtain a contribution of £14 400 [7200 × (£12 – £10)] from internal transfers of the intermediate product, whereas division B would obtain a contribution of £208 800 from converting the intermediate product and selling as a final product. Total contribution for the company as a whole would be £223 200. Note that division A would also earn a contribution of £190 000 from the sale of the intermediate product to the external market.

13.19 (a) See 'International transfer pricing' in Chapter 13 for the answer to this question. Besides the ethical issues and legal considerations other criticisms relate to the distortions in the divisional profit reporting system. Also divisional autonomy will be undermined if the transfer prices are imposed on the divisional managers.

(b) The ethical limitations relate to multinational companies using the transfer pricing system to reduce the amount paid in custom duties, taxation and the manipulation of dividends remitted. Furthermore, using the transfer prices for these purposes is likely to be illegal, although there is still likely to be some scope for manipulation that is within the law. It is important that multinational companies are seen to be acting in a socially responsible manner. Any bad publicity relating to using the transfer pricing system purely to avoid taxes and customs duties will be very harmful to the image of the organization. Nevertheless tax management and the ability to minimize corporate taxes is an important task for management if it is to maximize shareholder value. Thus it is important that management distinguish between tax avoidance and tax evasion. Adopting illegal practices is not acceptable and management must ensure that their transfer pricing policies do not contravene the regulations and laws of the host counties in which they operate.

Chapter 14

14.15 (a) (i)

	Units
Components worked on in the process	6120
Less: planned defective units	612
replacements to customers (2% × 5400)	108
Components invoiced to customers	5400

Therefore actual results agree with planned results.

(ii) Planned component cost = (3 × £18 for material A) + (2 × £9 for material B) + £15 variable cost = £87

Comparing with the data in the appendix:

Materials = £440 640/6120 = £72

Variable overhead = £91 800/6120 = £15

This indicates that prices were at the planned levels.

(b) Internal failure costs = £53 244 (612 units × £87)
External failure costs = £9396 (108 units × £87)

(c) (i)

	Period 2 (units)	Period 3 (units)
Components invoiced to customers	5500	5450
Planned replacement (2%)	110	109
Unplanned replacements	60 (170 – 110)	–69 (40 – 109)
Components delivered to customers	5670	5490
Planned process defects (10% of worked on in the process)	620	578
Unplanned defects (difference to agree with final row)	–90	–288
Components worked on in the process	6200	5780

(ii)

	Period 2 (£)	Period 3 (£)
Internal failure costs	46 110 (620 – 90) × £87	25 230 (578 – 288) × £87
External failure costs	14 790 (110 + 60) × £87	3 480 (109 – 69) × £87
Appraisal costs	10 000	15 000
Prevention costs	5 000	8 000

(iii) The following points should be included in the report:
1. Insufficient detail is provided in the statistics shown in the appendix, thus resulting in the need for an improvement in reporting.
2. The information presented in (c) (i) indicates that free replacements to customers were 60 greater than planned in period 2 but approximately 70 less than planned in period 3. In contrast, the in process defects were 90 less than planned (approximately 15 per cent) in period 2 and 288 less than plan (approximately 50 per cent) in period 3.
3. Internal failures costs show a downward trend from periods 1–3 with a substantial decline in period 3. External failure costs increased in period 2 but declined significantly in period 3.
4. The cost savings arising in periods 2 and 3 are as follows:

	Period 2 (£)	Period 3 (£)
Increase/decrease from previous period:		
Internal failure costs	–7134 (£53 244 – £46 110)	–20 880 (£46 110 – £25 230)
External failure costs	+5394 (£9396 – £14 790)	–11 310 (£14 790 – £3480)
Total decrease	–1740	–32 190

The above savings should be compared against the investment of £10 000 appraisal costs and £5000 prevention costs for period 2 and £15 000 and £8000 respectively in period 3. It can be seen that the costs exceed the savings in period 2 but the savings exceeded the costs in period 3. There has also been an increase in the external failure costs from period 1 to period 2. Investigations should be made relating to the likely time lag from incurring prevention/appraisal costs and their subsequent benefits.

5. The impact on customer goodwill from the reduction in replacements should also be examined.

14.16 (a) (i)   *Performance report for period ending 30 November (traditional analysis)*

Expenses

	Budget (£)	Actual (£)	Variance (£)
Salaries	600 000	667 800	67 800A
Supplies	60 000	53 000	7 000F
Travel cost	120 000	127 200	7 200A
Technology cost	100 000	74 200	25 800F
Occupancy cost	120 000	137 800	17 800A
Total	1 000 000	1 060 000	60 000A

Performance report for period ending 30 November (activity-based analysis)
Activities

	(£)	(£)	(£)
Routing/scheduling – new products	200 000	169 600	30 400F
Routing/scheduling – existing products	400 000	360 400	39 600F
Remedial re-routing/scheduling	50 000	127 200	77 200A
Special studies – specific orders	100 000	84 800	15 200F
Training	100 000	159 000	59 000A
Management and administration	150 000	159 000	9 000A
Total	1 000 000	1 060 000	60 000A

   (ii) See 'Activity-based budgeting' in Chapter 9 for the answer to this question. In particular, the answer should stress:
   (i)   The enhanced visibility of activity-based budgeting (ABB) by focusing on outcomes (activities) rather than a listing by expense categories.
   (ii) The cost of activities are highlighted thus identifying high-cost non-value-added activities that need to be investigated.
   (iii) ABB identifies resource requirements to meet the demand for activities whereas traditional budgeting adopts an incremental approach.
   (iv) Excess resources are identified that can be eliminated or redeployed.
   (v)   ABB enables more realistic budgets to be set.
   (vi) ABB avoids arbitrary cuts in specific budget areas in order to meet overall financial targets.
   (vii) It is claimed that ABB leads to increased management commitment to the budget process because it enables management to focus on the objectives of each activity and compare the outcomes with the costs that are allocated to the activity.

   (iii) The ABB statement shows a comparison of actual with budget by activities. All of the primary value-adding activities (i.e. the first, second and fourth activities in the budget statement) have favourable variances. Remedial re-routing is a non-value-added activity and has the highest adverse variance. Given the high cost, top priority should be given to investigating the activity with a view to eliminating it, or to substantially reducing the cost by adopting alternative working practices. Training and management and administration are secondary activities that support the primary activities. Actual training expenditure exceeds budget by 50 per cent and the reason for the over-spending should be investigated.
       For each activity it would be helpful if the costs were analysed by expense items (such as salaries, supplies, etc.) to pinpoint the cost build-up of the activities and to provide clues indicating why an overspending on some activities has occurred.
       Cost driver usage details should also be presented in a manner similar to that illustrated in Exhibit 9.1 in Chapter 9. Many organizations that have adopted ABC have found it useful to report budgeted and actual cost driver rates. The trend in cost driver rates is monitored and compared with similar activities undertaken within other divisions where a divisionalized structure applies. As indicated in Chapter 14, care must be taken when interpreting cost driver rates.

For additional points to be included in the answer see 'Activity-based management' in Chapter 14.

(b) The cost driver rates are as follows:

Product design = £250 per design hour (£2m/8000 hours)

Purchasing = £50 per purchase order (£200 000/4000 orders)

Production (excluding depreciation) = £100 per machine hour ((£1 500 000 – £300 000)/12 000 hours)

Packing = £20 per cubic metre (£400 000/20 000)

Distribution = £5 per kg (£600 000/120 000)

The activity-based overhead cost per unit is as follows:

		(£)
Product design	(400 design hours at £250 per hour = £100 000 divided by life-cycle output of 5000 units)	20.00
Purchasing	(5 purchase orders at 50 units per order costing a total of £250 for an output of 250 units)	1.00
Production	(0.75 machine hours at £100 per machine hour)	75.00
Depreciation	(Asset cost over life cycle of 4 years = 16 quarters' depreciation at £8000 per quarter divided by life-cycle output of 5000 units)	25.60
Packing	(0.4 cubic metres at £20)	8.00
Distribution	(3 kg at £5)	15.00
Total cost		144.60

14.17 See 'Cost of quality', 'Just-in-time systems' and 'Activity-based management' in Chapter 14 for the answer to this question. You should also refer to 'Activity-based budgeting' in Chapter 9. All of the approaches seek to eliminate waste and therefore when the principles are applied to budget preparation there should be a move away from incremental budgeting to the resources that are required to meet budgeted demand. For an explanation of this point see 'Activity-based budgeting' in Chapter 9. Within the budgeting process a total quality ethos would result in a move towards a zero-defects policy when the budgets are prepared. There would be reduced budget allocations for internal and external failure costs and an increase in the allocation for prevention and appraisal costs. The just-in-time philosophy would result in a substantial budgeted reduction in stocks and establishing physical targets that support JIT systems, such as manufacturing cycle efficiency and set-up times. See 'Operation processes' and 'Cycle time measures' in Chapter 15 for an explanation of some of the performance targets that are appropriate for JIT systems. The activity-based focus should result in the implementation of activity-based budgeting (see Chapter 9).

14.18 Benchmarking is a continuous process that involves comparing business processes and activities in an organization with those in other companies that represent world-class best practices in order to see how processes and activities can be improved. The comparison involves both financial and non-financial indicators.

Two different approaches are adopted in most organizations. Cost-driven benchmarking involves applying the principles of benchmarking from a distance and comparing some aspects of performance with those of competitors, usually using intermediaries such as consultants. The outcome of the exercise is cost reduction. The second approach involves process-driven benchmarking. It is a process involving the philosophy of continuous improvement. The focus is not necessarily on competitors but on a benchmarking partner. The aim is to obtain a better understanding of the processes and questions the reason why things take place, how they take place and how often they take place. The outcome should be superior performance through the strengthening of processes and business behaviour.

Inter-firm comparisons place much greater emphasis on the use of financial data and mostly involve comparisons at the company or strategic business unit level rather than at the business process or activity level. Inter-firm comparisons tend to compare data derived from published financial accounts whereas benchmarking also makes use of both internal and external data.

Benchmarking contributes to cost reduction by highlighting those areas where performance is inferior to competitors and where opportunities for cost reduction exist (e.g. elimination of non-value-added activities or more efficient ways of carrying out activities).

Activity-based budgeting (ABB) is an extension of ABC applied to the preparation of budgets. It focuses on the costs of activities necessary to produce and sell products and services by assigning costs to separate activity cost pools. The cause-and-effect criterion based on cost drivers is used to establish budgets for each cost pool.

ABB involves the following stages:

1   Determining the budgeted cost (i.e. the cost driver rate) of performing each unit of activity for all major activities.
2   Determining the required resources for each individual activity to meet sales and production requirements.
3   Computing the budgeted cost for each activity.

Note that ABB focuses on budgets for the cost of activities rather than functional departments.

Zero-based budgeting tends to be used more as a one-off cost reduction programme. The emphasis is on functional responsibility areas, rather than individual activities, with the aim of justifying all costs from a zero base.

Activity analysis is required prior to implementing ABB. This process can help to identify non-value-added activities that may be candidates for elimination or performing the activities in different ways with less resources. Activity performance measures can be established that enable the cost per unit of activity to be monitored and used as a basis for benchmarking. This information should highlight those activities where there is a potential for performing more efficiently by reducing resource consumption and future spending.

See 'Target costing' in Chapter 14 for an explanation of the objectives and workings of target costing.

Continuous cost improvement is a process whereby a firm gradually reduces costs without attempting to achieve a specific target. Target costing is emphasized more at a product's design and development stage whereas continuous cost improvement occurs throughout a product's life. The principles of target costing can also be applied to cost reduction exercises for existing products. Where this approach is applied there is little difference between the two methods. Both approaches clearly focus on reducing costs throughout a product's life cycle but target costing emphasizes cost reduction at the design and development stage. At this stage there is a greater potential for reducing costs throughout the product life cycle.

14.19 (a) The factors influencing the preferred costing system are different for every firm. The benefits from implementing ABC are likely to be influenced by the level of competition, the number of products sold, the diversity of the product range and the proportion of overheads and direct costs in the cost structure. Companies operating in a more competitive environment have a greater need for more accurate cost information, since competitors are more likely to take advantage of any errors arising from the use of distorted cost information generated by a traditional costing system. Where a company markets a small number of products special studies can be undertaken using the decision-relevant approach. Problems do not arise in determining which product or product combinations should be selected for undertaking special studies. Increased product diversity arising from the manufacture and sale of low-volume and high-volume products favours the use of ABC systems. As the level of diversity increases so does the level of distortion reported by traditional costing systems. Finally, organizations with a large proportion of overheads and a low proportion of direct costs are likely to benefit from ABC, because traditional costing systems can be relied upon only to report accurately direct product costs. Distorted product costs are likely to be reported where a large proportion of overheads are related to product variety rather than volume.

(b) For a more detailed answer to this question you should refer to 'Activity-based management' in Chapter 14. In particular, the answer should draw attention to the fact that ABM attaches costs to activities and identifies the cost drivers that cause the costs. Thus ABM provides a better understanding of what causes costs, and highlights ways of performing activities more efficiently by reducing cost driver transactions.

Costs can therefore be managed more effectively in the long run. Activities can be analysed into value-added and non-value-added activities and by highlighting the costs of non-value-added activities attention is drawn to areas where there is an opportunity for cost reduction, without reducing the products' service potentials to customers.

Finally, the cost of unused activity capacity is reported for each activity, thus drawing attention to where capacity can be reduced or utilized more effectively to expand future profitability.

(c) See 'Target costing' in Chapter 14 for the answer to this question.

Chapter 15

15.13 (a)

	Original budget based on 120 000 gross hours	Standard hours based on actual gross hours	Actual hours	Variance (hours)	Variance (£) at £75 per hour
Gross hours	120 000	132 000	132 000		
Contract negotiation	4 800 (4%)	5 280 (4%)	9 240 (7%)	3 960A	297 000A
Remedial advice	2 400 (2%)	2 640 (2%)	7 920 (6%)	5 280A	396 000A
Other non-chargeable	12 000 (10%)	13 200 (10%)	22 440 (17%)	9 240A	693 000A
Chargeable hours	100 800 (84%)	110 880 (84%)	92 400 (70%)	18 480A	1 386 000A

There was a capacity gain over budget of 10 080 (110 880 – 100 800) hours at a client value of £756 000 (10 080 hours at £75) but because all of this was not converted into actual chargeable hours there was a net fall in chargeable hours compared with the original budget of 8400 (100 800 – 92 400) hours at a client value of £630 000.

(b) *Financial performance*

Profit statement and financial ratios for year ending 30 April

	Budget (£000)	Actual (£000)
Revenue from client contracts (chargeable hours × £75)	7560	6930
Costs:		
Consultant salaries	1800	1980
Sundry operating costs	3500	4100
	5300	6080
Net profit	2260	850
Capital employed	6500	6500
Financial ratios:		
Net profit: Turnover	29.9%	12.3%
Turnover: Capital employed	1.16 times	1.07 times
Net profit: Capital employed	34.8%	13.1%

The above figures indicate a poor financial performance for the year. The statement in (a) indicates an increase in gross hours from 120 000 to 132 000 hours providing the potential for 110 880 chargeable hours compared with the budget of 100 800 hours. This should have increased fee income by £756 000 (10 080 × £75). However, of the potential 110 880 hours there were only 92 400 chargeable hours resulting in a shortfall of 18 480 hours at a lost fee income of £1 386 000. The difference between these two monetary figures of £630 000 represents the difference between budgeted and actual revenues.

Competitiveness
Competitiveness should be measured in terms of market share and sales growth. Sales are less than budget but the offer of free remedial advice to clients presumably

represents the allocation of staff time to improve longer-term competitiveness even though this has had an adverse impact on short-term profit.

Competitiveness may also be measured in terms of the relative success/failure in obtaining business from clients. The data shows that the budgeted uptake from clients is 40 per cent for new systems and 75 per cent for existing systems compared with actuals of 35 per cent and 80 per cent respectively. For new systems worked on there is a 16.7 per cent increase compared with the budget whereas for existing systems advice actual is 4 per cent less than budget.

Quality of service
The data indicate that client complaints were four times the budgeted level and that the number of clients requiring remedial advice was 75 compared with a budgeted level of 48. These items should be investigated.

Flexibility
Flexibility relates to the responsiveness to customer enquiries. For BS Ltd this relates to its ability to cope with changes in volume, delivery speed and the employment of staff who are able to meet changing customer demands. The company has retained 60 consultants in order to increase its flexibility in meeting demand. The data given show a change in the mix of consultancy specialists that may reflect an attempt to respond to changes in the marketing mix. The ratio of new systems to existing systems advice has changed and this may indicate a flexible response to market demands.

Resource utilization
The budget was based on chargeable hours of 84 per cent of gross hours but the actual percentage was 70 per cent (see part (a)). There was an increased level of remedial advice (6 per cent of gross hours compared with 2 per cent in the budget) and this may represent an investment with the aim of stimulating future demand.

Innovation
Innovation relates to the ability of the organization to provide new and better quality services. The company has established an innovative feature by allowing free remedial advice after completion of a contract. In the short term this is adversely affecting financial performance but it may have a beneficial long-term impact. The answer to part (a) indicates that remedial advice exceeded the adjusted budget by 5280 hours. This should be investigated to establish whether or not it was a deliberate policy decision.

Other points
Only budgeted data were given in the question. Ideally, external benchmarks ought to be established and the trend monitored over several periods rather than focusing only on a single period.

15.14 (a) The key areas of performance referred to in the question are listed in Exhibit 15.7 – financial, competitiveness, quality of service, flexibility, resource utilization and innovation.

Financial
- There has been a continuous growth in sales turnover during the period – increasing by 50 per cent in 2006, 10 per cent in 2007 and 35 per cent in 2008.
- Profits have increased at a higher rate than sales turnover – 84 per cent in 2006, 104 per cent in 2007 and 31 per cent in 2008.
- Profit margins (profit/sales) have increased from 14 per cent in 2005 to 31 per cent in 2008.

Competitiveness
Market share (total turnover/total turnover of all restaurants) has increased from 9.2 per cent in 2005 to 17.5 per cent in 2008. The proposals submitted to cater for special events has increased from 2 in 2005 to 38 in 2009. This has also been accompanied by an increase in the percentage of contracts won, which has increased over the years (20 per cent in 2005, 29 per cent in 2006, 52 per cent in 2007 and 66 per cent in 2008). Although all of the above measures suggest good performance in terms of this dimension, the

average service delay at peak times increased significantly in 2008. This area requires investigating.

Quality of service

The increasing number of regular customers attending weekly suggests that they are satisfied with the quality of service. Other factors pointing to a high-level quality of service are the increase in complimentary letters from satisfied customers. Conversely the number of letters of complaint and reported cases of food poisoning have not diminished over the years. Therefore the performance measures do not enable a definitive assessment to be made on the level of quality of service.

Innovation/flexibility

Each year the restaurant has attempted to introduce a significant number of new meals. There has also been an increase each year in the number of special theme evenings introduced and the turnover from special events has increased significantly over the years. These measures suggest that the restaurant has been fairly successful in terms of this dimension.

Resource utilization

The total meals served have increased each year. Idle time and annual operating hours with no customers have also decreased significantly each year. There has also been an increase in the average number of customers at peak times. The value of food wasted has varied over the years but was at the lowest level in 2008. All of the measures suggest that the restaurant has been particularly successful in terms of this dimension.

(b) *Financial*

Details of the value of business assets are required to measure profitability (e.g. return on investment). This is important because the seating capacity has been increased. This may have resulted in an additional investment in assets and there is a need to ascertain whether an adequate return has been generated. Analysis of expenditure by different categories (e.g. food, drinks, wages, etc.) is required to compare the trend in financial ratios (e.g. expense categories as a percentage of sales) and with other restaurants.

Competitiveness

Comparison with other restaurants should be made in respect of the measures described in (a) such as percentage of seats occupied and average service delay at peak times.

Quality of service

Consider using mystery shoppers (i.e. employment of outsiders) to visit this and competitor restaurants to assess the quality of service relative to competitors and to also identify areas for improvement.

Innovation/flexibility

Information relating to the expertise of the staff and their ability to perform multi-skill activities is required to assess the ability of the restaurant to cope with future demands.

Resource utilization

Data on the number of employees per customer served, and the percentage of tables occupied at peak and non-peak times would draw attention to areas where there may be a need to improve resource utilization.

15.15 (a) See 'The balanced scorecard' in Chapter 15 for the answer to this question. In particular, the answer should describe the four different perspectives of the balanced scorecard, the assumed cause-and-effect relationships and also provide illustrations of performance measures applicable to CM Ltd.

(b) See 'Benchmarking' in Chapter 14 for the answer to this question. The answer should stress the need to identify important activities or processes that may be common to other organizations (e.g. dispatching, invoicing or ordering activities) and to compare these activities with an organization that is considered to be a world leader in undertaking these activities.

15.16 See 'Cost of quality' in Chapter 14 and 'Quality measures' in the section relating to the balanced scorecard in Chapter 15 for the answer to this question. The answer could also draw off some of the content relating to performance measurement in service organizations described in Chapter 15 (note in particular the determinants of quality of service in Exhibit 15.7). The answer should also stress the need to monitor quality internally and externally. Internal controls and performance measures should be implemented as described in Chapters 14 and 15 so as to ensure that only products that meet customer quality requirements are despatched. To monitor quality externally customer feedback should be obtained and comparisons made with competitors. With service organizations the quality of the service can be assessed by using methods such as mystery shoppers. You should refer to Chapter 15 for a more detailed description of how quality can be monitored in service organizations.

15.17 (a) (i) Efficiency measures focus on the relationship between outputs and inputs. Optimum efficiency levels are achieved by maximizing the output from a given input or minimizing the resources used in order to achieve a particular output. Measures of effectiveness attempt to measure the extent to which the outputs of an organization achieve the latter's goals. An organization can be efficient but not effective. For example, it can use resources efficiently but fail to achieve its goals.

In organizations with a profit motive, effectiveness can be measured by return on investment. Inputs and outputs can be measured. Outputs represent the quality and amount of service offered. In profit-orientated organizations output can be measured in terms of sales revenues. This provides a useful proxy measure of the quality and amount of services offered. In non-profit-making organizations outputs cannot be easily measured in monetary terms. Consequently, it is difficult to state the objectives in quantitative terms and thus measure the extent to which objectives are being achieved.

If it is not possible to produce a statement of a particular objective in measurable terms, the objectives should be stated with sufficient clarity that there is some way of judging whether or not they have been achieved. However, the focus will tend to be on subjective judgements rather than quantitative measures of effectiveness. Because of the difficulty in measuring outputs, efficiency measures tend to focus entirely on input measures such as the amount of spending on services or the cost per unit of input.

(ii) Similar problems to those of measuring effectiveness and efficiency in non-profit-making organizations arise in measuring the performance of non-manufacturing activities in profit-orientated organizations. This is because it is extremely difficult to measure the output of non-manufacturing activities.

(b) (i) *Adherence to appointment times*
   1   Percentage meeting appointment times.
   2   Percentage within 15 minutes of appointment time.
   3   Percentage more than 15 minutes late.
   4   Average delay in meeting appointments.

Ability to contact and make appointments
It is not possible to obtain data on all those patients who have had difficulty in contacting the clinic to make appointments. However, an indication of the difficulties can be obtained by asking a sample of patients at periodic intervals to indicate on a scale (from no difficulty to considerable difficulty) the difficulty they experienced when making appointments. The number of complaints received and the average time taken to establish telephone contact with the clinic could also provide an indication of the difficulty patients experience when making appointments.

Monitoring programme
   1   Comparisons with programmes of other clinics located in different regions.
   2   Questionnaires asking respondents to indicate the extent to which they are aware of monitoring facilities currently offered.
   3   Responses on level of satisfaction from patients registered on the programme.
   4   Percentage of population undertaking the programme.

(ii) Combining the measures into a 'quality of care' measure requires that weights be attached to each selected performance measure. The sum of the performance measures multiplied by the weights would represent an overall performance measure. The problems with this approach are that the weights are set subjectively, and there is a danger that staff will focus on those performance measures with the higher weighting and pay little attention to those with the lower weighting.

15.18   (i)   The percentage of occupancy on flights to new destinations should provide feedback on how successful this policy is in terms of meeting the growth objective.

     (ii)   Measures of baggage loading/unloading times, aircraft cleaning times and fuel loading times can be used to implement a policy of continuous improvement and thus contribute to the achievement of the internal capabilities objective.

12
DECISION-MAKING UNDER CONDITIONS OF RISK AND UNCERTAINTY

LEARNING OBJECTIVES After studying this chapter, you should be able to:

- calculate and explain the meaning of expected values;

- explain the meaning of the terms standard deviation and coefficient of variation as measures of risk and outline their limitations;

- construct a decision tree when there is a range of alternatives and possible outcomes;

- describe and calculate the value of perfect and imperfect information;

- explain and apply the maximin, maximax and regret criteria;

- explain the implications of pursuing a diversification strategy.

In Chapters 8–11 we considered the use of a single representative set of estimates for predicting future costs and revenues when alternative courses of action are followed. For example, in Chapter 10 we used a single representative estimate of demand for each selling price. However, the outcome of a particular decision may be affected by an uncertain environment that cannot be predicted, and a single representative estimate does not therefore convey all the information that might reasonably influence a decision.

Let us now look at a more complicated example; consider a situation where a company has two mutually exclusive potential alternatives, A and B, which each yield receipts of £50 000. The estimated costs of alternative A can be predicted with considerable confidence, and are expected to fall in the range of £40 000–£42 000; £41 000 might be considered a reasonable estimate of cost. The estimate for alternative B is subject to much greater uncertainty, since this alternative requires high-precision work involving operations that are unfamiliar to the company's labour force. The estimated costs are between £35 000 and £45 000, but £40 000 is selected as a representative estimate. If we consider single representative estimates alternative B appears preferable, since the estimated profit is £10 000 compared with an estimated profit of £9000 for alternative A; but a different picture may emerge if we take into account the range of possible outcomes.

Alternative A is expected to yield a profit of between £8000 and £10 000 whereas the range of profits for alternative B is between £5000 and £15 000. Management may consider it preferable to opt for a fairly certain profit of between £8000 and £10 000 for alternative A rather than take the chance of earning a profit of £5000 from alternative B (even though there is the possibility of earning a profit of £15 000 at the other extreme).

This example demonstrates that there is a need to incorporate the uncertainty relating to each alternative into the decision-making process, and in this chapter we shall consider the various methods of doing this.

RISK AND UNCERTAINTY

A distinction is often drawn by decision theorists between risk and uncertainty. Risk is applied to a situation where there are several possible outcomes and there is relevant past experience to enable statistical evidence to be produced for predicting the possible outcomes. Uncertainty exists where there are several possible outcomes, but there is little previous statistical evidence to enable the possible outcomes to be predicted. Most business decisions can be classified in the uncertainty category, but the distinction between risk and uncertainty is not essential for our analysis and we shall use the terms interchangeably.

Probabilities

Because decision problems exist in an uncertain environment, it is necessary to consider those uncontrollable factors that are outside the decision-maker's control and that may occur for alternative courses of action. These uncontrollable factors are called events or states of nature. For example, in a product launch situation, possible states of nature could consist of events such as a similar product being

---

Risk and uncertainty – tracking business uncertainty

There are many ways to access the uncertainty in the general business environment. Two simple measures could be business activity (less will be sold in uncertain times) and levels of capital investment (firms, like individuals, save when the business environment is less favourable). Another way is to develop an index of business confidence, which measures the overall attitude of business towards their current situation and future prospects.

Take for example the IFO Business Climate Index (an index of German business confidence), which is calculated monthly by the IFO Institute for Economic Research in Munich, Germany. This index uses a survey of 7000 firms in construction, manufacturing, services, wholesale and retail. The firms are asked to assess their current business situation as poor, satisfactory or good. They are also asked to assess their prospects for the next six months. Combining these two measures into an index, an assessment is

made about how confident businesses feel. If the index is declining, confidence is lacking and businesses are effectively uncertain about the future. The IFO Index is an important measure in a European sense, as Germany is one of Europe largest economies. Most countries have similar indices. For example, the South African Chamber of Commerce and Industry reported in January 2011 that their business confidence index rose slightly towards the end of 2010. According to the Chamber, uncertainly over unemployment figures and industrial unrest still loomed, hence the small rise.

Questions

1. Would a management accountant use indices like those mentioned above in evaluating decisions or providing information?

2. What economic factors might reduce business uncertainty?

References

http://www.cesifo-group.de/portal/page/portal/ifoHome/a-winfo/d1index/10indexgsk
http://www.mg.co.za/article/2011-01-12-sa-business-confidence-rises-in-december

launched by a competitor at a lower price, at the same price, at a higher price or no similar product being launched.

The likelihood that an event or state of nature will occur is known as its probability, and this is normally expressed in decimal form with a value between 0 and 1. A value of 0 denotes a nil likelihood of occurrence, whereas a value of 1 signifies absolute certainty – a definite occurrence. A probability of 0.4 means that the event is expected to occur four times out of ten. The total of the probabilities for events that can possibly occur must sum to 1.0. For example, if a tutor indicates that the probability of a student passing an examination is 0.7 then this means that the student has a 70 per cent chance of passing the examination. Given that the pass/fail alternatives represent an exhaustive listing of all possible outcomes of the event, the probability of not passing the examination is 0.3.

The information can be presented in a probability distribution. A probability distribution is a list of all possible outcomes for an event and the probability that each will occur. The probability distribution for the above illustration is as follows:

Outcome	Probability
Pass examination	0.7
Do not pass examination	0.3
Total	1.0

Some probabilities are known as objective probabilities because they can be established mathematically or compiled from historical data. Tossing a coin and throwing a die are examples of objective probabilities. For example, the probability of heads occurring when tossing a coin logically must be 0.5. This can be proved by tossing the coin many times and observing the results. Similarly, the probability of obtaining number 1 when a die is thrown is 0.166 (i.e. one-sixth). This again can be ascertained from logical reasoning or recording the results obtained from repeated throws of the dice.

It is unlikely that objective probabilities can be established for business decisions, since many past observations or repeated experiments for particular decisions are not possible; the probabilities will have to be estimated based on managerial judgement. Probabilities established in this way are known as subjective probabilities because no two individuals will necessarily assign the same probabilities to a particular outcome. Subjective probabilities are based on an individual's expert knowledge, past experience and observations of current variables which are likely to have an impact on future events. Such probabilities are unlikely to be estimated correctly, but any estimate of a future uncertain event is bound to be subject to error.

The advantage of this approach is that it provides more meaningful information than stating the most likely outcome. Consider, for example, a situation where a tutor is asked to state whether student A and student B will pass an examination. The tutor may reply that both students are expected to pass the examination. This is the tutor's estimate of the most likely outcome. However, the following probability distributions are preferable:

Outcome	Student A probability	Student B probability
Pass examination	0.9	0.6
Do not pass examination	0.1	0.4
Total	1.0	1.0

Such a probability distribution requires the tutor to specify the degree of confidence in his or her estimate of the likely outcome of a future event. This information is clearly more meaningful than a mere estimate of the most likely outcome that both students are expected to pass the examination, because it indicates that it is most unlikely that A will fail, whereas there is a possibility that B will fail. Let us now apply the principles of probability theory to business decision-making.

PROBABILITY DISTRIBUTIONS AND EXPECTED VALUE

The presentation of a probability distribution for each alternative course of action can provide useful additional information to management, since the distribution indicates the degree of uncertainty that exists for each alternative course of action. Probability distributions enable management to consider not only the possible profits (i.e. the payoff) from each alternative course of action, but also the amount of uncertainty that applies to each alternative. Let us now consider the situation presented in Example 12.1.

From the probability distributions shown in Example 12.1 you will see that there is a 1 in 10 chance that profits will be £600 000 for product A, but there is also a 4 in 10 chance that profits will be £800 000. A more useful way of reading the probability distribution is to state that there is a 7 in 10 chance that

EXAMPLE 12.1

A manager is considering whether to make product A or product B, but only one can be produced. The estimated sales demand for each product is uncertain. A detailed investigation of the possible sales demand for each product gives the following probability distribution of the profits for each product.

Product A probability distribution

(1) Outcome	(2) Estimated probability	(3) Weighted (col. 1 amount × col. 2) (£)
Profits of £600 000	0.10	60 000
Profits of £700 000	0.20	140 000
Profits of £800 000	0.40	320 000
Profits of £900 000	0.20	180 000
Profits of £1 000 000	0.10	100 000
	1.00	
	Expected value	800 000

Product B probability distribution

(1) Outcome	(2) Estimated probability	(3) Weighted (col. 1 amount × col. 2) (£)
Profits of £400 000	0.05	20 000
Profits of £600 000	0.10	60 000
Profits of £800 000	0.40	320 000
Profits of £1 000 000	0.25	250 000
Profits of £1 200 000	0.20	240 000
	1.00	
	Expected value	890 000

Which product should the company make?

profits will be £800 000 or less. This is obtained by adding together the probabilities for profits of £600 000, £700 000 and £800 000. Similarly, there is a 3 in 10 chance that profits will be £900 000 or more.

Expected values

The expected value (sometimes called expected payoff) is calculated by weighting each of the profit levels (i.e. possible outcomes) in Example 12.1 by its associated probability. The sum of these weighted amounts is called the expected value of the probability distribution. In other words, the expected value is the weighted arithmetic mean of the possible outcomes. The expected values of £800 000 and £890 000 calculated for products A and B take into account a range of possible outcomes rather than using a single most likely estimate. For example, the single most likely estimate is the profit level with the highest probability attached to it. For both products A and B in Example 12.1 the single most likely estimate is £800 000, which appears to indicate that we may be indifferent as to which product should be made. However, the expected value calculation takes into account the possibility that a range of different profits are possible and weights these profits by the probability of their occurrence. The weighted calculation indicates that product B is expected to produce the highest average profits in the future.

The expected value of a decision represents the long-run average outcome that is expected to occur if a particular course of action is undertaken many times. For example, if the decision to make products A and B is repeated on, say, 100 occasions in the future then product A will be expected to give an average profit of £800 000 whereas product B would be expected to give an average profit of £890 000. The expected values are the averages of the possible outcomes based on management estimates. There is no guarantee that the actual outcome will equal the expected value. Indeed, the expected value for product B does not appear in the probability distribution.

MEASURING THE AMOUNT OF UNCERTAINTY

In addition to the expected values of the profits for the various alternatives, management is also interested in the degree of uncertainty of the expected future profits. For example, let us assume that another alternative course of action, say, product C, is added to the alternatives in Example 12.1 and that the probability distribution is as follows:

Product C probability distribution

Outcome	Estimated probability	Weighted amount (£)
Loss of £400 000	0.5	(200 000)
Profit of £2 200 000	0.5	1 100 000
	Expected value	900 000

Product C has a higher expected value than either product A or product B, but it is unlikely that management will prefer product C to product B, because of the greater variability of the possible outcomes. In other words, there is a greater degree of uncertainty attached to product C.

The conventional measure of the dispersion of a probability distribution is the standard deviation. The standard deviation (σ) is the square root of the mean of the squared deviations from the expected value and is calculated from the following formula:

$$\sigma = \sqrt{\sum_{x=1}^{n}(A_x - \overline{A})^2 P_x} \qquad (12.1)$$

where A_x are the profit-level observations, $\overline{A}$ is the expected or mean value, P_x is the probability of each outcome, and the summation is over all possible observations, where n is the total number of possibilities.

The calculations of the standard deviations are £109 540 for product A and £214 240 for product B. If we are comparing the standard deviations of two probability distributions with different expected values, we cannot make a direct comparison. Can you see why this should be so? Consider the following probability distribution for another product, say product D.

Product D probability distribution

Outcome (£ million)	Estimated probability	Weighted amount (£ million)
Profits of £4.0	0.05	0.2
Profits of £6.0	0.10	0.6
Profits of £8.0	0.40	3.2
Profits of £10.0	0.25	2.5
Profits of £12.0	0.20	2.4
	Expected value	8.9

The standard deviation for product D is £2 142 400, but all of the possible outcomes are ten times as large as the corresponding outcomes for product B. The outcomes for product D also have the same pattern of probabilities as product B so that the standard deviation for product D is ten times as large as that for product B. This scale effect can be removed be replacing the standard deviation with a relative measure of dispersion. The relative amount of dispersion can be expressed by the coefficient of variation, which is simply the standard deviation divided by the expected value. The coefficient of variation for product B is 214 240/890 000 = 0.241 (or 24.1 per cent), and for product D it is also 0.241 (2.1424m/8.9m), thus indicating that the relative amount of dispersion is the same for both products.

Measures such as expected values, standard deviations or coefficient of variations are used to summarize the characteristics of alternative courses of action, but they are poor substitutes for representing the probability distributions, since they do not provide the decision-maker with all the relevant information. There is an argument for presenting the entire probability distribution directly to the decision-maker. Such an approach is appropriate when management must select one from a small number of alternatives, but in situations where many alternatives need to be considered the examination of many probability distributions is likely to be difficult and time-consuming. In such situations management may have no alternative but to compare the expected values and coefficients of variation.

ATTITUDES TO RISK BY INDIVIDUALS

How do we determine whether or not a risky course of action should be undertaken? The answer to this question depends on the decision-maker's attitude to risk. We can identify three possible attitudes: an aversion to risk, a desire for risk and an indifference to risk. Consider two alternatives, A and B, which have the following possible outcomes, depending on the state of the economy (i.e. the state of nature):

Possible returns

State of the economy	A (£000)	B (£000)
Recession	90	0
Normal	100	100
Boom	110	200

If we assume that the three states of the economy are equally likely then the expected value for each alternative is £100 000. A risk-seeker is one who, given a choice between more or less risky alternatives with identical expected values, prefers the riskier alternative (alternative B). Faced with the same choice, a risk-averter would select the less risky alternative (alternative A). The person who is indifferent to risk (risk neutral) would be indifferent to both alternatives because they have the same expected values. With regard to investors in general, studies of the securities markets provide convincing evidence that the majority of investors are risk-averse.

Let us now reconsider how useful expected value calculations are for choosing between alternative courses of action. Expected values represent a long-run average solution, but decisions should not be made on the basis of expected values alone, since they do not enable the decision-maker's attitude towards risk to be taken into account. Consider for example, a situation where two individuals play a coin-tossing game, with the loser giving the winner £5000. The expected value to the player who calls heads is as follows:

Outcome	Cash flow (£)	Probability	Weighted amount (£)
Heads	+5000	0.5	+2500
Tails	−5000	0.5	−2500
		Expected value	0

The expected value is zero, but this will not be the actual outcome if only one game is played. The expected-value calculation represents the average outcome only if the game is repeated on many occasions. However, because the game is to be played only once, it is unlikely that each player will find the expected value calculation on its own to be a useful calculation for decision-making. In fact, the expected value calculation implies that each player is indifferent to playing the game, but this indifference will only apply if the two players are neutral to risk. However, a risk-averter will find the game most unattractive. As most business managers are unlikely to be neutral towards risk, and business decisions are rarely repeated, it is unwise for decisions to be made solely on the basis of expected values. At the very least, expected values should be supplemented with measures of dispersion and, where possible, decisions should be made after comparing the probability distributions of the various alternative courses of action.

REAL WORLD VIEWS 12.2

Risk and uncertainty – what risks do management accountants need to consider?

According to Gillian Lees, a blogger on **www.cimaglobal. com**, the typical risk assessment model for a management accountant reads like this: identify risks, assess their impact and probability and develop risk responses. This seems a reasonable approach, but Lees wonders how specific do management accountants need to be in their efforts to identify risks. Some risks are readily identifiable, for example risks of fire or flood. However, as Lees points out, not all risks are. The volcanic ash from an Icelandic volcano which caused major disruption to air traffic over Europe in 2010 was a risk not many could have foreseen. It probably was a surprise even to airlines which would include such risks in their 'risk register' as they fly close to or over volcanoes regularly. A key point raised by Lees based on the volcanic ash example is that all assessments of risk will have an element of 'unknown unknowns'. In other words, it is not possible to identity all risks. What is

important, according to Lees, is to try to think about the processes to deal with unknown risks. For example, a major disruption to fuel supplies would equally ground aircraft in the same way as a volcanic eruption. The risk assessment should, in the airline example, assess not what might cause aircraft to be grounded for a week or more, but how to deal with the event if it happened.

Questions

1 Do you think management accountants should spend a lot of time trying to evaluate different risks?

2 Do you think an assessment of *effects* would be a better approach to risk assessment and management?

References

http://community.cimaglobal.com/blogs/ gillian-lees-blog/did-you-have-volcanoes-your-risk- register

DECISION TREE ANALYSIS

In the examples earlier in this chapter we have assumed that profits were uncertain because of the uncertainty of sales demand. In practice, more than one variable may be uncertain (e.g. sales and costs), and also the value of some variables may be dependent on the values of other variables. Many outcomes may therefore be possible, and some outcomes may be dependent on previous outcomes. A useful analytical tool for clarifying the range of alternative courses of action and their possible outcomes is a decision tree.

A decision tree is a diagram showing several possible courses of action and possible events (i.e. states of nature) and the potential outcomes for each course of action. Each alternative course of action or event is represented by a branch, which leads to subsidiary branches for further courses of action or possible events. Decision trees are designed to illustrate the full range of alternatives and events that can occur, under all envisaged conditions. The value of a decision tree is that its logical analysis of a problem enables a complete strategy to be drawn up to cover all eventualities before a firm becomes committed to a scheme. Let us now consider Example 12.2. This will be used to illustrate how decision trees can be applied to decision-making under conditions of uncertainty.

The decision tree for Example 12.2 is set out in Figure 12.1. The box indicates the point at which decisions have to be taken, and the branches emanating from it indicate the available alternative courses of action. The circles indicate the points at which there are environmental changes that affect the consequences of prior decisions. The branches from these points indicate the possible types of environment (states of nature) that may occur.

Note that the joint probability of two events occurring together is the probability of one event times the probability of the other event. For example, the probability of the development effort succeeding and the product being very successful consists of the products of the probabilities of these two events, i.e. 0.75×0.4, giving a probability of 0.30. Similarly, the probability of the development effort being successful and the product being moderately successful is 0.225 (0.75×0.3). The total expected value for the decision to develop the product consists of the sum of all the items in the expected value column on the 'Develop product' branch of the decision tree, i.e. £49 500. If we assume that there are no other alternatives available, other than the decision not to develop, the expected value of £49 500 for developing the product can be compared with the expected value of zero for not developing the product. Decision theory would suggest that the product should be developed because a positive expected value occurs. However, this does not mean that an outcome of £49 500 profit is guaranteed. The expected-value calculation indicates that if the probabilities are correct and this decision was repeated on many occasions an average profit of £49 500 would result.

Unfortunately, the decision will not be repeated on many occasions, and a run of repeated losses could force a company out of business before it has the chance to repeat similar decisions. Management may

---

EXAMPLE 12.2

A company is considering whether to develop and market a new product. Development costs are estimated to be £180 000, and there is a 0.75 probability that the development effort will be successful and a 0.25 probability that the development effort will be unsuccessful. If the development is successful, the product will be marketed, and it is estimated that:

1 if the product is very successful profits will be £540 000;

2 if the product is moderately successful profits will be £100 000;

3 if the product is a failure, there will be a loss of £400 000.

Each of the above profit and loss calculations is after taking into account the development costs of £180 000. The estimated probabilities of each of the above events are as follows:

1 Very successful	0.4
2 Moderately successful	0.3
3 Failure	0.3

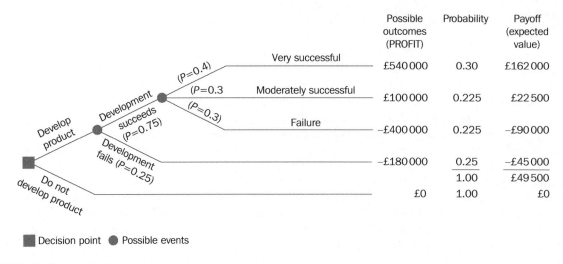

	Possible outcomes (PROFIT)	Probability	Payoff (expected value)
Very successful	£540 000	0.30	£162 000
Moderately successful	£100 000	0.225	£22 500
Failure	−£400 000	0.225	−£90 000
	−£180 000	0.25	−£45 000
		1.00	£49 500
	£0	1.00	£0

■ Decision point ● Possible events

FIGURE 12.1
A simple decision tree

therefore prefer to examine the following probability distribution for developing the product shown in Figure 12.1:

Outcome	Probability
Loss of £400 000	0.225
Loss of £180 000	0.25
Profit of £100 000	0.225
Profit of £540 000	0.30

Management may decide that the project is too risky, since there is nearly a 0.5 probability of a loss occurring.

The decision tree provides a convenient means of identifying all the possible alternative courses of action and their interdependencies. This approach is particularly useful for assisting in the construction of probability distributions when many combinations of events are possible.

BUYING PERFECT AND IMPERFECT INFORMATION

When a decision-maker is faced with a series of uncertain events that might occur, he or she should consider the possibility of obtaining additional information about which event is likely to occur. This section considers how we can calculate the maximum amount it would be worth paying to acquire additional information from a particular source. The approach we shall take is to compare the expected value of a decision if the information is acquired against the expected value with the absence of the information. The difference represents the maximum amount it is worth paying for the additional information. Consider Example 12.3.

Without the additional information, machine A will be purchased using the expected-value decision rule. If the additional information is obtained then this will give a perfect prediction of the level of demand, and the size of the machine can be matched with the level of demand. Therefore, if demand is predicted to be low, machine A will be purchased, whereas if demand is predicted to be high, machine B will be purchased. The revised expected value is:

$$(0.5 \times £500\,000) + (0.5 \times £1\,000\,000) = £750\,000$$

EXAMPLE 12.3

The Boston Company must choose between one of two machines – machine A has low fixed costs and high unit variable costs, whereas machine B has high fixed costs and low unit variable costs. Consequently, machine A is most suited to low-level demand whereas machine B is suited to high-level demand. For simplicity assume that there are only two possible demand levels – low and high – and the estimated probability of each of these events is 0.5. The estimated profits for each demand level are as follows:

	Low demand (£)	High demand (£)	Expected value (£)
Machine A	500 000	800 000	650 000
Machine B	50 000	1 000 000	525 000

There is a possibility of employing a firm of market consultants who would be able to provide a perfect prediction of the actual demand. What is the maximum amount the company should be prepared to pay the consultants for the additional information?

You can see that the expected value is calculated by taking the highest profit in the case of low and high demand. When the decision to employ the market consultants is being taken, it is not known which level of demand will be predicted. Therefore the best estimate of the outcome from obtaining the additional information is a 0.5 probability that it will predict a low demand and a 0.5 probability that it will predict a high demand. (These are the probabilities that are currently associated with low and high demand.) Note that without the survey the company will choose machine A resulting in an expected value of £650 000.

The value of the additional information is ascertained by deducting the expected value without the market survey (£650 000) from the expected value with the survey (£750 000). Thus the additional information increases expected value from £650 000 to £750 000 and the expected value of perfect information is £100 000. As long as the cost of obtaining the information is less than £100 000, the firm of market consultants should be employed.

In the above illustration it was assumed that the additional information would give a 100 per cent accurate prediction of the expected demand. In practice, it is unlikely that *perfect* information is obtainable, but *imperfect* information (for example, predictions of future demand may be only 80 per cent reliable) may still be worth obtaining. However, the value of imperfect information will always be less than the value of perfect information except when both equal zero. This would occur where the additional information would not change the decision. Note that the principles that are applied for calculating the value of imperfect information are the same as those we applied for calculating the value of perfect information, but the calculations are more complex. For an illustration see Scapens (1991).

MAXIMIN, MAXIMAX AND REGRET CRITERIA

In some situations it might not be possible to assign meaningful estimates of probabilities to possible outcomes. Where this situation occurs managers might use any of the following criteria to make decisions: maximin, maximax or the criterion of regret.

The assumption underlying the maximin criterion is that the worst possible outcome will always occur and the decision-maker should therefore select the largest payoff under this assumption. Consider the Boston Company in Example 12.3. You can see that the worst outcomes are £500 000 for machine A and £50 000 for machine B. Consequently, machine A should be purchased using the maximin decision rule.

The maximax criterion is the opposite of maximin, and is based on the assumption that the best payoff will occur. Referring again to Example 12.3, the highest payoffs are £800 000 for machine A and £1 000 000 for machine B. Therefore machine B will be selected under the maximax criterion.

The regret criterion is based on the fact that, having selected an alternative that does not turn out to be the best, the decision-maker will regret not having chosen another alternative when he or she had the opportunity. Thus if in Example 12.3 machine B has been selected on the assumption that the high level of demand would occur, and the high level of demand actually did occur, there would be no regret. However, if machine A has been selected, the company would lose £200 000 (£1 000 000 – £800 000). This measures the amount of the regret. Similarly, if machine A was selected on the assumption that demand would be low, and the low level of demand actually did occur, there would be no regret; but if machine B was selected, the amount of the regret would be £450 000 (£500 000 – £50 000). This information is summarized in the following regret matrix:

	State of nature	
	Low demand (£)	High demand (£)
Choose machine A	0	200 000
Choose machine B	450 000	0

REAL WORLD VIEWS 12.3

Risk reduction and diversification – risky innovations in financial services

Most businesses will try to minimize risk through a combination of risk assessment, risk management and, where possible, transfer the risk to another party. For businesses, risks like theft, fire damage, public liability and product indemnity can be covered by insurance. Insurance companies can estimate risks accurately. For example, they have detailed statistics on many kinds of accident, how frequent events happen and what the level of compensation may be. By insuring a large cross section of businesses, insurers can be fairly certain to make a profit as mass payouts due to risks being realized simultaneously are highly unlikely. However, as pointed out by Joseph Stiglitz in his book *Freefall* on the financial crisis which began in 2008, innovations in the financial services sector raised some new issues on risk. The world's largest insurer AIG had sold insurance' in the form of credit default swaps to cover events like the bankruptcy of banks like Lehman Brothers and Bear Stearns. Without going into the detail of complex financial instruments, Stiglitz outlines how a business is likely to hold an advantage over an insurer in cases when insurance against default on debts of bankruptcy is sought. Simply put, the business is likely to have a closer view on future prospect, and thus will not buy insurance which is too expensive. This in turn drives premiums down. In the case of AIG, it had taken on so many credit default swaps which all required pay outs at the same time (due to the financial crisis) that its cash resources dried up and the company was bailed out by the US government.

Questions

1 Based on the piece above, do you think it is possible to assess all business risks?

2 What effect might transferring risks have on decision-making and management controls?

References

Joseph Stiglitz (2010) *Freefall*, London: Penguin.

The aim of the regret criterion is to minimize the maximum possible regret. The maximum regret for machine A is £200 000 while that for Machine B is £450 000. Machine A would therefore be selected using the regret criterion.

RISK REDUCTION AND DIVERSIFICATION

It is unwise for a firm to invest all its funds in a single project, since an unfavourable event may occur that will affect this project and have a dramatic effect on the firm's total financial position. A better approach would be for the firm to adopt a diversification strategy and invest in a number of different projects. If this diversification strategy is followed, an unfavourable event that affects one project may have relatively less effect on the remaining projects and thus have only a small impact on the firm's overall financial position. That is, a firm should not put all of its eggs in one basket, but should try to minimize risk by spreading its investments over a variety of projects.

The objective in pursuing a diversification strategy is to achieve certain desirable characteristics regarding risk and expected return. Let us now consider Example 12.4. From Example 12.4 it can be seen that both the existing activities (umbrella manufacturing) and the proposed new project (ice-cream manufacturing) are risky when considered on their own, but when they are combined, the risk is eliminated because whatever the outcome the cash inflow will be £100 000. Example 12.4 tells us that we should not only consider the risk of individual projects but should also take into account how the risks of potential new projects and existing activities co-vary with each other. Risk is eliminated completely in Example 12.4 because perfect negative correlation (i.e. where the correlation coefficient is –1) exists between the cash flows of the proposed project and the cash flows of the existing activities. When the cash flows are perfectly positively correlated (where the correlation is +1), risk reduction cannot be achieved when the projects are combined. For all other correlation values risk reduction advantages can be obtained by investing in projects that are not perfectly correlated with existing activities.

The important point that emerges from the above discussion is that it is not the risk of individual projects in isolation that is of interest but rather the incremental risk that each project will contribute to the overall risk of the firm.

EXAMPLE 12.4

A firm which currently manufactures umbrellas is considering diversifying and investing in the manufacture of ice-cream. The predicted cash flows for the existing activities and the new project are shown below.

States of nature	Existing activities (Umbrella manufacturing) (£)	Proposed project (Ice-cream manufacturing) (£)	Combination of existing activities and the proposed project (£)
Sunshine	−200 000	+300 000	+100 000
Rain	+300 000	−200 000	+100 000

To simplify the illustration it is assumed that only two states of nature exist (rain or sunshine) and each has a probability of 0.5.

SUMMARY

The following items relate to the learning objectives listed at the beginning of the chapter.

● **Calculate and explain the meaning of expected values.**

The expected value is calculated by weighting each of the possible outcomes by its associated probability. The sum of these weighted outcomes is called the expected value of the probability distribution. In other words, the expected value is the weighted arithmetic mean of the possible outcomes.

● **Explain the meaning of the terms standard deviation and coefficient of variation as measures of risk and outline their limitations.**

Standard deviation measures the dispersion of the possible outcomes. It is an absolute measure. In contrast, the coefficient of variation is a relative measure derived from dividing the standard deviation by the expected value. Both measures attempt to summarize the risk associated with a probability distribution. They assume that risk is measured in terms of the spread of possible outcomes. Decision-makers are probably more interested in a downside measure of risk that measures the possibility of risk being less than the expected value. Because of this there are strong arguments for presenting the entire probability distribution to the decision-maker.

● **Construct a decision tree when there is a range of alternatives and possible outcomes.**

Where there are many possible outcomes for various alternatives, and some outcomes are dependent on previous outcomes, a decision tree is a useful analytical tool for clarifying the range of alternative courses of actions and their possible outcomes. A decision tree is a diagram that shows the possible courses of actions, the potential events (states of nature for each outcome) together with their potential outcomes and associated probabilities. A decision tree thus represents an analytical tool for deriving expected values and a probability distribution in more complex situations.

● **Describe and calculate the value of perfect and imperfect information.**

The value of perfect and imperfect information relates to determining the value of the maximum amount it is worth paying for additional information. The approach involves comparing the expected value of a decision if the information is acquired against the expected value with the absence of the information. The difference represents the maximum value that it is worth paying for the additional information. You should refer to the section in the chapter on buying perfect and imperfect information for an illustration of the calculation of the value of perfect information.

● **Explain and apply the maximin, maximax and regret criteria.**

In some situations it might not be possible to assign meaningful estimates of probabilities to possible outcomes. When this situation occurs, either the maximin, maximax or regret criteria may be used. The maximin criterion assumes that the worst possible outcome will occur and that the decision should be based on the largest payoff under this assumption. The maximax is the opposite to maximin, and is based on the assumption that the best possible payoff will occur. The regret criterion is based on the fact that, having selected an alternative that does not turn out to be the best, the decision-maker will regret not having chosen another alternative when he or she had the opportunity. The aim is to minimize the maximum possible regret. The application of the criteria was illustrated using Example 12.3.

● **Explain the implication of pursuing a diversification strategy.**

The implication of diversification is that the degree of uncertainty attached to various alternatives should not be considered in isolation. Instead, how an alternative interacts with existing activities should be considered. The aim should be to measure incremental, rather than the total risk, of a project.

KEY TERMS AND CONCEPTS

Coefficient of variation A ratio measure of dispersion derived by dividing the standard deviation divided by the expected value.

Decision tree A diagram showing several possible courses of action and possible events and the potential outcomes for each of them.

Diversification strategy A strategy of investing in a range of different projects in order to minimize risk.

Events In the context of risk and uncertainty, factors that are outside the decision-maker's control, also known as states of nature.

Expected value A figure calculated by weighting each of the possible outcomes by its associated probability.

Expected value of perfect information The maximum amount it is worth paying for additional information in an uncertain situation, calculated by comparing the expected value of a decision if the information is acquired against the expected value in the absence of the information.

Maximax criterion A decision rule based on the assumption that the best possible outcome will always occur and the decision-maker should therefore select the largest payoff.

Maximin criterion A decision rule based on the assumption that the worst possible outcome will always occur and the decision-maker should therefore select the largest payoff under this assumption.

Objective probabilities Probabilities that can be established mathematically or compiled from historical data.

Probability In the context of risk and uncertainty, the likelihood that an event or state of nature will occur, normally expressed in decimal form with a value between 0 and 1.

Probability distribution A list of all possible outcomes for an event and the probability that each will occur.

Regret criterion A decision rule based on the fact that if a decision-maker selects an alternative that does not turn out to be the best, he or she will experience regret and therefore decisions should be made that will minimize the maximum possible regret.

Risk A term applied to a situation where there are several possible outcomes and there is relevant past experience to enable statistical evidence to be produced for predicting the possible outcomes.

Risk-averter An individual who, given a choice between more or less risky alternatives with identical expected values, prefers the less risky option.

Risk neutral An individual who, given a choice between more or less risky alternatives with identical expected values, would be indifferent to both alternatives because they have the same expected values.

Risk-seeker An individual who, given a choice between more or less risky alternatives with identical expected values, prefers the riskier option.

Single most likely estimate The outcome with the highest probability attached to it.

Standard deviation The square root of the mean of the squared deviations from the expected value.

States of nature In the context of risk and uncertainty, factors that are outside the decision-maker's control, also known as events.

Subjective probabilities Probabilities that are based on an individual's expert knowledge, past experience, and on observations of current variables which are likely to affect future events.

Uncertainty A term applied to a situation where there are several possible outcomes and but there is little previous statistical evidence to enable possible outcomes to be predicted.

RECOMMENDED READING

For an explanation and illustration of how imperfect information can be valued you should refer to Chapter 7 of Scapens (1991).

KEY EXAMINATION POINTS

When you are faced with problems requiring an evaluation of alternatives with uncertain outcomes, you should calculate expected values and present probability distributions.

Note that expected values on their own are unlikely to be particularly useful and there is a need to supplement this measure with a probability distribution.

Avoid calculating standard deviations, since they are rarely required and are a poor substitute for probability distributions.

It is particularly important with this topic that you plan your answer carefully. Once you have started your answer, it is difficult to remedy the situation if you initially adopt the wrong approach. A rough sketch of a decision tree at the start of your answer will force you to analyze the problem and identify all the alternatives and possible outcomes.

Examination questions on this topic sometimes also include a requirement as to whether additional perfect information should be purchased. Do make sure that you understand how to calculate the value of perfect information.

ASSESSMENT MATERIAL

The review questions are short questions that enable you to assess your understanding of the main topics included in the chapter. The numbers in parentheses provide you with the page numbers to refer to if you cannot answer a specific question.

The review problems are more complex and require you to relate and apply the content to various business problems. The problems are graded by their level of difficulty. Solutions to review problems that are not preceded by the term 'IM' are provided in a separate section at the end of the book. Solutions to problems preceded by the term 'IM' are provided in the *Instructor's Manual* accompanying this book that can be downloaded from the lecturer's digital support resources. Additional review problems with fully worked solutions are provided in the *Student Manual* that accompanies this book.

REVIEW QUESTIONS

12.1 Distinguish between risk and uncertainty. (p. 279)
12.2 What is a probability distribution? (p. 280)
12.3 How do subjective probabilities differ from objective probabilities? (p. 280)
12.4 Distinguish between expected value and the single most likely estimate. (p. 282)
12.5 Distinguish between the standard deviation and the coefficient of variation. (pp. 282–283)
12.6 What are the disadvantages of the standard deviation as a measure of risk? (p. 283)

12.7 What is a decision tree and what purpose does it serve? (p. 285)
12.8 What is the expected value of perfect information and how can it be determined? (pp. 286–87)
12.9 Distinguish between maximin, maximax and regret criteria. When might it be appropriate to apply these criteria? (p. 288)
12.10 How does diversification impact on measuring risk? (p. 289)

REVIEW PROBLEMS

12.11 **Intermediate**. Darwin uses decision tree analysis in order to evaluate potential projects. The company has been looking at the launch of a new product which it believes has a 70 per cent probability of success. The company is, however, considering undertaking an advertising campaign costing £50 000, which would increase the probability of success to 95 per cent.

If successful the product would generate income of £200 000 otherwise £70 000 would be received.

What is the maximum that the company would be prepared to pay for the advertising?

(a) £32 500
(b) £29 000
(c) £17 500
(d) £50 000.

ACCA Paper 1.2 – Financial Information for Management

12.12 **Intermediate**. A company uses decision tree analysis to evaluate potential options. The management accountant for the company has established the following:

What would be the cost of the upgrade that would make the company financially indifferent between building new premises and upgrading the old one?

(a) £100 000
(b) £900 000
(c) £1 000 000
(d) £1 700 000

ACCA Paper 1.2 – Financial Information for Management

12.13 Intermediate. A company expects to sell 1000 units per month of a new product but there is uncertainty as to both the unit selling price and the unit variable cost of the product. The following estimates of selling price, variable costs and their related probabilities have been made:

Selling Price		Unit variance cost	
£ per unit	Probability	£ per unit	Probability
20	25%	8	20%
25	40%	10	50%
30	35%	12	30%

There are specific fixed costs of £5000 per month expected for the new product.

The expected value of monthly contribution is:

(a) £5890
(b) £10 300
(c) £10 890
(d) £15 300

12.14 Intermediate. Use the data presented in 12.13. The probability of the monthly contribution from the new product exceeding £13 500 is:

(a) 24.5%
(b) 30.5%
(c) 63.0%
(d) 92.5%

CIMA P2 Management Accounting: Decision Management

12.15 Intermediate - The following data are given for parts (i) and (ii) below:

The owner of a van selling hot take-away food has to decide how many burgers to purchase for sale at a forthcoming outdoor concert. The number of burgers sold will depend on the weather conditions and any unsold burgers will be thrown away at the end of the day. The table below details the profit that would be earned for each possible outcome:

	Number of burgers purchased			
Weather	1000	2000	3000	4000
Bad	$1 000	$0	($1 000)	($3 000)
Average	$3 000	$6 000	$7 000	$6 000
Good	$3 000	$6 000	$9 000	$12 000

(i) If the van owner applies the maximin rule he will purchase:

(A) 1 000 burgers
(B) 2 000 burgers
(C) 3 000 burgers
(D) 4 000 burgers   *(2 marks)*

(ii) If the van owner applies the minimax regret rule he will purchase:

(A) 1 000 burgers
(B) 2 000 burgers
(C) 3 000 burgers
(D) 4 000 burgers   *(2 marks)*

CIMA P1 Performance operations

12.16 Advanced. A company has decide which of three new mutually exclusive products to launch. The directors believe that demand for the products will vary depending on competitor reaction. There is a

30% chance that competitor reaction will be strong, a 20% chance that competitor reaction will be normal and a 50% chance that competitor reaction will be weak. The company uses expected value to make this type of decision.

The net present value for each of the possible outcomes is as follows:

Competitor reaction	Product A $000s	Product B $000s	Product C $000s
Strong	200	400	600
Normal	300	600	400
Weak	500	800	500

A market research company believes it can provide perfect information on potential competitor reaction in this market.

Required:
Calculate the maximum amount that should be paid for the information from the market research company.   *(5 marks)*

CIMA P1 Performance operations

12.17 Advanced. A company uses a third party delivery service to deliver goods to customers. The current average cost per delivery is $12.50. The company is trying to decide whether to establish an in-house delivery service. A number of factors could affect the average total cost per delivery for the in-house delivery service. The table below shows the possible average total costs and the probability of each one occurring:

Average total cost	Probability
$10.50	0.05
$10.70	0.10
$11.00	0.08
$12.10	0.12
$12.50	0.14
$12.60	0.16
$14.20	0.12
$15.60	0.18
$15.80	0.05

The expected value of the average total cost, based on the probability distribution above, is $13.

Required:
Explain the decision that the company manager is likely to make, based on the probability distribution and the current delivery cost of $12.50 per delivery, if the manager is:

(i) Risk neutral
(ii) Risk averse
(iii) Risk seeking   *(5 marks)*

CIMA P1 Performance operations

12.18 An events management company is trying to decide whether or not to advertise an outdoor concert. The sale of tickets is dependent on the weather. If the weather is poor it is expected that 5 000 tickets will be sold without advertising. There is a 70% chance that the weather will be poor. If the weather is good it is expected that 10 000 tickets will be sold without advertising. There is a 30% chance that the weather will be good.

If the concert is advertised and the weather is poor, there is a 60% chance that the advertising will stimulate further demand and ticket sales will increase to 7 000. If the weather is good there is a 25% chance the advertising will stimulate demand and ticket sales will increase to 13 000.

The profit expected, before deducting the cost of advertising, at different levels of ticket sales are as follows:

Number of tickets sold	Profit $
5 000	(20 000)
6 000	(5 000)
7 000	35 000
8 000	55 000
9 000	70 000
10 000	90 000
11 000	115 000
12 000	130 000
13 000	150 000

The cost of advertising the concert will be $15 000.
Required:
Demonstrate, using a decision tree, whether the concert should be advertised.
(5 marks)
CIMA P1 Performance operations

12.19 Advanced. Shifters Haulage (SH) is considering changing some of the vans it uses to transport crates for customers. The new vans come in three sizes; small, medium and large. SH is unsure about which type to buy. The capacity is 100 crates for the small van, 150 for the medium van and 200 for the large van.

Demand for crates varies and can be either 120 or 190 crates per period, with the probability of the higher demand figure being 0.6.

The sale price per crate is $10 and the variable cost $4 per crate for all van sizes subject to the fact that if the capacity of the van is greater than the demand for crates in a period then the variable cost will be lower by 10% to allow for the fact that the vans will be partly empty when transporting crates.

SH is concerned that if the demand for crates exceeds the capacity of the vans then customers will have to be turned away. SH estimates that in this case goodwill of $100 would be charged against profits per period to allow for lost future sales regardless of the number of customers that are turned away.

Depreciation charged would be $200 per period for the small, $300 for the medium and $400 for the large van.

SH has in the past been very aggressive in its decision-making, pressing ahead with rapid growth strategies. However, its managers have recently grown more cautious as the business has become more competitive.

Required:

(a) Explain the principles behind the maximax, maximin and expected value criteria that are sometimes used to make decisions in uncertain situations. (4 marks)
(b) Prepare a profits table showing the SIX possible profit figures per period. (9 marks)
(c) Using your profit table from (b) above discuss which type of van SH should buy taking into consideration the possible risk attitudes of the managers. (6 marks)
(d) Describe THREE methods other than those mentioned in (a) above, which businesses can use to analyze and assess the risk that exists in its decision-making. (6 marks)
(25 marks)
ACCA Performance Management

12.20 Advanced: Expected values, probability distributions and regret criterion. Central Ltd has developed a new product, and is currently considering the marketing and pricing policy it should employ for this. Specifically, it is considering whether the sales price should be set at £15 per unit or at the higher level of £24 per unit. Sales volumes at these two prices are shown in the following table:

Sales price £15 per unit		Sales price £24 per unit	
Forecast sales volume (000)	Probability	Forecast sales volume (000)	Probability
20	0.1	8	0.1
30	0.6	16	0.3
40	0.3	20	0.3
		24	0.3

The fixed production costs of the venture will be £38 000.

The level of the advertising and publicity costs will depend on the sales price and the market aimed for. With a sales price of £15 per unit, the advertising and publicity costs will amount to £12 000. With a sales price of £24 per unit, these costs will total £122 000.

Labour and variable overhead costs will amount to £5 per unit produced. Each unit produced requires 2 kg of raw material and the basic cost is expected to be £4 per kg. However, the suppliers of the raw materials are prepared to lower the price in return for a firm agreement to purchase a guaranteed minimum quantity. If Central Ltd contracts to purchase at least 40 000 kg then the price will be reduced to £3.75 per kg for *all* purchases. If Central contracts to purchase a minimum of 60 000 kg then the price will be reduced to £3.50 per kg for all purchases. It is only if Central Ltd guarantees either of the above minimum levels of purchases in advance that the appropriate reduced prices will be operative.

If Central Ltd were to enter into one of the agreements for the supply of raw material and was to find that it did not require to utilize the entire quantity of materials purchased then the excess could be sold. The sales price will depend upon the quantity that is offered for sale. If 16 000 kg or more are sold, the sales price will be £2.90 per kg for all sales. If less than 16 000 kg are offered, the sales price will be only £2.40 per kg.

Irrespective of amount sold, the costs incurred in selling the excess raw materials will be, per kg, as follows:

Packaging	£0.30
Delivery	£0.45
Insurance	£0.15

Central's management team feels that losses are undesirable, while high expected money values are desirable. Therefore it is considering the utilization of a formula that incorporated both aspects of the outcome to measure the desirability of each strategy. The formula to be used to measure the desirability is:

$$desirability = L + 3E$$

where L is the lowest outcome of the strategy and E is the expected monetary value of the strategy. The higher this measures, the more desirable the strategy.

The marketing manager seeks the advice of you, the management accountant, to assist in deciding the appropriate strategy. He says 'we need to make two decisions now:

(i) Which price per unit should be charged: £15 or £24?
(ii) Should all purchases of raw materials be at the price of £4 per kg, or should we enter into an agreement for a basic minimum quantity? If we enter into an agreement then what minimum level of purchases should we guarantee?

As you are the management accountant, I expect you to provide me with some useful relevant figures.'

Required:

(a) Provide statements that show the various expected outcomes of each of the choices open to Central Ltd. (10 marks)
(b) Advise on its best choice of strategies if Central Ltd's objective is:

(i)   to maximize the expected monetary value of the outcomes;

(ii) to minimize the harm done to the firm if the worst outcome of each choice were to eventuate;

(iii) to maximize the score on the above mentioned measure of desirability.   *(6 marks)*

(c) Briefly comment on either:

(i)   two other factors that may be relevant in reaching a decision;
OR

(ii) the decision criteria utilized in (b) above.   *(4 marks)*

ACCA P2 Management Accounting

12.21 Advanced: Decision tree, expected value and maximin criterion.

(a) The Alternative Sustenance Company is considering introducing a new franchised product, Wholefood Waffles.

Existing ovens now used for making some of the present 'Half-Baked' range of products could be used instead for baking the Wholefood Waffles. However, new special batch mixing equipment would be needed. This cannot be purchased, but can be hired from the franchiser in three alternative specifications, for batch sizes of 200, 300 and 600 units respectively. The annual cost of hiring the mixing equipment would be £5000, £15 000 and £21 500 respectively.

The 'Half-Baked' product which would be dropped from the range currently earns a contribution of £90 000 per annum, which it is confidently expected could be continued if the product were retained in the range.

The company's marketing manager considers that, at the market price for Wholefood Waffles of £0.40 per unit, it is equally probable that the demand for this product would be 600 000 or 1 000 000 units per annum.

The company's production manager has estimated the variable costs per unit of making Wholefood Waffles and the probabilities of those costs being incurred, as follows:

Batch size: Cost per unit (pence)	200 units Probability if annual sales are either 600 000 or 1 000 000 units	300 units Probability if annual sales are either 600 000 or 1 000 000 units	600 units Probability if annual sales are 600 000 units	600 units Probability if annual sales are 1 000 000
£0.20	0.1	0.2	0.3	0.5
£0.25	0.1	0.5	0.1	0.2
£0.30	0.8	0.3	0.6	0.3

You are required:

(i)   to draw a decision tree setting out the problem faced by the company,   *(12 marks)*

(ii) to show in each of the following three independent situations which size of mixing machine, if any, the company should hire:

1   to satisfy a 'maximin' (or 'minimax' criterion),

2   to maximize the expected value of contribution per annum,

3   to minimize the probability of earning an annual contribution of less than £100 000.   *(7 marks)*

(b) You are required to outline briefly the strengths and limitations of the methods of analysis which you have used in part (a) above.   *(6 marks)*

ICAEW Management Accounting

IM12.1 Advanced: Preparation of project statements for different demand levels and calculations of expected profit. Seeprint

Limited is negotiating an initial one year contract with an important customer for the supply of a specialized printed colour catalogue at a fixed contract price of £16 per catalogue. Seeprint's normal capacity for producing such catalogues is 50 000 per annum.

Last year Seeprint Limited earned £11 000 profit per month from a number of small accounts requiring specialized colour catalogues. If the contract under negotiation is not undertaken, then a similar profit might be obtained from these customers next year, but, if it is undertaken, there will be no profit from such customers.

The estimated costs of producing colour catalogues of a specialized nature are given below.

The costs below are considered certain with the exception of the direct materials price.

Cost data:

	(£)
Variable costs per catalogue	
Direct materials	4.50
Direct wages	3.00
Direct expenses	1.30

	80% *(£)*	*Output levels (capacity utilization)* 100% *(£)*	120% *(£)*
Semi-variable costs			
Indirect materials	46 800	47 000	74 400
Indirect wages	51 200	55 000	72 000
Indirect expenses	6 000	8 000	9 600

Estimated fixed costs per annum:

Depreciation of specialist equipment	£8 000
Supervisory and management salaries	£20 000
Other fixed costs allocated to specialist colour catalogues production	£32 000

You are required to:

(a) Tabulate the costs and profits per unit and in total and the annual profits, assuming that the contract orders in the year are:
(i) 40 000, (ii) 50 000 and (iii) 60 000 catalogues, at a direct material cost of £4.50 per catalogue. Comment on the tabulation you have prepared.   *(10 marks)*

(b) Calculate the expected profit for the year if it is assumed that the probability of the total order is:
0.4 for 40 000 catalogues
0.4 for 50 000 catalogues
0.1 for 60 000 catalogues
and that the probability of direct material cost is:
0.5 at £4.50 per catalogue
0.3 at £5.00 per catalogue
0.2 at £5.50 per catalogue.   *(6 marks)*

(c) Discuss the implications for Seeprint Limited of the acceptance or otherwise of the contract with the important customer.   *(6 marks)*

ACCA Level 2 Management Accounting

IM12.2 Advanced: CVP analysis and uncertainty. The accountant of Laburnum Ltd is preparing documents for a forthcoming meeting of the budget committee. Currently, variable cost is 40 per cent of selling price and total fixed costs are £40 000 per year.

The company uses an historical cost accounting system. There is concern that the level of costs may rise during the ensuing year and the chairman of the budget committee has expressed interest in a probabilistic approach to an investigation of the effect that this will have on historic cost profits. The accountant is attempting to prepare the documents in a way which will be most helpful to the committee members. He has obtained the following estimates from his colleagues:

	Average inflation rate over ensuing year	Probability
Pessimistic	10%	0.4
Most likely	5%	0.5
Optimistic	1%	0.1
		1.0

	Demand at current selling prices	Probability
Pessimistic	£50 000	0.3
Most likely	£75 000	0.6
Optimistic	£100 000	0.1
		1.0

The demand figures are given in terms of sales value at the current level of selling prices but it is considered that the company could adjust its selling prices in line with the inflation rate without affecting customer demand in real terms.

Some of the company's fixed costs are contractually fixed and some are apportionments of past costs; of the total fixed costs, an estimated 85 per cent will remain constant irrespective of the inflation rate.

You are required to analyze the foregoing information in a way which you consider will assist management with its budgeting problem. Although you should assume that the directors of Laburnum Ltd are solely interested in the effect of inflation on historic cost profits, you should comment on the validity of the accountant's intended approach. As part of your analysis you are required to calculate:

(i) the probability of at least breaking even, and
(ii) the probability of achieving a profit of at least £20 000.

(16 marks)
ACCA Level 2 Management Accounting

IM12.3 Advanced: Output decision based on expected values. A ticket agent has an arrangement with a concert hall that holds pop concerts on 60 nights a year whereby he receives discounts as follows per concert:

For purchase of:	He receives a discount of:
200 tickets	20%
300 tickets	25%
400 tickets	30%
500 tickets or more	40%

Purchases must be in full hundreds. The average price per ticket is £3.

He must decide in advance each year the number of tickets he will purchase. If he has any tickets unsold by the afternoon of the concert he must return them to the box office. If the box office sells any of these he receives 60 per cent of their price.

His sales records over a few years show that for a concert with extremely popular artistes he can be confident of selling 500 tickets, for one with lesser known artistes 350 tickets, and for one with relatively unknown artistes 200 tickets.

His records also show that 10 per cent of tickets he returns are sold by the box office.

His administration costs incurred in selling tickets are the same per concert irrespective of the popularity of the artistes.

There are two possible scenarios in which his sales records can be viewed:

Scenario 1: that, on average, he can expect concerts with lesser known artistes

Scenario 2: that the frequency of concerts will be:

	(%)
with popular artistes	45
with lesser known artistes	30
with unknown artistes	25
	100

You are required to calculate:

(a) separately for each of Scenarios 1 and 2:

(a) the expected demand for tickets per concert;

(b) (i) the level of his purchases of tickets per concert that will give him the largest profit over a long period of time;

(ii) the profit per concert that this level of purchases of tickets will yield;

(b) for Scenario 2 only: the maximum sum per annum that the ticket agent should pay to a pop concert specialist for 100 per cent correct predictions as to the likely success of each concert.

(25 marks)
CIMA P3 Management Accounting

IM12.4 Advanced: Contracting hotel accommodation based on uncertain demand. Crabbe, the owner of the Ocean Hotel, is concerned about the hotel's finances and has asked your advice. He gives you the following information:

We have rooms for 80 guests. When the hotel is open, whatever the level of business, we have to meet the following each month:

	(£)
Staff wages and benefits	12 500
General overheads (rates, electricity, etc)	8 000
Depreciation	2 200
Interest on mortgage and bank loan	1 800
Repayments on mortgage and bank loan	2 500
Drawings for my own needs	1 000
	28 000

'For our normal business we charge an average of £20 per night for each guest. Each guest-night involves variable costs of £4 for laundry and cleaning. Guests also spend money in the restaurant, which on average brings us another £5 per guest-night after meeting variable costs.

'I need advice on two problems; one concerns the month of September and the other relates to the winter.

1 'Normal business in September will depend on weather conditions, and the probabilities of occupancy from normal business are:

	For month of September		
Weather condition	A	B	C
Probability	0.3	0.4	0.3
Occupancy (total guest-nights)	1440	1680	1920

'Airtravel Tours has enquired about a block booking at a discount in September. I intend to quote a discount of 40 per cent on our normal guest-night charge. In the restaurant Airtravels package tourists will only bring us £3 per guest-night after variable costs. Airtravel could take all our capacity, but I have to decide how many guest-nights to offer. The contract will mean that I agree in advance to take the same number of Airtravel tourists every night throughout September. If they won't accept my price, I would be prepared to go as far as a 60 per cent discount.

2 'When we come to the winter, trade is usually so bad that we close for three months. We retain only a skeleton staff, costing £1500 per month, and general overheads are reduced from £8000 to £2000. I am trying to find ways of keeping open this winter, but staying open will incur the full monthly outgoings.

'If we remained open for all three months I estimate our basic winter trade at reduced prices, together with income from conferences, would be as follows:

	Average number of guests per night	Charge per guest-night (£)	Restaurant revenue per guest-night net of variable costs (£)
Basic winter trade	12	14	5
Conferences, etc.	30	13	4

'Alternatively, I am considering offering a series of language courses. We could not take any other guests, and I estimate the total demand for the three months as follows:

Market condition	X	Y	Z
Probability	0.3	0.4	0.3
Occupancy (total guest-nights)	2160	4320	6480

'If the courses are offered we shall have to run them for the full three months, irrespective of the take-up. The charge per night would be £24, and the revenue from the restaurant net of variable cost would only be £1 per guest-night.

We would have to spend about £5000 per month on tutors, and the courses would also have to be advertised beforehand at a cost of £1500.'

Assume 30-day months throughout.

Requirements:

(a) Calculate the number of guest-nights Crabbe should contract to Airtravel Tours at the quoted 40 per cent discount.

(6 marks)

(b) Determine the minimum price per guest-night at which it would be worthwhile for Crabbe to do business with Airtravel, and the maximum number of guest-nights it would be worthwhile to contract at this price. *(4 marks)*

(c) Assess which of the winter options Crabbe should undertake and state any reservation you may have about your assessment. *(9 marks)*

(d) Briefly explain the criteria on which you have identified costs to assess Crabbe's business options in requirements (a) to (c). *(6 marks)*

ICAEW P2 Management Accounting

IM12.5 Advanced: Pricing and purchase contract decisions based on uncertain demand and calculation of maximum price to pay for perfect information. Z Ltd is considering various product pricing and material purchasing options with regard to a new product it has in development. Estimates of demand and costs are as follows:

If selling price per unit is		£15 per unit Sales volume (000 units)	£20 per unit Sales volume (000 units)
Forecasts	Probability		
Optimistic	0.3	36	28
Most likely	0.5	28	23
Pessimistic	0.2	18	13
Variable manufacturing costs (excluding materials) per unit		£3	£3
Advertising and selling costs		£25 000	£96 000
General fixed costs		£40 000	£40 000

Each unit requires 3kg of material and because of storage problems any unused material must be sold at £1 per kg. The sole suppliers of the material offer three purchase options, which must be decided at the outset, as follows:

(i) any quantity at £3 per kg, or

(ii) a price of £2.75 per kg for a minimum quantity of 50 000 kg, or

(iii) a price of £2.50 per kg for a minimum quantity of 70 000 kg.

You are required, assuming that the company is risk neutral, to

(a) prepare calculations to show what pricing and purchasing decisions the company should make, clearly indicating the recommended decisions; *(15 marks)*

(b) calculate the maximum price you would pay for perfect information as to whether the demand would be optimistic or most likely pessimistic. *(5 marks)*

CIMA Stage 3 Management Accounting Techniques

IM12.6 Advanced: Selling price decision based on expected values and value of additional information. Warren Ltd is to produce a new product in a short-term venture which will utilize some obsolete materials and expected spare capacity. The new product will be advertised in quarter I with production and sales taking place in quarter II. No further production or sales are anticipated.

Sales volumes are uncertain but will, to some extent, be a function of sales price. The possible sales volumes and the advertising costs associated with each potential sales price are as follows:

Sales price £20 per unit		Sales price £25 per unit		Sales price £40 per unit	
Sales volume units (000)	Probability	Sales volume units (000)	Probability	Sales volume units (000)	Probability
4	0.1	2	0.1	0	0.2
6	0.4	5	0.2	3	0.5
8	0.5	6	0.2	10	0.2
		8	0.5	15	0.1
Advertising Costs	£20 000		£50 000		£100 000

The resources used in the production of each unit of the product are:

Production labour:	grade 1	0.4 hours
	grade 2	0.2 hour

Materials:	X	1 unit
	Y	2 units

The normal cost per hour of labour is

grade 1	£10
grade 2	£15

However, before considering the effects of the current venture, there is expected to be 800 hours of idle time for each grade of labour in quarter II. Idle time is paid at the normal rates.

Material X is in stock at a book value of £8 per unit, but is widely used within the firm and any usage for the purposes of this venture will require replacing. Replacement cost is £9 per unit.

Material Y is obsolete stock. There are 16 000 units in stock at a book value of £3.50 per unit and any stock not used will have to be disposed of at a cost, to Warren, of £2 per unit. Further quantities of Y can be purchased for £4 per unit.

Overhead recovery rates are

Variable overhead	£10 per direct labour hour worked
Fixed overhead	£3 per direct labour hour worked

Total fixed overheads will not alter as a result of the current venture.

Feedback from advertising will enable the exact demand to be determined at the end of quarter I and production in quarter II will be set to equal that demand. However, it is necessary to decide now on the sales price in order that it can be incorporated into the advertising campaign.

Required:

(a) Calculate the expected money value of the venture at each sales price and on the basis of this advise Warren of its best course of action. (12 marks)

(b) Briefly explain why the management of Warren might rationally reject the sales price leading to the highest expected money value and prefer one of the other sales prices. (4 marks)

(c) It will be possible, for the sales price of £40 per unit only, to ascertain which of the four levels of demand will eventuate. If the indications are that the demand will be low then the advertising campaign can be cancelled at a cost of £10 000 but it would then not be possible to continue the venture at another sales price. This accurate information concerning demand will cost £5000 to obtain.

Indicate whether it is worthwhile obtaining the information and ascertain whether it would alter the advice given in (a) above. (4 marks)

ACCA Level 2 Management Accounting

IM12.7 Advanced: Hire of machine based on uncertain demand and value of perfect information. The Ruddle Co. Ltd had planned to install and, with effect from next April, commence operating sophisticated machinery for the production of a new product – product Zed. However, the supplier of the machinery has just announced that delivery of the machinery will be delayed by six months and this will mean that Ruddle will not now be able to undertake production using that machinery until October.

'The first six months of production' stated the commercial manager of Ruddle, 'is particularly crucial as we have already contracted to supply several national supermarket groups with whatever quantities of Zed they require during that period at a price of £40 per unit. Their demand is, at this stage, uncertain but would have been well within the capacity of the permanent machinery we were to have installed. The best estimates of the total demand for the first period are thought to be:

Estimated demand – first six months

Quantity (000 units)	Probability
10	0.5
14	0.3
16	0.2

'Whatever the level of demand, we are going to meet it in full even if it means operating at a loss for the first half year. Therefore I suggest we consider the possibility of hiring equipment on which temporary production can take place.' Details of the only machines which could be hired are:

	Machine A	Machine B	Machine C
Productive capacity per six month period (units)	10 000	12 000	16 000
Variable production cost for each unit produced	£6.5	£6	£5
Other 'fixed' costs total for six months	£320 000	£350 000	£400 000

In addition to the above costs there will be a variable material cost of £5 per unit. For purchases greater than 10 000 units a discount of 20 per cent per unit will be given, but this only applies to the excess over 10 000 units.

Should production capacity be less than demand then Ruddle could subcontract production of up to 6000 units but would be required to supply raw materials. Subcontracting costs are:

up to 4000 units subcontracted £30 per unit
any excess over 4000 units subcontracted £35 per unit.

These subcontracting costs relate only to the work carried out by the subcontractor and exclude the costs of raw materials.

The commercial manager makes the following further points, 'Due to the lead time required for setting up production, the choice of which machine to hire must be made before the precise demand is known. However, demand will be known in time for production to be scheduled so that an equal number of units can be produced each month. We will, of course, only produce sufficient to meet demand.

'We need to decide which machine to hire. However, I wonder whether it would be worthwhile seeking the assistance of a firm of market researchers? Their reputation suggests that they are very accurate and they may be able to inform us whether demand is to be 10, 14 or 16 thousand units.'

Required:

(a) For each of the three machines which could be hired show the possible monetary outcomes and, using expected values, advise Ruddle on its best course of action. (12 marks)

(b) (i) Calculate the maximum amount which it would be worthwhile to pay to the firm of market researchers to ascertain details of demand. (You are required to assume that the market researchers will produce an absolutely accurate forecast and that demand will be exactly equal to one of the three demand figures given.) (4 marks)

(ii) Comment on the view that as perfect information is never obtainable the calculation of the expected value of perfect information is not worthwhile. Briefly explain any uses such a calculation may have. (4 marks)

Ignore taxation and the time value of money.

ACCA P2 Management Accounting

IM12.8 Advanced: Calculation of expected value of perfect and imperfect information. Butterfield Ltd manufactures a single brand of dog-food called 'Lots O Grissle' (LOG). Sales have stabilized for several years at a level of £20 million per annum at current prices. This level is not expected to change in the foreseeable future (except as indicated below). It is well below the capacity of the plant. The managing director, Mr Rover, is considering how to stimulate growth in the company's turnover and profits. After rejecting all of the alternative possibilities that he can imagine, or that have been suggested to him, he is reviewing a proposal to introduce a new luxury dog-food product. It would be called 'Before Eight Mince' (BEM), and would have a recommended retail price of £0.50 per tin. It would require no new investment, and would incur no additional fixed costs.

Mr Rover has decided that he will undertake this new development only if he can anticipate that it will at least break even in the first year of operation.

(a) Mr Rover estimates that BEM has a 75 per cent chance of gaining acceptance in the marketplace. His best estimate is that if the product gains acceptance it will have sales in the forthcoming year of £3.2 million at retail prices, given a contribution of £1 million after meeting the variable costs of manufacture and distribution. If, on the other hand, the product fails to gain acceptance, sales for the year will, he thinks, be only £800 000 at retail prices, and for various reasons there would be a negative contribution of £400 000 in that year.

You are required to show whether, on the basis of these preliminary estimates, Mr Rover should give the BEM project further consideration. (4 marks)

(b) Mr Rover discusses the new project informally with his sales director, Mr Khoo Chee Khoo, who suggests that some of the sales achieved for the new product would cause lost sales of LOG. In terms of retail values he estimates the likelihood of this as follows:

There is a 50 per cent chance that sales of LOG will fall by half of the sales of BEM.

There is a 25 per cent chance that sales of LOG will fall by one-quarter of the sales of BEM.

There is a 25 per cent chance that sales of LOG will fall by three-quarters of the sales of BEM.

The contribution margin ratio of LOG is 25 per cent at all relevant levels of sales and output. You are required to show whether, after accepting these further estimates, Mr Rover should give the BEM project further consideration. *(5 marks)*

(c) Mr Rover wonders also whether, before attempting to proceed any further, he should have some market research undertaken. He approaches Delphi Associates, a firm of market research consultants for whom he has a high regard. On previous occasions he has found them to be always right in their forecasts, and he considers that their advice will give him as near perfect information as it is possible to get. He decides to ask Delphi to advise him only on whether or not BEM will gain acceptance in the marketplace in the sense in which he has defined it; he will back Mr Khoo Chee Khoo's judgement about the effects of the introduction of BEM on the sales of LOG. If Delphi advise him that the product will not be accepted he will not proceed further. Delphi have told him that their fee for this work would be £100 000.

You are required to show whether Mr Rover should instruct Delphi Associates to carry out the market research proposals. *(5 marks)*

(d) Preliminary discussions with Delphi suggest that Delphi's forecast will not be entirely reliable. They believe that, if they indicate that BEM will gain acceptance, there is only a 90 per cent chance that they will be right; and, if they indicate failure to gain acceptance, there is only a 70 per cent chance that they will be right. This implies a 75 per cent chance overall that Delphi will indicate acceptance, in line with Mr Rover's estimate.

You are required to show the maximum amount that Mr Rover should be prepared to pay Delphi to undertake the market research, given the new estimates of the reliability of their advice. *(5 marks)*

(e) You are required to outline briefly the strengths and limitations of your methods of analysis in (a)–(d) above.

(6 marks)
ICAEW Management Accounting

21 STRATEGIC COST MANAGEMENT

LEARNING OBJECTIVES After studying this chapter, you should be able to:

- distinguish between the features of a traditional management accounting control system and cost management;

- explain life-cycle costing and describe the typical pattern of cost commitment and cost incurrence during the three stages of a product's life cycle;

- describe the target costing approach to cost management;

- describe reverse engineering, value analysis and functional analysis;

- distinguish between target costing and *kaizen* costing;

- describe activity-based cost management;

- distinguish between value added and non-value added activities;

- explain the role of benchmarking and business process engineering within the cost management framework;

- outline the main features of a just-in-time philosophy.

- explain the purpose of a cost of quality report;

- outline the main features of environmental cost management;

- describe how value chain analysis can be used to increase customer satisfaction and manage costs more effectively.

In Chapters 16–18 the major features of traditional management accounting control systems and the mechanisms that can be used to control costs were described. The focus was on comparing actual results against a pre-set standard (typically the budget), identifying and analyzing variances and taking remedial action to ensure that future outcomes conform with budgeted outcomes. Traditional cost control systems tend to be based on the preservation of the *status quo* and the ways of performing existing activities are not reviewed. The emphasis is on cost containment rather than cost reduction.

Cost management focuses on cost reduction and continuous improvement and change rather than cost containment. Indeed, the term cost reduction could be used instead of cost management but the former is an emotive term. Therefore cost management is preferred. Whereas traditional cost control systems are routinely applied on a continuous basis, cost management tends to be applied on an *ad hoc* basis when an opportunity for cost reduction is identified. Also many of the approaches that are incorporated within the area of cost management do not necessarily involve the use of accounting techniques. In contrast, cost control relies heavily on accounting techniques.

Cost management consists of those actions that are taken by managers to reduce costs, some of which are prioritized on the basis of information extracted from the accounting system. Other actions, however, are undertaken without the use of accounting information. They involve process improvements, where an opportunity has been identified to perform processes more effectively and efficiently, and which have obvious cost reduction outcomes. It is important that you are aware of all the approaches that can be used to reduce costs even if these methods do not rely mainly on accounting information. You should also note that although cost management seeks to reduce costs, it should not be at the expense of customer satisfaction. Ideally, the aim is to take actions that will both reduce costs and enhance customer satisfaction.

LIFE-CYCLE COSTING

Traditional management accounting control procedures have focused primarily on the manufacturing stage of a product's life cycle. Pre-manufacturing costs, such as research and development and design and post-manufacturing abandonment and disposal costs are treated as period costs. Therefore they are not incorporated in the product cost calculations, nor are they subject to the conventional management accounting control procedures.

Life-cycle costing estimates and accumulates costs over a product's entire life cycle in order to determine whether the profits earned during the manufacturing phase will cover the costs incurred during the pre- and post-manufacturing stages. Identifying the costs incurred during the different stages of a product's life cycle provides an insight into understanding and managing the total costs incurred throughout its life cycle. In particular, life-cycle costing helps management to understand the

REAL WORLD VIEWS 21.1

Target costing – target costing in agriculture
A CIMA 2009 report on the UK agriculture industry reports how farmers in general do not prioritize cost management. This may be partly due to EU subsidies, which distracts farmers from a business/cost focus, and partly due to a lack of product visibility through the supply chain to end consumers. The report cites earlier work by Prof. Lisa Jack, who found that farmers were in some cases 'designing to cost', which affected how farmers tilled their fields, organized their milking parlours and reduced waste. While farmers did not call it so, Jack points out that what they are doing is target cost management. She defines target cost simply as the anticipated price less the required return. While a simple concept, a number of problems are posed for agriculture. First, the price of agricultural produce fluctuates. Second, the concept of return is not something farmers frequently use in typical farm accounts. Jack

argues, however, that if farmers can get a better understanding of their costs, and what is a fair return, they may be able to increase their profits or cut costs to match the prevailing price for their produce.

Questions
1 Would a good understanding of the food supply chain help farmers embarking on a target costing exercise?
2 Could a collaborative approach, whereby farm costs are shared with others, help improve profit margins?

© kickers, iStock.com

References
CIMA (2009), *From gate to plate: strategic management accounting in the UK agriculture industry,* available at **http://www.cimaglobal.com/Documents/ImportedDocuments/cid_execrep_from_gate_to_plate_mar09.pdf**

ADVANCED READING

FIGURE 21.1

Product life-cycle phases: relationship between costs committed and costs incurred

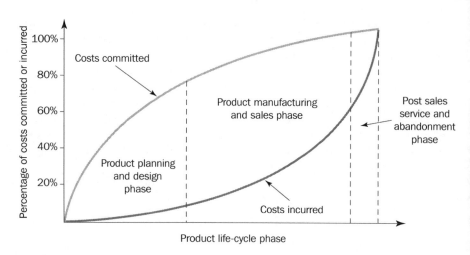

cost consequences of developing and making a product and to identify areas in which cost reduction efforts are likely to be most effective.

Figure 21.1 illustrates a typical pattern of cost commitment and cost incurrence during the three stages of a product's life cycle – the planning and design stage, the manufacturing stage and the service and abandonment stage. Committed or locked-in costs are those costs that have not been incurred but that will be incurred in the future on the basis of decisions that have already been made. Costs are incurred when a resource is used or sacrificed. Costing systems record costs only when they have been incurred. It is difficult to significantly alter costs after they have been committed. For example, the product design specifications determine a product's material and labour inputs and the production process. At this stage costs become committed and broadly determine the future costs that will be incurred during the manufacturing stage.

You will see from Figure 21.1 that the upper cost curve shows the costs that are committed and the lower curve shows the costs that are incurred. The graph shows the wide divergence between the time when the costs are committed and the time when they are incurred. Figure 21.1 shows that approximately 80 per cent of a product's costs are *committed* during the planning and design stage. At this stage product designers determine the product's design and the production process. In contrast, the majority of costs are *incurred* at the manufacturing stage, but they have already become locked-in at the planning and design stage and are difficult to alter. It is apparent from Figure 21.1 that cost management can be most effectively exercised during the planning and design stage and not at the manufacturing stage when the product design and processes have already been determined and costs have been committed. At this latter stage the focus is more on cost containment than cost management. An understanding of life-cycle costs and how they are committed and incurred at different stages throughout a product's life cycle led to the emergence of target costing, a technique that focuses on managing costs during a product's planning and design phase.

TARGET COSTING

In Chapter 10 we briefly looked at target costing as a mechanism for determining selling prices. We shall now consider how target costing can also be used as a cost management tool. Target costing involves the following stages:

Stage 1: Determine the target price which customers will be prepared to pay for the product.

Stage 2: Deduct a target profit margin from the target price to determine the target cost.

Stage 3: Estimate the actual cost of the product.

Stage 4: If estimated actual cost exceeds the target cost investigate ways of driving down the actual cost to the target cost.

The first stage requires market research to determine the customers' perceived value of the product, based on its functions and its attributes (i.e. its functionality), its differentiation value relative to competing products and the price of competing products. The target profit margin depends on the planned return on investment for the organization as a whole and profit as a percentage of sales. This is then decomposed into a target profit for each product which is subsequently deducted from the target price to give the target cost. The target cost is compared with the predicted actual cost. If the predicted actual cost is above the target cost intensive efforts are made to close the gap so that the predicted cost equals the target cost.

A major feature of target costing is that a team approach is adopted to achieve the target cost. The team members include designers, engineers, purchasing, manufacturing, marketing and management accounting personnel. Their aim is to achieve the target cost specified for the product at the prescribed level of functionality and quality. The discipline of a team approach ensures that no particular group is able to impose their functional preferences. For example, design engineers pursuing their flair for design may design into products features that increase a product's costs but which customers do not value, or features that require the use of unique parts when alternative designs requiring standardized parts may meet customer requirements. Similarly, without a multi-functional team approach a marketing emphasis might result in the introduction of product features that customers find attractive, but not essential, and so they are not prepared to pay to have them included in the product's design. Therefore, the aim during the product design process is to eliminate product functions that add cost but which do not increase the market price.

In some organizations representatives from the suppliers are included in the design team in order to obtain their expertise. They can often provide suggestions of design changes that will enable standard parts to replace custom-designed parts, thus reducing the product's cost. Alternatively, suppliers have the expertise to suggest alternative parts or components at the lowest cost for a given level of functionality.

The major advantage of adopting target costing is that it is deployed during a product's design and planning stage so that it can have a maximum impact in determining the level of the locked-in costs. It is an iterative process with the design team, which ideally should result in the design team continuing with its product and process design attempts until it finds designs that give an expected cost that is equal or less than the target cost. If the target cost cannot be attained then the product should not be launched. Design teams should not be allowed to achieve target costs by eliminating desirable product functions. Thus, the aim is to design a product with an expected cost that does not exceed target cost and that also meets the target level of functionality. Design teams use reverse engineering, value analysis and process improvements to achieve the target cost.

Reverse engineering

Reverse engineering (also known as tear down analysis) involves examining a competitor's product in order to identify opportunities for product improvement and/or cost reduction. The competitor's product is dismantled to identify its functionality and design and to provide insights about the processes that are used and the cost to make the product. The aim is to benchmark provisional product designs with the designs of competitors and to incorporate any observed relative advantages of the competitor's approach to product design.

Value analysis

Value analysis (also known as value engineering) is a systematic interdisciplinary examination of factors affecting the cost of a product or service in order to devise means of achieving the specified purpose at the required standard of quality and reliability at the target cost. The aim of value analysis is to achieve the assigned target cost by (i) identifying improved product designs that reduce the product's cost without sacrificing functionality and/or (ii) eliminating unnecessary functions that increase the product's costs and for which customers are not prepared to pay extra.

Value analysis requires the use of functional analysis. This process involves decomposing the product into its many elements or attributes. For example, in the case of automobiles, functions might consist of style, comfort, operability, reliability, quality, attractiveness and many others (Kato, 1993). A price, or value, for each element is determined which reflects the amount the customer is prepared to pay. To obtain this information companies normally conduct surveys and interviews with customers. The cost of each function of a product is compared with the benefits perceived by the customers. If the cost of the function exceeds the benefit to the customer, then the function should be either eliminated, modified to reduce its cost, or enhanced in terms of its perceived value so that its value exceeds the cost. Also by focusing on the product's functions, the design team will often consider components that perform the same function in other products, thus increasing the possibility of using standard components and reducing costs.

Process improvements

Both reverse engineering and value analysis focus on product design to achieve cost reductions. The business processes that will be used to produce and market the product are also potential sources of cost reduction. Therefore it is important that processes are intensively studied with a view to increasing their efficiency in order to achieve the needed cost reductions.

The need for accurate cost measurement systems

It is important that target costing is supported by an accurate cost system. In particular, cost drivers should be established that are the significant determinants of the costs of the activities so that cause-and-effect allocations are used. Arbitrary cost allocations should be avoided. If arbitrary cost allocations are used, the allocation base will not be a significant determinant of cost. Let us assume that an arbitrary allocation base, say direct labour hours, is used to allocate support costs to products. To reduce the projected cost towards the target cost the target costing team will be motivated to focus on reducing direct labour hours. Why? Because this will result in a smaller proportion of the support costs being assigned to the product. However, the support costs incurred by the organization will not be reduced because there is no cause-and-effect relationship between direct labour hours and the resulting costs. Therefore, the target costing exercise will merely result in a reduction in the costs that are allocated to the product but organizational costs will not be reduced. In contrast, if cause-and-effect allocation bases (i.e. cost drivers) are established, reductions in cost driver usage should be followed by a reduction in organizational support costs.

Therefore it is very important that cost systems use cost drivers that are the determinants of costs so that they will motivate designers to take actions that will reduce organizational costs. Decisions taken at the design stage lead to the committed usage of cost drivers which can be difficult to change in the future.

An illustration of target costing

Example 21.1 is used to illustrate the target costing process. You will note from reading the information presented in this example that the projected cost of the product is £700 compared with a target cost of £560. To achieve the target cost the company establishes a project team to undertake an intense target costing exercise. Example 21.1 indicates that the end result of the target costing exercise is a projected cost of £555 which is marginally below the target cost of £560. Let us now look at how the company has achieved the target cost and also how the costs shown in Example 21.1 have been derived.

In response to the need to reduce the projected cost the project team starts by purchasing similar types of camcorders from its main competitors and undertaking reverse engineering. This process involves dismantling the camcorders to provide insights into potential design improvements for the new camcorder that will be launched. Reverse engineering is undertaken with the project team working closely with the design engineers. Their objective is to identify new designs that will accomplish the same functions at a lower cost and also to eliminate any functions that are deemed to be unnecessary. This process results in a simplified design, the reduction in the number of parts and the replacement of some customized parts with standard parts. The outcome of the reverse engineering and value analysis activities is a significant reduction in the projected direct materials, labour and rework costs, but the revised cost estimates still indicate that the projected cost exceeds the target cost.

EXAMPLE 21.1

The Digital Electronics Company manufactures cameras and video equipment. It is in the process of introducing the world's smallest and lightest camcorder with 3D HD and SD recording modes. The company has undertaken market research to ascertain the customers' perceived value of the product, based on its special features and a comparison with competitors' products. The results of the survey, and a comparison of the new camcorder with competitors' products and market prices, have been used to establish a target selling price and projected lifetime volume. In addition, cost estimates have been prepared based on the proposed product specification. The company has set a target profit margin of 30 per cent on the proposed selling price and this has been deducted from the target selling price to determine the target cost. The following is a summary of the information that has been presented to management:

Projected lifetime sales volume	300 000 units
Target selling price	£800
Target profit margin (30% of selling price)	£240
Target cost (£800 – £240)	£560
Projected cost	£700

The excess of the projected cost over the target cost results in an intensive target costing exercise. After completing the target costing exercise the projected cost is £555 which is marginally below the target cost of £560. The analysis of the projected cost before and after the target costing exercise is as follows:

	Before (£)	Before (£)	After (£)	After (£)
Manufacturing cost				
Direct material (bought in parts)	390		325	
Direct labour	100		80	
Direct machining costs	20		20	
Ordering and receiving	8		2	
Quality assurance	60		50	
Rework	15		6	
Engineering and design	10	603	8	491
Non-manufacturing costs				
Marketing	40		25	
Distribution	30		20	
After-sales service and warranty costs	27	97	19	64
Total cost		700		555

Next the team engages in functional analysis. They identify the different elements, functions and attributes of the camcorder and potential customers are interviewed to ascertain the values that they place on each of the functions. This process indicates that several functions that have been included in the prototype are not valued by customers. The team therefore decide to eliminate these functions. The functional analysis results in further cost reductions being made, principally in the areas of materials and direct labour assembly costs but the revised cost estimates still indicate that the target cost has not been attained.

The team now turn their attention to redesigning the production and support processes. They decide to redesign the ordering and receiving process by reducing the number of suppliers and working closely with a smaller number of suppliers. The suppliers are prepared to enter into contractual arrangements whereby they are periodically given a pre-determined production schedule and in return they will inspect the shipments and guarantee quality prior to delivery. In addition, the marketing, distribution and customer after-sales services relating to the product are subject to an intensive review, and process improvements are made that result in further reductions in costs that are attributable to the camcorder. The projected cost after undertaking all of the above activities is £555 compared with the target cost of £560 and at this point the target costing exercise is concluded.

Having described the target costing approach that the Digital Electronics Company has used let us now turn our attention to the derivation of the projected costs shown in Example 21.1. The projected cost for direct materials prior to the target costing exercise is £390 but reverse engineering and the functional analysis have resulted in a reduction in the number of parts that are required to manufacture the camcorder. The elimination of most of the unique parts, and the use of standard parts that the company currently purchases in large volumes, also provides scope for further cost savings. The outcome of the redesign process is a direct material cost of £325.

The simplified product design enables the assembly time to be reduced thus resulting in the reduction of direct labour costs from £100 to £80. The direct machine costs relate to machinery that will be used exclusively for the production of the new product. The estimated cost of acquiring, maintaining and operating the machinery throughout the product's life cycle is £6 million. This is divided by the projected lifetime sales volume of the camera (300 000 units) giving a unit cost of £20. However, it has not been possible to reduce the unit cost because the machinery costs are committed, and fixed, and the target costing exercise has not resulted in a change in the predicted lifetime volume.

Prior to the target costing exercise 80 separate parts were included in the product specification. The estimated number of orders placed for each part throughout the product's life cycle is 150 and the predicted cost per order for the order and receiving activity is £200. Therefore the estimated lifetime costs are £2.4 million (80 parts × 150 orders × £200 per order) giving a unit cost of £8 (£2.4 million/300 000 units). The simplified design, and the parts standardization arising from the functional analysis and the value engineering activities, have enabled the number of parts to be reduced to 40. The redesign of the ordering and receiving process has also enabled the number of orders and the ordering cost to be reduced (the former from 150 to 100 and the latter from £200 to £150 per order). Thus the projected lifetime ordering and receiving costs after the target costing exercise are £600 000 (40 parts × 100 orders × £150 per order) giving a revised unit cost of £2 (£600 000/300 000 units).

Quality assurance involves inspecting and testing the camcorders. Prior to the target costing exercise the projected cost was £60 (12 hours at £5 per hour) but the simplified design means that the camcorder will be easier to test resulting in revised cost of £50 (10 hours at £5 per hour). Rework costs of £15 represent the average rework costs per camcorder. Past experience with manufacturing similar products suggests that 10 per cent of the output will require rework. Applying this rate to the estimated total lifetime volume of 300 000 camcorders results in 30 000 camcorders requiring rework at an estimated average cost of £150 per reworked camcorder. The total lifetime rework cost is therefore predicted to be £4.5 million (30 000 × £150) giving an average cost per unit of good output of £15 (£4.5 million/300 000). Because of the simplified product design the rework rate and the average rework cost will be reduced. The predicted rework rate is now 5 per cent and the average rework cost will be reduced from £150 to £120. Thus, the revised estimate of the total lifetime cost is £1.8 million (15 000 reworked units at £120 per unit) and the projected unit cost is £6 (£1.8 million/300 000 units).

The predicted total lifetime engineering and design costs and other product sustaining costs are predicted to be £3 million giving a unit cost of £10. The simplified design and reduced number of parts enables the lifetime cost to be reduced by 20 per cent, to £2.4 million, and the unit cost to £8. The planned process improvements have also enabled the predicted marketing, distribution and after-sales service costs to be reduced. In addition, the simplified product design and the use of fewer parts has contributed to the reduction to the after-sales warranty costs. However, to keep our example brief the derivation of the non-manufacturing costs will not be presented, other than to note that the company uses an activity-based-costing system. All costs are assigned using cost drivers that are based on established cause-and-effect relationships.

KAIZEN COSTING

In addition to target costing kaizen costing is widely used by Japanese organizations as a mechanism for reducing and managing costs. *Kaizen* is the Japanese term for making improvements to a process through small incremental amounts, rather than through large innovations. The major difference between target and *kaizen* costing is that target costing is normally applied during the design stage whereas *kaizen* costing is applied during the manufacturing stage of the product life cycle. With target costing the focus is on the product, and cost reductions are achieved primarily through product design. In contrast, *kaizen* costing focuses on the production processes and cost reductions are derived primarily through the increased efficiency of the production process. Therefore the potential cost reductions are smaller with kaizen costing because the products are already in the manufacturing stage of their life cycles and a significant proportion of the costs will have become locked-in.

The aim of *kaizen* costing is to reduce the cost of components and products by a pre-specified amount. Monden and Hamada (1991) describe the application of *kaizen* costing in a Japanese automobile plant. Each plant is assigned a target cost reduction ratio and this is applied to the previous year's actual costs to determine the target cost reduction. *Kaizen* costing relies heavily on employee empowerment. They are assumed to have superior knowledge about how to improve processes because they are closest to the manufacturing processes and customers and are likely to have greater insights into how costs can be reduced. Thus, a major feature of *kaizen* costing is that workers are given the responsibility to improve processes and reduce costs. Unlike target costing it is not accompanied by a set of techniques or procedures that are automatically applied to achieve the cost reductions.

ACTIVITY-BASED MANAGEMENT

The early adopters of activity-based costing (ABC) used it to produce more accurate product (or service) costs but it soon became apparent to the users that it could be extended beyond purely product costing to a range of budgeting (see activity-based budgeting in Chapter 15) and cost management applications. The terms activity-based management (ABM) or activity-based cost management (ABCM) are used to describe the cost management applications of ABC. To implement an ABM system only the first three of the four stages described in Chapter 11 for designing an activity-based product costing system are required. They are:

1 identifying the major activities that take place in an organization (i.e. activity analysis);
2 assigning costs to cost pools/cost centres for each activity;
3 determining the cost driver for each major activity.

Thus, firms can omit the final stage of assigning activity costs to products and adopt ABC solely for cost management without activity-based product costing. Where a firm does use an activity-based system for both cost management and product costing it may choose to create a large number of activity cost pools to monitor the costs of the many different activities but aggregate the pools so that a smaller number is used for product costing purposes.

ABM views the business as a set of linked activities that ultimately add value to the customer. It focuses on managing the business on the basis of the activities that make up the organization. ABM is based on the premise that activities consume costs. Therefore, by managing activities, costs will be managed in the long term. Managing activities requires an understanding of what factors cause activities to be performed and what causes activity costs to change. The goal of ABM is to enable customer needs to be satisfied while making fewer demands on organizational resources (i.e. cost reduction). Besides providing information on what activities are performed, ABM provides information on the cost of activities, why the activities are undertaken, and how well they are performed.

Traditional budget and control reports analyze costs by types of expense for each responsibility centre. In contrast, ABM analyzes costs by activities and thus provides management with information on why costs are incurred and the output from the activity (in terms of cost drivers). Exhibit 21.1

illustrates the difference between the conventional analysis and the activity-based analysis in respect of customer order processing. The major differences are that the ABM approach reports by *activities* whereas the traditional analysis is by *departments*. Also ABM reporting is by sub-activities but traditional reporting is by expense categories. Another distinguishing feature of ABM reporting is that it often reports information on activities that cross departmental boundaries. For example, different production departments and the distribution department might undertake customer processing activities. They may resolve customer problems by expediting late deliveries. The finance department may assess customer credit worthiness and the remaining customer processing activities might be undertaken by the customer service department. Therefore the total cost of the customer processing activity could be considerably in excess of the costs that are assigned to the customer service department. However, to simplify the presentation it is assumed in Exhibit 21.1 that the departmental and activity costs are identical but if the cost of the customer order processing activity was found to be, say, three times the amount assigned to the customer service department, this would be important information because it may change the way in which the managers view the activity. For example, the managers may give more attention to reducing the costs of the customer processing activity.

It is apparent from an examination of Exhibit 21.1 that the ABM approach provides more meaningful information. It gives more visibility to the cost of undertaking the activities that make up the organization and may raise issues for management action that are not highlighted by the traditional analysis. For example, why is £90 000 spent on resolving customer problems? Attention-directing information such as this is important for managing the cost of the activities.

Knowing costs by activities is a catalyst that eventually triggers the action necessary to become competitive. Consider a situation where salespersons, as a result of costing activities, are informed that it costs £50 to process a customer's order. They therefore become aware that it is questionable to pursue orders with a low sales value. By eliminating many small orders, and concentrating on larger value orders, the demand for customer-processing activities should decrease, and future spending on this activity should be reduced.

Prior to the introduction of ABM most organizations have been unaware of the cost of undertaking the activities that make up the organization. Knowing the cost of activities enables those activities with the highest cost to be highlighted so that they can be prioritized for detailed studies to ascertain whether they can be eliminated or performed more efficiently. In a study of a UK-based multinational bank Soin, Seal and Cullen (2002) reported that ABM was used to establish which activities were expensive and why they were being used, and to ascertain whether increased volumes would or would not increase costs. No attempt was made to link costs to products or customers.

To identify and prioritize the potential for cost reduction many organizations have found it useful to classify activities as either value added or non-value added. Definitions of what constitutes value added and non-value added activities vary. A common definition is that a value added activity is an activity that customers perceive as adding usefulness to the product or service they purchase. For example, painting a car would be a value added activity in an organization that manufactures cars. Other definitions are an activity that is being performed as efficiently as possible or an activity that supports the primary objective of producing outputs.

In contrast, a non-value added activity is an activity where there is an opportunity for cost reduction without reducing the product's service potential to the customer. Examples of non-value added activities include inspecting, storing and moving raw materials and performing set-ups. The cost of these activities can be reduced without reducing the value of the products to the customers. Non-value added activities are essentially those activities that customers should not be expected to pay for. Reporting the cost of non-value added activities draws management's attention to the vast amount of waste that has been tolerated by the organization. This should prioritize those activities with the greatest potential for cost reduction by eliminating or carrying them out more effectively. For example, the activity of inspecting incoming materials is necessary only because of the poor quality of deliveries by suppliers. By establishing strong relationships with nominated suppliers who can guarantee high quality deliveries, incoming inspections can be eventually eliminated. Activities can be undertaken more effectively at a lower cost by finding ways of reducing set-up times, material movements and inventory levels and also improving production flows. Taking action to reduce or eliminate non-value added activities is given top priority

The impact of ABC at Insteel Industries

In 1996 Insteel Industries decided to implement ABC at the Andrews, South Carolina plant. The ABC team analyzed operations and identified 12 business processes involving a total of 146 activities. The ABC study revealed that the 20 most expensive activities accounted for 87 per cent of Andrew's total physical and people resource of $21.4 million. Within the top 20 activities, almost $5 million pertained to quality-related activities such as reactive maintenance, management of by-products and scrap and preventive maintenance. The analysis also revealed that material-handling costs, including freight costs, consumed $4.6 million. Activities were further classified into value-added and non-value added. Nearly $4.9 million was spent on non-value added activities such as reactive maintenance, dealing with scrap, moving materials, reworking products and managing customer complaints. Those activities, within the 20 most expensive, were targeted for cost reduction and process improvement.

The company estimates that within a year of the first ABC study, $1.8 million had been saved in quality costs, mainly through a reduction of scrap and reactive maintenance costs. Freight costs were reduced $555 000 in a year in the Andrews plant alone. Non-value added activities were reduced from 22 per cent of activity costs to 17 per cent.

Insteel focused on freight because delivering products to customers represented 16 per cent of the total people and physical resources cost at the Andrews plant. As a part of the ABC study, Insteel started tracking freight cost per pound shipped. This directed attention to ways in which these costs could be reduced. In 1997, by changing the layout of boxes within each truck, the Andrews plant was able to ship 7400 pounds more per truckload. This represented a 20 per cent reduction in freight expense. When Insteel realized how much they were actually incurring in quality costs, the team probed deeper into understanding better what was causing the quality costs to be incurred and for suggesting steps to reduce them. Insteel realized that certain foreign suppliers of rods were lower in price but supplied poorer-quality rods that caused breakdowns in Insteel's manufacturing process. The lower price of those suppliers did not compensate for the quality costs. Insteel switched to higher-quality rod suppliers. Insteel also realized that smaller diameter wire products were more likely to break and disrupt the manufacturing process. Insteel migrated its product mix to more large diameter wire products. Such initiatives led to reduction in quality costs from $6.7 million in 1996 to $4.9 million in 1997. It is hard to estimate how much of these savings would have been realized had Insteel not conducted an ABC analysis. The activity analysis gave them an appreciation of the scope and quantified the magnitude of the improvement potential, thereby allowing them to prioritize among various process improvement possibilities. Clearly ABC served as a focusing device by providing cost data by activities, directing attention to the top 20 activities, and by labelling some of them as non-value added activities.

Question

1 How might activity costs for Insteel differ from departmental costs?

References

Narayanan, V.G and Sarkar, R.G. (2002), 'The impact of activity-based costing on managerial decisions at Insteel Industries: a field study', *Journal of Economics and Management Strategy*, 11(2), pp.257–288.

because by doing so the organization permanently reduces the cost it incurs without reducing the value of the product to the customer.

Kaplan and Cooper (1998) criticize the classification of activities by simplistic value added and non-value added categories. They point out, that apart from the extreme examples similar to the ones illustrated above, people cannot consistently define what constitutes a value added or non-value added activity. Many items fall within an uncertain area that cannot easily be specified as being value added or non-value added. To reinforce this point they discuss whether the activity of setting up a machine is value added or non-value added. One view is that customers do not perceive performing set-ups as adding usefulness to products and the activity is non-value added. However, without set-ups a plant can only produce single products. If customers value customized or diverse products, changing machine

EXHIBIT 21.1 Customer order processing activity

	(£000s)
Traditional analysis	
Salaries	320
Stationery	40
Travel	140
Telephone	40
Depreciation of equipment	40
	580
ABM analysis	
Preparing quotations	120
Receiving customer orders	190
Assessing the creditworthiness of customers	100
Expediting	80
Resolving customer problems	90
	580

settings to produce different product varieties creates value for customers. Kaplan and Cooper also point out the demotivating impact when employees are informed that they are performing non-value added activities.

To overcome the above problems Kaplan and Cooper advocate that instead of using a value added/ non-value added classification the following simple five point scale should be used to summarize an ABC project team's initial judgement about the current efficiency of an activity:

1 highly efficient, with little (less than 5 per cent) apparent opportunity for improvement;

2 modestly efficient, some (5–15 per cent) opportunity for improvement;

3 average efficiency, good opportunities (15–25 per cent) for improvement;

4 inefficient, major opportunities (25–50 per cent) for improvement;

5 highly inefficient, perhaps should not be done at all; 50–100 per cent opportunity for improvement.

By identifying the cost of activities that make up their organization and classifying them into the above five categories, opportunities for cost reduction can be prioritized. Cost reduction can be achieved by either eliminating the activities, performing them more efficiently with fewer organizational resources or redesigning them so that they are performed in an entirely different and more cost efficient way. We shall consider how activities can be redesigned later in the chapter.

Our discussion so far has related to the application of ABM during the manufacturing or service phase of a product's life cycle. However, some organizations have used their activity-based costing systems to influence future costs at the design stage within the target costing process. In particular, they have opted for behaviourally orientated cost systems that are less accurate than costing technology allows in order to induce desired behavioural responses (Merchant and Shields, 1993). For example, the Portable Instruments Division of Tektronix, Inc. in the USA, assigned material support expenses using a single cost driver – number of part numbers. The company wanted to encourage design engineers to focus their attention on reducing the number of part numbers, parts and suppliers in future generations of products. Product timeliness was seen as a critical success factor and this was facilitated by designs that simplified parts procurement and production processes. The cost system motivated engineers to design simpler products requiring less development time because they had fewer parts and part numbers. The cost system designers knew that most of the material support expenses were not incurred in direct proportion to the single cost driver chosen, but the simplified and imprecise cost system focused attention on factors deemed to be most critical to the division's future success.

BENCHMARKING

In order to identify the best way of performing activities and business processes, organizations are turning their attention to benchmarking, which involves comparing key activities with best practices found within and outside the organization. External benchmarking attempts to identify an activity, such as customer order processing, that needs to be improved and finding a non-rival organization that is considered to represent world-class best practice for the activity and studying how it performs the activity. The objective is to find out how the activity can be improved and ensure that the improvements are implemented. In contrast, with internal benchmarking different business units within an organization that perform the same activities are compared. The unit that is considered to represent best practice becomes the target to achieve.

Benchmarking is cost beneficial since an organization can save time and money avoiding mistakes that other companies have made and/or the organization can avoid duplicating the efforts of other companies. The overall aim should be to find and implement best practice.

BUSINESS PROCESS RE-ENGINEERING

Business process re-engineering involves examining business processes and making substantial changes to how the organization currently operates. It involves the redesign of how work is done through activities. A business process consists of a collection of activities that are linked together in a co-ordinated manner to achieve a specific objective. For example, material handling might be classed as a business process consisting of separate activities relating to scheduling production, storing materials, processing purchase orders, inspecting materials and paying suppliers.

The aim of business process re-engineering is to improve the key business processes in an organization by focusing on simplification, cost reduction, improved quality and enhanced customer satisfaction. Consider the materials handling process outlined in the above paragraph. The process might be re-engineered by sending the production schedule direct to nominated suppliers and entering into contractual agreements to deliver the materials in accordance with the production schedule and also guaranteeing their quality by inspecting them prior to delivery. The end result might be the elimination, or a permanent reduction, of the storing, purchasing and inspection activities. These activities are non-value added activities since they represent an opportunity for cost reduction without reducing the products' service potentials to customers.

A distinguishing feature of business process re-engineering is that it involves radical and dramatic changes in processes by abandoning current practices and reinventing completely new methods of performing business processes. The focus is on major changes rather than marginal improvements. A further example of business process re-engineering is moving from a traditional functional plant layout to a just-in-time cellular product layout and adopting a just-in-time philosophy. Adopting a just-in-time (JIT) system and philosophy has important implications for cost management and performance reporting. It is therefore important that you understand the nature of such systems and how they differ from traditional systems. This topic is discussed in the next section.

JUST-IN-TIME SYSTEMS

In the previous section it was pointed out that re-organizing business processes and adopting a just-in-time (JIT) system was an illustration of business process engineering. Given that implementing a JIT system is a mechanism for reducing non-value added costs and long-run costs it is important that you understand the nature of such a system and its cost management implications.

The success of Japanese firms in international markets in the 1980s and 1990s generated interest among many Western companies as to how this success was achieved. The implementation of just-in-time (JIT) production methods was considered to be one of the major factors contributing to this success. The aims of JIT are to reduce waste by producing the required items, at the required quality and in the required quantities, at the precise time they are required. JIT manufacturing is a demand pull manufacturing system that pulls products through the manufacturing process. Each operation produces only what is necessary to meet the demand of the following operation. Production is not undertaken until there is a signal from the following process indicating a need to produce. The demand pull process starts with customer demand for a finished product and works all the way back to the demand for direct materials that arrive just in time to be used in the production process. JIT production aims to keep the materials moving in a continuous flow with no stoppages and no storage.

The major features of a JIT production system are:

1 The rearrangement of the production process into production cells consisting of different types of equipment that are used to manufacture a given product.

2 Reducing set-up times (i.e. the amount of time required to adjust equipment settings and to retool for the production of a different product).

3 Increased emphasis on total quality management that seeks to eliminate defective production.

4 Production cell workers are trained to multi-task so that they can perform a variety of operations and tasks.

5 The adoption of JIT purchasing techniques, whereby the delivery of materials immediately precedes demand or use.

6 The modification of management accounting performance measures and product costing systems so that they support the JIT production systems.

Rearrangement of the production process

The first stage in implementing JIT manufacturing techniques is to rearrange the production process away from a batch production functional layout towards a product layout using flow lines. With a batch production functional plant layout, products pass through a number of specialist departments that normally contain a group of similar machines. Products are processed in large batches so as to minimize the set-up times when machine settings are changed between processing batches of different products. Batches move via different and complex routes through the various departments, travelling over much of the plant before they are completed. Each process normally involves a considerable amount of waiting time. In addition, much time is taken transporting items from one process to another. A further problem is that it is not easy at any point in time to determine what progress has been made on individual batches. Therefore detailed cost accumulation records are necessary to track work in progress. The consequences of this complex routing process are high work in progress inventory levels, long manufacturing cycle times and high material handling costs.

The JIT solution is to reorganize the production process by dividing the many different products that an organization makes into families of similar products or components. All of the products in a particular group will have similar production requirements and routings. Production is rearranged so that each product family is manufactured in a well-defined production cell based on flow line principles. In a product flow line, specialist departments containing *similar* machines no longer exist. Instead groups of *dissimilar* machines are organized into product or component family flow lines that function like an assembly line. For each product line the machines are placed close together in the order in which they are required by the group of products to be processed. Items in each product family can now move, one at a time, from process to process more easily, thereby reducing work in progress inventories and lead times. The ideal layout of each flow line is normally U-shaped. This layout is called cellular manufacturing.

JIT manufacturing aims to produce the right parts at the right time, only when they are needed, and only in the quantity needed, using a pull manufacturing system. The pull system is implemented by monitoring the consumption of parts at each operation stage and using various types of visible signalling systems (known as Kanbans) to authorize production and movement of the part to the using location. The producing cell cannot run the parts until authorized to do so. The signalling mechanism usually involves the use of *Kanban* containers. These containers hold materials or parts for movement from one work centre to another. The capacity of *Kanban* containers tends to vary from two to five units. They are just big enough to permit the production line to operate smoothly despite minor interruptions to individual work centres within the cell. To illustrate how the system works consider three machines forming part of a cell where the parts are first processed by machine A before being further processed on machine B and then machine C. The *Kanbans* are located between the machines. As long as the *Kanban* container is not full, the worker at machine A continues to produce parts, placing them in the *Kanban* container. When the container is full the worker stops producing and recommences when a part has been removed from the container by the worker operating machine B. A similar process applies between the operations of machines B and C. This process can result in idle time within certain locations within the cell, but the JIT philosophy considers that it is more beneficial to absorb short-run idle time rather than add to inventory during these periods. During idle time the workers perform preventive maintenance on the machines.

With a pull system problems arising in any part of the system will immediately halt the production line because work centres at the earlier stages will not receive the pull signal (because the *Kanban* container is full) if a problem arises at a later stage. Alternatively, work centres at a later stage will not have their pull signal answered (because of empty *Kanban* containers) when problems arise with work centres at the earlier stages of the production cycle. Thus attention is drawn immediately to production problems so that appropriate remedial action can be taken. This is deemed to be preferable to the approach adopted in a traditional manufacturing system where large inventory levels provide a cushion for production to continue.

In contrast, the traditional manufacturing environment is based on a push manufacturing system. With this system, machines are grouped into work centres based on the similarity of their functional capabilities. Each manufactured part has a designated routing, and the preceding process supplies parts to the subsequent process without any consideration being given to whether the next process is ready to work on the parts or not. Hence the use of the term 'push-through system'.

Demand-pull JIT systems are also applied in non-manufacturing organizations. For example, fast food restaurants such as McDonald's and Burger King use a demand-pull system to control their finished inventories. When a customer orders a burger, it is taken from the shelf of completed burgers and the chef does not cook any new burgers until the inventories begin to run out. Customer demand thus pulls the burgers through the system.

Reduced set-up times

Set-up time is the amount of time required to adjust equipment settings and to retool for the production of a different product. Long set-up and changeover times make the production of batches with a small number of units uneconomic. Why? Because larger batches enable the costs of a set-up to be spread over a larger number of units thus reducing the set-up cost per unit. However, the production of large batches leads to substantial throughput delays and the creation of high inventory levels. Throughput delays arise because several lengthy production runs are required to process larger batches through the factory. A further problem with large batches is that they often have to wait for lengthy periods before they are processed by the next process or before they are sold.

The JIT philosophy is to substantially reduce or eliminate the need for set-ups. Set-up times can be reduced by training workers to perform set-ups more quickly. Alternatively, set-ups can be minimized or eliminated entirely by establishing manufacturing cells that are dedicated to the manufacture of a single product or a family of single products rather than multiple dissimilar products. Many firms have also reduced set-up times by investing in advanced manufacturing technologies that enable machine settings to be adjusted automatically instead of manually. By significantly reducing set-up times, small batch sizes become economical. Small batch sizes, combined with short throughput times, also enable a firm to adapt more readily to short-term fluctuations in market demand and respond faster to customer requests, since production is not dependent on long planning lead times.

Total quality management

With a JIT system a defective part can stop the entire demand pull production flow line. Defective parts cannot be tolerated in a production environment that operates without inventories. Therefore total quality management with a never-ending quest of zero-defects is an essential part of a JIT production system. In contrast, with a traditional batch production system WIP inventories are available at each production stage to meet the demands of succeeding operations so defective units are unlikely to halt the production process. Compared with a JIT system there is less need to eliminate defective output and therefore the same emphasis may not be placed on total quality management.

Multiple-task workforce

Producing on demand can result in workers having free time when there is no demand pull signal from the following operation. There is also a need to respond quickly to any production problems in the flow line. Therefore workers are trained to perform multiple tasks by undertaking support activities such as duties relating to set-ups, minor repairs, preventive maintenance, quality testing and inspection. Workers are also trained to operate different machines within the cell. The ability of workers to multi-task enables a smooth production flow within the cell to be achieved.

JIT purchasing arrangements

The JIT philosophy also extends to adopting JIT purchasing techniques, whereby the delivery of materials immediately precedes demand or use. By arranging with suppliers for more frequent deliveries, inventories can be cut to a minimum. Considerable savings in material handling expenses can be obtained by requiring suppliers to inspect materials before their delivery and guaranteeing their quality. This improved service is obtained by giving more business to fewer suppliers and placing longer-term purchasing orders. Therefore the supplier has an assurance of long-term sales, and can plan to meet this demand. Thus, a critical component of JIT purchasing is that strong relationships are established with suppliers.

Companies that have implemented JIT purchasing techniques claim to have substantially reduced their investment in raw materials and work in progress inventories. Other advantages include a substantial saving in factory space, large quantity discounts, savings in time from negotiating with fewer suppliers and a reduction in paperwork arising from issuing blanket long-term orders to a few suppliers rather than individual purchase orders to many suppliers.

JIT and management accounting

Management accountants in many organizations have been strongly criticized because of their failure to alter the management accounting system to reflect the move from a traditional manufacturing to a just-in-time manufacturing system. Conventional management accounting systems can encourage behaviour that is inconsistent with a just-in-time manufacturing philosophy. Management accounting must support just-in-time manufacturing by monitoring, identifying and communicating to decision-makers any delay, error and waste in the system. Modern management accounting systems are now placing greater emphasis on providing information on supplier reliability, set-up times, throughput cycle times, percentage of deliveries that are on time and defect rates. All of these measures are critical to supporting a just-in-time manufacturing philosophy and are discussed in more detail in the next chapter.

In a traditional manufacturing environment many different unrelated products may be subject to processing in a single department. After the products have been processed they are transferred to other processes located in different departments. Because many products are processed in each department the costs of each department are common to all products passing through each department. These departmental costs are mostly indirect product costs that are allocated to products using the approaches described in Chapter 3. In a JIT manufacturing system all of the processes necessary for the manufacture of a single product (or family of similar products) are undertaken in a single cell. Therefore the costs of operating the cell can be directly assigned to the cell's product or family of similar products.

Also with traditional manufacturing systems support departments provide services for all products manufactured by an organization and support costs represent indirect product costs which are allocated to products using the approaches described in Chapter 3. In contrast, we have noted that workers within production cells multi-task by performing multiple support activities that are performed by support departments in traditional manufacturing systems. Because production cells are dedicated to the manufacturing of a single product or a family of similar products, many of the support activities can now be directly traced to the product dedicated cells. Thus, with a JIT system a higher proportion of costs can be directly assigned to products compared with a traditional batch production systems. Therefore the benefits from implementing ABC product costing may be lower in JIT organizations.

QUALITY COST MANAGEMENT

To compete successfully in today's global competitive environment companies have become 'customer-driven' and have made customer satisfaction an overriding priority. Customers now demand ever-improving levels of service regarding cost, quality, reliability, delivery and the choice of innovative new products. Quality has become a key competitive variable in both service and manufacturing organizations and this has created the need for management accountants to become more involved in the provision of information relating to the quality of products and services and activities that produce them. Various studies suggest that costs of quality can be substantial. In the UK quality related costs have been reported to range from 5 per cent to 15 per cent of total company sales revenue (Plunkett, Dale and Tyrrell, 1985) and in the USA Ostrenga (1991) reported that in American companies costs of quality are typically 20 to 30 per cent of total sales. Eliminating inferior quality by implementing quality improvement initiatives can therefore result in substantial cost savings and higher revenues. Companies that do not focus on continuous quality improvement programmes are likely to suffer a decline in market shares and revenues. Some writers now argue that the emphasis on quality has been a key competitive weapon for many years, resulting quality having now shifted from a source of strategic advantage to a competitive necessity (Kaplan and Norton, 1996b).

Total quality management (TQM), a term used to describe a situation where all business functions are involved in a process of continuous quality improvement, has been adopted by many companies. TQM is a customer-oriented process of continuous improvement that focuses on delivering products or services of consistent high quality in a timely fashion. In the past most European and American companies considered quality to be an additional cost of manufacturing, but in the 1990s they realized that focusing on TQM saves money. Prior to the 1990s companies focused on emphasizing production volume over quality resulting in high levels of inventories at each production stage in order to protect against shortages caused by inferior quality at previous stages. This approach results in excessive expenditure on inspection,

Cost of quality: bad quality and high costs – BP and Toyota

In recent years, two global companies have had to deal with some quite large costs as a result of quality control failures. First, take the example of Toyota cars in the US. In late 2009 and early 2010, Toyota recalled several of its US models, the Camry in particular, after several accidents occurred due to a faulty accelerator pedal. The recall involved over 5 million vehicles and sales and production were suspended for a time in the US. According to author Paul Ingrassia, the problem occurred because Toyota broke one of their key principles called the 'three nevers' at its US manufacturing plants: never build a new product, in a new facility, with a new workforce. In the case of the Camry in the US, all three were broken. A report by the Forbes.com put the estimated cost of the problem at $2 billion as of February 2010.

In April 2010, the *Deepwater Horizon* drilling rig, which was ultimately under the control of British Petroleum (BP), exploded in the Gulf of Mexico. An oil slick resulted, which lasted for approximately three months and caused extensive damage to the environment and coastlines around the Gulf of Mexico. By June 2010, the costs to BP had racked up to $1.25 billion. By September 2010, the total costs had risen to almost $10 billion, with BP setting aside a provision

of $20 billion. In January 2011, a US presidential commission squarely laid the blame for the disaster at the door of BP and its contractors. The report cited several systemic failures, short-cuts and sub-standard materials and workmanship as the cause, all of which it attributed to management failures.

Questions

1 Can management accountants do anything to help engineers and designers focus more on considering the cost of failures in quality and quality control?

2 Can you list some of the internal and external failure costs for the two issues described above?

© Donald Johansson, iStock

References

http://www.forbes.com/2010/02/04/toyota-earnings-recall-markets-equities-prius.html
http://www.guardian.co.uk/business/2010/jun/07/bp-deepwater-horizon-costs-soar
http://www.guardian.co.uk/environment/2010/sep/20/bp-oil-spill-deepwater-horizon-costs-10bn
http://www.telegraph.co.uk/earth/energy/oil/8242717/Systemic-failures-to-blame-for-BP-Deepwater-Horizon-spill-US-commission-finds.html
Ingrassia, P. (2010), *Crash Course: The American Automobile Industry's Road from Glory to Disaster*, Random House, New York.

rework, scrap and warranty repairs. In the 1990s many companies discovered that it was cheaper to produce the items correctly the first time rather than wasting resources by making substandard items that have to be detected, reworked, scrapped or returned by customers.

In recent years international quality standards have been introduced. The International Organization for Standardization has introduced five standards known as the ISO 9000 family of standards that provide a certification that a company's quality systems meets certain quality standards. The process of obtaining certification is subject to a detailed audit of quality systems and is lengthy and expensive. Many companies now require their suppliers to hold ISO certification and certification has become necessary to compete in the global market. The ISO quality standards have been adopted worldwide by over one million companies. The top ten countries for ISO 9001 certifications were China, Italy, Japan, Spain, Russia, Germany, UK, India, USA and Korea [ISO survey (2009)]. China now accounts for approximately one quarter of global certifications.

Cost of quality reports

Management accounting systems can help organizations achieve their quality goals by providing a variety of reports and measures that motivate and evaluate managerial efforts to improve quality. These include financial and non-financial measures. Many companies are currently not aware of how much they are spending on quality because it is incurred across many different departments and not accumulated as a separate cost object within the costing system. Managers need to know the costs of quality and how they are changing over time. A cost of quality report should be prepared to indicate the total cost to the organization of producing products or services that do not conform with quality requirements. Four categories of costs should be reported:

1 Prevention costs are the costs incurred in preventing the production of products or services that do not conform to specification. They include the costs of preventive maintenance, quality planning and training, quality reporting and supplier evaluation and selection.

2 Appraisal costs are the costs incurred to ensure that materials, products and services meet quality conformance standards. They include the costs of inspecting purchased parts, work in process and finished goods, quality audits and field tests.

3 Internal failure costs are the costs incurred when products and services fail to meet quality standards or customer needs. They include costs incurred before the product is despatched to the customer, such as the costs of scrap, repair, downtime and work stoppages caused by defects.

4 External failure costs are the costs incurred when products or services fail to conform to requirements or satisfy customer needs after they have been delivered. They include the costs of handling customer complaints, warranty replacement, repairs of returned products, lost market share and the costs arising from a damaged company reputation. Costs within this category can have a dramatic impact on future sales.

Exhibit 21.2 presents a typical cost of quality report. Note that some of the items in the report will have to be estimated. For example, included in the external failure costs category is the forgone contribution from lost sales arising from poor quality. This cost is extremely difficult to estimate. Nevertheless, the lost contribution can be substantial and it is preferable to include an estimate rather than omit it from the report. Because of the difficulty in estimating the opportunity cost of lost sales arising from poor quality, many companies omit this cost from their cost of quality reports. The total costs of quality in these firms will be significantly higher than the costs that are reported in the cost of quality reports. By expressing each category of costs as a percentage of sales revenues comparisons can be made with previous periods, other organizations and divisions within the same group. Such comparisons can highlight problem areas. For example, comparisons of external failure costs with other companies can provide an indication of the current level of customer satisfaction.

The cost of quality report can be used as an attention-directing device to make the top management of a company aware of how much is being spent on quality-related costs and the areas where they should focus their attention. Exhibit 21.2 shows that significant savings can be made by reducing the costs of scrap and rework. The report can also draw management's attention to the possibility of reducing total quality costs by a wiser allocation of costs among the four quality categories. For example, by spending more on the prevention costs, the amount of spending in the internal and external failure categories can be substantially reduced, and therefore total spending can be lowered. Also, by designing quality into the products and processes, appraisal costs can be reduced, since far less inspection is required.

Prevention and appraisal costs are sometimes referred to as the costs of quality conformance or compliance and internal and external failure costs are also known as the costs of non-conformance or non-compliance. Costs of compliance are incurred with the intention of eliminating the costs of failure. They are discretionary in the sense that they do not have to be incurred, whereas costs of non-compliance are the result of production imperfections and can only be reduced by increasing compliance expenditure. The optimal investment in compliance costs is when total costs of quality reach a minimum. This can occur when 100 per cent quality compliance has not been achieved. It is virtually impossible to measure accurately all quality costs (particularly the lost contribution from forgone sales) and determine the optimal investment in conformance costs. However, some people argue that a failure to achieve 100 per cent quality compliance is non-optimal and that a zero-defects policy is optimal. With a zero-defects policy the focus is on continuous improvement with the ultimate aim of achieving zero-defects and eliminating all internal and external failure costs.

EXHIBIT 21.2 Cost of quality report

	(£000s)		% of sales (£100 million)
Prevention costs			
Quality training	1 000		
Supplier reviews	300		
Quality engineering	400		
Preventive maintenance	500		
		2 200	2.2
Appraisal costs			
Inspection of materials received	500		
Inspection of WIP and completed units	1 000		
Testing equipment	300		
Quality audits	800		
		2 600	2.6
Internal failure costs			
Scrap	800		
Rework	1 000		
Downtime due to quality problems	600		
Retesting	400	2 800	2.8
External failure costs			
Returns	2 000		
Recalls	1 000		
Warranty repairs	800		
Handling customer complaints	500		
Foregone contribution from lost sales	3 000		
		7 300	7.3
		14 900	14.9

A zero-defects policy does not use percentages as the unit of measurement because a small percentage defect rate can result in a large number of defects. For example, a 1 per cent defect rate from an output of 1 million units results in 10 000 defective units. To overcome this problem the attainment of a zero-defects goal is measured in parts per million (PPM) so that seemingly small numbers can be transferred into large numbers. Thus, instead of reporting a 1 per cent defect rate, a measure of 10 000 PPM is more likely to create pressure for action and highlight the trend in defect rates. Cost of quality reports provide a useful summary of quality efforts and progress to top management, but at lower management levels non-financial quality measures provide more timely and appropriate target measures for quality improvement.

Non-financial measures of quality and customer satisfaction

In addition to financial measures organizations need non-financial measures relating to the quality of the products and services and the activities that produce them. Typical measures provided by the management accounting information system relating to internal processes include:

- process parts per million (PPM) defect rates for each product line;
- the number and percentage of defects for each product line;
- process yields (ratio of good items produced to good items entering the process);
- supplier performance measures such as percentage of defects of incoming materials and the number of late deliveries.

Non-financial measures relating to customer satisfaction include:

- number and percentage of defective goods delivered to customers;
- number and percentage of customer complaints;
- percentage of products that do not meet the warranty requirements;
- percentage of deliveries that are not on time.

In addition, many companies conduct surveys to measure customer satisfaction in relation to product or service quality. In general, cost of quality reports are produced annually but non-financial measures should be reported at more frequent intervals. Managers should examine trends over time and use the measures to highlight areas that require action to improve quality performance.

Control charts

Cost of quality reports and the above non-financial measures provide top management with an overview of the cost of quality and quality performance but they must be supplemented by techniques for the detailed daily control of the quality of operations and processes. Statistical quality control charts are used as a mechanism for distinguishing between random and non-random variations in operating processes. A control chart is a graph of a series of successive observations of operations taken at regular intervals of time to test whether a batch of produced items is within pre-set tolerance limits. Usually, samples from a particular production process are taken at hourly or daily intervals. The mean, and sometimes the range, of the sampled items are calculated and plotted on a quality control chart (see Figure 21.2). Each observation is plotted relative to pre-set points on the expected distribution. Only observations beyond specified pre-set control limits are regarded as worthy of investigation.

The control limits are based on a series of past observations of a process when it is under control, and thus working efficiently. It is assumed that the past observations can be represented by a normal distribution. The past observations are used to estimate the population mean and the population standard deviation. Assuming that the distribution of possible outcomes is normal, then, when the process is under control, we should expect:

68.27 per cent of the observation to fall within the range $+1\sigma$ from the mean;

95.45 per cent of the observation to fall within the range $+2\sigma$ from the mean.

Control limits are now set. For example, if control limits are set based on two standard deviations from the mean then this would indicate 4.55 per cent (100 per cent – 95.45 per cent) of future observations would result from pure chance when the process is under control. Therefore there is a high probability that an observation outside the 2σ control limits is out of control.

Figure 21.2 shows three control charts, with the outer horizontal lines representing a possible control limit of 2σ so that all observations outside this range are investigated. You will see that for operation A the

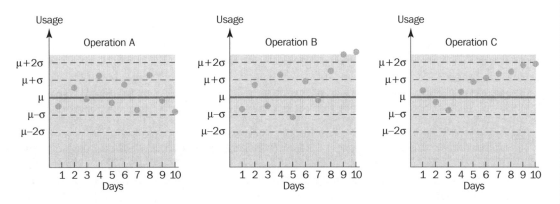

FIGURE 21.2

Statistical quality control charts

process is deemed to be in control because all observations fall within the control limits. For operation B the last two observations suggest that the operation is out of control. Therefore both observations should be investigated. With operation C the observations would not prompt an investigation because all the observations are within the control limits. However, the last six observations show a steadily increasing usage in excess of the mean, and the process may be out of control. Statistical procedures (called casum procedures) that consider the trend in recent usage as well as daily usage can also be used.

ENVIRONMENTAL COST MANAGEMENT

Environmental cost management is becoming increasingly important in many organizations. There are several reasons for this. First, environmental costs can be large for some industrial sectors. For example, Ranganathan and Ditz (1996) reported that Amoco's environmental costs at its Yorktown refinery were at least 22 per cent of operating costs. Second, regulatory requirements involving huge fines for non-compliance have increased significantly over the past decade. Therefore, selecting the least costly method of compliance has become a major objective. Third, society is demanding that companies focus on becoming more environmentally friendly. Companies are finding that becoming a good social citizen and being environmentally responsible improves their image and enhances their ability to sell their products and services. These developments have created the need for companies to develop a system of measuring, reporting and monitoring environmental costs. In 2005 the International Federation of Accountants (IFAC) issued a guidance document that provides a general framework and set of definitions for environmental management accounting (see **http://www.ifac.org**).

According to Epstein and Roy (1997) many companies cannot identify their total environmental costs and do not recognize that they can be controlled and reduced. Environmental costs can be a significant percentage of total operating costs but the reporting of these costs and their causes provides the potential for them to be reduced by redesigning processes in order to reduce hazardous materials used or pollutants emitted to the environment. In most cost accounting systems, environmental costs are hidden within general overheads and are either not allocated to cost objects, or they are allocated on an arbitrary basis within the allocation of general overheads. Thus, crucial relationships are not identified between environmental costs and the responsible products, processes and underlying activities. For example, Ranganathan and Ditz point out that the principal environmental issue facing Spectrum Glass, a major manufacturer of speciality sheet glass, is the use and release of cadmium. It discovered that only one product (Ruby red glass) was responsible for all of its cadmium emissions but the cost accounting system allocated a portion of this cost to all products. This process resulted in ruby red glass being undercosted and other products being overcosted.

Environmental costs should be accumulated by separate cost pools, analyzed by appropriate categories and traced to the products or processes that caused the costs using ABC concepts. Knowledge of the amount and categories of environmental costs, and their causes, provides the information that managers need to not only manage environmental costs more effectively by process redesign but to also reduce the pollutants emitted to the environment.

Hansen and Mendoza (1999) point out that environmental costs are incurred because poor environmental quality exists and thus are similar in nature to quality costs discussed earlier in this chapter. They advocate that an environmental cost report should be periodically produced, based on the principles of a cost of quality report (see Exhibit 21.2) to indicate the total environmental costs to the organization associated with the creation, detection, remedy and prevention of environmental degradation. Adopting a similar classification as that used for quality costs, the following four categories of environmental costs can be reported:

1. **Environmental prevention costs** are the costs of activities undertaken to prevent the production of waste that could cause damage to the environment. Examples include the costs associated with the design and operation of processes to reduce contaminants, training employees, recycling products and obtaining certification relating to meeting the requirements of international and national standards.

2. **Environmental detection costs** are the costs incurred to ensure that a firm's activities, products and processes conform to regulatory laws and voluntary standards. Examples include inspection

REAL WORLD VIEWS 21.5

Environmental accounting

Most businesses are concerned with their effect on the environment. Many businesses portray themselves as being friendly to the environment or carbon neutral. Lever Brothers, for example, developed a 'Small & Mighty' detergent range that has half the packaging, uses half the water and needs half the lorries to deliver it. BSkyB claimed to be a carbon neutral company in 2006. Reporting on environmental performance is even recognized in the UK Companies Act 2006, which increased the narrative reporting requirements of UK companies. Thus, with legal and practical recognition it would seem environmental issues are integral to business strategy.

Management accounting plays an important role in ensuring companies take environmental factors into account when making decisions. According to Gray and Bebbington (2001, p. 9), a management accountant's job changes somewhat:

1 planning will include new costs and capital expenditures – for example clean-up or recycling costs;

2 investment appraisal will incorporate environmental costs and benefits;

3 decisions on costs and benefits of environmental improvements will be undertaken;

4 environmental performance reporting will be required;

5 five cost analysis and efficiency improvement programmes will consider environmental issues.

At an operational level, management are ideally placed to play a role in a number of areas, including: accounting for and controlling energy costs; reducing packaging and waste material and product life-cycle analysis. Additionally, many governments now issue carbon credits to companies based on national carbon emission targets. Such credits are not free and companies are under pressure to reduce carbon emissions to reduce costs. Here again, management accountants can help analyze business processes to determine operational and cost efficient methods of operating.

Questions

1 Do you think environmental costs and benefits can be accurately determined?

2 Do issues such as the environment help management accountants to become more strategically important members of an organization?

References

http://www.persil.com/formatsmallandmighty.aspx

http://media.corporate-ir.net/media_files/irol/10/104016/SkyCNPressRelease_18052006.pdf

Gray, R. and Bebbington, J. (2001) *Accounting for the Environment*, Sage Publications.

of products and processes to ensure regulatory compliance, auditing environmental activities and performing contamination tests.

3 *Environmental internal failure costs* are the costs incurred from performing activities that have produced contaminants and waste that have not been discharged into the environment. Such costs are incurred to eliminate or reduce waste to levels that comply with regulatory requirements. Examples include the costs of disposing of toxic materials and recycling scrap.

4 *Environmental external failure costs* are the costs incurred on activities performed after discharging waste into the environment. Examples include the costs of cleaning up contaminated soil, restoring land to its natural state and cleaning up oil spills and waste discharges. Clearly this category of costs has the greatest impact on a company in terms of adverse publicity. For example, in late 2010 it was reported that BP expects the cost of the oil leak arising from the Deepwater Horizon oil disaster to be nearly $40bn. The disaster has had a dramatic negative impact on BP's image.

The environmental cost report should be similar in format to the cost of quality report (see Exhibit 21.2) with each category of costs expressed as a percentage of sales revenues (or operating costs) so that comparisons can be made with previous periods, other organizations and divisions within the same group. The environmental cost report should be used as an attention-directing device to make top management aware of how much is being spent on environmental costs and the relative amount in each category. The report also draws management's attention to those areas that have the greatest potential for cost reduction. The same principles as those described for quality cost reporting also apply. That is, investing more in prevention and detection activities has the potential to significantly reduce environmental failure costs. A major limitation of environmental cost reports is that they only report those environmental costs for which the company is responsible. The report does not include costs that are caused by a firm but borne by society. Examples include losing land for recreational use and damaging ecosystems from solid waste disposal. Attempts should be made to develop non-financial and/or qualitative measures that draw attention to how an organization is contributing to becoming environmentally responsible and a good social citizen.

In addition to the approaches described above, the environmental consequences of products should be evaluated using the life-cycle costing approach described at the beginning of this chapter. In other words, the environmental consequences should be managed at the planning and design stage and not at the manufacturing stage when a substantial proportion of the environmental costs and outcomes will already have been determined. Finally, you should note at this point that incorporating an environmental perspective within a balanced scorecard framework has been adopted by some companies to link their environmental strategy to concrete performance measures. The balanced scorecard framework requires that within the scorecard the environmental objectives are clearly specified. Typical objectives include minimizing the use of hazardous materials, minimizing energy requirements and minimizing the release of pollutants. These objectives should be translated into specific performance measures. In addition, within the scorecard, firms should describe the major initiatives for achieving each objective and also establish targets for each performance measure. For feedback reporting, actual performance measures should also be added. The balanced scorecard framework is described in the next chapter.

COST MANAGEMENT AND THE VALUE CHAIN

Increasing attention is now being given to value-chain analysis as a means of increasing customer satisfaction and managing costs more effectively. The value chain is illustrated in Figure 21.3. It is the linked set of value-creating activities all the way from basic raw material sources for component suppliers through to the ultimate end-use product or service delivered to the customer. A value-chain analysis is used to analyze, coordinate and optimize linkages in the value chain. Coordinating the individual parts of the value chain together creates the conditions to improve customer satisfaction, particularly in terms of cost efficiency, quality and delivery. A firm which performs the value chain activities more efficiently, and at a lower cost than its competitors, will gain a competitive advantage. Therefore it is necessary to understand how value chain activities are performed and how they interact with each other. The activities are not just a collection of independent activities but a system of inter-dependent activities in which the performance of one activity affects the performance and cost of other activities.

FIGURE 21.3
The value chain

REAL WORLD VIEWS 21.6

Value chain analysis in interfirm relationships

The following presents extracts from a case study on the use of an ABC cost model by a large UK retail firm (Sainsbury's) and a group of suppliers for supporting their supply chain management practices. This cost model was based on the principles of value chain analysis and integrated cost information across the supply chain. It was used to improve supply chain operations by performing benchmark analyses, strategic what-if analyses and cost monitoring. The model was used to identify opportunities to reduce supply chain costs.

To be able to analyze the supply chain costs, cost and cost driver data were required from both Sainsbury and suppliers. Suppliers who chose to participate in the initiative were required to deliver cost data and cost driver quantities to Sainsbury for feeding the supplier section of the model. Benchmarking was used to compare suppliers' activity costs with the average of their network. In addition, cost comparisons were made between networks, regions and store types. By clustering suppliers into different networks the most important differences between their operations were eliminated, as suppliers within a network performed fairly comparable activities. The most important measure for the benchmark analysis was the cost per cost driver (i.e. the cost driver rate), as this measure could be compared directly with other

suppliers. The benchmark analysis revealed the suppliers' relative performance against the network average. When a supplier deviated significantly from the average, the logistics operations department would initiate a discussion with the supplier to find out the cause(s) of the difference, by analyzing the underlying activities, and to assess whether and how performance could be improved. In addition, comparing the costs of their activities and analyzing the differences in their operations could be used to transfer efficient supply chain practices across networks.

Strategic what-if analyses were performed to analyze the effects of changes in the supply chain on supply chain costs. When, for example, as a result of a benchmark analysis, Sainsbury and a supplier developed ideas or scenarios for improving supply chain processes, the model was used to calculate the expected changes in costs of each scenario.

Questions

1 What kinds of activities might be included in the benchmark analysis?

2 What cost drivers might be used within the benchmark analysis?

References

Dekker, H.C. (2003), 'Value chain analysis in interfirm relationships: a field study' *Management Accounting Research*, 14(1).

The linkages in the value chain express the relationships between the performance of one activity and its effects on the performance of another activity. A linkage occurs when interdependence exists between activities and the higher the interdependence between activities the greater is the required coordination. Thus, it is appropriate to view the value chain from the customer's perspective, with each link being seen as the customer of the previous link. If each link in the value chain is designed to meet the needs of its customers, then end-customer satisfaction should ensue. Furthermore, by viewing each link in the value chain as a supplier–customer relationship, the opinions of the customers can be used to provide useful feedback information on assessing the quality of service provided by the supplier. Opportunities are thus identified for improving activities throughout the entire value chain.

In the value chain shown in Figure 21.3 the design process activities occur before the production process. Product designs affect production costs and production costs are determined by product cost drivers so that knowing the cost driver rates of the activities required to produce the products is essential for exploiting the linkages between design and production. If designers are made aware that the number of parts is a major cost driver of the various product-related activities, then they will focus on producing products with standard parts and thus reduce the costs of the production activities. A further example relates to the materials procurement process which in Figure 21.3 is assumed to be one of the processes within the overall production process. Providing high quality materials and parts that are delivered when required may be just as important to a company as a whole in terms of ensuring good internal supplier-customer relationships as is providing high quality goods delivered on a timely basis to external customers.

Shank and Govindarajan (1992) argue that traditional management accounting adopts an internal focus which, in terms of the value chain, starts too late and stops too soon. Starting cost analysis with purchases misses all the opportunities for exploiting linkages with the firm's suppliers and stopping cost analysis at the point of sale eliminates all opportunities for exploiting linkages with customers. Shank (1989) illustrates how an American automobile company failed to use the value chain approach to exploit links with suppliers and enhance profitability. The company had made significant internal savings from introducing JIT manufacturing techniques, but, at the same time, price increases from suppliers more than offset these internal cost savings. A value chain perspective revealed that 50 per cent of the firm's costs related to purchases from parts suppliers. As the automobile company reduced its own need for buffer inventories, it placed major new strains on the manufacturing responsiveness of suppliers. The increase in the suppliers' manufacturing costs was greater than the decrease in the automobile company's internal costs. Shank states:

> For every dollar of manufacturing cost the assembly plants saved by moving towards JIT management concepts, the suppliers' plant spent much more than one dollar extra because of schedule instability arising from the introduction of JIT. Because of its narrow value added perspective, the auto company had ignored the impact of its changes on its suppliers' costs. Management had ignored the idea that JIT involves a partnership with suppliers (Shank, 1989: 51).

Managing linkages in the value chain is also the central idea of the concept of supply chain management. By examining potential linkages with suppliers and understanding supplier costs it may be possible for the buying organization to change its activities in order to reduce the supplier's costs. For example, cost generating activities in the supplying organizations are often triggered by purchasing parameters (e.g. design specifications, lot size, delivery schedule, number of shipments, design changes and level of documentation). However, the buying organization can only be sensitive to these issues if it understands how supplier costs are generated (Seal et al., 1999). In many organizations materials purchased from suppliers account for more than 60 per cent of total manufacturing costs (Drury et al., 1993) and therefore managing supply chain costs has become a critical element in overall cost management. Because of this some companies have established strategic supply partnerships. Seal et al. describe the attempt at a strategic supply partnership between two UK companies and how the buying company was seeking information sharing and research and development collaboration with the supplier for strategic components. In return the supplier was wishing to develop a higher level of cooperation and trust. Such developments represent an attempt to apply cost management throughout the entire value chain.

Similarly, by developing linkages with customers mutually beneficial relationships can be established. For example, Shank and Govindarajan (1992), drawing off research by Hergert and Morris (1989) point out that some container producers in the USA have constructed manufacturing facilities near beer breweries and deliver the containers through overhead conveyers directly onto the customers' assembly lines. This practice results in significant cost reductions for both the container producers and their customers by expediting the transport of empty containers, which are bulky and heavy.

SUMMARY

The following items relate to the learning objectives listed at the beginning of the chapter.

● **Distinguish between the features of a traditional management accounting control system and cost management.**

A traditional management accounting control system tends to be based on the preservation of the status quo and the ways of performing existing activities are not reviewed. The emphasis is on cost containment rather than cost reduction. Cost management focuses on cost reduction rather than cost containment. Whereas traditional cost control systems are routinely applied on a continuous basis, cost management tends to be applied on an *ad hoc* basis when an opportunity for cost reduction is identified. Also many of the approaches that are incorporated within the area of cost management do not involve the use of accounting techniques. In contrast, cost control relies heavily on accounting techniques.

● **Explain life-cycle costing and describe the typical pattern of cost commitment and cost incurrence during the three stages of a product's life cycle.**

Life-cycle costing estimates and accumulates costs over a product's entire life cycle in order to determine whether the profits earned during the manufacturing phase will cover the costs incurred during the pre- and post-manufacturing stages. Three stages of a product's life cycle can be identified – the planning and design stage, the manufacturing stage and the service and abandonment stage. Approximately 80 per cent of a product's costs are committed during the planning and design stage. At this stage product designers determine the product's design and the production process. In contrast, the majority of costs are incurred at the manufacturing stage, but they have already become locked-in at the planning and design stage and are difficult to alter. Cost management can be most effectively exercised during the planning and design stage and not at the manufacturing stage when the product design and processes have already been determined and costs have been committed.

● **Describe the target costing approach to cost management.**

Target costing is a customer-oriented technique that is widely used by Japanese companies and which has recently been adopted by companies in Europe and the USA. The first stage requires market research to determine the target selling price for a product. Next a standard or desired profit margin is deducted to establish a target cost for the product. The target cost is compared with the predicted actual cost. If the predicted actual cost is above the target cost intensive efforts are made to close the gap. Value engineering and functional analysis are used to drive the predicted actual cost down to the target cost. The major advantage of adopting target costing is that it is deployed during a product's design and planning stage so that it can have a maximum impact in determining the level of the locked-in costs.

● **Describe tear-down analysis, value engineering and functional analysis.**

Tear-down analysis involves examining a competitor's product in order to identify opportunities for product improvement and/or cost reduction. The aim of value engineering is to achieve the assigned target cost by (a) identifying improved product designs that reduce the product's cost without sacrificing functionality and/or (b) eliminating unnecessary functions that increase the product's costs and for which customers are not prepared to pay extra. Value engineering requires the use of functional analysis. This involves decomposing the product into its many elements or attributes. A value for each element is determined which reflects the amount the customer is prepared to pay. The cost of each function of a product is compared with the benefits perceived by the customers. If the cost of the function exceeds the benefit to the customer, then the function is either eliminated, modified to reduce its cost or enhanced in terms of its perceived value so that its value exceeds the cost.

● **Distinguish between target costing and *kaizen* costing.**

The major difference between target and *kaizen* costing is that target costing is normally applied during the design stage whereas *kaizen* costing is applied during the manufacturing stage of the product life cycle. With target costing, the focus is on the product and cost reductions are achieved primarily through product design. In contrast, *kaizen* costing focuses on the production processes and cost reductions are derived primarily through the increased efficiency of the production process. The aim of *kaizen* costing is to reduce the cost of components and products by a pre-specified amount. A major feature is that workers are given the responsibility to improve processes and reduce costs.

Describe activity-based cost management.

Activity-based management (ABM) focuses on managing the business on the basis of the activities that make up the organization. It is based on the premise that activities consume costs. Therefore, by managing activities, costs will be managed in the long term. The goal of ABM is to enable customer needs to be satisfied while making fewer demands on organization resources. Knowing the cost of activities enables those activities with the highest cost to be highlighted so that they can be prioritized for detailed studies to ascertain whether they can be eliminated or performed more efficiently.

Distinguish between value added and non-value added activities.

To identify and prioritize the potential for cost reduction using ABM, many organizations have found it useful to classify activities as either value added or non-value added. A value added activity is an activity that customers perceive as adding usefulness to the product or service they purchase, whereas a non-value added activity is an activity where there is an opportunity for cost reduction without reducing the product's service potential to the customer. Taking action to reduce or eliminate non-value added activities is given top priority because by doing so the organization permanently reduces the cost it incurs without reducing the value of the product to the customer.

Explain the role of benchmarking and business-process engineering within the cost management framework.

Benchmarking involves comparing key activities with world-class best practices by identifying an activity that needs to be improved, finding a non-rival organization that is considered to represent world-class best practice for the activity, and studying how it performs the activity. The objective is to establish how the activity can be improved and ensure that the improvements are implemented. The outcome should be reduced costs for the activity or process or performing the activity more effectively, thus increasing customer satisfaction. The aim of business process re-engineering is to improve the key business processes in an organization by focusing on simplification, cost reduction, improved quality and enhanced customer satisfaction. A distinguishing feature of business process re-engineering is that it involves radical and dramatic changes in processes by abandoning current practices and reinventing completely new methods of performing business processes.

Outline the main features of a just-in-time philosophy.

Many companies seek to eliminate and/or reduce the costs of non-value added activities by introducing just-in-time (JIT) systems. The aims of a JIT system are to produce the required items, at the required quality and in the required quantities, at the precise time they are required. In particular, JIT aims to eliminate waste by minimizing inventories and reducing cycle or throughput times (i.e. the time elapsed from when customers place an order until the time when they receive the desired product or service). Adopting a JIT manufacturing system involves moving from a batch production functional layout to a cellular flow line manufacturing system. The JIT philosophy also extends to adopting JIT purchasing techniques, whereby the delivery of materials immediately precedes their use. By arranging with suppliers for more frequent deliveries, inventories can be cut to a minimum.

Explain the purpose of a cost of quality report.

A cost of quality report indicates the total cost to the organization of producing products or services that do not conform with quality requirements. Quality costs are analyzed by four categories for reporting purposes (prevention, appraisal, and internal and external failure costs). The report draws management's attention to the possibility of reducing total quality costs by a wiser allocation of costs among the four quality categories.

● **Outline the main features of environmental cost management.**

Environmental cost management is becoming increasingly important in many organizations because: (1) environmental costs are large for some industrial sectors; (2) regulatory requirements have increased significantly over the past decade; and (3) society is demanding that companies focus on becoming more environmentally friendly. The reporting of environmental costs and their causes provides the potential for them to be reduced by redesigning processes in order to reduce hazardous materials used or pollutants emitted to the environment. An environmental cost report should be periodically produced that indicates the total environmental costs analyzed by four categories for reporting purposes (prevention, detection, and internal and external failure costs). The report draws management's attention to the possibility of reducing environmental costs by a wiser allocation of costs among the four categories. The environmental cost report should be used as an attention-directing device to make top management aware of how much is being spent on environmental costs and the relative amount in each category. The report also draws management's attention to those areas that have the greatest potential for cost reduction.

● **Describe how value chain analysis can be used to increase customer satisfaction and manage costs more effectively.**

Increasing attention is now being given to value chain analysis as a means of increasing customer satisfaction and managing costs more effectively. The value chain is the linked set of value-creating activities all the way from basic raw material sources from component suppliers through to the ultimate end-use product or service delivered to the customer. Understanding how value chain activities are performed and how they interact with each other creates the conditions to improve customer satisfaction, particularly in terms of cost efficiency, quality and delivery.

KEY TERMS AND CONCEPTS

Activity-based cost management (ABCM) The cost management applications applied to activity-based costing, without the need to assign activity costs to products, also known as activity-based management.

Activity-based management (ABM) The cost management applications applied to activity-based costing, without the need to assign activity costs to products, also known as activity-based cost management.

Appraisal costs The costs incurred to ensure that materials, products and services meet quality conformance standards.

Batch production functional layout A plant layout in which products pass in batches through a number of specialist departments that normally contain a group of similar machines.

Benchmarking A mechanism for achieving continuous improvement by measuring products, services or activities against those of other best performing organizations.

Business process re-engineering Examining business processes and making substantial changes to how the organization operates and the redesign of how work is done through activities.

Cellular manufacturing A plant layout based on product flow lines, which are normally U-shaped.

Committed costs Costs that have not yet been incurred but that will be incurred in the future on the basis of decisions that have already been made, also known as locked-in costs.

Cost of quality report A report indicating the total cost to the organization of producing products or services that do not conform with quality requirements.

Costs of non-compliance Internal and external failure costs, also known as costs of non-conformance.

Costs of non-conformance Internal and external failure costs, also known as costs of non-complicance.

Costs of quality compliance Prevention and appraisal costs, also known as costs of quality conformance.

Costs of quality conformance Prevention and appraisal costs, also known as costs of quality compliance.

Environmental detection costs The costs incurred to ensure that a firm's activities, products and processes conform to regulatory laws and voluntary standards.

Environmental external failure costs The costs incurred on activities performed after discharging waste into the environment.

Environmental internal failure costs The costs incurred from performing activities that have produced contaminants and waste that have not been discharged into the environment

Environmental prevention costs The costs of activities undertaken to prevent the production of waste that could cause damage to the environment.

External failure costs The costs incurred when products or services fail to conform to requirements or satisfy customer needs after they have been delivered.

Functional analysis A process that involves decomposing a product into its many elements or attributes and determining a price or value for each element that reflects the amount the customer is prepared to pay.

Internal failure costs The internal costs incurred when products and services fail to meet quality standards or customer needs.

Just-in-time (JIT) production methods The design of the production process that involves producing the required items, at the required quality and in the required quantities, at the precise time they are required.

Kaizen costing Making improvements to a process during the manufacturing phase of the product life cycle through small incremental amounts, rather than through large innovations.

Kanbans Visible signalling systems that authorize the production of parts and their movement to the location where they will be used.

Life-cycle costing The estimation of costs over a product's entire life cycle in order to determine whether profits made during the manufacturing phase will cover the costs incurred during the pre- and post-manufacturing stages.

Locked-in costs Costs that have not yet been incurred but that will be incurred in the future on the basis of decisions that have already been made, also known as committed costs.

Non-value added activity An activity where there is an opportunity for cost reduction without reducing the product's service potential to the customer.

Prevention costs The costs incurred in preventing the production of products or services that do not conform to specification.

Product flow line A plant layout in which groups of dissimilar machines are organized into product or component family flow lines so that individual items can move from process to process more easily.

Production cell A self-contained area in which a team works on a product family.

Pull manufacturing system A system that pulls products through the manufacturing process so that each operation produces only what is necessary to meet the demand of the following operation.

Push manufacturing system A system in which machines are grouped into work centres based on the similarity of their functional capabilities and one process supplies parts to the subsequent process without any consideration as to whether the next process is ready to work on the parts or not.

Reverse engineering The dismantling and examination of a competitor's product in order to identify opportunities for product improvement and/or cost reduction, also known as tear-down analysis.

Statistical quality control charts A graph of a series of successive observations of operations taken at regular intervals to test whether a batch of produced items is within pre-set tolerance limits.

Supply chain management Managing linkages in the supply chain by examining supplier costs and modifying activities to reduce these costs.

Target costing A technique that focuses on managing costs during a product's planning and design phase by establishing the target cost for a product or service that is derived from starting with the target selling price and deducting a desired profit margin.

Tear down analysis The dismantling and examination of a competitor's product in order to identify opportunities for product improvement and/or cost reduction, also known as reverse engineering.

Total quality management (TQM) A customer-oriented process of continuous improvement that focuses on delivering products or services of consistent high quality in a timely fashion.

Value added activity An activity that customers perceive as adding usefulness to the product or service they purchase.

Value analysis A systematic interdisciplinary examination of factors affecting the cost of a product or service in order to devise means of achieving the specified purpose at the required standard of quality and reliability at the target cost, also known as value engineering.

Value engineering A systematic interdisciplinary examination of factors affecting the cost of a product or service in order to devise means of achieving the specified purpose at the required standard of quality and reliability at the target cost, also known as value analysis.

Value-chain analysis The analysis, coordination and optimization of the linked set of value-creating activities all the way from basic raw material sources for component suppliers through to the ultimate end-use product or service delivered to the customer.

Zero-defects policy A focus on continuous improvement with the ultimate aim of achieving zero-defects and eliminating all internal and external failure costs.

RECOMMENDED READING

You should refer to Kato (1993) and Tani *et al.* (1994) for a description of target costing in Japanese companies. For a survey of target costing in Dutch firms you should refer to Dekker and Smidt (2003). A more detailed description of activity-based cost management can be found in Chapter 8 of Kaplan and Cooper (1998). You should refer to Shank and Govindarajan (1992) for a description of the application of value chain analysis to cost management and Soonawalla (2006) for a more detailed discussion of environmental cost management. The International Federation of Accountants (IFAC) also provides a guidance document that gives a general framework and set of definitions for environmental management accounting (see **http://www.ifac.org**).

KEY EXAMINATION POINTS

Much of the content of this chapter relates to relatively new topics. Therefore fewer examination questions have been set by the professional examining bodies on the content of this chapter. The questions that follow provide an illustration of the type of questions that have been set.

It is likely that most of the questions that will be set on cost management topics will be essays and will require students to demonstrate that they have read widely on the various topics covered in this chapter. Questions set are likely to be open-ended and there will be no ideal answer.

ASSESSMENT MATERIAL

The review questions are short questions that enable you to assess your understanding of the main topics included in the chapter. The numbers in parentheses provide you with the page numbers to refer to if you cannot answer a specific question.

The review problems are more complex and require you to relate and apply the content to various business problems. The problems are graded by their level of difficulty. Solutions to review problems that are not preceded by the term 'IM' are provided in a separate section at the end of the book. Solutions to problems preceded by the term 'IM' are provided in the *Instructor's Manual* accompanying this book that can be downloaded from the lecturer's digital support resources. Additional review problems with fully worked solutions are provided in the *Student Manual* that accompanies this book.

REVIEW QUESTIONS

21.1 How does cost management differ from traditional management accounting control systems? (pp. 542–543)

21.2 What are committed (locked-in) costs? (p. 544)

21.3 Explain the essential features of life-cycle costing. (pp. 543–544)

21.4 Describe the stages involved with target costing. Describe how costs are reduced so that the target cost can be achieved. (pp. 544–546)

21.5 What is *kaizen* costing? (p. 549)

21.6 What are the distinguishing features of activity-based management? (pp. 549–552)

21.7 Distinguish between value added and non-value added activities. (p. 550)

21.8 What is business process re-engineering? (p. 553)

21.9 Identify and discuss the four kinds of quality costs that are included in a cost of quality report. Give examples of costs that fall within each category. (p. 559)

21.10 Discuss the value of a cost of quality report. (p. 559)

21.11 Describe what is meant by a zero-defects policy. (p. 559)

21.12 Explain what is meant by value-chain analysis. Illustrate how value-chain analysis can be applied. (pp. 564–565)

21.13 Explain how benchmarking can be used to manage costs and improve activity performance. What are the major features of a just-in-time manufacturing philosophy? (p. 553, pp. 553–557)

21.14 Distinguish between a pull and push manufacturing system. (pp. 554–555)

21.15 What are the essential features of just-in-time purchasing arrangements? (p. 556)

REVIEW PROBLEMS

21.16 Advanced: Calculation of cost of quality. CAL manufactures and sells solar panels for garden lights. Components are bought in and assembled into metal frames that are machine manufactured by CAL. There are a number of alternative suppliers of these solar panels. Some of CAL's competitors charge a lower price, but supply lower quality panels; whereas others supply higher quality panels than CAL but for a much higher price.

CAL is preparing its budgets for the coming year and has estimated that the market demand for its type of solar panels will be 100 000 units and that its share will be 20 000 units (i.e. 20 per cent of the available market). The standard cost details of each solar panel are as follows:

		$ per unit
Selling price		60
Bought-in components (1 set)	15	
Assembly & machining cost	25	
Delivery cost	5	45
Contribution		15

An analysis of CAL's recent performance revealed that 2 per cent of the solar panels supplied to customers were returned for free replacement, because the customer found that they were faulty. Investigation of these returned items shows that the components had been damaged when they had been assembled into the metal frame. These returned panels cannot be repaired and have no scrap value. If the supply of faulty solar panels to customers could be eliminated then, due to improved customer perception, CAL's market share would increase to 25 per cent.

Required:

(a) Explain, with reference to CAL, quality conformance costs and quality non-conformance costs and the relationship between them. *(4 marks)*

(b) Assuming that CAL continues with its present systems and that the percentage of quality failings is as stated above:

(i) Calculate, based on the budgeted figures and sales returns rate, the total relevant costs of quality for the coming year. *(4 marks)*

(ii) Calculate the maximum saving that could be made by implementing an inspection process for the solar panels, immediately before the goods are delivered. *(2 marks)*

CIMA P2 Performance Management

21.17 Advanced: Preparations of a cost of quality statement. Telecoms At Work (TAW) manufactures and markets office communications systems. During the year ended 31 May TAW made an operating profit of $30 million on sales of $360 million. However, the directors are concerned that products do not conform to the required level of quality and TAW is therefore not fulfilling its full potential in terms of turnover and profits achieved.

The following information is available in respect of the year ended 31 May:

1   Production data:

Units manufactured and sold	18 000
Units requiring rework	2 100
Units requiring warranty repair service	2 700
Design engineering hours	48 000
Process engineering hours	54 000
Inspection hours (manufacturing)	288 000

2   Cost data:

	$
Design engineering per hour	96
Process engineering per hour	70
Inspection per hour (manufacturing)	50
Rework per communication system reworked (manufacturing)	4 800
Customer support per repaired unit (marketing)	240
Transportation costs per repaired unit (distribution)	280
Warranty repairs per repaired unit (customer service)	4 600

3   Staff training costs amounted to $180 000 and additional product testing costs of $72 000.

4   The marketing director has estimated that sales of 1 800 units were lost as a result of public knowledge of poor quality at TAW. The average contribution per communication system is estimated at $7 200.

Required:

(a) Prepare a cost analysis which shows actual prevention costs, appraisal costs, internal failure costs, and external failure costs for the year ended 31 May. Your statement should show each cost heading as a per cent of turnover and clearly show the total cost of quality. Comment briefly on the inclusion of opportunity costs in such an analysis.

(11 marks)

(b) A detailed analysis has revealed that the casings in which the communications systems are housed are often subject to mishandling in transit to TAW's manufacturing premises. The directors are considering two alternative solutions proposed by the design engineering team which are aimed at reducing the quality problems that are currently being experienced. These are as follows:

Option 1 – Increase the number of immediate physical inspections of the casings when they are received from the supplier. This will require an additional 10 000 inspection hours.

Option 2 – Redesign and strengthen the casings and the containers used to transport them to better withstand mishandling during transportation. Redesign will require an additional 2 000 hours of design engineering and an additional 5 000 hours of process engineering.

Internal failure costs of rework for each reworked communication system are as follows:

		$
Variable costs	(including direct materials, direct labour rework and supplies)	1 920
Allocated fixed costs	(equipment, space and allocated overhead)	2 880
Total costs (as per note 2 on cost data)		4 800

The directors of TAW believe that, even if it is able to achieve improvements in quality, it will be unable to save any of the fixed costs of internal and external failure.

If TAW chooses to inspect the casings more carefully, it expects to eliminate re-work on 720 communication systems whereas if it redesigns the casings it expects to eliminate rework on 960 communication systems.

If incoming casings are inspected more carefully, TAW estimates that 600 fewer communication systems will require warranty repair and that it will be able to sell an additional 300 communication systems. If the casing is redesigned, the directors estimate that

840 fewer communication systems will require warranty repair and that an additional 360 communication systems will be sold.

External failure costs of repair for each repaired communication system are as follows:

	Variable costs $	Fixed costs $	Total costs $
Customer support costs	96	144	240
Transportation costs	210	70	280
Warranty repair costs	1 700	2 900	4 600

Required:

Prepare an estimate of the financial consequences of each option and advise the directors of TAW which option should be chosen.

(9 marks)

ACCA P5 Advanced Performance Management

21.18 Advanced: Cost of quality reporting. Burdoy plc has a dedicated set of production facilities for component X. A just-in-time system is in place such that no stock of materials; work-in-progress or finished goods are held.

At the beginning of period 1, the planned information relating to the production of component X through the dedicated facilities is as follows:

(i)   Each unit of component X has input materials: 3 units of material A at £18 per unit and 2 units of material B at £9 per unit.

(ii) Variable cost per unit of component X (excluding materials) is £15 per unit worked on.

(iii) Fixed costs of the dedicated facilities for the period: £162 000.

(iv) It is anticipated that 10 per cent of the units of X worked on in the process will be defective and will be scrapped.

It is estimated that customers will require replacement (free of charge) of faulty units of component X at the rate of 2 per cent of the quantity invoiced to them in fulfilment of orders.

Burdoy plc is pursuing a total quality management philosophy. Consequently all losses will be treated as abnormal in recognition of a zero-defect policy and will be valued at variable cost of production.

Actual statistics for each periods 1 to 3 for component X are shown in Appendix 3.1. No changes have occurred from the planned price levels for materials, variable overhead or fixed overhead costs.

Required:

(a) Prepare an analysis of the relevant figures provided in Appendix 3.1 to show that the period 1 actual results were achieved at the planned level in respect of (i) quantities and losses and (ii) unit cost levels for materials and variable costs.

(5 marks)

(b) Use your analysis from (a) in order to calculate the value of the planned level of each of internal and external failure costs for period 1.

(3 marks)

(c) Actual free replacements of component X to customers were 170 units and 40 units in periods 2 and 3 respectively. Other data relating to periods 2 and 3 is shown in Appendix 3.1.

Burdoy plc authorized additional expenditure during periods 2 and 3 as follows:

Period 2: Equipment accuracy checks of £10 000 and staff training of £5000.

Period 3: Equipment accuracy checks of £10 000 plus £5000 of inspection costs; also staff training costs of £5000 plus £3000 on extra planned maintenance of equipment.

Required:

(i)   Prepare an analysis for EACH of periods 2 and 3 which reconciles the number of components invoiced to customers with those worked-on in the production process. The analysis should show the changes from the planned quantity of process losses and changes from the planned quantity of replacement of faulty components in customer hands;

(All relevant working notes should be shown)   (8 marks)

(ii) Prepare a cost analysis for EACH of periods 2 and 3 which shows actual internal failure costs, external failure costs, appraisal costs and prevention costs;   (6 marks)

(iii) Prepare a report which explains the meaning and inter-relationship of the figures in Appendix 3.1 and in the analysis in (a), (b) and (c) (i)/(ii). The report should also give examples of each cost type and comment on their use in the monitoring and progressing of the TQM policy being pursued by Burdoy plc.   (13 marks)

Appendix 3.1
Actual statistics for component X

	Period 1	Period 2	Period 3
Invoiced to customers (units)	5 400	5 500	5 450
Worked-on in the process (units)	6 120	6 200	5 780
Total costs:			
Materials A and B (£)	440 640	446 400	416 160
Variable cost of production (£) (excluding material cost)	91 800	93 000	86 700
Fixed cost (£)	162 000	177 000	185 000

ACCA Information for Control and Decision Making

21.19 Advanced: Calculation of total savings from introducing a JIT system and determination of optimal selling price. X Ltd manufactures and distributes three types of car (the C1, C2 and C3). Each type of car has its own production line. The company is worried by extremely difficult market conditions and forecasts losses for the forthcoming year.

Current operations
The budgeted details for next year are as follows:

	C1 £	C2 £	C3 £
Direct materials	2 520	2 924	3 960
Direct labour	1 120	1 292	1 980
Total direct cost per car	3 640	4 216	5 940
Budgeted production (cars)	75 000	75 000	75 000
Number of production runs	1 000	1 000	1 500
Number of orders executed	4 000	5 000	5 600
Machine hours	1 080 000	1 800 000	1 680 000

Annual overheads

	Fixed £000	Variable £
Set ups	42 660	13 000 per production run
Materials handling	52 890	4 000 per order executed
Inspection	59 880	18 000 per production run
Machining	144 540	40 per machine hour
Distribution and warehousing	42 900	3 000 per order executed

Proposed JIT system
Management has hired a consultant to advise them on how to reduce costs. The consultant has suggested that the company adopts a just-in-time (JIT) manufacturing system. The introduction

of the JIT system would have the following impact on costs (fixed and variable):

Direct labour	Increase by 20%
Set ups	Decrease by 30%
Materials handling	Decrease by 30%
Inspection	Decrease by 30%
Machining	Decrease by 15%
Distribution and warehousing	Eliminated

Required:

(a) Based on the budgeted production levels, calculate the total annual savings that would be achieved by introducing the JIT system. *(6 marks)*

The following table shows the price/demand relationship for each type of car per annum.

C1		C2		C3	
Price £	Demand	Price £	Demand	Price £	Demand
5000	75 000	5750	75 000	6500	75 000
5750	65 000	6250	60 000	6750	60 000
6000	50 000	6500	45 000	7750	45 000
6500	35 000	7500	35 000	8000	30 000

Required:

(b) Assuming that X Ltd adopts the JIT system and that the revised variable overhead cost per car remains constant (as per the proposed JIT system budget), calculate the profit-maximizing price and output level for each type of car. *(12 marks)*

Investigations have revealed that some of the fixed costs are directly attributable to the individual production lines and could be avoided if a line is closed down for the year. The specific fixed costs for each of the production lines, expressed as a percentage of the total fixed costs, are:

C1	4%
C2	5%
C3	8%

Required:

(c) Determine the optimum production plan for the forthcoming year (based on the JIT cost structure and the prices and output levels you recommended in answer to requirement (b)). *(4 marks)*

(d) Write a report to the management of X Ltd which explains the conditions that are necessary for the successful implementation of a JIT manufacturing system. *(8 marks)*

CIMA Management Accounting – Decision Making

21.20 Advanced: Traditional and activity-based budget statements and life-cycle costing. The budget for the production, planning and development department of Obba plc, is currently prepared as part of a traditional budgetary planning and control system. The analysis of costs by expense type for the period ended 30 November where this system is in use is as follows:

Expense type	Budget %	Actual %
Salaries	60	63
Supplies	6	5
Travel cost	12	12
Technology cost	10	7
Occupancy cost	12	13

The total budget and actual costs for the department for the period ended 30 November are £1 000 000 and £1 060 000 respectively.

The company now feels that an activity based budgeting approach should be used. A number of activities have been identified for the production, planning and development department. An investigation has indicated that total budget and actual costs should be attributed to the activities on the following basis:

	Budget %	Actual %
Activities		
1. Routing/scheduling – new products	20	16
2. Routing/scheduling – existing products	40	34
3. Remedial re-routing/scheduling	5	12
4. Special studies – specific orders	10	8
5. Training	10	15
6. Management and administration	15	15

Required:

(a) (i) Prepare *two* budget control statements for the production planning and development department for the period ended 30 November which compare budget with actual cost and show variances using:

   1 a traditional expense based analysis and

   2 an activity based analysis. *(6 marks)*

(ii) Identify and comment on *four* advantages claimed for the use of activity based budgeting over traditional budgeting using the production planning and development example to illustrate your answer. *(12 marks)*

(iii) Comment on the use of the information provided in the activity based statement which you prepared in (i) in activity based performance measurement and suggest additional information which would assist in such performance measurement. *(8 marks)*

(b) Other activities have been identified and the budget quantified for the three months ended 31 March as follows:

Activities	Cost driver unit basis	Units of Cost driver	Cost (£000)
Product design	design hours	8 000	2000 (see note 1)
Purchasing	purchase orders	4 000	200
Production	machine hours	12 000	1500 (see note 2)
Packing	volume (cu.m.)	20 000	400
Distribution	weight (kg)	120 000	600

Note 1: this includes all design costs for new products released this period.
Note 2: this includes a depreciation provision of £300 000 of which £8000 applies to 3 months' depreciation on a straight line basis for a new product (NPD). The remainder applies to other products.

New product NPD is included in the above budget. The following additional information applies to NPD:

(i) Estimated total output over the product life cycle: 5000 units (4 years life cycle).

(ii) Product design requirement: 400 design hours

(iii) Output in quarter ended 31 March : 250 units

(iv) Equivalent batch size per purchase order: 50 units

(v) Other product unit data: production time 0.75 machine hours: volume 0.4 cu. metres; weight 3 kg.

Required:
Prepare a unit overhead cost for product NPD using an activity based approach which includes an appropriate share of life cycle costs using the information provided in (b) above. *(9 marks)*

ACCA Information for Control and Decision Making

21.21 Advanced. The implementation of budgeting in a world class manufacturing environment may be affected by the impact of (i) a total quality ethos (ii) a just-in-time philosophy and (iii) an activity based focus.

Briefly describe the principles incorporated in EACH of (i) to (iii) and discuss ways in which each may result in changes in the way in which budgets are prepared as compared to a traditional incremental budgeting system.

(15 marks)

ACCA Information for Control and Decision Making

21.22 Advanced. HT manufactures and sells consumer goods. The market in which it operates is highly competitive and HT is constantly designing new products in order to maintain its market share. The life cycle of products in the market is extremely short with all of the manufacturers constantly introducing new products or variations on existing products.

Consumers consider two main factors when buying these products: price and quality. HT uses a penetration pricing policy when launching its products and is always striving to improve its quality from product design stage through to customer care. As a result it has a 15 per cent market share, and its largest competitor has a 6 per cent market share with around 30 other companies sharing the remainder of the market.

Required:

(a) Compare and contrast:

- Costs of quality conformance; and
- Costs of quality non-conformance. *(3 marks)*

(b) Discuss the relationship between quality conformance costs and product selling prices in HT. *(4 marks)*

(c) Explain how Kaizen principles could be used by HT to extend the life or its products. *(3 marks)*

CIMA Performance Management

21.23 Advanced.

(a) Contrast the features of organizations which would benefit from ABC with those which would not; *(8 marks)*

(b) explain in what ways ABC may be used to manage costs, and the limitations of these approaches; *(11 marks)*

(c) explain and discuss the use of target costing to control product costs. *(6 marks)*

CIMA Stage 4 Management Accounting

21.24 Advanced. You are financial controller of a medium-sized engineering business. This business was family-owned and managed for many years but has recently been acquired by a large group to become its engineering division.

The first meeting of the management board with the newly appointed divisional managing director has not gone well.

He commented on the results of the division:

- sales and profits were well below budget for the month and cumulatively for the year, and the forecast for the rest of the year suggested no improvement;
- working capital was well over budget;
- even if budget were achieved the return on capital employed was well below group standards.

He proposed a total quality management (TQM) programme to change attitudes and improve results.

The initial responses of the managers to these comments were:

- the production director said there was a limit to what was possible with obsolete machines and facilities and only a very short-term order book;
- the sales director commented that it was impossible to get volume business when deliveries and quality were unreliable and designs out of date;

- the technical director said that there was little point in considering product improvements when the factory could not be bothered to update designs and the sales executives were reluctant to discuss new ideas with new potential customers.

You have been asked to prepare reports for the next management board meeting to enable a more constructive discussion.

You are required:

(a) to explain the critical success factors for the implementation of a programme of total quality management. Emphasize the factors that are crucial in changing attitudes from those quoted; *(11 marks)*

(b) to explain how you would measure quality cost, and how the establishment of a system of measuring quality costs would contribute to a TQM programme. *(9 marks)*

CIMA Stage 4 Management Accounting

IM21.1 Advanced. Your managing director, after hearing a talk at a branch meeting on just-in-time (JIT) manufacturing would like the management to consider introducing JIT at your unit which manufactures typewriters and also keyboards for computing systems.

You are required as the assistant management accountant, to prepare a discussion paper for circulation to the directors and senior management, describing just-in-time manufacturing, the likely benefits which would follow its introduction and the effect its introduction would probably have on the cost accounting system.

(13 marks)

CIMA Stage 2 Cost Accounting

IM21.2 Advanced.

(a) Life-cycle costing normally refers to costs incurred by the user of major capital equipment over the whole of the useful equipment life. Explain the determination and calculation of these costs and the problems in their calculation.

(8 marks)

(b) In the strategy and marketing literature there is continual discussion of the product life cycle. You are required to explain, for *each* of the *four* stages of the product life cycle:

- start-up
- growth
- maturity
- harvest,

which system of product costing would be most useful for decision making and control, and why.

Explain briefly in your answer possible alternative organizational structures at each stage in the life cycle.

(12 marks)

CIMA Stage 4 Management Accounting – Control and Audit

IM21.3 Advanced. Kaplan ('Relevance regained', *Management Accounting*, September 1988) states the view that the 'time-honoured traditions of cost accounting' are 'irrelevant, misleading and wrong'. Variance analysis, product costing and operational control are cited as examples of areas where information provided by management accountants along traditional lines could well fail to meet today's needs of management in industry.

You are required to:

(a) state what you consider to be the main requirements for effective operational control and product costing in modern industry; *(10 marks)*

(b) identify which 'traditional cost accounting' methods in the areas quoted in (a) *may be considered* to be failing to supply the appropriate information to management, and explain why; *(9 marks)*

(c) recommend changes to the 'traditional cost accounting' methods and information which would serve to meet the problems identified in (b).   *(6 marks)*
    CIMA Stage 4 Management Accounting – Control and Audit

IM21.4 Advanced. A company is proposing the introduction of an activity-based costing (ABC) system as a basis for much of its management accounting information.

(a) Briefly describe how ABC is different from a traditional absorption approach to costing and explain why it was developed.   *(8 marks)*
(b) Discuss the advantages and limitations of this 'approach based on activities' for management accounting information in the context of:

  (i) preparing plans and budgets
  (ii) monitoring and controlling operations
  (iii) decision-making, for example, product deletion decisions.   *(12 marks)*
    ACCA Paper 8 Managerial Finance

IM21.5 Advanced. 'Japanese companies that have used just-in-time (JIT) for five or more years are reporting close to a 30 per cent increase in labour productivity, a 60 per cent reduction in inventories, a 90 per cent reduction in quality rejection rates, and a 15 per cent reduction in necessary plant space. However, implementing a just-in-time system does not occur overnight. It took Toyota over twenty years to develop its system and realize significant benefits from it.' *Source:* Sumer C. Aggrawal, *Harvard Business Review* (9/85).

Requirements:

(a) explain how the benefits claimed for JIT in the above quotation are achieved and why it takes so long to achieve those benefits;   *(15 marks)*
(b) explain how management information systems in general (and management accounting systems in particular) should be developed in order to facilitate and make best use of JIT.   *(10 marks)*
    CIMA Stage 3 Management Accounting Applications

IM21.6 Advanced: Feedback control theory and product quality measurement.

(a) In control theory, a 'feedback control' mechanism is one which supplies information to determine whether corrective action should be taken to re-establish control of a system.

You are required to:

  (i) illustrate by means of a diagram how the feedback mechanism operates within a control system, adding a commentary describing how the system functions;   *(9 marks)*
  (ii) distinguish 'feedforward' from 'feedback' control, giving two examples of each from within management accounting.   *(4 marks)*

(b) Achievement of a high standard of product quality has become a major issue in modern manufacturing industry.

In support of programmes aimed at achieving acceptable quality standards, some companies have introduced detailed 'quality cost' measurement schemes.

In others, the philosophy has been that no measurement procedures should be devoted especially to the measurement of quality costs: quality cost schemes designed to measure performance in this area are considered to add to administrative burdens; in reality 'quality' should be the expected achievement of the required product specification.

(i) set out a classification of quality costs which would be useful for reporting purposes. Give examples of actual costs which would be represented in each classification;   *(7 marks)*
(ii) discuss the reality of the differences of philosophy expressed in the opening statement. Do they represent fundamental differences or may they be reconciled?   *(5 marks)*
    CIMA Stage 4 Management Accounting – Control and Audit

IM21.7 Advanced: Financial evaluation of implementing a quality management programme. Bushworks Ltd convert synthetic slabs into components AX and BX for use in the car industry. Bushworks Ltd is planning a quality management programme at a cost of £250 000. The following information relates to the costs incurred by Bushworks Ltd both before and after the implementation of the quality management programme:

1. *Synthetic slabs*
   Synthetic slabs cost £40 per hundred. On average 2.5 per cent of synthetic slabs received are returned to the supplier as scrap because of deterioration in stores. The supplier allows a credit of £1 per hundred slabs for such returns. In addition, on receipt in stores, checks to ensure that the slabs received conform to specification costs £14 000 per annum.
   A move to a just-in-time purchasing system will eliminate the holding of stocks of synthetic slabs. This has been negotiated with the supplier who will deliver slabs of guaranteed design specification for £44 per hundred units, eliminating all stockholding costs.

2. *Curing/moulding process*
   The synthetic slabs are issued to a curing/holding process which has variable conversion costs of £20 per hundred slabs input. This process produces sub-components A and B which have the same cost structure. Losses of 10 per cent of input to the process because of incorrect temperature control during the process are sold as scrap at £5 per hundred units. The quality programme will rectify the temperature control problem thus reducing losses to 1 per cent of input to the process.

3. *Finishing process*
   The finishing process has a bank of machines which perform additional operations on type A and B sub-components as required and converts them into final components AX and BX respectively. The variable conversion costs in the finishing process for AX and BX are £15 and £25 per hundred units respectively. At the end of the finishing process 15 per cent of units are found to be defective.
   Defective units are sold for scrap at £10 per hundred units. The quality programme will convert the finishing process into two dedicated cells, one for each of component types AX and BX. The dedicated cell variable costs per hundred sub-components A and B processed will be £12 and £20 respectively. Defective units of components AX and BX are expected to fall to 2.5 per cent of the input to each cell. Defective components will be sold as scrap as at present.

4. *Finished goods*
   A finished goods stock of components AX and BX of 15 000 and 30 000 units respectively is held throughout the year in order to allow for customer demand fluctuations and free replacement of units returned by customers due to specification faults. Customer returns are currently 2.5 per cent of components delivered to customers. Variable stock holding costs are £15 per thousand component units.
   The proposed dedicated cell layout of the finishing process will eliminate the need to hold stocks of finished components, other than sufficient to allow for the free replacement of those found to be defective in customer

hands. This stock level will be set at one month's free replacement to customers which is estimated at 500 and 1000 units for types AX and BX respectively. Variable stockholding costs will remain at £15 per thousand component units.

5 *Quantitative data*

Some preliminary work has already been carried out in calculating the number of units of synthetic slabs, sub-components A and B and components AX and BX which will be required both before and after the implementation of the quality management programme, making use of the information in the question. Table 1 summarizes the relevant figures.

Table 1

	Existing situation		Amended situation	
	Type A/AX (units)	Type B/BX (units)	Type A/AX (units)	Type B/BX (units)
Sales	800 000	1 200 000	800 000	1 200 000
Customer returns	20 000	30 000	6 000	12 000
Finished goods delivered	820 000	1 230 000	806 000	1 212 000
Finished process losses	144 706	217 059	20 667	31 077
Input to finishing process	964 706	1 447 059	826 667	1 243 077
	2 411 765		2 069 744	
Curing/moulding losses	267 974		20 907	
Input to curing/moulding	2 679 739		2 090 651	
Stores losses	68 711		—	
Purchase of synthetic slabs	2 748 450		2 090 651	

Required:

(a) Evaluate and present a statement showing the net financial benefit or loss per annum of implementing the quality management programme, using the information in the question and the data in Table 1.
(All relevant workings must be shown)   *(27 marks)*

(b) Explain the meaning of the terms internal failure costs, external failure costs, appraisal costs and prevention costs giving examples of each.   *(8 marks)*

22
STRATEGIC MANAGEMENT ACCOUNTING

LEARNING OBJECTIVES After studying this chapter, you should be able to:

- describe the different elements of strategic management accounting;

- describe three competitive strategies that a firm can adopt to achieve sustainable competitive advantage and explain how they influence management accounting practices;

- describe the balanced scorecard;

- explain each of the four perspectives of the balanced scorecard;

- provide illustrations of performance measures for each of the four perspectives;

- explain how the balanced scorecard links strategy formulation to financial outcomes.

During the late 1980s and early 1990s criticisms of traditional management accounting practices were widely publicized and new approaches were advocated which are more in tune with today's competitive and business environment. In particular, strategic management accounting has been identified as a way forward. However, there is still no comprehensive framework as to what constitutes strategic management accounting. In this chapter we shall examine the elements of strategic management accounting and describe the different contributions that have been made to its development.

One of the elements of strategic management accounting involves the provision of information for the formulation of an organization's strategy and managing strategy implementation. To encourage behaviour that is consistent with an organization's strategy, many companies have developed an integrated framework of performance measurement that can be used to clarify, communicate and manage strategy. In the latter part of this chapter recent developments that seek to incorporate performance measurement within the strategic management process are described.

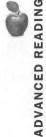

ADVANCED READING

WHAT IS STRATEGIC MANAGEMENT ACCOUNTING?

For many years strategic management accounting has been advocated as a potential area of development that would enhance the future contribution of management accounting. In the late 1980s the UK Chartered Institute of Management Accountants commissioned an investigation to review the current state of development of management accounting. The findings were published in a report entitled *Management Accounting: Evolution not Revolution*, authoured by Bromwich and Bhimani (1989). In the report, and a follow-up report (*Management Accounting: Pathways to Progress*, 1994) Bromwich and Bhimani drew attention to strategic management accounting as an area for future development.

Despite the publicity that strategic management accounting has received there is still no comprehensive conceptual framework of what strategic management accounting is (Tomkins and Carr, 1996). For example, Coad (1996) states:

> Strategic management accounting is an emerging field whose boundaries are loose and, as yet, there is no unified view of what it is or how it might develop. The existing literature in the field is both disparate and disjointed (Coad, 1996: 392)

Innes (1998) defines strategic management accounting as the provision of information to support the strategic decisions in organizations. Strategic decisions usually involve the longer term, have a significant effect on the organization and, although they may have an internal element, they also have an external element. Adopting this definition suggests that the provision of information that supports an organization's major long-term decisions, such as investment appraisal, the strategic planning and budgeting process and the use of activity-based costing information for providing information relating to product mix, introduction and abandonment decisions, falls within the domain of strategic management accounting. This view is supported by Cooper and Kaplan (1988) who state that strategic accounting techniques are designed to support the overall competitive strategy of the organization, principally by the power of using information technology to develop more refined product and service costs. In the previous chapter strategic cost management was examined. Adding the term 'strategic' to cost management implies that strategic cost management should be included within the domain of strategic management accounting.

Other writers, however, have adopted a narrower definition that emphasizes that the distinguishing feature of strategic management accounting is its external focus. Simmonds (1981, 1982), who first coined the term strategic management accounting, views it as the provision and analysis of management accounting data about a business and its competitors which is of use in the development and monitoring

---

REAL WORLD VIEWS 22.1

What is strategic management accounting? Long term sustainability in South Africa

The term corporate social responsibility (CSR) emerged in the 1990s. Today, this term has largely been supplanted by the term *sustainability*. The sustainability of a business refers of course to its longer term economic prospects, but also to social and environment sustainability. A CIMA (2010) report on sustainability highlights how some emerging market countries are more focused on sustainability reporting than many leading economies. According to the report, South Africa scored best on corporate level sustainability reporting among the BRICS[1] economies (p. 9). This is attributed to South Africa's broad corporate governance code, which encompasses themes like leadership, sustainability and corporate citizenship. The CIMA report provides some examples of what South African firms are doing. One textile company, Impahla Clothing, which is a supplier to sportswear giant Puma, has developed a rigorous sustainability report. Puma were so impressed with

the report that they are asking all suppliers to voluntarily report in a similar way. Impahla Clothing is a private company, with 176 employees according to its 2009 sustainability report – which extends to more than 50 pages. The report provides performance data under headings like occupational health and safety, environmental management, governance and risk management and human rights. For small business, the company seems to be leading the way.

Questions

1 Can you think of some basic management accounting techniques/principles which may be useful when incorporating sustainability into business decisions?

2 Do you think any sustainability initiatives directly impact profits?

References

http://www.cimaglobal.com/Thought-leadership/Research-topics/Sustainability/Sustainability-in-emerging-markets-lessons-from-South-Africa/

http://safe.puma.com/us/en/wp-content/uploads/imphala_2009.pdf

[1]Brazil, India, Russia, China and South Africa.

of the strategy of that business. He views profits as emerging not from internal efficiencies but from the firm's competitive position in its markets. More recently, Bromwich (1990), a principal advocate of strategic management accounting, has provided the following definition:

> The provision and analysis of financial information on the firm's product markets and competitors' costs and cost structures and the monitoring of the enterprise's strategies and those of its competitors in these markets over a number of periods (Bromwich, 1990: 28).

The Chartered Institute of Management Accountants (CIMA) in the UK defines strategic management accounting as:

> A form of management accounting in which emphasis is placed on information which relates to factors external to the firm, as well as non-financial information and internally generated information (Chartered Institute of Management Accountants (CIMA) Official Terminology, 2005: 54).

Because of the lack of consensus on what constitutes strategic management accounting, Lord (1996) reviewed the literature and identified several strands that have been used to characterize strategic management accounting. They include:

1 The extension of traditional management accounting's internal focus to include external information about competitors.

2 The relationship between the strategic position chosen by a firm and the expected emphasis on management accounting (i.e. accounting in relation to strategic positioning).

3 Gaining competitive advantage by analyzing ways to decrease costs and/or enhance the differentiation of a firm's products, through exploiting linkages in the value chain and optimizing cost drivers.

Let us now examine each of the above characteristics in more detail.

External information about competitors

Much of the early work relating to strategic management accounting can be attributed to the writings of Simmonds (1981, 1982 and 1986). He argued that management accounting should be more outward looking and should help the firm evaluate its competitive position relative to the rest of the industry by collecting data on costs and prices, sales volumes and market shares and cash flows and resources availability for its main competitors. To protect an organization's strategic position and determine strategies to improve its future competitiveness, managers require information that indicates by whom, by how much and why they are gaining or being beaten. This information provides advance warning of the need for a change in competitive strategy. Simmonds advocated that market share statements should be incorporated into management accounts. In addition, budgets could be routinely presented in a strategic format with columns for Ourselves, Competitor A, Competitor B, etc. Competitive information is available from public sources such as company annual reports, press, official institutions and informal sources (e.g. sales personnel, analyzing competitors' products, industry specialists, consultants, etc.).

Accounting in relation to strategic positioning

Various classifications of strategic positions that firms may choose have been identified in the strategic management literature. Porter (1985) suggests that a firm has a choice of three generic strategies in order to achieve sustainable competitive advantage. They are:

- *cost leadership*, whereby an enterprise aims to be the lowest-cost producer within the industry thus enabling it to compete on the basis of lower selling prices rather than providing unique products or services. The source of this competitive advantage may arise from factors such as economies of scale, access to favourable raw materials prices and superior technology (Langfield-Smith, 1997).

- *differentiation*, whereby the enterprise seeks to offer products or services that are considered by its customers to be superior and unique relative to its competitors. Examples include the quality or dependability of the product, after-sales service, the wide availability of the product and product flexibility (Langfield-Smith, 1997).

- A *focusing strategy*, which involves seeking competitive advantage by focusing on a narrow segment of the market that has special needs that are poorly served by other competitors in the industry. A focusing strategy recognizes that differences can exist within segments (e.g. customers and geographical regions) of the same market. Competitive advantage is based on adopting either a cost leadership or product differentiation strategy within the chosen segment.

In practice firms may choose a combination of the three strategies within the different markets in which they operate. Strategic positioning relates to the choice of the optimal mix of the three general strategies.

Miles and Snow (1978) distinguish between *defenders* and *prospector* strategies. Defenders operate in relatively stable areas, have limited product lines and employ a mass production routine technology. They compete by making operations efficient through cost, quality and service leadership, and engage in little product/market development. Prospectors compete through new product innovations and market development and are constantly looking for new market opportunities. Hence, they face a more uncertain task environment.

Firms should place more emphasis on particular accounting techniques, depending on which strategic position they adopt. For example, firms pursuing a cost leadership strategy will place more emphasis on the importance of standard costing variance analysis, flexible budgets, using tightly controlled budgets and strategic cost management. Firms pursuing a differentiation strategy place greater emphasis on seeking ways to differentiate their products and services from those provided by competitors. This frequently results in a greater number of products and services offered and also increased customer segmentation. Companies that pursue a differentiation strategy need more sophisticated product costing systems (e.g. ABC systems) that have the potential to more accurately measure the costs of product and volume diversity that stem from pursuing this strategy. Without such a system they run the risk of not being able to determine whether the higher revenues generated from their products or services exceed the extra costs associated with differentiation.

Several studies have examined the relationship between the strategic positioning that they adopt and the emphasis placed on accounting techniques. Simons (1987) found that business units that follow a defender strategy tend to place a greater emphasis on the use of financial measures (e.g., short-term budget targets) for compensating financial managers. Prospector firms placed a greater emphasis on forecast data and reduced importance on cost control. Ittner, Larcker and Rajan (1997) also found that the use of non-financial measures for determining executive's bonuses increases with the extent to which firms follow an innovation-oriented prospector strategy. Shank (1989) stresses the need for management accounting to support a firm's competitive strategies, and illustrates how two different competitive strategies – cost leadership and product differentiation – demand different cost analysis perspectives. For example, carefully engineered product cost standards are likely to be a very important management control tool for a firm that pursues a cost leadership strategy in a mature commodity business. In contrast, carefully engineered manufacturing cost standards are likely to be less important for a firm following a product differentiation strategy in a market-driven, rapidly changing and fast-growing business. A firm pursuing a product differentiation strategy is likely to require more information than a cost leader about new product innovations, design cycle times, research and development expenditures and marketing cost analysis. Exhibit 22.1 illustrates some potential differences in cost management emphasis, depending on the primary strategic thrust of the firm.

Gaining competitive advantage using value-chain analysis

Porter (1985) advocated using value-chain analysis (see Chapter 21) to gain competitive advantage. The aim of value chain analysis is to find linkages between value-creating activities which result in lower cost and/or enhanced differentiation. These linkages can be within the firm or between the firm and its suppliers, and customers. The previous chapter illustrated how an American automobile company initially failed to use the value chain approach to exploit links with suppliers and enhance profitability. The company had made significant internal savings from introducing JIT manufacturing techniques, but, at the same time, price increases from suppliers more than offset these internal cost savings. A value chain

EXHIBIT 22.1 Relationship between strategies and cost management emphasis

	Product differentiation	Cost leadership
Role of standard costs in assessing performance	Not very important	Very important
Importance of such concepts as flexible budgeting for manufacturing cost control	Moderate to low	High to very high
Perceived importance of meeting budgets	Moderate to low	High to very high
Importance of marketing cost analysis	Critical to success	Often not done at all on a formal basis
Importance of product cost as an input to pricing decisions	Low	High
Importance of competitor cost analysis	Low	High

Source: Shank (1989) Strategic cost management: New wine, or just new bottles? *Journal of Management Accounting Research* (1): 47–65.

perspective revealed that 50 per cent of the firm's costs related to purchases from parts suppliers. As the automobile company reduced its own need for buffer inventories, it placed major new strains on the manufacturing responsiveness of suppliers. The increase in the suppliers' manufacturing costs was greater than the decrease in the automobile company's internal costs. Shank (1989) states:

> For every dollar of manufacturing cost the assembly plants saved by moving towards JIT management concepts, the suppliers' plant spent much more than one dollar extra because of schedule instability arising from the introduction of JIT. Because of its narrow value added perspective, the auto company had ignored the impact of its changes on its suppliers' costs. Management had ignored the idea that JIT involves a partnership with suppliers (Shank, 1989: 51).

SURVEYS OF STRATEGIC MANAGEMENT ACCOUNTING PRACTICES

Little research has been undertaken on the extent to which companies use strategic management accounting practices. A notable exception is a survey undertaken by Guilding, Craven and Tayles (2000). The survey consisted of a sample of 314 large companies comprising 63 from the UK, 127 from the USA and 124 from New Zealand.

Guilding, Craven and Tayles acknowledge the difficulty in identifying what are generally accepted as constituting strategic management accounting practices. Based on a review of the literature they identified 12 strategic management accounting practices. The criteria that they used for identifying the practices were that they must exhibit one or more of the following characteristics: environmental or marketing orientation; focus on competitors; and long-term, forward-looking orientation. The average usage of the identified practices and their perceived merits are reported in Exhibit 22.2. Three of the 12 listed practices, namely quality costing (involving the use of cost of quality reports), life-cycle costing and target costing were described in the previous chapter. Although some of the remaining nine practices have been described in this chapter they can be subject to different interpretations and definitions. The following represent the definitions of these nine terms given to the respondents participating in the survey:

- *Competitive position monitoring* The analysis of competitor positions within the industry by assessing and monitoring trends in competitor sales, market share, volume, unit costs and return on sales. This information can provide a basis for the assessment of a competitor's market strategy.

- *Strategic pricing* The analysis of strategic factors in the pricing decision process. These factors may include: competitor price reaction; price elasticity; market growth; economies of scale and experience.

EXHIBIT 22.2 Usage and perceived merit of strategic management accounting practices

Strategic management accounting practice	Average usage score[a]	Ranking	Average perceived merit score[b]	Ranking
Competitive position monitoring	4.99	1	5.73	1
Strategic pricing	4.54	2	5.45	2
Competitor performance appraisal based on published financial statements	4.42	3	5.31	3
Competitor cost assessment	4.07	4	5.27	4
Strategic costing	3.49	5	4.91	5
Quality costing	3.22	6	4.29	6
Target costing	3.12	7	3.94	8
Value-chain costing	3.04	8	4.27	7
Brand value monitoring	2.73	9	3.38	11
Life-cycle costing	2.60	10	3.58	9
Attribute costing	2.33	11	3.49	10
Brand value budgeting	2.32	12	3.33	12

Notes
[a] All items scored on a Likert scale where 1 denotes used 'not at all' and 7 denotes used 'to a great extent'.
[b] All items scored on a Likert scale where 1 denotes 'not at all helpful' and 7 denotes 'helpful to a great extent'.

- *Competitor performance appraisal based on published financial statements.* The numerical analysis of a competitor's published statements as part of an assessment of the competitor's key sources of competitive advantage.

- *Competitor cost assessment* The provision of regularly updated estimates of a competitor's costs based on, for example, appraisal of facilities, technology, economies of scale. Sources include direct observation, mutual suppliers, mutual customers and ex-employees.

- *Strategic costing* The use of cost data based on strategic and marketing information to develop and identify superior strategies that will sustain a competitive advantage.

- *Value-chain costing* An activity-based costing approach where costs are allocated to activities required to design, procure, produce, market, distribute and service a product or service.

- *Brand value monitoring* The financial valuation of a brand through the assessment of brand strength factors such as: leadership; stability; market; internationality; trend; support; and protection combined with historical brand profits.

- *Attribute costing* The costing of specific product attributes that appeal to customers. Attributes that may be costed include: operating performance variables; reliability; warranty arrangements; the degree of finish and trim; assurance of supply and after sales service.

- *Brand value budgeting* The use of brand value as a basis for managerial decisions on the allocation of resources to support/enhance a brand position, thus placing attention on management dialogue on brand issues.

It is apparent from Exhibit 22.2 that the three competitor accounting practices and strategic pricing are the most popular strategic management accounting practices. They all have average scores above the mid-point on the seven-point scale for the 'not at all/to a large extent' used measure. You will also see from Exhibit 22.2 that the usage rates for the remaining eight strategic management accounting practices are below the mid-point of the '1–7' measurement scale used, thus suggesting that these practices are not widely used by the responding organizations.

In terms of the perceived merit of the 12 practices, the rankings shown in Exhibit 22.2 are similar to those reported for the extent of usage. Guilding, Craven and Tayles conclude that while usage rates for most of the practices appraised scored relatively lowly, two factors suggest that it would be inappropriate to dismiss their potential. First, for all of the strategic management accounting practices appraised, the perceived merit scores are significantly greater than the usage rate scores. Second, for the eight strategic management accounting practices where relatively low usage rates were observed, three (strategic costing, quality costing and value-chain costing) scored above the mid-point with respect to perceived merit. These observations suggest that there is a gap between what is needed and what is reported by an accounting system.

Guilding, Craven and Tayles also examined the familiarity of practising accountants with the term 'strategic management accounting'. The responses suggest that there was negligible use of the term in organizations and practising accountants have a limited appreciation of what the term means. This provides some support for Lord's (1996) assertion that:

> ... the characteristics that have been ascribed to strategic management accounting are likely to be operating in many firms. However, it appears that the management accountant does not need to be involved in their operation, nor do they need to be quantified in management accounting figures. Perhaps the widely touted 'strategic management accounting' is but a figment of academic imagination.

More recently a study by Langfield-Smith (2008) reported that strategic management accounting techniques have not been adopted widely, nor is the term strategic management accounting widely understood or used. However, aspects of strategic management accounting have had an impact, influencing the thinking and language of business, and the way in which various business processes are undertaken. Strategic management accounting issues cut across the wider domain of management, and are not just the province of management accountants.

THE BALANCED SCORECARD

A more recent contribution to strategic management accounting that emphasizes the role of management accounting in formulating and supporting the overall competitive strategy of an organization is the balanced scorecard. The balanced scorecard seeks to encourage behaviour that is consistent with an organization's strategy. It comprises of an integrated framework of performance measurements that aim to clarify, communicate and manage strategy implementation. The financial performance measures that have been described in Chapters 16–19 tend to be used primarily as a financial control mechanism whereas the balanced scorecard integrates both financial and non-financial measures and incorporates performance measurement within the strategic management process.

Prior to the 1980s, management accounting control systems tended to focus mainly on financial measures of performance. The inclusion of only those items that could be expressed in monetary terms motivated managers to focus excessively on cost reduction and ignore other important variables which were necessary to compete in the global competitive environment that emerged during the 1980s. Product quality, delivery, reliability, after-sales service and customer satisfaction became key competitive variables but none of these were given sufficient importance measured by the traditional management accounting performance measurement system.

During the 1980s much greater emphasis was given to incorporating into the management reporting system those non-financial performance measures that provided feedback on the key variables that are required to compete successfully in a global economic environment. However, a proliferation of performance measures emerged. This resulted in confusion when some of the measures conflicted with each other and it was possible to enhance one measure at the expense of another. It was also not clear to managers how the non-financial measures they were evaluated on contributed to the whole picture of achieving success in financial terms. According to Kaplan and Norton (2001a) previous performance measurement systems that incorporated non-financial measurements used *ad hoc* collections of such measures, more like checklists of measures for managers to keep track of and improve than a comprehensive system of linked measurements.

The need to integrate financial and non-financial measures of performance and identify key performance measures that link measurements to strategy led to the emergence of the balanced scorecard. The balanced scorecard was devised by Kaplan and Norton (1992) and refined in later

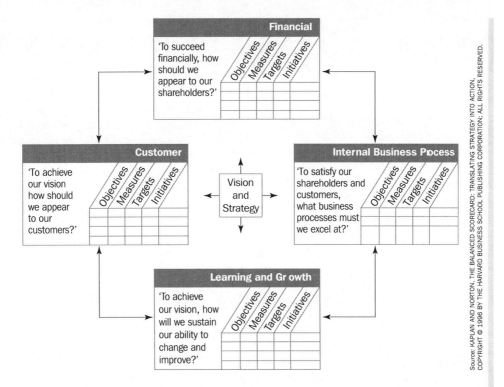

FIGURE 22.1
The balanced
scorecard

publications (Kaplan and Norton, 1993, 1996a, 1996b, 2001a, 2001b). The following discussion is a summary of Kaplan and Norton's writings on this topic. They use the diagram reproduced in Figure 22.1 to illustrate how the balanced scorecard translates strategy into tangible objectives and linked performance measures.

Figure 22.1 emphasizes that the balanced scorecard philosophy creates a strategic focus by translating an organization's vision and strategy into operational objectives and performance measures for the following four perspectives:

1 Financial perspective (How do we look to shareholders?)

2 Customer perspective (How do customers see us?)

3 Internal business perspective (What must we excel at?)

4 Learning and growth perspective (Can we continue to improve and create value?)

The balanced scorecard is a strategic management technique for communicating and evaluating the achievement of the mission and strategy of the organization. Kaplan and Norton define strategy as:

> Choosing the market and customer segments the business unit intends to serve, identifying the critical internal and business processes that the unit must excel at to deliver the value propositions to customers in the targeted market segments, and selecting the individual and organizational capabilities required for the internal and financial objectives.

You will see by referring to Figure 22.1 that strategy is implemented by specifying the major objectives for each of the four perspectives and translating them into specific performance measures, targets and initiatives. There may be one or more objectives for each perspective and one or more performance measures linked to each objective. Only the critical performance measures are incorporated in the scorecard. To minimize information overload and avoid a proliferation of measures, each perspective ought to comprise four to five separate measures. Thus, the scorecard can provide *top* management with a fast but comprehensive view of the organizational unit (i.e. a division/strategic business unit). Let us now examine each of the four perspectives. The following discussion presents generic core objectives and measures applicable to each perspective. In practice each organization will customize the objectives and performance measures to fit their own specific strategies.

REAL WORLD VIEWS 22.2

How Southwest Airlines developed its balanced scorecard analysis

Southwest Airlines set 'operating efficiency' as its strategic theme. The four perspectives embodied in the balanced scorecard were linked together by a series of relatively simple questions and answers:

Financial: What will drive operating efficiency? *Answer:* More customers on fewer planes.

Customer: How will we get more customers on fewer planes? *Answer:* Attract targeted segments of customers who value price and on-time arrivals.

Internal: What must our internal focus be? *Answer:* Fast aircraft turnaround time.

Learning: How will our people accomplish fast turnaround? *Answer:* Educate and compensate the ground crew regarding how they contribute to the firm's success. Also, use the employee stockholder programme.

The chart below shows how Southwest used this framework to lay out its balanced scorecard model. The first column of the chart contains the 'strategy map', that illustrates the cause-and-effect relationships between strategic objectives. The Objectives column shows what each strategy must achieve and what is critical to its success. The Measurement column shows how success in achieving each strat-

egy will be measured and tracked. The Target column spells out the level of performance or rate of improvement that is needed. The Initiative column contains key action programmes required to achieve objectives. Note that all of the measures, targets and initiatives are all aligned to each objective.

The company extended the effort to the department level, and the degree of development varied between departments. The goal was to identify key performance measures in each segment for the operating personnel. Some of the non-financial metrics that have emerged on a departmental level include: load factor (percentage of seats occupied); utilization factors on aircraft and personnel; on-time performance; available seat miles; denied-boarding rate; lost-bag reports per 10 000 passengers; flight cancellation rate; employee head count; and customer complaints per 10 000 passengers filed with the Department of Transportation.

Questions

1 Looking at the internal key answer of "fast turnaround time", can Southwest always control this?

2 Do you think performance measures like those in the Southwest scorecard are more useful to non-accountants and managers?

References

Institute of Management & Administration Report on Financial Analysis Planning and Reporting, July 2002

Southwest Airlines' Balanced Scorecard Framework

Strategic Theme: Operating Efficiency	Objectives	Measurement	Target	Initiative
Financial Profitability Fewer planes More customers	Profitability More customers Fewer planes	Market value Seat revenue Plane lease cost	30% CAGR 20% CAGR 5% CAGR	
Customer Flight is on time Lowest prices	Flight is on time Lowest prices	FAA on time arrival rating Customer ranking (market survey)	#1 #1	Quality management Customer loyalty program
Internal Fast ground turnaround	Fast ground turnaround	On ground time On time departure	30 minutes 90%	Cycle time optimization
Learning Ground crew alignment	Ground crew alignment	% Ground crew trained % Ground crew stockholders	Yr. 1 70% Yr. 3 90% Yr. 5 100%	ESOP Ground crew training

(Source: Balanced Scorecard Collaborative)

EXHIBIT 22.3 Financial perspective objectives and measures

Objectives	Measures
Revenue growth:	
Increase the number of new products	Percentage of revenues from new products
Develop new customers and markets	Percentage of revenues from new customers/markets
Change to a more profitable product (or service) mix	
	Sales growth percentage for targeted segments
Cost reduction:	
Reduce product/service cost per unit	Percentage reduction in cost per unit
Reduce selling/general administration costs	Percentage to total revenues of selling and administration costs
Asset utilization:	
Improve asset utilization	Return on investment
	Economic value-added

The financial perspective

The financial perspective specifies the financial performance objectives anticipated from pursuing the organization's strategy and also the economic consequences of the outcomes expected from achieving the objectives specified from the other three perspectives. Therefore the objectives and measures from the other perspectives should be selected to ensure that the financial outcomes will be achieved. Kaplan and Norton state that they have observed three core financial themes that drive the business strategy: revenue growth and mix, cost reduction and asset utilization.

Generic objectives and possible measures for these themes are shown in Exhibit 22.3. Typical *revenue growth* objectives for a business pursuing a growth strategy include increasing the number of new products, developing new customers and markets and changing to a more profitable product or service mix. Once the objectives have been determined, performance measures should be established that are linked to each objective. Possible measures are listed against each objective in Exhibit 22.3. They are percentage revenues from new products, percentage revenues from new customers/markets and growth of sales in the targeted segments.

The *cost reduction* objectives may include reduction in unit product costs and a reduction in selling and general and administration costs. Thus the percentage reduction in costs per unit of output for the selected cost objects and the percentage to total revenues of selling and administrative costs represent possible performance measures.

Exhibit 22.3 lists the improvement of *asset utilization* as the major objective of the asset utilization theme. Financial performance measures such as return on investment and economic value-added that were described in Chapter 19 provide overall outcome measures of success for the overall financial objectives of revenue growth, cost reduction and asset utilization.

The customer perspective

The customer perspective should identify the customer and market segments in which the business unit will compete. The customer perspective underpins the revenue element for the financial perspective objectives. Therefore the achievement of customer objectives should ensure that target revenues will be generated. Exhibit 22.4 lists five typical core or generic objectives. They are: increasing market share, increasing customer retention, increasing customer acquisition, increasing customer satisfaction and increasing customer profitability. Typical core measures for these objectives (see Exhibit 22.4) are respectively: percentage market share, percentage growth of business with existing customers, number of new customers or total sales to new customers, ratings from customer satisfaction surveys and

EXHIBIT 22.4 Customer perspective objectives and measures

Objectives	Measures
Core:	
Increase market share	Percentage market share
Increase customer retention	Percentage growth in business from existing customers
Increase customer acquisition	Total sales to new customers
Increase customer satisfaction	Customer survey satisfaction ratings
Increase customer profitability	Customer profitability analysis
Customer value propositions:	
Improve product functionality	Customer survey product functionality rating scores
Decrease price relative to competitors	Price relative to competitors
Improve product/service quality	Percentage returns from customers
Improve delivery time	Percentage on-time deliveries

profitability analysis by customer segments. The first four measures relate to the means required to achieve customer profitability but they do not measure the outcome. Customer profitability measures meet this requirement. In other words, a company does not want just satisfied customers, it also wants profitable customers.

Kaplan and Norton state that there is also a need to focus on customer value propositions that represent the attributes that drive core objectives and measures relating to the customer perspective. They identify common product/service attributes as encompassing the functionality of the products/services, their price and quality and for the customer dimension they identify the delivery time attribute. Focusing on these attributes has the potential to increase customer value and thus have a favourable impact on the core objectives. Typical objectives relating to the above attributes are listed in Exhibit 22.4. They are respectively: improve product functionality, decrease price relative to competitors, improve quality and improve delivery time. Possible measures for these objectives include, respectively, customer surveys satisfaction scores relating to product functionality, price relative to competitors, percentage of returns from customers and percentage of on-time deliveries.

The internal business perspective

The internal business perspective requires that managers identify the critical internal processes for which the organization must excel in implementing its strategy. Critical processes should be identified that are required to achieve the organization's customer and financial objectives. Kaplan and Norton identify a generic process value chain that provides guidance for companies applying the internal process perspective. The process value chain consists of three processes: the innovation process, the operations process and the post-sales process.

In the *innovation process*, managers research the needs of customers and then create the products or services that will meet those needs. It represents the long wave of value creation in which companies first identify new markets, new customers, and the emerging and latent needs of existing customers. Then continuing on this long wave of value creation companies design and develop new products and services that enable them to reach these new markets and customers. Typical objectives for the innovation process are listed in Exhibit 22.5. They are increasing the number of new products, developing new markets and customers and decreasing the time taken to develop new products. Supporting performance measures are, respectively: percentage of sales from new products (also new product introductions versus competitors), percentage of sales from new markets and development cycle time (e.g. time to the market).

The *operations process* represents the short wave of value creation. It is concerned with producing and delivering existing products and services to customers. Objectives of the operation process listed in Exhibit 22.5 include, increasing process efficiency, increasing process quality, decreasing process

EXHIBIT 22.5 Internal business perspective objectives and measures

Objectives	Measures
Innovation:	
Increase the number of new products	Percentage of sales from new products
	New product introductions versus competitors
Develop new markets and customers	Percentage of sales from new markets
Decrease the time taken to develop new products	Development cycle time (time to the market)
Operations:	
Increase process efficiency	Output/inputs ratios
Increase process quality	Total quality costs as a percentage of sales
	Percentage of defective output
Decrease process cost	Unit cost trends
Decrease process time	Manufacturing cycle efficiency
Post-sales service:	
Increase service quality	Percentage of customer requests that are handled with a single call
Increase service efficiency	Output/inputs ratios
Decrease service time	Cycle time in resolving customer problems
Decrease service cost	Unit cost trends

cost and decreasing process time. Historically, the operations process has been the major focus of most of an organization's performance measurement system and many possible measures exist. Typical measures associated with each of the objectives for the operations process are listed in Exhibit 22.5.

Process efficiency measures tend to focus on output/input measures such as the production efficiency ratio (standard hours of output/actual hours of input) or capacity measures such as the capacity usage ratio (actual hours utilized/budgeted hours to be utilized). Quality measures include total quality costs as a percentage of sales derived from the cost of quality report (see Chapter 21), process parts per million defect rates, percentage of defective units and percentage of processes under statistical control. Process cost measures include unit cost trend measures relating to key processes and cycle time measures have evolved that support the objective of decreasing process time.

The total manufacturing cycle time consists of the sum of processing time, inspection time, wait time and move time. Only processing time adds value, and the remaining activities are non-value added activities. The aim is to reduce the time spent on non-value added activities and thus minimize manufacturing cycle time. A measure of cycle time that has been adopted is manufacturing cycle efficiency (MCE):

$$MCE = \frac{\text{processing time}}{\text{processing time} + \text{inspection time} + \text{wait time} + \text{move time}}$$

The generic performance measures that have been illustrated above relate to manufacturing operations but similar measures can be adopted for service companies. For example, many customers are forced to queue to receive a service. Companies that can eliminate waiting time for a service will find it easier to attract customers. The time taken to process mortgage and loan applications by financial institutions can involve a considerable amount of non-value added waiting time. Thus, reducing the time to process the applications enhances customer satisfaction and creates the potential for increasing sales revenues. Therefore service companies should also develop cycle time measures that support their specific customer processing activity objectives.

The *post-sales service process* represents the final item in the process value chain for the operations process perspective. It focuses on how responsive the organization is to customers after the product or service has been delivered. Post-sales services include warranty and repair activities, treatment of defects and returns and the process and administration of customer payments. Increasing quality, increasing efficiency and decreasing process time and cost are also objectives that apply to the post-sales service. Performance can be measured by some of the time, quality and cost measurements that have been suggested for the operations process. For example, service quality can be measured by first-pass yields defined as the percentage of customer requests that are handled with a single service call, rather than requiring multiple calls to resolve the problem. Increasing efficiency can be measured by appropriate output/input ratios and decreasing process time can be measured by cycle time where the process starts with the receipt of a customer request and ends with the ultimate resolution of the problem. Finally, the trend in unit costs can be used to measure the key post-sale service processes.

The learning and growth perspective

To ensure that an organization will continue to have loyal and satisfied customers in the future and continue to make excellent use of its resources, the organization and its employees must keep learning and developing. Hence there is a need for a perspective that focuses on the capabilities that an organization needs to create long-term growth and improvement. This perspective stresses the importance of organizations investing in their infrastructure (people, systems and organizational procedures) to provide the capabilities that enable the accomplishment of the other three perspectives' objectives. Kaplan and Norton have identified three major enabling factors for this perspective. They are: employee capabilities, information systems capabilities and the organizational climate for motivation, empowerment and alignment. Thus this perspective has three major core objectives: increase employee capabilities, increase information system capabilities and increase motivation, empowerment and alignment. The objectives and associated performance measures for this perspective are listed in Exhibit 22.6.

Core measures for the *employee capabilities* objective are concerned with employee satisfaction, employee retention and employee productivity. Many companies periodically measure employee satisfaction using surveys to derive employee satisfaction ratings. Employee retention can be measured by the annual percentage of key staff that resigns and many different methods can be used to measure employee productivity. A generic measure of employee productivity that can be applied throughout the organization and compared with different divisions is the sales revenue per employee.

For employees to be effective in today's competitive environment they need accurate and timely information on customers, internal processes and the financial consequences of their decisions. Measures of *strategic information system capabilities* suggested by Kaplan and Norton include

EXHIBIT 22.6 Learning and growth perspective objectives and measures

Objectives	Measures
Increase employee capabilities	Employee satisfaction survey ratings
	Annual percentage of key staff leaving
	Sales revenue per employee
Increase information system capabilities	Percentage of processes with real time feedback capabilities
	Percentage of customer-facing employees having on-line access to customer and product information
Increase motivation, empowerment and alignment	Number of suggested improvements per employee
	Number of suggestions implemented per employee
	Percentage of employees with personal goals aligned to the balanced scorecard
	Percentage of employees who achieve personal goals

THE BALANCED SCORECARD   **537**

REAL WORLD VIEWS 22.3

Balanced scorecard – a balanced scorecard variant at Siemens

The term 'balanced scorecard' may have been popularized by Kaplan and Norton, but their four perspectives on performance are not the only ones used by organizations in practice. For example, Siemens uses a balanced scorecard type approach to evaluate its performance. The company calls their reporting framework *One Siemens*. A summary of the framework on the company's website shows similar characteristics to a balanced scorecard. The first step shown is the company's vision: Siemens – The pioneer in: energy efficiency; industrial productivity; affordable and personalized healthcare; intelligent infrastructure solutions. This is followed by an approach which focuses on three strategic directions: 1 Focus on innovation-driven growth markets; 2 Get closer to our customers; and 3 Use the power of Siemens. Finally, performance measures are used to monitor progress. The graphic below depicts the frameworks as shown on the Siemens website (see the link below).

The three external sides of the framework show three metrics which are primarily financial, revenue growth, capital efficiency and capital structure. The internal portions show areas where non-financial metrics are likely to be more prevalent.

Questions

1 Can you think of a suitable performance metric under the heading 'Strengthen our portfolio'?

2 And a suitable metric under the heading 'Encourage lifelong learning and development'

References

http://www.siemens.com/about/pool/de/vision/one_siemens_brochure_e.pdf

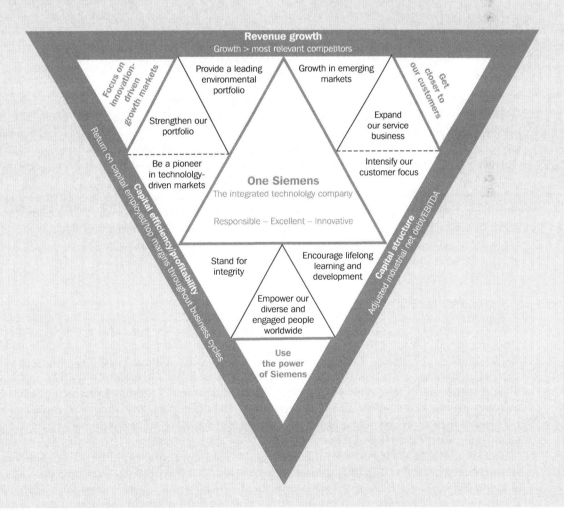

Courtesey of Siemens

percentage of processes with real time quality, cycle time and cost feedback capabilities available and the percentage of customer-facing employees having on-line access to customer and product information.

The number of suggested improvements per employee and the number of suggestions implemented per employee are proposed measures relating to the objective having *motivated and empowered employees*. Suggested measures relating to the objective of increasing individual and organizational alignment are the percentage of employees with personal goals aligned to the balanced scorecard and the percentage of employees who achieve personal goals.

Communicating and implementing the strategy

Look at Figure 22.1. You will see that, besides objectives and measures, targets and initiatives are also incorporated in the balanced scorecard. Target values should be established for the measures associated with each objective. In addition, the major initiatives for each objective should be described. The scorecard objectives, initiatives and measures become the means for conveying the strategy of the organization to its employees and managers. Responsibility centre objectives and measures should also be aligned with the scorecard objectives and measures.

For feedback reporting actual performance measures should also be added. The reward system should also be linked to the achievement of the scorecard objectives and measures. Failure to change the reward system may result in managers continuing to focus on short-term financial performance at the expense of concentrating on the strategic objectives of the scorecard. A USA study indicates that the balanced scorecard approach is linked to incentive compensation schemes. Epstein and Manzoni (1998) reported that 60 per cent of the 100 large USA organizations surveyed linked the balanced scorecard approach to incentive pay for their senior executives.

Lag and lead measures

The balanced scorecard is not simply a collection of critical performance measures. The performance measures are derived from a company's strategy and objectives. The balanced scorecard consists of two types of performance measures. The first consists of lag measures. These are the outcome measures that mostly fall within the financial perspective and are the results of past actions. Outcome (lag) measures are important because they indicate whether strategy is being implemented successfully with the desired financial consequences. Lag measures generally do not incorporate the effect of decisions when they are made. Instead, they show the financial impact of the decisions as their impact materializes and this can be long after the decisions were made. The second type of performance measures are lead measures that are the drivers of future financial performance. They cause the outcome. These tend to be the non-financial measures relating to the customer, internal business process and learning and growth perspectives.

Cause-and-effect relationships

A critical assumption of the balanced scorecard is that each performance measure is part of a cause-and-effect relationship involving a linkage from strategy formulation to financial outcomes. The chain of cause and effect should permeate all four perspectives of the balanced scorecard. Measures of organizational learning and growth are assumed to be the drivers of the internal business processes. The measures of these processes are in turn assumed to be the drivers of measures of customer perspective, while these measures are the driver of the financial perspective. The assumption that there is a cause-and-effect relationship is necessary because it allows the measurements relating to the non-financial perspectives to be used to predict future financial performance.

Kaplan and Norton (1996b) state that strategy can be viewed as a set of hypotheses about cause-and-effect, thus enabling a scorecard to tell the story of a business unit's strategy through a sequence of cause-and-effect relationships. The measurement system should make relationships (hypotheses) among objectives (and measures) in the various perspectives explicit so that they can be managed

FIGURE 22.2

Strategy map

and validated. Every measure selected for a balanced scorecard should be an element of a chain of cause-and-effect relationships that communicates the meaning of the business unit's strategy to the organization.

Cause-and-effect relationships can be expressed by a sequence of if-then statements. For example, a link between improved training of workers to perform multiple tasks and higher profits can be established through the following sequence of if-then statements:

> If employee skills are upgraded to perform multiple tasks by undertaking support activities such as duties relating to set-ups, minor repairs, preventive maintenance, quality inspection and operating different machines within the cell, then manufacturing processes can be redesigned by moving from a batch production functional layout to a cellular JIT manufacturing system. If the manufacturing processes are redesigned then cycle time will decrease; if cycle time decreases, then delivery time will decrease; if delivery time decreases, then customer satisfaction will increase; if customer satisfaction increases, then market share will increase; if market share increases, then sales revenues will increase; if sales revenues increase then profits will increase.

The strategy map shown in Figure 22.2 illustrates the process redesign strategy as described by the above sequence of if-then statements, and indicates that the chain of cause-and-effect relationships encompasses all four perspectives of the balanced scorecard. Also note that a performance measure can serve as both a lag indicator and a lead indicator. For example, cycle time is an outcome measure (i.e. a lag measure) arising from improving employee skills and redesigning processes. Improvements in cycle times also serve as a lead indicator in terms of its influence on delivery time measures.

Benefits and limitations of the balanced scorecard approach

The following is a summary of the major benefits that can be attributed to the balanced scorecard approach:

1 The scorecard brings together in a single report four different perspectives on a company's performance that relate to many of the disparate elements of the company's competitive agenda such as becoming customer oriented, shortening response time, improving quality, emphasizing teamwork, reducing new product launch times and managing for the long-term. Many organizations collect some performance measures relating to each of the four

perspectives but they are typically presented in several different large reports that often prove to be unhelpful because they suffer from information overload.

2 The approach provides a comprehensive framework for translating company's strategic goals into a coherent set of performance measures by developing the major goals for the four perspectives and then translating these goals into specific performance measures.

3 The scorecard helps managers to consider all the important operational measures together. It enables managers to see whether improvements in one area may have been at the expense of another.

4 The approach improves communications within the organization and promotes the active formulation and implementation of organizational strategy by making it highly visible through the linkage of performance measures to business unit strategy.

The balanced scorecard has also been subject to frequent criticisms. Most of them question the assumption of the cause-and-effect relationship on the grounds that they are too ambiguous and lack a theoretical underpinning or empirical support. The empirical studies that have been undertaken have failed to provide evidence on the underlying linkages between non-financial data and future financial performance (American Accounting Association Financial Accounting Standards Committee, 2002). Other criticisms relate to the omission of important perspectives, the most notable being the environmental/impact on society perspective (see Chapter 21) and an employee perspective. It should be noted, however, that Kaplan and Norton presented the four perspectives as a suggested framework rather than a constraining straitjacket. There is nothing to prevent companies adding additional perspectives to meet their own requirements but they must avoid the temptation of creating too many perspectives and performance measures since one of the major benefits of the balanced scorecard is its conciseness and clarity of presentation.

Our discussion relating to the core objectives and measures of the four perspectives has concentrated mainly on the manufacturing organizations. The balance scorecard, however, has been widely adopted in

EXHIBIT 22.7 Surveys of practice relating to balanced scorecard usage

Surveys indicate that even though the balanced scorecard did not emerge until the early 1990s it is now widely used in many countries throughout the world. A USA survey by Silk (1998) estimated that 60 per cent of Fortune 1000 firms have experimented with the balanced scorecard. In the UK a survey of 163 manufacturing companies (annual sales turnover in excess of £50 million) by Zuriekat (2005) reported that 30 per cent had implemented the balanced scorecard. Other studies in mainland Europe indicate significant usage. Pere (1999) reported a 31 per cent usage rate of companies in Finland with a further 30 per cent in the process of implementing it. In Sweden Kald and Nilsson (2000) reported that 27 per cent of major Swedish companies have implemented the approach. Oliveras and Amat (2002) report widespread usage in Spain and and Speckbacher, Bischof and Pfeiffer (2003) report a usage rate of 24 per cent in German-speaking countries (Germany, Austria and Switzerland). Major companies adopting the balanced scorecard include KPMG Peat Marwick, Allstate Insurance and AT&T (Chow, Haddad and Williamson, 1997).

In terms of the perspectives used Malmi (2001) conducted a study involving semi-structured interviews in 17 companies in Finland. He found that 15 companies used the four perspectives identified by Kaplan and Norton and two companies added a fifth – an employee's perspective. The UK study by Zuriekat (2005) reported that virtually all of the balanced scorecard respondents used the financial, customer and internal business process perspectives. Other perspectives used were learning and growth, employee, supplier and the environment. The respective percentage usage rates for the balance scorecard adopters were 39 per cent, 45 per cent, 65 per cent and 26 per cent. The study also reported that 35 per cent of the adopters linked their reward systems to the balanced scorecard. A study by Olve, Roy and Wetter (2000) found that 15–20 performance measures are customarily used.

service organizations. Exhibit 22.8 provides an illustration of potential balanced scorecard performance measures for different types of service organizations. You will also find it appropriate at this point to refer to Exhibit 22.7 which summarizes surveys of practice relating to the usage of the balanced scorecard. For a discussion of an alternative system of performance measurement in service organizations you should refer to Learning Note 22.1 in the digital support resources accompanying this book (see Preface for details).

EXHIBIT 22.8 Potential scorecard measures in different business sectors

	Generic	Health care	Airlines	Banking
Financial Strength (Looking back)	Market share Revenue growth Operating profits Return on equity Stock market performance Growth in margin	Patient census Unit profitability Funds raised for capital improvements Cost per care Per cent of revenue – new programmes	Revenue/cost per available passenger mile Mix of freight Mix of full fare to discounted Average age of fleet Available seat miles and related yields	Outstanding loan balances Deposit balances Non-interest income
Customer service and satisfaction (Looking from the outside in)	Customer satisfaction Customer retention Quality customer service Sales from new products/ services	Patient satisfaction survey Patient retention Patient referral rate Admittance or discharge timeliness Medical plan awareness	Lost bag reports per 10 000 passengers Denied boarding rate Flight cancellation rate Customer complaints filed with the DOT	Customer retention Number of new customers Number of products per customer Face time spent between loan officers and customers
Internal operating efficiency (Looking from the inside out)	Delivery time Cost Process quality Error rates on shipments Supplier satisfaction	Weekly patient complaints Patient loads Breakthroughs in treatments and medicines Infection rates Readmission rate Length of stay	Load factors (percentage of seats occupied) Utilization factors on aircraft and personnel On-time performance	Sales calls to potential customers Thank you calls or cards to new and existing customers Cross selling statistics
Learning and growth (Looking ahead)	Employee skill level Training availability Employee satisfaction Job retention Amount of overtime worked Amount of vacation time taken	Training hours per caregiver Number of peer reviewed papers published Number of grants awarded (NIH) Referring MDs Employee turnover rate	Employee absenteeism Worker safety statistics Performance appraisals completed Training programme hours per employee	Test results from training knowledge of product offerings, sales and service Employee satisfaction survey

SUMMARY

The following items relate to the learning objectives listed at the beginning of the chapter.

● **Describe the different elements of strategic management accounting.**

Despite the publicity that strategic management accounting has received there is still no comprehensive conceptual framework of what strategic management accounting is. Because of the lack of consensus on what constitutes strategic management accounting the elements that have been identified in the literature to characterize strategic management accounting have been described. Three elements can be identified: (a) the extension of traditional management accounting's internal focus to include external information about competitors; (b) the relationship between the strategic position chosen by a firm and the expected emphasis on management accounting; and (c) gaining competitive advantage by analyzing ways to decrease costs and/or enhance the differentiation of a firm's products through exploiting linkages in the value chain and optimizing cost drivers. Some authors have adopted a broader view of strategic management accounting that encompasses activity-based costing and the strategic cost management approaches described in the previous chapter.

● **Describe three competitive strategies that a firm can adopt to achieve sustainable competitive advantage and explain how they influence management accounting practices.**

Porter suggests that a firm has a choice of three generic strategies to achieve sustainable competitive advantage. A firm adopting a cost leadership strategy seeks to be the lowest-cost producer within the industry thus enabling it to compete on the basis of lower selling prices. A differentiation strategy applies when a firm seeks to offer products or services that are considered by its customers to be superior and unique relative to its competitors. Finally, a firm can adopt a focus strategy, which involves focusing on a narrow segment of the market that has special needs that are poorly served by other competitors. More emphasis is likely to be given to cost controls (e.g. standard costing) in firms pursing a low cost strategy whereas firms following a product differentiation strategy are likely to have a greater need for information about new product innovations, design cycle times and marketing cost analysis.

● **Describe the balanced scorecard.**

Recent developments in performance evaluation have sought to integrate financial and non-financial measures and assist in clarifying, communicating and managing strategy. The balanced scorecard attempts to meet these requirements. It requires that managers view the business from the following four different perspectives: (a) customer perspective (how do customers see us?); (b) internal business process perspective (what must we excel at?); (c) learning and growth perspective (can we continue to improve and create value?) and (d) financial perspective (how do we look to shareholders?). Organizations should articulate the major goals for each of the four perspectives and then translate these goals into specific performance measures. Each organization must decide what are its critical performance measures. The choice will vary over time and should be linked to the strategy that the organization is following.

● **Explain each of the four perspectives of the balanced scorecard.**

The financial perspective provides objectives and associated performance measures relating to the financial outcomes of past actions. Thus, it provides feedback on the success of pursuing the objectives identified for the other three perspectives. In the customer perspective managers identify the customer and market segments in which the businesses unit will compete. Objectives and performance measures should be developed within this perspective that track a business unit's ability to create satisfied and loyal customers in the targeted segments. They relate to market share, customer retention, new customer acquisition, customer satisfaction and customer profitability. In the internal business perspective, managers identify the critical internal processes for which the organization must excel in implementing its strategy. The internal business process objectives and measures should focus on the internal processes that will have the greatest impact on customer satisfaction and achieving the organization's financial objectives. The principal internal business processes include the innovation processes, operation processes and post-service sales processes. The final perspective on the balanced scorecard identifies the infrastructure that the business must build to create long-term growth and improvement. The following three categories have been identified as falling within this perspective: employee capabilities, information system capabilities and motivation, empowerment and alignment.

Provide illustrations of performance measures for each of the four perspectives.

Within the financial perspective examples include economic value added and residual income. Market share and customer satisfaction ratings are generic measures within the customer perspective. Typical internal business perspective measures include percentage of sales from new products (innovation processes), cycle time measures such as manufacturing cycle efficiency (operation processes) and percentage returns from customers (post-service sales processes). Measures of employee satisfaction represent generic measures within the learning and growth satisfaction.

Explain how the balanced scorecard links strategy formulation to financial outcomes.

The balanced scorecard philosophy translates an organization's vision and strategy into operational objectives and performance measures for each of the four perspectives. Each performance measure is part of a cause-and-effect relationship involving a linkage from strategy formulation to financial outcomes. Measures of organizational learning and growth are assumed to be the drivers of the internal business processes. The measures of these processes are in turn assumed to be the drivers of measures of customer perspective, while these measures are the driver of the financial perspective. Measurements relating to the non-financial perspectives are assumed to be predictors of future financial performance.

KEY TERMS AND CONCEPTS

Attribute costing The costing of specific product attributes that appeal to customers.

Balanced scorecard A strategic management tool that integrates financial and non-financial measures of performance in a single concise report, with the aim of incorporating performance measurement within the strategic management process.

Brand value budgeting The use of brand value as a basis for managerial decisions on the allocation of resources to support/enhance a brand position.

Brand value monitoring The financial valuation of a brand through the assessment of brand strength factors such as: leadership; stability; market; internationality; trend; support; and protection combined with historical brand profits.

Capacity usage ratio A measure of capacity calculated by dividing the actual hours utilized by the budgeted hours to be utilized.

Competitive position monitoring The analysis of competitor positions within an industry by assessing and monitoring trends in competitor sales, market shares and unit costs.

Competitor cost assessment The appraisal of a competitor's costs based on direct observation, mutual suppliers, mutual customers and ex-employees.

Competitor performance appraisal The appraisal of competitor performance based on published financial statements.

Customer perspective One of the perspectives considered on the balanced scorecard, focusing on how the organization appears to its customers.

Customer value propositions The attributes that drive core objectives and measures relating to the customer perspective of an organization.

Financial perspective One of the perspectives considered on the balanced scorecard, focusing on how the organization looks to shareholders.

Internal business perspective One of the perspectives considered on the balanced scorecard, focusing on what the organization needs to excel at.

Lag measures Outcome measures that mostly fall within the financial perspective and are the results of past actions

Lead measures Non-financial measures that are the drivers of future financial performance.

Learning and growth perspective One of the perspectives considered on the balanced scorecard, focusing on how the organization can continue to improve and create value.

Manufacturing cycle efficiency (MCE) A measure of cycle time that is calculated by dividing processing time by processing time plus the non-value-added activities of inspection time, wait time and move time.

Production efficiency ratio A process efficiency measure calculated by dividing the standard hours of output by the actual hours of input.

Strategic costing The use of cost data based on strategic and marketing information to develop and identify superior strategies that will sustain a competitive advantage.

Strategic management accounting The provision of information to support the strategic decisions in organizations.

Strategic positioning The choice of strategies an organization uses to achieve sustainable competitive advantage.

Strategic pricing The analysis of competitor positions within the industry by assessing and monitoring trends in competitor sales, market share, volume, unit costs and return on sales.

Value-chain analysis The analysis, coordination and optimization of the linked set of value-creating activities all the way from basic raw material sources for component suppliers through to the ultimate end-use product or service delivered to the customer.

Value-chain costing An activity-based costing approach where costs are allocated to activities required to design, procure, produce, market, distribute and service a product or service.

RECOMMENDED READING

For a more detailed discussion of strategic management accounting you should refer to the articles by Lord (1996), Roslender (1995, 1996), Roslender and Hart (2002, 2003) and Langfield-Smith (2008). Research relating to a survey of strategic management accounting practices is presented in Guilding, Craven and Tayles (2000). Kaplan and Norton designed the balanced scorecard and in their writings they describe its development and the experiences of companies that have implemented it. This chapter has summarized Kaplan and Norton's writings but for a more detailed description of their work you should refer to

the books they have written on the balance scorecard – *Translating Strategy into Action: The Balance Scorecard* (1996b) and *The Strategy-Focused Organization* (2001a). See also Kaplan and Norton (2001b) and Epstein and Manzoni (1998) for shorter articles on the balanced scorecard. You should refer to the writings of Norreklit (2000, 2003) for a critique of the balanced scorecard. For a broader description of performance measurement linked to strategy you should refer to Simons (1998). Finally, for a study of the purposes for which managers use the balanced scorecard see Wiersma (2009).

KEY EXAMINATION POINTS

Strategic management accounting and the balanced scorecard are relatively new topics so they have not been extensively examined in the past. Consequently, fewer past examination questions are included in this chapter. Strategic management accounting can be viewed as incorporating a wide range of topics. In addition, other approaches to performance measurement have been examined that do

not adopt a balanced scorecard perspective. Therefore some questions are included that do not relate directly to the chapter content. However, where questions are set on performance measurement you should try and adopt a balanced scorecard approach by emphasizing the need to integrate financial and non-financial measures and link performance measurement to an organization's strategies.

ASSESSMENT MATERIAL

The review questions are short questions that enable you to assess your understanding of the main topics included in the chapter. The numbers in parentheses provide you with the page numbers to refer to if you cannot answer a specific question.

The review problems are more complex and require you to relate and apply the content to various business problems. The problems are graded by their level of difficulty. Solutions to review problems that are not preceded by the term 'IM' are provided in a separate section at the end of the book. Solutions to problems preceded by the term 'IM' are provided in the *Instructor's Manual* accompanying this book that can be downloaded from the lecturer's digital support resources. Additional review problems with fully worked solutions are provided in the *Student Manual* that accompanies this book.

The digital support resources also include over 30 case study problems. The Brunswick Plastics case is relevant to the content of this chapter.

REVIEW QUESTIONS

22.1 Provide a definition of strategic management accounting. (p. 579)

22.2 Describe the three major strands of strategic management accounting that can be identified from the literature. (pp. 580–582)

22.3 How do different competitive strategies influence the emphasis that is given to particular management accounting techniques? (p. 581)

22.4 What is the purpose of a balanced scorecard? (p. 585)

22.5 Describe the four perspectives of the balanced scorecard. (pp. 584–585)

22.6 Explain the differences between lag measures and lead measures. (p. 592)

22.7 Explain what is meant by cause-and-effect relationships within the balanced scorecard. (p. 592)

22.8 Discuss the benefits and limitations of the balanced scorecard. (pp. 593–594)

22.9 Identify and describe the core objectives of the customer perspective. (pp. 587–588)

22.10 Describe the three principal internal business processes that can be included within the internal business perspective. (pp. 588–590)

22.11 What is manufacturing cycle efficiency? (p. 589)

22.12 Describe three principal categories within the learning and growth perspective. (pp. 590–592)

22.13 Provide examples of performance measures within each of the four perspectives of the balanced scorecard. (pp. 587–590)

REVIEW PROBLEMS

22.14 **Intermediate**. ZY is an airline operator. It is implementing a balanced scorecard to measure the success of its strategy to expand its operations. It has identified two perspectives and two associated objectives. They are:

Perspective	Objective
Growth	Fly to new destinations
Internal capabilities	Reduce time between touch down and take off

(i) For the 'growth perspective' of ZY, recommend a performance measure and briefly justify your choice of the measure by explaining how it will reflect the success of the strategy. *(2 marks)*

(ii) (For the 'internal capabilities perspective' of ZY, state data that you would gather and explain how this could be used to ensure the objective is met. *(2 marks)*

CIMA P1 Management Accounting: Performance Evaluation

22.15 **Advanced: Financial and non-financial performance measures**. BS Ltd provides consultancy services to small and medium sized businesses. Three types of consultants are employed offering administrative, data processing and marketing advice respectively. The consultants work partly on the client's premises and partly in BS Ltd premises, where chargeable development work in relation to each client contract will be undertaken. Consultants spend some time negotiating with potential clients attempting to secure contracts from them. BS Ltd has recently implemented a policy change which allows for a number of follow-up (remedial) hours at the client's premises after completion of the contract in order to eliminate any problems which have arisen in the initial stages of operation of the system.

Contract negotiation and remedial work hours are not charged directly to each client. BS Ltd carries out consultancy for new systems and also offers advice on existing systems which a client

may have introduced before BS Ltd became involved. BS Ltd has a policy of retaining its consultancy staff at a level of 60 consultants on an ongoing basis.

Additional information for the year ended 30 April is as follows:

(i) BS Ltd invoices clients £75 per chargeable consultant hour.

(ii) Consultant salaries are budgeted at an average per consultant of £30 000 per annum. Actual salaries include a bonus for hours in excess of budget paid for at the budgeted average rate per hour.

(iii) Sundry operating costs (other than consultant salaries) were budgeted at £3 500 000. Actual was £4 100 000.

(iv) BS Ltd capital employed (start year) was £6 500 000.

(v) Table 1 shows an analysis of sundry budgeted and actual quantitative data.

Required:

(a) (i) Prepare an analysis of actual consultancy hours for the year ended 30 April which shows the increase or decrease from the standard/allowed non-chargeable hours. This increase or decrease should be analyzed to show the extent to which it may be shown to be attributable to a change from standard in: 1. standard chargeable hours; 2. remedial advice hours; 3. contract negotiation hours; 4. other non-chargeable hours. *(13 marks)*

(ii) Calculate the total value of each of 1 to 4 in (a) above in terms of chargeable client income per hour. *(4 marks)*

(b) BS Ltd measure business performance in a number of ways. For each of the undernoted measures, comment on the performance of BS Ltd using quantitative data from the question and your answer to (a) to assist in illustrating your answer:

(i) Financial performance

(ii) Competitive performance

(iii) Quality of service
(iv) Flexibility
(v) Resource utilization
(vi) Innovation. *(18 marks)*

Table 1: BS Ltd Sundry statistics for year ended 30 April

	Budget	Actual
Number of consultants:		
Administration	30	23
Data processing	12	20
Marketing	18	17
Consultants hours analysis:		
contract negotiation hours	4 800	9 240
remedial advice hours	2 400	7 920
other non-chargeable hours	12 000	22 440
general development work hours (chargeable)	12 000	6 600
customer premises contract hours	88 800	85 800
Gross hours	120 000	132 000
Chargeable hours analysis:		
new systems	70%	60%
existing systems advice	30%	40%
Number of clients enquiries received:		
new systems	450	600
existing systems advice	400	360
Number of client contracts worked on:		
new systems	180	210
existing systems advice	300	288
Number of client complaints	5	20
Contracts requiring remedial advice	48	75

ACCA Information for Control and Decision Making

22.16 Advanced: Financial and non-financial performance measurement in a service organization. The owners of *The Eatwell Restaurant* have diversified business interests and operate in a wide range of commercial areas. Since buying the restaurant in 2007 they have carefully recorded the data below.

Recorded data for The Eatwell Restaurant (2008–2011)

	2008	2009	2010	2011
Total meals served	3 750	5 100	6 200	6 700
Regular customers attending weekly	5	11	15	26
Number of items on offer per day	4	4	7	9
Reported cases of food poisoning	4	5	7	7
Special theme evenings introduced	0	3	9	13
Annual operating hours with no customers	380	307	187	126
Proposals submitted to cater for special events	10	17	29	38
Contracts won to cater for special events	2	5	15	25
Complimentary letters from satisfied customers	0	4	3	6
Average number of customers at peak times	18	23	37	39
Average service delay at peak time (mins)	32	47	15	35
Maximum seating capacity	25	25	40	40
Weekly opening hours	36	36	40	36
Written complaints received	8	12	14	14
Idle time	570	540	465	187
New meals introduced during the year	16	8	27	11

Financial data	£	£	£	£
Average customer spend on wine	3	4	4	7
Total turnover	83 000	124 500	137 000	185 000
Turnover from special events	2 000	13 000	25 000	55 000
Profit	11 600	21 400	43 700	57 200
Value of food wasted in preparation	1 700	1 900	3 600	1 450
Total turnover of all restaurants in locality	895 000	1 234 000	980 000	1 056 000

Required:

(a) Assess the overall performance of the business and submit your comments to the owners. They wish to compare the performance of the restaurant with their other business interests and require your comments to be grouped into the key areas of performance such as those described by Fitzgerald and Moon.
(See Learning Note 22.1 on the digital support resources.) *(14 marks)*

(b) Identify any additional information that you would consider of assistance in assessing the performance of *The Eatwell Restaurant* in comparison with another restaurant. Give reasons for your selection and explain how they would relate to the key performance area categories used in (a). *(6 marks)*

ACCA Advanced Performance Management

22.17 Advanced: Performance evaluation and the balanced scorecard. The Royal Laurel Hospital (RLH) and The King Hardy Hospital (KHH) are government funded institutions which are managed by the Glasburgh Trust. The following information is available for the year ended 31 May.

	RLH Actual	RLH Budget	KHH Actual
Total inpatients	37 000	36 500	40 000
Number of inpatients waiting >5 weeks for admission	3 330	365	320
Number of inpatients waiting >11 weeks for admission	740	0	0
Total outpatients	44 000	43 800	44 000
Number of outpatients waiting >5 weeks for treatment	4 400	2 190	352
Number of outpatients waiting >11 weeks for treatment	1 320	438	220
Number of outpatients waiting >13 weeks for treatment	220	0	0
Achievement (per cent) of target maximum waiting time of 2 weeks for admission to Rapid Access Chest Pains Clinic	70	98	100
Number of emergency admissions	300	400	300
Number of 12 hour 'trolley' waits for emergency admissions	4	0	0
Achievement (per cent) of target of 4 hours or less time spent in accident and Emergency ward	96	98	100
Number of complaints received	1 620	803	420
Number of complaints responded to within 25 days	1 539	803	416
Number of deaths (all inpatients)	600	730	800
Infection control – number of instances of infections reported	2	6	0
Number of drug administration errors	80	100	20

Number of staff shortages	80	60	20
Staff productivity measure (number of patient days per staff member)	8.4	7.4	9.2
Number of times of Government or agency staff usage	80	60	20
Bed occupancy (number of inpatient bed days)	138 750	146 000	134 320
Theatre utilization (per cent)	?	?	?
Per cent of inpatients requiring a single operation	80%	80%	80%
Number of operations performed	29 008	?	31 840
Revenue from clinical and non-clinical activities ($m)	54.2	55.2	60.2
Medical staff costs ($m)	22.3	22.2	19.6
Other staff costs ($m)	5.5	5.5	4.0
Income and expenditure surplus margin	(1.0)	0.0	4.0
Number of days cash in hand	31	30	35

Additional information

1. Both hospitals were in operation for 365 days during the year
2. Each hospital has 42 wards, each of which accommodates 10 beds
3. RLH budgeted that each inpatient would require a stay of four days and nights in hospital.
4. Each hospital has ten operating theatres in each of which an average of nine operations per day were undertaken.
5. No outpatient required an operation during the year.
6. The management of the trust uses a 'balanced scorecard' approach in order to assess the performance of each hospital. Their balanced scorecard has four dimensions which are as follows:
   (i) Access to services
   (ii) Clinical
   (iii) Efficiency
   (iv) Financial management.

Required:
Prepare a report to the management of the Glasburgh Trust which:

(a) Critically assesses, on the basis of the above information, the performance of both hospitals for the year ended 31 May. You should use the four dimensions to perform your assessment as per note (6) above; *(20 marks)*
(b) Evaluates the balanced scorecard used by the Glasburgh Trust and provides recommendations which would improve its usefulness as a performance measurement tool. *(11 marks)*

4 professional marks will be awarded in question 1 for the appropriateness of the format and presentation of the report and the quality of its content. *(4 marks)*

ACCA Advanced Performance Management

22.18 Advanced: Critical success factors. The 'Care For Dogs Company' (CFD) is a very profitable organization which was established in 1998. CFD offers accommodation, care and supervision for pet dogs owned by inhabitants of Barkland.

CFD provides temporary accommodation for dogs whose owners are unable to care for them due to holidays, work commitments, illness etc. As part of the service offered to dog owners, CFD collects and returns dogs at the beginning and end of all dog stays.

When CFD was formed, the directors created a mission statement which was 'to provide very high value for money to all of our clients'.

The directors have always attempted to manage CFD in a socially responsible manner. Indeed, they are now considering the creation of a 'Dog Sanctuary' for homeless dogs which would involve an allocation of 20 per cent of the total accommodation available for dogs to the Dog Sanctuary. The Dog Sanctuary would accommodate homeless dogs until such time as a new owner was found for them. CFD would not receive any revenue whatsoever in respect of any homeless dog.

Required:

(a) (i) Discuss the purpose, potential benefits and potential problems of mission statements; *(8 marks)*
(ii) Advise the directors of CFD regarding the appropriateness of its mission statement. *(3 marks)*
(b) Explain the term 'critical success factor' and discuss THREE critical success factors for CFD clearly highlighting a key performance indicator for each critical success factor. *(6 marks)*
(c) Excluding the number of complaints by clients, identify and briefly explain THREE quantitative non-financial performance measures that could be used to assess the 'quality of service' provided by CFD. *(3 marks)*

ACCA Advanced Performance Management

22.19 Advanced; Strategic factors influencing an investment decision. The Global Hotel Group (GHG) operates hotels in most of the developed countries throughout the world. The directors of GHG are committed to a policy of achieving 'growth' in terms of geographical coverage and are now considering building and operating another hotel in Tomorrowland. Tomorrowland is a developing country which is situated 3 000 kilometres from the county in which GHG's nearest hotel is located.

The managing director of GHG recently attended a seminar on 'the use of strategic and economic information in planning organizational performance'.

He has called a board meeting to discuss the strategic and economic factors which should be considered before a decision is made to build the hotel in Tomorrowland.

Required:

(a) Discuss the strategic and economic factors which should be considered before a decision is made to build the hotel. *(14 marks)*
(b) GHG has always used local labour to build and subsequently operate hotels. The directors of GHG are again considering employing a local workforce not only to build the hotel but also to operate it on a daily basis.

Required:
Explain TWO ways in which the possibility of cultural differences might impact on the performance of a local workforce in building and operating a hotel in Tomorrowland. *(6 marks)*
(20 marks)

ACCA Advanced Performance Management

22.20 Advanced: Performance measurement in non-profit organizations.

(a) The absence of the profit measure in not-for-profit (NFP) organizations causes problems for the measurement of their efficiency and effectiveness.

You are required to explain:

(i) Why the absence of the profit measure should be a cause of the problems referred to? *(9 marks)*
(ii) How these problems extend to activities within business entities which have a profit motive. Support your answer with examples. *(4 marks)*
(b) A public health clinic is the subject of a scheme to measure its efficiency and effectiveness. Amongst a number of factors, the 'quality of care provided' has been included as an aspect of the clinic's service to be measured. Three features of 'quality of care provided' have been listed:

clinic's adherence to appointment times;

patients' ability to contact the clinic and make appointments without difficulty;

the provision of a comprehensive patient health monitoring programme.

You are required to:

(i) suggest a set of quantitative measures which can be used to identify the effective level of achievement of each of the features listed; *(9 marks)*

(ii) indicate how these measures could be combined into a single 'quality of care' measure. *(3 marks)*

CIMA Stage 4 Management Accounting – Control and Audit

22.21 Advanced. You are responsible for managing the preparation of all revenue and cost budgets for a motor component manufacturer. You are aware that the external environment has a significant impact on the business activity and financial performance of your company and that the current information systems are underdeveloped and ineffective in this respect.

Required:

(a) identify which aspects of the external environment you are likely to consider and give reasons for your choice; *(10 marks)*

(b) identify where you might find the relevant sources of information; *(5 marks)*

(c) suggest how an external environment information system could be introduced into your company. *(5 marks)*

ACCA P3 Performance Measurement

IM22.1 Advanced. Management accounting practice has traditionally focused on techniques to assist organizational decision-making and cost control. In concentrating on the internal environment, the management accounting function has been criticized for not addressing the needs of senior management to enable effective strategic planning. In particular, the criticism has focused on inadequate provision of information which analyses the organization's exposure to environmental change and its progress towards the achievement of corporate objectives.

Requirement:

Explain how strategic management accounting can provide information which meets the requirements of senior managers in seeking to realize corporate objectives. *(20 marks)*

CIMA Stage 4 Strategic Management Accountancy and Marketing

IM22.2 Advanced. The new manufacturing environment is characterized by more flexibility, a readiness to meet customers' requirements, smaller batches, continuous improvements and an emphasis on quality.

In such circumstances, traditional management accounting performance measures are, at best, irrelevant and, at worst, misleading.

You are required:

(a) to discuss the above statement, citing specific examples to support or refute the views expressed; *(10 marks)*

(b) to explain in what ways management accountants can adapt the services they provide to the new environment.

(7 marks)

CIMA Stage 3 Management Accounting Techniques

IM22.3 Advanced. Research on performance measurement in service businesses, reported in *Management Accounting*, found that 'performance measurement often focuses on easily quantifiable aspects such as cost and productivity whilst neglecting other dimensions which are important to competitive success'.

You are required:

(a) to explain what 'other dimensions' you think are important measures of performance; *(8 marks)*

(b) to describe what changes would be required to traditional information systems to deal with these 'other dimensions'.

(9 marks)

CIMA Stage 3 Management Accounting

IM22.4 Advanced. The 'balanced scorecard' approach aims to provide information to management to assist strategic policy formulation and achievement. It emphasizes the need to provide the user with a set of information which addresses all relevant areas of performance in an objective and unbiased fashion.

Requirements:

(i) Discuss in general terms the main types of information which would be required by a manager to implement this approach to measuring performance; and

(ii) comment on three specific examples of performance measures which could be used in a company in a service industry, for example a firm of consultants. *(10 marks)*

CIMA Stage 4 Strategic Financial Management

IM22.5 Advanced: Design and discussion of key performance indicators for DIY outlets and regional companies. Duit plc has recently acquired Ucando Ltd which is a regional builders' merchants/DIY company with three outlets all within a radius of 40 miles. Duit plc is building up its national coverage of outlets. Duit plc has set up regional companies each with its own board of directors responsible to the main board situated in London.

It is expected that eventually each regional company will have between 10 and 20 outlets under its control. A regional company will take over control of the three Ucando Ltd outlets. Each outlet will have its own manager, and new ones have just been appointed to the three Ucando Ltd outlets.

The outlets' managers will be allowed to hire and fire whatever staff they need and the introduction of a head count budget is being considered by head office. Each outlet manager is responsible for his own sales policy, pricing, store layout, advertising, the general running of the outlet and the purchasing of goods for resale, subject to the recommendations below. Duit plc's policy is that all outlet managers have to apply to the regional board for all items of capital expenditure greater than £500, while the regional board can sanction up to £100 000 per capital expenditure project.

The outlets will vary in size of operations, and this will determine the number of trade sales representatives employed per outlet. There will be a minimum of one trade sales representative per outlet under the direction of the outlet manager. Each manager and representative will be entitled to a company car.

Outlet sales are made to both retail and trade on either cash or credit terms. Debtor and cash control is the responsibility of regional office. Cash received is banked locally, and immediately credited to the head office account. Credit sales invoices are raised by the outlet with a copy sent to regional office. Within each outlet it is possible to identify the sales origin, e.g. timber yard, saw mill, building supplies, kitchen furniture, etc.

Timber for resale is supplied to an outlet on request from stocks held at regional office or direct from the ports where Duit (Timber Importers) Ltd has further stocks. Duit Kitchens Ltd provides kitchen furniture that the outlets sell. Duit plc also has a small factory making windows, doors and frames which are sold through the outlets. When purchasing other products for resale, the outlet is requested to use suppliers with which head office has negotiated discount buying arrangements. All invoices for outlet purchases and overheads are passed by the respective outlet manager before being paid by regional office. In existing Duit outlets a perpetual inventory system is used, with a complete physical check once a year.

Information concerning last year's actual results for one of Ucando Ltd's outlets situated at Birport is given below:

Birport DIY outlet
Trading and profit and loss account for year to 31 March

	(£)	(£)
Sales (1)		1 543 000
Less cost of sales		1 095 530
Prime gross margin (29%)		447 470
Less:		
Wages (2)	87 400	
Salaries (3)	45 000	
Depreciation:		
equipment (4)	9 100	
buildings	3 500	
vehicles (3 cars)	6 500	
Vehicle running expenses	6 170	
Leasing of delivery lorry	6 510	
Lorry running expenses	3 100	
Energy costs	9 350	
Telephone/stationery	9 180	
Travel and entertaining	3 490	
Commission on sales	7 770	
Bad debts written off	9 440	
Advertising	25 160	
Repairs	6 000	
Rates, insurance	13 420	
Sundry expenses	10 580	
Delivery expenses	7 400	269 070
	Net profit	£178 400
	(11.56%)	

Position at 31 March

	(£)
Debtors	100 900
Stock	512 000

Notes:

1 Sales can be identified by till code: cash/credit, trade/retail, timber, kitchen furniture, frames, heavy building supplies, light building supplies, sawmill etc.
2 Workforce distributed as follows: timber yard (3), sawmill (1), sales (7), general duties (1), administration (3).
3 Paid to sales representatives (2), assistant manager, manager.
4 Equipment used in sales area, sawmill, yard.

Requirements:

(a) Describe a cost centre, a profit centre and an investment centre and discuss the problems of and benefits from using them for management accounting purposes. *(7 marks)*
(b) Suggest key performance indicators which can be used either individually or jointly by each member of the management team for the regional outlet network, i.e. those in the regional office, the outlets and their departments, in a responsibility reporting system for their evaluation purposes. *(6 marks)*
(c) Justify the key performance indicators that you have suggested in (b) incorporating, where appropriate, reference to whether the individuals or entities are being treated as cost, profit or investment centres. *(6 marks)*
(d) Design a pro forma monthly report without figures which can be used by both the outlet manager for his management and

control needs and by the regional board to evaluate the outlet. The report can include two or more sections if you wish. Provide a brief explanation for the format chosen. *(6 marks)*

Note: The manufacturing companies and the importing company report direct to the main board.

ICAEW Management Accounting

IM22.6 **Advanced: Financial and non-financial performance measures**. Scotia Health Consultants Ltd provides advice to clients in medical, dietary and fitness matters by offering consultation with specialist staff.

The budget information for the year ended 31 May is as follows:

(i) Quantitative data as per Appendix.
(ii) Clients are charged a fee per consultation at the rate of: medical £75; dietary £50 and fitness £50.
(iii) Health foods are recommended and provided only to dietary clients at an average cost to the company of £10 per consultation. Clients are charged for such health foods at cost plus 100 per cent mark-up.
(iv) Each customer enquiry incurs a variable cost of £3, whether or not it is converted into a consultation.
(v) Consultants are *each* paid a fixed annual salary as follows: medical £40 000; dietary £28 000; fitness £25 000.
(vi) Sundry other fixed cost: £300 000.

Actual results for the year to 31 May incorporate the following additional information:

(i) Quantitative data as per Appendix.
(ii) A reduction of 10 per cent in health food costs to the company per consultation was achieved through a rationalization of the range of foods made available.
(iii) Medical salary costs were altered through dispensing with the services of two full-time consultants and sub-contracting outside specialists as required. A total of 1900 consultations were sub-contracted to outside specialists who were paid £50 per consultation.
(iv) Fitness costs were increased by £80 000 through the hire of equipment to allow sophisticated cardiovascular testing of clients.
(v) New computer software has been installed to provide detailed records and scheduling of all client enquiries and consultations. This software has an annual operating cost (including depreciation) of £50 000.

Required:

(a) Prepare a statement showing the financial results for the year to 31 May in tabular format. This should show:

(i) the budget and actual gross margin for each type of consultation and for the company;
(ii) the actual net profit for the company;
(iii) the budget and actual margin (£) per consultation for each type of consultation. (Expenditure for each expense heading should be shown in (i) and (ii) as relevant.)

(15 marks)

(b) Suggest ways in which each of the undernoted performance measures (1 to 5) could be used to supplement the financial results calculated in (a). You should include relevant quantitative analysis from the Appendix below for each performance measure:

1. Competitiveness; 2 Flexibility; 3. Resource utilization;
4. Quality; 5. Innovation. *(20 marks)*

Appendix
Statistics relating to the year ended 31 May

	Budget	Actual
Total client enquiries:		
new business	50 000	80 000
repeat business	30 000	20 000
Number of client consultations:		
new business	15 000	20 000
repeat business	12 000	10 000
Mix of client consultations:		
medical	6 000	5 500
		(note 1)
dietary	12 000	10 000
fitness	9 000	14 500
Number of consultants employed:		
medical	6	4
		(note 1)
dietary	12	12
fitness	9	12
Number of client complaints:	270	600

Note 1: Client consultations *includes* those carried out by outside specialists. There are now four full-time consultants carrying out the remainder of client consultations.

ACCA Paper 9 Information for Control and Decision Making

IM22.7 Advanced: Critical success factors. The directors of The Healthy Eating Group (HEG), a successful restaurant chain, which commenced trading in 1998, have decided to enter the sandwich market in Homeland, its country of operation. It has set up a separate operation under the name of Healthy Sandwiches Co (HSC). A management team for HSC has been recruited via a recruitment consultancy which specializes in food sector appointments. Homeland has very high unemployment and the vast majority of its workforce has no experience in a food manufacturing environment. HSC will commence trading on 1 January 2013.

The following information is available:

1 HSC has agreed to make and supply sandwiches to agreed recipes for the Superior Food Group (SFG) which owns a chain of supermarkets in all towns and cities within Homeland. SFG insists that it selects the suppliers of the ingredients that are used in making the sandwiches it sells and therefore HSC would be unable to reduce the costs of the ingredients used in the sandwiches. HSC will be the sole supplier for SFG.

2 The number of sandwiches sold per year in Homeland is 625 million. SFG has a market share of 4 per cent.

3 The average selling price of all sandwiches sold by SFG is $2.40. SFG wishes to make a mark-up of $33\frac{1}{3}$ per cent on all sandwiches sold. 90 per cent of all sandwiches sold by SFG are sold before 2 pm each day. The majority of the remaining 10 per cent are sold after 8 pm. It is the intention that all sandwiches are sold on the day that they are delivered into SFG's supermarkets.

4 The finance director of HSC has estimated that the average cost of ingredients per sandwich is $0.70. All sandwiches are made by hand.

5 Packaging and labelling costs amount to $0.15 per sandwich.

6 Fixed overheads have been estimated to amount to $5 401 000 per annum. Note that fixed overheads include all wages and salaries costs as all employees are subject to fixed term employment contracts.

7 Distribution costs are expected to amount to 8 per cent of HSC's revenue.

8 The finance director of HSC has stated that he believes the target sales margin of 32 per cent can be achieved, although he is concerned about the effect that an increase in the cost of all ingredients would have on the forecast profits (assuming that all other revenue/cost data remains unchanged).

9 The existing management information system of HEG was purchased at the time that HEG commenced trading. The directors are now considering investing in an enterprise resource planning system (ERPS).

Required:

(a) Using only the above information, show how the finance director of HSC reached his conclusion regarding the expected sales margin and also state whether he was correct to be concerned about an increase in the price of ingredients.
(5 marks)

(b) Explain FIVE critical success factors to the performance of HSC on which the directors must focus if HSC is to achieve success in its marketplace.
(10 marks)

(c) Explain how the introduction of an ERPS could impact on the role of management accountants.
(5 marks)

(20 marks)
ACCA P5 Performance Management

25
THE APPLICATION OF LINEAR PROGRAMMING TO MANAGEMENT ACCOUNTING

LEARNING OBJECTIVES   After studying this chapter you should be able to:

- describe the situations when it may be appropriate to use linear programming;

- explain the circumstances when the graphical method can be used;

- use graphical linear programming to find the optimum output levels;

- formulate the initial linear programming model using the simplex method;

- explain the meaning of the term shadow prices.

In Chapter 9 we considered how accounting information should be used to ensure that scarce resources (also known as bottleneck activities) are efficiently allocated. To refresh your memory you should now refer back to Example 9.3 and Appendix 9.1, relating to throughput accounting and the optimum use of bottleneck activities, to ascertain how the optimum production programme was determined. You will see that where a scarce resource exists, that has alternative uses, the contribution per unit should be calculated for each of these uses. The available capacity of this resource is then allocated to the alternative uses on the basis of the contribution per scarce resource.

Where more than one scarce resource exists, the optimum production programme cannot easily be established by the process described in Chapter 9. In such circumstances there is a need to resort to linear programming techniques to establish the optimum production programme. Our objective in this chapter is to examine how linear programming techniques can be applied to determine the optimum production programme in situations where more than one scarce resource exists. Initially we shall assume that only two products are produced so that the optimum output can be determined using a two-dimensional graph. Where more than two products are produced the optimal output cannot easily be determined using the graphical method. Instead, the optimal output can be determined using a non-graphical approach that is known as the simplex method.

Linear programming is a topic that is sometimes included in operational management courses rather than management accounting courses. You should therefore check your course content to ascertain if you will need to read this chapter.

LINEAR PROGRAMMING

Linear programming is a powerful mathematical technique that can be applied to the problem of rationing limited facilities and resources among many alternative uses in such a way that the optimum benefits can be derived from their utilization. It seeks to find a feasible combination of output that will maximize or minimize the objective function. The objective function refers to the quantification of an objective, and usually takes the form of maximizing profits or minimizing costs. Linear programming may be used when relationships can be assumed to be linear and where an optimal solution does in fact exist.

To comply with the linearity assumption, it must be assumed that the contribution per unit for each product and the utilization of resources per unit are the same whatever quantity of output is produced and sold within the output range being considered. It must also be assumed that units produced and resources allocated are infinitely divisible. This means that an optimal plan that suggests we should produce 94.38 units is possible. However, it will be necessary to interpret the plan as a production of 94 units.

Let us now apply this technique to the problem outlined in Example 25.1, where there is a labour restriction plus a limitation on the availability of materials and machine hours. The contributions per scarce resource are as follows:

	Product Y (£)	Product Z (£)
Labour	2.33 (£14/6 hours)	2.00 (£16/8 hours)
Material	1.75 (£14/8 units)	4.00 (£16/4 units)
Machine capacity	3.50 (£14/4 hours)	2.67 (£16/6 hours)

EXAMPLE 25.1
Multiple resource constraint problem

The LP company currently makes two products. The standards per unit of product are as follows:

Product Y	(£)	(£)	Product Z	(£)	(£)
Product Y			Product Z		
Standard selling price		110	Standard selling price		118
Less standard costs:			Less standard costs:		
Materials (8 units at £4)	32		Materials (4 units at £4)	16	
Labour (6 hours at £10)	60		Labour (8 hours at £10)	80	
Variable overhead			Variable overhead		
(4 machine hours at £1)	4		(6 machine hours at £1)	6	
		96			102
Contribution		14	Contribution		16

During the next accounting period, the availability of resources are expected to be subject to the following limitations:

Labour	2880 hours
Materials	3440 units
Machine capacity	2760 hours

The marketing manager estimates that the maximum sales potential for product Y is limited to 420 units. There is no sales limitation for product Z. You are asked to advise how these limited facilities and resources can best be used so as to gain the optimum benefit from them.

This analysis shows that product Y yields the largest contribution per labour hour, and product Z yields the largest contribution per unit of scarce materials, but there is no clear indication of how the quantity of scarce resources should be allocated to each product. Linear programming should be used in such circumstances.

The procedure is first, to formulate the problem algebraically, with Y denoting the number of units of product Y and Z the number of units of product Z that are manufactured by the company. Second, we must specify the objective function, which in this example is to maximize contribution (denoted by C), followed by the input constraints. We can now formulate the linear programming model as follows:

$$\text{Maximize } C = 14Y + 16Z \text{ subject to}$$
$$8Y + 4Z \leq 3440 \text{ (material constraint)}$$
$$6Y + 8Z \leq 2880 \text{ (labour constraint)}$$
$$4Y + 6Z \leq 2760 \text{ (machine capacity constraint)}$$
$$0 \leq Y \leq 420 \text{ (maximum and minimum sales limitation)}$$
$$Z \geq 0 \text{ (minimum sales limitation)}$$

In this model, 'maximize C' indicates that we wish to maximize contribution with an unknown number of units of Y produced, each yielding a contribution of £14 per unit, and an unknown number of units of Z produced, each yielding a contribution of £16. The labour constraint indicates that six hours of labour are required for each unit of product Y that is made, and eight hours for each unit of product Z. Thus (6 hours × Y) + (8 hours × Z) cannot exceed 2880 hours. Similar reasoning applies to the other inputs.

Because linear programming is nothing more than a mathematical tool for solving constrained optimization problems, nothing in the technique itself ensures that an answer will 'make sense'. For example, in a production problem, for some very unprofitable product, the optimal output level may be a negative quantity, which is clearly an impossible solution. To prevent such nonsensical results, we must include a non-negativity requirement, which is a statement that all variables in the problem must be equal to or greater than zero. We must therefore add to the model in our example the constraint that Y and Z must be greater than or equal to zero, i.e. $Z \geq 0$ and $0 \leq Y \leq 420$. The latter expression indicates that sales of Y cannot be less than zero or greater than 420 units. The model can be solved graphically, or by the simplex method. When no more than two products are manufactured, the graphical method can be used, but this becomes impracticable where more than two products are involved, and it is then necessary to resort to the simplex method.

GRAPHICAL METHOD

Taking the first *constraint for the materials* input $8Y + 4Z \leq 3440$ means that we can make a maximum of 860 units of product Z when production of product Y is zero. The 860 units is arrived at by dividing the 3440 units of materials by the four units of material required for each unit of product Z. Alternatively, a maximum of 430 units of product Y can be made (3440 units divided by eight units of materials) if no materials are allocated to product Z. We can therefore state that

$$\text{when } Y = 0, \ Z = 860$$
$$\text{when } Z = 0, \ Y = 430$$

These items are plotted in Figure 25.1, with a straight line running from $Z = 0, Y = 430$ to $Y = 0, Z = 860$. Note that the vertical axis represents the number of units of Y produced and the horizontal axis the number of units of Z produced.

The area to the left of line $8Y + 4Z \leq 3440$ contains all possible solutions for Y and Z in this particular situation, and any point along the line connecting these two outputs represents the maximum combinations of Y and Z that can be produced with not more than 3440 units of materials. Every point to the right of the line violates the material constraint.

The *labour constraint* $6Y + 8Z \leq 2880$ indicates that if production of product Z is zero, then a maximum of 480 units of product Y can be produced (2880/6), and if the output of Y is zero then 360 units of Z (2880/8) can be produced. We can now draw a second line Y = 480, Z = 0 to Y = 0, Z = 360, and this is illustrated in Figure 25.2. The area to the left of line $6Y + 8Z \leq 2880$ in this figure represents all the possible solutions that will satisfy the labour constraint.

The *machine input constraint* is represented by Z = 0, Y = 690 and Y = 0, Z = 460, and the line indicating this constraint is illustrated in Figure 25.3. The area to the left of the line $4Y + 6Z \leq 2760$ in this figure represents all the possible solutions that will satisfy the machine capacity constraint.

The final constraint is that the *sales output* of product Y cannot exceed 420 units. This is represented by the line $Y \leq 420$ in Figure 25.4, and all the items below this line represent all the possible solutions that will satisfy this sales limitation.

FIGURE 25.1

Constraint imposed by limitations of materials

FIGURE 25.2

Constraint imposed by limitations of labour

FIGURE 25.3

Constraint imposed by machine capacity

It is clear that any solution that is to fit *all* the constraints must occur in the shaded area ABCDE in Figure 25.5, which represents Figures 25.1–25.4 combined together. The point must now be found within the shaded area *ABCDE* where the contribution C is the greatest. The maximum will occur at one of the corner points *ABCDE*. The objective function is $C = 14Y + 16Z$, and a random contribution value is chosen that will result in a line for the objective function falling within the area *ABCDE*.

If we choose a random total contribution value equal to £2240, this could be obtained from producing 160 units (£2240/£14) of Y at £14 contribution per unit or 140 units of Z (£2240/£16) at a contribution of £16 per unit. We can therefore draw a line $Z = 0$, $Y = 160$ to $Y = 0$, $Z = 140$. This is represented by the dashed line in Figure 25.5. Each point on the dashed line represents all the output combinations of Z and Y that will yield a total contribution of £2240. The dashed line is extended to the right until it touches the last corner of the boundary *ABCDE*. This is the optimal solution and is at point *C*, which indicates an output of 400 units of Y (contribution £5600) and 60 units of Z (contribution £960), giving a total contribution of £6560.

The logic in the previous paragraph is illustrated in Figure 25.6. The shaded area represents the feasible production area *ABCDE* that is outlined in Figure 25.5, and parallel lines represent possible contributions,

FIGURE 25.4

Constraint imposed by sales limitation of product Y

FIGURE 25.5

Combination of Figures 25.1–25.4

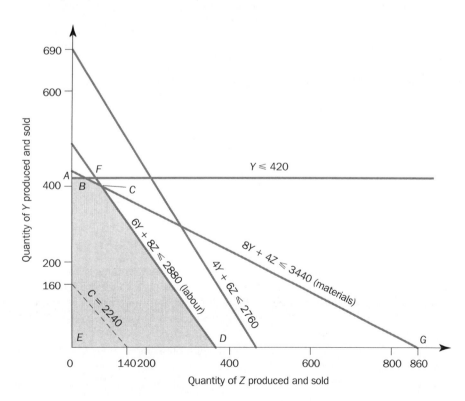

FIGURE 25.6

Combination levels from different potential
combinations of products Y and Z

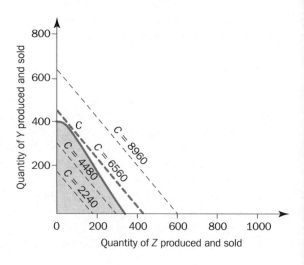

which take on higher values as we move to the right. If we assume that the firm's objective is to maximize total contribution, it should operate on the highest contribution curve obtainable. At the same time, it is necessary to satisfy the production constraints, which are indicated by the shaded area in Figure 25.6. You will see that point C indicates the solution to the problem, since no other point within the feasible area touches such a high contribution line.

It is difficult to ascertain from Figure 25.5 the exact output of each product at point C. The optimum output can be determined exactly by solving the simultaneous equations for the constraints that intersect at point C:

$$8Y + 4Z = 3440 \qquad (25.1)$$

$$6Y + 8Z = 2880 \qquad (25.2)$$

We can now multiply equation (25.1) by 2 and equation (25.2) by 1, giving

$$16Y + 8Z = 6880 \qquad (25.3)$$

$$6Y + 8Z = 2880 \qquad (25.4)$$

Subtracting equation (25.4) from equation (25.3) gives

$$10Y = 4000$$

and so

$$Y = 400$$

We can now substitute this value for Y onto equation (25.3), giving

$$(16 \times 400) + 8Z = 6880$$

and so

$$Z = 60$$

You will see from Figure 25.5 that the constraints that are binding at point C are materials and labour. It might be possible to remove these constraints and acquire additional labour and materials resources by paying a premium over and above the existing acquisition cost. How much should the company be prepared to pay? To answer this question, it is necessary to determine the optimal use from an additional unit of a scarce resource.

We shall now consider how the optimum solution would change if an additional unit of materials were obtained. You can see that if we obtain additional materials, the line $8Y + 4Z \leq 3440$ in Figure 25.5 will shift upwards and the revised optimum point will fall on line CF. If one extra unit of materials is obtained, the constraints $8Y + 4Z \leq 3440$ and $6Y + 8Z \leq 2880$ will still be binding, and the new optimum plan can be determined by solving the following simultaneous equations:

$$8Y + 4Z = 3441 \text{ (revised materials constraint)}$$
$$6Y + 8Z = 2880 \text{ (unchanged labour constraint)}$$

The revised optimal output when the above equations are solved is 400.2 units of Y and 59.85 units of Z. Therefore the planned output of product Y should be increased by 0.2 units, and planned production of Z should be reduced by 0.15 units. This optimal response from an independent marginal increase in a resource is called the marginal rate of substitution. The change in contribution arising from obtaining one additional unit of materials is as follows:

	(£)
Increase in contribution from Y (0.2 × £14)	2.80
Decrease in contribution of Z (0.15 × £16)	(2.40)
Increase in contribution	0.40

Therefore the value of an additional unit of materials is £0.40. The value of an independent marginal increase of scarce resource is called the opportunity cost or shadow price. We shall be considering these terms in more detail later in the chapter. You should note at this stage that for materials purchased in excess of 3440 units the company can pay up to £0.40 over and above the present acquisition cost of materials of £4 and still obtain a contribution towards fixed costs from the additional output.

From a practical point of view, it is not possible to produce 400.2 units of Y and 59.85 units of Z. Output must be expressed in single whole units. Nevertheless, the output from the model can be used to calculate the revised optimal output if additional units of materials are obtained. Assume that 100 additional units of materials can be purchased at £4.20 per unit from an overseas supplier. Because the opportunity cost (£0.40) is in excess of the additional acquisition cost of £0.20 per unit (£4.20 – £4), the company should purchase the extra materials. The marginal rates of substitution can be used to calculate the revised optimum output. The calculation is:

$$\text{Increase } Y \text{ by 20 units } (100 \times 0.2 \text{ units})$$
$$\text{Decrease } Z \text{ by 15 units } (100 \times 0.15 \text{ units})$$

Therefore the revised optimal output is 420 outputs (400 + 20) of Y and 35 units (60 – 15) of Z. You will see later in this chapter that the substitution process outlined above is applicable only within a particular range of material usage.

We can apply the same approach to calculate the opportunity cost of labour. If an additional labour hour is obtained, the line $6Y + 8Z = 2880$ in Figure 25.5 will shift to the right, and the revised optimal point will fall on line CG. The constraints $8Y + 4Z = 3440$ and $6Y + 8Z = 2880$ will still be binding, and the new optimum plan can be determined by solving the following simultaneous equations:

$$8Y + 4Z = 3440 \text{ (unchanged materials constraint)}$$
$$6Y + 8Z = 2881 \text{ (revised labour constraint)}$$

The revised optimal output when the above equations are solved is 399.9 units of Y and 60.2 units of Z. Therefore the planned output of product Y should be decreased by 0.1 units and planned production of Z should be increased by 0.2 units. The opportunity cost of a scarce labour hour is:

	(£)
Decrease in contribution from Y (0.1 × £14)	(1.40)
Increase in contribution from Z (0.2 × £16)	3.20
Increase in contribution (opportunity cost)	1.80

SIMPLEX METHOD

Where more than two products can be manufactured using the scarce resources available, the optimum solution cannot be established from the graphical method. In this situation a mathematical programming technique known as the simplex method must be used. This method also provides additional information on opportunity costs and marginal rates of substitution that is particularly useful for decision-making, and also for planning and control. Some courses only include the graphical method in their curriculum so you should check your course curriculum to ascertain whether you need to read the following sections that relate to the simplex method.

The simplex method involves many tedious calculations, but there are standard spreadsheet packages that will complete the task within a few minutes. The aim of this chapter is not therefore to delve into these tedious calculations but to provide you with an understanding of how the simplex linear programming model should be formulated for an input into a spreadsheet package and also how to interpret the optimal solution from the output from the spreadsheet package. However, if you are interested in how the optimal solution is derived you should refer to Learning Note 25.1 in the digital support resources accompanying this book (see Preface for details) but do note that examination questions do not require you to undertake the calculations. They merely require you to formulate the initial model and interpret the output derived from the model. Example 25.1 is now used to illustrate the simplex method.

To apply the simplex method, we must first formulate a model that does not include any *inequalities*. This is done by introducing what are called slack variables to the model. Slack variables are added to a linear programming problem to account for any constraint that is unused at the point of optimality, and one slack variable is introduced for each constraint. In our example, the company is faced with constraints on materials, labour, machine capacity and maximum sales for product Y. Therefore S_1 is introduced to represent unused material resources, S_2 represents unused labour hours, S_3 represents unused machine capacity and S_4 represents unused potential sales output. We can now express the model for Example 25.1 in terms of equalities rather than inequalities:

$$\text{Maximize } C = 14Y + 16Z$$
$$8Y + 4Z + S_1 = 3440 \text{ (materials constraint)}$$
$$6Y + 8Z + S_2 = 2880 \text{ (labour constraint)}$$
$$4Y + 6Z + S_3 = 2760 \text{ (machine capacity constraint)}$$
$$1Y + S_4 = 420 \text{ (sales constraint for product } Y)$$

For labour (6 hours × Y) + (8 hours × Z) plus any unused labour hours (S_2) will equal 2880 hours when the optimum solution is reached. Similar reasoning applies to the other production constraints. The sales limitation indicates that the number of units of Y sold plus any shortfall on maximum demand will equal 420 units.

We shall now express all the above equations in matrix form (sometimes described as in tableau form), with the slack variables on the left-hand side:

Initial matrix

Quantity	Y	Z	
$S_1 = 3440$	−8	−4	(1) (material constraint)
$S_2 = 2880$	−6	−8	(2) (labour constraint)
$S_3 = 2760$	−4	−6	(3) (machine hours constraint)
$S_4 = 420$	−1	0	(4) (sales constraint)
$C = 0$	+14	+16	(5) contribution

Note that the quantity column in the matrix indicates the resources available or the slack that is not taken up when production is zero. For example, the S_1 row of the matrix indicates that 3440 units of materials are available when production is zero. Column Y indicates that eight units of materials, six labour hours and four machine hours are required to produce one unit of product Y, and this will reduce the potential sales of Y by one. You will also see from column Y that the production of one unit of Y will yield

£14 contribution. Similar reasoning applies to column Z. Note that the entry in the contribution row (i.e. the C row) for the quantity column is zero because this first matrix is based on nil production, which gives a contribution of zero.

The simplex method involves the application of matrix algebra to generate a series of matrices until a final matrix emerges that represents the optimal solution based on the initial model. The final matrix containing the optimal solution is shown below.

Final matrix

Quantity	S_1	S_2	
$Y = 400$	$-\frac{1}{5}$	$+\frac{1}{10}$	(1)
$Z = 60$	$+\frac{3}{20}$	$-\frac{1}{5}$	(2)
$S_3 = 800$	$-\frac{1}{10}$	$+\frac{4}{5}$	(3)
$S_4 = 20$	$+\frac{1}{5}$	$-\frac{1}{10}$	(4)
$C = 6560$	$-\frac{2}{5}$	$-1\frac{4}{5}$	(5)

Interpreting the final matrix

The final matrix can be interpreted using the same approach that was used for the initial matrix but the interpretation is more complex. The contribution row (equation 5) of the final matrix contains only negative items, which signifies that the optimal solution has been reached. The quantity column for any products listed on the left hand side of the matrix indicates the number of units of the product that should be manufactured when the optimum solution is reached. 400 units of Y and 60 units of Z should therefore be produced, giving a total contribution of £6560. This agrees with the results we obtained using the graphical method. *When an equation appears for a slack variable, this indicates that unused resources exist.* The final matrix therefore indicates that the optimal plan will result in 800 unused machine hours (S_3) and an unused sales potential of 20 units for product Y (S_4). The fact that there is no equation for S_1 and S_2 means that these are the inputs that are fully utilized and that limit further increases in output and profit.

The S_1 column (materials) of the final matrix indicates that the materials are fully utilized. (*Whenever resources appear as column headings in the final matrix, this indicates that they are fully utilized.*) So, to obtain a unit of materials, the column for S_1 indicates that we must alter the optimum production programme by increasing production of product Z by $\frac{3}{20}$ of a unit and decreasing production of product Y by $\frac{1}{5}$ of a unit. The effect of removing one scarce unit of material from the production process is summarized in Exhibit 25.1.

Look at the machine capacity column of Exhibit 25.1. If we increase production of product Z by $\frac{3}{20}$ of a unit then more machine hours will be required, leading to the available capacity being reduced by $\frac{9}{10}$ of an hour. Each unit of product Z requires six machine hours, so $\frac{3}{20}$ of a unit will require $\frac{9}{10}$ of an hour

EXHIBIT 25.1 The effect of removing 1 unit of material from the optimum production programme

	S_3 Machine capacity	S_4 Sales of Y	S_1 Materials	S_2 Labour	Contribution (£)
Increase product Z by $\frac{3}{20}$ of a unit	$-\frac{9}{10}(\frac{3}{20}\times 6)$	–	$-\frac{3}{5}(\frac{3}{20}\times 4)$	$-1\frac{1}{5}(\frac{3}{20}\times 8)$	$+2\frac{2}{5}(\frac{3}{20}\times 16)$
Decrease product Y by $\frac{1}{5}$ of a unit	$+\frac{4}{5}(\frac{1}{5}\times 4)$	$+\frac{1}{5}$	$+1\frac{3}{5}(\frac{1}{5}\times 8)$	$+1\frac{1}{5}(\frac{1}{5}\times 6)$	$-2\frac{4}{5}(\frac{1}{5}\times 14)$
Net effect	$-\frac{1}{10}$	$+\frac{1}{5}$	$+1$	Nil	$-\frac{2}{5}$

($\frac{3}{20} \times 6$). Decreasing production of product Y by $\frac{1}{5}$ unit will release $\frac{4}{5}$ of a machine hour, given that one unit of product Y requires four machine hours. The overall effect of this process is to reduce the available machine capacity by $\frac{1}{10}$ of a machine hour. Similar principles apply to the other calculations presented in Exhibit 25.1.

Let us now reconcile the information set out in Exhibit 25.1 with the materials column (S_1) of the final matrix. The S_1 column of the final matrix indicates that to release one unit of materials from the optimum production programme we should increase the output of product Z by $\frac{3}{20}$, and decrease product Y by $\frac{1}{5}$ of a unit. This substitution process will lead to the unused machine capacity being reduced by $\frac{1}{10}$ of a machine hour, an increase in the unfulfilled sales demand of product Y (S_4) by $\frac{1}{5}$ of a unit and a reduction in contribution of £$\frac{2}{5}$. All this information is obtained from column S_1 of the final matrix, and Exhibit 25.1 provides the proof. Note that Exhibit 25.1 also proves that the substitution process that is required to obtain an additional unit of materials releases exactly 1 unit. In addition, Exhibit 25.1 indicates that the substitution process for labour gives a net effect of zero, and so no entries appear in the S_1 column of the final matrix in respect of the labour row (i.e. S_2).

The contribution row of the final matrix contains some vital information for the accountant. The figures in this row represent opportunity costs (also known as shadow prices) for the scarce factors of materials and labour. For example, the reduction in contribution from the loss of one unit of materials is £$\frac{2}{5}$ (£0.40) and from the loss of one labour hour is £$1\frac{4}{5}$ (£1.80). Our earlier studies have indicated that this information is vital for decision-making, and we shall use this information again shortly to establish the relevant costs of the resources.

The proof of the opportunity costs can be found in Exhibit 25.1. From the contribution column we can see that the loss of one unit of materials leads to a loss of contribution of £0.40.

Substitution process when additional resources are obtained

Management may be able to act to remove a constraint which is imposed by the shortage of a scarce resource. For example, the company might obtain substitute materials or it may purchase the materials from an overseas supplier. A situation may therefore occur where resources additional to those included in the model used to derive the optimum solution are available. In such circumstances the marginal rates of substitution specified in the final matrix can indicate the optimum use of the additional resources. However, when additional resources are available it is necessary to *reverse* the signs in the final matrix. The reason is that the removal of one unit of materials from the optimum production programme requires that product Z be increased by $\frac{3}{20}$ of a unit and product Y decreased by $\frac{1}{5}$ of a unit.

If we then decide to return released materials to the optimum production programme, we must reverse this process – that is, increase product Y by $\frac{1}{5}$ of a unit and reduce product Z by $\frac{3}{20}$ of a unit. The important point to remember is that *when considering the response to obtaining additional resources over and above those specified in the initial model, the signs of all the items in the final matrix must be reversed.*

We can now establish how we should best use an additional unit of scarce materials. Inspection of the final matrix indicates that product Y should be increased by $\frac{1}{5}$ of a unit and product Z reduced by $\frac{3}{20}$, giving an additional contribution of £0.40. Note that this is identical with the solution we obtained using the graphical method.

Note that this process will lead to an increase in machine hours of $\frac{1}{10}$ hour (S_3) and a decrease in potential sales of product Y by $\frac{1}{5}$ (S_4). Similarly, if we were to obtain an additional labour hour, we should increase production of Z by $\frac{1}{5}$ of a unit and decrease production of product Y by $\frac{1}{10}$ of a unit, which would yield an additional contribution of £1.80. These are the most efficient uses that can be obtained from additional labour and material resources. From a practical point of view, decisions will not involve the use of fractions; for example, the LP company considered here might be able to obtain 200 additional labour hours; the final matrix indicates that optimal production plan should be altered by increasing production of product Z by 40 units (200 × $\frac{1}{5}$ of a unit) and decreasing production of product Y by 20 units. This process will lead to machine capacity being reduced by 160 hours and potential sales of product Y being increased by 20 units.

Note that examination questions often present the final matrix in a different format to the approach illustrated in this chapter. You should refer to the Key examination points section at the end of the chapter for an explanation of how you can reconcile the alternative approaches.

USES OF LINEAR PROGRAMMING

Calculation of relevant costs

The calculation of relevant costs is essential for decision-making. When a resource is scarce, alternative uses exist that provide a contribution. An opportunity cost is therefore incurred whenever the resource is used. The relevant cost for a scarce resource is calculated as:

$$acquisition\ cost\ of\ resource + opportunity\ cost.$$

When more than one scarce resource exists, the opportunity cost should be established using linear programming techniques. Note that the opportunity costs of materials and labour are derived from the final row (monetary figures expressed in fractions) of the third and final matrix. Let us now calculate the relevant costs for the resources used by the LP company. The costs are as follows:

$$materials = £4.40\,(£4\ acquisition\ cost\ plus\ £0.40\ opportunity\ cost)$$
$$labour = £11.80\,(£10\ acquisition\ cost\ plus\ £1.80\ opportunity\ cost)$$
$$variable\ overheads = £1.00\,(£1\ acquisition\ cost\ plus\ zero\ opportunity\ cost)$$
$$fixed\ overheads = nil$$

Because variable overheads are assumed to vary in proportion to machine hours, and because machine hours are not scarce, no opportunity costs arise for variable overheads. Fixed overheads have not been included in the model, since they do not vary in the short term with changes in activity. The relevant cost for fixed overheads is therefore zero.

REAL WORLD VIEWS 25.1

Uses of linear programming – linear programming in the supply chain

SAP, the global leader in enterprise resource planning (ERP) systems, offers several tools to help a business find an optimal solution to scheduling and planning problems. The advanced planner and optimizer (APO) offers solutions to help firms find the best and most cost effective solution in areas like demand planning, production planning, transportation planning and supply network planning. The later module, Supply network planning (SNP) allows planners to determine optimal production plans, distribution plans and purchasing plans. According to SAP's documentation, the SNP module offer an optimizer which will obtain the most cost effective solution based on the following criteria:

- production, procurement, storage and transportation costs;
- costs for increasing the production capacity, storage capacity, transportation capacity and handling capacity;
- costs for violating (falling below) the safety stock level;
- costs for late delivery;
- stock-out costs.

The optimizer uses linear programming method to take account of all planning factors simultaneously. According to the SAP's documentation, as more constraints are activated, the optimization problem becomes more complex and takes more time to complete. The SNP module offers several variants on linear programming to allow maximum applicability to varying problem scenarios.

Questions

1 Can you think of factors that might affect production, procurement, storage or transportation costs as referred to above?

2 Given the apparently large number of factors taken into account by the optimizer in SNP, do you think the business and/or the system can run the optimizer programme frequently?

References

http://help.sap.com/saphelp_apo/helpdata/en/36/2eb514a309102de10000009b38f9b6/content.htm
http://help.sap.com/saphelp_scm41/helpdata/en/09/707b37db6bcd66e10000009b38f889/content.htm

Selling different products

Let us now assume that the company is contemplating selling a modified version of product Y (called product L) in a new market. The market price is £160 and the product requires ten units input of each resource. Should this product L be manufactured? Conventional accounting information does not provide us with the information necessary to make this decision. Product L can be made only by restricting output of Y and Z, because of the input constraints, and we need to know the opportunity costs of releasing the scarce resources to this new product. Opportunity costs were incorporated in our calculation of the relevant costs for each of the resources, and so the relevant information for the decision is as follows:

	(£)	(£)
Selling price of product L		160
Less relevant costs:		
Materials (10 × 4.40)	44	
Labour (10 × 11.80)	118	
Variable overhead (10 × 1.00)	10	
Contribution		172
		(−12)

Total planned contribution will be reduced by £12 for each unit produced of product L.

Maximum payment for additional scarce resources

Opportunity costs provide important information in situations where a company can obtain additional scarce resources, but only at a premium. How much should the company be prepared to pay? For example, the company may be able to remove the labour constraint by paying overtime. The final matrix indicates that the company can pay up to an additional £1.80 over and above the standard wage rate for each hour worked in excess of 2880 hours and still obtain a contribution from the use of this labour hour. The total contribution will therefore be improved by any additional payment below £1.80 per hour. Similarly, LP will improve the total contribution by paying up to £0.40 in excess of the standard material cost for units obtained in excess of 3440 units. Hence the company will increase short-term profits by paying up to £11.80 for each additional labour hour in excess of 2880 hours and up to £4.40 for units of material that are acquired in excess of 3440 units.

Control

Opportunity costs are also important for cost control. For example, material wastage is reflected in an adverse material usage variance. The responsibility centre should therefore be identified not only with the acquisition cost of £4 per unit but also with the opportunity cost of £0.40 from the loss of one scarce unit of materials. This process highlights the true cost of the inefficient usage of scarce resources and encourages responsibility heads to pay special attention to the control of scarce factors of production. This approach is particularly appropriate where a firm has adopted an optimized production technology (OPT) strategy (see Chapter 9) because variance arising from bottleneck operations will be reported in terms of opportunity cost rather than acquisition cost.

Managing constraints

When scarce resources are fully utilized they are referred to as bottleneck operations/resources. It is important that managers seek to increase the efficiency and capacity of bottleneck operations. Capacity can be increased by working overtime on the bottleneck, subcontracting some of the work that is undertaken by bottleneck operations, investing in additional capacity at the bottleneck and implementing business process improvements such as business process engineering and total quality management processes described in Chapter 21.

Capital budgeting

Linear programming can be used to determine the optimal investment programme when capital rationing exists. This topic tends not to form part of the management accounting curriculum for most courses. You should refer to Learning Note 25.2 if you wish to study how linear programming can be used in capital investment appraisal.

Sensitivity analysis

Opportunity costs are of vital importance in making management decisions, but production constraints do not exist permanently, and therefore opportunity costs cannot be regarded as permanent. There is a need to ascertain the range over which the opportunity cost applies for each input. This information can be obtained from the final matrix. For materials we merely examine the negative items for column S_1 in the final matrix and divide each item into the quantity column as follows:

$$Y = 400/(-\tfrac{1}{5}) = -2000$$
$$S_3 = 800/(-\tfrac{1}{10}) = -8000$$

The number closest to zero in this calculation (namely −2000) indicates by how much the availability of materials used in the model can be reduced. Given that the model was established using 3440 units of materials, the lower limit of the range is 1440 units (3440 − 2000). The upper limit is determined in a similar way. We divide the positive items in column S_4 into the quantity column as follows:

$$Z = 60/\tfrac{3}{20} = 400$$
$$S_4 = 20/\tfrac{1}{5} = 100$$

The lower number in the calculation (namely 100) indicates by how much the materials can be increased. Adding this to the 3440 units of materials indicates that the upper limit of the range is 3540 units. The opportunity cost and marginal rates of substitution for materials therefore apply over the range of 1440 to 3540 units.

Let us now consider the logic on which these calculations are based. The lower limit is determined by removing materials from the optimum production programme. We have previously established from the final matrix and Exhibit 25.1 that removing one unit of material from the optimum production programme means that product Y will be reduced by $\tfrac{1}{5}$ and machine capacity will be reduced by $\tfrac{1}{10}$ of an hour. Since the final matrix indicates an output of 400 units of product Y, this reduction can only be carried out 2000 times (400/$\tfrac{1}{5}$) before the process must stop. Similarly, 800 hours of machine capacity are still unused, and the reduction process can only be carried out 8000 times (800/$\tfrac{1}{10}$) before the process must stop. Given the two constraints on reducing materials, the first constraint that is reached is the reduction of product Y. The planned usage of materials can therefore be reduced by 2000 units before the substitution process must stop. The same reasoning applies (with the signs reversed) in understanding the principles for establishing the upper limit of the range.

Similar reasoning can be applied to establish that the opportunity cost and marginal rates of substitution apply for labour hours over a range of 2680 to 3880 hours. For any decisions based on scarce inputs outside the ranges specified a revised model must be formulated and a revised final matrix produced. From this matrix revised opportunity costs and marginal rates of substitution can be established.

SUMMARY

The following items relate to the learning objectives listed at the beginning of the chapter.

● **Describe the situations when it may be appropriate to use linear programming.**

Conventional limiting factor analysis (see Chapter 9) should be used when there is only one scarce factor. Linear programming can be used to determine the production programme that maximizes total contribution when there is more than one scarce input factor.

● **Explain the circumstances when the graphical method can be used.**

The graphical method can be used with two products. Where more than two products are involved the simplex method should be used.

● **Use graphical linear programming to find the optimum output levels.**

Production/sales quantities for one of the two products are labelled on the horizontal axis and the vertical axis is used for the other product. Combinations of the maximum output (based on the two products) from fully utilizing each resource, and any sales volume limitations, are plotted on the graph. A series of contribution lines are plotted based on the potential output levels for each product that will achieve a selected total contribution. The optimum output levels are derived at the point where the feasible production region touches the highest contribution line. The process is illustrated in Figure 25.5 using the data presented in Example 25.1.

● **Formulate the initial linear programming model using the simplex method.**

Assuming that the objective function is to maximize total contribution the objective function should initially be specified expressed in terms of the contributions per unit for each product. Next the constraints should be listed in equation form with slack variables introduced to ensure that model is specified in terms of equalities rather than inequalities. The initial matrix is prepared by converting the linear programming model into a matrix format. The process is illustrated using Example 25.1.

● **Explain the meaning of the term shadow prices.**

The simplex method of linear programming generates shadow prices (also known as opportunity costs) for each of those scarce resources that are fully utilized in the optimum production programme. The shadow prices represent the reduction in total contribution that will occur from the loss of one unit of a scarce resource. Conversely, they represent the increase in total contribution that will occur if an additional unit of the scarce resource can be obtained.

KEY TERMS AND CONCEPTS

Bottleneck activities Activities or operations where constraints apply arising from demand exceeding available capacity.

Bottleneck operations/resources Scarce resources that are fully utilized and therefore can present limiting factors.

Linear programming A mathematical technique used to determine how to employ limited resources to achieve optimum benefits.

Marginal rate of substitution The optimal response from an independent marginal increase in a resource.

Objective function In linear programming, the objective to be minimized or maximized.

Opportunity cost The value of an independent marginal increase of scarce resource, also known as the shadow price.

Shadow price The value of an independent marginal increase of scarce resource, also known as the opportunity cost.

Simplex method A mathematical technique used in linear programming to solve optimization problems.

Slack variable A variable that is added to a linear programming problem to account for any constraint that is unused at the point of optimality, and so turn an inequality into an equality.

KEY EXAMINATION POINTS

A common error is to state the objective function in terms of profit per unit. This is incorrect, because the fixed cost per unit is not constant. The objective function should be expressed in terms of contribution per unit. You should note that there are several ways of formulating the matrices for a linear program-

ming model. The approach adopted in this chapter was to formulate the first matrix with positive contribution signs and negative signs for the slack variable equations. The optimal solution occurs when the signs in the contribution row are all negative. Sometimes examination questions are set that adopt the opposite procedure. That is, the signs are the reverse of the approach presented in this chapter.

For an illustration of this approach see review problem IM 25.7. A more recent approach is to present the output from the model as a computer printout. You should refer to the solution to review problem 25.14 to make sure you understand this approach.

Most examination questions include the final matrix and require you to interpret the figures. You may also be required to formulate the initial model. It is most unlikely that you will be required to complete the calculations and prepare the final matrix. However, you may be asked to construct a graph and calculate the marginal rates of substitution and opportunity costs.

ASSESSMENT MATERIAL

The review questions are short questions that enable you to assess your understanding of the main topics included in the chapter. The numbers in parentheses provide you with the page numbers to refer to if you cannot answer a specific question.

The review problems are more complex and require you to relate and apply the content to various business problems. The problems are graded by their level of difficulty. Solutions to review problems that are not preceded by the term 'IM' are provided in a separate section at the end of the book. Solutions to problems preceded by the term 'IM' are provided in the *Instructor's Manual* accompanying this book that can be downloaded from the lecturer's digital support resources. Additional review problems with fully worked solutions are provided in the *Student Manual* that accompanies this book.

REVIEW QUESTIONS

25.1 Describe the situations when it may be appropriate to use linear programming. (pp. 655–656)

25.2 Explain what is meant by the term 'objective function'. (p. 656)

25.3 What is the feasible production area? (p. 659)

25.4 What is the marginal rate of substitution? (p. 661)

25.5 Explain what is meant by the term 'shadow price'. (p. 661)

25.6 Explain the circumstances when it is appropriate to use the simplex method. (p. 662)

25.7 What are slack variables? (p. 662)

25.8 Provide illustrations of how the information derived from linear programming can be applied to a variety of management accounting problems. (pp. 665–667)

25.9 Explain how sensitivity analysis can be applied to the output of a linear programming model. (p. 667)

REVIEW PROBLEMS

25.10 Intermediate. Taree Limited uses linear programming to establish the optimal production plan for the production of its two products, A and U, given that it has the objective of minimizing costs. The following graph has been established bearing in mind the various constraints of the business. The clear area indicates the feasible region.

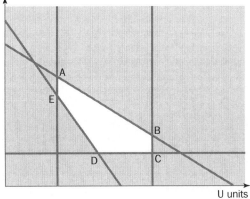

A units

U units

Which points are most likely to give the optimal solution?

(a) A and B only
(b) A, B and C only
(c) D and E only
(d) B, D and E only.

ACCA – Financial Information for Management

25.11 Advanced: Optimal output and calculation of shadow prices using graphical approach. Brass Ltd produces two products, the Masso and the Russo. Budgeted data relating to these products on a unit basis for August are as follows:

	Masso (£)	Russo (£)
Selling price	150	100
Materials	80	30
Salesmen's commission	30	20

Each unit of product incurs costs of machining and assembly. The total capacity available in August is budgeted to be 700 hours of machining and 1000 hours of assembly, the cost of this capacity being fixed at £7000 and £10 000 respectively for the month, whatever the level of usage made of it. The number of hours required in each of these departments to complete one unit of output is as follows:

	Masso	Russo
Machining	1.0	2.0
Assembly	2.5	2.0

Under the terms of special controls recently introduced by the government in accordance with EEC requirements, selling prices are fixed and the maximum permitted output of either product in August is 400 units (i.e. Brass Ltd may produce a maximum of 800 units of product). At the present controlled selling prices the demand for the products exceeds this considerably.

You are required:

(a) to calculate Brass Ltd's optimal production plan for August, and the profit earned; *(10 marks)*

(b) to calculate the value to Brass Ltd of an independent marginal increase in the available capacity for each of machining and assembly, assuming that the capacity of the other department is not altered and the output maxima continue to apply; *(10 marks)*

(c) to state the principal assumptions underlying your calculations in (a) above, and to assess their general significance. *(5 marks)*

ICAEW Management Accounting

25.12 Advanced: Optimal output and calculation of shadow prices using graphical approach. Higgins Co (HC) manufactures and sells pool cues and snooker cues. The cues both use the same type of good quality wood (ash) which can be difficult to source in sufficient quantity. The supply of ash is restricted to 5 400 kg per period. Ash costs $40 per kg.

The cues are made by skilled craftsmen (highly skilled labour) who are well known for their workmanship. The skilled craftsmen take years to train and are difficult to recruit. HC's craftsmen are generally only able to work for 12 000 hours in a period. The craftsmen are paid $18 per hour.

HC sells the cues to a large market. Demand for the cues is strong, and in any period, up to 15 000 pool cues and 12 000 snooker cues could be sold. The selling price for pool cues is $41 and the selling price for snooker cues is $69.

Manufacturing details for the two products are as follows:

	Pool cues	Snooker cues
Craftsmen time per cue	0.5 hours	0.75 hours
Ash per cue	270 g	270 g
Other variable costs per cue	$1.20	$4.70

HC does not keep inventory.

Required:

(a) Calculate the contribution earned from each cue. *(2 marks)*

(b) Determine the optimal production plan for a typical period assuming that HC is seeking to maximise the contribution earned. You should use a linear programming graph (using the graph paper provided), identify the feasible region and the optimal point and accurately calculate the maximum contribution that could be earned using whichever equations you need. *(12 marks)*

Some of the craftsmen have offered to work overtime, provided that they are paid double time for the extra hours over the contracted 12 000 hours. HC has estimated that up to 1 200 hours per period could be gained in this way.

Required:

(a) Explain the meaning of a shadow price (dual price) and calculate the shadow price of both the labour (craftsmen) and the materials (ash). *(5 marks)*

(b) Advise HC whether to accept the craftsmens' initial offer of working overtime, discussing the rate of pay requested, the quantity of hours and one other factor that HC should consider. *(6 marks)*

(25 marks)
ACCA Performance Management

25.13 Advanced: optimum production programme and interpretation of the solution of a linear programming model. LM produces two products from different quantities of the same resources using a just-in-time (JIT) production system. The selling price and resource requirements of each of these two products are as follows:

Product	L	M
Unit selling price ($)	70	90
Variable costs per unit:		
Direct labour ($7 per hour)	28	14
Direct material ($5 per kg)	10	45
Machine hours ($10 per hour)	10	20
Fixed overheads absorbed	12	6
Profit per unit	10	5

Fixed overheads are absorbed at the rate of $3 per direct labour hour.

Market research shows that the maximum demand for products L and M during December 2010 will be 400 units and 700 units respectively.

At a recent meeting of the purchasing and production managers to discuss the company's production plans for December 2010, the following resource availability for December 2010 was identified:

Direct labour	3 500 hours
Direct material	6 000 kg
Machine hours	2 000 hours

Required:

(a) Prepare calculations to show, from a financial perspective, the optimum production plan for December 2010 and the contribution that would result from adopting your plan. *(6 marks)*

(b) You have now presented your optimum plan to the purchasing and production managers of LM. During the presentation, the following additional information became available:

(i) The company has agreed to an order for 250 units of product M For a selling price of $90 per unit from a new overseas customer. This order is in addition to the maximum demand that was previously predicted and must be produced and delivered in December 2010;

(ii) The originally predicted resource restrictions were optimistic. The managers now agree that the availability of all resources will be 20 per cent lower than their original predictions.

Required:
Construct the revised resource constraints and the objective function to be used to identify, given the additional information above, the revised optimum production plan for December 2010. *(6 marks)*

(c) The resource constraints and objective function requested in part *(b)* above have now been processed in a simplex linear programming model and the following solution has been printed:

Product L	400	Product L other value	0
Product M	194	Product M other value	506
Direct labour	312		
Direct material ($)	1.22		
Machine hours	312		
Contribution ($)	10 934.00		

Required:
Analyze the meaning of each of the above eight values in the solution to the problem. Your answer should include a proof of the five individual values highlighted n bold. *(13 marks)*
CIMA P5 Performance Management

25.14 Advanced: Interpretation of the linear programming solution.
Woodalt plc has two automated machine groups X and Y, through which timber is passed in order to produce two models of an item of sports equipment. The models are called 'Traditional' and 'Hightech'.

The following forecast information is available for the year to 31 December:

	'Traditional'	'Hightech'
(i) Maximum sales potential (units)	6000	10 000
(ii) Equipment unit data:		
Selling price	£100	£90
Machine time: group X (hours)	0.5	0.3
group Y (hours)	0.4	0.45

(iii) Machine groups X and Y have maximum operating hours of 3400 and 3840 respectively. The sports equipment production is the sole use available for the production capacity.
(iv) The maximum quantity of timber available is 34 000 metres. Each product unit requires four metres of timber. Timber may be purchased in lengths as required at £5 per metre.
(v) Variable machine overhead cost for machine groups X and Y is estimated at £25 and £30 per machine hour respectively.
(vi) All units are sold in the year in which they are produced.

A linear programme of the situation has been prepared in order to determine the strategy which will maximize the contribution for the year to 31 December and to provide additional decision making information. Appendix 3.1 below shows a print-out of the solution to the LP model.

Required:

(a) Formulate the mathematical model from which the input to the LP programme would be obtained. *(4 marks)*
(b) Using the linear programme solution In Appendix 3.1 where appropriate, answer the following in respect of the year to 31 December :

(i) State the maximum contribution and its distribution between the two models; *(3 marks)*

(ii) Explain the effect on contribution of the limits placed on the availability of timber and machine time; *(3 marks)*

(iii) In addition to the sports equipment models, Woodalt plc has identified additional products which could earn contribution at the rate of £20 and £30 per machine hour for machine groups X and Y respectively. Such additional products would be taken up only to utilize any surplus hours not required for the sports equipment production.
Prepare figures which show the additional contribution which could be obtained in the year to 31 December from the additional sales outlets for each of machine groups X and Y; *(4 marks)*

(iv) Explain the sensitivity of the plan to changes in contribution per unit for each sports equipment product type; *(2 marks)*

(v) Woodalt plc expects to be able to overcome the timber availability constraint. All other parameters in the model remain unchanged. (*The additional products suggested in (iii) above do not apply.*)
Calculate the increase in contribution which this would provide; *(2 marks)*

(vi) You are told that the amended contribution maximizing solution arising from (v) will result in the production and sale of the 'Traditional' product being 3600 units.
Determine how many units of the 'Hightech' product will be produced and sold. *(2 marks)*
(c) Suggest ways in which Woodalt plc may overcome the capacity constraints which limit the opportunities available to it in the year to 31 December. Indicate the types of cost which may be incurred in overcoming each constraint. *(6 marks)*
(d) Explain why Woodalt plc should consider each of the following items before implementing the profit maximizing strategy indicated in Appendix 3.1:

(i) product specific costs;
(ii) customer specific costs;
(iii) life cycle costs.

Your answer should include relevant examples for each of (i) to (iii). *(9 marks)*

Appendix 3.1
Forecast strategy evaluation for the year to 31 December

Target cell (max) (£)

Cell	Name	Final Value
C2	Contribution	444 125

Adjustable cells (units)

Cell	Name	Final Value
A1	Traditional	4250
B1	Hightech	4250

Adjustable cells (units and £)

Cell	Name	Final value	Reduced cost	Objective coefficient	Allowable increase	Allowable decrease
A1	Traditional	4250	0	55.50	26.17	6.50
B1	Hightech	4250	0	49.00	6.50	15.70

Constraints (quantities and £)

Cell	Name	Final value	Shadow price	Constraint R.H. side	Allowable increase	Allowable decrease
C3	Timber	34 000	9.8125	34 000	1733.33	6800
C4	Machines X	3 400	32.5	3 400	850	850
C5	Machines Y	3 612.5	0	3 840	IE+30	227.5

ACCA Information for Control and Decision Making

IM25.1 Intermediate: Optimal output using the graphical approach.
G Limited, manufacturers of superior garden ornaments, is preparing its production budget for the coming period. The company makes four types of ornament, the data for which are as follows:

Product	Pixie (£ per unit)	Elf (£ per unit)	Queen (£ per unit)	King (£ per unit)
Direct materials	25	35	22	25
Variable overhead	17	18	15	16
Selling price	111	98	122	326

Direct labour hours:	Hours per unit	Hours per unit	Hours per unit	Hours per unit
Type 1	8	6	—	—
Type 2	—	—	10	10
Type 3	—	—	5	25

Fixed overhead amounts to £15 000 per period.

Each type of labour is paid £5 per hour but because of the skills involved, an employee of one type cannot be used for work normally done by another type.

The maximum hours available in each type are:

Type 1	8 000 hours
Type 2	20 000 hours
Type 3	25 000 hours

The marketing department judges that, at the present selling prices, the demand for the products is likely to be:

Pixie	Unlimited demand
Elf	Unlimited demand
Queen	1500 units
King	1000 units

You are required:

(a) to calculate the product mix that will maximize profit, and the amount of the profit; *(14 marks)*

(b) to determine whether it would be worthwhile paying Type 1 Labour for overtime working at time and a half and, if so, to calculate the extra profit for each 1000 hours of overtime; *(2 marks)*

(c) to comment on the principles used to find the optimum product mix in part (a), pointing out any possible limitations; *(3 marks)*

(d) to explain how a computer could assist in providing a solution for the data shown above. *(3 marks)*

CIMA Stage 3 Management Accounting Techniques

IM25.2 Advanced: Optimal output using the graphical approach and the impact of an increase in capacity. A company makes two products, X and Y. Product X has a contribution of £124 per unit and product Y £80 per unit. Both products pass through two departments for processing and the times in minutes per unit are:

	Product X	Product Y
Department 1	150	90
Department 2	100	120

Currently there is a maximum of 225 hours per week available in department 1 and 200 hours in department 2. The company can sell all it can produce of X but EEC quotas restrict the sale of Y to a maximum of 75 units per week.

The company, which wishes to maximize contribution, currently makes and sells 30 units of X and 75 units of Y per week.

The company is considering several possibilities including:

(i) altering the production plan if it could be proved that there is a better plan than the current one;

(ii) increasing the availability of either department 1 or department 2 hours. The extra costs involved in increasing capacity are £0.5 per hour for each department;

(iii) transferring some of their allowed sales quota for Product Y to another company. Because of commitments the company would always retain a minimum sales level of 30 units.

You are required to

(a) calculate the optimum production plan using the existing capacities and state the extra contribution that would be achieved compared with the existing plan; *(8 marks)*

(b) advise management whether they should increase the capacity of either department 1 or department 2 and, if so, by how many hours and what the resulting increase in contribution would be over that calculated in the improved production plan; *(7 marks)*

(c) calculate the minimum price per unit for which they could sell the rights to their quota, down to the minimum level, given the plan in (a) as a starting point. *(5 marks)*

CIMA Stage 3 Management Accounting Techniques

IM25.3 Advanced: Maximizing profit and sales revenue using the graphical approach. Goode, Billings and Prosper plc manufactures two products, Razzle and Dazzle. Unit selling prices and variable costs, and daily fixed costs are:

	Razzle (£)	Dazzle (£)
Selling price per unit	20	30
Variable costs per unit	8	20
Contribution margin per unit	12	10
Joint fixed costs per day		£60

Production of the two products is restricted by limited supplies of three essential inputs: Raz, Ma, and Taz. All other inputs are available at prevailing prices without any restriction. The quantities of Raz, Ma, and Taz necessary to produce single units of Razzle and Dazzle, together with the total supplies available each day, are:

	kg per unit required		Total available
	Razzle	Dazzle	(kg per day)
Raz	5	12.5	75
Ma	8	10	80
Taz	2	0	15

William Billings, the sales director, advises that any combination of Razzle and/or Dazzle can be sold without affecting their market prices. He also argues very strongly that the company should seek to maximize its sales revenues subject to a minimum acceptable profit of £44 per day in total from these two products.

In contrast, the financial director, Silas Prosper, has told the managing director, Henry Goode, that he believes in a policy of profit maximization at all times.

You are required to:

(a) calculate:

(i) the profit and total sales revenue per day, assuming a policy of profit maximization, *(10 marks)*

(ii) the total sales revenue per day, assuming a policy of sales revenue maximization subject to a minimum acceptable profit of £44 per day, *(10 marks)*

(b) suggest why businessmen might choose to follow an objective of maximizing sales revenue subject to a minimum profit constraint. *(5 marks)*

(Total 25 marks)
ICAEW Management Accounting

IM25.4 Advanced: Optimal output and shadow prices using the graphical approach. Usine Ltd is a company whose objective is to maximize profits. It manufactures two speciality chemical powders, gamma and delta, using three processes: heating, refining and blending. The powders can be produced and sold in infinitely divisible quantities.

The following are the estimated production hours for each process per kilo of output for each of the two chemical powders during the period 1 June to 31 August:

	Gamma (hours)	Delta (hours)
Heating	400	120
Refining	100	90
Blending	100	250

During the same period, revenues and costs per kilo of output are budgeted as

	Gamma (£ per kilo)	Delta (£ per kilo)
Selling price	16 000	25 000
Variable costs	12 000	17 000
Contribution	4 000	8 000

It is anticipated that the company will be able to sell all it can produce at the above prices, and that at any level of output fixed costs for the three month period will total £36 000.

The company's management accountant is under the impression that there will only be one scarce factor during the budget period, namely blending hours, which cannot exceed a total of 1050 hours during the period 1 June to 31 August. He therefore correctly draws up an optimum production plan on this basis.

However, when the factory manager sees the figures he points out that over the three-month period there will not only be a restriction on blending hours, but in addition the heating and refining hours cannot exceed 1200 and 450 respectively during the three month period.

Requirements:

(a) Calculate the initial production plan for the period 1 June to 31 August as prepared by the management accountant, assuming blending hours are the only scarce factor. Indicate the budgeted profit or loss, and explain why the solution is the optimum. *(4 marks)*

(b) Calculate the optimum production plan for the period 1 June to 31 August, allowing for both the constraint on blending hours and the additional restrictions identified by the factory manager, and indicate the budgeted profit or loss. *(8 marks)*

(c) State the implications of your answer in (b) in terms of the decisions that will have to be made by Usine Ltd with respect to production during the period 1 June to 31 August after taking into account all relevant costs. *(2 marks)*

(d) Under the restrictions identified by the management accountant and the factory manager, the shadow (or dual) price of one extra hour of blending time on the optimum production plan is £27.50. Calculate the shadow (or dual) price of one extra hour of refining time. Explain how such information might be used by management, and in so doing indicate the limitations inherent in the figures. *(6 marks)*

Note: Ignore taxation.

Show all calculations clearly.

ICAEW Management Accounting and Financial Management I Part Two

IM25.5 Advanced: Formulation of initial tableau and interpretation of final tableau. The Alphab Group has five divisions A, B, C, D and E. Group management wish to increase overall group production capacity per year by up to 30 000 hours. Part of the strategy will be to require that the minimum increase at any one division must be equal to 5 per cent of its current capacity. The maximum funds available for the expansion programme are £3 000 000. Additional information relating to each division is as follows:

Division	Existing capacity (hours)	Investment cost per hour (£)	Average contribution per hour (£)
A	20 000	90	12.50
B	40 000	75	9.50
C	24 000	100	11
D	50 000	120	8
E	12 000	200	14

A linear programme of the plan has been prepared in order to determine the strategy which will maximize additional contribution

per annum and to provide additional decision-making information. The Appendix to this question shows a print-out of the LP model of the situation.

Required:

(a) Formulate the mathematical model from which the input to the LP programme would be obtained. *(6 marks)*

(b) Use the linear programme solution in the Appendix in order to answer the following:

(i) State the maximum additional contribution from the expansion strategy and the distribution of the extra capacity between the divisions. *(3 marks)*

(ii) Explain the cost to the company of providing the minimum 5 per cent increase in capacity at each division. *(3 marks)*

(iii) Explain the effect on contribution of the limits placed on capacity and investment. *(2 marks)*

(iv) Explain the sensitivity of the plan to changes in contribution per hour. *(4 marks)*

(v) Group management decide to relax the 30 000 hours capacity constraint. All other parameters of the model remain unchanged. Determine the change in strategy which will then maximize the increase in group contribution. You should calculate the increase in contribution which this change in strategy will provide. *(6 marks)*

(vi) Group management wish to decrease the level of investment while leaving all other parameters of the model (as per the Appendix) unchanged.

Determine and quantify the change in strategy which is required indicating the fall in contribution which will occur. *(6 marks)*

(c) Explain the limitations of the use of linear programming for planning purposes. *(5 marks)*

Appendix
Divisional investment evaluation
Optimal solution – detailed report

Variable	Value
1 DIV A	22 090.91
2 DIV B	2 000.00
3 DIV C	1 200.00
4 DIV D	2 500.00
5 DIV E	2 209.09

	Constraint	Type	RHS	Slack	Shadow price
1	Max. hours	<=	30 000.00	0.00	11.2727
2	DIV A	>=	1 000.00	21 090.91	0.0000
3	DIV B	>=	2 000.00	0.00	-2.7955
4	DIV C	>=	1 200.00	0.00	-1.6364
5	DIV D	>=	2 500.00	0.00	-4.9091
6	DIV E	>=	600.00	1 609.09	0.0000
7	Max. funds	<=	3 000 000.00	0.00	0.0136

Objective function value = 359 263.6

Sensitivity analysis of objective function coefficients

Variable	Current coefficient	Allowable minimum	Allowable maximum
1 DIV A	12.50	10.7000	14.0000
2 DIV B	9.50	-Infinity	12.2955
3 DIV C	11.00	-Infinity	12.6364
4 DIV D	8.00	-Infinity	12.9091
5 DIV E	14.00	12.5000	27.7778

Sensitivity Analysis of right-hand side values

Constraint	Type	Current value	Allowable minimum	Allowable maximum
1 Max. hours	<=	30 000.00	18 400.00	31 966.67
2 DIV A	>=	1 000.00	–Infinity	22 090.91
3 DIV B	>=	2 000.00	0.00	20 560.00
4 DIV C	>=	1 200.00	0.00	18 900.00
5 DIV D	>=	2 500.00	0.00	8 400.00
6 DIV E	>=	600.00	–Infinity	2 209.09
7 Max. funds	<=	3 000 000.00	2 823 000.00	5 320 000.00

Note: RHS = Right-hand side

ACCA Paper 9 Information for Control and Decision Making

IM25.6 **Formulation of initial tableau and interpretation of final tableau using the simplex method.**

(a) The Argonaut Company makes three products, Xylos, Yo-yos and Zicons. These are assembled from two components, Agrons and Bovons, which can be produced internally at a variable cost of £5 and £8 each respectively. A limited quantity of each of these components may be available for purchase from an external supplier at a quoted price which varies from week to week.

The production of Agrons and Bovons is subject to several limitations. Both components require the same three production processes (L, M and N), the first two of which have limited availabilities of 9600 minutes per week and 7000 minutes per week respectively. The final process (N) has effectively unlimited availability but for technical reasons must produce at least one Agron for each Bovon produced. The processing times are as follows:

Process	L	M	N
Time (mins) required to produce			
1 Agron	6	5	7
1 Bovon	8	5	9

The component requirements of each of the three final products are:

Product	Xylo	Yo-yo	Zicon
Number of components required			
Agrons	1	1	3
Bovons	2	1	2

The ex-factory selling prices of the final products are given below, together with the standard direct labour hours involved in their assembly and details of other assembly costs incurred:

Product	Xylo	Yo-yo	Zicon
Selling price	£70	£60	£150
Direct labour hours used	3	3.5	8
Other assembly costs	£4	£5	£15

The standard direct labour rate is £10 per hour. Factory overhead costs amount to £4350 per week and are absorbed to products on the basis of the direct labour costs incurred in their assembly. The current production plan is to produce 100 units of each of the three products each week.

Requirements:

(i) Present a budgeted weekly profit and loss account, by product, for the factory. *(4 marks)*

(ii) Formulate the production problem facing the factory manager as a linear program:

1 assuming there is no external availability of Agrons and Bovons; *(5 marks)*

and

2 assuming that 200 Agrons and 300 Bovons are available at prices of £10 and £12 each respectively. *(4 marks)*

(b) In a week when no external availability of Agrons and Bovons was expected, the optimal solution to the linear program and the shadow prices associated with each constraint were as follows:

Production of Xylos	50 units
Production of Yo-yos	0 units; shadow price £2.75
Production of Zicons	250 units

Shadow price associated with:

Process L	£0.375 per minute
Process M	£0.450 per minute
Process N	£0.000 per minute
Agron availability	£9.50 each
Bovon availability	£13.25 each

If sufficient Bovons were to become available on the external market at a price of £12 each, a revised linear programming solution indicated that only Xylos should be made.

Requirement:

Interpret this output from the linear program in a report to the factory manager. Include calculations of revised shadow prices in your report and indicate the actions the manager should take and the benefits that would accrue if the various constraints could be overcome. *(12 marks)*

ICAEW P2 Management Accounting

IM25.7 **Advanced: Formulation of an initial tableau and interpretation of a final tableau using the simplex method.**

Hint: Reverse the signs and ignore entries of 0 and 1.

The Kaolene Co. Ltd has six different products all made from fabricated steel. Each product passes through a combination of five production operations: cutting, forming, drilling, welding and coating.

Steel is cut to the length required, formed into the appropriate shapes, drilled if necessary, welded together if the product is made up of more than one part, and then passed through the coating machine. Each operation is separate and independent, except for the cutting and forming operations, when, if needed, forming follows continuously after cutting. Some products do not require every production operation.

The output rates from each production operations, based on a standard measure for each product, are set out in the tableau below, along with the total hours of work available for each operation. The contribution per unit of each product is also given. It is estimated that three of the products have sales ceilings and these are also given below:

Products	X_1	X_2	X_3	X_4	X_5	X_6
Contribution per unit (£)	5.7	10.1	12.3	9.8	17.2	14.0
Output rate per hour:						
Cutting	650	700	370	450	300	420
Forming	450	450	—	520	180	380
Drilling	—	200	380	—	300	—
Welding	—	—	380	670	400	720
Coating	500	—	540	480	600	450
Maximum sales units (000)	—	—	150	—	20	70

	Cutting	Forming	Drilling	Welding	Coating
Production hours available	12 000	16 000	4000	4000	16 000

The production and sales for the year were found using a linear programming algorithm. The final tableau is given below.

Variables X_7 to X_{11} are the slack variables relating to the production constraints, expressed in the order of production. Variables X_{12} to X_{14} are the slack variables relating to the sales ceilings of X_3, X_5 and X_6 respectively.

After analysis of the above results, the production manager believes that further mechanical work on the cutting and forming machines costing £200 can improve their hourly output rates as follows:

Products	X_1	X_2	X_3	X_4	X_5	X_6
Cutting	700	770	410	500	330	470
Forming	540	540	—	620	220	460

The optimal solution to the new situation indicates the shadow prices of the cutting, drilling and welding sections to be £59.3, £14.2 and £71.5 per hour respectively.

Requirements:

(a) Explain the meaning of the seven items ringed in the final tableau. *(9 marks)*

(b) Show the range of values within which the following variables or resources can change without changing the optimal mix indicated in the final tableau

(i) c_4: contribution of $X4$

(ii) b_5: available coating time. *(4 marks)*

(c) Formulate the revised linear programming problem taking note of the revised output rates for cutting and forming. *(5 marks)*

(d) Determine whether the changes in the cutting and forming rates will increase profitability. *(3 marks)*

(e) Using the above information discuss the usefulness of linear programming to managers in solving this type of problem. *(4 marks)*

ICAEW P2 Management Accounting

X_1	X_2	X_3	X_4	X_5	X_6	X_7	X_8	X_9	X_{10}	X_{11}	X_{12}	X_{13}	X_{14}	Variable in basic solution	Value of variable in basic solution
1	0	−1.6	−0.22	−0.99	0	10.8	0	−3.0	−18.5	0	0	0	0	X_1	43 287.0 units
0	0	−0.15	−0.02	0.12	0	−1.4	1	−0.3	0.58	0	0	0	0	X_8	15 747.81 hours
0	1	0.53	0	0.67	0	0	0	3.33	0	0	0	0	0	X_2	13 333.3 units
0	0	1.9	1.08	1.64	1	0	0	0	12	0	0	0	0	X_6	48 019.2 units
0	0	0.06	0.01	0	0	−1.3	0	0.37	0.63	1	0	0	0	X_{11}	150 806.72 hours
0	0	1	0	0	0	0	0	0	0	0	1	0	0	X_{12}	150 000.0 units
0	0	0	0	1	0	0	0	0	0	0	0	1	0	X_{13}	20 000.0 units
0	0	−1.9	−1.0	−1.6	0	0	0	0	−12	0	0	0	1	X_{14}	21 980.8 units
0	0	10.0	4	6.83	0	61.7	0	16.0	62.1	0	0	0	0	$(Z_i - C_i)$	£1 053 617.4

15
THE BUDGETING PROCESS

In the previous seven chapters we have considered how management accounting can assist managers in making decisions. The actions that follow managerial decisions normally involve several aspects of the business, such as the marketing, production, purchasing and finance functions, and it is important that management should coordinate these various interrelated aspects of decision-making. If they fail to do this, there is a danger that managers may each make decisions that they believe are in the best interests of the organization when, in fact, taken together they are not; for example, the marketing department may introduce a promotional campaign that is designed to increase sales demand to a level beyond that which the production department can handle. The various activities within a company should be coordinated by the preparation of plans of actions for future periods. These detailed plans are usually referred to as budgets. Our objective in this chapter is to focus on the planning process within a business organization and to consider the role of budgeting within this process.

THE STRATEGIC PLANNING, BUDGETING AND CONTROL PROCESS

To help you understand the budgetary process we shall begin by looking at how it fits into an overall general framework of planning and control. The framework outlined in Figure 15.1 provides an overview of an organization's planning and control process. The first stage involves establishing the objectives and supporting strategies of the organization within the strategic planning process.

Strategic planning process

Before the budgeting process begins, an organization should have prepared a long-term plan (also known as a strategic plan). Strategic planning begins with the specification of objectives towards which future operations should be directed. Johnson, Scholes and Whittington (2010) identify a hierarchy of objectives – the mission of an organization, corporate objectives and unit objectives.[1]

The mission of an organization (see Exhibit 15.1 for an illustration) describes in very general terms the broad purpose and reason for an organization's existence, the nature of the business(es) it is in and the customers it seeks to serve and satisfy. It is a visionary projection of the central and over-riding concepts on which the organization is based. Corporate objectives relate to the organization as a whole. Objectives tend to be more specific, and represent desired states or results to be achieved. They are normally measurable and are expressed in financial terms such as desired profits or sales levels, return on capital employed, rates of growth or market share. Objectives must also be developed for the different parts of an organization. Unit objectives relate to the specific objectives of individual units within the organization, such as a division or one company within a holding company. Corporate objectives are normally set for the organization as a whole and are then translated into unit objectives, which become the targets for the individual units. It is important that senior managers in an organization understand clearly where their company is going, and why and how their own role contributes to the attainment of corporate objectives. The strategic planning process should also specify how the objectives of the organization will be achieved.

FIGURE 15.1

Strategic planning, budgeting and control process

EXHIBIT 15.1 **EasyJet mission statement**

> 'To provide our customers with safe, good value, point-to-point air services. To effect and to offer a consistent and reliable product and fares appealing to leisure and business markets on a range of European routes. To achieve this we will develop our people and establish lasting relationships with our suppliers.'
>
> **Source:** Easyjet.co.uk/en/about/index.html

Creation of long-term plan

The term strategy is used to describe the courses of action that need to be taken to achieve the objectives set. When management has identified those strategic options that have the greatest potential for achieving the company's objectives, long-term plans should be created to implement the strategies. A long-term plan is a statement of the preliminary targets and activities required by an organization to achieve its strategic plan, together with a broad estimate for each year of the resources required and revenues expected. Because long-term planning involves 'looking into the future' for several years ahead (typically at least five years) the plans tend to be uncertain, general in nature, imprecise and subject to change.

Preparation of the annual budget within the context of the long-term plan

Budgeting is concerned with the implementation of the long-term plan for the year ahead. Because of the shorter planning horizon, budgets are more precise and detailed. Budgets are a clear indication of what is expected to be achieved during the budget period, whereas long-term plans represent the broad directions that top management intend to follow.

The budget is not something that originates 'from nothing' each year – it is developed within the context of ongoing business and is ruled by previous decisions that have been taken within the long-term planning process. When the activities are initially approved for inclusion in the long-term plan, they are based on uncertain estimates that are projected for several years. These proposals must be reviewed and revised in the light of more recent information. This review and revision process frequently takes place as part of the annual budgeting process, and it may result in important decisions being taken on possible activity adjustments within the current budget period. The budgeting process cannot therefore be viewed as being purely concerned with the current year – it must be considered as an integrated part of the long-term planning process.

Monitor actual outcomes and respond to deviations from planned outcomes

The final stages in the strategic planning, budgeting and control process outlined in Figure 15.1 are to compare the actual and the planned outcomes, and to respond to any deviations from the plan. These stages represent the control process of budgeting. Planning and control are closely linked. Planning involves looking ahead to determine the actions required to achieve the objectives of the organization. Control involves looking back to ascertain what actually happened and comparing it with the planned outcomes. Effective control requires that corrective action is taken so that actual outcomes conform to planned outcomes. Alternatively, the plans may require modification if the comparisons indicate that the plans are no longer attainable. The corrective action is indicated by the arrowed lines in Figure 15.1 linking stages 5 and 2 and 5 and 3. These arrowed lines represent feedback loops. They signify that the process is dynamic and stress the interdependencies between the various stages in the process. The feedback loops between the stages indicate that the plans should be regularly reviewed, and if they are no longer attainable then alternative courses of action must be considered for achieving the organization's objectives. The loop between stages 5 and 3 also stresses the corrective action that may be taken so that actual outcomes conform to planned outcomes.

A detailed discussion of the control process will be deferred until the next chapter. Let us now consider the short-term budgeting process in more detail.

THE MULTIPLE FUNCTIONS OF BUDGETS

Budgets serve a number of useful purposes. They include:

1 *planning* annual operations;
2 *coordinating* the activities of the various parts of the organization and ensuring that the parts are in harmony with each other;
3 *communicating* plans to the various responsibility centre managers;
4 *motivating* managers to strive to achieve the organizational goals;
5 *controlling* activities;
6 *evaluating* the performance of managers.

Let us now examine each of these six factors.

Planning

The major planning decisions will already have been made as part of the long-term planning process. However, the annual budgeting process leads to the refinement of those plans, since managers must produce detailed plans for the implementation of the long-range plan. Without the annual budgeting process, the pressures of day-to-day operating problems may tempt managers not to plan for future operations. The budgeting process ensures that managers do plan for future operations, and that they consider how conditions in the next year might change and what steps they should take now to respond to these changed conditions. This process encourages managers to anticipate problems before they arise, and hasty decisions that are made on the spur of the moment, based on expediency rather than reasoned judgement, will be minimized.

Coordination

The budget serves as a vehicle through which the actions of the different parts of an organization can be brought together and reconciled into a common plan. Without any guidance, managers may each make their own decisions, believing that they are working in the best interests of the organization. For example, the purchasing manager may prefer to place large orders so as to obtain large discounts; the production manager will be concerned with avoiding high inventory levels; and the accountant will be concerned with the impact of the decision on the cash resources of the business. It is the aim of budgeting to reconcile these differences for the good of the organization as a whole, rather than for the benefit of any individual area. Budgeting therefore compels managers to examine the relationship between their own operations and those of other departments, and, in the process, to identify and resolve conflicts.

Communication

If an organization is to function effectively, there must be definite lines of communication so that all the parts will be kept fully informed of the plans and the policies, and constraints, to which the organization is expected to conform. Everyone in the organization should have a clear understanding of the part they are expected to play in achieving the annual budget. This process will ensure that the appropriate individuals are made accountable for implementing the budget. Through the budget, top management communicates its expectations to lower level management, so that all members of the organization may understand these expectations and can coordinate their activities to attain them. It is not just the budget itself that facilitates communication – much vital information is communicated in the actual act of preparing it.

Motivation

The budget can be a useful device for influencing managerial behaviour and motivating managers to perform in line with the organizational objectives. A budget provides a standard that under certain circumstances, a manager may be motivated to strive to achieve. However, budgets can also encourage inefficiency and conflict between managers. If individuals have actively participated in preparing the budget, and it is used as a tool to assist managers in managing their departments, it can act as a strong motivational device by providing a challenge. Alternatively, if the budget is dictated from above, and imposes a threat rather than a challenge, it may be resisted and do more harm than good. We shall discuss the dysfunctional motivational consequence of budgets in Chapter 16.

Control

A budget assists managers in managing and controlling the activities for which they are responsible. By comparing the actual results with the budgeted amounts for different categories of expenses, managers can ascertain which costs do not conform to the original plan and thus require their attention. This process enables management to operate a system of management by exception which means that a manager's attention and effort can be concentrated on significant deviations from the expected results. By investigating the reasons for the deviations, managers may be able to identify inefficiencies such as the purchase of inferior quality materials. When the reasons for the inefficiencies have been found, appropriate control action should be taken to remedy the situation.

Performance evaluation

A manager's performance is often evaluated by measuring his or her success in meeting the budgets. In some companies bonuses are awarded on the basis of an employee's ability to achieve the targets specified in the periodic budgets, or promotion may be partly dependent upon a manager's budget record. In addition, the manager may wish to evaluate his or her own performance. The budget thus provides a useful means of informing managers of how well they are performing in meeting targets that they have previously helped to set. The use of budgets as a method of performance evaluation also influences human behaviour, and for this reason we shall consider the behavioural aspects of performance evaluation in Chapter 16.

CONFLICTING ROLES OF BUDGETS

Because a single budget system is normally used to serve several purposes there is a danger that they may conflict with each other. For instance, the planning and motivation roles may be in conflict with each other. Demanding budgets that may not be achieved may be appropriate to motivate maximum performance, but they are unsuitable for planning purposes. For these a budget should be set based on easier targets that are expected to be met.

There is also a conflict between the planning and performance evaluation roles. For planning purposes budgets are set in advance of the budget period based on an anticipated set of circumstances or environment. Performance evaluation should be based on a comparison of actual performance with an adjusted budget to reflect the circumstances under which managers actually operated. In practice, many firms compare actual performance with the original budget (adjusted to the actual level of activity, i.e. a flexible budget), but if the circumstances envisaged when the original budget was set have changed then there will be a planning and evaluation conflict.

THE BUDGET PERIOD

The conventional approach is that once per year the manager of each budget centre prepares a detailed budget for one year. The budget is divided into either twelve monthly or thirteen four-weekly periods for control purposes. The preparation of budgets on an annual basis has been strongly criticized on the grounds that it is too rigid and ties a company to a 12-month commitment, which can be risky because the budget is based on uncertain forecasts.

An alternative approach is for the annual budget to be broken down by months for the first three months, and by quarters for the remaining nine months. The quarterly budgets are then developed on a monthly basis as the year proceeds. For example, during the first quarter, the monthly budgets for the second quarter will be prepared; and during the second quarter, the monthly budgets for the third quarter will be prepared. The quarterly budgets may also be reviewed as the year unfolds. For example, during the first quarter, the budget for the next three quarters may be changed as new information becomes available. A new budget for a fifth quarter will also be prepared. This process is known as continuous or rolling budgeting, and ensures that a 12-month budget is always available by adding a quarter in the future as the quarter just ended is dropped. Contrast this with a budget prepared once per year. As the year goes by, the period for which a budget is available will shorten until the budget for next year is prepared. Rolling budgets also ensure that planning is not something that takes place once a year when the budget is being formulated. Instead, budgeting is a continuous process, and managers are encouraged to constantly look ahead and review future plans. Furthermore, it is likely that actual performance will be compared with a more realistic target, because budgets are being constantly reviewed and updated. The main disadvantage of a rolling budget is that it can create uncertainty for managers because the budget is constantly being changed.

Irrespective of whether the budget is prepared on an annual or a continuous basis, it is important that monthly or four-weekly budgets are normally used for *control* purposes.

ADMINISTRATION OF THE BUDGETING PROCESS

It is important that suitable administration procedures be introduced to ensure that the budget process works effectively. In practice, the procedures should be tailor-made to the requirements of the organization, but as a general rule a firm should ensure that procedures are established for approving the budgets and that the appropriate staff support is available for assisting managers in preparing their budgets.

The budget committee

The budget committee should consist of high-level executives who represent the major segments of the business. Its major task is to ensure that budgets are realistically established and that they are coordinated satisfactorily. The normal procedure is for the functional heads to present their budget to the committee for approval. If the budget does not reflect a reasonable level of performance, it will not be approved and the functional head will be required to adjust the budget and re-submit it for approval. It is important that the person whose performance is being measured should agree that the revised budget can be achieved; otherwise, if it is considered to be impossible to achieve, it will not act as a motivational device. If budget revisions are made, the budgetees should at least feel that they were given a fair hearing by the committee. We shall discuss budget negotiation in more detail later in this chapter.

The budget committee should appoint a budget officer, who will normally be the accountant. The role of the budget officer is to coordinate the individual budgets into a budget for the whole organization, so that the budget committee and the budgetee can see the impact of an individual budget on the organization as a whole.

Accounting staff

The accounting staff will normally assist managers in the preparation of their budgets; they will, for example, circulate and advise on the instructions about budget preparation, provide past information that may be useful for preparing the present budget, and ensure that managers submit their budgets on time. The accounting staff do not determine the content of the various budgets, but they do provide a valuable advisory service for the line managers.

Budget manual

A budget manual should be prepared by the accountant. It will describe the objectives and procedures involved in the budgeting process and will provide a useful reference source for managers responsible for budget preparation. In addition, the manual may include a timetable specifying the order in which the budgets should be prepared and the dates when they should be presented to the budget committee. The manual should be circulated to all individuals who are responsible for preparing budgets.

STAGES IN THE BUDGETING PROCESS

The important stages are as follows:

1 communicating details of budget policy and guidelines to those people responsible for the preparation of budgets;
2 determining the factor that restricts output;
3 preparation of the sales budget;
4 initial preparation of various budgets;
5 negotiation of budgets with superiors;
6 coordination and review of budgets;
7 final acceptance of budgets;
8 ongoing review of budgets.

Let us now consider each of these stages in more detail.

Communicating details of the budget policy

Many decisions affecting the budget year will have been taken previously as part of the long-term planning process. The long-range plan is therefore the starting point for the preparation of the annual budget. Thus, top management must communicate the policy effects of the long-term plan to those responsible for preparing the current year's budgets. Policy effects might include planned changes in sales mix, or the expansion or contraction of certain activities. In addition, other important guidelines that are to govern the preparation of the budget should be specified – for example the allowances that are to be made for price and wage increases, and the expected changes in productivity. Also, any expected changes in industry demand and output should be communicated by top management to the managers responsible for budget preparation. It is essential that all managers be made aware of the policy of top management for implementing the long-term plan in the current year's budget so that common guidelines can be established. The process also indicates to the managers responsible for preparing the budgets how they should respond to any expected environmental changes.

Determining the factor that restricts performance

In every organization there is some factor that restricts performance for a given period. In the majority of organizations this factor is sales demand. However, it is possible for production capacity to restrict performance when sales demand is in excess of available capacity. Prior to the preparation of the budgets, it is necessary for top management to determine the factor that restricts performance, since this factor determines the point at which the annual budgeting process should begin.

Preparation of the sales budget

The volume of sales and the sales mix determine the level of a company's operations, when sales demand is the factor that restricts output. For this reason, the sales budget is the most important plan in the annual budgeting process. This budget is also the most difficult plan to produce, because total sales revenue depends on the actions of customers. In addition, sales demand may be influenced by the state of the economy or the actions of competitors.

Initial preparation of budgets

The managers who are responsible for meeting the budgeted performance should prepare the budget for those areas for which they are responsible. The preparation of the budget should be a 'bottom-up' process. This means that the budget should originate at the lowest levels of management and be refined and coordinated at higher levels. The justification for this approach is that it enables managers to participate in the preparation of their budgets and increases the probability that they will accept the budget and strive to achieve the budget targets.

There is no single way in which the appropriate quantity for a particular budget item is determined. Past data may be used as the starting point for producing the budgets, but this does not mean that budgeting is based on the assumption that what has happened in the past will occur in the future. Changes in future conditions must be taken into account, but past information may provide useful guidance for the future. In addition, managers may look to the guidelines provided by top management for determining the content of their budgets. For example, the guidelines may provide specific instructions as to the content of their budgets and the permitted changes that can be made in the prices of purchases of materials and services. For production activities standard costs (see Chapter 17) may be used as the basis for costing activity volumes which are planned in the budget.

Negotiation of budgets

To implement a participative approach to budgeting, the budget should be originated at the lowest level of management. The managers at this level should submit their budget to their superiors for approval. The superior should then incorporate this budget with other budgets for which he or she is responsible and then submit this budget for approval to his or her superior. The manager who is the superior then becomes the budgetee at the next higher level. The process is illustrated in Figure 15.2. Sizer (1989) describes this approach as a two-way process of a top-down statement of objectives and strategies, bottom-up budget preparation and top-down approval by senior management.

The lower-level managers are represented by boxes 1–8. Managers 1 and 2 will prepare their budgets in accordance with the budget policy and the guidelines laid down by top management. The managers will submit their budget to their supervisor, who is in charge of the whole department (department A). Once these budgets have been agreed by the manager of department A, they will be combined by the departmental manager, who will then present this budget to his or her superior (manager of plant 1) for approval. The manager of plant 1 is also responsible for department B, and will combine the agreed budgets for departments A and B before presenting the combined budget to his or her supervisor (the production manager). The production manager will merge the budget for plants 1 and 2, and this final budget will represent the production budget that will be presented to the budget committee for approval.

At each of these stages the budgets will be negotiated between the budgetees and their superiors, and eventually they will be agreed by both parties. Hence the figures that are included in the budget are the result of a bargaining process between a manager and his or her superior. It is important that the budgetees should participate in arriving at the final budget and that the superior does not revise the budget without giving full consideration to the subordinates' arguments for including any of the budgeted items. Otherwise, real participation will not be taking place, and it is unlikely that the subordinate will be motivated to achieve a budget that he or she did not accept.

It is also necessary to be watchful that budgetees do not deliberately attempt to obtain approval for easily attainable budgets, or attempt to deliberately understate budgets in the hope that the budget that is finally agreed will represent an easily attainable target. It is equally unsatisfactory for a superior to impose difficult targets in the hope that an authoritarian approach will produce the desired results. The desired results may be achieved in the short term, but only at the cost of a loss of morale and increased labour turnover in the future.

The negotiation process is of vital importance in the budgeting process, and can determine whether the budget becomes a really effective management tool or just a routine to follow. If managers are successful

REAL WORLD VIEWS 15.1

Sales budget – budgeting revenues at BAA
The BAA group (**www.baa.com**) is the leading airport management company in the UK, managing six of the countries airports, including London Heathrow, one of the world's busiest airports. The company is engaged in all aspects of airport operation, including passenger security, retail and baggage handling. The company generates revenue from some of these sectors, but the key revenue source is the passenger charge levied on each passenger using the airport. These charges are approved by the Civil Aviation Authority and are currently agreed at £12.80 plus a retail price index adjustment until March 2013. For the year to December 2010, BAA reported passenger numbers at 84.4 million for all its airports, approximately 66 million of which related to London Heathrow.

Flight passenger numbers have faced several setbacks in recent years. Terror attacks in 2001 reduced numbers globally, and more recently in 2010 volcanic ash caused disruptions across Europe. Such events, added to economic recession in many developed countries, leaves forecasting passenger numbers dif-

ficult. While BAA does not publish how it budgets for passenger revenues, it is likely to have had to adjust its forecasting of passenger numbers to take account of such factors. Additionally, the seasonality of the sector needs to be taken into account when forecasting. The actual passenger numbers from 2003 to 2010 at London Heathrow remained relatively stable however, as shown in the graphic below.

Questions

1 Would the historical information/trend shown in the chart be useful in forecasting revenues from passenger charges?

2 In general, the global economy was in a boom period between 2003 and 2007. Why do you think the passenger numbers at London Heathrow remain relatively static?

References
http://www.baa.com/assets/Internet/BAA%20Airports/Downloads/Static%20files/BAA_(SP)_Ltd_FY_2010_results_announcement.pdf
http://www.baa.com/portal/page/Investor/BAA+Airports%5EInvestor+centre%5EResults+and+performance%5ETraffic+statistics/6571e5ca9ceee110VgnVCM10000036821c0a___/448c6a4c7f1b0010VgnVCM200000357e120a/%20centre

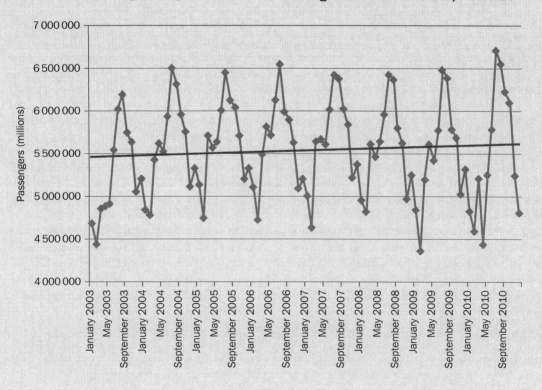

FIGURE 15.2

An illustration of budgets
moving up the organization
hierarchy

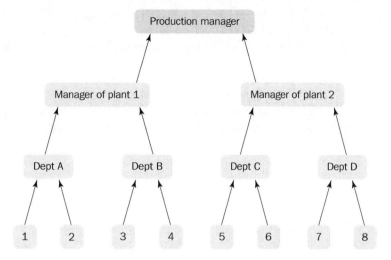

FIGURE 15.2

An illustration of budgets
moving up the organization
hierarchy

in establishing a position of trust and confidence with their subordinates, the negotiation process will
produce a meaningful improvement in the budgetary process and outcomes for the period.

Coordination and review of budgets

As the individual budgets move up the organizational hierarchy in the negotiation process, they must be
examined in relation to each other. This examination may indicate that some budgets are out of balance
with other budgets and need modifying so that they will be compatible with other conditions, constraints
and plans that are beyond a manager's knowledge or control. For example, a plant manager may include
equipment replacement in his or her budget when funds are simply not available. The accountant must
identify such inconsistencies and bring them to the attention of the appropriate manager. Any changes in
the budgets should be made by the responsible managers, and this may require that the budgets be
recycled from the bottom to the top for a second or even a third time until all the budgets are coordinated
and are acceptable to all the parties involved. During the coordination process, a budgeted profit and loss
account, a balance sheet and a cash flow statement should be prepared to ensure that all the parts
combine to produce an acceptable whole. Otherwise, further adjustments and budget recycling will be
necessary until the budgeted profit and loss account, the balance sheet and the cash flow statement prove
to be acceptable.

Final acceptance of the budgets

When all the budgets are in harmony with each other, they are summarized into a master budget
consisting of a budgeted profit and loss account, a balance sheet and a cash flow statement. After the
master budget has been approved, the budgets are then passed down through the organization to the
appropriate responsibility centres. The approval of the master budget is the authority for the manager of
each responsibility centre to carry out the plans contained in each budget.

Budget review

The budget process should not stop when the budgets have been agreed. Periodically, the actual results
should be compared with the budgeted results. These comparisons should normally be made on a
monthly basis and a report should be available online in the first week of the following month, so that
it has the maximum motivational impact. This will enable management to identify the items that are not
proceeding according to plan and to investigate the reasons for the differences. If these differences are
within the control of management, corrective action can be taken to avoid similar inefficiencies occurring
again in the future. However, the differences may be due to the fact that the budget was unrealistic to

begin with, or that the actual conditions during the budget year were different from those anticipated; the budget for the remainder of the year would then be invalid.

During the budget year, the budget committee should periodically evaluate the actual performance and reappraise the company's future plans. If there are any changes in the actual conditions from those originally expected, this will normally mean that the budget plans should be adjusted. This revised budget then represents a revised statement of formal operating plans for the remaining portion of the budget period. The important point to note is that the budgetary process does not end for the current year once the budget has begun; budgeting should be seen as a continuous and dynamic process.

A DETAILED ILLUSTRATION

Let us now look at an illustration of the procedure for constructing budgets in a manufacturing company, using the information contained in Example 15.1. Note that the level of detail included here is much less than that which would be presented in practice. A truly realistic illustration would fill many pages, with detailed budgets being analyzed in various ways. We shall consider an annual budget, whereas a realistic illustration would analyze the annual budget into twelve monthly periods. Monthly analysis would considerably increase the size of the illustration, but would not give any further insight into the basic concepts or procedures. In addition, we shall assume in this example that the budgets are prepared for only two responsibility centres (namely departments 1 and 2). In practice, many responsibility centres are likely to exist.

EXAMPLE 15.1

The Enterprise Company manufactures two products, known as alpha and sigma. Alpha is produced in department 1 and sigma in department 2. The following information is available for 200X.
Standard material and labour costs:

	(£)
Material X	7.20 per unit
Material Y	16.00 per unit
Direct labour	12.00 per hour

Overhead is recovered on a direct labour hour basis.
The standard material and labour usage for each product is as follows:

	Model alpha	Model sigma
Material X	10 units	8 units
Material Y	5 units	9 units
Direct labour	10 hours	15 hours

The balance sheet for the previous year end 200X was as follows:

	(£)	(£)	(£)
Fixed assets:			
Land		170 000	
Buildings and equipment	1 292 000		
Less depreciation	255 000	1 037 000	1 207 000
Current assets:			
Inventories, finished goods	99 076		
raw materials	189 200		
Debtors	289 000		
Cash	34 000		
	611 276		
Less current liabilities			
Creditors	248 800		362 476
Net assets			1 569 476
Represented by shareholder's interest:			
1 200 000 ordinary shares of £1 each		1 200 000	
Reserves		369 476	
			1 569 476

Other relevant data is as follows for the year 200X:

	Finished product	
	Model alpha	Model sigma
Forecast sales (units)	8500	1600
Selling price per unit	£400	£560
Ending inventory required (units)	1870	90
Beginning inventory (units)	170	85

	Direct material	
	Material X	Material Y
Beginning inventory (units)	8 500	8 000
Ending inventory required (units)	10 200	1 700

	Department 1 (£)	Department 2 (£)
Budgeted variable overhead rates (per direct labour hour):		
Indirect materials	1.20	0.80
Indirect labour	1.20	1.20
Power (variable portion)	0.60	0.40
Maintenance (variable portion)	0.20	0.40
Budgeted fixed overheads		
Depreciation	100 000	80 000
Supervision	100 000	40 000
Power (fixed portion)	40 000	2 000
Maintenance (fixed portion)	45 600	3 196

	(£)
Estimated non-manufacturing overheads: Stationery etc. (Administration)	4 000
Salaries	
Sales	74 000
Office	28 000
Commissions	60 000
Car expenses (Sales)	22 000
Advertising	80 000
Miscellaneous (Office)	8 000
	276 000

Budgeted cash flows are as follows:

	Quarter 1 (£)	Quarter 2 (£)	Quarter 3 (£)	Quarter 4 (£)
Receipts from customers	1 000 000	1 200 000	1 120 000	985 000
Payments:				
Materials	400 000	480 000	440 000	547 984
Payments for wages	400 000	440 000	480 000	646 188
Other costs and expenses	120 000	100 000	72 016	13 642

You are required to prepare a master budget for the year 200X and the following budgets:

1 sales budget;

2 production budget;

3 direct materials usage budget;

4 direct materials purchase budget;

5 direct labour budget;

6 factory overhead budget;

7 selling and administration budget;

8 cash budget.

SALES BUDGET

The sales budget shows the quantities of each product that the company plans to sell and the intended selling price. It provides the predictions of total revenue from which cash receipts from customers will be estimated, and it also supplies the basic data for constructing budgets for production costs, and for selling, distribution and administrative expenses. The sales budget is therefore the foundation of all other budgets, since all expenditure is ultimately dependent on the volume of sales. If the sales budget is not accurate, the other budget estimates will be unreliable. We will assume that the Enterprise Company has completed a marketing analysis and that the following annual sales budget is based on the result:

Schedule 1 – Sales budget for year ending 200X

Product	Units sold	Selling price (£)	Total revenue (£)
Alpha	8500	400	3 400 000
Sigma	1600	560	896 000
			4 296 000

Schedule 1 represents the *total* sales budget for the year. In practice, the *total* sales budget will be supported by detailed *subsidiary* sales budgets where sales are analyzed by areas of responsibility, such as sales territories, and into monthly periods analyzed by products.

PRODUCTION BUDGET AND BUDGETED INVENTORY LEVELS

When the sales budget has been completed, the next stage is to prepare the production budget. This budget is expressed in *quantities only* and is the responsibility of the production manager. The objective is to ensure that production is sufficient to meet sales demand and that economic inventory levels are maintained. The production budget (schedule 2) for the year will be as follows:

Schedule 2 – Annual production budget

	Department 1 (alpha)	Department 2 (sigma)
Units to be sold	8 500	1600
Planned closing inventory	1 870	90
Total units required for sales and inventories	10 370	1690
Less planned opening inventories	170	85
Units to be produced	10 200	1605

The total production for each department should also be analyzed on a monthly basis.

DIRECT MATERIALS USAGE BUDGET

The supervisors of departments 1 and 2 will prepare estimates of the materials which are required to meet the production budget. The materials usage budget for the year will be as follows:

Schedule 3 – Annual direct material usage budget

	Department 1			Department 2					
	Units	Unit price (£)	Total (£)	Units	Unit price (£)	Total (£)	Total units	Total unit price (£)	Total (£)
Material X	102 000[a]	7.20	734 400	12 840[c]	7.20	92 448	114 840	7.20	826 848
Material Y	51 000[b]	16.00	816 000	14 445[d]	16.00	231 120	65 445	16.00	1 047 120
			1 550 400			323 568			1 873 968

[a] 10 200 units production at 10 units per unit of production.
[b] 10 200 units production at 5 units per unit of production.
[c] 1605 units production at 8 units per unit of production.
[d] 1605 units production at 9 units per unit of production.

DIRECT MATERIALS PURCHASE BUDGET

The direct materials purchase budget is the responsibility of the purchasing manager, since it will be he or she who is responsible for obtaining the planned quantities of raw materials to meet the production requirements. The objective is to purchase these materials at the right time at the planned purchase price. In addition, it is necessary to take into account the planned raw material inventory levels. The annual materials purchase budget for the year will be as follows:

Schedule 4 – Direct materials purchase budget

	Material X (units)	Material Y (units)
Quantity necessary to meet production requirements as per material usage budget	114 840	65 445
Planned closing inventory	10 200	1 700
	125 040	67 145
Less planned opening inventory	8 500	8 000
Total units to be purchased	116 540	59 145
Planned unit purchase price	£7.20	£16
Total purchases	£839 088	£946 320

Note that this budget is a summary budget for the year, but for detailed planning and control it will be necessary to analyze the annual budget on a monthly basis.

DIRECT LABOUR BUDGET

The direct labour budget is the responsibility of the respective managers of departments 1 and 2. They will prepare estimates of the departments' labour hours required to meet the planned production. Where different grades of labour exist, these should be specified separately in the budget. The budget rate per hour should be determined by the industrial relations department. The direct labour budget will be as follows:

Schedule 5 – Annual direct labour budget

	Department 1	Department 2	Total
Budgeted production (units)	10 200	1 605	
Hours per unit	10	15	
Total budgeted hours	102 000	24 075	126 075
Budgeted wage rate per hour	£12	£12	
Total wages	£1 224 000	£288 900	£1 512 900

FACTORY OVERHEAD BUDGET

The factory overhead budget is also the responsibility of the respective production department managers. The total of the overhead budget will depend on the behaviour of the costs of the individual overhead items in relation to the anticipated level of production. The overheads must also be analyzed according to whether they are controllable or non-controllable for the purpose of cost control. The factory overhead budget will be as follows:

Schedule 6 – Annual factory overhead budget
Anticipated activity – 102 000 direct labour hours (department 1)
24 075 direct labour hours (department 2)

| | Variable overhead rate per direct labour hour | | Overheads | | |
	Department 1 (£)	Department 2 (£)	Department 1 (£)	Department 2 (£)	Total (£)
Controllable overheads:					
Indirect material	1.20	0.80	122 400	19 260	
Indirect labour	1.20	1.20	122 400	28 890	
Power (variable portion)	0.60	0.40	61 200	9 630	
Maintenance (variable portion)	0.20	0.40	20 400	9 630	
			326 400	67 410	393 810
Non-controllable overheads:					
Depreciation			100 000	80 000	
Supervision			100 000	40 000	
Power (fixed portion)			40 000	2 000	
Maintenance (fixed portion)			45 600	3 196	
			285 600	125 196	410 796
Total overhead			612 000	192 606	804 606
Budgeted departmental overhead rate			£6.00[a]	8.00[b]	

[a]£612 000 total overheads divided by 102 000 direct labour hours.
[b]£192 606 total overheads divided by 24 075 direct labour hours.

The budgeted expenditure for the variable overhead items is determined by multiplying the budgeted direct labour hours for each department by the budgeted variable overhead rate per hour. It is assumed that all variable overheads vary in relation to direct labour hours.

SELLING AND ADMINISTRATION BUDGET

The selling and administration budgets have been combined here to simplify the presentation. In practice, separate budgets should be prepared: the sales manager will be responsible for the selling budget, the distribution manager will be responsible for the distribution expenses and the chief administrative officer will be responsible for the administration budget.

Schedule 7 – Annual selling and administration budget

	(£)	(£)
Selling:		
Salaries	74 000	
Commission	60 000	
Car expenses	22 000	
Advertising	80 000	236 000
Administration:		
Stationery	4 000	
Salaries	28 000	
Miscellaneous	8 000	40 000
		276 000

DEPARTMENTAL BUDGETS

For cost control the direct labour budget, materials usage budget and factory overhead budget are combined into separate departmental budgets. These budgets are normally broken down into twelve separate monthly budgets, and the actual monthly expenditure is compared with the budgeted amounts for each of the items concerned. This comparison is used for judging how effective managers are in controlling the expenditure for which they are responsible. The departmental budget for department 1 will be as follows:

Department 1 – Annual departmental operating budget

	(£)	Budget (£)	Actual (£)
Direct labour (from schedule 5):			
102 000 hours at £12		1 224 000	
Direct materials (from schedule 3):			
102 000 units of material X at £7.20 per unit	734 400		
51 000 units of material Y at £16 per unit	816 000	1 550 400	
Controllable overheads (from schedule 6):			
Indirect materials	122 400		
Indirect labour	122 400		
Power (variable portion)	61 200		
Maintenance (variable portion)	20 400	326 400	
Uncontrollable overheads (from schedule 6):			
Depreciation	100 000		
Supervision	100 000		
Power (fixed portion)	40 000		
Maintenance (fixed portion)	45 600	285 600	
		3 386 400	

MASTER BUDGET

When all the budgets have been prepared, the budgeted profit and loss account and balance sheet provide the overall picture of the planned performance for the budget period.

Budgeted profit and loss account for the year ending 200X

	(£)	(£)
Sales (schedule 1)		4 296 000
Opening inventory of raw materials	189 200	
(from opening balance sheet)		
Purchases (schedule 4)	1 785 408[a]	
	1 974 608	
Less closing inventory of raw materials (schedule 4)	100 640[b]	
Cost of raw materials consumed	1 873 968	
Direct labour (schedule 5)	1 512 900	
Factory overheads (schedule 6)	804 606	
Total manufacturing cost	4 191 474	

Add opening inventory of finished goods (from opening balance sheet)	99 076	
Less closing inventory of finished goods	665 984[c]	
		(566 908)
Cost of sales		3 624 566
Gross profit		671 434
Selling and administration expenses (schedule 7)		276 000
Budgeted operating profit for the year		395 434

[a]£839 088 (X) + £946 320 (Y) from schedule 4.
[b]10 200 units at £7.20 plus 1700 units at £16 from schedule 4.
[c]1870 units of alpha valued at £332 per unit, 90 units of sigma valued at £501.60 per unit. The product unit costs are calculated as follows:

	Alpha		Sigma	
	Units	*(£)*	*Units*	*(£)*
Direct materials				
X	10	72.00	8	57.60
Y	5	80.00	9	144.00
Direct labour	10	120.00	15	180.00
Factory overheads:				
Department 1	10	60.00	—	—
Department 2	—	—	15	120.00
		332.00		501.60

Budgeted balance sheet as at 31 December

	(£)	*(£)*
Fixed assets:		
Land		170 000
Building and equipment	1 292 000	
Less depreciation[a]	435 000	857 000
		1 027 000
Current assets:		
Raw material inventory	100 640	
Finished good inventory	665 984	
Debtors[b]	280 000	
Cash[c]	199 170	
	1 245 794	
Current liabilities:		
Creditors[d]	307 884	937 910
		1 964 910
Represented by shareholders' interest:		
1 200 000 ordinary shares of £1 each	1 200 000	
Reserves	369 476	
Profit and loss account	395 434	1 964 910

[a]£255 000 + £180 000 (schedule 6) = £435 000.
[b]£289 000 opening balance + £4 296 000 sales − £4 305 000 cash.
[c]Closing balance as per cash budget.
[d]£248 800 opening balance + £1 785 408 purchases + £141 660 indirect materials − £1 876 984 cash.

CASH BUDGETS

The objective of the cash budget is to ensure that sufficient cash is available at all times to meet the level of operations that are outlined in the various budgets. The cash budget for Example 15.1 is presented below and is analyzed by quarters, but in practice monthly or weekly budgets will be necessary. Because cash budgeting is subject to uncertainty, it is necessary to provide for more than the minimum amount required, to allow for some margin of error in planning. Cash budgets can help a firm to avoid cash balances that are surplus to its requirements by enabling management to take steps in advance to invest the surplus cash in short-term investments. Alternatively, cash deficiencies can be identified in advance, and steps can be taken to ensure that bank loans will be available to meet any temporary cash deficiencies. For example, by looking at the cash budget for the Enterprise Company, management may consider that the cash balances are higher than necessary in the second and third quarters of the year, and they may invest part of the cash balance in short-term investments.

The overall aim should be to manage the cash of the firm to attain maximum cash availability and maximum interest income on any idle funds.

Cash budget for year ending 200X

	Quarter 1 (£)	Quarter 2 (£)	Quarter 3 (£)	Quarter 4 (£)	Total (£)
Opening balance	34 000	114 000	294 000	421 984	34 000
Receipts from debtors	1 000 000	1 200 000	1 120 000	985 000	4 305 000
	1 034 000	1 314 000	1 414 000	1 406 984	4 339 000
Payments:					
Purchase of materials	400 000	480 000	440 000	547 984	1 867 984
Payment of wages	400 000	440 000	480 000	646 188	1 966 188
Other costs and expenses	120 000	100 000	72 016	13 642	305 658
	920 000	1 020 000	992 016	1 207 814	4 139 830
Closing balance	114 000	294 000	421 984	199 170	199 170

FINAL REVIEW

The budgeted profit and loss account, the balance sheet and the cash budget will be submitted by the accountant to the budget committee, together with a number of budgeted financial ratios such as the return on capital employed, working capital, liquidity and gearing ratios. If these ratios prove to be acceptable, the budgets will be approved. In Example 15.1 the return on capital employed is approximately 20 per cent, but the working capital ratio (current assets : current liabilities) is over 4:1, so management should consider alternative ways of reducing investment in working capital before finally approving the budgets.

COMPUTERIZED BUDGETING

In the past, budgeting was a task dreaded by many management accountants. You will have noted from Example 15.1 that many numerical manipulations are necessary to prepare the budget. In the real world the process is far more complex, and, as the budget is being formulated, it is altered many times since some budgets are found to be out of balance with each other or the master budget proves to be unacceptable.

In today's world, the budgeting process is computerized instead of being primarily concerned with numerical manipulations, the accounting staff can now become more involved in the real planning process. Computer-based financial models normally consist of mathematical statements of inputs and outputs. By simply altering the mathematical statements budgets can be quickly revised with little effort.

Computerized budgeting – demand planning at AmBev

AmBev is Latin America's largest beverage company. The company has 49 beverage plants in Brazil alone, and it distributes its products to over 1 million points of sale throughout the country. Keeping all these outlets stocked is a mammoth operation. According to Tiago Rino, a demand planning specialist at AmBev, the company does not want to produce too much or too little, while simultaneously maximizing the distribution of its products.

In 2003, the company started using SAS, a leading business analytics software provider. The SAS forecasting solution used by AmBev combines historical data from company locations, including sales and distribution data for more than 180 products. The software automatically analyzes the data and provides in-depth information on demand by connecting production levels, distribution plans and all other

processes related to demand and replenishment planning. The results speak for themselves. According to Rino, product turnover (i.e. days held in inventory in a factory) has decreased by 50 per cent to 7–8 days. Production planning, distribution planning and sales forecasts have all improved too.

Questions

1   How useful is the detailed demand planning information obtained from systems like SAS for the annual budgeting process?

2   Is an annual sales/demand budgeting process still necessary when such detailed and complex systems are in place?

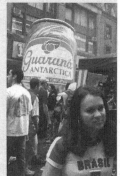

© Richard Levine / Alamy

References

http://www.sas.com/success/ambev.html
http://www.ambev.com.br/pt-br

However, the major advantage of computerized budgeting is that management can evaluate many different options before the budget is finally agreed. Establishing a model enables 'What-if?' analysis to be employed. For example, answers to the following questions can be displayed in the form of a master budget: What if sales increase or decrease by 10 per cent? What if unit costs increase or decrease by 5 per cent? What if the credit terms for sales were reduced from 30 to 20 days?

In addition, computerized models can incorporate actual results, period by period, and carry out the necessary calculations to produce budgetary *control* reports. It is also possible to adjust the budgets for the remainder of the year when it is clear that the circumstances on which the budget was originally set have changed.

ACTIVITY-BASED BUDGETING

The conventional approach to budgeting works fine for unit level activity costs where the consumption of resources varies proportionately with the volume of the final output of products or services. However, for those indirect costs and support activities where there are no clearly defined input–output relationships, and the consumption of resources does not vary with the final output of products or services, conventional budgets merely serve as authorization levels for certain levels of spending for each budgeted item of expense. Budgets that are not based on well-understood relationships between activities and costs are poor indicators of performance, and performance reporting normally implies little more than checking whether the budget has been exceeded. Conventional budgets therefore provide little relevant information for managing the costs of support activities.

With conventional budgeting, indirect costs and support activities are prepared on an incremental basis. This means that existing operations and the current budgeted allowance for existing activities are taken as the starting point for preparing the next annual budget. The base is then adjusted for changes (such as changes in product mix, volumes and prices) which are expected to occur during the new budget period. This approach is called incremental budgeting, since the budget process is concerned mainly with the increment in operations or expenditure that will occur during the forthcoming budget period. For example, the allowance for budgeted expenses may be based on the previous budgeted allowance plus an increase to cover higher prices caused by inflation. The major disadvantage of the incremental approach is that the majority of expenditure, which is associated with the 'base level' of activity, remains unchanged. Thus, the cost of non-unit level activities becomes fixed and past inefficiencies and waste inherent in the current way of doing things is perpetuated.

To manage costs more effectively organizations that have implemented activity-based costing (ABC) have also adopted activity-based budgeting (ABB). The aim of ABB is to authorize the supply of only those resources that are needed to perform activities required to meet the budgeted production and sales volume. Whereas ABC assigns resource expenses to activities and then uses activity cost drivers to assign activity costs to cost objects (such as products, services or customers), ABB is the reverse of this process. Cost objects are the starting point. Their budgeted output determines the necessary activities which are then used to estimate the resources that are required for the budget period. ABB involves the following stages:

1 estimate the production and sales volume by individual products and customers;
2 estimate the demand for organizational activities;
3 determine the resources that are required to perform organizational activities;
4 estimate for each resource the quantity that must be supplied to meet the demand;
5 take action to adjust the capacity of resources to match the projected supply.

The first stage is identical to conventional budgeting. Details of budgeted production and sales volumes for individual products and customer types will be contained in the sales and production budgets. Next, ABC extends conventional budgeting to support activities such as ordering, receiving, scheduling production and processing customers' orders. To implement ABB the activities that are necessary to produce and sell the products and services and service customers must be identified. Estimates of the quantity of activity cost drivers must be derived for each activity. For example, the number of purchase orders, the number of receipts, the number of set-ups and the number of customer orders processed are estimated using the same approach as that used by conventional budgeting to determine the quantity of direct labour and materials that are incorporated into the direct labour and materials purchase budgets. Standard cost data incorporating a bill of activities is maintained for each product indicating the different activities, and the quantity of activity drivers that are required, to produce a specified number of products. Such documentation provides the basic information for building up the activity-based budgets.

The third stage is to estimate the resources that are required for performing the quantity of activity drivers demanded. In particular, estimates are required of each type of resource, and their quantities required, to meet the demanded quantity of activities. For example, if the number of customer orders to be processed is estimated to be 5000 and each order takes 30 minutes processing time then 2500 labour hours of the customer processing activity must be supplied.

In the fourth stage the resources demanded (derived from the third stage) are converted into an estimate of the total resources that must be supplied for each type of resource used by an activity. The quantity of resources supplied depends on the cost behaviour of the resource. For flexible resources where the supply can be matched exactly to meet demand, such as direct materials and energy costs, the quantity of resources supplied will be identical to the quantity demanded. For example, if customer processing were a flexible resource exactly 2500 hours would be purchased. However, a more likely assumption is that customer processing labour will be a step cost function in relation to the volume of the activity (see Chapter 2 for a description of step cost functions). Assuming that each person employed is contracted to work 1500 hours per year then 1.67 persons (2500/1500) represents the quantity of resources required, but because resources must be acquired in uneven amounts, two persons must be employed. For other resources, such as equipment, resources will tend to be fixed and committed over a very wide range of volume for the activity. As long as demand is less than the capacity supplied by the committed resource no additional spending will be required.

EXHIBIT 15.2 Activity-based budget for an order receiving process

Activities →	Handle import goods	Execute express orders	Special deliveries	Distribution administration	Order receiving (standard products)	Order receiving (non-standard products)	Execute rush orders	Total cost
Resource expense accounts:								
Office supplies								
Telephone expenses								
Salaries								
Travel Training								
Total cost								
Activity cost driver → measures	Number of customs documents	Number of customer bills	Number of letters of credit	Number of consignment notes	Number of standard orders	Number of non-standard orders	Number of rush orders	

The final stage is to compare the estimates of the quantity of resources to be supplied for each resource with the quantity of resources that are currently committed. If the estimated demand for a resource exceeds the current capacity additional spending must be authorized within the budgeting process to acquire additional resources. Alternatively, if the demand for resources is less than the projected supply, the budgeting process should result in management taking action to either redeploy or reduce those resources that are no longer required.

Exhibit 15.2 illustrates an activity-based budget for an order receiving process or department. You will see that the budget is presented in a matrix format with the major activities being shown for each of the columns and the resource inputs are listed by rows. The cost driver activity levels are also highlighted. A major feature of ABB is the enhanced visibility arising from showing the outcomes, in terms of cost drivers, from the budgeted expenditure. This information is particularly useful for planning and estimating future expenditure.

Let us now look at how ABB can be applied using the information presented in Exhibit 15.2. Assume that ABB stages one and two as outlined above result in an estimated annual demand of 2800 orders for the processing of the receipt of the standard customers' order activity (column 6 in Exhibit 15.2). For the staff salaries row (that is, the processing of customers' orders labour resource) assume that each member of staff can process on average 50 orders per month, or 600 per year. Therefore 4.67 (2800 orders/600 orders) persons are required for the supply of this resource (that is, stage three as outlined above). The fourth stage converts the 4.67 staff resources into the amount that must be supplied, that is five members of staff. Let us assume that the current capacity or supply of resources committed to the activity is six members of staff at £25 000 per annum, giving a total annual cost of £150 000. Management is therefore made aware that staff resources can be reduced by £25 000 per annum by transferring one member of staff to other activities where staff resources need to be expanded or, more drastically, making them redundant.

Some of the other resource expenses (such as office supplies and telephone expenses) listed in Exhibit 15.2 for the processing of customers' order activity represent flexible resources which are likely to vary in the short-term with the number of orders processed. Assuming that the budget for the forthcoming period represents 80 per cent of the number of orders processed during the previous budget period, then the budget for those resource expenses that vary in the short-term with the number of orders processed should be reduced by 20 per cent.

With conventional budgeting the budgeted expenses for the forthcoming budget for support activities are normally based on the previous year's budget plus an adjustment for inflation. Support costs are therefore considered to be fixed in relation to activity volume. In contrast, ABB provides a framework for understanding the amount of resources that are required to achieve the budgeted level of activity. By comparing the amount of resources that are required with the amount of resources that are in place, upwards or downwards adjustments can be made during the budget setting phase.

THE BUDGETING PROCESS IN NON-PROFIT-MAKING ORGANIZATIONS

The budgeting process in a non-profit-making organization normally begins with the managers of the various activities calculating the expected costs of maintaining current ongoing activities and then adding to those costs any further developments of the services that are considered desirable. For example, the education, health, housing and social services departments of a municipal authority will propose specific activities and related costs for the coming year. These budgets are coordinated by the accounting department into an overall budget proposal.

The available resources for financing the proposed level of public services should be sufficient to cover the total costs of such services. In the case of a municipal authority the resources will be raised by local taxes and government grants. Similar procedures are followed by churches, hospitals, charities and other non-profit-making organizations, in that they produce estimates for undertaking their activities and then find the means to finance them, or reduce the activities to realistic levels so that they can be financed from available financial resources.

One difficulty encountered in non-profit-making organizations is that precise objectives are difficult to define in a quantifiable way, and the actual accomplishments are even more difficult to measure. In most situations outputs cannot be measured in monetary terms. By 'outputs' we mean the quality and amount of the services rendered. In profit-oriented organizations output can be measured in terms of sales revenues. The effect of this is that budgets in non-profit organizations, tend to be mainly concerned with the input of resources (i.e. expenditure), whereas budgets in profit organizations focus on the relationships between inputs (expenditure) and outputs (sales revenue). In non-profit organizations there is not the same emphasis on what was intended to be achieved for a given input of resources. The budgeting process tends to compare what is happening in cash input terms with the estimated cash inputs. In other words, there is little emphasis on measures of managerial performance in terms of the results achieved. The reason for this is that there is no clear relationship between resource inputs and the benefits flowing from the use of these resources.

Line item budgets

The traditional format for budgets in non-profit organizations is referred to as line item budgets. A line item budget is one in which the expenditures are expressed in considerable detail, but the activities being undertaken are given little attention. In other words, line item budgeting shows the nature of the spending but not the purpose. A typical line item budget is illustrated in Exhibit 15.3.

EXHIBIT 15.3 Typical line item budget

	Actual 20X2 (£)	Original budget 20X3 (£)	Revised budget 20X3 (£)	Proposed budget 20X4 (£)
Employees	1 292 000	1 400 000	1 441 000	1 830 000
Premises	3 239	12 000	10 800	14 200
Supplies and services	34 735	43 200	44 900	147 700
Transport	25 778	28 500	28 700	30 700
Establishment expenses	123 691	120 000	116 000	158 600
Agency charges	10 120	10 000	9 800	13 300
Financing charges	2 357	2 700	2 800	114 800
Other expenses	1 260	1 350	1 400	1 600
	1 493 180	1 617 750	1 655 400	2 310 900

The amounts in this type of budget are frequently established on the basis of historical costs that have been adjusted for anticipated changes in costs and activity levels. When they are compared with the actual expenditures, line item budgets provide a basis for comparing whether or not the authorized budgeted expenditure has been exceeded or whether underspending has occurred. Note that data for the current year and for the previous year are included to indicate how the proposed budget differs from current spending patterns. However, such line item budgets fail to identify the costs of *activities* and the *programmes* to be implemented. In addition, compliance with line item budgets provides no assurance that resources are used wisely, effectively or efficiently in financing the various activities in a non-profit organization. Planning, programming budgeting systems (PPBS) are intended to overcome these deficiencies. For a description and illustration of PPBS you should refer to Learning Note 15.1 on the digital support resources accompanying this book (see Preface for details).

ZERO-BASED BUDGETING

Zero-based budgeting (also known as priority-based budgeting) emerged as an attempt to overcome the limitations of incremental budgets. This approach requires that projected expenditure for existing activities should start from base zero rather than last year's budget. In other words, managers are required to justify all budgeted expenditure rather than just the changes from the previous year. Besides adopting a 'zero-based' approach, zero-based budgeting (ZBB) also focuses on programmes or activities instead of functional departments based on line-items which is a feature of traditional budgeting. Programmes normally relate to various activities undertaken by municipal or government organizations. Examples include extending childcare facilities, improvement of health care for senior citizens and the extension of nursing facilities.

REAL WORLD VIEWS 15.3

Zero-based budgeting – zero-based budgeting in local communities

Michael Portillo (a British MP) hosted a BBC documentary called 'Power to the People', which looks at ways democracy can empower people. In an episode in March 2010, Portillo described what is, in effect, an example of zero-based budgeting (ZBB). In the documentary, Portillo visits a 'You Decide' session organized by the local council in Tower Hamlets, London. At this session, local people decide what is to be done with £250 000 of council money. They are given fully costed options under headings such as healthcare, the elderly and local policing. The options in each category can be debated for a time, then all present 'vote' for their preferred option using an electronic voting system like used those on popular TV shows. This process continues until all funds are

allocated. What in effect has happened here is that the local residents are undertaking the ranking and deciding part of ZBB. This saves the council a bit of time and allocates resources to where residents decide is best. Of course £250 000 is a long way off a council's full budget. The Tower Hamlets Borough Council terms the You Decide process 'participatory budgeting', but what it does at these community sessions applies the principles of ZBB.

Questions

1 What are the key advantages of allowing local people to decide where to allocate money?

2 How do you think the local council decided what service offerings were offered to residents at the sessions?

References

http://wp.me/pxcli-4s
http://www.participatorybudgeting.org.uk/case-studies/you-decide-tower-hamlets-london

ZBB is best suited to discretionary costs and support activities. With discretionary costs management has some discretion as to the amount it will budget for the particular activity in question. Examples of discretionary costs include advertising, research and development and training costs. There is no optimum relationship between inputs (as measured by the costs) and outputs (measured by revenues or some other objective function) for these costs. Furthermore, they are not predetermined by some previous commitment. In effect, management can determine what quantity of service it wishes to purchase and there is no established method for determining the appropriate amount to be spent in particular periods. ZBB has mostly been applied in municipal and government organizations where the predominant costs are of a discretionary nature.

ZBB involves the following three stages:

- a description of each organizational activity in a decision package;
- the evaluation and ranking of decision packages in order of priority;
- allocation of resources based on order of priority up to the spending cut-off level.

Decision packages are identified for each decision unit. Decision units represent separate programmes or groups of activities that an organization undertakes. A decision package represents the operation of a particular programme with incremental packages reflecting different levels of effort that may be expended on a specific function. One package is usually prepared at the 'base' level for each programme. This package represents the minimum level of service or support consistent with the organization's objectives. Service or support higher than the base level is described in one or more incremental packages. For example, managers might be asked to specify the base package in terms of level of service that can be provided at 70 per cent of the current cost level and incremental packages identify higher activity or cost levels.

Once the decision packages have been completed, management is ready to start to review the process. To determine how much to spend and where to spend it, management will rank all packages in order of decreasing benefits to the organization. Theoretically, once management has set the budgeted level of spending, the packages should be accepted down to the spending level based on cost–benefit principles.

The benefits of ZBB over traditional methods of budgeting are claimed to be as follows:

1 Traditional budgeting tends to extrapolate the past by adding a percentage increase to the current year. ZBB avoids the deficiencies of incremental budgeting and represents a move towards the allocation of resources by need or benefit. Thus, unlike traditional budgeting the level of previous funding is not taken for granted.

2 ZBB creates a questioning attitude rather than one that assumes that current practice represents value for money.

3 ZBB focuses attention on outputs in relation to value for money.

ZBB was first applied in Texas Instruments. It quickly became one of the fashionable management tools of the 1970s and, according to Phyrr (1976), there were 100 users in the USA in the early 1970s. ZBB never achieved the widespread adoption that its proponents envisaged. The major reason for its lack of success would appear to be that it is too costly and time-consuming. The process of identifying decision packages and determining their purpose, cost and benefits is extremely time-consuming. Furthermore, there are often too many decision packages to evaluate and there is frequently insufficient information to enable them to be ranked.

Research suggests that many organizations tend to approximate the principles of ZBB rather than applying the full-scale approach outlined in the literature. For example, it does not have to be applied throughout the organization. It can be applied selectively to those areas about which management is most concerned and used as a one-off cost reduction programme. Some of the benefits of ZBB can be captured by using priority-based incremental budgets. Priority incremental budgets require managers to specify what incremental activities or changes would occur if their budgets were increased or decreased by a specified percentage (say 10 per cent). Budget allocations are made by comparing the change in costs with the change in benefits. Priority incremental budgets thus represent an economical compromise between ZBB and incremental budgeting.

CRITICISMS OF BUDGETING

In recent years criticisms of traditional budgeting have attracted much publicity. Indeed, in a series of articles Hope and Fraser (1999a, 1999b, 2001, 2003) have argued that companies should abandon traditional budgeting. They advocate that companies should move beyond budgeting. According to Hope and Fraser (1999a) a number of innovative companies, such as Svenska Handelsbanken (a Swedish bank) and Volvo, are in the process of abandoning traditional budgeting. The major criticism is that the annual budgeting process is incapable of meeting the demands of the competitive environment in today's information age. Ekholm and Wallin (2000) and Dugdale and Lyne (2006) have reviewed the literature relating to annual budgets. They have identified the following criticisms relating to the annual budgeting process:

- encouraging rigid planning and incremental thinking;
- being time-consuming;
- ignoring key drivers of shareholder value by focusing too much attention on short-term financial numbers;
- being a yearly rigid ritual that impedes firms from being flexible and adaptive in the increasingly unpredictable environment facing contemporary organizations;
- tying the company to a 12-month commitment, which is risky since it is based on uncertain forecasts;
- meeting only the lowest targets and not attempting to beat the targets;
- spending what is in the budget even if this is not necessary in order to guard against next year's budget being reduced;
- achieving the budget even if this results in undesirable actions;
- being disconnected from strategy.

The term beyond budgeting is used by Hope and Fraser to relate to alternative approaches that should be used instead of annual budgeting. Rolling forecasts, produced on a monthly or quarterly basis, are suggested as the main alternative to the annual budget. Such rolling forecasts should embrace key performance indicators based on balanced scorecards (see Chapter 22) that are necessary to achieve the objectives of the organization and should also incorporate exception-based monitoring and benchmarking (see Chapter 21). Rolling forecasts are advocated because they do not have the same compulsory and stifling image when compared with the annual budget.

Because of the criticisms of budgeting, and the beyond budgeting movement, Dugdale and Lyne (2006) surveyed financial and non-financial managers in 40 UK companies. Their main conclusion was that budgeting is alive and well. All of the companies surveyed used budgets and, generally, both financial and non-financial managers thought they were important for planning, control, performance measurement, coordination and communication. To find out how problematic the respondents viewed their budgets, they were asked whether they agreed with 20 critical propositions. The respondents tended to disagree with the propositions. Ekholm and Wallin also surveyed 168 Finnish companies. They reported that relatively few companies were planning to abandon the annual budget. However, in contrast to the UK findings by Dugdale and Lyne there was strong agreement with many of the criticisms relating to budgeting. Comments by several respondents also indicated that complementary systems, such as rolling forecasts and monitoring systems similar to the balanced scorecard already exist, and are run in parallel with the annual budget.

A more recent study of budgeting practices in North American organizations was undertaken by Libby and Lindsay (2010). Their findings indicate that budgeting systems continue to play a key role in firms' control systems and that only 5 per cent of the 558 surveyed firms were considering possibly abandoning budgeting, although many were taking steps to improve their systems to overcome some of the common criticisms. They also found that:

- subjective considerations for uncontrollable events were frequently taken into account when using the budget to evaluate performance;
- budgets were revised much more often than expected, and
- the budget process was explicitly linked to strategy implementation in the majority of firms surveyed.

SUMMARY

The following items relate to the learning objectives listed at the beginning of the chapter.

Explain how budgeting fits into the overall planning and control framework.

The annual budget should be set within the context of longer-term plans, which are likely to exist even if they have not been made explicit. A long-term plan is a statement of the preliminary targets and activities required by an organization to achieve its strategic plans, together with a broad estimate for each year of the resources required. Because long-term planning involves 'looking into the future' for several years, the plans tend to be uncertain, general in nature, imprecise and subject to change. Annual budgeting is concerned with the detailed implementation of the long-term plan for the year ahead.

Identify and describe the six different purposes of budgeting.

Budgets are used for the following purposes: (a) planning annual operations; (b) coordinating the activities of the various parts of the organization and ensuring that the parts are in harmony with each other; (c) communicating the plans to the managers of the various responsibility centres; (d) motivating managers to strive to achieve organizational goals; (e) controlling activities; and (f) evaluating the performance of managers.

Identify and describe the various stages in the budget process.

The important stages are as follows: (a) communicating details of the budget policy and guidelines to those people responsible for the preparation of the budgets; (b) determining the factor that restricts output (normally sales volume); (c) preparation of the sales budget (assuming that sales demand is the factor that restricts output); (d) initial preparation of the various budgets; (e) negotiation of budgets with superiors; (f) coordination and review of budgets; (g) final acceptance of budgets; and (h) ongoing review of budgets. Each of the above stages is described in the chapter.

Prepare functional and master budgets.

When all of the budgets have been prepared they are summarized into a master budget consisting in a budgeted profit and loss account, a balance sheet and a cash budget statement. The preparation of functional and master budgets was illustrated using Example 15.1.

Describe the use of computer-based financial models for budgeting.

Computer-based financial models are mathematical statements of the inputs and output relationships that affect the budget. These models allow management to conduct sensitivity analysis to ascertain the effects on the master budget of changes in the original predicted data or changes in the assumptions that were used to prepare the budgets.

Describe the limitations of incremental budgeting.

With incremental budgeting indirect costs and support activities are prepared on an incremental basis. This means that existing operations and the current budgeted allowance for existing activities are taken as the starting point for preparing the next annual budget. The base is then adjusted for changes (such as changes in product mix, volumes and prices) which are expected to occur during the new budget period. When this approach is adopted the concern is mainly with the increment in operations or expenditure that will occur during the forthcoming budget period. The major disadvantage of the incremental approach is that the majority of expenditure, which is associated with the 'base level' of activity, remains unchanged. Thus, past inefficiencies and waste inherent in the current way of doing things are perpetuated.

● **Describe activity-based budgeting.**

With conventional budgeting the budgeted expenses for the forthcoming budget for support activities are normally based on the previous year's budget plus an adjustment for inflation. Support costs are therefore considered to be fixed in relation to activity volume. Activity-based budgeting (ABB) aims to manage costs more effectively by authorizing the supply of only those resources that are needed to perform activities required to meet the budgeted production and sales volume. Whereas ABC assigns resource expenses to activities and then uses activity cost drivers to assign activity costs to cost objects (such as products, services or customers) ABB is the reverse of this process. Cost objects are the starting point. Their budgeted output determines the necessary activities which are then used to estimate the resources that are required for the budget period. ABB involves the following stages: (a) estimate the production and sales volume by individual products and customers; (b) estimate the demand for organizational activities; (c) determine the resources that are required to perform organizational activities; (d) estimate for each resource the quantity that must be supplied to meet the demand; and (e) take action to adjust the capacity of resources to match the projected supply.

● **Describe zero-based budgeting (ZBB).**

ZBB is a method of budgeting that is mainly used in non-profit organizations but it can also be applied to discretionary costs and support activities in profit organizations. It seeks to overcome the deficiencies of incremental budgeting. ZBB works from the premise that projected expenditure for existing programmes should start from base zero, with each year's budgets being compiled as if the programmes were being launched for the first time. The budgetees should present their requirements for appropriations in such a fashion that all funds can be allocated on the basis of cost–benefit or some similar kind of evaluative analysis. The cost–benefit approach is an attempt to ensure 'value for money'; it questions long-standing assumptions and serves as a tool for systematically examining and perhaps abandoning any unproductive projects.

● **Describe the criticisms relating to traditional budgeting.**

Criticisms relating to traditional budgeting include encouraging rigid planning and incremental thinking, being time-consuming, a failure to encourage continuous improvement, achieving the target even if this results in undesirable actions and being a yearly rigid ritual. The beyond budgeting movement advocates that budgeting should be replaced with rolling forecasts that embrace key performance indicators and also incorporate exception-based monitoring and benchmarking.

NOTE

1   The criteria specified are derived from Johnson, Scholes and Whittington (2010).

KEY TERMS AND CONCEPTS

Activity-based budgeting (ABB) An approach to budgeting that takes cost objects as the starting point, determines the necessary activities and then estimates the resources that are required for the budget period.

Beyond budgeting A term used to describe alternative approaches, such as rolling forecasts, that can be used instead of annual budgeting.

Budgeting The implementation of the long-term plan for the year ahead through the development of detailed financial plans.

Budget A financial plan for implementing management decisions.

Cash budget A budget that aims to ensure that sufficient cash is available at all times to meet the level of operations that are outlined in all other budgets.

Continuous budgeting An approach to budgeting in which the annual budget is broken down into months for the first three months and into quarters for the rest of the year, with a new quarter being added as each quarter ends, also known as rolling budgeting.

Control process The process of comparing actual and planned outcomes, and responding to any deviations from the plan.

Corporate objectives Specific, measurable statements, often expressed in financial terms, of what the organization as a whole wishes to achieve.

Decision packages In zero-based budgeting, alternative versions of activities that are described and costed for review by management.

Discretionary costs Costs such as advertising and research where management has some discretion as to the amount it will budget.

Feedback loops Parts of a control system that allow for review and corrective action to ensure that actual outcomes conform with planned outcomes.

Incremental budgeting An approach to budgeting in which existing operations and the current budgeted allowance for existing activities are taken as the starting point for preparing the next annual budget and are then adjusted for anticipated changes.

Incremental budgets Budgets in which existing operations and the current budgeted allowance for existing activities are taken as the starting point for preparing the next annual budget

Line item budgets The traditional format for budgets in non-profit organizations, in which expenditures are expressed in considerable detail, but the activities being undertaken are given little attention.

Long-term plan A top level plan that sets out the objectives that an organization's future activities will be directed towards, also known as a strategic plan.

Management by exception A system in which a manager's attention and effort can be concentrated on significant deviations from the expected results.

Master budget A document that brings together and summarizes all lower level budgets and which consists of a budgeted profit and loss account, a balance sheet and cash flow statement.

Mission A general statement of an organization's purpose, its reason for existence, the nature of the business(es) it is in and the customers it seeks to serve.

Priority-based budgeting An approach to budgeting in which projected expenditure for existing activities starts from base zero rather than last year's budget, forcing managers to justify all budget expenditure, also known as zero-based budgeting.

Priority-based incremental budgets Budgets in which managers specify what incremental activities or changes would occur if their budgets were increased or decreased by a specified percentage, leading to budget allocations being made by comparing the change in costs with the change in benefits.

Rolling budgeting An approach to budgeting in which the annual budget is broken down into months for the first three months and into quarters for the rest of the year, with a new quarter being added as each quarter ends, also known as continuous budgeting.

Strategic plan A top level plan that sets out the objectives that an organization's future activities will be directed towards, also known as a long-term plan.

Strategy The courses of action that must be taken to achieve an organization's overall objectives.

Unit objectives Specific, measurable statements, often expressed in financial terms, of what individual units within an organization wish to achieve.

Zero-based budgeting An approach to budgeting in which projected expenditure for existing activities starts from base zero rather than last year's budget, forcing managers to justify all budget expenditure, also known as priority-based budgeting.

RECOMMENDED READING

In this chapter we have provided a very brief summary of the process for selecting alternative strategies. A detailed explanation of strategy formulation can be found in the corporate strategy literature. Predominant texts on this area include Johnson, Scholes and Whittington (2011) and Thompson and Martin (2010). For a more detailed discussion of budgeting in the public sector see Jones and Pendlebury (2010).

You should refer to Kennedy and Dugdale (1999) for a discussion of the reasons for the dissatisfaction with the budgeting process and suggestions for ways in which they can be eliminated. Other relevant articles relating to the criticisms of budgeting include Ekholm and Wallin (2000), Hope and Fraser (2001) and Dugdale and Lyne (2006).

KEY EXAMINATION POINTS

Examination questions on budgeting frequently require the preparation of functional or cash budgets. A common mistake is to incorrectly deduct closing inventories and add opening inventories when preparing production and material purchase budgets. Examination questions are also set frequently on zero-based budgeting (ZBB). Do make sure that you can describe and discuss the advantages and disadvantages of ZBB and distinguish between incremental budgeting and ZBB. You should refer to the solution to Review Problem 15.22 for the application of activity-based budgeting.

ASSESSMENT MATERIAL

The review questions are short questions that enable you to assess your understanding of the main topics included in the chapter. The numbers in parentheses provide you with the page numbers to refer to if you cannot answer a specific question.

The review problems are more complex and require you to relate and apply the content to various business problems. The problems are graded by their level of difficulty. Solutions to review problems that are not preceded by the term 'IM' are provided in a separate section at the end of the book. Solutions to problems preceded by the term 'IM' are provided in the *Instructor's Manual* accompanying this book that can be downloaded from the lecturer's digital support resources. Additional review problems with fully worked solutions are provided in the *Student Manual* that accompanies this book.

The digital support resources also include over 30 case problems. A list of these cases is provided on pages 676–680. Several cases are relevant to the content of this chapter. Examples include Endeavour Twoplise Ltd, Global Ltd and Integrated Technology Ltd.

REVIEW QUESTIONS

15.1 Define the term 'budget'. How are budgets used in planning? (pp. 358–361)

15.2 Describe the different stages in the planning and control process. (pp. 359–660)

15.3 Distinguish between budgeting and long-range planning. How are they related? (p. 360)

15.4 Describe the different purposes of budgeting. (pp. 361–362)

15.5 Explain what is meant by the term 'management by exception'. (p. 362)

15.6 Describe how the different roles of budgets can conflict with each other. (p. 362)

15.7 Distinguish between continuous and rolling budgets. (p. 363)

15.8 Describe the different stages in the budgeting process. (pp. 364–367)

15.9 All budgets depend on the sales budget. Do you agree? Explain. (p. 364)

15.10 What is a master budget? (p. 367)

15.11 Define incremental budgeting. (pp. 377–378)

15.12 What are the distinguishing features of activity-based budgeting? (pp. 377–379)

15.13 Describe the five different stages that are involved with activity-based-budgeting. (pp. 378–379)

15.14 What are the distinguishing features of budgeting in non-profit-making organizations? (pp. 380–381)

15.15 What are line item budgets? (p. 380)

15.16 How does zero-based budgeting differ from traditional budgeting? (pp. 381–382)

15.17 What are discretionary costs? (p. 382)

15.18 Distinguish between zero-based budgeting and priority-based incremental budgeting. (p. 382)

REVIEW PROBLEMS

15.19 **Basic**. H has a budgeted production for the next budget year of 12 000 units spread evenly over the year. It expects the same production level to continue for the next two years. Each unit uses 4 kg of material.

The estimated opening raw material inventory at the start of the next budget year is 3 000 kg. H's future policy will be to hold sufficient raw material inventory at the end of each month to cover 110% of the following month's production.

The budgeted material cost is $8 per kg for purchases up to 49 000 kg. The excess of purchases over 49 000 kg in a year will be at cost of $7.50 per kg.

Calculate the material purchases budget for the year is $.

(3 marks)
CIMA P1 Performance operations

15.20 **Intermediate: Budget preparation and flexible budgets**. X Plc manufactures specialist insulating products that are used in both residential and commercial buildings. One of the products, Product W, is made using two different raw materials and two types of labour. The company operates a standard absorption costing system and is now preparing its budgets for the next four quarters. The following information has been identified for Product W:

Sales

Selling price	£220 per unit
Sales demand	
Quarter 1	2250 units
Quarter 2	2050 units
Quarter 3	1650 units
Quarter 4	2050 units
Quarter 5	1250 units
Quarter 6	2050 units

Costs

Materials

A	5 kgs per unit @ £4 per kg
B	3 kgs per unit @ £7 per kg

Labour

Skilled	4 hours per unit @ £15 per hour
Semi-skilled	6 hours per unit @ £9 per hour
Annual overheads	£280 000

40 per cent of these overheads are fixed and the remainder varies with total labour hours. Fixed overheads are absorbed on a unit basis.

Inventory holiday policy

Closing inventory of finished goods	30 per cent of the following quarter's sales demand
Closing inventory of materials	45 per cent of the following quarter's materials usage

The management team are concerned that X Plc has recently faced increasing competition in the market place for Product W. As a consequence there have been issues concerning the availability and costs of the specialized materials and employees needed to manufacture Product W, and there is concern that these might cause problems in the current budget setting process.

(a) Prepare the following budgets for each quarter for X Plc:
   (i) Production budget in units;
   (ii) Raw material purchases budget in kgs and value for Material B. *(5 Marks)*

(b) X Plc has just been informed that Material A may be in short supply during the year for which it is preparing budgets. Discuss the impact this will have on budget preparation and other areas of X Plc. *(5 Marks)*

(c) Assuming that the budgeted production of Product W was 7700 units and that the following actual results were incurred for labour and overheads in the year:

Actual production	7250 units
Actual overheads	
Variable	£185 000
Fixed	£105 000
Actual labour costs	
Skilled – £16.25 per hour	£568 750
Semi-skilled – £8 per hour	£332 400

Prepare a flexible budget statement for X Plc showing the total variances that have occurred for the above four costs only. *(5 Marks)*

(d) X Plc currently uses incremental budgeting. Explain how zero based budgeting could overcome the problems that might be faced as a result of the continued use of the current system. *(5 Marks)*

(e) Explain how rolling budgets are used and why they would be suitable for X Plc. *(5 Marks)*
   CIMA P1 Management Accounting: Performance Evaluation

15.21 Intermediate: Cash budgets. Thorne Co. values, advertises and sells residential property on behalf of its customers. The company has been in business for only a short time and is preparing a cash budget for the first four months of 2013. Expected sales of residential properties are as follows.

	2012	2013	2013	2013	2013
Month	December	January	February	March	April
Units sold	10	10	15	25	30

The average price of each property is £180 000 and Thorne Co. charges a fee of 3 per cent of the value of each property sold. Thorne Co. receives 1 per cent in the month of sale and the remaining 2 per cent in the month after sale. The company has nine employees who are paid on a monthly basis. The average salary per employee is

£35 000 per year. If more than 20 properties are sold in a given month, each employee is paid in that month a bonus of £140 for each additional property sold.

Variable expenses are incurred at the rate of 0.5 per cent of the value of each property sold and these expenses are paid in the month of sale. Fixed overheads of £4300 per month are paid in the month in which they arise. Thorne Co. pays interest every three months on a loan of £200 000 at a rate of 6 per cent per year. The last interest payment in each year is paid in December.

An outstanding tax liability of £95 800 is due to be paid in April. In the same month Thorne Co. intends to dispose of surplus vehicles, with a net book value of £15 000, for £20 000. The cash balance at the start of January 2012 is expected to be a deficit of £40 000.

Required:

(a) Prepare a monthly cash budget for the period from January to April. Your budget must clearly indicate each item of income and expenditure, and the opening and closing monthly cash balances. *(10 marks)*

(b) Discuss the factors to be considered by Thorne Co. when planning ways to invest any cash surplus forecast by its cash budgets. *(5 marks)*

(c) Discuss the advantages and disadvantages to Thorne Co. of using overdraft finance to fund any cash shortages forecast by its cash budgets. *(5 marks)*
   ACCA 2.4 Financial Management and Control

15.22 Advanced: Activity-based budgeting. Flosun plc makes and sells a range of products. Management has carried out an analysis of the total cost of production. The information in Appendix 3.1 reflects this analysis of budgeted costs for the six month period to 30 June. The analysis has identified that the factory is organized in order to permit the operation of three production lines X, Y and Z. Each production line facilitates the production of two or more products. Production line X is only used for the production of products A and B. The products are manufactured in batches on a just-in-time basis in order to fulfil orders from customers. Only one product can be manufactured on the production line at any one time. Materials are purchased and received on a just-in-time basis. Additional information is available for production line X as follows:

(i)   Production line machine costs including labour, power, etc., vary in proportion to machine hours.

(ii) Costs incurred for production scheduling, WIP movement, purchasing and receipt of materials are assumed to be incurred in proportion to the number of batches of product which are manufactured. Machine set-up costs vary in proportion to the number of set-ups required and are linked to a batch throughput system.

(iii) Costs for material scheduling systems and design/testing routines are assumed to be incurred by each product in proportion to the total quantity of components purchased and the total number of types of component used respectively. The number of different components designed/tested for products A and B are 12 and 8 respectively.

(iv) Product line development cost is identified with changes in product design and production method. At present such costs for production line X are apportioned 80 per cent: 20 per cent to products A and B respectively. Production line maintenance costs are assumed to vary in proportion to the maintenance hours required for each product.

(v)   General factory costs are apportioned to each of production lines X, Y and Z in the ratio 25 per cent: 30 per cent: 45 per cent respectively. Such costs are absorbed by product units at an average rate per unit through each production line.

Required:

(a) Prepare an activity based budget for production line X for the six-month period to 30 June analyzed into sub-sets for activities which are product unit based, batch based, product sustaining, production line sustaining and factory sustaining.

The budget should show:

(i) Total cost for each activity sub-set grouped to reflect the differing operational levels at which each sub-set is incurred/controlled.

(ii) Average cost per unit for each of products A and B analyzed by activity sub-set. *(24 marks)*

(b) Discuss the incidence and use of each of the following terms in relation to Flosun plc, giving examples from the question to illustrate your answer:

(i) hierarchy of activities;
(ii) cost pools;
(iii) cost drivers. *(6 marks)*

(c) Prepare a sequential set of steps which may be included in an investigation of activities in order to improve company profitability.

This should be a general list of steps and not specifically relating to Flosun plc. *(5 marks)*
ACCA Paper 9 Information for Control and Decision Making

Appendix 3.1

Flosun plc – Budget data six months to 30 June

	Product A	Product B
Material cost per product unit	£60	£45
Production line X – machine hours per unit	0.8	0.5
Production batch size (units)	100	200
Total production (units)	9 000	15 000
Components per product unit (quantity)	20	12
Number of customers	5	10
Number of production line set-ups	15	25
Production line X – maintenance hours	300	150

Cost category	Production line X £	Factory total £
Labour, power, etc.	294 000	
Set-up of machines	40 000	
Production scheduling	29 600	
WIP movement	36 400	
Purchasing and receipt of material	49 500	
Material scheduling system	18 000	
Design/testing routine	16 000	
Production line development	25 000	
Production line maintenance	9 000	
General factory administration		500 000
General factory occupancy		268 000

15.23 Advanced. You are the management accountant of a group of companies and your managing director has asked you to explore the possibilities of introducing a zero-based budgeting system experimentally in one of the operating companies in place of its existing orthodox system. You are required to prepare notes for a paper for submission to the board that sets out:

(a) how zero-based budgeting would work within the company chosen; *(6 marks)*

(b) what advantages it might offer over the existing system; *(5 marks)*

(c) what problems might be faced in introducing a zero-based budgeting scheme; *(5 marks)*

(d) the features you would look for in selecting the operating company for the introduction in order to obtain the most beneficial results from the experiment. *(4 marks)*
CIMA P3 Management Accounting

15.24 Advanced. Various attempts have been made in the public sector to achieve a more stable, long-term planning base in contrast to the traditional short-term annual budgeting approach, with its emphasis on 'flexibility'.

You are required to:

(a) explain the deficiencies of the traditional approach to planning which led to the attempts to introduce PPBS (programme budgeting); *(6 marks)*

(b) give an illustration of how a PPBS plan could be drawn up in respect of one sector of public authority activity; *(8 marks)*

(c) discuss the problems which have made it difficult in practice to introduce PPBS. *(6 marks)*
CIMA Stage 4: Management Accounting

15.25 Advanced. DW, a transport company, operates three depots. Each depot has a manager who reports directly to the Operations Director.

For many years the depot managers have been asked by the Operations Director to prepare a budget for their depot as part of the company's annual budgeting process. A new depot manager has been appointed to the Southern region and he has concerns about the validity of these annual budgets. He argues that they soon become out of date as operational circumstances change. At a recent manager's meeting he said, "They are restrictive. They do not permit the depot managers to make decisions in response to operational changes, or change working practices for next year until that year's budget has been approved."

Required:

(a) Explain the differences between the above annual budgeting system and a rolling budget system. *(4 marks)*

(b) Discuss how the Southern region depot manager could use a rolling budget system to address his concerns. *(6 marks)*
CIMA P2 Performance Management

IM15.1 Intermediate. Outline:

(a) the objectives of budgetary planning and control systems;

(b) the organization required for the preparation of a master budget. *(10 marks)*
ACCA Level 1 Costing

IM15.2 Intermediate. The preparation of budgets is a lengthy process which requires great care if the ultimate master budget is to be useful for the purposes of management control within an organization.

You are required:

(a) to identify and to explain briefly the stages involved in the preparation of budgets identifying separately the roles of managers and the budget committee; *(8 marks)*

(b) to explain how the use of spreadsheets may improve the efficiency of the budget preparation process. *(7 marks)*
CIMA Stage 1 Accounting

IM15.3 Advanced. What is zero-based budgeting and how does it differ from other more traditional forms of budgeting? Discuss the applicability of zero-based budgeting to profit-orientated organizations. *ACCA Level 2 Management Accounting*

IM15.4 Advanced. The chief executive of your organization has recently seen a reference to zero-based budgeting. He has asked for more details of the technique.

You are required to prepare a report for him explaining:

(a) what zero-based budgeting is and to which areas it can best be applied;

(b) what advantages the technique has over traditional type budgeting systems; and

(c) how the organization might introduce such a technique.

(20 marks)
CIMA P3 Management Accounting

IM15.5 Advanced. Prepare brief notes about zero-based budgeting covering the following topics:

(a) what zero-based budgeting means;
(b) how zero-based budgeting would operate;
(c) what problems might be met in introducing zero-based budgeting;
(d) what special advantages could be expected from zero-base budgeting, as compared with more traditional budgeting methods, for an organization operating in an economic recession.   *(20 marks)*
CIMA P3 Management Accounting

IM15.6 Advanced. A budgetary planning and control system may include many individual budgets which are integrated into a 'master budget'.

You are required to outline and briefly explain with reasons the steps which should normally be taken in the preparation of master budgets in a manufacturing company, indicating the main budgets which you think should normally be prepared.   *(12 marks)*
ICAEW Management Accounting

IM15.7 Advanced. The managing director of your company believes that the existing annual budget system is costly to operate and produces unsatisfactory results due to: long preparation period; business decisions being made throughout the year; unpredictable changes in the rate of general inflation; sudden changes in the availability and price of raw materials. He has read about rolling budgets and wonders whether these might be more useful for his decision-making.

You are required, as the management accountant, to prepare a paper for him covering the following areas.

(a) a brief explanation of rolling budgets;   *(4 marks)*
(b) how a rolling budget system would operate;   *(4 marks)*
(c) *three* significant advantages of a rolling budget system;
(6 marks)
(d) *three* problems likely to be encountered in using a rolling budget system.   *(6 marks)*
CIMA P3 Management Accounting

IM15.8 Advanced. Explain the specific roles of planning, motivation and evaluation in a system of budgetary control.   *(7 marks)*
ACCA Level 2 Management Accounting

IM15.9 Intermediate: Preparation of functional budgets. X plc manufactures Product X using three different raw materials. The product details are as follows:

Selling price per unit £250

Material A	3 kgs	material price £3.50 per kg
Material B	2 kgs	material price £5.00 per kg
Material C	4 kgs	material price £4.50 per kg
Direct labour	8 hours	labour rate £8.00 per hour

The company is considering its budgets for next year and has made the following estimates of sales demand for Product X for July to October:

July	August	September	October
400 units	*300 units*	*600 units*	*450 units*

It is company policy to hold stocks of finished goods at the end of each month equal to 50 per cent of the following month's sales demand, and it is expected that the stock at the start of the budget period will meet this policy.

At the end of the production process the products are tested: it is usual for 10 per cent of those tested to be faulty. It is not possible to rectify these faulty units.

Raw material stocks are expected to be as follows on 1 July:

Material A	1000 kgs
Material B	400 kgs
Material C	600 kgs

Stocks are to be increased by 20 per cent in July, and then remain at their new level for the foreseeable future.

Labour is paid on an hourly rate based on attendance. In addition to the unit direct labour hours shown above, 20 per cent of *attendance time* is spent on tasks which support production activity.

Requirements:

(a) Prepare the following budgets for the quarter from July to September inclusive:

(i)   sales budget in quantity and value;
(ii) production budget in units;
(iii) raw material usage budget in kgs;
(iv) raw material purchases budget in kgs and value;
(v)   labour requirements budget in hours and value.

(16 marks)

(b) Explain the term '*principal budget factor*' and why its identification is an important part of the budget preparation process.   *(3 marks)*
(c) Explain clearly, using data from part (a) above, how you would construct a spreadsheet to produce the labour requirements budget for August. Include a specimen cell layout diagram containing formulae which would illustrate the basis for the spreadsheet.   *(6 marks)*
CIMA Stage 2 Operational Cost Accounting

IM15.10 Intermediate: Preparation of functional budgets. D Limited is preparing its annual budgets for the year to 31 December 2013. It manufactures and sells one product, which has a selling price of £150. The marketing director believes that the price can be increased to £160 with effect from 1 July 2013 and that at this price the sales volume for each quarter of 2013 will be as follows:

	Sales volume
Quarter 1	40 000
Quarter 2	50 000
Quarter 3	30 000
Quarter 4	45 000

Sales for each quarter of 2014 are expected to be 40 000 units.

Each unit of the finished product which is manufactured requires four units of component R and three units of component T, together with a body shell S. These items are purchased from an outside supplier. Currently prices are:

Component R	£8.00 each
Component T	5.00 each
Shell S	£30.00 each

The components are expected to increase in price by 10 per cent with effect from 1 April 2013; no change is expected in the price of the shell.

Assembly of the shell and components into the finished product requires 6 labour hours: labour is currently paid at £10.00 per hour. A 4 per cent increase in wage costs is anticipated to take effect from 1 October 2013.

Variable overhead costs are expected to be £10 per unit for the whole of 2013; fixed production overhead costs are expected to be £240 000 for the year, and are absorbed on a per unit basis. Stocks on 31 December 2012 are expected to be as follows:

Finished units	9000 units
Component R	3000 units
Component T	5500 units
Shell S	500 units

Closing stocks at the end of each quarter are to be as follows:

Finished units	10% of next quarter's sales
Component R	20% of next quarter's production requirements
Component T	15% of next quarter's production requirements
Shell S	10% of next quarter's production requirements

Requirement:

(a) Prepare the following budgets of D Limited for the year ending 31 December 2013, showing values for each quarter and the year in total:

  (i) sales budget (in £s and units)
  (ii) production budget (in units)
  (iii) material usage budget (in units)
  (iv) production cost budget (in £s). *(15 marks)*

(b) Sales are often considered to be the principal budget factor of an organization.

Requirement:
Explain the meaning of the 'principal budget factor' and, assuming that it is sales, explain how sales may be forecast making appropriate reference to the use of statistical techniques and the use of microcomputers. *(10 marks)*
CIMA Stage 2 Operational Cost Accounting

IM15.11 Intermediate: Preparation of cash budgets. A company is to carry out a major modernization of its factory commencing in two weeks time. During the modernization, which is expected to take four weeks to complete, no production of the company's single product will be possible.
  The following additional information is available:

  (i) *Sales/Debtors:* Demand for the product at £100 per unit is expected to continue at 800 units per week, the level of sales achieved for the last four weeks, for one further week. It is then expected to reduce to 700 units per week for three weeks, before rising to a level of 900 units per week where it is expected to remain for several weeks. All sales are on credit, 50 per cent being received in cash in the week following the week of sale and 50 per cent in the week after that.
  (ii) *Production/Finished goods stock:* Production will be at a level of 1200 units per week for the next two weeks. Finished goods stock is 2800 units at the beginning of week 1.
  (iii) *Raw material stock:* Raw material stock is £36 000 at the beginning of week 1. This will be increased by the end of week 1 to £40 000 and reduced to £10 000 by the end of week 2.
  (iv) *Costs*

	(£ per unit)
Variable:	
Raw material	35
Direct labour	20
Overhead	10
Fixed:	
Overhead	25

Fixed overheads have been apportioned to units on the basis of the normal output level of 800 units per week and include depreciation of £4000 per week.
  In addition to the above unit costs, overtime premiums of £5000 per week will be incurred in weeks 1 and 2. During the modernization variable costs will be avoided, apart from direct labour which will be incurred at the level equivalent to 800 units production per week. Outlays on fixed overheads will be reduced by £4000 per week.

  (v) *Payments:* Creditors for raw materials, which stand at £27 000 at the beginning of week 1, are paid in the week

following purchase. All other payments are made in the week in which the liability is incurred.
  (vi) *Liquidity:* The company has a bank overdraft balance of £39 000 at the beginning of week 1 and an overdraft limit of £50 000.

The company is anxious to establish the liquidity situation over the modernization period, excluding the requirements for finance for the modernization itself.

Required:

(a) Prepare a weekly cash budget covering the six-week period up to the planned completion of the modernization.
(15 marks)

(b) Comment briefly upon any matters concerning the liquidity situation which you feel should be drawn to the attention of management. *(7 marks)*
ACCA Level 1 Costing

IM15.12 Advanced: Preparation of a cash budget and a decision whether to close a department and subcontract. The Rosrock Housing Association has two types of housing estate in the Rosburgh area (A and B).
  The following information is available:

  (i) The association has its own squad of painters who carry out painting and decorating work on the housing estates. The estimated cost for each house in which the work will be done in 2013 is as follows:

Painting	
	(£)
(a) Direct material cost	75
(b) Direct labour cost	270

  (c) In 2013 overhead cost is absorbed at 20 per cent on direct material cost plus 100 per cent on direct labour cost. Only 30 per cent of material related overhead and $33^1/3$ per cent of labour related overhead is variable, the remainder is fixed overhead and the absorption rate is arrived at using the budgeted number of houses which require painting and decorating each year.

  (d) Fixed overhead may be analyzed into:

1	Items avoidable on cessation of the service	30%
2	Depreciation of equipment and premises	20%
3	Apportionment of head office costs	50%

  (e) Direct material and direct labour cost are wholly variable.

  (ii) The total number of houses of each type and the percentage requiring painting and decorating each year is as follows:

	Estate Type A	Estate Type B
Total number of houses	500	600
Percentage of houses requiring maintenance each year:	30%	20%

  (iii) Where relevant, all future costs are expected to increase each year by a fixed percentage of the previous year's level due to changes in prices and wage rates as follows:

Direct material cost	5%
Direct labour cost	7%
Overhead cost	6%

  (iv) Forecast balances at 31 December 2012 and other cash flow timing information is as follows:

  (a) Creditors for materials: £2100. Credit purchases are 90 per cent of purchases, the remainder being cash purchases. The credit purchases outstanding at a year end are estimated at 10 per cent of the annual materials purchased on credit. There are no materials on hand on 31 December 2012.

(b) Labour costs accrued: £2800. Labour costs outstanding at a year end are estimated at 4 per cent of the annual total earnings for the year.

(c) Creditors for variable overheads: £600. Variable overheads are paid 60 per cent in the month of incidence and 40 per cent in the month following. Variable overheads are deemed to accrue evenly each month throughout the year.

(d) Fixed overheads are paid in twelve equal amounts with no accruals or prepayments.

Required:

(a) Prepare a cash budget for the existing painting and decorating function for the period 1 January 2013 to 31 December 2015 which shows the cash flows for each of the years 2013, 2014 and 2015. (Calculations should be rounded to the nearest whole £.)   (14 marks)

(b) An outside company has offered to undertake all painting and decorating work for a three year period 2013 to 2015 for a fixed fee of £135 000 per annum.

(i) Calculate whether the offer should be accepted on financial grounds using the information available in the question.   (2 marks)

(ii) List and comment upon other factors which should be taken into account by Rosrock Housing Association management when considering this offer.   (6 marks)

ACCA Level 2 Cost and Management Accounting

16
MANAGEMENT CONTROL SYSTEMS

LEARNING OBJECTIVES After studying this chapter you should be able to:

- describe the three different types of controls used in organizations;

- distinguish between feedback and feed-forward controls;

- explain the potential harmful side-effects of results controls;

- define the four different types of responsibility centres;

- explain the different elements of management accounting control systems;

- describe the controllability principle and the methods of implementing it;

- describe the different approaches that can be used to determine financial performance targets and discuss the impact of their level of difficulty on motivation and performance;

- describe the influence of participation in the budgeting process;

- distinguish between the three different styles of evaluating performance and identify the circumstances when a particular style is most appropriate.

Control is the process of ensuring that a firm's activities conform to its plan and that its objectives are achieved. There can be no control without objectives and plans, since these predetermine and specify the desirable behaviour and set out the procedures that should be followed by members of the organization to ensure that a firm is operated in a desired manner.

In an article published many years ago Drucker (1964) distinguished between 'controls' and 'control'. Controls are measurement and information, whereas control means direction. In other words, 'controls' are purely a means to an end; the end is control. 'Control' is the function that makes sure that actual work is done to fulfil the original intention, and 'controls' are used to provide information to assist in determining the control action to be taken. For example, material costs may be greater than budget. 'Controls' will indicate that costs exceed budget and that this may be because the purchase of inferior quality materials causes excessive wastage. 'Control' is the action that is taken to purchase the correct quality materials in the future to reduce excessive wastage. 'Controls' encompasses all the methods and procedures that direct employees towards achieving the organization objectives. Many different control mechanisms are used in organizations and the management accounting control system represents only one aspect of the various control mechanisms that companies use to control their managers and employees. To fully understand the role that management accounting control systems play in the control process, it is necessary to be aware of how they relate to the entire array of control mechanisms used by organizations. Note that the term management control system is used to refer to the entire array of controls used by an organization.

This chapter begins by describing the different types of controls that are used by companies. The elements of management accounting control systems will then be described within the context of the overall control process.

CONTROL AT DIFFERENT ORGANIZATIONAL LEVELS

Control is applied at different levels within an organization. Merchant and Van der Stede (2007) distinguish between strategic control and management control. Strategic control has an external focus. The emphasis is on how a firm, given its strengths and weaknesses and limitations, can compete with other firms in the same industry. We shall explore some of these issues in Chapter 22 within the context of strategic management accounting. In this, and the next four chapters, our emphasis will be on management control systems which consist of a collection of control mechanisms that primarily have an internal focus. The aim of management control systems is to influence employee behaviours in desirable ways in order to increase the probability that an organization's objectives will be achieved. Merchant and Van der Stede define management control as dealing with employees' behaviour. They state:

> It is people in the organization that make things happen. Management controls are necessary to guard against the possibilities that people will do something the organizations do not want them to do or fail to do something they should do.... If all employees could always be relied on to do what is best for the organization there would be no need for management control systems.

The terms 'management accounting control systems', 'accounting control systems' and 'management control systems' are often used interchangeably. Both management accounting and accounting control systems refer to the collection of practices such as budgeting, standard costing and periodic performance reporting that are normally administered by the management accounting function. Management control systems represent a broader term that encompasses management accounting/accounting control systems but it also includes other controls such as action, personnel and social controls. These controls are described in the following section.

DIFFERENT TYPES OF CONTROLS

Companies use many different control mechanisms to cope with the problem of organizational control. To make sense of the vast number of controls that are used we shall classify them into three categories using approaches that have been adopted by Ouchi (1979) and Merchant and Van der Stede. They are:

1 action (or behavioural) controls;

2 personnel, cultural and social controls;

3 results (or output) controls.

You should note that management accounting systems are normally synonymous with output controls whereas management control systems encompass all of the above categories of controls.

Action or behavioural controls

Behavioural controls (also known as action controls) involve observing the actions of individuals as they go about their work. They are appropriate where cause and effect relationships are well understood, so that if the correct actions are followed, the desired outcomes will occur. Under these circumstances effective control can be achieved by having superiors watch and guide the actions of subordinates. For example, if the supervisor watches the workers on the assembly line and ensures that the work is done exactly as prescribed, then the expected quality and quantity of work should ensue. Forms of action controls described by Merchant and Van der Stede include behavioural constraints, preaction reviews and action accountability.

The aim of *behavioural constraints* is to prevent people from doing things that should not be done. They include physical constraints, such as computer passwords that restrict accessing or updating information sources to authorized personnel, and administrative constraints such as imposing ceilings on the amount of capital expenditure that managers may authorize is an example of an administrative constraint.

Preaction reviews involve the scrutiny and approval of action plans of the individuals being controlled before they can undertake a course of action. Examples include the approval by municipal authorities of plans for the construction of properties prior to building commencing, or the approval by a tutor of a dissertation plan prior to the student being authorized to embark on the dissertation.

Action accountability involves defining actions that are acceptable or unacceptable, observing the actions and rewarding acceptable or punishing unacceptable actions. Examples of action accountability include establishing work rules and procedures and company codes of conduct that employees must follow. Line item budgets that were described in the previous chapter are another form of action accountability whereby an upper limit on an expense category is given for the budget period. If managers exceed these limits they are held accountable and are required to justify their actions.

Action controls that focus on *preventing* undesirable behaviour are the ideal form of control because their aim is to prevent the behaviour from occurring. They are preferable to *detection* controls that are applied after the occurrence of the actions because they avoid the costs of undesirable behaviour. Nevertheless, detection controls can still be useful if they are applied in a timely manner so that they can lead to the early cessation of undesirable actions. Their existence also discourages individuals from engaging in such actions.

Personnel, cultural and social controls

Social controls involve the selection of people who have already been socialized into adopting particular norms and patterns of behaviour to perform particular tasks. For example, if the only staff promoted to managerial level are those who display a high commitment to the firm's objectives then the need for other forms of controls can be reduced.

Personnel controls involve helping employees do a good job by building on employees' natural tendencies to control themselves. In particular, they ensure that the employees have the capabilities (in terms of intelligence, qualifications and experience) and the resources needed to do a good job. Merchant identifies three major methods of implementing personnel controls. They are selection and placement, training and job design and the provision of the necessary resources. Selection and placement involves finding the right people to do a specified job. Training can be used to ensure that employees know how to perform the assigned tasks and to make them fully aware of the results and actions that are expected from them. Job design entails designing jobs in such a way that employees are able to undertake their tasks with a high degree of success. This requires that jobs are not made too complex, onerous or badly defined so that employees do not know what is expected of them.

Cultural controls represent a set of values, social norms and beliefs that are shared by members of the organization and that influence their actions. Cultural controls are exercised by individuals over one another – for example, procedures used by groups within an organization to regulate performance of their own members and to bring them into line when they deviate from group norms. Cultural controls are virtually the same as social controls.

Results or output controls

Output or results controls involve collecting and reporting information about the outcomes of work effort. The major advantage of results controls is that senior managers do not have to be knowledgeable about the means required to achieve the desired results or be involved in directly observing the actions of subordinates. They merely rely on output reports to ascertain whether or not the desired outcomes have been achieved. Management accounting control systems can be described as a form of output controls. They are mostly defined in monetary terms such as revenues, costs, profits and ratios such as return on investment. Results measures also include non-accounting measures such as the number of units of defective production, the number of loan applications processed or ratio measures such as the number of customer deliveries on time as a percentage of total deliveries.

Results controls involve the following stages:

1 establishing results (i.e. performance) measures that minimize undesirable behaviour;

2 establishing performance targets;

3 measuring performance;

4 providing rewards or punishment.

The *first stage* involves selecting performance measures for those aspects of activities that the organization wishes to monitor. Ideally, desirable behaviour should improve the performance measure and undesirable behaviour should have a detrimental effect on the measure. A performance measure that is not a good indicator of what is desirable to achieve the organization's objectives might actually encourage employees to take actions that are detrimental to the organization. The term 'What you measure is what you get' can apply whereby employees concentrate on improving the performance measures even when they are aware that their actions are not in the firm's best interests. For example, a divisional manager whose current return on investment (ROI) is 30 per cent might reject a project which yields an ROI of 25 per cent because it will lower the division's average ROI, even though the project has a positive NPV, and acceptance is in the best interests of the organization.

The *second-stage* requirement of a preset performance target informs individuals what to aim for and enables employees or their superiors to interpret performance. The *third stage* specified above relates to measuring performance. Ability to measure some outputs effectively constrains the use of results measures. In the previous chapter you will remember that it was pointed out that the outputs in non-profit organizations are extremely difficult to measure and inhibit the use of results controls. Another example relates to measuring the performance of support departments. Consider a personnel department. The accomplishments of the department can be difficult to measure and other forms of control might be preferable. To encourage the right behaviours results, measures should be timely and understandable. Significant delays in reporting will result in the measures losing most of their motivational impact and a lengthy delay in taking remedial action when outcomes deviate from target. If measures are not under-standable it is unlikely that managers will know how their actions will effect the measure and there is a danger that the measures will lose their motivational impact.

The *final stage* of results controls involves encouraging employees to achieve organizational goals by having rewards (or punishments) linked to their success (or failure) in achieving the results measures. Organizational rewards include salary increases, bonuses, promotions and recognition. Employees can also derive intrinsic rewards through a sense of accomplishment and achievement. Punishments include demotions, failure to obtain the rewards and possibly the loss of one's job.

FEEDBACK AND FEED-FORWARD CONTROLS

Feedback control involves monitoring outputs achieved against desired outputs and taking whatever corrective action is necessary if a deviation exists. In feed-forward control instead of actual outputs being compared against desired outputs, predictions are made of what outputs are expected to be at some future time. If these expectations differ from what is desired, control actions are taken that will minimize these differences. The objective is for control to be achieved before any deviations from desired outputs actually occur. In other words, with feed-forward controls, likely errors can be anticipated and steps taken to avoid them, whereas with feedback controls actual errors are identified after the event and corrective action is taken to implement future actions to achieve the desired outputs.

A major limitation of feedback control is that errors are allowed to occur. This is not a significant problem when there is a short time lag between the occurrence of an error and the identification and implementation of corrective action. Feed-forward control is therefore preferable when a significant time lag occurs. The budgeting process is a feed-forward control system. To the extent that outcomes

Feed-forward control – the virtual engineer and fault prevention

Maintaining manufacturing and process equipment is always a delicate balance between preventative maintenance and repairing faults after they occur. Spare parts and maintenance staff pay is a substantial cost. Most manufacturers engage in preventive maintenance programmes. This usually implies a mixture of following guidelines from equipment manufacturers and the experience of the maintenance staff. Preventative maintenance comes at a cost too, but this needs to be compared to the consequences of letting a piece of equipment go unmaintained. A business needs to avoid its main manufacturing process being down – losses of revenue per day (or even per hour) rack up very quickly.

Modern process equipment typically comes complete with many fault sensors and even remote engineer access via the internet. However, these sensors only report reasons for faults after they occur, i.e.

they feed back information. An article in *The Economist* reports on research being conducted at the University of Portsmouth. The research centres on the idea of a 'virtual engineer'. The idea is that a sensor can spot tell-tale signs of likely failure in electrical equipment. This could mean that preventive maintenance happens less frequently as equipment may be perfectly fine beyond its normal maintenance period. The virtual engineer is thus acting as a feed-forward control measure, as it is measuring the performance of electrical components and trying to predict if they will fail.

Questions

1 Why is the type of predictive control mentioned above superior? List some reasons why.

2 What kinds of cost savings may be possible with a system like a 'virtual engineer'?

References

http://wp.me/pxcli-bl
http://www.economist.com/node/17408466?
story_id=E1_TSQDRQGG

fall short of what is desired, alternatives are considered until a budget is produced that is expected to achieve what is desired. The comparison of actual results with budget, in identifying variances and taking remedial action to ensure that future outcomes will conform with budgeted outcomes, is an illustration of a feedback control system. Thus, accounting control systems consist of both feedback and feed-forward controls.

HARMFUL SIDE-EFFECTS OF CONTROLS

Harmful side-effects occur when the controls motivate employees to engage in behaviour that is not organizationally desirable. In this situation the control system leads to a lack of goal congruence. Alternatively, when controls motivate behaviour that is organizationally desirable they are described as encouraging goal congruence.

Results controls can lead to a lack of goal congruence if the results that are required can only be partially specified. Here there is a danger that employees will concentrate only on what is monitored by the control system, regardless of whether or not it is organizationally desirable. In other words, they will seek to maximize their individual performance according to the rules of the control system, irrespective of whether their actions contribute to the organization's objectives. In addition, they may ignore other important areas if they are not monitored by the control system. The term 'What you measure is what you get' applies in these circumstances.

Figure 16.1, derived from Emmanual, Otley and Merchant (1990) illustrates the problems that can arise when the required results can only be partially specified. You will see that those aspects of behaviour on which subordinates are likely to concentrate to achieve their personal goals (circle B) do not necessarily correspond with those necessary for achieving the wider organizational goals (circle A). In an ideal system the measured behaviour (represented by circle C) should completely cover the area of

FIGURE 16.1

FIGURE 16.1

The measurement and reward process with imperfect measures

A Behaviour necessary to achieve organizational goals
B Behaviour actually engaged in by an individual manager
C Behaviour formally measured by control systems

desired behaviour (represented by circle A). Therefore if a manager maximizes the performance measure, he or she will also maximize his or her contribution to the goals of the organization. In other words, the performance measures encourage goal congruence. In practice, it is unlikely that perfect performance measures can be constructed that measure all desirable organizational behaviour, and so it is unlikely that all of circle C will cover circle A. Assuming that managers desire the rewards offered by circle C, their actual behaviour (represented by circle B) will be altered to include more of circle C and, to the extent that C coincides with A, more of circle A.

However, organizational performance will be improved only to the extent that the performance measure is a good indicator of what is desirable to achieve the firm's goals. Unfortunately, performance measures are not perfect and, as an ideal measure of overall performance, are unlikely to exist. Some measures may encourage goal congruence or organizationally desirable behaviour (the part of circle C that coincides with A), but other measures will not encourage goal congruence (the part of circle C that does not coincide with A). Consequently, there is a danger that subordinates will concentrate only on what is measured, regardless of whether or not it is organizationally desirable. Furthermore, actual behaviour may be modified so that desired results appear to be obtained, although they may have been achieved in an undesirable manner which is detrimental to the firm.

It is clear that flaws in the performance measurement systems used by banks contributed to the financial crisis in the banking sector. Bonuses and performance measures were based on short-term, rather than long-term performance, that did not take risk into account. These performance measures encouraged managers to take actions to increase sales or profits when such actions resulted in providing high risk loans. The performance measures motivated managers to increase the reported sales revenues and profits, and thus their bonus, without considering the adverse long-term implications of their actions. They were not engaging in organizationally desirable behaviour because the performance measurement and reward system strongly encouraged them not to do so. Many would argue that the managers were acting in an unethical manner but clearly the performance measurement and the reward system was also at fault. We shall discuss how such dysfunctional behaviour may be reduced in Chapters 19 and 22.

ADVANTAGES AND DISADVANTAGES OF DIFFERENT TYPES OF CONTROLS

Merchant and Van der Stede suggest that when deciding on the control alternatives managers should start by considering whether *personnel* or *cultural controls* will be sufficient on their own because they have relatively few harmful side-effects. Also in small organizations they may be completely effective

REAL WORLD VIEWS 16.2

Crime-fighting targets lead to 'dysfunctional' policing says police chief

Government crime-fighting targets are a shambles and should be scrapped, claims Chief Superintendent Ian Johnston. Mr Johnston was speaking ahead of the Police Superintendents' Association's 2007 annual conference, when he will ask the police minister to scrap the current targets regime.

'I believe we should abolish the performance framework in its entirety,' Mr Johnston said. 'It sounds radical, but it would be very warmly welcomed by the police service and would allow us, the professionals, to make judgements. We want to reclaim policing for the police.' He added: 'Centrally imposed targets are preventing senior police officers from delivering the policing that the public wants and deserves. We need to restore discretion to senior police officers enabling them to make decisions that relate to local policing issues, ensuring that we deliver a high standard of quality policing.'

In May 2007, the leaders of rank-and-file police officers made a similar demand to reverse the target-driven culture that has forced them to make 'ludicrous' decisions such as a case in Kent where a child was arrested for throwing cream buns at a bus. The Police Federation said judging officers purely on how many arrests, cautions or on-the-spot fines they can deliver was making a mockery of the criminal justice system. The drive to meet Whitehall performance targets was compelling officers to criminalize middle England, they added.

The organization published a dossier of ridiculous cases they claimed resulted from Home Office targets placed on beat bobbies. The cases included a Cheshire man who was cautioned by police for being found in possession of an egg with intent to throw, and a West Midlands woman arrested on her wedding day for criminal damage to a car park barrier when her foot slipped on her accelerator.

Today, Mr Johnston said, 'current Home Office targets have made some senior officers seriously ill from the stress of managing a wide range of competing demands. More than 70 per cent of basic command unit commanders believe national targets have had a negative impact on service delivery. We are obliged to count everything and in order to account for our performance we are not addressing a lot of the issues that the public see as far more important.' He added: 'The time has come for someone to say that the performance framework and the red tape and the bureaucracy have got to go. The government's focus on volume crime targets is skewing all police activity in a way that our members see as increasingly dysfunctional.'

Question

1 How might the dysfunctional effects of the performance system in the police force be minimized?

© alxpin, iStock.com

References

www.dailymail.co.uk/news 7th September 2007

without the need to supplement them with other forms of controls. If personnel/cultural controls are not sufficient on their own it will be necessary to supplement them with other forms of control.

Action controls are the most effective form of control because there is a direct link between the control mechanism and the action and also a high probability that desirable outcomes will occur. They dispense with the need to measure the results but their major limitation is that they are dependent on cause-and-effect work relationships that are well understood and this does not apply in many situations.

The major attraction of *results controls* is that they can be applied where knowledge of what actions are desirable is lacking. This situation applies in most organizations. A second attraction of results controls is that their application does not restrict individual autonomy. The focus is on the outcomes thus giving individuals the freedom to determine how they can best achieve the outcomes. Individuals are not burdened with having to follow prescribed rules and procedures. The major disadvantages of results controls are that in many cases the results required can only be partially specified and there can be difficulties in separating controllable and uncontrollable factors.

MANAGEMENT ACCOUNTING CONTROL SYSTEMS

Up to this point in the chapter we have been looking at the broad context of management control systems. We shall now concentrate on management accounting control systems which represent the predominant controls in most organizations.

Why are accounting controls the predominant controls? There are several reasons. First, all organizations need to express and aggregate the results of a wide range of dissimilar activities using a common measure. The monetary measure meets this requirement. Second, profitability and liquidity are essential to the success of all organizations and financial measures relating to these and other areas are closely monitored by stakeholders. It is therefore natural that managers will wish to monitor performance in monetary terms. Third, financial measures also enable a common decision rule to be applied by all managers when considering alternative courses of action. That is, a course of action will normally benefit a firm only if it results in an improvement in its financial performance. Fourth, measuring results in financial terms enables managers to be given more autonomy. Focusing on the outcomes of managerial actions, summarized in financial terms, gives managers the freedom to take whatever actions they consider to be appropriate to achieve the desired results. Finally, outputs expressed in financial terms continue to be effective in uncertain environments even when it is unclear what course of action should be taken. Financial results provide a mechanism to indicate whether the actions benefited the organization.

RESPONSIBILITY CENTRES

The complex environment in which most businesses operate today makes it virtually impossible for most firms to be controlled centrally. This is because it is not possible for central management to have all the relevant information and time to determine the detailed plans for all the organization. Some degree of decentralization is essential for all but the smallest firms. Organizations decentralize by creating responsibility centres. A responsibility centre may be defined as a unit of a firm where an individual manager is held responsible for the unit's performance. There are four types of responsibility centres. They are:

1 cost or expense centres;
2 revenue centres;
3 profit centres;
4 investment centres.

The creation of responsibility centres is a fundamental part of management accounting control systems. It is therefore important that you can distinguish between the various forms of responsibility centres.

Cost or expense centres

Cost or expense centres are responsibility centres whose managers are normally accountable for only those costs that are under their control. We can distinguish between two types of cost centres – standard cost centres and discretionary cost centres. The main features of standard cost centres are that output can be measured and the input required to produce each unit of output can be specified. Control is exercised by comparing the standard cost (that is, the cost of the inputs that *should* have been consumed in producing the output) with the cost that was *actually* incurred. The difference between the actual cost and the standard cost is described as the variance. Standard cost centres and variance analysis will be discussed extensively in the next chapter.

Standard cost centres are best suited to units within manufacturing firms but they can also be established in service industries such as units within banks, where output can be measured in terms of the number of cheques or the number of loan applications processed, and there are also well defined input–output relationships. Although cost centre managers are not accountable for sales revenues they can affect the amount of sales revenue generated if quality standards are not met and outputs are not produced according to schedule. Therefore quality and timeliness non-financial performance measures are also required besides financial measures.

Responsibility centres – cost centre accounting in SAP

SAP is the global leader in the provision of enterprise resource planning (ERP) systems. While SAP is designed to process many business transactions, it also acts as a key source of information for management control. At the centre of its management control functions is a 'cost centre accounting' (CCA) subsystem, that, according to the SAP website 'enables you to check the profitability of individual functional areas and provide decision-making data for management.' CCA needs to have cost, profit and investment centres defined by the user organization, and is one of the earlier items to be configured in the system. This is because the CCA links other component of SAP, such as product cost controlling and profitability analysis. According to SAP, using CCA offers several advantages:

- Assigning costs to cost centres lets you determine where costs are incurred within the organization.

- If you plan costs at cost centre level, you can check cost efficiency at the point where costs are incurred.

- If you want to assign overhead costs accurately to individual products, services or market segments, you need to further allocate the costs to those cost centres directly involved in the creation of the products or services. From these cost centres you can then use different methods to assign the activities and costs to the relevant products, services and market segments. The 'activities' of cost centres represent 'internal resources' for business processes in activity-based costing.

Questions

1   Can you give an example of how a cost would be captured/recorded and allocated to a cost centre?

2   Do you think cost centre accounting data is useful for budgeting/planning?

References

http://help.sap.com/saphelp_46c/helpdata/en/5b/d2200743c611d182b30000e829fbfe/frameset.htm

Discretionary expense centres are those responsibility cost centres where output cannot be measured in financial terms and there are no clearly observable relationships between inputs (the resources consumed) and the outputs (the results achieved). Control normally takes the form of ensuring that actual expenditure adheres to budgeted expenditure for each expense category and also ensuring that the tasks assigned to each centre have been successfully accomplished. Examples of discretionary centres include advertising and publicity and research and development departments. One of the major problems arising in discretionary expense centres is measuring the effectiveness of expenditures. For example, the marketing support department may not have exceeded an advertising budget but this does not mean that the advertising expenditure has been effective. The advertising may have been incorrectly timed, it may have been directed to the wrong audience, or it may have contained the wrong message. Determining the effectiveness and efficiency of discretionary expense centres is one of the most difficult areas of management control.

Revenue centres

Revenue centres are responsibility centres where managers are mainly accountable for financial outputs in the form of generating sales revenues. Typical examples of revenue centres are where regional sales managers are accountable for sales within their regions. Revenue centre managers may also be held accountable for selling expenses, such as salesperson salaries, commissions and order-getting costs. They are not, however, made accountable for the cost of the goods and services that they sell.

Profit centres

Both cost and revenue centre managers have limited decision-making authority. Cost centre managers are accountable only for managing inputs of their centres, and decisions relating to outputs are made by other units within the firm. Revenue centres are accountable for selling the products or services but they have no control over their manufacture. A significant increase in managerial autonomy occurs when unit managers are given responsibility for both production and sales. In this situation managers are normally free to set selling prices, choose which markets to sell in, make product-mix and output decisions and select suppliers. Units within an organization whose managers are accountable for both revenues and costs are called profit centres.

Investment centres

Investment centres are responsibility centres whose managers are responsible for both sales revenues and costs and, in addition, have responsibility and authority to make capital investment decisions. Typical investment centre performance measures include return on investment and economic value added. These measures are influenced by revenues, costs and assets employed and thus reflect the responsibility that managers have for both generating profits and managing the investment base.

Investment centres represent the highest level of managerial autonomy. They include the company as a whole, operating subsidiaries, operating groups and divisions. You will find that many firms are not precise in their terminology and call their investment centres profit centres. Profit and investment centres will be discussed extensively in Chapter 19.

THE NATURE OF MANAGEMENT ACCOUNTING CONTROL SYSTEMS

Management accounting control systems have two core elements. The first is the formal planning processes such as budgeting and long-term planning that were described in the previous chapter. These processes are used for establishing performance expectations for evaluating performance. The second is responsibility accounting which involves the creation of responsibility centres. Responsibility centres enable accountability for financial results and outcomes to be allocated to individuals throughout the organization. The objective of responsibility accounting is to accumulate costs and revenues for each individual responsibility centre so that the deviations from a performance target (typically the budget) can be attributed to the individual who is accountable for the responsibility centre. For each responsibility centre the process involves setting a performance target, measuring performance, comparing performance against the target, analyzing the variances and taking action where significant variances exist between actual and target performance. Financial performance targets for profit or investment centres are typically in terms of profits, return on investment or economic value added, whereas performance targets for cost centres are defined in terms of costs.

Responsibility accounting is implemented by issuing performance reports at frequent intervals (normally monthly) that inform responsibility centre managers of the deviations from budgets for which they are accountable and are required to take action. An example of a performance report issued to a cost centre manager is presented in the lower section of Exhibit 16.1. You should note that at successively higher levels of management less detailed information is reported. You can see from the upper sections of Exhibit 16.1 that the information is condensed and summarized as the results relating to the responsibility centre are reported at higher levels. Exhibit 16.1 only includes financial information. In addition, non-financial measures such as those relating to quality and timeliness may be reported. We shall look at non-financial measures in more detail in Chapter 22.

Responsibility accounting involves:

- distinguishing between those items which managers can control and for which they should be held accountable and those items over which they have no control and for which they are not held accountable (i.e. applying the controllability principle);
- setting financial performance targets and determining how challenging the financial targets should be;
- determining how much influence managers should have in the setting of financial targets.

We shall now examine each of these items in detail.

XHIBIT 16.1   Responsibility accounting monthly performance reports

Performance report to managing director

| | | Budget | | Variance[a] F (A) | |
		Current month (£)	Year to date (£)	This month (£)	Year to date (£)
Managing director	→ Factory A	453 900	6 386 640	80 000(A)	98 000(A)
	Factory B	X	X	X	X
	Factory C	X	X	X	X
	Administration costs	X	X	X	X
	Selling costs	X	X	X	X
	Distribution costs	X	X	X	X
		2 500 000	30 000 000	400 000(A)	600 000(A)

Performance report to production manager of factory A

| | | Budget | | Variance[a] F (A) | |
		Current month (£)	Year to date (£)	This month (£)	Year to date (£)
Production manager	Works manager's office	X	X	X	X
	→ Machining department 1	165 600	717 600	32 760(A)	89 180(A)
	Machining department 2	X	X	X	X
	Assembly department	X	X	X	X
	Finishing department	X	X	X	X
		453 900	6 386 640	80 000(A)	98 000(A)

Performance report to head of responsibility centre

| | | Budget | | Variance[a] F (A) | |
		Current month (£)	Year to date (£)	This month (£)	Year to date (£)
Head of responsibility centre	Direct materials	X	X	X	X
	Direct labour	X	X	X	X
	Indirect labour	X	X	X	X
	Indirect materials	X	X	X	X
	Power	X	X	X	X
	Maintenance	X	X	X	X
	Idle time	X	X	X	X
	Other	X	X	X	X
		165 600	717 600	32 760(A)	89 180(A)

[a] F indicates a favourable variance (actual cost less than budgeted cost) and (A) indicates an adverse budget (actual cost greater than budget cost). Note that, at the lowest level of reporting, the responsibility centre head's performance report contains detailed information on operating costs. At successively higher levels of management less detail is reported. For example, the managing director's information on the control of activities consists of examining those variances that represent significant departures from the budget for each factory and functional area of the business and requesting explanations from the appropriate managers.

THE CONTROLLABILITY PRINCIPLE

Responsibility accounting is based on the application of the controllability principle which means that it is appropriate to charge to an area of responsibility only those costs that are significantly influenced by the manager of that responsibility centre. The controllability principle can be implemented by either eliminating the uncontrollable items from the areas for which managers are held accountable or calculating their effects so that the reports distinguish between controllable and uncontrollable items.

Applying the controllability principle is difficult in practice because many areas do not fit neatly into either controllable and uncontrollable categories. Instead, they are partially controllable. For example, even when outcomes may be affected by occurrences outside a manager's control, such as competitors' actions, price changes and supply shortages, managers can take action to reduce their adverse effects.

They can substitute alternative materials where the prices of raw materials change or they can monitor and respond to competitors' actions. If these factors are categorized as uncontrollable, managers will not be motivated to try and influence them.

Dealing with the distorting effects of uncontrollable factors before the measurement period

Management can attempt to deal with the distorting effects of uncontrollables by making adjustments either before or after the measurement period. Uncontrollable and controllable factors can be determined prior to the measurement period by specifying which budget line items are to be regarded as controllable and uncontrollable. Uncontrollable items can either be excluded from performance reports or shown in a separate section within the performance report so that they are clearly distinguishable from controllable items. The latter approach has the advantage of drawing managerial attention to those costs that a company incurs to support their activities. Managers may be able to indirectly influence these costs if they are made aware of the sums involved.

How do we distinguish between controllable and uncontrollable items? Merchant and Van der Stede suggest that the following general rule should be applied to all employees: 'Hold employees accountable for the performance areas you want them to pay attention to.' Applying this rule explains why some organizations assign the costs of shared resource pools, such as administrative costs relating to personnel and data processing departments, to responsibility centres. Assigning these costs authorizes managers of the user responsibility centres to question the amount of the costs and the quantity and quality of services supplied. In addition, responsibility centres are discouraged from making unnecessary requests for the use of these services when they are aware that increases in costs will be assigned to the users of the services.

Dealing with the distorting effects of uncontrollable factors after the measurement period

Merchant and Van der Stede identify four methods of removing the effects of uncontrollable factors from the results measures after the measurement period and before the rewards are assigned. They are:

1 variance analysis;
2 flexible performance standards;
3 relative performance evaluations;
4 subjective performance evaluations.

Variance analysis seeks to analyze the factors that cause the actual results to differ from pre-determined budgeted targets. In particular, variance analysis helps to distinguish between controllable and uncontrollable items and identify those individuals who are accountable for the variances. For example, variances analyzed by each type of cost, and by their price and quantity effects, enables variances to be traced to accountable individuals and also to isolate those variances that are due to uncontrollable factors. Variance analysis will be discussed extensively in Chapters 17 and 18.

Flexible performance standards apply when targets are adjusted to reflect variations in uncontrollable factors arising from the circumstances not envisaged when the targets were set. The most widely used flexible performance standard is to use flexible budgets whereby the uncontrollable volume effects on cost behaviour are removed from the manager's performance reports. Because some costs vary with changes in the level of activity, it is essential when applying the controllability principle to take into account the variability of costs. For example, if the actual level of activity is greater than the budgeted level of activity, then those costs that vary with activity will be greater than the budgeted costs purely because of changes in activity. Let us consider the simplified situation presented in Example 16.1.

Assuming that the increase in activity was due to an increase in sales volume greater than that anticipated when the budget was set, then the increases in costs arising from the volume change are beyond the control of the responsibility centre manager. It is clearly inappropriate to compare actual *variable* costs of £105 000 from an activity level of 24 000 units with budgeted *variable* costs of £100 000

EXAMPLE 16.1

An item of expense that is included in the budget for a responsibility centre varies directly in relation to activity at an estimated cost of £5 per unit of output. The budgeted monthly level of activity was 20 000 units and the actual level of activity was 24 000 units at a cost of £105 000.

from an activity level of 20 000 units. This would incorrectly suggest an overspending of £5000. If managers are to be made responsible for their costs, it is essential that they are responsible for performance under the conditions in which they worked, and not for a performance based on conditions when the budget was drawn up. In other words, it is misleading to compare actual costs at one level of activity with budgeted costs at another level of activity. At the end of the period the original budget must be adjusted to the actual level of activity to take into account the impact of the uncontrollable volume change on costs. This procedure is called flexible budgeting. In Example 16.1 the performance report should be as follows:

Budgeted expenditure	Actual expenditure
(flexed to 24 000 units)	(24 000 units)
£120 000	£105 000

The budget is adjusted to reflect what the costs should have been for an actual activity of 24 000 units. This indicates that the manager has incurred £15 000 less expenditure than would have been expected for the actual level of activity, and a favourable variance of £15 000 should be recorded on the performance report, not an adverse variance of £5000, which would have been recorded if the original budget had not been adjusted.

In Example 16.1 it was assumed that there was only one variable item of expense, but in practice the budget will include many different expenses including fixed, semi-variable and variable expenses. You should note that fixed expenses do not vary in the short-term with activity and therefore the budget should remain unchanged for these expenses. The budget should be flexed only for variable and semi-variable expenses.

Budgets may also be adjusted to reflect other uncontrollable factors besides volume changes. Budgets are normally set based on the environment that is anticipated during the budget setting process. If the budget targets are then used throughout the duration of the annual budget period for performance evaluation the managers will be held accountable for uncontrollable factors arising from forecasting errors. To remove the managerial exposure to uncontrollable risks arising from forecasting errors ex post budget adjustments can be made whereby the budget is adjusted to the environmental and economic conditions that the manager's actually faced during the period.

Relative performance evaluation relates to the situations where the performance of a responsibility centre is evaluated relative to the performance of similar centres within the same company or to similar units outside the organization. To be effective, responsibility centres must perform similar tasks and face similar environmental and business conditions with the units that they are being benchmarked against. Such relative comparisons with units facing similar environmental conditions neutralizes the uncontrollable factors because they are in effect held constant when making the relative comparisons. The major difficulty relating to relative performance evaluations is finding benchmark units that face similar conditions and uncertainties.

Instead of making the formal and quantitative adjustments that are a feature of the methods that have been described so far, subjective judgements can be made in the evaluation process based on the knowledge of the outcome measures and the circumstances faced by the responsibility centre heads. The major advantage of subjective evaluations is that they can alleviate some of the defects of the measures used by accounting control systems. The disadvantages of subjective evaluations are that they are not objective, they tend not to provide the person being evaluated with a clear indication of how performance has been evaluated, they can create conflict with superiors resulting in a loss of morale and a decline in motivation and they are expensive in terms of management time.

Guidelines for applying the controllability principle

Dealing with uncontrollables represents one of the most difficult areas for the design and operation of management accounting control systems. The following guidelines published by the Report of the Committee of Cost Concepts and Standards by the American Accounting Association in the United States in 1957 still continues to provide useful guidance:

1. If a manager *can control the quantity and price paid* for a service then the manager is responsible for all the expenditure incurred for the service.

2. If the manager *can control the quantity of the service but not the price paid* for the service then only that amount of difference between actual and budgeted expenditure that is due to usage should be identified with the manager.

3. If the manager *cannot control either the quantity or the price paid* for the service then the expenditure is uncontrollable and should not be identified with the manager.

An example of the latter situation is when the costs of an industrial relations department are apportioned to a department on some arbitrary basis; such arbitrary apportionments are likely to result in an allocation of expenses that the managers of responsibility centres may not be able to influence. In addition to the above guidelines Merchant and Van der Stede's general rule should also be used as a guide – 'Hold employees accountable for the performance areas you want them to pay attention to.'

REAL WORLD VIEWS 16.4

Responsibility cost control systems in China

Because of the previous lack of effective control of expenditure by the Han Dan Company a system of responsibility accounting and standard costing was introduced in 1990. The basic principles underlying the responsibility cost control system included: (1) setting cost and profit targets (responsibility standards) that take into account market pressures; (2) assigning target costs to various levels of responsibility centre; (3) evaluating performance based on fulfilment of the responsibility targets; and (4) implementing a reward scheme with built-in incentive mechanisms. In order to facilitate performance measurement and evaluation, non-controllable common costs were excluded from the responsibility costs decomposed within primary production factories. Responsibility contracts between factory managers and managers at lower levels must also be signed. Breakdown of the aggregated responsibility targets to all profit centres and their subordi-

nates are conducted by the Department of Finance and Accounting. In addition, the department is responsible for monthly and yearly reporting of the execution results of the responsibility cost control system. It also reports and analyzes the variances between actual outcomes and responsibility targets, and determines the necessary bonus rewards (or penalty) for each responsibility centre in terms of the fulfilment of the cost and profit targets signed by managers. If a responsibility centre or individual worker fails to meet the cost targets specified in the responsibility contracts, all bonus and other benefits relating to the responsibility unit or worker will be forfeited.

Question

1. What are the limitations of linking bonuses to meeting cost targets?

References

Jun Lin, Z. and Yu, Z. (2002), 'Responsibility, cost control system in China: A case of management accounting application', Management Accounting Research, *13*(4), 447–67.

SETTING FINANCIAL PERFORMANCE TARGETS AND DETERMINING HOW CHALLENGING THEY SHOULD BE

There is substantial evidence from a large number of studies that the existence of a defined, quantitative goal or target is likely to motivate higher levels of performance than when no such target is stated. People perform better when they have a clearly defined goal to aim for and are aware of the standards that will be used to interpret their performance. There are three approaches that can be used to set financial targets. They are targets derived from engineering studies of input–output relationships, targets derived from historical data and targets derived from negotiations between superiors and subordinates.

Engineered targets can be used when there are clearly defined and stable input–output relationships such that the inputs required can be estimated directly from product specifications. For example, in a fast-food restaurant for a given output of hamburgers it is possible to estimate the inputs required because there is a physical relationship between the ingredients such as meats, buns, condiments and packaging and the number of hamburgers made. Input–output relationships can also be established for labour by closely observing the processes to determine the quantity of labour that will be required for a given output.

Where clearly defined input–output relationships do not exist other approaches must be used to set financial targets. One approach is to use historical targets derived directly from the results of previous periods. Previous results plus an increase for expected price changes may form the basis for setting the targets, or an improvement factor may be incorporated into the estimate, such as previous period costs less a reduction of 10 per cent. The disadvantage of using historical targets is that they may include past inefficiencies or may encourage employees to underperform if the outcome of efficient performance in a previous period is used as a basis for setting a more demanding target in the next period.

Negotiated targets are set based on negotiations between superiors and subordinates. The major advantage of negotiated targets is that they address the information asymmetry gap that can exist between superior and subordinate. This gap arises because subordinates have more information than their superiors on the relationships between outputs and inputs and the constraints that exist at the operating level, whereas superiors have a broader view of the organization as a whole and the resource constraints that apply. Negotiated targets enable the information asymmetry gap to be reduced so that the targets set incorporate the constraints applying at both the operational level and the firm as a whole. You should refer back to the previous chapter for a more detailed discussion of the negotiation process.

The effect of the level of budget difficulty on motivation and performance

The fact that a financial target represents a specific quantitative goal gives it a strong motivational potential, but the targets set must be accepted if managers are to be motivated to achieve higher levels of performance. Unfortunately, it is not possible to specify exactly the optimal degree of difficulty for financial targets, since task uncertainty and cultural, organizational and personality factors all affect an individual manager's reaction to a financial target.

Figure 16.2, derived from Emmanuel, Otley and Merchant (1990), shows the theoretical relationship between budget difficulty, aspiration levels and performance. In Figure 16.2 it is *assumed that performance and aspiration levels are identical*. Note that the aspiration level relates to the personal goal of the budgetee (that is, the person who is responsible for the budget). In other words, it is the level of performance that they hope to attain. You will see from Figure 16.2 that as the level of budget difficulty is increased, both the budgetees' aspiration level and performance increases. However, there becomes a point where the budget is perceived as impossible to achieve and the aspiration level and performance decline dramatically. It can be seen from Figure 16.2 that the budget level that motivates the best level of performance may not be achievable. In contrast, the budget that is expected to be achieved (that is, the expectations budget in Figure 16.2) motivates a lower level of performance.

To motivate the highest level of actual performance, demanding budgets should be set and small adverse variances should be regarded as a healthy sign and not as something to be avoided. If budgets are always achieved with no adverse variances, this indicates that the standards are too loose to motivate the best possible results.

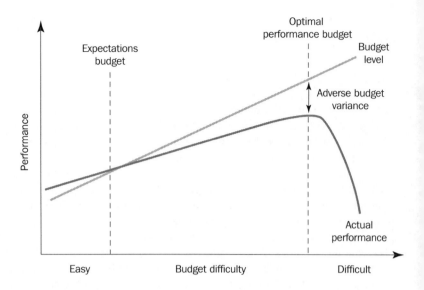

FIGURE 16.2

The effect of budget
difficulty on performance

Source: Otley (1987) copyright
elsevier 1987 reproduced with
permission

Arguments in favour of setting highly achievable budgets

It appears from our previous discussion that tight budgets should be established to motivate maximum performance, although this may mean that the budget has a high probability of not being achieved. However, budgets are not used purely as a motivational device to maximize performance. They are also used for planning purposes and it is most unlikely that tight budgets will be suitable for planning purposes. Why? Tight budgets that have a high probability of not being achieved are most unsuitable for cash budgeting and for harmonizing the company plans in the form of a master budget. Most companies use the same budgets for planning and motivational purposes. If only one set of budgets is used it is most unlikely that one set can, at the same time, perfectly meet both the planning and the motivational requirements.

Budgets with a high probability of being achieved are widely used in practice. They provide managers with a sense of achievement and self-esteem which can be beneficial to the organization in terms of increased levels of commitment and aspirations. Rewards such as bonuses, promotions and job security are normally linked to budget achievement so that the costs of failing to meet budget targets can be high. The greater the probability of the failure to meet budget targets the greater is the probability that managers will be motivated to distort their performance by engaging in behaviour that will result in the harmful side-effects described earlier in this chapter.

PARTICIPATION IN THE BUDGETING AND TARGET SETTING PROCESS

Participation relates to the extent that subordinates or budgetees are able to influence the figures that are incorporated in their budgets or targets. Participation is sometimes referred to as bottom-up budget setting whereas a non-participatory approach whereby subordinates have little influence on the target setting process is sometimes called top-down budget setting.

Allowing individuals to participate in the setting of performance targets has several advantages. First, individuals are more likely to accept the targets and be committed to achieving them if they have been involved in the target setting process. Second, participation can reduce the information asymmetry gap that applies when standards are imposed from above. Earlier in this chapter it was pointed out that subordinates have more information than their superiors on the relationships between outputs and inputs and the constraints that exist at the operating level whereas the superiors have a broader view of the organization as a whole and the resource constraints that apply. This information sharing process enables more effective targets to be set that attempt to deal with both operational and organizational constraints.

Finally, imposed standards can encourage negative attitudes and result in demotivation and alienation. This in turn can lead to a rejection of the targets and poor performance.

Participation has been advocated by many writers as a means of making tasks more challenging and giving individuals a greater sense of responsibility. For many years participation in decision-making was thought to be a panacea for effective organizational effort but this school of thought was later challenged. The debate has never been resolved. The believers have never been able to demonstrate that participation really does have a positive effect on productivity and the sceptics have never been able to prove the opposite (Macintosh, 1985).

Because of the conflicting findings relating to the effectiveness of participation research has tended to concentrate on studying how various factors influence the effectiveness of participation. If participation is used selectively in the right circumstances, it has an enormous potential for encouraging the commitment to organizational goals, improving attitudes towards the budgeting system and increasing subsequent performance. Note, however, at this stage that there are some limitations on the positive effects of participation in standard setting and circumstances where top-down budget setting is preferable. They are:

1. Performance is measured by precisely the same standard that the budgetee has been involved in setting. This gives the budgetee the opportunity to negotiate lower targets that increase the probability of target achievement and the accompanying rewards. Therefore an improvement in performance – in terms of comparison with the budget – may result merely from a lowering of the standard.

2. Participation by itself is not adequate in ensuring commitment to standards. The manager must also believe that he or she can significantly influence the results and be given the necessary feedback about them.

3. A top-down approach to budget setting is likely to be preferable where a process is highly programmable, and there are clear and stable input–output relationships, so that engineered studies can be used to set the targets. Here there is no need to negotiate targets using a bottom-up process.

SIDE-EFFECTS ARISING FROM USING ACCOUNTING INFORMATION FOR PERFORMANCE EVALUATION

Earlier in this chapter we discussed some of the harmful side-effects that can arise from the use of results controls. Some of these effects can be due to the ways in which the output measures are used. A number of studies have been undertaken that examine the side-effects arising from the ways that accounting information is used in performance evaluation. A pioneering study that is widely cited of how budgets are used in performance evaluation was undertaken many years ago by Hopwood (1976), based on observations in a manufacturing division of a large US company. Three distinct styles of using budget and actual cost information in performance evaluation were observed and were described as follows:

1. **Budget-constrained style**: Despite the many problems in using accounting data as comprehensive measures of managerial performance, the evaluation is based primarily upon the cost centre head's ability continually to meet the budget on a short-term basis. This criterion of performance is stressed at the expense of other valued and important criteria, and a cost centre head will tend to receive an unfavourable evaluation if his or her actual costs exceed the budgeted costs, regardless of other considerations. Budget data are therefore used in a rigid manner in performance evaluation.

2. **Profit-conscious style**: The performance of the cost centre head is evaluated on the basis of his or her ability to increase the general effectiveness of his or her unit's operations in relation to the long-term goals of the organization. One important aspect of this at the cost centre level is the head's concern with the minimization of long-run costs. The accounting data must be used with some care and in a rather flexible manner, with the emphasis for performance evaluation in contributing to long-term profitability.

3. **Non-accounting style**: Accounting data plays a relatively unimportant part in the supervisor's evaluation of the cost centre head's performance.

EXHIBIT 16.2 Hopwood's findings on the effect of different styles of evaluating budget performance

	Style of evaluation		
	Budget-constrained	Profit-conscious	Non-accounting
Involvement with costs	High	High	Low
Job-related tension	High	Medium	Medium
Manipulation of accounting information	Extensive	Little	Little
Relations with superior	Poor	Good	Good
Relations with colleagues	Poor	Good	Good

The evidence from Hopwood's study indicated that both the budget-constrained and the profit-conscious styles of evaluation led to a higher degree of involvement with costs than the non-accounting style. Only the profit-conscious style, however, succeeded in attaining this involvement without incurring either emotional costs for the managers in charge of the cost centres or defensive behaviour that was undesirable from the company's point of view.

The budget-constrained style gave rise to a belief that the evaluation was unjust, and caused widespread worry and tension on the job. Hopwood provides evidence of manipulation of information and undesirable decision behaviour as methods of relieving tension when a budget-constrained style of evaluation is used. In contrast, Hopwood found that the profit-conscious style avoided these problems, while at the same time it ensured that there was an active involvement with the financial aspects of the operations. A summary of the effect of the three styles of evaluation is given in Exhibit 16.2.

Hopwood's study was based on cost centres having a high degree of interdependence. Rigid measures of performance become less appropriate as the degree of interdependence increases, and therefore the managers used the accounting information in a more flexible manner to ensure that the information remained effective. Otley (1978) replicated Hopwood's study in a British firm that consisted of profit centres with a high degree of independence and where accounting information represented a more adequate basis of performance evaluation. He found no significant differences in the levels of job tension and performance reported by managers evaluated on styles initially used by Hopwood. Possible explanations for the differences included the fact that in Otley's study, managers operated more independently of other units within the same organization and the managers in Hopwood's study operated in a less predictable environment than those in Otley's study.

Otley's study suggested that when managers face high levels of managerial interdependency[1] or uncertainty, they may perceive themselves as having less than full control over performance outcomes. Using budget data in a rigid manner in such situations may be dysfunctional for performance, since a rigid use of budget data assumes that most of the factors that have an effect on task outcomes are within the control of the managers being evaluated (Ansari, 1979). On the other hand, Imoisili (1989) suggests that a rigid use of budget data may be more acceptable to managers if they perceive they are able to exercise control over their performance outcomes. This would be the case with task uncertainty where tasks are characterized by low uncertainty or interdependency.[2] In other words, it is not budget style per se that may lead to higher stress or lower performance. Rather, it is the mismatch of budget style and task contexts that may enhance stress or reduce managerial performance.

CONTINGENCY THEORY

To design effective management accounting control systems it is necessary to consider the circumstances in which they will be used. It should be apparent from this chapter that there is no universally best management accounting control system which can be applied to all organizations. The applicability of a management accounting control system is contingent on the situational factors faced by organizations. This approach is known as the contingency theory approach to management accounting. The situational factors represent the contingent factors (also known as contingent variables or contextual factors).

Examples of the contingent factors that have been examined in the literature include the external environment faced by organizations, the type of competitive strategy they adopt, organizational structure and the nature of the production process. The aspects of the management accounting control systems that contingency theory research has focused on include dimensions of budgeting (participation, importance of meeting budgets), reliance on accounting information for performance evaluation and dimensions of information (e.g. timeliness and level of aggregation). For example, in this chapter it has been pointed out that the appropriateness of participation is dependent on the nature of the production process. In the previous section it was also suggested that the appropriate style of performance evaluation was influenced by organizational structure and environmental uncertainty.

A considerable amount of literature has emerged focusing on the contingency theory of management accounting. For a detailed summary of this literature you should refer to Learning Note 16.1 in the Digital Support Resources accompanying this book (see Preface for details).

ALTERNATIVE USES OF MANAGEMENT ACCOUNTING INFORMATION

Throughout this book it is generally assumed that one of the major purposes of management accounting is to aid rational economic decision-making. However, at this stage it is important that you are aware that accounting information can also be used for other purposes that are not necessarily consistent with rational economic behaviour. Managers can find value in accounting information for symbolic purposes even when the information has little or no relation to decision-making. For example, instead of the information actually being used for decision-making or control purposes it may be used as a means of signalling to others inside and outside the organization that decisions are being taken rationally and that managers in an organization are accountable. Accounting information is also used for political purposes. Interested parties use the information to promote their own vested interests to achieve political power or a bargaining position. Finally, accounting information may be used for legitimizing purposes in order to justify and legitimize actions that have already been decided upon, rather than the information being used as a decision input. For a more detailed discussion of the different purposes for which accounting information is used you should refer to Learning Note 16.2 in the digital support resources accompanying this book.

SUMMARY

The following items relate to the learning objectives listed at the beginning of the chapter.

Describe the three different types of controls used in organizations.

Three different categories of controls are used – action/behavioural controls, personnel and cultural controls and results/output controls. With action controls the actions themselves are the focus of controls. Personnel controls help employees do a good job by building on employees' natural tendencies to control themselves. They include selection and placement, training and job design. Cultural controls represent a set of values, social norms and beliefs that are shared by members of the organization and that influence their actions. Output or results controls involve collecting and reporting information about the outcomes of work effort.

Distinguish between feedback and feed-forward controls.

Feedback control involves monitoring outputs achieved against desired outputs and taking whatever corrective action is necessary if a deviation exists. In feed-forward control, instead of actual outputs being compared against desired outputs, predictions are made of what outputs are expected to be at some future time. If these expectations differ from what is desired, control actions are taken that will minimize these differences. The objective is for control to be achieved before any deviations from desired outputs actually occur. The *budgeting planning* process is a feed-forward control system. The budgetary *control* process consisting of the comparison of actual results with budget, identifying variances and taking remedial action to ensure future outcomes will conform with budgeted outcomes, is an illustration of a feedback control system.

Explain the potential harmful side-effects of results controls.

Results controls can promote a number of harmful side-effects. They can lead to a lack of goal congruence when employees seek to achieve the performance targets in a way that is not organizationally desirable. They can also lead to data manipulation and negative attitudes, which can result in a decline in morale and a lack of motivation.

Define the four different types of responsibility centres.

A responsibility centre may be defined as a unit of a firm where an individual manager is held accountable for the unit's performance. There are four types of responsibility centres – cost or expense centres, revenue centres, profit centres and investment centres. Cost or expense centres are responsibility centres where managers are normally accountable for only those costs that are under their control. Revenue centres are responsibility centres where managers are accountable only for financial outputs in the form of generating sales revenues. A significant increase in managerial autonomy occurs when unit managers are given responsibility for both production and sales. Units within an organization whose managers are accountable for both revenues and costs are called profit centres. Investment centres are responsibility centres whose managers are responsible for both sales revenues and costs and, in addition, have responsibility and authority to make working capital and capital investment decisions.

Explain the different elements of management accounting control systems.

Management accounting control systems have two core elements. The first is the formal planning processes such as budgeting and long-term planning. These processes are used for establishing performance expectations for evaluating performance. The second is responsibility accounting, which involves the creation of responsibility centres. Responsibility centres enable accountability for financial results/outcomes to be allocated to individuals throughout the organization. Responsibility accounting involves: (a) distinguishing between those items which managers can control and for which they should be held accountable, and those items over which they have no control and for which they are not held accountable; (b) determining how challenging the financial targets should be; and (c) determining how much influence managers should have in the setting of financial targets.

Describe the controllability principle and the methods of implementing it.

The controllability principle states that it is appropriate to charge to an area of responsibility only those costs that are significantly influenced by the manager of that responsibility centre. The controllability principle can be implemented by either eliminating the uncontrollable items from the areas that managers are held accountable for or calculating their effects so that the reports distinguish between controllable and uncontrollable items.

Describe the different approaches that can be used to determine financial performance targets and discuss the impact of their level of difficulty on motivation and performance.

There are three approaches that can be used to set financial targets. They involve targets derived from engineering studies of input–output relationships, targets derived from historical data and targets derived from negotiations between superiors and subordinates. Different types of financial performance targets can be set ranging from easily achievable to difficult to achieve. Targets that are considered moderately difficult to achieve (called highly achievable targets) are recommended because they can be used for planning purposes and they also have a motivational impact.

● Describe the influence of participation in the budgeting process.

Participation relates to the extent that budgetees are able to influence the figures that are incorporated in their budgets or targets. Allowing individuals to participate in the setting of performance targets has the following advantages: (a) individuals are more likely to accept the targets and be committed to achieving them if they have been involved in the target setting process; (b) participation can reduce the information asymmetry gap that applies when standards are imposed from above; and (c) imposed standards can encourage negative attitudes and result in demotivation and alienation. Participation, however, is subject to the following limitations: (a) performance is measured by precisely the same standard that the budgetee has been involved in setting; and (b) a top-down approach to budget setting is likely to be preferable where a process is highly programmable. Participation must be used selectively; but if it is used in the right circumstances, it has an enormous potential for encouraging the commitment to organizational goals.

● Distinguish between the three different styles of evaluating performance and identify the circumstances when a particular style is most appropriate.

Three distinct styles of performance evaluation have been identified – a budget-constrained style, a profit-conscious style and a non-accounting style. With a budget-constrained style, budget data are used in a rigid manner in performance evaluation. A profit-conscious style uses accounting data in a more flexible manner, with the emphasis for performance evaluation on a unit's contribution to long-term profitability. With a non-accounting style, accounting data play a relatively unimportant part in performance evaluation. Using a budget-constrained style when managers face high levels of interdependence or uncertainty is likely to be inappropriate because the rigid use of budget data assumes that most of the factors that have an effect on task outcomes are within the control of the managers being evaluated. In contrast, the rigid use of budget data may be more acceptable where managers perceive that they are able to exercise control over their performance outcomes. This applies where low uncertainty or interdependency characterizes tasks.

NOTES

1 Managerial interdependency is the extent to which each manager perceives his or her work-related activities to require the joint or cooperative effort of other managers within the organization.

2 Task uncertainty is the extent to which managers can predict confidently the factors that have effects on their work-related activities.

KEY TERMS AND CONCEPTS

Action controls Observing the actions of individuals as they go about their work, also known as behavioural controls.

Aspiration level The level of performance that the person responsible for the budget hopes to attain.

Behavioural controls Controls that involve observing the actions of individuals as they go about their work, also known as action controls.

Bottom-up budget setting Allowing individuals to participate in the setting of budgets and targets.

Contingency theory An approach to management accounting that takes account of situational factors faced by organizations.

Control The process of ensuring that a firm's activities conform to its plan and that its objectives are achieved.

Controllability principle The principle that it is appropriate to charge to an area of responsibility only those costs that are significantly influenced by the manager of that responsibility centre.

Controls Measurement and information used to help determine what control action needs to be taken.

Cost centres Responsibility centres whose managers are normally accountable for only those costs that are under their control, also known as expense centres.

Cultural controls A set of values, social norms and beliefs that are shared by members of the organization and that influence their actions.

Discretionary expense centres Cost centres where output cannot be measured in financial terms and there are no clearly observable relationships between inputs and outputs.

Engineered targets Targets derived from engineering studies of input-output relationships.

Ex post budget adjustments The adjustment of a budget to the environmental and economic conditions that the manager's actually faced during the period.

Expense centres Responsibility centres whose managers are normally accountable for only those costs that are under their control, also known as cost centres.

Feedback control Monitoring outputs achieved against desired outputs and taking whatever corrective action is necessary if a deviation exists.

Feed-forward control Comparing predictions of expected outputs with the desired outputs and taking corrective action to minimize any differences.

Flexible budgets Budgets in which the uncontrollable volume effects on cost behaviour are removed from the manager's performance reports.

Goal congruence The situation that exists when controls motivate employees to behave in a way that is in tune with the organization's goals.

Historical targets Targets derived directly from the results of previous periods.

Investment centres Responsibility centres whose managers are responsible for both sales revenues and costs and also have responsibility and authority to make capital investment decisions.

Management control system The entire array of controls used by an organization.

Managerial interdependency The extent to which each manager perceives his or her work-related activities to require the joint or cooperative effort of other managers within the organization.

Negotiated targets Targets based on negotiations between superiors and subordinates.

Output controls Collecting and reporting information about the outcomes of work effort, also known as results controls.

Participation The extent that individuals are able to influence the figures that are incorporated in their budgets or targets.

Personnel controls Helping employees to perform well through the use of selection and placement, training, job design and the provision of necessary resources.

Profit centres Responsibility centres where managers are accountable for both revenues and costs.

Relative performance evaluation The evaluation of the performance of a responsibility centre relative to the performance of similar centres within the same company or of similar units outside the organization.

Responsibility accounting The creation of responsibility centres and the accumulation of costs and revenues so that the deviations from budget can be attributed to the individual who is accountable for the responsibility centre.

Responsibility centre A unit of a firm where an individual manager is held responsible for the unit's performance.

Results controls Collecting and reporting information about the outcomes of work effort, also known as output controls.

Revenue centres Responsibility centres where managers are mainly accountable for financial outputs in the form of generating sales revenues.

Social controls The selection of people who have already been socialized into adopting particular norms and patterns of behaviour to perform particular tasks.

Standard cost centres Cost centres where output can be measured and the input required to produce each unit of output can be specified.

Strategic control Control that focuses outside the organization, looking at how a firm can compete with other firms in the same industry.

Subjective judgements Judgements made in the evaluation process based on the knowledge of the outcome measures and the circumstances faced by the responsibility centre heads.

Task uncertainty The extent to which managers can predict confidently the factors that have effects on their work-related activities.

Top-down budget setting Imposing budgets and targets from above, without the participation of the individuals involved.

Variance The difference between the actual cost and the standard cost.

Variance analysis The analysis of factors that cause the actual results to differ from pre-determined budgeted targets.

RECOMMENDED READING

There are a number of important textbooks that specialize in management control. If you wish to study management control in more depth you are recommended to read Merchant and Van der Stede (2007). For a broader discussion of how the array of different controls should be viewed as a single package you should refer to Malmi and Brown (2008). With regard to performance sector in the service industries you should read Fitzgerald and Moon (1996).

KEY EXAMINATION POINTS

Essay questions are extensively used in second year management accounting courses. They tend not to be widely used for first year courses. The most frequently examined topic on first year courses is to prepare flexible budgets (see Solutions to Review problem 16.20). If you are required to prepare flexible budgets, remember to flex the budget on the basis of target cost for actual output rather than input measures, such as direct labour or input hours. Also questions requiring you to comment on, or redraft performance reports, are frequently set at all levels (e.g. Review problem 16.22). It is important that you distinguish between controllable and non-controllable expenses and stress the need to incorporate non-financial measures. A common error is to compare actual performance with an unflexed budget.

ASSESSMENT MATERIAL

The review questions are short questions that enable you to assess your understanding of the main topics included in the chapter. The numbers in parentheses provide you with the page numbers to refer to if you cannot answer a specific question.

The review problems are more complex and require you to relate and apply the chapter content to various business problems. The problems are graded by their level of difficulty. Solutions to review problems that are not preceded by the term 'IM' are provided in a separate section at the end of the book. Solutions to problems preceded by the term 'IM' are provided in the *Instructor's Manual* accompanying this book that can be downloaded from the lecturer's digital support resources. Additional review problems with fully worked solutions are provided in the *Student Manual* that accompanies this book.

The digital support resources also include over 30 case study problems. Several cases are relevant to the content of this chapter. Examples include Airport Complex and Integrated Technology Services Ltd.

REVIEW QUESTIONS

16.1 Distinguish between 'controls' and 'control'. (p. 393)
16.2 Identify and describe three different types of control mechanisms used by companies. (pp. 394–396)
16.3 Provide examples of behavioural, action, social, personnel and cultural controls. (pp. 394–395)
16.4 Describe the different stages that are involved with output/results controls. (pp. 395–396)
16.5 Distinguish between feedback and feed-forward controls. Provide an example of each type of control. (p. 396)
16.6 Describe some of the harmful side-effects that can occur with output/results controls. (pp. 397–398)
16.7 Explain the circumstances when it is appropriate or inappropriate to use personnel/cultural, behavioural/action and results/output controls. (pp. 398–399)
16.8 Describe the four different types of responsibility centres. (pp. 400–402)
16.9 Explain what is meant by the term 'responsibility accounting'. (p. 402)
16.10 What factors must be taken into account when operating a responsibility accounting system? (p. 402)

16.11 What is the 'controllability principle'? Describe the different ways in which the principle can be applied. (pp. 403–406)
16.12 What are flexible budgets? Why are they preferred to fixed (static budgets)? (p. 404)
16.13 What is meant by the term 'aspiration level'? (p. 407)
16.14 Describe the effect of the level of budget difficulty on motivation and performance. (pp. 407–408)
16.15 Distinguish between participation and top-down budget setting. (pp. 408–409)
16.16 Describe the factors influencing the effectiveness of participation in the budget process. (pp. 408–409)
16.17 What are the limitations of participation in the budget process? (p. 409)
16.18 Distinguish between budget-constrained, profit-conscious and non-accounting styles of performance evaluation. (p. 409)
16.19 Under what circumstances is it considered appropriate to use (a) the budget constrained and (b) the profit-conscious style of performance evaluation? (p. 410)

REVIEW PROBLEMS

16.20 **Intermediate: Performance reporting.** M plc designs, manufactures and assembles furniture. The furniture is for home use and therefore varies considerably in size, complexity and value. One of the departments in the company is the Assembly Department. This department is labour intensive; the workers travel to various locations to assemble and fit the furniture using the packs of finished timbers that have been sent to them.

Budgets are set centrally and they are then given to the managers of the various departments who then have the responsibility of achieving their respective targets. Actual costs are compared against the budgets and the managers are then asked to comment on the budgetary control statement. The statement for April for the Assembly Department is shown below.

	Budget	Actual	Variances	
Assembly labour				
hours	6 400	7 140		
	$	$	$	
Assembly labour	51 970	58 227	6 257	Adverse
Furniture packs	224 000	205 000	19 000	Favourable
Other materials	23 040	24 100	1 060	Adverse
Overheads	62 060	112 340	50 280	Adverse
Total	361 070	399 667	38 597	Adverse

Note: the costs shown are for assembling and fitting the furniture (they do not include time spent travelling to jobs and the related costs). The hours worked by the manager are not included in the figure given for the assembly labour hours.

The manager of the Assembly Department is new to the job and has very little previous experience of working with budgets, but he does have many years' experience as a supervisor in assembly departments. Based on that experience he was sure that the department had performed well. He has asked for your help in replying to a memo he has just received asking him to 'explain the serious overspending in his department'. He has sent you some additional information about the budget.

1 The budgeted and actual assembly labour costs include the fixed salary of $2050 for the manager of the Assembly Department. All of the other labour is paid for the hours they work.

2 The cost of furniture packs and other materials is assumed by the central finance office of M plc to vary in proportion to the number of assembly labour hours worked.

3 The budgeted overhead costs are made up of three elements: a fixed cost of $9000 for services from central headquarters, a stepped fixed cost which changes when the assembly hours exceed 7000 hours, and some variable overheads. The variable overheads are assumed to vary in proportion to the number of assembly labour hours. Working papers for the budget showed the impact on the overhead costs of differing amounts of assembly labour hours:

Assembly labour hours	5 000	7 500	10 000
Overhead costs	$54 500	$76 500	$90 000

The actual fixed costs for April were as budgeted.

(a) Prepare, using the additional information that the Manager of the Assembly Department has given you, a budgetary control statement that would be more helpful to him. *(7 marks)*

(b) (i) Discuss the differences between the format of the statement that you have produced and that supplied by M plc. *(4 marks)*

(ii) Discuss the assumption made by the central office of M plc that costs vary in proportion to assembly labour hours. *(3 marks)*

(c) Discuss whether M plc should change to a system of participative budgeting. *(6 marks)*

CIMA P1 Management Accounting: Performance Evaluation

16.21 Intermediate: Flexible budgets and the motivational role of budgets. Club Atlantic is an all-weather holiday complex providing holidays throughout the year. The fee charged to guests is fully inclusive of accommodation and all meals. However, because the holiday industry is so competitive, Club Atlantic is only able to generate profits by maintaining strict financial control of all activities.

The club's restaurant is one area where there is a constant need to monitor costs. Susan Green is the manager of the restaurant. At the beginning of each year she is given an annual budget which is then broken down into months. Each month she receives a statement monitoring actual costs against the annual budget and highlighting any variances. The statement for the month ended 31 October is reproduced below along with a list of assumptions:

Club Atlantic Restaurant Performance Statement Month to 31 October

	Actual	Budget	Variance (over)/under
Number of guest days	11 160	9 600	(1 560)
	(£)	(£)	(£)
Food	20 500	20 160	(340)
Cleaning materials	2 232	1 920	(312)
Heat, light and power	2 050	2 400	350
Catering wages	8 400	7 200	(1 200)
Rent rates, insurance and depreciation	1 860	1 800	(60)
	35 042	33 480	(1 562)

Assumptions:

(a) The budget has been calculated on the basis of a 30-day calendar month with the cost of rents, insurance and depreciation being an apportionment of the fixed annual charge.

(b) The budgeted catering wages assume that:

(i) there is one member of the catering staff for every 40 guests staying at the complex;

(ii) the daily cost of a member of the catering staff is £30.

(c) All other budgeted costs are variable costs based on the number of guest days.

Task 1

Using the data above, prepare a revised performance statement using flexible budgeting. Your statement should show both the revised budget and the revised variances. Club Atlantic uses the existing budgets and performance statements to motivate its managers as well as for financial control. If managers keep expenses below budget they receive a bonus in addition to their salaries. A colleague of Susan is Brian Hilton. Brian is in charge of the swimming pool and golf course, both of which have high levels of fixed costs. Each month he manages to keep expenses below budget and in return enjoys regular bonuses. Under the current reporting system, Susan Green only rarely receives a bonus.

At a recent meeting with Club Atlantic's directors Susan Green expressed concern that the performance statement was not a valid reflection of her management of the restaurant. You are currently employed by Hall and Co., the club's auditors, and the directors of Club Atlantic have asked you to advise them whether there is any justification for Susan Green's concern.

At the meeting with the Club's directors, you were asked the following questions:

(a) Do budgets motivate managers to achieve objectives?

(b) Does motivating managers lead to improved performance?

(c) Does the current method of reporting performance motivate Susan Green and Brian Hilton to be more efficient?

Task 2

Write a *brief* letter to the directors of Club Atlantic addressing their question and justifying your answers.

Note: You should make use of the data given in this task plus your findings in Task 1.

AAT Technicians Stage

16.22 Advanced: Recommendations for improvements to a performance report and a review of the management control system. Your firm has been consulted by the managing director of Inzone plc, which owns a chain of retail stores. Each store has departments selling furniture, tableware and kitchenware. Departmental managers are responsible to a store manager, who is in turn responsible to head office (HO).

All goods for sale are ordered centrally and stores sell at prices fixed by HO. Store managers (aided by departmental managers) order stocks from HO and stores are charged interest based on month-end stock levels. HO appoints all permanent staff and sets all pay levels. Store managers can engage or dismiss temporary workers, and are responsible for store running expenses.

The introduction to Inzone plc's management accounting manual states:

'Budgeting starts three months before the budget year, with product sales projections which are developed by HO buyers in consultation with each store's departmental managers. Expense budgets, adjusted for expected inflation, are then prepared by HO for each store. Inzone plc's accounting year is divided into 13 four-weekly control periods, and the budgeted sales and expenses are assigned to periods with due regard to seasonal factors. The budgets are completed one month before the year begins on 1st January.

'All HO expenses are recharged to stores in order to give the clearest indication of the "bottom line" profit of each store. These HO costs are mainly buying expenses, which are recharged to stores according to their square footage.

'Store reports comparing actual results with budgets are on the desks of HO and store management one week after the end of each control period. Significant variations in performance are then investigated, and appropriate action taken.'

Ms Lewis is manager of an Inzone plc store. She is eligible for a bonus equal to 5 per cent of the amount by which her store's 'bottom-line' profit exceeds the year's budget. However, Ms Lewis sees no chance of a bonus this year, because major roadworks near the store are disrupting trade. Her store report for the four weeks ending 21 June is as follows:

	Actual (£)	Budget (£)
Sales	98 850	110 000
Costs:		
Cost of goods (including stock losses)	63 100	70 200
Wages and salaries	5 300	5 500
Rent	11 000	11 000
Depreciation of store fittings	500	500
Distribution costs	4 220	4 500
Other store running expenses	1 970	2 000
Interest charge on stocks	3 410	3 500
Store's share of HO costs	2 050	2 000
Store profit	7 300	10 800
	98 850	110 000
Stocks held at end of period	341 000	350 000
Store fittings at written down value	58 000	58 000

Requirements:

(a) Make recommendations for the improvement of Inzone plc's store report, briefly justifying each recommendation.
(11 marks)

(b) Prepare a report for the managing director of Inzone plc reviewing the company's responsibility delegation, identifying the major strengths and weaknesses of Inzone plc's management control system, and recommending any changes you consider appropriate. *(14 marks)*

ICAEW P2 Management Accounting

16.23 Advanced: Comments on budget and control practices.
The Rubber Group (TRG) manufactures and sells a number of rubber-based products. Its strategic focus is channelled through profit centres which sell products transferred from production divisions that are operated as cost centres. The profit centres are the primary value-adding part of the business, whose commercial profit centre managers are responsible for the generation of a contribution margin sufficient to earn the target return of TRG. The target return is calculated after allowing for the sum of the agreed budgeted cost of production at production divisions, plus the cost of marketing, selling and distribution costs and central services costs.

The Bettamould Division is part of TRG and manufactures moulded products that it transfers to profit centres at an agreed cost per tonne. The agreed cost per tonne is set following discussion between management of the Bettaniould Division and senior management of TRG.

The following information relates to the agreed budget for the Bettamould Division for the year ending 30 June 2009:

1 The budgeted output of moulded products to be transferred to profit centres is 100 000 tonnes. The budgeted transfer cost has been agreed on a two-part basis as follows:

(i) A standard variable cost of $200 per tonne of moulded products;

(ii) A lump sum annual charge of $50 000 000 in respect of fixed costs, which is charged to profit centres, at $500 per tonne of moulded products.

2 Budgeted standard variable costs (as quoted in 1 above) have been set after incorporating each of the following:

(i) A provision in respect of processing losses amounting to 15% of material inputs. Materials are sourced on a JIT basis from chosen suppliers who have been used for some years. It is felt that the 15% level of losses is necessary because the ageing of the machinery will lead to a reduction in the efficiency of output levels.

(ii) A provision in respect of machine idle time amounting to 5%. This is incorporated into variable machine costs. The idle time allowance is held at the 5% level partly through elements of 'real-time' maintenance undertaken by the machine operating teams as part of their job specification.

3 Quality checks are carried out on a daily basis on 25% of throughput tonnes of moulded products.

4 All employees and management have contracts based on fixed annual salary agreements. In addition, a bonus of 5% of salary is payable as long as the budgeted output of 100 000 tonnes has been achieved;

5 Additional information relating to the points in (2) above (but NOT included in the budget for the year ending 30 June 2009) is as follows:

(i) There is evidence that materials of an equivalent specification could be sourced for 40% of the annual requirement at the Bettamould Division, from another division within TRG which has spare capacity.

(ii) There is evidence that a move to machine maintenance being outsourced from a specialist company could help reduce machine idle time and hence allow the possibility of annual output in excess of 100 000 tonnes of moulded products.

(iii) It is thought that the current level of quality checks (25% of throughput on a daily basis) is vital, although current evidence shows that some competitor companies are able to achieve consistent acceptable quality with a quality check level of only 10% of throughput on a daily basis.

The directors of TRG have decided to investigate claims relating to the use of budgeting within organizations which have featured in recent literature. A summary of relevant points from the literature is contained in the following statement

'The use of budgets as part of a 'performance contract' between an organization and its managers may be seen as a practice that causes management action which might lead to the following problems:

(a) Meeting only the lowest targets
(b) Using more resources than necessary
(c) Making the bonus — whatever it takes
(d) Competing against other divisions, business units and departments
(e) Ensuring that what is in the budget is spent
(f) Providing inaccurate forecasts
(g) Meeting the target, but not beating it
(h) Avoiding risks,'

Required:

(a) Explain the nature of any SIX of the eight problems listed above relating to the use of budgeting; *(12 marks)*
(b) Illustrate EACH of the six problems chosen in (a) using the data from the Bettamould division TRG scenario; and *(6 marks)*
(c) Suggest ways in which each of the six problems chosen in (a) above may be overcome. *(6 marks)*

ACCA Advanced Performance Management

16.24 Advanced. A college is preparing its budget for 2012. In previous years the director of the college has prepared the college budget without the participation of senior staff and presented it to the college board for approval.

Last year the college board criticised the director over the lack of participation of his senior staff in the preparation of the budget for 2011 and requested that for the 2012 budget the senior staff were to be involved.

Required:
Discuss the potential advantages and disadvantages to the college of involving the senior staff in the budget preparation process.
CIMA P2 Performance Management

16.25 Advanced. 'Responsibility accounting is based on the application of the controllability principle.'

Required:

(a) Explain the 'controllability' principle and why its application is difficult in practice. *(6 marks)*
(b) Explain how the management of an organization can attempt to overcome the difficulties inherent in the practical application of the controllability principle. *(8 marks)*
(c) Explain the following approaches that can be used to set financial targets within an organization:

(i)   Engineered approach
(ii) Historical approach
(iii) Negotiated approach. *(6 marks)*

ACCA P3 Performance Measurement

16.26 Advanced. 'A competent management accounting system should endeavour to enhance the performance of a company. It should, in particular, consider the behavioural consequences of the system.'

Required:

(a) Explain why it is necessary when designing a management accounting system to consider the behavioural consequences of its application. *(5 marks)*
(b) Explain the potential behavioural issues that may arise in the application of performance monitoring, budgeting and transfer pricing and suggest how problems may be overcome.

(15 marks)
ACCA P3 Performance Measurement

16.27 Advanced. A firm of solicitors is using budgetary control during 2010. The senior partner estimated the demand for the year for each of the firm's four divisions: Civil, Criminal, Corporate. and Property. A separate partner is responsible for each division.

Each divisional partner then prepared a cost budget based on the senior partner's demand estimate for the division. These budgets were then submitted to the senior partner for his approval. He then amended them as he thought appropriate before issuing each divisional partner with the final budget for the division. He did not discuss these amendments with the respective divisional partners. Actual performance is then measured against the final budgets for each month and each divisional partner's performance is appraised by asking the divisional partner to explain the reasons for any variances that occur.

The Corporate partner has been asked to explain why her staff costs exceeded the budgeted costs for last month while the chargeable time was less than budgeted. Her reply is below:

'My own original estimate of staff costs was higher than the final budgeted costs shown on my divisional performance report. In my own cost budget I allowed for time to be spent developing new services for the firm's corporate clients and improving the clients access to their own case files. This would improve the quality of our services to clients and therefore increase client satisfaction. The trouble with our present system is that it focuses on financial performance and ignores the other performance indicators found in modem performance management systems.'

Required:

(a) Discuss the present budgeting system and its likely effect on divisional partner motivation. *(6 marks)*
(b) Explain two non-financial performance indicators (other than client satisfaction and service quality) that could be used by the firm. *(4 marks)*

CIMA P2 Performance Management

IM16.1 Intermediate. Explain the meaning of each of the undernoted terms, comment on their likely impact on cash budgeting and profit planning and suggest ways in which any adverse effects of each may be reduced.

(a) Budgetary slack. *(7 marks)*
(b) Incremental budgets. *(7 marks)*
(c) Fixed budgets. *(6 marks)*

ACCA Level 2 Cost and Management Accounting II

IM16.2 Advanced.

(a) Discuss the use of the following as aids to *each* of planning and control:

(i)   rolling budgets;
(ii) flexible budgets;
(iii) planning and operational variances. *(9 marks)*

(b) Discuss the extent to which the incidence of budgetary slack is likely to be affected by the use of each of the techniques listed in (a). *(6 marks)*

ACCA Paper 9 Information for Control and Decision Making

IM16.3 Advanced. In the context of budgetary control, certain costs are not amenable to the use of flexible budgets. These include some costs which are often called 'discretionary' (or 'programmed').
You are required to explain:

(a) the nature of discretionary (or programmed) costs and give *two* examples;
(b) how the treatment of these costs differs from that of other types of cost in the process of preparing and using budgets for control purposes. *(20 marks)*

CIMA P3 Management Accounting

IM16.4 Advanced.

(a) In the context of budgeting, provide definitions for *four* of the following terms:
aspiration level;
budgetary slack;
feedback;
zero-base budgeting;
responsibility accounting. *(8 marks)*

(b) Discuss the motivational implications of the level of efficiency assumed in establishing a budget. *(9 marks)*

ACCA Level 2 Management Accounting

IM16.5 Advanced. 'Budgeting is too often looked upon from a purely mechanistic viewpoint. The human factors in budgeting are more important than the accounting techniques. The success of a budgetary system depends upon its acceptance by the company members who are affected by the budgets.'

Discuss the validity of the above statement from the viewpoint of both the planning and the control aspects of budgeting. In the course of your discussion present at least one practical illustration to support your conclusions. *(20 marks)*

ACCA P2 Management Accounting

IM16.6 Advanced. 'The major reason for introducing budgetary control and standard costing systems is to influence human behaviour and to motivate the managers to achieve the goals of the organization. However, the accounting literature provides many illustrations of accounting control systems that fail to give sufficient attention to influencing human behaviour towards the achievement of organization goals.'

You are required:

(a) To identify and discuss four situations where accounting control systems might not motivate desirable behaviour.

(b) To briefly discuss the improvements you would suggest in order to ensure that some of the dysfunctional behavioural consequences of accounting control systems are avoided.

IM16.7 Advanced. 'The final impact which any accounting system has on managerial and employee behaviour is dependent not only upon its design and technical characteristics but also in the precise manner in which the resulting information is used.' (A. Hopwood, *Accountancy and Human Behaviour*)

Discuss this statement in relation to budgeting and standard costing.

IM16.8 Advanced. 'Motivation is the over-riding consideration that should influence management in formulating and using performance measures, and in designing management control systems.'

Discuss this statement in relation to the design and implementation of budgetary control systems.

IM16.9 Advanced.

(a) Discuss the behavioural arguments for and against involving those members of management who are responsible for the implementation of the budget in the annual budget setting process. *(10 marks)*

(b) Explain how the methods by which annual budgets are formulated might help to overcome behavioural factors likely to limit the efficiency and effectiveness of the budget.

(7 marks)

IM16.10 Advanced. An article in *Management Accounting* concluded that there will always be some budgetary padding in any organization.

Requirements:

(a) As management accountant, write a report to your finance director, explaining what steps can be taken by you, and by senior management when approving budgets, to minimize budgetary slack. *(8 marks)*

(b) The finance director, having read the report referred to in part (a), discussed the problem with the managing director and suggested that appropriate action be taken to reduce budgetary slack.

The managing director expressed doubts, stating that in his opinion removing all budget padding could cause considerable problems.

Requirement:
Explain the arguments that can be advanced for accepting some budgetary slack, and the advantages of this to the manager being appraised and to the organization. Discuss whether the budget review and approval process should permit managers to build in some budgetary slack. *(12 marks)*

CIMA Stage 4 Management Accounting Control Systems

IM16.11 Intermediate: Preparation of flexible budgets and an explanation of variances. You have been provided with the following operating statement, which represents an attempt to compare the actual performance for the quarter which has just ended with the budget:

	Budget	Actual	Variance
Number of units sold (000s)	640	720	80
	£000	£000	£000
Sales	1024	1071	47
Cost of sales (all variable)			
Materials	168	144	
Labour	240	288	
Overheads	32	36	
	440	468	(28)
Fixed labour cost	100	94	6
Selling and distribution costs:			
Fixed	72	83	(11)
Variable	144	153	(9)
Administration costs:			
Fixed	184	176	8
Variable	48	54	(6)
	548	560	(12)
Net profit	36	43	7

Required:

(a) Using a flexible budgeting approach, re-draft the operating statement so as to provide a more realistic indication of the variances and comment briefly on the possible reasons (other than inflation) why they have occurred. *(12 marks)*

(b) Explain why the original operating statement was of little use to management. *(2 marks)*

(c) Discuss the problems associated with the forecasting of figures which are to be used in flexible budgeting. *(6 marks)*

ACCA Paper 8 Managerial Finance

IM16.12 Intermediate: Responsibility centre performance reports.
Data
Jim Smith has recently been appointed as the head teacher of Mayfield School in Midshire. The age of the pupils ranges from 11 years to 18 years. For many years, Midshire County Council was responsible for preparing and reporting on the school budget. From June, however, these responsibilities passed to the head teacher of Mayfield School.

You have recently accepted a part-time appointment as the accountant to Mayfield School, although your previous accounting experience has been gained in commercial organizations. Jim Smith is hoping that you will be able to apply that experience to improving the financial reporting procedures at Mayfield School.

The last budget statement prepared by Midshire County Council is reproduced below. It covers the ten months to the end of May and all figures refer to cash *payments* made.

Midshire County Council Mayfield School
Statement of school expenditure against budget: 10 months ending May

	Expenditure to date	Budget to date	Under/ over spend	Total budget for year
Teachers full-time	1 680 250	1 682 500	2 250 Cr	2 019 000
Teachers part-time	35 238	34 600	638	41 520
Other employee expenses	5 792	15 000	9 208 Cr	18 000
Administrative staff	69 137	68 450	687	82 140
Caretaker and cleaning	49 267	57 205	7 938 Cr	68 646
Resources (books, etc.)	120 673	100 000	20 673	120 000
Repairs and maintenance	458	0	458	0
Lighting and heating	59 720	66 720	7 000 Cr	80 064
Rates	23 826	19 855	3 971	23 826
Fixed assets: furniture and equipment	84 721	100 000	15 279 Cr	120 000
Stationery, postage and phone	1 945	0	1 945	0
Miscellaneous expenses	9 450	6 750	2 700	8 100
Total	2 140 477	2 151 080	10 603 Cr	2 581 296

Task 1

Write a memo to Jim Smith. Your memo should:

(a) identify *four* weaknesses of the existing statement as a management report;

(b) include an improved *outline* statement format showing revised column headings and a more meaningful classification of costs which will help Jim Smith to manage his school effectively (figures are not required);

(c) give *two* advantages of your proposed format over the existing format.

Data

The income of Mayfield School is based on the number of pupils at the school. Jim Smith provides you with the following breakdown of student numbers.

Mayfield School:
Student numbers as at 31 May

School year	Age range	Current number of pupils
1	11–12	300
2	12–13	350
3	13–14	325
4	14–15	360
5	15–16	380
6	16–17	240
7	17–18	220
Total number of students		2175

Jim also provides you with the following information relating to existing pupils:

- pupils move up one school-year at the end of July;
- for those pupils entering year 6, there is an option to leave the school. As a result, only 80 per cent of the current school-year 5 pupils go on to enter school-year 6;
- of those currently in school-year 6 only 95 per cent continue into school-year 7;
- pupils currently in school-year 7 leave to go on to higher education or employment;
- the annual income per pupil is £1200 in years 1 to 5 and £1500 in years 6 to 7.

The new year 1 pupils come from the final year at four junior schools. Not all pupils, however, elect to go to Mayfield School. Jim has investigated this matter and derived accurate estimates of the proportion of final year pupils at each of the four junior schools who go on to attend Mayfield School.

The number of pupils in the final year at each of the four junior schools is given below along with Jim's estimate of the proportion likely to choose Mayfield School.

Junior School	Number in final year at 31 May	Proportion choosing Mayfield School
Ranmoor	60	0.9
Hallamshire	120	0.8
Broomhill	140	0.9
Endcliffe	80	0.5

Task 2

(a) Forecast the number of pupils and the income of Mayfield School for the next year from August to July.

(b) Assuming expenditure next year is 5 per cent more than the current annual budgeted expenditure, calculate the budgeted surplus or deficit of Mayfield School for next year.

AAT Technicians Stage

IM16.13 Advanced: Comments on an existing performance measurement and bonus system and recommendations for improvement. 1. You are the group management accountant of a large divisionalized group.

There has been extensive board discussion of the existing system of rewarding Divisional General Managers with substantial bonuses based on the comparison of the divisional profit with budget.

The scheme is simple: the divisional profit (PBIT) is compared with the budget for the year. If budget is not achieved no bonus is paid. If budget is achieved a bonus of 20 per cent of salary is earned. If twice budgeted profit is achieved, a bonus of 100 per cent of salary is paid, which is the upper limit of the bonus scheme. Intermediate achievements are calculated *pro rata*.

The finance director has been asked to prepare a number of reports on the issues involved, and has asked you to prepare some of these.

He has decided to use the results for Division X as an example on which the various discussions could be based. A schedule of summary available data is given below.

Division X
Summary of management accounting data

	Strategic plan 2013 Prepared Aug 2012	Budget 2013 Prepared Oct 2012	Latest estimate 2013 Prepared April 2013
Sales of units by Division X	35 000	36 000	35 800
Sales	28 000	28 800	28 100
Marginal costs	14 350	15 300	14 900
Fixed factory cost	6 500	6 800	7 200
Product development	2 000	2 000	1 400
Marketing	3 500	3 200	2 600
PBIT	1 650	1 500	2 000

Division X manufactures and sells branded consumer durables in competitive markets. High expenditure is required on product development and advertising, as the maintenance of market share depends on a flow of well-promoted new models.

Reliable statistics on market size are available annually. Based on the market size for 2012, where stronger than anticipated growth had occurred, a revised market estimate of 165 000 units for 2013 is agreed by group and divisional staff in May 2013. This is a significant increase on the estimate of 150 000 units made in May 2012 and used since.

The divisional general manager has commented that action now, almost half way through the year, is unlikely to produce significant results during this year. However, had he known last year, at the time of producing the budget, that the market was growing faster, he could have taken the necessary action to maintain the strategic plan market share. The actions would have been:

- cutting prices by £10 per unit below the price at present charged and used in the latest estimate for 2013;
- increasing marketing expenditure by £300 000 compared with the strategic plan.

The group managing director, commenting on the same data, said that the divisional general manager could have maintained both strategic plan market share and selling prices by an alternative approach.

The approach, he thought, should have been:

- maintaining expenditure on product development and marketing at 20 per cent of sales over the years;
- spending his time controlling production costs instead of worrying about annual bonuses.

You are required:

(a) to analyze and comment on the results of Division X, making appropriate comparisons with Budget, with Plan and with new available data. Present the results in such a form that the Board can easily understand the problems involved;
(17 marks)

(b) to comment on the advantages and problems of the existing bonus system for the Divisional General Manager and the way in which the present bonus scheme may motivate the Divisional General Manager; *(8 marks)*

(c) to make specific proposals, showing calculations if appropriate, for an alternative bonus scheme, reflecting your analysis in (a). *(8 marks)*

A non-executive director has commented that he can understand the case for linking executive directors' rewards to group results. He is not convinced that this should be extended to divisional managers, and certainly not to senior managers below this level in divisions and head office.

(d) Explain and discuss the case for extending bonus schemes widely throughout the organization. *(7 marks)*

CIMA Stage 4 Management Accounting – Control and Audit

IM16.14 Advanced: Budget use and performance reporting. A new private hospital of 100 beds was opened to receive patients on 2 January though many senior staff members including the supervisor of the laundry department had been *in situ* for some time previously. The first months were expected to be a settling-in period; the hospital facilities being used to full capacity only in the second and subsequent months.

In May the supervisor of the laundry department received her first monthly performance report from the hospital administrator, together with an explanatory memorandum. Copies of both documents are set out below.

The supervisor had never seen the original budget, nor had she been informed that there would be a monthly performance report. She knew she was responsible for her department and had made every endeavour to run it as efficiently as possible. It had been made clear to her that there would be a slow build up in the number of patients accepted by the hospital and so she would need only three members of staff, but she had had to take on a fourth during the month due to the extra work. This extra hiring had been anticipated for May, not late February.

Rockingham Private Patients Hospital Ltd

MEMORANDUM   30 April

To: All Department Heads/Supervisors
From: Hospital Administrator

Attached is the Monthly Performance Report for your department. The hospital has adopted a responsibility accounting system so you will be receiving one of these reports monthly. Responsibility accounting means that you are accountable for ensuring that the expenses of running your department are kept in line with the budget. Each report compares the actual expenses of running your department for the month with our budget for the same period. The difference between the actual and forecast will be highlighted so that you can identify the important variations from budget and take corrective action to get back on budget. Any variation in excess of 5 per cent from budget should be investigated and an explanatory memo sent to me giving reasons for the variations and the proposed corrective actions.

Performance report – laundry department
month ending to 31 March

	Actual	Budget	Variation (Over) Under	% Variation
Patient days	8 000	6 500	(1 500)	(23)
Weight of laundry processed (kg)	101 170	81 250	(19 920)	(24.5)
	(£)	(£)	(£)	
Department expenses				
Wages	4 125	3 450	(675)	(19.5)
Supervisor salary	1 490	1 495	5	—
Washing materials	920	770	(150)	(19.5)
Heating and power	560	510	(50)	(10)
Equipment depreciation	250	250	—	—
Allocated administration costs	2 460	2 000	(460)	(23)
Equipment maintenance	10	45	35	78
	9 815	8 520	(1 295)	(15)

Comment: We need to have a discussion about the overexpenditure of the department.

You are required to:

(a) discuss in detail the various possible effects on the behaviour of the laundry supervisor of the way that her budget was prepared and the form and content of the performance report, having in mind the published research findings in this area, *(15 marks)*

(b) re-draft, giving explanations, the performance report and supporting memorandum in a way which, in your opinion, would make them more effective management tools.

(10 marks)
ICAEW P2 Management Accounting

IM16.15 Advanced: Advantages and disadvantages of participation and comments on a new performance measurement and evaluation system. Incorporated Finance plc is a finance company having one hundred branch offices in major towns and cities throughout the UK. These offer a variety of hire purchase and loan facilities to personal customers both directly and through schemes operated on behalf of major retailers. The main function of the branches is to sell loans and to ensure that repayments are collected; the head office is responsible for raising the capital required, which it provides to branches at a current rate of interest.

Each year branch managers are invited to provide estimates of the following items for the forthcoming year, as the start of the budgetary process:

Value of new loans (by category e.g. direct, retail, motor)
Margin percentage (i.e. loan rate of interest less cost of capital provided by head office)
Gross margin (i.e. value of new loans × margin percentage)
Branch operating expenses
Net margin (i.e. gross margin less operating expenses).

The main branch expenses relate to the cost of sales and administrative staff, and to the cost of renting and maintaining branch premises, but also include the cost of bad debts on outstanding loans.

These estimates are then passed to headquarters by area and regional managers and are used, together with other information such as that relating to general economic conditions, to set an overall company budget. This is then broken down by headquarters into regional figures; regional managers then set the area budgets and area managers finally set branch budgets. However, a common complaint of branch managers is that the budgets they are set often bear little resemblance to the estimates they originally submitted.

Budget targets are set for the five items specified above, with managers receiving a bonus based on the average percentage achievement of all five targets, weighted equally.

Requirements

(a) Discuss the advantages and disadvantages of allowing managers to participate in budget-setting, and suggest how Incorporated Finance plc should operate its budgetary system.   (15 marks)

(b) The managing director is considering changing the performance evaluation and bonus scheme so that branch managers are set only a net margin target. Prepare a report for him outlining the advantages and disadvantages of making such a change.   (10 marks)

ICAEW P2 Management Accounting